MW01632564

Das Reich

III

1941-1943

The 2. SS-Panzer-Division "Das Reich"
The History of the Original Division of the
Waffen-SS

Otto Weidinger

Translated by
Fred Steinhardt

Das Reich III

1941-1943

The 2. SS-Panzer-Division "Das Reich"
The History of the Original Division of the Waffen-SS

Franz Kurowski

Translated by
Fred Steinhardt

Published by
J.J. Fedorowicz Publishing, Inc.
104 Browning Boulevard
Winnipeg, Manitoba
Canada R3K 0L7
Web: www.jjfpub.mb.ca
E-Mail: jjfpub@jjfpub.mb.ca
Telephone: (204) 837-6080
Fax: (204) 889-1960

Printed in Canada
ISBN 0 - 921991 - 67-3

Printed by
Friesens Printers
Altona, Manitoba, Canada

Publishers' Acknowledgements

We wish to thank you, the reader, for purchasing this book and all of you who have written us with kind words of praise and encouragement. It gives us the impetus to continue translating the best available German-language books and producing original titles. Our catalog of books is listed on the following pages and can be viewed on our web site at www.jjfpub.mb.ca. We have also listed titles which are near production and can be expected in the near future. Many of these are due to your helpful proposals.

For this edition, we wish to thank Matt Lukes for another excellently rendered signing box. Fred Steinhardt turned in another fine translation. Shawn Biettner assisted with fact checking. They have all helped make this book another enjoyable project.

John Fedorowicz, Mike Olive, Bob Edwards and Ian Clunie

Editors' Notes

Modern American Army terminology is generally used wherever an equivalent term is applicable. In cases where there may be nuances where we think the reader might enjoy learning the German term, we have included it with an explanation

In cases where the German term is commonly understood or there is no good, direct English equivalent, we have tended to retain the original German term, e.g., *Schwerpunkt* (point of main effort), *Auftragstaktik* (mission-type orders) etc.

In an attempt to highlight the specific German terminology, we have italicized German-language terms and expressions. Since most of the terms are repeated several times, we have not included a glossary. There is a rank -comparison table at the back of the book listing German Army, *Waffen-SS* and US Army equivalents.

Unit designations follow standard German practise, i.e., an Arabic numeral before the slash (e.g., *1./SS-Aufklärungs-Abteilung 1*) indicates a company or battery formation. A Roman numeral indicates the battalion within the regiment.

The same also holds true when discussing *Luftwaffe* formations. An Arabic numeral before the slash (e.g., *1./Schlachtgeschwader 3*) refers to the first squadron (Staffel) of the wing. A Roman numeral would indicate the group (Gruppe) within the wing (Geschwader).

Other Titles by J.J. Fedorowicz Publishing

The Leibstandarte (1. SS-Panzer-Division): Volumes I, II, III, IV/1 and IV/2
European Volunteers (5. SS-Panzer-Division)
Das Reich (2. SS-Panzer-Division): Volumes I and II
The History of Panzerkorps "Großdeutschland": Volumes 1, 2 and 3
Panzer Soldiers for "God, Honor, Fatherland": The History of Panzerregiment "Großdeutschland"
Otto Weidinger
Otto Kumm
Manhay, The Ardennes: Christmas 1944
Armor Battles of the Waffen-SS, 1943-1945
Tiger: The History of a Legendary Weapon, 1942-1945
Hitler Moves East
Tigers in the Mud
Panzer Aces
Footsteps of the Hunter
History of the 12. SS-Panzer-Division "Hitlerjugend"
Grenadiers, the Autobiography of Kurt Meyer
Field Uniforms of German Army Panzer Forces in World War 2
Tigers in Combat, Volumes I and II
Infanterie Aces
Freineaux and Lamormenil—The Ardennes
The Caucasus and the Oil
East Front Drama — 1944
The History of the Fallschirm-Panzer-Korps "Hermann Göring"
Michael Wittmann and the Tiger Commanders of the Leibstandarte
The Western Front 1944: Memoirs of a Panzer Lehr Officer

Luftwaffe Aces
Quiet Flows the Rhine
Decision in the Ukraine: Summer 1943
Combat History of the schwere Panzer-Jäger-Abteilung 653
The Brandenburgers—Global Mission
Field Uniforms of Germany's Panzer Elite
Soldiers of the Waffen-SS: Many Nations, One Motto
In the Firestorm of the Last Years of the War
The Meuse First and Then Antwerp
Jochen Peiper: Commander, Panzerregiment "Leibstandarte"
Sturmgeschütze vor! Assault Guns to the Front!
Karl Baur: A Pilot's Pilot
Kharkov
Panzer Aces 2
Panzertaktik! Armor Tactics of the German Armed Forces
The Combat History of schwere Panzer-Abteilung 503
The Combat History of Sturmgeschutz-Brigade 276, Assault Gun Fighting on the Eastern Front
Normandy 1944
Funklenkpanzer, A History of German Remote- and Radio-Controlled Armor Units
Tragedy of the Faithful, The History of the III. SS-Panzer-Korps
Ju-88, The A and H Series
Sd. Kfz. 166 Sturmpanzer Brummbär (Volume 1)
7,000 Kilometers in a Sturmgeschütz, The Wartime Diaries and Photo Album of Knight's Cross Recipient Heinrich Engel
Das Reich (2. SS-Panzer-Division), Volume III
The Combat History of schwere Panzerjäger Abteilung 654
Bridgehead Kurland

In Preparation (Working Titles)

Kursk 1943, The Southern Salient, A Photo Album
History of the 3. SS-Panzer-Division "Totenkopf"
Operation "Zitadelle", July 1943

J.J. Fedorowicz Publishing

Table of Contents

Introduction

(To the original German edition of 1973)

Publication of the third volume of the division's history has been delayed for more two years by unforeseen circumstances and a long illness of the author. In the meantime, death has opened a gap in our ranks that can never be closed.

On 21 December 1972 our unforgettable senior member of the *Waffen-SS*, the founder and first commander of *SS-Division "Reich", SS-Oberstgruppenführer und Generaloberst der Waffen-SS* Paul Hausser died in the 93rd year of his life. He died on the same day that the German *Reich*, which had existed for more than one hundred years, ceased to exist. It was destroyed as a state with the conclusion of the *Grundvertrag* — the so-called basic treaty — between the federal Republic of Germany and the German Democratic Republic.

None of those who took part in the moving burial service at the cemetery at Ludwigsburg will ever forget how, at the close of the funeral ceremony, the national anthem and the loyalty song sounded. They were sung by approximately 3,500 soldiers of the former *Waffen-SS*.

With the death of our senior member an epoch of German history also came to a symbolic end. (See also the appendices.)

Four weeks before his death, the author spoke with him. He had no idea that the conversation would be the last one. In the course of the conversation, our senior member emphasized that he would like to live long enough to see the completion of the history of the division. Up to the last day of his life he preferred to busy himself with studying the two first volumes of the history. His family wrote to the author that they were in his hands at the very end.

SS-Division "Reich" was at the heart of his life work — the military formation of the *Waffen-SS* as an elite formation in the framework of the German frontline army.

Years before, he had turned over his handwritten notes on the individual combat activities of the division to the author. In particular, he included notes on the overall situation surrounding the division at the time that was being considered within the setting of these volumes. His notes were often cited verbatim.

Through his notes, our senior member remained active in contributing to this division history. It is regrettable that he did not survive to see the completion of the history of what was, so truly, *his* division.

The introduction to volume two of the division history covered the monstrous campaign of calumniation against *SS-Division "Reich"* associated with the ostensible "recovery" of *SS* wartime files from the Black Lake in Czechoslovakia. The "recovery" was alleged to consist of "documents from the wartime archives of *SS-Division 'Reich'.*"

Since then, a broadcast of *ZDF-Magazin* by Gerhard Löwenthal on 18 April 1973 [a German television news program] revealed that this affair was a cunning fabrication of the Czechoslovakian Secret Service's "Bureau of Dis-Information". That bureau's deputy chief, Ladislav Bittman had, in meantime, defected to the west. He revealed all the details and background of that action. With that, the campaign of defamation was exposed, essentially by one of its own perpetrators.

The notarized sworn statement of former *SS-Hauptscharführer* Georg Streicher (see the appendices) has, in the intervening time, made clear that the entire wartime files of *SS-Division "Reich"* were burned by members of the *Waffen-SS*. With a degree of probability approaching absolute certainty, they are neither in Czechoslovakian or Russian archives. Otherwise, the files would long since have been placed at the disposal of German authorities if they had contained any damaging material.

This third volume continues to detail the history of *SS-Division "Reich"* as a permanent component of the German frontline army. It details its employment in the winter campaign of 1942/43 as one of the three oldest divisions of the *Waffen-SS* and within the framework of the first *SS-Panzer-Korps* under the command of our first division commander, *SS-Obergruppenführer und Generalleutnant der Waffen-SS* Hausser.

This section of the history of the division will also make an additional contribution to historical truth and form the basis for a later, objective writing of history.

Otto Weidinger
Aalen, September 1973

The Situation in the Central Sector of the Eastern Front after the Withdrawal of SS-Division "Reich" from the Front in the Jelnja Salient

A Look Back

SS-Oberstgruppenführer und Generaloberst der Waffen-SS Hausser, who commanded the division at the time, wrote the following in his personal notes:

The operational *Schwerpunkt* on the Eastern Front lay in the center with *Heeresgruppe von Bock*, with *Panzergruppen 2* (Guderian) and *3* (Hoth).

The advance of those armored forces led to multiple battles of encirclement on the land-bridge between the Dnjepr and Düna, first as far as the Mogilew — Witebsk line, then to the upper course of the Desna: Jelnja — Jargewo, east of Smolensk.

That was the first decisive point!

From the Russian viewpoint — after the defense at the "Stalin Line" had miscarried — that was the place where the attacker would have to be stopped in order to protect Moscow.

According to statements by Werth, Smolensk was "the first check to the *Blitzkrieg*". There, for the first time, Stalin introduced strong new troop units from the east. The German front held. (See Alexander Werth, *Russia at War*, New York: E. P. Dutton & Co., 1964.)

It would have been a check if the German front had given way, which it did not. Therefore, it was not a success. After brief refitting and provision of replacements, the German forces were ready for new missions.

However, Soviet morale was also firmed up. The feeling was that Moscow was in danger. Stalin's speeches referring to the "fatherland war" had their effect. They were singing a new song!

Their efforts for the defense were strengthened.

In his memoirs, Marshal Zhukov, Stalin's chief of general staff at the time, wrote that on 29 July 1941, at the time of the heaviest fighting, he reported the following to Stalin: "The weakest and most dangerous sector of our fronts is the Central Front. It would have to be reinforced. The Southwest

Front would have to be pulled back behind the Dnjepr and, in so doing, Kiev would have to be surrendered. In the Western sector a counter-attack would have to be mounted without delay in order to liquidate the Yelnya salient. Moscow was in danger." (G. K. Zhukov (in German: Schukow), *Erinnerungen und Gedanken*, p. 287 ff. Stuttgart: Deutsche Verlagsanstalt, 1969.)

Stalin did not agree. Zhukov was relieved as chief of staff and assumed command of the Reserve Front at Gshatsk. The next day he familiarized himself with the 24th Army in the Jelnja area. He noted the well-organized German defenses which had transformed the Jelnja bridgehead into a "fortified area". Marshal Zhukov mentioned *SS-Division "Reich"* and the *10. Panzer-Division*.

Werner Haupt wrote:

The Russian high command committed the Reserve Front that it had employed in the central sector in the south. Using strong air support, the 28th and 43rd Armies were employed against the Jelnja bridgehead.

SS-Division "Reich" (*SS-Gruppenführer Hausser*) took extensive casualties for the first time and, [starting] on 17 August, had to be relieved by infantry divisions...

In succession, the following divisions fought, suffered and bled in the trenches of Jelnja: the *10. Panzer-Division*, the *SS-Division "Reich"*, the *268. Infanterie-Division*, the *263. Infanterie-Division*, the *137. Infanterie-Division*, the 87. *Infanterie-Division*, the *15. Infanterie-Division*, the *78. Infanterie-Division* and *Infanterie-Regiment (mot.) "Großdeutschland"*.

Feldmarschall von Bock called the headquarters of the German High Command (*Oberkommando des Heeres = OKH*) on 28 August at 1030 hours and reported: "The end of the army group's resistance is in sight! It is impossible to hold the Eastern Front."

While the chief of the general staff of the *OKH*, *Generaloberst* Halder, made it clear that consideration would have to be given to the possibility that an evacuation of the Jelnja Salient might become necessary, the battle of Jelnja went on. The Soviets then brought in their 24th Army and also employed it against the Jelnja salient. With that, three Russian armies were attacking the exposed position.

On 30 August the Russian 50th and 64th Rifle Divisions, supported by the 48th Air Division and several armored regiments, achieved a deep penetration. Three days later — on 2 September 1941 — the OKH decided, under great pressure from the army group command, to evacuate the Jelnja salient.

The Soviet 24th Army entered the ruined city on 6 September. (Werner Haupt, *Heeresgruppe Mitte*, p. 78. Bad Nauheim: Podzun-Pallas-Verlag, 1968.)

The General Situation

The situation along the front of *Heeresgruppe Mitte* (Army Group Center) was anything but rosy. The Jelnja bridgehead had developed into a first magnitude crisis. The divisions employed there were bled white in a defensive battle comparable to the battle of Verdun in the First World War.

The army group had sacrificed its freedom of movement to the east. It had become bogged down and, at the beginning of September 1941, had neither the manpower or materiel resources to conduct offensive operations to the east.

In mid-September it had to go over to positional warfare. The defensive front stretched for 120 kilometers east of Smolensk. Six Soviet armies maintained a continuous assault without being able to affect the overall situation at the front to any degree.

The operational *Schwerpunkt* had clearly moved to the south, where *Panzergruppe Guderian* had regained its freedom of movement starting on 8 August. By 13 August the *XXIV. Panzer-Korps* destroyed or scattered four Russian armored divisions and strong cavalry and airborne brigades in a battle of encirclement in the Miloslawitschi — Klimowitschi area.

The government in Moscow preached a "National War of Liberation" to the Russian people. Every effort was made to arouse the varied peoples of that giant land in a united battle against the German armies. Stalin hastened to evoke the traditions of Czarist Russia. The concept of "Mother Russia" and "Papa Stalin" were made a part of the daily language of the Russian people.

Section G
The Campaign Against Russia
Part II: 19 August 1941 - 18 February 1943

The Operational Possibilities

How was the fighting to be conducted at this point?

There were three major options: Advance on Moscow, Eliminate the deep flank at Kiev or Attack Leningrad. The latter option, however, lacked decisive significance to the outcome of the war.

Hitler had favored the Kiev option early on. In a *Führer* directive of 21 August 1941 it stated:

> The most important objective to be attained before the onset of winter is not the capture of Moscow but the capture of the Crimea, the industrial and coal region on the Donez and the cutting off of the Russian supply of oil from the Caucasus. In the north [the most important objective to be obtained is] the encirclement of Leningrad and physical contact with the Finns. (Heinz Guderian, *Erinnerungen eines Soldaten*, p. 183. Heidelberg: Kurt-Vowinckel-Verlag, 1960. Also available in English translation as *Panzer Leader*, New York: E.P. Dutton (and reprinted by Zenger Pub. Co.), ?)

Philippi and Heim state: "The creative spark for the battle of Kiev did not arise from Hitler's order, nor did it come from the intentions of the senior army command. It stemmed from *Heeresgruppe Süd*. (See Philippi and Heim, Der Feldzug gegen Sowjetrußland", Stuttgart: Verlag W. Kohlhammer GmbH, ?)

As a result, the *OKH* was forced to conduct a battle against its will.

The *OKH* — with von Brauchitsch and Halder and the commander of *Panzergruppe 2*, Guderian — repeatedly pushed for continuation of the attack on Moscow. Moscow was not only the capital of Russia, but also the central nodal point for the road and rail network. If Moscow were to fall, then only the limited number of north-south railroads and roads would be available to the Russians for operational transfers of forces.

There was still time before the fall mud season and winter to hope to reach Moscow. *Heeresgruppe Mitte* and also *Generaloberst* Guderian had made appropriate forceful proposals. They were turned down by Hitler because, for military-economic reasons, the occupation of the industrial region on the Donez had first priority.

Therefore, *Armeeabteilung Guderian* (= army detachment = 2 to 3 corps formations) — initially minus the *XXXXVI. Panzer-Korps* — was sent south and committed to the battle of Kiev.

That was the big picture as *SS-Division "Reich"* was being refitted near the front in the final days of August 1941 in the area east of Smolensk.

Chapter II: From Jelnja to Lenino (Outside of Moscow) 19 August 1941 - 21 December 1941

Army Group Reserve while Refitting Near the Front in the Area East of Smolensk 19 August - 1 September 1941

After the withdrawal of *SS-Division "Reich"* from the Jelnja front it was moved in six march groups to the refitting area west of the Dankowo — Roslawl road, south of the Polujewo — Rudnja Nowaja line.

The last units of the division had barely arrived at their refitting area — the roads had been turned to total mud by cloudbursts — when, on 20 August, the order arrived from the *XXXXVI. Panzer-Korps* moving the division. The order called for it to move out immediately to a new refitting area east of Smolensk as a reserve for *Heeresgruppe Mitte.* The divisional elements, which had just set up for a period of rest and had begun maintaining weapons and vehicles, had to immediately prepare to march again. From 20 to 22 August they marched back again incrementally along the same route by which they had just arrived. The command post of the division was set up in Ilinja,

15 kilometers northeast of Smolensk.

According to the division's order regarding refitting, an approximately seven-day stay in the same area was expected. All arrangements were made on that basis. The divisional units generally rested in bivouac areas. Repair and maintenance of weapons, clothing, vehicles and equipment was begun immediately. Individual units were employed to assist in the local harvest. On 25 August the commanding general, von Vietinghoff, visited *SS-Infanterie-Regiment "Deutschland"* and *SS-Infanterie-Regiment 11*.

During the time from 26 to 28 August, about 320 army replacements from *Panzergruppe 2* and 1,372 *Waffen-SS* replacements arrived and were assigned to the units of the division. This, however, covered only about one third of the losses. After the incorporation of these replacements, the division was considered only conditionally operational.

The men recuperated both mentally and physically after the long weeks of unbroken combat, deprivation and exertion. In the evenings, groups sat in front of the tents, singing and making music. Many heard Lale Andersen singing "Lili Marlene" for the first time on the army radio stations. She had originally sung it on the Belgrade military broadcast station. It was a song that formed a strong bridge to the homeland and that was just as popular with Allied soldiers as it was with the German ones. A number of units watched the feature films *Reitet für Deutschland...* (*Ride for Germany*) and *Friedrich Schiller* in the movie theater in Smolensk.

In addition to this, training details had to bring the newly arrived replacements to the training level of the frontline troops, roads had to be improved, bridges secured and patrols had to be sent out in response to reported drops of Russian paratroops.

On 28 August all commanders were ordered to report to the division headquarters. The operations officer, *SS-Obersturmbannführer* Ostendorff, presented a comprehensive outline of the overall situation. The German army in the East and *SS-Division "Reich"* had definitely achieved combat successes that they could take pride in. The fighting had, however, been intense and bloody, exacting heavy losses. The enemy situation which the operations officer briefed left no doubts as to the current and steadily growing strength of the Red Army.

The need for the security measures that had been ordered was illustrated when a platoon of the *14. (Panzer-Jäger)/SS-Infanterie-Regiment "Deutschland"* acted on information from local inhabitants. On 30 August, outside the billeting area of the regiment, the platoon surprised and captured armed Russian paratroops, including a lieutenant and a noncommissioned officer. Interrogation of the lieutenant elicited important information for the division.

The breather only lasted for a few days until the division had again been made conditionally operational and prepared for new missions. On 31 August the division was alerted. On that day it was detached from the *XXXXVI. Panzer-Korps* and was immediately attached directly to *Panzergruppe 2*. At that point *Panzergruppe 2* was redesignated as *Armeeabteilung Guderian*. As soon as the bridge in Smolensk was cleared, the division was to start its march south.

The Battle of Kiev: 4-18 September 1941

Organization of Heeresgruppe Mitte

As ordered, *Heeresgruppe Mitte* — minus the *XXXXVI. Panzer-Korps* — was to begin advancing south with its right wing. That wing was organized as follows:

On the right was the *2. Armee*:

Höheres Kommando XXXV (a corps-level equivalent) with the *112.* and *45. Infanterie-Divisionen*
XIII. Armee-Korps with the *134.*, *17.* and *260. Infanterie-Divisionen*
XXXXIII. Armee-Korps with the *131.* and *293. Infanterie-Divisionen*

On the left was *Armeeabteilung Guderian*:

XXIV. Panzer-Korps with the *3.* and *4. Panzer-Divisionen*, the *10. Infanterie-Division (mot.)* and, effective 4 September 1941, *SS-Division "Reich"* and *Infanterie-Regiment "Großdeutschland" (mot.)*
XXXXVII. Panzer-Korps with the *17.* and *18. Panzer-Divisionen* and the *29. Infanterie-Division (mot.)*

The *XXXXVI. Panzer-Korps* (with *SS-Division "Reich"*) was initially withheld by *Heeresgruppe Mitte* as army-group reserve because *Feldmarschall* von Bock still counted on a timely assault on Moscow. When, however, *Armeeabteilung Guderian* encountered a difficult situation against superior enemy forces north of the Desna, *SS-Division "Reich"* was also sent up front to reinforce the drive south.

March via Smolensk to the Staging Area at Awdejewka

On 1 September the division set out in cool, rainy weather. Five march groups marched in the following order: *SS-Kradschützen-Bataillon "Reich"* (motorcycle), *SS-Aufklärungs-Abteilung "Reich"* (reconnaissance), *SS-Infanterie-Regiment "Der Führer"*, *SS-Pionier-Bataillon "Reich"* (combat engineer), *SS-Infanterie-Regiment 11* and *SS-Infanterie-Regiment "Deutschland"*. The divisional elements were distributed among the march groups on the road leading through Smolensk, Roslawl, Mglin, Unetscha and Starodub to Awdeyewka, a combined distance of about 500 kilometers.

The march proceeded over good asphalt roads as far as Roslawl. It then continued on corduroy roads and rutted, wooded trails. On 2 September cloudbursts with subsequent steady rains transformed the march route into a bottomless morass through which only tracked vehicles could move. There were stretches where all of the wheeled vehicles had to be towed by the prime movers. Again and again they had to pull out vehicles that had sunk in to the axles. Extreme demands were placed on the drivers. The march was greatly delayed and the march columns of the division became separated by as much as six days. As a result, only individual elements of the division could take part in the fighting on the way to the Desna.

Low-flying *Ju 52* aircraft and heavy oncoming traffic consisting of army supply columns showed that the fighting was already going full blast. Reports that had already reached the division gave the following picture of the situation:

Kiev formed the apex of a long and continually narrowing salient in the Russian front extending toward the west. On 3 September the front line extended from the area north of Tschernigow generally to the northeast. West of Nowgorod Sewerssk it bent sharply south to Krolowetz and, from there, went directly north through Woronesh and Schostka back to Nowgorod Sewerssk.

The *10. Infanterie-Division (mot.)* had gone through heavy fighting against a Russian armored brigade and four divisions, with bitter losses, in the area south of Awdejewka during the preceding few days . Enemy forces remained firmly on the division's right flank at the boundary with the *2. Armee*. In some cases, the *10. Infanterie-Division (mot.)* screened against those forces with its rear-echelon elements such as its bakery company and the like.

SS-Aufklärungs-Abteilung "Reich" moved against that enemy.

In the early hours of the morning, the leading elements of the division passed Starodub and *SS-Infanterie-Regiment "Der Führer"* engaged in brief fighting with withdrawing Russians. In the afternoon the regiment (minus the *I./SS-Infanterie-Regiment "Der Führer"*) reached Awdejewka and initially screened toward the south while, to its west, *SS-Kradschützen-Bataillon "Reich"* screened toward the southwest. *Generaloberst* Guderian greeted the formations of the division that were arriving when he toured the front.

The Russians probed the lines of *SS-Kradschützen-Bataillon "Reich"* with a few light tanks, two of which were knocked out. The others fell back. In addition, the battalion sent a combat patrol against the Russian flank. In the course of the day, elements of the *10. Infanterie-Division (mot.)* were relieved by the division at Awdejewka.

In the afternoon *SS-Gruppenführer* Hausser met with *Generaloberst* Guderian and received the following verbal order:

SS-Division "Reich" is attached to the *XXIV. Panzer-Korps* as of 4 September and will be employed on its right flank at the boundary with the *2. Armee*.

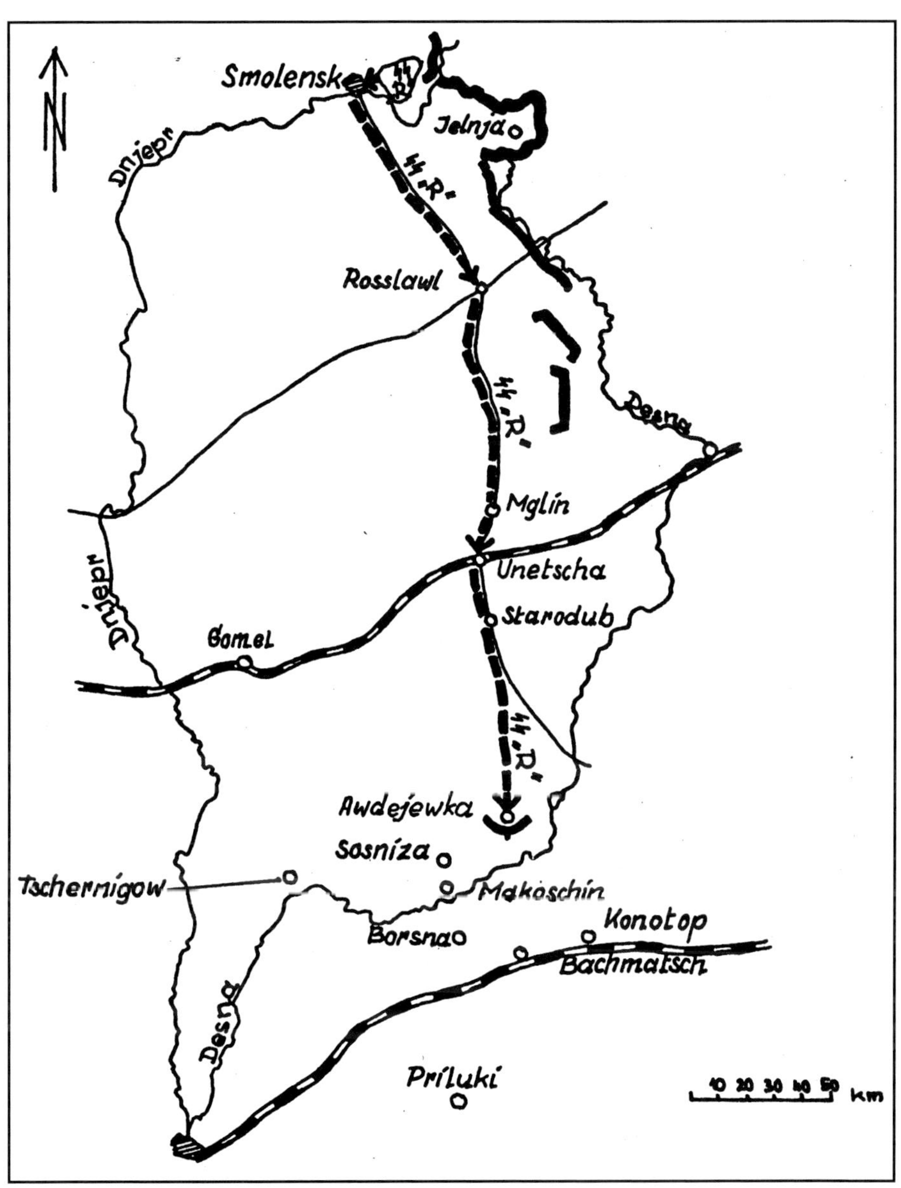

Approach March of *SS-Division "Reich"* (1 - 4 September 1941) from the area east of Smolensk to the Battle of Kiev in the Awdejewka area north of the Desna

SS-Infanterie-Regiment "Der Führer" and *SS-Kradschützen-Bataillon "Reich"* are to attack at 0600 hours toward the southwest without waiting for the arrival of additional elements of the division.

The division's mission is to advance to the southwest and cut off the route of retreat of enemy withdrawing to the southeast in front of the left wing of the *2. Armee*. *MG-Bataillon 5* (machine gun) is attached to the division, effective immediately.

In the early evening hours the battalions assembled for the attack at the southern edge of Awdejewka with the *III./SS-Infanterie-Regiment "Der Führer"* on the right, the *II./SS-Infanterie-Regiment "Der Führer"* on the left and *SS-Kradschützen-Bataillon "Reich"* as the friendly forces on the right.

The commander of the *III./SS-Infanterie-Regiment "Der Führer"*, *SS-Sturmbannführer* Kempin, was wounded in a sudden artillery concentration during the night and *SS-Hauptsturmführer* Lingner, assumed temporary command of the battalion. He had been the regiment's adjutant.

The following additional units of March Group 2 (*SS-Infanterie-Regiment "Der Führer"*) also reached the assembly area along with the regiment: The division command echelon, *Sturmgeschütz-Batterie "Reich"*, *I./SS-Artillerie-Regiment "Reich"*, *SS-Nachrichten-Abteilung "Reich"* (signals), the *2./SS-Flak-Abteilung "Reich"* and a medical company.

Sub-Section f)

Pursuit in the Battle of Kiev
4 - 18 September 1941

4 September 1941

At 0600 hours *SS-Infanterie-Regiment "Der Führer"* — directly reinforced with assault guns and light *Flak* and supported by the *I./SS-Artillerie-Regiment "Reich"* and *MG-Bataillon 5* — set out through the German combat outposts to attack south. *SS-Kradschützen-Bataillon "Reich"* also moved out at the same time. The regiment had an open left flank.

At first, ground gains were slow, but soon the attack started moving smoothly forward.

The *II./SS-Infanterie-Regiment "Der Führer"* attacked and captured the village of Lusik with its *7. Kompanie*. During the attack two *Sturmgeschütze* — *"Seydlitz"* and *"Prinz Eugen"* — knocked out two Russian tanks and engaged field positions on the western edge of the village. After the capture of Lusik the attack moved on briskly.

In the afternoon, the *II./SS-Infanterie-Regiment "Der Führer"*, under *SS-Sturmbannführer* Harmel, vigorously carried the assault on to the south, staying so close on the heels of the fleeing enemy that the Red soldiers never even succeeded in halting long enough to fight. Late in the afternoon the bridge at Rudnja over the Ubedy was captured intact and the high ground south of the village was occupied. During that engagement, the assault guns destroyed four enemy guns.

The *III./SS-Infanterie-Regiment "Der Führer"* advanced toward

Chlopeniki, during which the *Sturmgeschütze "Blücher"* and *"Lützow"* destroyed three guns, one observation post and several machine-gun nests. As noon approached, the attack reached Chlopeniki and cleared it. The battalion fired on fleeing Russian columns and advanced as far as the *II./SS-Infanterie-Regiment "Der Führer"* in the afternoon.

The *15. (Kradschützen)/SS-Infanterie-Regiment "Der Führer"* — employed with the *II. Bataillon* of the regiment — set out in pursuit of the enemy from Rudnja toward Tschernotitschi with some assault guns. It surprised a fleeing Russian column, which surrendered outside the town. Numerous prisoners were collected and ten guns and a dozen trucks were captured.

SS-Kradschützen-Bataillon "Reich", which attacked along with *SS-Infanterie-Regiment "Der Führer"*, had the mission of rolling up the front southwest of Awdejewka. In the process, it was to comb the woods and thus screen the right flank of the regiment. It carried out that mission with a flanking attack on the Russian west flank with the *1./SS-Kradschützen-Bataillon "Reich"* as lead company. It was followed by the *4. (MG)/SS-Kradschützen-Bataillon "Reich"*, which had the *2./SS-Kradschützen-Bataillon "Reich"* echeloned to its right rear. At the same time, the *3./SS-Kradschützen-Bataillon "Reich"* frontally attacked the woods to the southwest from the outskirts of the village of Awdejewka. The attack proceeded so quickly that the specified attack objective had already been reached by 0830 hours.

The enemy in front of the division only offered organized resistance in places. He appeared to be falling back to the southwest in front of *SS-Division "Reich"* and the *10. Infanterie-Division (mot.)*, which had closed up to the left of the division's attack. In the wooded area northwest of Awdejewka there were still numerically strong enemy forces. However, they lacked unified command.

While this was going on, the remaining elements of the division struggled forward to the south along roads made almost impassable by repeated cloudbursts. As a result, the march group of *SS-Infanterie-Regiment 11* was again stuck fast in the afternoon outside of Starodub with the march group of *SS-Infanterie-Regiment "Deutschland"* closed up behind it.

5 September 1941

Panzergruppe Guderian intended to advance farther to the south from bridgeheads south of the Desna in order to close the pocket northwest of Sosniza. It would work with the *2. Armee* to accomplish that mission.

While the *1. Kavallerie-Division* (cavalry) advanced farther south to the right of the division in order to clear the area of enemy, the *10. Infanterie-Division (mot.)* cleared the enemy in the area between the Bogatschka River, the Uberty River and the Desna River.

The division's mission was to continue the advance to Sosniza, capture it and take and occupy the high ground west of Sosniza and screen to the west.

The Russians attacked Chlopeniki at about 0430 hours. The attack was repulsed by the assault guns, however, which destroyed one gun and one antitank gun in the process.

The reinforced *SS-Infanterie-Regiment "Der Führer"* advanced by motor march farther to the south. Strong Russian elements retreating in various directions were effectively taken under fire by the *I./SS-Artillerie-Regiment "Reich"*.

During a halt the *I./SS-Infanterie-Regiment "Der Führer"* reached the regiment again. It immediately took over the lead and advanced vigorously farther south while the *III./SS-Infanterie-Regiment "Der Führer"* was placed under the operational control of the division.

During the advance, *Generaloberst* Guderian drove along the columns of the regiment and greeted the troops with words of praise. At about 1530 hours in the afternoon the *II./SS-Infanterie-Regiment "Der Führer"* continued the advance to Tschernotitschi. During the night of 4/5 September the Russians had reoccupied the town and attempted to haul away the guns that they had earlier left behind.

Before night had fallen, the field positions on both sides of Tschernotitschi had been overwhelmed. The *15.(Kradschützen)/SS-Infanterie-Regiment "Der Führer"* attacked the town one more time with two assault guns and took it. In conjunction with that attack, Hill 846 and Point 79.0 were attacked and taken, during which the assault guns knocked out a gun and an antitank gun. Withdrawing enemy columns were taken under fire from there.

The enemy pulled back out of Sosniza and was followed. During the pursuit, three more enemy guns fell victim to the *Sturmgeschütze*. Sosniza was attacked and captured.

During that advance the field-telephone company of *SS-Nachrichten-Abteilung "Reich"* maintained continuous contact among the leading battalions and with the division command post by continuously laying field telephone wire behind the spearhead of the attack. For that accomplishment, the company was commended in the division order for 5 September 1941.

After the advance of the *I./* and *II./SS-Infanterie-Regiment "Der Führer"*, the *III./SS-Infanterie-Regiment "Der Führer"* was brought forward to Rudnja, where it screened from the hills south of the town as well as the wooded terrain to the north. The combat outposts that had been put out by *SS-Kradschützen-Bataillon "Reich"* remained without enemy contact until they were relieved in the morning by *MG-Bataillon 5*. The battalion then marched only a few kilometers to Chlopeniki and screened the town from all directions.

SS-Aufklärungs-Abteilung "Reich" conducted reconnaissance in the area north of Rudnja as far as the line: Rejmentorowka — Dolschok — Chawdejewka — Alexandrowka — Mjna — Sosniza.

Establishing a Bridgehead over the Desna at Makoschin

6 September 1941

The enemy units that were surrounded in the wooded terrain northwest of Awdejewka attempted to break out to the south. Increased enemy pressure from the northwest had to be expected as a result of the successful advance of the *2. Armee.* The *1. Kavallerie-Division* (on the right) was to secure the right flank of the division by advancing to Walynka. It was also to clear the enemy out of the woods in the Dolshok — Awdejewka — Cholmy area.

The *10. Infanterie-Division (mot.)* (on the left) had reached the area west of Progny with *Infanterie-Regiment 41.* Its reinforced *Kradschützen-Bataillon 40* cleared out the area between the Desna and Ubety Rivers.

SS-Division "Reich" had the mission of completing the encirclement of the enemy with a continued advance to the south and capture of the important bridge over the Desna southwest of Sosniza. In addition, the division was also to attempt to link up with the *2. Armee* by advancing through Mjena.

It was necessary to determine which of the four bridges over the Desna that were in the division's sector was the best bridge with the most favorable access and exit roads. A small bridgehead would then be established on the south bank of the Desna at that bridge.

In addition, the Gonscharoff Estate — Sosniza — Makoschin sector was to be occupied orienting northwest. It was to consist of strongpoints so as to prevent an enemy breakthrough to the southeast.

During the morning, leading elements of *SS-Infanterie-Regiment "Der Führer"* reached the Desna south of Sosniza. The *III./SS-Infanterie-Regiment "Der Führer"* was reattached to the regiment. A platoon of assault guns was also placed under the regiment's operations control and the *I./SS-Artillerie-Regiment "Reich"* was placed in direct support. The *I./SS-Infanterie-Regiment "Der Führer"* advanced into an enemy column near Mena during the morning and caused disastrous losses. The enemy then started to feel signs of the impending encirclement. Strong Russian formations fell back from the northwest across the railroad bridge over the Desna at Makoschin. They were fleeing from the *2. Armee,* which was attacking from the west. The Soviets set up a strong defense at the northern and eastern outskirts of Makoschin. The cornerstone of the defense consisted of two Russian armored trains, which were to hold open the crossing over the approximately 60-meter-wide river.

While the *I./SS-Infanterie-Regiment "Der Führer"* remained fully committed in bitter fighting east of Mjena, the *II./* and the *III./SS-Infanterie-*

Regiment "Der Führer" screened at the Desna east of Makoschin. *SS-Kradschützen-Bataillon "Reich"* — minus the *1./SS-Kradschützen-Bataillon "Reich"*, which was attached to *MG-Bataillon 5* — moved out of Chlopeniki at 0700 hours. It passed through Rudnja and Tshernotitschi to become available to the division at Sosniza.

The following is a first-hand account of that operation by motorcycle messenger, *SS-Sturmmann* Helmut Günther, *SS-Kradschützen-Bataillon "Reich"* (Taken from Helmut Günther, *Heiße Motoren — Kalte Füße,* p. 142. Neckargemünd: Kurt Vowinckel-Verlag, 1963)

The Advance on Makoschin

"Start your engines!"

The battalion moved out on a relatively good road. The sixth of September 1941 had begun. It was to be one of the most tragic days in the motorcycle battalion's history. The first platoon of the *2./SS-Kradschützen-Bataillon "Reich"* took the lead. It was followed by the company commander and the battalion commander. We messengers rode beside and behind the "old man". The remainder of the company and battalion followed behind the radio vehicle.

After about fifteen kilometers we left the road and moved on field trails, as was our custom. The god of weather granted us a singularly beautiful day. It was warm with the sun showing us its best side. The sandy ground prevented the previous day's continuous rain from producing excessive mud, so the battalion advanced at a really good clip.

We came to a large town. The local inhabitants stared at us in amazement. They had never seen German soldiers. I was sent back to the trains elements with an order directing them to come forward and establish themselves in Sosniza. Only the combat elements of the battalion were to move on. I had an inkling that the battalion was faced with a mission that was more than a bit dicey...

***

I made a quick visit to Ewald, who was muddling around with the heavy field-kitchen vehicle, to direct him to the right place.

"Ewald, where's my chow been for the last few days?" I gave him a wink. "Give me the Schnaps! You can polish your boots with the rest!"

"Hey, punk, you don't need to get fresh with me. I dumped your Schnaps out."

We both laughed. That would have been the last thing that Ewald would have done. I knew that the special goodies had already been issued. Nickel would have taken my Schnaps and long since drunk it. That rascal knew no limits! But Ewald would not really know just which of the messengers had already received his share. Without grumbling, he filled my canteen. He shouted out "Break a leg!" and I took off. I wanted to get away from Ewald before the *Spieß* (first sergeant) could stop me. I saw him heading for us from across the village street.

For Werner and Albert there was no break when we got to the battalion. The two of them had to escort about a hundred Russians who had surrendered to the battalion along the way to a collecting point. The thought that two men were a bit on the minimal side for such an mission left the "old man" cold. Albert crouched on the sidecar with his submachine gun ready to fire. They circled like a sheep dog, always at a proper distance, alongside the march group. It goes without saying that the two of them were more than nervous. Small groups of Ivans were often sent off to the rear with a wave in that direction and no guards at all. Most arrived, but a few took off. No doubt it was irresponsible, but where were guards to come from when every man was needed elsewhere? The buddies to the rear would have to stay awake. Certainly, the combat zone was no amusement park like the one in Düsseldorf.

A massive dust cloud in the distance showed the route that the battalion had taken. It led over clear, open terrain. The only ground cover was the short grass of the steppe. With a silent prayer that I would not run into a hole, I lifted myself up a bit off the saddle, clamped the fuel tank firmly between my thighs and opened the throttle. The machine bucked like a circus nag, but it ran. Soon I caught up with the rearmost motorcycles and slowly worked my way forward. The sidecar machines had also set a good tempo.

The battalion swept over the steppe deeply echeloned like the mounted horde of a king of the Huns. After the mud-bound drudgery of the previous day, the attack was a relief. Russian field positions emerged to the right and left of our wild ride. We could even make out individual soldiers. We dashed on by like a phantom, shrouded in dust. Not a single shot was fired. Did the Ivans think we were their comrades?

Slowly and surely I had worked my way forward to the point. There, Klingenberg and *SS-Obersturmführer* Wagner vied for the lead. Werner and Albert, who had been fortunate in getting rid of their prisoners while I went back to the trains elements, had already made it back to the battalion and were driving right behind the "old man". I spotted Nickel over on the right. He was bent low over his motorcycle. Loisl had to be somewhere between the companies. On through another village. An old granny was drawing water at a well. On seeing us, she let the full bucket drop and disappeared in a flash into a house. What a fright the old woman must have had when we dashed by! Without pausing, we swept on.

Nobody stopped to maybe determine if the village were actually free of the enemy or whether some Ivans were lurking somewhere. The air was filled with the thunder of the engines. We rounded the corners of the houses with squealing tires. The only thing I knew was that I didn't want to break down at that moment. We were all possessed with the frenzy — enlisted, noncommissioned officers and officers alike. Nothing like this had ever happened to us before. Without reconnaissance, no point squad — the "old man" was the point. There was no screening to the flanks. The whole band swept forward like a wild horde.

Beyond the village the open steppe resumed. More field positions could be spotted. A harmless shot whizzed past us into the ground.

"Forward!" Klingenberg shouted.

Standing in his staff car, his body tensed like a hunter, that wild man charged on at the head of his motorcyclists.

Bang — a pop — the staff car began to swerve and came to a halt. Flat tire! Without wasting a lot of words, Klingenberg swung onto Werner's bike.

"Keep going! What's holding you up? What's your problem?" he shouted. It was his luck that *SS-Obersturmführer* Wagner drove on without a pause. The "old man" thought nothing of passing Wagner a cigar, right then and there.

The outlines of a larger town emerged from the horizon. The first sidecar drivers roared into the city at top speed with the "old man" in their midst. Only when they got to the middle of the town did Klingenberg have them halt. While one platoon of motorcyclists with *SS-Obersturmführer* Rentrop at the lead swept past, Wagner stopped with the commander. The adjutant was also there, and there was a short conference among the officers.

Capture of the Railroad Bridge at Makoschin

SS-Kradschützen-Bataillon "Reich" was given the mission in Sosniza of capturing the railroad bridge at Makoschin in a *coup de main* and establishing a bridgehead on the south bank of the Desna.

The reinforced motorcycle battalion set out for the attack on Makoschin with its attached units in the following order of march: the *2./SS-Kradschützen-Bataillon "Reich"* (reinforced with two *Sturmgeschütze*, two *Pak*, one antiaircraft machine-gun platoon, one combat-engineer platoon and one section of heavy mortars); the battalion command section; the *4./SS-Kradschützen-Bataillon "Reich"*; the *3./SS-Kradschützen-Bataillon "Reich"*; remainder of the *5./SS-Kradschützen-Bataillon "Reich"*; and, one battery of the *II./SS-Artillerie-Regiment "Reich"*.

A *Stuka* attack on Makoschin and on the north and south bank at the railroad bridge had been promised by *Panzergruppe 2* for 1330 hours. However, *Kampfgruppe Klingenberg* waited in vain for the *Stukas*.

Finally, when there was still no sign of approaching German aircraft at

1445 hours, *Generaloberst* Guderian personally issued the order to the motorcycle battalion from the command post of *SS-Infanterie-Regiment "Der Führer"* to attack Makoschin.

Because the sudden onset of nice weather rapidly dried the sandy roads and farm paths, *SS-Kradschützen-Bataillon "Reich"* was able to launch its assault on Makoschin through unreconnoitered enemy territory at top speed. The first enemy contact came at the Slobtka — Makoschin road fork and several prisoners were taken.

The advance into the enemy-held town succeeded relatively rapidly, thanks to surprise and in spite of heavy fire from a Russian armored train. The antiaircraft machine-gun platoon went into position against the armored train. Then, however, enemy fire came from everywhere. The enemy had pulled himself together and defended doggedly. The men chewed their way through the town with hand grenades and submachine guns in hand-to-hand combat.

The motorcyclists of the *2./SS-Kradschützen-Bataillon "Reich"*, under *SS-Hauptsturmführer* Heinz Wagner, advanced through the town to the railroad line. They were supported by two assault guns and two armored cars of *SS-Infanterie-Regiment "Der Führer"* as well as the regiment's motorcycle company, which were employed against the eastern outskirts of Makoschin. Russian units crossed the Desna bridge to the south in a steady stream. The *Sturmgeschütze "Derfflinger"* and *"Prinz Eugen"* pushed immediately forward to the bridge. One of the assault guns opened fire on a Russian tank on the opposite bank and destroyed it. An armored train withdrew when it was fired on. Since another attack by the armored train was expected, the two assault guns fell back a bit.

During the fighting, the commander of the *2./SS-Flak-Abteilung "Reich"*, *SS-Obersturmführer* Rentrop, who happened to be at the point, and the commander of the *14. (Panzer-Jäger)/SS-Infanterie-Regiment "Der Führer"*, *SS-Untersturmführer* Frank, advanced forward with a few men of Frank's company along the edge of the town of Makoschin. They crossed the large railroad bridge in a single, bold rush, tore the fuses from the demolition charges, wiped out the Russian demolition party and, with a few men, established a foothold on the southern bank of the Desna. In so doing, that assault troop succeeded in preventing demolition of the bridge over the Desna at the last moment that was critically important for the continued advance.

Thereupon the two assault guns again moved forward to the bridge. When they were within 50 meters of the bridge, the *Stukas* that had been promised for 1330 hours, but which were no longer expected, appeared in three squadrons with a total of 27 aircraft. In spite of signal flags and signal flares, they attacked Makoschin and both north and south banks of the Desna at the bridge.

The town then disappeared in an inferno of swelling smoke and fire as the howling *Stuka* bombs burst in mighty detonations. The bombs not only hit the enemy, but also had a devastating effect on the *Kradschützen* fighting in the center of the town. The shocking outcome of that *Stuka* attack for the motorcycle battalion was 10 dead and 30 severely wounded, mostly from the signals platoon and the battalion's motorcycle messenger section.

SS-Obersturmführer Schädlich, commander of the *5./SS-Kradschützen-Bataillon "Reich"*, who was on his way to the battalion command post, was also killed in the attack. Many curses were screamed at the *Stukas*. In the meantime, *SS-Hauptsturmführer* Tychsen, commander of the *3./SS-Kradschützen-Bataillon "Reich"*, replaced *SS-Sturmbannführer* Klingenberg, who had fallen ill, in command of the battalion. The exact time of the change in command can no longer be determined from the available records.

A combination of tragic circumstances and misunderstandings had evidently led to this misfortune. No unit carries a charm that guarantees protection from such accidents in a war of movement with rapidly changing fronts. The *Stukas* had just done an outstanding job of supporting the men of *SS-Division "Reich"* in the difficult days of the battle at Jelnja. Frequently their support had been decisive. Presumably, the tragic error arose in passing on the time of attack for the *Stukas*. It goes along with the unique nature of their form of attack that, once they are into the dive, there is no more stopping them with signal flares or ground-marking panels. Since the ground troops were no longer expecting the *Stukas*, it is likely that the German air-ground recognition signals were not displayed until it was already too late.

Some good did, however, result from the *Stuka* attack. It considerably aided the advance across the bridge and the defense of the small bridgehead on the south bank. With it, the last resistance in Makoschin was broken and both of the armored trains were finally eliminated.

As a result of one bomb, the bridge was partially hit and burned. However, the 1st and 2nd platoons of the *2./SS-Kradschützen-Bataillon "Reich"* with the company commander, *SS-Obersturmführer* Heinz Wagner, charged over the bridge to strengthen Rentrop's assault troop. The 3rd and 4th platoons immediately followed, so that the entire company was engaged in heavy fighting at the bridgehead by 1540 hours.

The enemy recognized the threat and launched an immediate counterattack, which he continually reinforced. He laid down such concentrated artillery fire on the bridge that, for a time, it was impossible to cross. No more help could be brought to the courageous men in the bridgehead during the day. They had to hold out on their own and defend the small bridgehead against all of the Russian attacks. The company commander of the *14. (Panzer-Jäger)/SS-Infanterie-Regiment "Der Führer"* was killed in the heavy fighting.

The combat-engineer platoon of the *5./SS-Kradschützen-Bataillon "Reich"* improved the bridge under heavy enemy artillery fire, and *Sturmgeschütz*

"Prinz Eugen" was brought over into the bridgehead. As a result of a damaged track, *Sturmgeschütz "Derfflinger"* did not come over into the bridgehead until later.

The other assault guns and the *15. (Kradschützen)/SS-Infanterie-Regiment "Der Führer"* had entered the fight from the east. They started to provide covering fire to the northwest and repulsed several enemy advances.

The crews of the two Russian armored trains fought with astounding stubbornness. Before the *Stuka* attack they had repeatedly moved forward and joined the firefight, even though they were fired on by the *Sturmgeschütze*, antiaircraft machine guns and *Pak*. One time, after the armored train pulled back, the combat-engineer platoon blew up the rails. The armored train then advanced again. It derailed and, after unhitching the derailed car, pulled back again. When one of the armored trains started to burn as a result of the concentrated fire, the crews of both trains abandoned them. Shortly thereafter, the *Stukas* attacked again and completely destroyed the trains.

During that fighting the *3./* and *4./SS-Kradschützen-Bataillon "Reich"* were employed screening the right flank to the west and northwest.

During the night, two *Sturmgeschütze* and the entire *4.(MG)/SS-Kradschützen-Bataillon "Reich"* were brought up to reinforce the bridgehead on the south bank of the Desna. They took position there on both sides of the bridge.

SS-Obersturmführer Fritz Rentrop, who had assumed command of the assault troop in a dangerous situation on his own initiative and had captured the important Desna railroad bridge undamaged in a *coup de main*, made possible the continued advance of *SS-Division "Reich"* across the Desna and to the south. As a result, the retreat route east was cut off for strong enemy formations. *SS-Obersturmführer* Rentrop was awarded the Knight's Cross on 13 October 1941 in recognition of that decisive action by the courageous assault troop. He was killed in action in February 1945 as *SS-Sturmbannführer* and operations officer of the *IV. SS-Panzer-Korps*.

During the course of the day, *SS-Infanterie-Regiment 11* — with the attached *II./SS-Artillerie-Regiment "Reich"* (minus one battery) and the elements that had arrived in the meanwhile — occupied the following sectors to defend toward the northwest: Bridge at Rudnja (inclusive) — Hill 84.6 (2 kilometers southwest of Tschernotitschi). It also screened the Tschernotitschi — Gontscharoff road continuously with strong combat patrols.

MG-Bataillon 5 (reinforced with the *1./SS-Kradschützen-Bataillon "Reich"*) spent the entire day clearing up the Nowenjkij — Shuklja — Lusk — Korbin Estate wooded area.

Generaloberst Guderian wrote the following in his memoirs for 6 September 1941:

Another visit with *SS-Division "Reich"*. It was engaged in attacking the railway bridge over the Desna at Makoschin. I went to some trouble to provide air support for this. As a result of the bad roads the whole division was not yet assembled. On the way there I passed a number of its units, some on the march, others resting in the woods. The excellent discipline of the troops made a first-class impression, and they loudly expressed their satisfaction at once again forming part of the *Panzergruppe*.

The bridge was captured during the afternoon and a further crossing place over the Desna thus secured. My vehicle section was compelled on several occasions to drive through hostile artillery fire but suffered no casualties or damage. On the way back we encountered....*SS* units moving up on foot because of the bad condition of the roads. (Heinz Guderian, *Erinnerungen eines Soldaten*, p. 193.)

When *Generaloberst* Guderian got to the division command post on his return journey, he issued the order to extend the bridgehead over the Desna so that the division could stage from there to launch an attack on the west bank of the Sejm. That would facilitate the advance of the *XXIV. Panzer-Korps* through that sector.

(On that day the Jelnja salient, which had been so hotly contested for weeks, was evacuated by the German divisions as ordered and occupied by units of the Russian 24th Army.)

7 September 1941

In spite of the shortage of ammunition, heavy Russian attacks during the night were repulsed by the *2./SS-Kradschützen-Bataillon "Reich"* and Rentrop's assault troop fighting in the bridgehead.

In the gray dawn light, *Sturmgeschütz "Derfflinger"* was hit by a round from an antitank gun and had to pull back. However, it got stuck on the rails on the railroad embankment. Since *Sturmgeschütz "Prinz Eugen"* soon ran out of ammunition, it also had to head back over the bridge. It was unable to get past *"Derfflinger"*, so both assault guns were stuck on the railroad embankment under heavy artillery fire, since it was impossible to get them going right away.

During the course of the day, the Russians again attacked doggedly in order to reduce the bridgehead and recapture the Desna bridge, which was also very important for them. All of the attacks were repulsed, however, by the reinforced *2./SS-Kradschützen-Bataillon "Reich"*. Heavy artillery and mortar fire of all calibers up to and including 21-centimeter covered the bridge throughout the day. In spite of varied damage, the bridge remained passable.

Because of inadequate room to assemble for the attack, there was no likelihood for a German attack to be successfully launched from within the small bridgehead. The Russians had also reinforced their forces in the Desna sector and, in addition, weak enemy units that had been dispersed were still in the wooded terrain north and south of Chlopeniki. The enemy was still present in strength northwest of Mjena and in the Desna sector east of Makoschin.

Thus, enemy pressure from the northwest and the arrival of enemy forces on the route of the division's advance march were probable.

Accordingly, *Panzergruppe 2* assigned *SS-Division "Reich"* the mission on 7 September of completing the encirclement of the enemy forces on the right flank north of the Desna and extending the bridgehead across the river to the south.

SS-Infanterie-Regiment "Der Führer" warded off all attacks from the northwest on its positions and, at the same time during the course of the morning, prepared to cross the Desna on a broad front with inflatable rubber boats on both sides of Makoschin. To do this, it employed the help of the *16.(Pionier)/SS-Infanterie-Regiment "Der Führer"* and the divisional combat-engineer battalion, *SS-Pionier-Bataillon ""Reich"*. The crossing was to be made with the *I./SS-Infanterie-Regiment "Der Führer"* west of the railroad bridge and the *III./SS-Infanterie-Regiment "Der Führer"* east of it. It was intended to form a second, broader bridgehead around the previously formed smaller bridgehead, to destroy the Russian units that would be encircled in the formation of the enlarged bridgehead and, finally, to relieve *SS-Kradschützen-Bataillon "Reich"*.

At the same time the *II./SS-Infanterie-Regiment "Der Führer"* crossed about six kilometers east of Makoschin, captured a small village on the south bank and held it against minor enemy attacks. That covered the regiment's left flank.

SS-Infanterie-Regiment 11 continued to screen at the Rudnja and Tschernotitschi strongpoints and reconnoitered to the northwest and west.

SS-Infanterie-Regiment "Deutschland", whose reinforced first battalion had reached Tschernotitschi in an exhausting advance the previous evening, set out again at 0630 hours. Its foremost units reached Mjena at 1115 hours and secured the Mjena — Baba area. *SS-Aufklärungs-Abteilung "Reich"* was to its south.

The Russians had renewed their attack on the small Makoschin bridgehead at midday in approximately regiment size and had support from five batteries of artillery. They were, however, courageously repulsed by the reinforced *2./SS-Kradschützen-Bataillon "Reich"*.

SS-Infanterie-Regiment "Der Führer" started the crossing and attack of its two battalions across the Desna on both sides of Makoschin at 1600 hours. The operation proceeded according to plan. By the time darkness fell, both battalions were, for the most part, on the south bank of the Desna. As far as possible, they made preparations to form a second, larger bridgehead the following morning.

It is no longer possible to provide a more exact review of the German situation south of the Desna on that evening.

Extension of the Bridgehead Over the Desna and Continued Advance to the South

8 September 1941

With the first light of day it was finally possible to free the two *Sturmgeschütze* that had become stuck on the railroad bridge and tow them over the bridge for repairs.

As dawn broke, the two battalions of *SS-Infanterie-Regiment "Der Führer"* that were on the south bank of the Desna carried on their attack.

The *I./SS-Infanterie-Regiment "Der Führer"*, which attacked into broken-up terrain, ran into tough fighting but was able to reach the railroad embankment south of the railway bridge in the early morning hours.

The *III./SS-Infanterie-Regiment "Der Führer"* advanced into the Desna lowlands in thick fog. About three kilometers in front of it was the large community of Slobotka. The battalion advanced silently on foot, reached the high ground without being spotted and advanced into the town with such complete surprise that the enemy was unable to put up significant resistance. Numerous prisoners, including an entire artillery battalion with guns, were captured.

The enlarged bridgehead closed at the railroad embankment during the morning. The enemy forces that had been encircled by it were completely wiped out by *SS-Kradschützen-Bataillon "Reich"* and *SS-Infanterie-Regiment "Deutschland"*, which was moving into the bridgehead. During that operation, 11 guns, numerous other weapons, ammunition and other equipment were captured and 1,400 prisoners were taken.

The commander of the division particularly praised the commander of the *2./SS-Kradschützen-Bataillon "Reich"*, *SS-Obersturmführer* Heinz Wagner, for the fight in the bridgehead. Wagner was submitted for advanced promotion to *SS-Hauptsturmführer*, which was announced on 9 November 1941. With that, the accomplishment of the entire company in the bridgehead was recognized.

After *SS-Infanterie-Regiment "Deutschland"* had passed its combat outposts, *SS-Infanterie-Regiment "Der Führer"* was to assemble its battalions. The vehicle sections were to fall in behind the motorcycle battalion. The regiment was to be prepared to follow *SS-Infanterie-Regiment "Deutschland"*, probably echeloned to the right.

The enemy facing the division appeared to be withdrawing. However, strong resistance was to be expected, including armor, along the general line Borsna — Baturin.

The *XXIV. Panzer-Korps,* to which the division was once again attached, advanced toward the Bachmatsch — Konotop line, where it would then con-

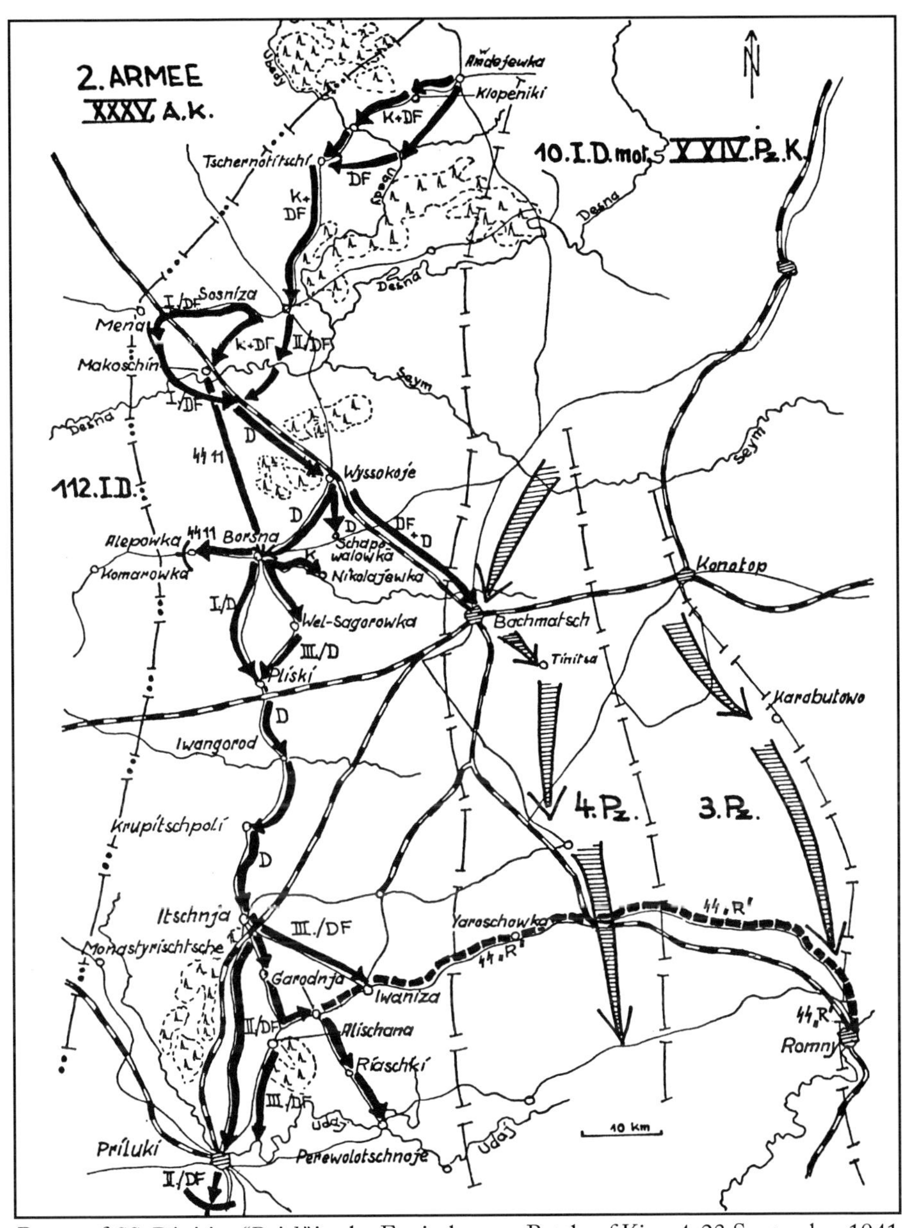

Route of *SS-Division "Reich"* in the Encirclement Battle of Kiev, 4-23 September 1941

---

tinue the advance to the southwest.

The *4. Panzer-Division* on the left moved out of the bridgehead six kilometers east of Baturin toward Bachmatsch.

The *10. Infanterie-Division (mot.)* screened the area between *SS-Division "Reich"* and the *4. Panzer-Division* north of the Sejm River.

SS-Division "Reich" also had the mission of advancing from the Desna bridgehead toward Bachmatsch. Some elements were to advance towards Borsna.

SS-Aufklärungs-Abteilung "Reich" set out to the southwest toward Jaduty as soon as *SS-Pionier-Bataillon "Reich"* had repaired the Makoschin railroad bridge. It reconnoitered to the line Komarowka — Pliska — Bachmatsch railroad station.

Clearance for crossing the bridge was then given to the units in the order: *SS-Aufklärungs-Abteilung "Reich"*, the *II./SS-Artillerie-Regiment "Reich"*, the reinforced *SS-Infanterie-Regiment "Deutschland"* and *SS-Kradschützen-Bataillon "Reich"*.

At 1400 hours *SS-Infanterie-Regiment "Deutschland"* was given the mission of advancing dismounted over the Desna bridge to Butowka with the reinforced *I./SS-Infanterie-Regiment "Deutschland"*. The battalion was to clear the rear of the *II./SS-Infanterie-Regiment "Der Führer"* which was positioned there and oriented southeast. It was then to advance with the reinforced *III./SS-Infanterie-Regiment "Deutschland"* on both sides of the railroad line on the right wing of the *III./SS-Infanterie-Regiment "Der Führer"*.

When *SS-Aufklärungs-Abteilung "Reich"* reported that the enemy was falling back with both motorized and horse-drawn units toward Jaduty, the division approved the recommendation of the commander of *SS-Infanterie-Regiment "Deutschland"*, *SS-Oberführer* Bittrich, to advance on both sides of the railroad line with the *I./SS-Infanterie-Regiment "Deutschland"* to Pratschi and have the *III./SS-Infanterie-Regiment "Deutschland"* follow.

Due to damaged bridges, it was not initially possible to bring the heavy weapons forward, especially the artillery. The *II./SS-Infanterie-Regiment "Deutschland"* remained for the time being mounted up in its vehicles in Baba.

The *15. (Kradschützen)/SS-Infanterie-Regiment "Deutschland"* advanced toward Bonderewka and reconnoitered to the west. It reported at 1745 hours that it had reached Bonderewka and that the wooded areas west of Bonderewka were occupied by weak enemy infantry. The *I./SS-Infanterie-Regiment "Deutschland"* reached the Bonderewka railroad station at 1800 hours. The *III./SS-Infanterie-Regiment "Deutschland"* reached the Strdnje estate at 2145 hours and screened to the east and west.

The Kiev Pocket begins to Form

9 September 1941

The *2. Armee*, attacking from the right, reached the Desna on the full width of its front and occupied Tschernigow.

The *XXIV. Panzer-Korps* had crossed the area between Korop and

Krolewetz and was attacking Konotop. With that, the Soviet 5th Army, which had been courageously and successfully defending itself in the Pripjet region, was in danger of encirclement.

Starting 9 September the Russian front in the bend of the Dnjepr began to fall apart. The Russians also had their problems with how to conduct the battle. When the German movements first alerted the Russian command of the Southwest Front to the planned encirclement, Marshal Budjenny issued orders on 9 September for preparations for retreat. He requested permission from Stalin for the evacuation of Kiev and the bend of the Dnjepr. The dictator, however, had a fit of rage and issued his notorious order: "Stand and hold and, if necessary, die!"

Marshal Budjenny was, as a result, soon replaced by Marshal Timoschenko. The difference of opinions remained. The enemy, who still had powerful formations north of the Krassnostaff — Wyssokoje sector, had constructed and occupied field fortifications northwest of Borsna and north of the Dotsch railroad station in the *SS-Division "Reich"* sector. (The division had its command post at Makoschin.) Strong enemy forces were expected south of that sector.

All results of observation and reconnaissance indicated that Jaduty and Bratschi were strongly held by the enemy. Various enemy attacks were repulsed.

The division was to capture the field fortifications on the south bank of the Dotsch sector before darkness fell. It had the mission of clearing the positions required to assemble for the attack by that afternoon. *SS-Aufklärungs-Abteilung "Reich"* was employed for reconnaissance from Jaduty to the south and on the right flank through Ssidorowka toward the area designated in the orders.

The task of *SS-Infanterie-Regiment "Deutschland"* was to attack along the railroad line and to the south of it to the southeast. It was to reach a new staging area northwest of Wyssokoje and conduct reconnaissance there.

At 1400 hours, SS-Infanterie-Regiment "Deutschland" set out to Bratschi with the reinforced I./SS-Infanterie-Regiment "Deutschland" in the lead, followed by the III./SS-Infanterie-Regiment "Deutschland". With outstanding support from the Sturmgeschütze "Lützow" and "Yorck", the Russian field fortifications were overwhelmed in spite of strong resistance and heavy artillery fire. Bratschi was captured at 1630 hours. The II./SS-Infanterie-Regiment "Deutschland" was brought forward at that time and employed along the railroad line.

As evening approached, the attack went on through swamps and over moors. Impacting enemy rounds disappeared almost soundlessly into the swamp. The enemy, however, also occasionally fired shrapnel. An assault gun destroyed one Russian battery with four guns.

In spite of falling darkness, the regiment continued pushing forward. At about 2115 hours, the *I./* and *III./SS-Infanterie-Regiment "Deutschland"* reached the southern portion of Wyssokoje and the *II./SS-Infanterie-Regiment "Deutschland"* reached the eastern portion, where the battalion set up outposts.

The *II./* and *III./SS-Infanterie-Regiment "Der Führer"* continued to hold their positions. After *SS-Infanterie-Regiment 11* advanced through Ostanowka, the regiment had the *I./SS-Infanterie-Regiment "Der Führer"* move over the railroad bridge to the area northeast of Bondarewka. As soon as enemy resistance slackened, the battalion was to pursue in the general direction of the Zerkownyj estate and destroy the enemy.

When, in fact, enemy resistance did slacken during the course of the day, the commander of *SS-Infanterie-Regiment "Der Führer"*, *SS-Sturmbannführer* Kumm, attacked along the railroad line with his regiment. The *III./SS-Infanterie-Regiment "Der Führer"* was in the lead. Continuing its advance, the regiment caught up with *SS-Infanterie-Regiment "Deutschland"* during the night. The latter regiment had established combat outposts in the Wyssokoje area.

SS-Infanterie-Regiment 11 crossed the Desna bridge to Jaduty with the *II./SS-Infanterie-Regiment 11* in the lead and two *Sturmgeschütze*. The infantry was dismounted, since the routes were impassable for motorized columns. Jaduty was captured late in the evening. As a result of the marshy terrain and strong enemy resistance, however, it was not possible to reach the day's objective — Borsna.

Within the context of *Panzergruppe Guderian*, the situation had developed as follows:

Kradschützen-Bataillon 34 of the *4. Panzer-Division* attacked from Mittschenki and, supported by a *Stuka* attack, made such good progress that it captured Baturin shortly after midday.

Schützen-Regiment 12 (of the *4. Panzer-Division*) attacked along with a tank battalion. Supported by a very successful *Stuka* attack, it reached and captured Gorodischtsche.

The *3. Panzer-Division* (*Generalleutnant* Model) advanced farther to the south and reached the railroad line west of Konotop, the city still being held by the enemy. An advance guard of the *3. Panzer-Division* was able to capture Korabutowo and both of the crossings there undamaged.

The *10. Infanterie-Division (mot.)* screened the east flank of the *XXIV. Panzer-Korps* and advanced past Konotop.

By doing so, the *XXIV. Panzer-Korps* had hit upon the Achilles' Heel in the Russian front between Baturin and Konotop. On receipt of reports of the rapid advance of the *3. Panzer-Division*, *Panzergruppe Guderian* ordered the immediate advance on Romny with the strongest possible forces and formation there of bridgeheads over the Romen and Ssula rivers.

At midnight the *3. Panzer-Division* set out toward Romny with an advance guard that was followed by *Gruppe Manteuffel* which, in turn, was followed by *Gruppe Kleemann*. This was the decisive step in the formation of the gigantic pocket of Kiev!

10 September 1941

SS-Infanterie-Regiment "Der Führer advanced farther south during the night. In the morning it was fighting at the railroad junction of Bachmatsch with greatly superior enemy forces that were falling back to the west as a result of the attack of the *4. Panzer-Division*. The Russians suffered heavy losses. In that operation the regiment lost one of its best and bravest officers, the commander of the *11./SS-Infanterie-Regiment "Der Führer"*, *SS-Hauptsturmführer* Ney.

During the night and throughout the following day it rained in torrents and the roads of the advance route dissolved into mud.

Following the capture of Jaduty the previous evening, during which one bridge had been destroyed and the second captured intact, the right-hand group of the division — *SS-Infanterie-Regiment 11, SS-Aufklärungs-Abteilung "Reich"* and *SS-Kradschützen-Bataillon "Reich"* — continued the attack. *SS-Infanterie-Regiment 11* advanced on foot in steady rain and conditions that were physically punishing. It ejected the enemy from his field fortifications on the high ground at Klenussof. By evening, the ongoing attack captured Konoschewka, where the enemy still offered strong resistance at the Dotsch sector.

SS-Kradschützen-Bataillon "Reich", with two attached *Sturmgeschütze*, was unable to carry out its mission of advancing to Borsna because of the bottomless roads. The motorcycles sank to the axles. The second mission that had been ordered, an advance on Alepowka, also had to be rescinded. For the time being, *SS-Kradschützen-Bataillon "Reich"* remained stuck in the mud.

SS-Infanterie-Regiment "Deutschland" set out at 0510 hours. The *I./SS-Infanterie-Regiment "Deutschland"* was on the right and the *III./SS-Infanterie-Regiment "Deutschland"* on the left. It advanced to reach the Dotsch railroad station — Schapowalowka road and the high ground directly to its north.

At 0620 hours strong enemy columns were reported marching from Schapowalowka to Borsna. The division therefore ordered the *III./SS-Infanterie-Regiment "Deutschland"* to block that road by advancing to Wel. Sagorowka and west of it.

In the meantime, the *4. Panzer-Division* attacked Bachmatsch from the northeast. Schapowalowka was strongly held by the enemy. For the time being, the advance on Wel. Sagorowka was impossible, since all of the battalions of *SS-Infanterie-Regiment "Deutschland"* were engaged in heavy defensive fighting to the east and south. Some companies had not received any rations for 36 hours.

Strong enemy pressure on the *III./SS-Infanterie-Regiment "Deutschland"* from Nosilewka became evident, but a relief attack by the *6./SS-Infanterie-Regiment "Deutschland"* to the southern outskirts of Nosilewka eased the pressure.

The *I./SS-Infanterie-Regiment "Deutschland"* reached its attack objective by 0945 hours and blocked the road from Schapowalowka toward the east. This scattered the strong enemy column. A defensive front was formed on both sides of the road.

At 1130 hours, *SS-Infanterie-Regiment "Deutschland"* ordered an advance west of the Wyssokoje — Bachmatsch railroad line with the reinforced *15.(Kradschützen)/SS-Infanterie-Regiment "Deutschland"* as the advance guard. The order of march: Reinforced *II./SS-Infanterie-Regiment "Deutschland"*, reinforced *III./SS-Infanterie-Regiment "Deutschland"*, reinforced *I./SS-Regiment "Deutschland"*. Hill 200, northeast of Klenusoff, was reached by midday. There were still Russians in the village.

The division's order for 10 September 1941 stated, among other things:

> In spite of locally strong enemy resistance and difficult terrain conditions, the division gained 20 kilometers to the southeast and south on 9 September, advancing untiringly from the Makoschin bridgehead with its three infantry regiments. After a night advance, it was able to attack and destroy significant portions of the enemy that was retreating before the *4. Panzer-Division*.

The *15./SS-Infanterie-regiment "Deutschland"* established contact with the *4. Panzer-Division* at Tschessnakoff, 6 kilometers north of Bachmatsch.

When the advance guard reached Bachmatsch around 1500 hours, it had already been taken by the *4. Panzer-Division*. In accordance with its orders, *SS-Infanterie-Regiment "Deutschland"* took and held the line along the road from the western outskirts of Schapowalowka to Bachmatsch (exclusive). It screened in the direction of Borsna and maintained contact with the *4. Panzer-Division*. The night passed quietly.

The following radio message was received by the division at 2355 hours from the *XXIV. Panzer-Korps*:

> Complete recognition for the performance by the leadership and the soldiers on 10 September.
> /signed/ *Freiherr* von Geyr

Great demands had been made of the men on that day, since the entire advance had taken place on foot, including weapons, ammunition and equipment. Whoever has had to carry a machine gun with ammunition or a mortar or its base plate will know what it meant for those soldiers to have covered 20 kilometers in a bottomless morass in streaming rain against continual enemy resistance and the attendant reoccurring setting up and taking down of positions.

SS-Schütze Ludwig Hümmer of the *3./SS-Infanterie-Regiment "Deutschland"* recorded the following in his diary on 10 September 1941:

> The *I./SS-Infanterie-Regiment "Deutschland"* continued to advance. Several villages were taken. We stopped for a while in the morning after we had passed through burning villages. We continued to advance at the railway embankment. It started to rain in buckets. Everyone breathed a sigh of relief when a halt was made in the evening. We established contact with the *4. Panzer-Division.* We were drenched to the bone as we dug in and established security. In the blink of an eye the foxholes were filled with water, since it never stopped raining. During the night we were in the water-filled holes. Our feet were in terrible shape. Almost everyone had some sort of foot disease after the difficult march through the moors.

The situation in the area of operations around Kiev had developed as follows in the meantime:

The *4. Panzer-Division* had taken Bachmatsch and had advanced in the direction of Tiniza until evening.

The *3. Panzer-Division* had already entered Romny by 0850 hours and had taken both northern bridges intact. By 1200 hours the entire city, including the southern bridge, was in friendly hands. Despite this, scattered enemy forces were still lurking about so that one could only cross through the city in an armored vehicle.

The *10. Infanterie-Division (mot.)* had taken Konotop.

The commanding general of the neighboring army (*2. Armee*), *Generaloberst Freiherr* von Weichs, released an order of the day which stated, among other things:

> You have created the prerequisites for a battle of annihilation of the greatest magnitude with this attack. It will begin shortly. The enemy has been surrounded by us on all sides and will be eliminated…

Heeresgruppe Süd was preparing to cross the Dnjepr at Krementschug. From there it would advance to the north in order to establish contact with *Armeeabteilung Guderian* at Romny. Once that was done, the huge Kiev pocket would be complete.

Prisoner statements revealed that the Russian formations fighting in the Ukraine still had the strength to defend themselves but that their offensive capabilities had been shattered. Starting that day Marshall Budjenny, the commander-in-chief of all Soviet forces in the Southwest Front, lost his ability to control his units north and east of Kiev.

The mission for *SS-Division "Reich"* for 11 September 1941 read:

SS-Division "Reich" is to take Borsna, clear the area between the rail line and the Ssejm in conjunction with the *4. Panzer-Division*, cover the west flank of the corps by advancing into the Itschnja — Parafejewka area and establish contact with the right wing of the *2. Armee.*

The continued advance of the division was undertaken initially by *SS-Infanterie-Regiment "Deutschland"* from Bachmatsch. *SS-Infanterie-Regiment "Der Führer"* advanced incrementally and conducted operations again on 15 September.

11 September 1941

SS-Infanterie-Regiment "Deutschland" and assault guns continued the advance on Golowenjki and occupied the village. Overcoming weak enemy resistance, Borsna was captured at about 0900 hours by *SS-Infanterie-Regiment 11*, which had been reinforced with one platoon of *Sturmgeschütze.* An enemy column comprised of different combat arms forces marched from the west to Alepowka. The *III./SS-Infanterie-Regiment 11* was directed against the enemy to defeat him.

The combat outposts which *SS-Kradschützen-Bataillon "Reich"* had set up at Golowniki brought in 160 prisoners. In pouring rain the march set out in the afternoon to Schapowalowka. The *1./SS-Kradschützen-Bataillon "Reich"* advanced to Nikolajewka, where it attacked the enemy.

The *III./SS-Infanterie-Regiment 11* (*SS-Sturmbannführer* Ax) and *Sturmgeschütze* attacked Alepowka in the afternoon of 11 September, succeeding in capturing the town in the morning of 12 September.

It was not possible for *SS-Division "Reich"* to continue moving south since the miserable weather and the catastrophic road conditions ruled out a motorized advance. The situation was no different for the other divisions of the corps.

Panzer-Regiment 35 of the *4. Panzer-Division* captured the Potrowsky estate against weak enemy resistance. Although there was no enemy worth mentioning facing the division to the south, a shortage of fuel prevented any continued advance.

The *3. Panzer-Division* extended its bridgehead at Romny. Bobrik, south of Romny, was still held by the enemy, but the division had no other enemy in front of it. Since the fuel column had not reached Romny, the combat reconnaissance that was to head south was unable to move out.

MG-Bataillon 5, which had been attached to *SS-Division "Reich"*, was attached to the *10. Infanterie-Division (mot.)* in order to secure the airfield at Konotop. However, it was also unable to reach its objective that day.

The mission assigned by the corps to *SS-Division "Reich"* for the coming day stated:

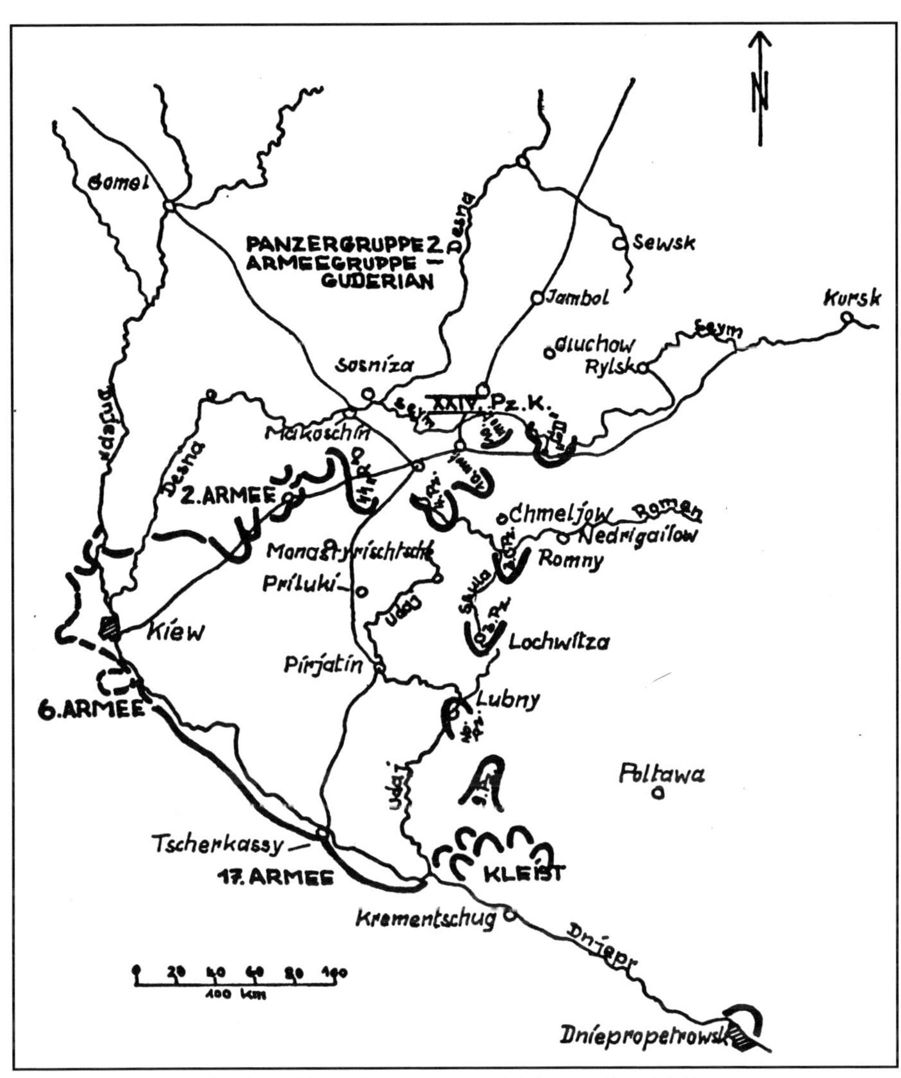

Battle of Kiev. Situation on 14 September 1941.
The pocket is nearly closed by the *3. Panzer-Division* in the north and the *16. Panzer-Division* in the south.

SS-Division "Reich" is to advance through Itschnja to Monastyrischtsche, block the Udaj sector to the west and, with rear-area units, eliminate enemy units in the former main battle area.

The Southern Arm of the Encirclement is Formed

In the sector of *Heeresgruppe Süd*, elements of the *16. Panzer-Division* under *General* Hube in *General* Kempf's *XXXXVIII. Panzer-Korps* rolled over the military bridge at Krementschug to the north. The bridge had been finished the day before. In 12 hours the division forced its way 70 kilometers forward over bottomless roads against a stubbornly defending enemy.

Since the start of *Heeresgruppe Kleist's* attack from the south had been delayed, *Generaloberst* Guderian gave orders to advance as far as the Monastyischtsche — Kustowzy (Priluki) — Lochwiza line and block there.

12 September 1941

Defeated enemy units had marched west since 11 September through Alepowka, then turned south toward Iwangorod. Some were still to the east before the combat-outpost line of the division. Strong enemy forces screened his southward withdrawal to the northeast.

While the *112. Infanterie-Division* attacked on the right from the Sanki — Britani line to the southeast in order to reach the Komarowka — Prochory line, the friendly forces on the left, the *4. Panzer-Division*, launched its attack at 0600 hours south from the Kuren — Tiniza line.

In carrying out its mission, the divisional order for 12 September 1941 stated, among other things:

> *SS-Division "Reich"*, with leading elements moving out south at 0900 hours from Borsna, is to pursue the withdrawing enemy to the south, break through his outposts and advance through Iwangorod and Itschnja to Monstyrischtsche. The crossing there over the Udaj River is to be blocked toward the west.
>
> It is essential that, as a minimum, a strong advance guard reaches the attack objective despite the road conditions.

SS-Infanterie-Regiment 11 launched its attack on Alepowka in the first light of dawn against the enemy approaching from the west. It took possession of the municipality at 0600 hours and blocked to the west and south. Two hundred prisoners were taken and two light batteries were captured in the engagement.

SS-Aufklärungs-Abteilung "Reich" and *SS-Kradschützen-Bataillon "Reich"* reconnoitered southward along the route of the advance and the roads parallel to it. The enemy was withdrawing along the same route.

SS-Infanterie-Regiment "Deutschland" set out southward from Borsna toward the Kossikoff estate at 0730 hours. The advance presented great physical hardships to the troops. It was possible to advance mounted for a short stretch, but the enemy, who had reestablished himself, soon forced the troops to dismount. One could see many men marching barefoot, since their boots were repeatedly pulled off in the bottomless morass. Several kilometers south of Borsna the leading battalion, the *I./SS-Infanterie-Regiment "Deutschland"*, ran into strong enemy resistance, which was broken with the help of artillery support.

While the *III./SS-Infanterie-Regiment "Deutschland"* was diverted from

Borsna through Wel. Sagorowka, where weaker enemy forces had been reported, the *I./SS-Infanterie-Regiment "Deutschland"* continued to advance to the south. The *Sturmgeschütze "Blücher"* and *"Schill"*, arrived. They were directed to support the battalion. *SS-Obersturmführer* Telkamp took over the platoon after its platoon leader, *SS-Oberscharführer* Muscheid, was injured by fragments from antitank fire. The platoon provided outstanding support for the infantry.

The assault guns engaged enemy field fortifications and observation posts from positions with the forward-most infantry elements. The *"Schill"* knocked out one antitank gun. Again and again, infantrymen could be heard saying: "What would we do without the *Sturmgeschütze*?" The *"Blücher"* ran over a mine at a small bridge and had to be towed away with a broken track. The Russians fell back.

As the force was about to enter the Lendin estate at 1600 hours, the Russians blew up the bridge. The *16. (Pionier)/SS-Infanterie-Regiment "Deutschland"* and the *3./SS-Pionier-Bataillon "Reich"* were quickly brought forward to repair the bridge, a task that lasted until daybreak.

In the meantime, the command post of *SS-Infanterie-Regiment "Deutschland"* moved forward on foot.

At 2300 hours the following radio message arrived at the division:

> Leading elements of the *4. Panzer-Division* are at Gajworon. The *3. Panzer-Division* is at Lochwiza. The enemy is in wild flight to the east. Continue the advance. Every hour is important!

As a result, an assault troop of the *I./SS-Infanterie-Regiment "Deutschland"* immediately crossed the river to the south toward Pliska. However, it ran into strong enemy resistance on both sides of the route of advance about four kilometers south of the Lendin estate. Since Russian snipers made their presence known in most unpleasant fashion at short range, the unit had to dig in and provide security for the night.

On 12 September 1941, the commander of *SS-Division "Reich"* released the following order of the day:

> 1.) The *Führer* and supreme commander has awarded the Knight's Cross of the Iron Cross to *SS-Unterscharführer* Rossner, *2./SS-Panzer-Jäger-Abteilung "Reich"*, for his courageous action in the destruction of several enemy tanks during the fighting in the Jelnja salient. *SS-Unterscharführer* Rossner has since died as a result of his serious wounds. We dip our flags and banners in memory of this brave man.
>
> 2.) The Commander-in-Chief of the Army has sent letters of commendation to *SS-Untersturmführer* Weisenbach and *SS-Unterscharführer* Ehm, *14./SS-Infanterie-Regiment "Deutschland"*, for successfully combating enemy armor in the Jelnja salient. Their names are listed in the Honor Roll of the German Army.
>
> 3.) On 1 September 1941 the division left the Smolensk area for employment on the right wing of *Panzergruppe Guderian* in the fighting for the crossing of the Desna.

As a result of terrible weather and heavy downpours, the movement made unheard of demands on men and equipment. For six days the division was stretched apart.

It was possible to smash the Russian formations north of the Desna and capture numerous guns and much equipment in a rapid advance. This was in large part thanks to *SS-Aufklärungs-Abteilung "Reich"*, *SS-Kradschützen-Bataillon "Reich"*, *SS-Infanterie-Regiment "Der Führer"* and elements of divisional formations. The *II./SS-Infanterie-Regiment "Der Führer"* particularly distinguished itself in its bold advance.

The fighting for the Makoschin Railroad Bridge, which the enemy intended to hold at any price, added an honorable page to the history of the division. *SS-Obersturmführer* Rentrop of *SS-Flak-Abteilung "Reich"*, *SS-Untersturmführer* Frank, *SS-Untersturmführer* Burmeister, *SS-Oberscharführer* Ruhland and *SS-Rottenführer* Fredel of the *14./SS-Infanterie-Regiment "Der Führer"* were the first at the bridge on 6 September. They were followed by the *Sturmgeschütze*, the *15./SS-Infanterie-Regiment "Der Führer"* and *SS-Kradschützen-Bataillon "Reich"*.

SS-Obersturmführer Rentrop and his four men succeeded in a textbook assault in removing the prepared demolition charges from the bridge, extinguishing a fire that had broken out on the bridge, capturing an enemy antitank gun and preventing the enemy from recapturing the bridge. *SS-Untersturmführer* Frank was killed in that action.

The *Sturmgeschütze* that followed engaged an armored train on the south bank and, together with a platoon of medium *Pak*, knocked out three armored trains on the north bank. It is thanks to their timely arrival that a small bridgehead could be built on the south bank by the motorcycle battalion. Those units of the motorcycle battalion that were employed there courageously held the bridgehead on the following day against continuous heavy artillery fire and repeated attacks.

The bridgehead was significantly expanded by the employment of *SS-Infanterie-Regiment "Der Führer"*. *SS-Infanterie-Regiment 11*, *SS-Infanterie-Regiment "Deutschland"* and the rest of *SS-Infanterie-Regiment "Der Führer"*, supported by artillery and division units, attacked from their bridgehead to the south. In an unstoppable advance that continued even at night, the Russians south of the Desna were smashed. The operational objective, the railroad west of Bachmatsch, was attained on 11 September. Contact was established with the *4. Panzer-Division* and the left wing of the neighboring army on the right. Continued advance was made possible south of the Desna.

Most of the march and fighting was carried out on foot. The motorized advance was extraordinarily complicated by the bottomless roads and the fact that only limited numbers of vehicles could be brought forward on the railroad embankment. Both officers and men have earned full recognition from the commanding general of the *XXIV. Panzer-Korps.*

The advance continues!

/signed/ Hausser

Development of the Situation within the XXIV. Panzer-Korps

Within the framework of the *XXIV. Panzer-Korps* the situation had, in the meantime, developed as follows:

The *4. Panzer-Division*, on the left, found all the bridges in Gajworon had been destroyed and had to stop the advance for the day.

The *3. Panzer-Division* continued to form the point of main effort for *Panzergruppe Guderian*. *General* Model sent an advance guard, *Vorausabteilung Frank*, south with the mission of establishing contact with *Heeresgruppe Süd*. The advance guard encountered only weak enemy resistance. Advancing through Andrejewka, the battalion captured three intact bridges at Meiny and surprised enemy motorized and horse-drawn columns. By evening it reached the area north of Lochwiza. The spearhead of *Heeresgruppe Süd* was no more than 40 kilometers south of that point! The other elements of the division were not able to move out since no fuel had made it forward as a result of the mud-bound routes.

According to information from *Panzergruppe 2*, the *16. Panzer-Division* of *Panzergruppe 1*, coming from the south, had reached the area 30 kilometers south of Choroly. *Panzergruppe 2* directed the *XXIV. Panzer-Korps* to advance south with the strongest possible forces — as a minimum, to Lochwiza — so as to prevent the enemy from escaping past there to the east. This was, however, complicated by the fact that the bad condition of the roads prevented bringing stronger units and fuel forward for the time being.

The *10. Infanterie-Division (mot.)*, which had attacked with *Infanterie-Regiment 41* to the east to secure the left flank of the corps, made good forward progress in combat with enemy advance guards and captured Swetschkino.

On 12 September German air reconnaissance determined for the first time that Soviet units were falling back along the entire front.

Feldmarschall von Rundstedt, the commander-in-chief of *Heeresgruppe Süd*, asked the *OKH* to subordinate *Armeegruppe Guderian* and the *2. Armee* to him for the purpose of unity of command. The *OKH*, however, turned down his request because of its own future plans. Thus, both *Armeegruppe Guderian* and the *2. Armee* remained under the command of *Heeresgruppe Mitte*.

13 September 1941

Panzergruppe Guderian's advance to the south continued the encirclement of the enemy. The mission of *SS-Division "Reich"* remained unchanged. The division's 13 September 1941 order stated:

> *SS-Division "Reich"* on the right inner wing is to continue the advance begun on 12 September on 13 September. It will rapidly break all resistance and achieve its attack objective, even under difficult circumstances: The Udaj River at Monastyrischtsche, where it will block the crossing to the west.

During the early morning hours, *SS-Infanterie-Regiment "Deutschland"* moved out, with the first battalion in the lead. It broke through the Russian resistance north of Pliska, where it reached and pushed on through the village. The bridge at Pliska had not been blown.

The *III./SS-Infanterie-Regiment "Deutschland"*, which had changed its direction of movement in order to break light enemy resistance, also reached Pliska. The bridge at Pliska collapsed under the weight of the *Sturmgeschütze*. Emergency repairs made it possible for empty vehicles, at least, to again cross the bridge.

At 1000 hours, *SS-Infanterie-Regiment "Deutschland"* reached Iwangorod, where the enemy continued his resistance. At about 1120 hours the leading units of the *I./Regiment "Deutschland"* spotted a new enemy column approaching Machnorka from Bar. The column was several hundred meters long. It was possible to engage part of the column from the flank.

The Udaj sector south of Krupitschpoli was reached in the evening. Shortage of fuel prevented stronger elements of the division from being brought forward. Numerous abandoned Russian vehicles lined the road. Increasing numbers of prisoners were sent to the rear. One of the men of the *3./SS-Infanterie-Regiment "Deutschland"* wrote in his personal notes concerning that day: "If only I did not have raw feet that make each step a separate agony..."

For *SS-Kradschützen-Bataillon "Reich"*, the day of fighting went as follows:

During the night of 12/13 September the rest of the motorcycle battalion was brought forward to Nikolajewka. The *2./SS-Artillerie-Regiment "Reich"*, an antiaircraft machine-gun platoon and an assault-gun platoon with *Sturmgeschütze "Derfflinger"* and *"Prinz Eugen"* were attached.

The motorcycle battalion set out toward Streljniki at 0415 hours with the *2./* and *3./SS-Kradschützen-Bataillon "Reich"* dismounted and the *4./SS-Kradschützen-Bataillon "Reich"* providing flank security. The *1./SS-Kradschützen-Bataillon "Reich"* — with attached *Sturmgeschütz* platoon, antiaircraft machine-gun platoon and mortar section — remained ready to move out immediately as soon as the two other companies reached Streljniki.

Streljniki was held by no more than weak enemy forces and was rapidly captured. After the bridge there had been strengthened so that it was negotiable for all vehicles, the reinforced *1./SS-Kradschützen-Bataillon "Reich"* continued the southward advance.

Weak enemy resistance was crushed outside of Krassilowka. The enemy abandoned his field fortifications and fell back to the south. The advance was seriously impeded by roads that had turned to mud. Strong enemy columns were identified and engaged. However, because of the catastrophic condition of the roads, it was impossible to take advantage of the success. Russian 7.6-cm guns were engaged and destroyed south of the railroad line.

As the advance continued to Chwastowzy, an antitank gun and a 7.6-cm gun were knocked out at the outskirts of the village. Russian artillery that had approached west of the village was driven off by fire from the *Sturmgeschütze*. One element of the *1./SS-Kradschützen-Bataillon "Reich"* reached Chastowzy mounted on the *Sturmgeschütze*. That operation resulted in the capture of two guns and a large number of trucks and the taking of numerous prisoners.

At 1600 hours the advance continued to the south, cutting through Biljmatschewka. South of Biljmatschewka Russian columns were surprised and overrun. The *SS* motorcycle troops, riding in captured vehicles and on the *Sturmgeschütze*, continued the advance to the south. The enemy offered renewed resistance outside of Maximowka, which was rapidly crushed in a short firefight. Numerous prisoners were taken. During the night the lead group set up security in the village while the main body of the motorcycle battalion remained in Chwaswajowy.

During the day, *SS-Aufklärungs-Abteilung "Reich"* reconnoitered the area northwest of Iwangorod toward the west and southwest, giving a running commentary on enemy movements.

Further development of the situation with respect to the corps included:

The *4. Panzer-Division* captured Grigorowka by noon after fighting in the town. The tank brigade of the *4. Panzer-Division* reported the capture of Dimitrowka early in the afternoon.

The advance guard of the *3. Panzer-Division* reported late in the afternoon of 12 September that it had captured the bridges at Lochwiza in a *coup de main*. Air reconnaissance reported strong enemy columns, generally moving from the west. Apparently the enemy wanted to withdraw to the east and was not yet aware that Lochwiza had been captured. *Gruppe Frank* held Lochwiza for the entire day against strong enemy pressure from the west, while *Gruppe von Lewinski* set out from Romny with infantry, armor and artillery at about noon. It reached Lochwiza by evening with the mission of reconnoitering toward Lubny.

Leading elements of *Infanterie-Regiment 41* of the *10. Infanterie-Division (mot.)* reached Karabutowo as night fell. At 1000 hours the division's reconnaissance spotted an enemy motorized column coming from the east. Its leading elements had reached Beskowka and the end was not in sight.

According to a report from *Panzergruppe 1*, the *16. Panzer-Division*, coming from the south, had occupied Lubny by 1100 hours. With that, the central Russian army group was encircled for all intents and purposes, that is, all roads and railroad lines had been cut.

The *XXIV. Panzer-Korps* received the mission to attack onward with *SS-Division "Reich"* on the following day to Itschnja. Elements of the division that were freed up were to advance to Kustowzy and eastward and, on 15 September, attack the enemy between the Udaj and Ssula Rivers along with the other divisions of the corps. Accordingly, *SS-Division "Reich"* was to attack to the southeast since there were strong enemy forces there.

The intention of the corps for the employment of the division on 14 September stated:

> *SS-Division "Reich"* is to attack initially as far as Itschnja, mop up the area as far as the boundary with the *4. Panzer-Division* and close up to that division. A later advance to Kustowzy and eastward of it is intended.

14 September 1941

The bad weather continued. After scouting the route, the *III./SS-Infanterie-Regiment "Deutschland"* set out from Iwangorod through the Udaj sector to Krupitschpoli to build a bridgehead.

At 0550 hours the *I./* and *II./SS-Infanterie-Regiment "Deutschland"* attacked from Bjilmatschibka via Maximowka with one battalion against Krupitschpoli and one battalion via the Bushkari estate to the fork in the road 1.5 kilometers south of Krupitschpoli.

During the course of the morning, the *III./SS-Infanterie-Regiment "Deutschland"* defeated a Russian battalion. In a bold advance, the *9./* and *10./SS-Infanterie-Regiment "Deutschland"* captured the bridge at Krupitschpoli. Ten demolition charges had been affixed to the bridge, some of which were almost ready for detonation. The enemy was scattered to the south, east and west. The bridge was negotiable for vehicles. Fleeing enemy columns were continually fired on by the attached *Sturmgeschütze*. Nevertheless, the enemy continued his efforts.

The enemy resisted north of Itschnja with infantry and two batteries of artillery. After stubborn fighting, the eastern outskirts of Itschnja was reached by 1435 hours. Early in the afternoon *SS-Infanterie-Regiment "Deutschland"* was the target of repeated Russian bombing attacks. By 1530 hours the regiment had reached the southern outskirts of Itschnja and firmly held the place. The enemy fell back to the south.

Late in the afternoon, the commander of the division, *SS-Gruppenführer und Generalleutnant der Waffen-SS* Hausser, radioed the regiment with his commendation for what it had so far achieved. In its southward advance — with poor road conditions and against repeated enemy resistance — the regiment had captured the following on 13 and 14 September: 4 15-cm guns, 1 heavy antiaircraft gun, 6 7.62-cm guns, 5 heavy machine guns, 2 armored cars and 307 motor vehicles. In addition, it had taken 730 prisoners.

Continued pursuit of the enemy by night was impossible because of mine obstacles south of Itschnja and because of the lack of vehicles. It had been impossible to bring the vehicles forward due to the mud conditions on the roads.

The reinforced *SS-Kradschützen-Bataillon "Reich"*, echeloned to the left, mopped up the area between *SS-Infanterie-Regiment "Deutschland"* and the boundary of the *4. Panzer-Division* during the day. It got as far as Maximowka.

***

What did the "big picture" look like in the eastern area of operations of the pocket as it was closing?

The enemy fell back to the south along the entire front. He pulled back a sector at a time,. Bad weather prevented friendly air reconnaissance. Ground reconnaissance was stuck in the mud. Those formations of the *XXXXVI.* and *XXXXVII. Panzer-Korps* which were employed to secure the flanks were nearly immobilized.

Uncertainty regarding the long southeast flank grew daily. Enemy forces seeking safety by slipping through the gap between *Panzergruppe 1*, which was coming from the south, and *Panzergruppe 2*, coming from the north, piled up at Lochwiza and south of it. The *3. Panzer-Division*, at that point, had only brought one regiment forward to Lochwiza. The remainder of the division was still struggling through the mud, far to the rear.

The large Russian concentration west of Lochwiza consisted largely of supply units. During the course of the day, *Stuka* formations were very successful in attacking and destroying it.

The *10. Infanterie-Division (mot.)* set out to the south from Korabotowo behind the last elements of the *3. Panzer-Division*. The enemy, however, advanced from the east on both sides of the railroad and was already exerting pressure on elements of the division. *Infanterie-Regiment 20* was employed in attacking the enemy south of the railroad.

Paul Carell wrote about 14 September 1941 in his book *Unternehmen Barbarossa*:

> ...In the evening, the reconnaissance battalion of the division (the *16. Panzer-Division*) was still a hundred kilometers from the spearhead of the *3. Panzer-Division*. In the meantime, the Russians had recognized the developing danger. Aerial reconnaissance by *Luftflotten 2* and *4* reported enemy combat-arms formations moving from the Dnjepr front toward Guderian's and Kleist's formations in the direction of the open gap. The gap had to be closed or major formations of the Soviet army would escape...
>
> ...There were still fifty kilometers separating the two *Panzergruppen*. Fifty kilometers were still open! Russian reconnaissance aircraft circled over the gap. They guided the supply columns that were attempting to get through the German lines. Hastily assembled packs of tanks moved forward to clear the way for them. *General* Geyr von Schweppenburg was suddenly faced with an attack on his own forward command post by just such a Russian column that was breaking through. The staff

formed a strong point...At the last moment *Oberleutnant* Vopel's 2nd Company saved the commander and the staff of the *XXIV. Panzer-Korps* from an untimely end...(Paul Carell, *Unternehmen Barbarossa"*, page 110. Frankfurt am Main/Berlin (West): Verlag Ullstein GmbH, 1963)

Werner Haupt wrote:

General Model, however, did not let up. A tiny *Kampfgruppe* consisting of two officers and 45 men set out from the *3. Panzer-Division* in the morning of 14 September on a bold raid to the south. At 1820 hours it established contact with the *2./Pionier-Bataillon 16* of the *16. Panzer-Division.* With that, the Kiev pocket was closed! The battle of Kiev began. It was the greatest pocket battle in military history. (Werner Haupt, *Heeresgruppe Mitte*, page 81. Bad Nauheim: Podzun-Pallas-Verlag, 1968)

15 September 1941

The division order for 15 September read as follows (excerpt):

1.) The commander-in-chief of *Heeresgruppe Mitte, Feldmarschall* von Bock, telegraphed his special commendation to *SS-Division "Reich"* for the achievements of its officers and men.

Reinforced *SS-Infanterie-Regiment "Deutschland"*, in two days of aggressive pursuit behind the fleeing enemy, captured Itschnja in the afternoon of 14 September.

Reinforced *SS-Kradschützen-Bataillon "Reich"* , echeloned to the left, reached Maximowka at the same time.

Both have covered more than 40 kilometers on foot in spite of extremely bad road conditions and repeated fighting.

The encirclement of the Russian armies approaches its completion. Until then all of us must exert our utmost.

2.) The enemy facing *Panzergruppe 2* is attempting to escape the impending encirclement in forced marches. Rearguard actions have been weak.

3.) *Panzergruppe 2*, continuing its advance to the south, will close the pocket east of Kiev. The division is to close up with the advance guards and plug any gaps while orienting to the west.

The *XXXV. Korps*, on the left wing of the *2. Armee,* is to maintain contact with the right wing of *Panzergruppe 2.*

4.) *SS-Division "Reich"*, as the right-hand attack unit of *Panzergruppe 2* is to continue pursuing the enemy to the south on 15 September and reach Priluki with at least one advance-guard detachment. The units that are following are to close up as soon as possible.

5.) *SS-Infanterie-Regiment "Der Führer"* — with attached *I./SS-Artillerie-Regiment "Reich"*, one *Pak* company, one light *Flak* battery (minus one platoon), one heavy battery and a *Sturmgeschütz* platoon — is to move out at 0500 hours from the northern outskirts of Iwangorod, proceed to Itschnja and advance from there on a suitable road, paralleling the railroad as far as Priluki. The regiment is to capture

Priluki and screen to the south and west.

Since considerable delays are to be expected in the marshy terrain south of Iwangorod, the regiment is to form an advance-guard detachment for the mission. The main body of the regiment is to concentrate north of Itschnja and follow behind the advance guard.

Attached units of the artillery regiment are to move forward to Itschnja, as is the light *Flak* battery (via *SS-Infanterie-Regiment "Deutschland"*).

6.) *SS-Infanterie-Regiment "Deutschland"* is to secure Itschnja and the designated line to its northwest. It is to hold a reinforced battalion on standby so that, if strong enemy forces appear in the wooded area southwest of Itschnja, the regiment will be able to clear the enemy out of the area.

The *III./SS-Artillerie-Regiment "Reich"* and one heavy battery remain attached to the regiment. The motor vehicle elements that have not yet been brought forward to the Itschnja area are to remain in their present position until the rest of the division has finished moving. With the exception of supply vehicles, it is expressly forbidden for those vehicles to be brought forward.

7.) *SS-Infanterie-Regiment 11* is to secure the route of advance on its western side in the sector of the estate 3 kilometers southwest of Iwangorod — Krupitschpoli. The main body of the regiment is to be in Machnowka initially. The regiment is to be prepared to advance behind *SS-Infanterie-Regiment "Der Führer"* and the motorized elements of the motorcycle battalion via Itschnja and Iwaniza to the south. It will be echeloned to the left behind *SS-Infanterie-Regiment "Der Führer"*.

8.) *SS-Kradschützen-Bataillon "Reich"* is to extend the bridgehead south of Maximowka and, from there, advance to the Gushowka area. Battalion motor vehicles are to move forward behind *SS-Infanterie-Regiment "Der Führer"* over the Iwangorod bridge to Maximowka and then concentrate in Gushowka via the reconnoitered bridge.

From there the battalion is to advance via the previously reconnoitered route via Iwaniza to Gardnja. Orders for continued advance will follow. The battalion is to screen the flank of the division and maintain contact.

9.) *SS-Aufklärungs-Abteilung "Reich"* is to remain until further orders with the main body in Pliska and to reconnoiter with a few patrols in the areas: Ombisch — Tomaschowka — Priluki — section of railroad to Itschnja (exclusive). Is the enemy approaching from the northwest or the west? Where are strong enemy elements in that area? The *Schwerpunkt* for the reconnaissance is the bridges over the Udaj River.

The division command post is at the school in Iwangorod.

At 1015 hours the corps ordered *SS-Division "Reich"* to turn to the east with all available units and advance via Turkenowka and Joroschewka to Romny, thus reinforcing the east wing of the corps. By order of *Panzergruppe 2*, however, that order was rescinded. *SS-Division "Reich"* was to continue the advance south.

That day *SS-Infanterie-Regiment "Der Führer"* again joined the fighting. The commander of the regiment, *SS-Sturmbannführer* Kumm, described that day's fighting as follows:

SS-Infanterie-Regiment "Der Führer" received the mission of attacking and capturing Priluki.

It increasingly appeared that *SS-Division "Reich"* was advancing as the point of a wedge toward the center of the Kiev pocket with enemy formations flowing back on both sides.

At 1345 hours the regiment was involved in woodland fighting five kilometers southwest of Itschnja. When that was finished, it continued to advance. By evening the enemy in Matischowka had renewed his firm stand, particularly on the high ground south of the town. The *II./SS-Infanterie-Regiment "Der Führer"*, attacking from the line of march, suffered sad losses. The splendid commander of the *6./SS-Infanterie-Regiment "Der Führer"*, *SS-Hauptsturmführer* Grund, was killed there. Two officers and 95 soldiers were captured. The battalion had to halt the attack when darkness fell in order to regroup.

At the same time, the *III./SS-Infanterie-Regiment "Der Führer* was also engaged in hard fighting on a road running three kilometers east of where the *II./SS-Infanterie-Regiment "Der Führer"* was engaged.

The *I./SS-Infanterie-Regiment "Der Führer"* was again held at the disposal of the *XXIV. Panzer-Korps*. In spite of repeated reconnaissance during the night, the enemy withdrew unnoticed. The high level of training and the instinctive, confident behavior of Soviet soldiers and officers was repeatedly observed. (Otto Weidinger, *Kameraden bis zum Ende*, page 85. Göttingen: Plesse Verlag, 1962)

During the night of 14/15 September, *SS-Infanterie-Regiment "Deutschland"* formed a pursuit group and prepared for its employment. However, that operation was superseded by the division order.

At 0500 hours, the reinforced *6./SS-Infanterie-Regiment "Der Führer"* attacked the high ground near Schajenki, two kilometers west of Istschnja, with two *Sturmgeschütze* under the command of *SS-Obersturmführer* Telkamp. The enemy, however, had fled from the field fortifications. The *6./SS-Infanterie-Regiment "Der Führer"* and the assault guns then attacked and captured Schajenki, where it then bivouacked. With that, the enemy was forced back to the Udaj sector.

The enemy repeatedly offered opposition to *SS-Infanterie-Regiment "Der Führer"*. By evening, the southern outskirts of Kolesskiki had been captured. The continued attack on Kustowzy was halted until the following morning.

The intention of the corps for *SS-Division "Reich"* on 16 September 1941 read:

The *XXIV. Panzer-Korps* will continue to reduce the pocket.

SS-Division "Reich", advancing on a broad front, will force the enemy back over the Udaj sector: Kustowzy (Priluki) — Iwankowzy (inclusive).

(Author's note: The name Priluki was also used for Kustowzy, presumably due to different ways that it was written on Russian maps. Priluki was the name preferred by the units.)

General Situation: Elements of five Russian armies are contained in the vast Kiev pocket — the 21st, 5th, 37th, 26th and 38th Armies.

The *3. Panzer-Division* established contact with the advance guard of the *9. Panzer-Division,* which was coming from the south. With that, the pocket containing approximately 50 Russian divisions was closed.

The Fighting for Priluki

16 September 1941

Since the enemy evacuated his positions in front of the *II./SS-Infanterie-Regiment "Der Führer"* during the night, the battalion advanced rapidly on Priluki at daybreak. It deployed on both sides of the road.

The *II./SS-Infanterie-Regiment "Der Führer"* advanced into the northern outskirts of Priluki in the early hours of morning. The city was on both sides of the Udaj River with a small portion on the northern bank and a section on the southern bank extending for 2-3 kilometers.

The enemy had organized his defense in the houses and gardens of the northern part of the city. An armored train took part in the fighting from the western outskirts. "Not one step back! Hold and, if necessary, die where you are!" was the order the Soviet high command issued to its soldiers. The *II./SS-Infanterie-Regiment "Der Führer"*, attacking from the line of march, got bogged down in the northern part of the city. Every house, every bit of garden was bitterly fought over in a struggle conducted mostly with hand grenades and submachine guns.

The *Sturmgeschütze "Lützow", "Yorck"* and *"Schill"*, led by *SS-Obersturmführer* Telkamp, attacked Priluki with the *15. (Kradschützen)/SS-Infanterie-Regiment "Der Führer"*. The attack reached the bridge at the entrance to Priluki without opposition. The *Sturmgeschütze* penetrated about a kilometer into the city. Since the infantry made only slow progress in the house-to-house fighting, the assault guns were forced to stop at times. Thanks to the time lost in this way, the Russians succeeded in fleeing over the bridge to the other part of the city and blowing it up.

There were also mines securing the approach to the bridge. *"Lützow"* ran over a mine and was immobilized. *SS-Obersturmführer* Telkamp and his crew bailed out and proceeded to the command post of the *7./SS-Infanterie-Regiment "Der Führer"*. The *"Yorck"* and *"Schill"* remained in position in front of the mine obstacle and supported the infantry.

During the night, the *III./SS-Infanterie-Regiment "Der Führer* broke through an enemy position while mounted. In the process, it caused the enemy substantial losses. The battalion continued the attack, reaching the course of the Udaj River a few kilometers east of the *II./SS-Infanterie-Regiment "Der Führer"*. The attack then came to a temporary halt under heavy enemy fire from the southern portion of Priluki.

The command post of *SS-Infanterie-Regiment "Der Führer"* had been located on a commanding hill about 300 meters north of the city since the early morning hours. It had excellent opportunities for observation from there. Friendly artillery could be effectively directed from that location and the armored train was forced to withdraw.

At about 0900 hours the commander of the regiment, *SS-Sturmbannführer* Kumm, was surprised to spot two battalions of enemy infantry attacking the rear of the *II./SS-Infanterie-Regiment "Der Führer"* and advancing on the command post of the regiment. At the same time, the command post was under fire from Russian artillery.

Hour by hour the enemy fire increased in intensity while the Russians strengthened their infantry attacks. By employing every available man, the attack was stopped. The *5./SS-Artillerie-Regiment "Reich"* under *SS-Hauptsturmführer* Johst, provided vital support. It fired round after round over open sights into the attacking Russians.

While this was happening, the *Sturmgeschütze* and the *II./SS-Infanterie-Regiment "Der Führer"* were temporarily unable to contact the command post of the regiment. The crew that had bailed out of *"Lützow"* after it had run over the mine proceeded from the command post of the *7./SS-Infanterie-Regiment "Der Führer"* toward the rear to disable captured Russian antiaircraft guns. In so doing, *SS-Obersturmführer* Telkamp saw a large Russian column approaching from the north and threatening the rear of the *II./SS-Infanterie-Regiment "Der Führer"*. A messenger immediately informed the *II./SS-Infanterie-Regiment "Der Führer"* and brought the *Sturmgeschütze*. Two additional Russian battalions were identified advancing on the eastern part of the city from the north.

When the first column had advanced about 300 meters past the bridge at the northern outskirts of the city, *Sturmgeschütz "Yorck"* arrived and immediately opened fire. The column, which had an armored car and a machine-gun vehicle at the lead, had already passed the regimental command post. The armored vehicles were destroyed first, followed by the remainder of the column.

After that threat had been eliminated, the *II./SS-Infanterie-Regiment "Der Führer"* turned and counterattacked with a reversed front. The commander of the regiment then sent the *5./SS-Infanterie-Regiment "Der Führer"* under *SS-Hauptsturmführer* Stadler with *Sturmgeschütze "Yorck"* and *"Schill"* in an attack to the rear. It was oriented to the northwest.

The *5./SS-Infanterie-Regiment "Der Führer"* put in an outstanding performance in the fighting. The enemy column was totally wiped out in an engagement that lasted about two hours. Approximately 900 dead and 30 guns, 13 tanks and 150 vehicles of all sorts were scattered on the field of battle. Innumerable Russians sank into the morass and drowned in the swampy lowlands as they attempted to escape to the south across the river.

The suburb of Priluki was firmly in the hands of *SS-Infanterie-Regiment "Der Führer"* at that point. Fighting in the western portion of the city continued in the evening. The combat engineers immediately commenced restoring the bridge.

During the day the reinforced *SS-Infanterie-Regiment 11* started to advance south from the Borsna area. Two *Sturmgeschütze* — the *"Derfflinger"* and *Blücher"* — were attached to the regiment while it was already moving. Echeloned to the left rear of *SS-Infanterie-Regiment "Der Führer"*, the advance proceeded via Itschnja and Iwaniza toward the hills east of Dedowzy. The advance reached the Udaj east of Priluki without opposition. The enemy had taken positions on the far side of the river. The *Sturmgeschütze* engaged the enemy positions, making it possible for the *II./* and *III./SS-Infanterie-Regiment 11* to cross the river. The *Sturmgeschütze* were unable to cross. During the night they went back to Mazejewka for fuel and ammunition.

Because strong enemy forces had entered the division's area, the *III./SS-Infanterie-Regiment "Deutschland"* was positioned at 1400 hours at Kolosseki near the division command post as the division reserve.

From there, the division sent it south via Ssorotschnizy. The battalion reached Jarowda — Beleschtschina without enemy contact. The command post of the battalion was set up in the village, where a destroyed enemy artillery, antitank gun and vehicle column were found. The *III./SS-Infanterie-Regiment "Deutschland"* was employed there to screen the right flank of *SS-Infanterie-Regiment "Der Führer"* and to the northwest. The enemy was falling back to the south.

The *4./SS-Kradschützen-Bataillon "Reich"* had the mission of advancing during the night of 15/16 September to a Russian ammunition and fuel dump located 7 kilometers south of Itschnja. It was supposed to secure it. The company reached the dump in the morning. Among other things, the company found six *MG-34's*, which the company used to increase its firepower. The main body of *SS-Kradschützen-Bataillon "Reich"* advanced farther to Garodnja. By evening it reached Rjaschki during its advance on Perwolotschnoje.

The overall situation at the time: The giant pocket was being further reduced. The Russian fighting power dropped off markedly. Strong rearguards still fought extremely stubbornly in some places. The enemy no longer made decisive decisions. Breakout attempts were uncoordinated. Only scattered units escaped.

Panzergruppe Guderian established contact with von Kleist's approaching

Panzergruppe.

The *10. Infanterie-Division (mot.)* secured the area around Romny. The forward command post of *Panzergruppe 2* was shifted to Romny. (In December 1708, before the battle of Poltawa, Romny was the headquarters of King Charles XII of Sweden for a few days.)

When *OKH* transferred the headquarters of the *2. Armee* to the east front of *Heeresgruppe Mitte*, the staff of *Armeegruppe Guderian* was left as the highest command on the southern wing of *Heeresgruppe Mitte.*

17 September 1941

The intentions of the corps for 17 September 1941:

SS-Division "Reich" is to advance over the Udaj on a broad front, secure the bend of the Udaj River and advance as far as the Priluki (Kustowzy) — Shorowka road.

The *4. Panzer-Division* is to force the enemy back over the Udaj River between Iwankowzy and Antonowka and hold the Udaj sector between Schurawka and Antonowka.

The *3. Panzer-Division* is to force the enemy back over the Udaj along the line Antonowka — Tischki.

The *10. Motorized Division (mot.)* is to attack the enemy east of Konotop in cooperation with the *XXXXVI. Panzer-Korps* and screen the Chmeljow — Romny area to the east.

The division order for 17 September (excerpts):

1.) The reinforced *SS-Infanterie-Regiment "Der Führer"* forced the enemy back from Itschnja to the south in repeated fighting on 15 September 1941 and, on 16 September, captured the eastern part of Priluki after crushing bitter resistance. *SS-Infanterie-Regiment 11* made that success possible by advancing on the left flank of *SS-Infanterie-Regiment "Der Führer".*

The reinforced *SS-Kradschützen-Bataillon "Reich"* repeatedly attacked the enemy as he withdrew to the south. By advancing to Garodnja, it protected the division's deep left flank.

Vast amounts of guns, motor vehicles and materiel have been captured, particularly by *SS-Infanterie-Regiment "Der Führer".*

2.) The enemy is fleeing to the south and southwest. Strong rearguards are defending some positions with extraordinary stubbornness.

3.) The left wing of the *3. Armee* is advancing to the south, echeloned to the rear, behind the right wing of *SS-Division "Reich".*

The *4. Panzer-Division*, the friendly force to the left of *SS-Division "Reich"*, is advancing from the area of Ssekirenzy and to its east toward the south, swinging with its right wing along the Udaj River to the west so as to reach Schurawka with its right wing.

4.) *SS-Division "Reich"* is to mop up the north bank of the Udaj River, cross to the south bank on a broad front and advance along the line: High ground southwest of Priluki — high ground southwest of Iwkowzy...

During the night of 16/17 September the *III./SS-Infanterie-Regiment "Der Führer"* successfully crossed the Udaj into the southern section of the city, which was burning in many parts.

In the morning, the assault guns that were in Priluki provided covering fire for the *II./SS-Infanterie-Regiment "Der Führer"* at the demolished bridge and made it possible for the infantry to cross the Udaj. The enemy offered stubborn resistance, especially in the railroad and factory areas. *SS-Infanterie-Regiment 11* continued the attack to the south and captured the high ground on both sides of Glubowka. The battalion on the right swung right from Glubowka and supported *SS-Infanterie-Regiment "Der Führer"* in its fight at the Priluki railroad station.

SS-Kradschützen-Bataillon "Reich" reached Perewolotschnoje, fought for a crossing over the Udaj River and built a small bridgehead for *SS-Infanterie-Regiment "Deutschland"*, which was following it. While the men were still fighting for the bridge, *Generaloberst* Guderian showed up on one of his trips to the front and was an eyewitness to the fight of the *SS-Kradschützen.*

SS-Infanterie-Regiment "Deutschland", whose *I./SS-Infanterie-Regiment "Deutschland"* remained as corps reserve and whose *III./SS-Infanterie-Regiment "Deutschland"* was temporarily at the disposal of the division, initially screened the division's right flank.

At 0700 hours, the *II./SS-Infanterie-Regiment "Deutschland"*, reinforced through the fires of the *III./SS-Artillerie-Regiment "Reich"*, set out for Iwaniza. The commander of the regiment, *SS-Oberführer* Bittrich, reached the bridge over the Udaj at Perewolotschnoje at 1245 hours. The bridge had been blown up. The enemy still offered resistance with one or two companies and a troop of cavalry. Enemy artillery fire was minimal.

The *II./SS-Infanterie-Regiment "Deutschland"* was quickly brought up and the *III./SS-Artillerie-Regiment "Reich"* employed in support to strengthen the small bridgehead that the *SS-Kradschützen* had built. The men of the *II./SS-Infanterie-Regiment "Deutschland"* climbed over the bridge under the extremely effective covering fire of the supporting artillery battalion.

SS-Oberführer Bittrich brought *Generaloberst* Guderian, who was at the bridge, up to date on the fighting.

After passing through Perewolotschnoje, the *II./SS-Infanterie-Regiment "Deutschland"* advanced to Hill 158, arriving there at 1600 hours. It did not encounter any appreciable resistance. From there the battalion continued via Hill 171 and, at nightfall, was on both sides of Besubowka.

In the evening dusk, enemy rear-area troops that had been dispersed engaged the command post of the regiment close to the edge of some woods. Rapid response by several machine guns of the *15./SS-Infanterie-Regiment "Deutschland"* wiped out the attackers.

Starting at daybreak, *SS-Aufklärungs-Abteilung "Reich"* reached Lewki and reconnoitered in the area southwest of Kolessniki, establishing contact with the *45. Infanterie-Division.*

In the evening of 17 September 1941 the *III./SS-Infanterie-Regiment 11* reached the Priluki railroad station. The battalion secured the high ground south of the city.

The *II./SS-Infanterie-Regiment "Der Führer"*, supported by the *III./SS-Infanterie-Regiment "Der Führer"*, also crossed the Udaj River.

In the overall situation of *Panzergruppe 2*, strong Russian attacks against the outer front of the pocket foreshadowed the impending involvement of the *XXIV. Panzer-Korps*. It would strengthen the defense in the area from Romny to the east and counterattack. The *3.* and *4. Panzer-Divisionen* had already organized their uncommitted elements for departure.

***

On 18 September, the corps intended to advance to the line Priluki — Bogelanowka — Machnowka with *SS-Division "Reich"*. After establishing contact with the *4. Panzer-Division*, the division was to clear up the Udaj bend northeast of that line.

In the evening, the commander of *SS-Infanterie-Regiment "Der Führer"*, *SS-Sturmbannführer* Kumm, reported to the commander of the division, *SS-Gruppenführer* Hausser, on a hill south of the city. He stated "Priluki is firmly in the regiment's hands!"

The commander of the division praised *SS-Infanterie-Regiment "Der Führer"* for that success.

18 September 1941

The division's order for 18 September (excerpt):

1.)The reinforced *SS-Infanterie-Regiment "Der Führer"* captured the city of Priluki after two days of bitter fighting with a stubborn enemy. In so doing it has eliminated a cornerstone of the enemy resistance.

The other units of the division, particularly *SS-Infanterie-Regiment 11*, contributed to the success by advancing east of Priluki.

Only small groups of the enemy remain facing the division...

...

4.) *SS-Division "Reich"* is to cross the combat-outpost line specified on 17

September as far as the following line: western outskirts of Priluki — Bogdanowka — Machnowka.

The enemy is to be cleared out of the bend in the Udaj east of that line...

By evening elements of the division had cleared out the Udaj bend as ordered, thus accomplishing the mission of *SS-Division "Reich"* in that area. The division was promised a few days of rest.

***

In the meantime, however, the situation on the eastern flank of *Armeegruppe Guderian* had reached crisis proportions.

A flank attack by three Russian rifle divisions, two cavalry divisions and two armored brigades struck the *10. Infanterie-Division (mot.)* at Romny. The division was providing all of the flank protection for the army group between Romny and Lochwiza. Only with the help of several antiaircraft batteries of *Flak-Regiment 104* and *Flak-Regiment "Hermann Göring"* could the attack be brought to a halt with difficulty. The Russians reached the outskirts of the city of Romny.

The Russians had formed two battle groups which were to seal the gap between the Briansk Front and the Southwest Front. The students of the Kharkov Military School charged against the positions of the *17. Panzer-Division* and *Infanterie-Regiment "Großdeutschland"* at Putiwl. They sang as they ran, and they were killed, to the very last man. It was a Russian "Langemarck", as Paul Carell described the attack.

Generaloberst Guderian described that day in his memoirs:

> Crisis in Romny. The sounds of fighting could be heard since early in the morning from the eastern flank. They increased in intensity during the course of the morning. A newly introduced enemy — the Russian 9th Cavalry Division and another division with tanks — was moving on Romny from the east in three columns. He managed to penetrate to within 800 meters of the outskirts of the town. From one of the high watchtowers of the prison on the outskirts of Romny, I had an uninterrupted view of the enemy attack.
>
> The *XXIV. Panzer-Korps* was made responsible for the defense. Available were two battalions of the *10. Infanterie-Division (mot.)* and a few *Flak* batteries. Our air reconnaissance was suffering from enemy local air superiority. There was a heavy aerial attack on Romny. Finally, however, we succeeded in holding the town and our forward headquarters.
>
> At the same time Russian reinforcements were moving up on the line Kharkov — Sumy and were being unloaded at Sumy and Shurawka. To defend against this new threat the *XXIV. Panzer-Korps* was instructed to withdraw part of *SS-Division "Reich"* and the *4. Panzer-Division* from the encirclement front and send them off towards Konotop and Putiwl.
>
> The dangerous situation forced us to move the army-group command post back

to Konotop.

The *XXIV. Panzer-Korps* wanted to postpone the attack on this newly introduced enemy from the east until the corps was in a position to strike with all its force. I sympathized with this view but could not approve the plan since the availability of *SS-Division "Reich"* for this operation might not last for more than a few days; it was destined to form part of the *XLVI. Panzer-Korps*, together with *Infanterie-Regiment "Großdeutschland"*, and to return to the Roslawl area.

Besides, recent detrainings at Seredina Buda and more transports moving through Sumy to the north were strong incentives to hurry.

Kiev fell on this day.... (Heinz Guderian, *Erinnerungen eines Soldaten*, p. ?. Heidelberg: Kurt-Vowinckel-Verlag, 1960)

Because of that alarming situation, the division's expectation of some days of rest came to naught.

SS-Division "Reich" received orders from the corps to set out with all elements early in the morning of 19 September via Jaroschowka to Romny and to hold the area around Romny. The reinforced *Infanterie-Regiment 41* of the *10. Infanterie-Division (mot.)* would hold Romny until the arrival of *SS-Division "Reich"*, to which it would then be attached.

***

On that 18 September 1941 Stalin revived the old Czarist designation of "Guards Division". The first four Russian rifle divisions were redesignated as "Guards Divisions". They were all divisions that had fought *Heeresgruppe Mitte* since the beginning of the war, namely the 100th, 127th, 153rd and 161st Rifle Divisions.

Report of SS-Division "Reich"

At the close of that period of fighting, the division sent a report on 18 September 1941 — "Report of *SS-Division 'Reich'* from 11-18 September 1941" — to the headquarters of the *Waffen-SS* in Berlin. It briefly summarized the employment of the division after establishing the bridgehead south of Makoschin. It read:

After building a strong bridgehead south of Makoschin, the division advanced with *SS-Infanterie-Regiment "Deutschland"* in the lead along the railroad to the transportation nodal point of Bachmatsch. Strong enemy resistance, difficult road conditions and weather conditions made the advance difficult.

On 11 September 1941 the division reached the line Borsna (*SS-Infanterie-Regiment 11*) — Bachmatsch (*SS-Infanterie-Regiment "Deutschland"*) and contact was established on the left flank at Bachmatsch with the *4. Panzer-Division*. As a result of continuous rain, all roads apart from the railroad line became seas of bottomless mud. The railroad embankment, on which a controlled traffic system had to be set up, offered the only possibility to bring up ammunition and, above all, heavy weapons.

In spite of all difficulties, contact with the enemy was continuously maintained.

With its last reserves of strength, pursuit was carried forward to the south via Iwangorod — Ischnja with the objective of reaching Priluki (also called Kustowzy) and eliminating that vital road intersection for the enemy by building a broad bridgehead south of the Udaj River. As a result of pushing to the limits of what was physically possible, particularly by the infantry, the division's spearhead reached the Udaj at Priluki on 16 September 1941.

The enemy attempted to stop the advance with mine obstacles and by fighting from hurriedly built field fortifications across the front. In the afternoon of 16 September the division crossed the Udaj on a broad front with the right wing (*SS-Infanterie-Regiment "Der Führer"*) at the bridge at Priluki and the left wing (*SS-Infanterie Regiment 11*) at and east of Borsna. All of the bridges had been blown up at the last moment.

Enemy resistance from the south bank, especially in Priluki, was particularly stubborn. Heavy losses to our own units were unavoidable. Early on 18 September a large bridgehead was built south of Priluki. With that, the mission of the division in that operation was accomplished.

Generalfeldmarschall von Bock sent the division a Teletype on 13 September with his praise for the leadership and the soldiers for their achievements.

Details

The loss in combat-experienced company commanders, platoon leaders and noncommissioned officers has become alarmingly evident. Many of the platoons are led by noncommissioned officers. In one battalion (*II./SS-Infanterie-Regiment "Deutschland"*), four young *SS-Untersturmführer* are leading companies.

Panzergruppe 2 has submitted the names of the members of *Stoßtrupp Rentrop* (assault-troop) for mention in the Honor Roll of the German Army. The names are:

SS-Untersturmführer der Reserve Frank (killed)
SS Untersturmführer Burmeister
SS-Oberscharführer Ruhland
SS-Rottenführer Frodel

All of them were from the *14./SS-Infanterie-Regiment "Der Führer"*. *SS-Obersturmführer* Rentrop has been recommended for the Knight's Cross of the Iron Cross.

In accordance with its latest orders, the division is to be moved to take part in a new operation. It is to move out early on 19 September 1941 to the east for employment.

/signed/ Hausser

Appended to the end of the report was the following list of enemy losses. (See next page.)

Prisoners and Material Captured by *SS-Division "Reich"*

from 3 - 9 September 1941

1.) Prisoners: 12,951

2.) Materiel captured:

a) Guns: 243
b) Antitank guns: 28
c) Heavy mortars: 37
d) 9 tanks and 4 armored trains put out of action
e) Numerous infantry weapons
f) 25 heavy tractors
g) Several ammunition dumps, weapons dumps and one army medical park

The End of the Battle of Kiev

While the division moved to the area west of Roslawl, the battle of Kiev came to an end on 26 September 1941.

Paul Carell wrote the following concerning the end of the fighting:

Five Soviet armies were completely smashed, two more destroyed for the most part. A million men were killed, wounded, dispersed or captured. Marshal Budjenny, Stalin's old fighting buddy and former noncommissioned officer in the Czarist army, was flown out of the pocket by order of the supreme commander. Budjenny was not to fall into German hands. Stalin also wanted to avoid the death of that hero of the revolution. Colonel General M. P. Kirponos took over Budjenny's command. He and his chief of staff, Lieutenant General Tupikow, were killed in a breakout attempt.

The battle resulted in 665,000 prisoners (approximately six times as many as in the Tannenberg battle of annihilation). Three thousand seven hundred eighteen guns, eight hundred eighty-four armored vehicles and vast amounts of additional military materiel were captured or destroyed...

History had not yet known a battle with such numbers: Five armies destroyed. Five armies! The victory was rooted in the superior leadership, bold movement and rugged endurance of the German soldiers.

It was an immense blow to Stalin. His order — "Win or die!" — cost a million soldiers...it cost the entire Ukraine. And, with that, the entrance to the Crimea and to the Soviet industrial area, the Donez basin, was open. (Paul Carell, *Unternehmen Barbarossa,* p. 114. Frankfurt am Main / Berlin (West): Verlag Ullstein GmbH, 1963)

19 September 1941

The commander of *SS-Infanterie-Regiment "Der Führer"* at that time, *SS-Sturmbannführer* Kumm:

During the night of 19 September the regiment was alerted for new employment and received the following order:

"The enemy is advancing with a newly assembled corps consisting of one rifle division, one cavalry division and an armored brigade from Kharkov toward Romny to break open the pocket. The friendly force there, the *10. Infanterie-Division (mot.),* is not sufficient to defend against the attack. *SS-Division "Reich"*, with *SS-Aufklärungs-Abteilung "Reich"* and *SS-Infanterie-Regiment "Der Führer"* in the lead, is to move to Romny by forced march, It is to attack those enemy forces by advancing through friendly security lines and destroy them."

While the *3.* and *4. Panzer-Divisionen* were still busy mopping up the captured territory in their assigned sectors, *SS-Division "Reich"* set out in the early morning hours. Its order of march: *SS-Aufklärungs-Abteilung "Reich"; SS-Infanterie-Regiment "Der Führer"*; *SS-Kradschützen-Bataillon "Reich"*; *SS-Infanterie-Regiment "Deutschland"*; and, *SS-Infanterie-Regiment 11.*

The march groups advanced via Olischana, Iwaniza, Jaroschewka and Fol. Bubny to Romny.

The intention of the corps was to defeat the enemy east of Romny. The *3.* and *4. Panzer-Divisionen* were to attack from the south, *SS-Division "Reich"* from the west and the *10. Infanterie-Division (mot.)* from the north.

Panzergruppe 2 ordered the attack take place on 20 September. However, since the *3. Panzer-Division* was still engaged north of the Udaj River and the *4. Panzer-Division* had almost no fuel, only weak units of the *4. Panzer-Division* initially attacked from the south.

As a result, the *10. Infanterie-Division (mot.)* was to attack with the strongest forces possible from the north via Beshowka, Chorushewka and Nedrigailow into the enemy's deep flank. *SS-Division "Reich"* was to attack with strong forces in the general direction of Nedrigailow. The *4. Panzer-Division* was to attack with units — as it turned out, only a reinforced company — via Lipowaja Dolinea in the general direction of Nedrigailow.

The commander of *SS-Infanterie-Regiment "Der Führer"* moved forward to link up with the combat outposts that were already there and to reconnoiter for the employment of the regiment.

There was an excellent view of the terrain of the upcoming fighting from the command post of a regiment of the *10. Infanterie-Division (mot.)* in the church steeple in Romny.

Situated on a hill, Romny was bounded by the Romen River, which flowed toward the southwest. The terrain rose gradually to a ridgeline that was approximately five kilometers wide on the far side of the river. Elements of the *10. Infanterie-Division (mot.)* were positioned there in a bridgehead.

At that time nothing was to be seen of the enemy. However, reports of the approach of the Russian units named above caused discomfort.

SS-Aufklärungs-Abteilung "Reich" and the reinforced *SS-Infanterie-Regiment "Der Führer"* arrived in Romny in the afternoon. Repeated enemy air attacks had taken place on the division's columns around 1555 hours about 8 kilometers west of Romny.

The *I.* and *II./SS-Infanterie-Regiment "Der Führer"* immediately crossed the river and staged themselves for the attack in the large bridgehead. The high ground around Sidorenkow and the village itself were to be captured with support of the *Sturmgeschütze.*

The *II./SS-Infanterie-Regiment "Der Führer"* was moved about five kilometers further to the northeast.

The Russians attacked the assembly positions of the *I.* and *II./SS-Infanterie-Regiment "Der Führer"* with about thirty tanks, some of them being heavy. The security forces in the bridgehead began to give way. With support from the *Sturmgeschütze "Derrflinger"* and *"Yorck"*, which were employed in the attack sector of the *I./SS-Infanterie-Regiment "Der Führer"*, both battalions launched a counterattack.

Effective support was provided by the crew of an 8.8-cm *Flak* that was positioned south of the river. With great fighting spirit, the men went for the Russian tanks. Any that did not fall victim to the *Flak* and the *Sturmgeschütze* were eliminated with *Teller* mines and concentrated charges made of bundled hand grenades.

Within an hour, 28 Russian tanks were in flames. Two of the heaviest tanks succeeded in fleeing. The *II./SS-Infanterie-Regiment "Der Führer"* attacked a village across the river with the onset of darkness. The companies succeeded in surprising and almost completely destroying an enemy cavalry regiment. Taking advantage of that success, the *I./* and *III./SS-Infanterie-Regiment "Der Führer"* were pushed forward as far as the *II./SS-Infanterie-regiment "Der Führer"* during the night of 20 September.

An enemy group of about 300 cavalrymen with infantry and antitank guns advanced on the road south of Romny and occupied Bobrik. A reinforced company of *Infanterie-Regiment 41* that attacked them was unable to drive off the enemy. (Otto Weidinger, personal notes)

Sub-Section g)

Fighting in the Area East of Kiev
20 - 24 September 1941

20 September 1941

In accordance with the division's order for the attack on 20 September 1941, *SS-Division "Reich"* was to attack the enemy facing the bridgehead position with the attached *Infanterie-Regiment 41* and available elements, capture the commanding heights east of the position and advance via Karowinzy to Nedrigailow.

At 1100 hours *SS-Division "Reich"* set out to the east with *Infanterie-Regiment 41*. The attack made good forward progress. The enemy offered minimal resistance from either infantry or artillery.

At midday, the *III./SS-Infanterie-Regiment "Deutschland"*, which was placed under the direct control of the division, attacked Bobrik and captured it by evening. During that fighting, numerous Russian tanks appeared, however. Ten of the first twelve Russian tanks that appeared were knocked out. By evening the number of enemy tanks that were knocked out rose to 15, including two heavy 52-ton tanks.

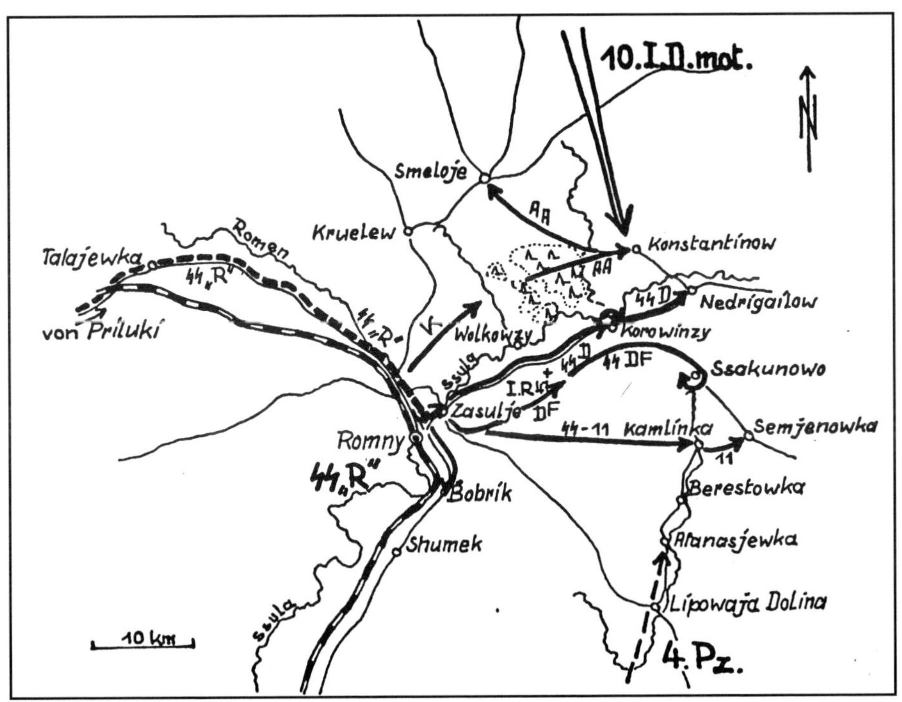

Defensive and Offensive operations of *SS-Divison "Das Reich"* in the Area East of Romny, 19 - 23 September 1941.

SS-Infanterie-Regiment "Der Führer" joined the attack in the afternoon between the Nedrigailow road to the Ssule River. *SS-Kradschützen-Bataillon "Reich"* and *SS-Aufklärungs-Abteilung "Reich"* advanced north of the Ssule. Wolkowzy was captured by evening. From there, the line ran south.

The *2./* and *4./SS-Kradschützen-Bataillon "Reich"* relieved *Kradschützen-Bataillon 40* (*10. Infanterie-Division (mot.)*) in Basowka, northeast of Romny. The enemy, who was located south of the Ssule River, had accurately registered his mortars on the positions and disrupted the relief with his fire. The *3./SS-Kradschützen-Bataillon "Reich"* built a bridgehead at Pustowojtowka in spite of strong enemy defense.

Heavy enemy bombing attacks on *SS-Division "Reich"* continued throughout the day with resultant casualties.

***

The war diary of *SS-Sturmgeschütz-Batterie "Reich"* describes an engagement of the battery's assault guns at the time:

Sturmgeschütz Against a 52-ton Tank

The *"Derfflinger"* and the *"Yorck"* were attached to the *I./SS-Infanterie-Regiment "Der Führer"* around 1200 hours. They moved out from Romny towards the high ground at Ssidorenkoff and the village proper.

Russian tanks attacked from the vicinity of the nearby oil rigs. Both of the assault guns took the tanks under fire. One T 34 drove into a ditch and was immobilized. The others turned off and disappeared behind a hill. Both of the assault guns moved back a short distance.

SS-Oberscharführer Klaffke and *SS-Unterscharführer* Roos dismounted to discuss the situation. At that moment a new Russian tank appeared. It fired at both assault guns and then disappeared again. *SS-Oberscharführer* Klaffke was mortally wounded; *SS-Unterscharführer* Roos was slightly wounded.

The *"Derfflinger"* moved back with the dead *SS-Oberscharführer* Klaffke. At that point the Russian tank, a 52-ton heavy model, appeared once more and moved directly towards the *"Yorck"*. Roos immediately jumped into his vehicle. He succeeded in hitting the turret three times at the shortest possible distance, so that the tank stopped firing. Despite that, the tank continued to move and rammed the assault gun. The crew of the *"Yorck"* immediately bailed out. Frankenbusch was slightly wounded. The hope that the crew of the Russian tank would likewise bail out did not materialize. Instead, the tank pulled back a bit and then moved past the rammed assault gun. It was then immobilized by a round from a 88-mm *Flak*.

Around 1200 hours *SS-Untersturmführer* Kneissl returned with the "Derfflinger". An attack on Ssidorenkoff was jointly conducted with the *I./SS-Infanterie-Regiment "Der Fuuhrer"* at 1600 hours. The *"Derfflinger"* destroyed one gun and captured another; the *"Yorck"* eliminated a field piece and several machine-gun nests. The village was taken.

***

The division passed on to the troops a copy of instructions from *Heeresgruppe Mitte* on how to deal with phosphorus bombs dropped in large numbers in Russian low-level aerial attacks.

The 20th of September did, indeed, bring successes against the enemy in the east, but the fighting continued on the pocket front for the *3. Panzer-Division*. The staff of the Russian 5th Army was located in front of it. The *Kradschützen* of the *3. Panzer-Division* captured the brave commander-in-chief of that army, Major General Potapow, finally putting an end to the fighting in their sector.

For *Armeegruppe Guderian*, the battle of Kiev came to an end. In the days that followed the divisions were to be withdrawn in succession from the front and then assembled to prepare for new employment. Since 13 September *Armeegruppe Guderian* had taken 30,000 prisoners.

21 September 1941

After the Romny bridgehead had been extended by the attack on 20 September, *SS-Division "Reich"* continued the attack on Nedrigailow and south of it as far as the line Kamlitschka — Olschana with strong forces. It also extended the right wing of the bridgehead.

***

The enemy facing the division at that time was identified as two cavalry divisions and strong armored forces. Russian aerial forces played a substantial part in the previous day's operations in the Romny area.

The *4. Panzer-Division* was to advance with its reconnaissance battalion (reinforced with one battery) via Lipowaja Dolina and Beresnowka against the deep southern flank of the enemy and cover the right flank of the corps to the south.

SS-Division "Reich" attacked the enemy in Bobrik at 0600 hours with the *III./SS-Infanterie-Regiment "Deutschland"* and captured the northern portion of the town. Relatively strong enemy forces with armor support remained in the southern portion. Plesski (west of Bobrik) was reported to be clear of the enemy.

Enemy resistance strengthened during the course of the day. *SS-Infanterie-Regiment "Deutschland"* (minus the *III./SS-Infanterie-Regiment "Deutschland"*) attacked on both sides of the Romny — Nedrigailow road. Initially the attack made good progress. However, the southern flank was threatened, so *SS-Infanterie-Regiment "Der Führer"* was employed to attack Hill 91.55 with an attached *Sturmgeschütz* platoon. However, the attack failed to take the hill.

By evening the hills directly southwest of Korowinzy had been captured. North of the Ssula *SS-Aufklärungs-Abteilung "Reich"*, which was in Konstantinowka, had to be pulled back to the Smeloje area in the face of strong enemy forces with armor.

At 1700 hours *SS-Infanterie-Regiment 11* relieved *Infanterie-Regiment 41*, which proceeded via Smeloje to the *10. Infanterie-Division (mot.)*.

The enemy attacked in the large forested area southeast of Smeloje. *SS-Kradschützen-Bataillon "Reich"* screened against them and reconnoitered at Bassowka and south of it. *Pionier-Bataillon 45* reconnoitered from Cmeljow and *Aufklärungs-Abteilung 10* from Beshowka.

The operation against the enemy east of Romny was disrupted by the fact that the *4. Panzer-Division*, as a result of fuel shortage, could not be brought south in time. That brought in question the possibility of encircling the Russian forces at Nedrigailow. In addition, the *3. Panzer-Division* was still tied up in a mission in the Udaj sector that was actually the business of the *XXXXVIII. Panzer-Korps*. It was ordered to depart on 22 September.

The *XXIV. Panzer-Korps* intended to defeat the enemy at Nedrigailow on 22 September 1941 with *SS-Division "Reich"*, the *10. Infanterie-Division (mot.)* and the *4. Panzer-Division*. In order to put a speedy end to the fighting, the *4. Panzer-Division* was to attack the flank and rear of the enemy facing *SS-Division "Reich"*. It was to advance with strong forces via Lipowaja and

Dolino, while *SS-Division "Reich"* was to carry on the attack on Nedrigailow with a strong left wing. At the same time, *SS-Division "Reich"* was to screen to the south. The *10. Infanterie-Division (mot.)* was to attack the enemy north of the Ssula while screening the east flank. *SS-Kradschützen-Bataillon "Reich"* was attached to the division.

While that group of forces operated offensively to defend against a strong enemy relief effort on the outer front of the pocket, the fighting on the inner front of the pocket gradually came to an end.

Werner Haupt cited the 21 September 1941 diary entry of a medical officer of the *3. Panzer-Division* regarding the conclusion of the fighting in the battle of the Kiev Pocket:

> It was a portrait of horror. Corpses of men and horses lay between wagons and equipment of all sorts. Ambulances were overturned, (as well as) heavy antiaircraft guns, cannon, howitzers, tanks, trucks. Some were stuck in the marshlands, some were rammed into houses or trees. Some had plunged down slopes, run into each other or burned up...leaving a scene of utter chaos. (Werner Haupt, *Heeresgruppe Mitte*, p. 82. Bad Nauheim: Podzun-Pallas-Verlag, 1968)

The Southwest Front of the Red Army had met its end in gruesome chaos. The classic pocket battle of the Second World War was over. *Armeegruppe Guderian* alone reported taking 82,000 prisoners.

22 September 1941

SS-Infanterie-Regiment "Deutschland" continued to be at the *Schwerpunkt* of the fighting.

At 0600 hours the regiment attacked with the reinforced *I./SS-Infanterie-Regiment "Deutschland"*, followed by the reinforced *II./SS-Infanterie-Regiment "Deutschland"* and *Sturmgeschütze*. It moved north past Korowinzy to the east while pinning the enemy in the western part of the town. The *I./SS-Infanterie-Regiment "Deutschland"* reached the hill 1200 meters east of Hill 91.5 without significant enemy contact.

The *II./SS-Infanterie-Regiment "Deutschland"*, supported by flanking fire of heavy weapons and by the *Sturmgeschütze* advancing with the battalion, captured the brickyard 500 meters east of Korowinzy in a rapid advance. Concentrated fire exacted heavy losses on the enemy.

SS-Infanterie-Regiment "Der Führer", with its leading elements on the hill near Balturinoff, followed *SS-Infanterie-Regiment "Deutschland"*. It was echeloned to the right rear.

The commanding general of the *XXIV. Panzer-Korps* and the commander of *SS-Division "Reich"* arrived at the command post of *SS-Infanterie-Regiment "Deutschland"* at 1130 hours.

At 1430 hours the *16. (Pionier)/SS-Infanterie-Regiment "Deutschland"* received orders to mop up Korowinzy. Up to that point, it had been bypassed. It carried out the mission during the afternoon. It captured ten guns, two tanks and three antitank guns and brought in about 150 prisoners.

Late in the afternoon *SS-Infanterie-Regiment "Deutschland"* reached the ridgeline 1.5 kilometers southwest of Nedrigailow with the *I./SS-Infanterie-Regiment "Deutschland"* on the right and the *II./SS-Infanterie-Regiment "Deutschland"* on the left. By evening it had advanced to Nedrigailow, initially occupying the western and southern outskirts and penetrating into the western part of the town. The enemy, who had been outflanked in the north by the *10. Infanterie-Division (mot.)*, attempted to break out to the south but was repulsed by the *II./SS-Infanterie-Regiment "Deutschland"*.

The *III./SS-Infanterie-Regiment "Deutschland"* was brought forward to Korowinzy, by truck. The day's report of enemy losses included: 12 guns, six trucks, four heavy machine guns, seven light machine guns, two heavy mortars, three antitank guns, three tanks (44 ton) and one light infantry gun. Five hundred twenty prisoners were taken.

In the course of the day *SS-Infanterie-Regiment 11* attacked east via Bobrik and, supported by *Sturmgeschütze*, reached the Glubokoj estate by evening. The enemy there pulled back rapidly. Isolated enemy tanks remained in the southern portion of Bobrik. They were apparently covering the enemy's retreat.

During the morning *SS-Infanterie-Regiment "Der Führer"* captured the hills southeast of Korowinzy. The enemy, who was retreating from Korowinzy and Kermany toward Nedrigailow, was decimated by *SS-Infanterie-Regiment "Der Führer"* and the *10. Infanterie-Division (mot.)*, which was positioned on the hills north of the Ssula.

SS-Infanterie-Regiment "Der Führer" turned to the south in the afternoon in order to attack strong enemy forces that were reported to be advancing from that direction. In the evening, the *I./* and *II./SS-Infanterie-Regiment "Der Führer"* halted close to Sakunowo, while the *III./SS-Infanterie-Regiment "Der Führer"* was left behind to screen the right flank. Reconnaissance sent out by both battalions during the night reported that Sakunowo was only weakly held by the enemy.

The strength of the strong enemy relief attacks from the east notably abated. However, the German forces were unable to outflank and encircle the enemy.

23 September 1941

At 0030 hours *SS-Infanterie-Regiment "Deutschland"* received orders to move after being relieved by *SS-Kradschützen-Bataillon "Reich"*. It was to assemble and follow *SS-Infanterie-Regiment "Der Führer"*, which was launching an attack at 0600 hours from Hill 86 toward Ssemjonowka. The regiment was to be echeloned to the right rear. *SS-Infanterie-Regiment "Deutschland"* was to proceed to Ssakunowo, attack the enemy there and establish a blocking position facing west on both sides of the town.

During the course of the morning — until 1030 hours — a variety of missions were assigned in response to varied enemy activities. None of these were actually carried out. At 1040 hours the regiment received a verbal order from the division: "*SS-Infanterie-Regiment "Deutschland"* is to be prepared to depart toward the west on its previous approach route effective 1300 hours."

After being relieved by *SS-Kradschützen-Bataillon 11*, the regiment marched at 1300 hours via Romny to the new billeting area in Tschernigow, where it was quartered at 2050 hours.

SS-Infanterie-Regiment 11 continued to attack toward Kamlinke (Kamlitschka) and occupied it by noon. In the afternoon it continued its attack on Semjonowka, which was captured by evening.

Farther to the north, *SS-Aufklärungs-Abteilung "Reich"* mopped up dispersed enemy units in the area between Kamlinke (Kamlitschka) and Ssakunowo.

SS-Infanterie-Regiment "Der Führer" launched an attack in the early morning hours against Ssakunowo (8 kilometers north of Kamlinke) without artillery preparation. The attack continued through Ssakunowo without significant enemy resistance and a hill on the far side was occupied.

Suddenly, heavy firing broke out in the rear of both battalions in which all of the enemy's weapons participated. As was later determined, the enemy had superbly concealed himself in the houses, gardens and cornfields on both sides of Ssakunowo. An enemy regiment-sized formation was involved. The enemy forces were then located between the battalions and the regiment's command post, which had moved up close to the battalions. The enemy attempted to attack the companies from the rear.

The battalions quickly turned and attacked Ssakunowo again from the south, while heavy infantry weapons, especially infantry guns, joined in the fight from the regiment's command post. Extremely heavy fighting developed which lasted throughout the entire day. The enemy joined in from the west with Stalin organs (multiple-rocket launchers). The *III./SS-Infanterie-Regiment "Der Führer"* later captured one of the multiple-rocket launchers.

The fighting in Ssakunowo ended that evening. The enemy left about 1,200 dead behind. German losses were also substantial but bore no relation to the enemy losses.

With that, the Russian relief attack finally ended. It was the last fighting of *SS-Infanterie-Regiment "Der Führer"* in the battle of Kiev. During the fighting the regiment brought in about 15,000 prisoners and captured more than 200 guns. The numbers of destroyed tanks, motor vehicles and other materiel of war are no longer available.

This day of fighting ended the difficult operations of *SS-Division "Reich"* in the pocket battle of Kiev. The division had an outstanding share in the successes on the inner front of the pocket as far as the Priluki area and also in the defense against strong Russian relief attacks from the east in the area east of Romny.

The achievements of the men in the infantry regiments, *SS-Aufklärungs-Abteilung "Reich"* and *SS-Kradschützen-Bataillon "Reich"* were beyond all praise. In addition to the frequent, sometimes heavy fighting, they had to cover great distances on bottomless roads and through mud-bound terrain. They were loaded with weapons, equipment and ammunition and had to march through days of continuous rain. For long periods of time they did not have a stitch of dry clothing on their bodies. Their raw feet were covered with blisters in perpetually sodden boots, so that every step was a fresh agony.

The entire supply services of the division also put in an outstanding performance in supplying the fighting troops with ammunition, fuel and rations. They also repaired and maintained and brought forward weapons, equipment and motor vehicles. Not to be forgotten were the recovery sections of the various units. They were on the go day and night recovering damaged vehicles and freeing those that had become stuck.

The achievements of the supply services during this period, under the supervision of the divisional logistics officer, *SS-Sturmbannführer* Fritz Steinbeck, rank among the greatest logistical accomplishments during the entire campaign in Russia. They succeeded in meeting supply objectives that changed daily during an offensive war of movement in spite of truly catastrophic road conditions resulting from the periods of rain. Many drivers of supply vehicles spent extremely cold nights in their vehicles that were bogged down to the axles as they waited for one of the division's tracked vehicles to come and pull them out of the mire. Yet, it might be only a short interval before they were stuck again and the same, familiar song was repeated from the beginning. The combat troops only had to cover the route from Roslawl to Priluki and to Romny a single time, while the supply services had to cover it many times, often daily, under extremely difficult conditions.

Thanks to the self-sacrificing efforts of the military surgeons and their medical personnel, the ambulance drivers, the doctors and their assistants in the dressing stations and the field hospitals, the medical care of the numerous wounded was constantly assured in spite of extreme difficulties. Many comrades in the division owe their lives to those men.

All members of the division's supply services made possible the division's successful fighting through their exhausting and nerve-racking service. This was an impressive accomplishment.

Regrouping for the new operation began on 23 September. The staging area for *Panzergruppe 2* was moved to Gluchow and the area north of it.

SS-Division "Reich" departed that day from the control of *Armeegruppe Guderian*. It was attached to the *XXXX. Panzer-Korps* under *General der Kavallerie* Stumme.

It was the last time during the war that the division fought under the command of *Generaloberst* Guderian. From the commander of the division to the youngest soldier, the departure from the trustworthy *Panzergruppe 2* was sincerely regretted. Guderian was a sincere friend of the young *Waffen-SS* and always knew how to appraise and acknowledge its accomplishments.

Guderian wrote:

I personally saw the *Leibstandarte SS "Adolf Hitler"* and *SS-Division "Reich"* in combat. Later, as Inspector-General of Armored Troops, I observed numerous *SS* divisions. I can summarize my judgement of them as follows: The *SS* divisions always distinguished themselves with a high standard of discipline, of *esprit de corps*, and conduct in the face of the enemy, They fought shoulder to shoulder with the armored divisions of the Army and, the longer the war went on, the more they became one of us. (Heinz Guderian, *Erinnerungen eines Soldaten*, p. 406. Heidelberg: Verlag Kurt Vowinckel, 1960)

SS-Oberstgruppenführer und Generaloberst der Waffen-SS Paul Hausser wrote in his personal notes:

In spite of the Russian defeat in the pocket battle of Kiev, the Russian history of the war states that the German victory in the Ukraine contributed to the "bankruptcy of the fascist *Blitzkrieg* plans". Was Stalin correct in that?

The German success in that pocket battle was the basis "for the delayed attack on Moscow".

The commander of the division, *SS-Gruppenführer* Hausser, released the following order of the day on 23 September 1941 at the conclusion of the fighting:

Order of the Day

1.) The *Führer* and Supreme Commander has awarded the Knight's Cross of the Iron Cross to *SS-Obersturmbannführer* Ostendorff. That award was not for his service on the general staff but for his personal involvement during the critical night at Uschakowa.

After an enemy penetration on 25 July 1941, *SS-Obersturmbannführer* Ostendorff personally scouted the enemy, prepared for the employment of heavy weapons and then launched and led the immediate counterattack. The enemy was forced back and the former position recaptured. The danger of an enemy breakthrough was eliminated for the division and corps. In so doing, *SS-Obersturmbannführer* Ostendorff personally made an essential contribution to the fact that, after the close of the fighting in the Jelnja salient, the division was able to report that it had held all of its positions without loss of ground.

2.) The *Reichsführer SS* has summoned *SS-Oberführer* Hansen to a new duty position. With that, the first artillery regiment commander of the *Waffen-SS* leaves the division. His accomplishment was the organization and training of the regiment as the cadre for the entire artillery of the *Waffen-SS*. May his credo — "The fastest possible response to fire in support of the infantry" — continue in effect. *SS-Oberführer* Merk will assume temporary command of *SS-Artillerie-Regiment "Reich"*.

3.) After sealing the great pocket east of Kiev, *SS-Division "Reich"* was rapidly moved to the Romny area to stop a strong enemy relief attack as part of the *XXIV. Panzer-Korps* and then destroy those enemy forces.

In carrying out that mission, all the elements of the division again gave their best.

SS-Infanterie-Regiment "Der Führer" initially attacked with *Infanterie-Regiment 41* to extend the bridgehead. During that fighting the antitank forces and heavy *Flak* destroyed numerous medium and heavy tanks.

During the days that followed, *SS-Infanterie-Regiment "Deutschland"* and *SS-Infanterie-Regiment "Der Führer"* advanced rapidly to the east, quickly gaining ground in hard fighting. After destroying strong enemy forces, *SS-Infanterie-Regiment "Deutschland"* was able to penetrate into Nedrigailow in the evening of 22 September and destroy an enemy motorized column. *SS-Infanterie-Regiment "Der Führer"* simultaneously advanced to the southeast to pursue the fleeing enemy. Enemy forces were smashed in bitter fighting on 23 September.

SS-Infanterie-Regiment 11 advanced from the right wing of the bridgehead after the enemy and, in a speedy attack, captured Ssemjonowka. Several tanks were knocked out in that engagement.

SS-Aufklärungs-Abteilung "Reich" and *SS-Kradschützen-Bataillon "Reich"* established the prerequisites for the successful employment of the division in their tireless reconnaissance into broken terrain on the northern flank.

While elements of the division are still fighting, the lead regiment is on the march again to new employment. The demands are great. But we must not forget that it is only when each gives the utmost which a good soldier is capable of giving that the larger objective can be attained.

We follow the *Führer* onward to the final victory.

/signed/ Hausser

The commanding general of the *XXIV. Panzer-Korps*, *General der Panzertruppen* Geyr von Schweppenburg, sent his farewell to the division on 23 September 1941 with the following:

To
SS-Division "Reich"

The outstanding combat performance of *SS-Division "Reich"* as part of the *XXIV. Panzer-Korps* and the style of its command leave me sincerely sorry at its departure.

My thanks, praise and wishes for continued professional good fortune go with this outstanding unit.

/signed/ *Freiherr* von Geyr

The commander-in-chief of *Panzergruppe 2, Generaloberst* Guderian, released the following communique on the departure of the division from his command on 23 September 1941:

Order of the Day

Soldiers of SS-Division "*Reich*"!

On 1 September 1941 the division set out from the Smolensk area for employment on the right wing of the *Panzergruppe* in fighting for the crossing of the Desna. As a consequence of terrible roads and massive downpours, the march placed unheard of demands on men and equipment. The division was strung out for six days.

The enemy front was breached in heavy fighting, the Desna and Seim Rivers crossed and, on 13 September, the ring around the enemy east of Kiev was closed by establishing contact with a *Panzergruppe* that was advancing from the south. The commander-in-chief of the Russian 5th Army fell into our hands. The entire Russian southern front has been shattered. In these weeks you have, yet again, done your duty in full measure and taken all difficulties in stride, even though you have not had a single break since 22 June 1941.

The fighting for the railroad bridge in Makoschin added a page of honor to the history of the Division.

I thank you for your spirit that has been proven so often in fighting and in offensive operations. My best wishes for your future go with the division as it now departs from the *Panzergruppe*.

Hail Germany and Hail to our *Führer*!
/signed/ Guderian

A situation report to the *SS* Main Office in Berlin on 27 September 1941 stated the following regarding the fighting that had just come to an end:

The fighting that resulted in the destruction of the Russian relief attack of a cavalry corps (two cavalry divisions, one infantry division, one armored brigade) east of Romny ended on 24 September. The final advances of *SS-Infanterie-Regiment "Der Führer"* and *SS-Infanterie-Regiment 11* caused the enemy significant losses in men and equipment. It was largely due to the efforts of the division that the relief attack was repulsed...

...Losses since the start of fighting as part of the *XXIV. Panzer-Korps*: 1,700 men. We hope that replacements will arrive in time for the new employment.

The situation with respect to motor vehicles is, naturally, getting worse. Probably 60% are in service.

/signed/ Hausser

Movement to the Area West of Roslawl and Short Refitting: 24 September - 2 October 1941

After relief of the elements that were in contact with the enemy in the area of operations east of Romny, *SS-Division "Reich"* set out to the west on

24 September 1941. *SS-Infanterie-Regiment "Deutschland"* had already been moved in the evening of 23 September to the Timoschewskago estate — Welikije Bubny area.

The route of march led via Romny, Itschnja and Tschernigow and then northward via Gomel and Dowsk to the area west of Roslawl. The following order of march was established: March serial Klingenberg; march serial *SS-Infanterie-Regiment "Der Führer"*; march serial *SS-Infanterie-Regiment "Deutschland"* with integrated division weapons; and, march serial *SS-Artillerie-Regiment "Reich"* with integrated division weapons.

On 26 September the *XXXX. Panzer-Korps* broke through the enemy positions far to the east toward Mosalk — Juchnow. To do that required the complete efforts of the *258. Infanterie-Division*, which placed its main effort on the left. *SS-Division "Reich"* would be attached to the corps a few days later.

It was intended that *SS-Division "Reich"* be brought forward behind the right wing of the *XXXX. Panzer-Korps.*

The division reached its new billeting area on both sides of the Propoisk — Tscherikow — Kritschew road west of Roslawl by 28 September 1941. It traveled under conditions of nighttime frost and cold weather. The division staff quarters were in Usztjz.

The division was only granted a few days rest and refitting in that area — until 2 October — after weeks of heavy fighting. Replacement personnel arrived at the last minute. Noncommissioned officers with experience at the front made use of every free moment to put the final polish on the new arrivals before the impending operations. Vehicles, weapons and equipment were thoroughly overhauled. *SS-Infanterie-Regiment "Deutschland"* received 750 men as replacements. Other formations of the division received similar personnel replenishments.

Just as important were the few hours of leisure provided for physical and mental recovery after the immense strains of the employment that had just been completed.

On 1 October the commander of the division, *SS-Obergruppenführer* Hausser, established contact with the *XXXX. Panzer-Korps.*

***

The war diary of *SS-Infanterie-Regiment "Deutschland"* lists the following losses to the regiment during the period from 24 June 1941 to 30 September 1941:

	Killed	Wounded	Missing	Ill
Officers:	16	37	8	2
Noncommissioned officers and enlisted personnel:	355	963	24	114
Total:	371	1,000	32	116

Total losses: 1,519 officers, noncommissioned officers and enlisted personnel.

The Attack on Moscow – Operation "Taifun": 2 October – 4 December 1941

Overall Situation

The commander of the division at the time, *SS-Oberstgruppenführer und Generaloberst der Waffen-SS* Paul Hausser, wrote in his personal notes:

The German army was roughly aligned from the Sea of Asow to the Gulf of Finland. Every forward step broadened the area as if one were walking out the large end of a funnel.

Was it still possible to make up for the time lost during the Kiev offensive?

The motorized formations had covered approximately 1,000 kilometers, to which the average distance to Kiev and back added another 600 kilometers. The distance to Moscow was yet another 500 kilometers.

The mobility of the motorized units was precarious. The combat strengths were notably reduced but the feeling of superiority was still complete. The *Luftwaffe* was still superior to that of the enemy.

Strong enemy groups faced the front, particularly along the main roads. The Juchnow, Wjasma, Gshatsk and Rshew groups were subordinated to the staff of Timoschenko's West Front.

Preparations for Operation "Taifun"

Even at the start of the Battle of Kiev, the *OKH* had included in its directives on 6 September 1941 the order for *Heeresgruppe Mitte* to attack to the east as soon as possible. It had the mission of eliminating the enemy east of Smolensk in a double envelopment toward Wjasma. It was to employ strong armored forces on both wings.

Only after the completion of the Kiev encirclement operation was *Heeresgruppe Mitte* to start the pursuit toward Moscow with its right wing on the Oka River and its left on the upper Volga.

In accordance with that order, *Heeresgruppe Mitte* had to regroup its forces even during the course of the battle of Kiev.

Panzergruppe 4 (Commander-in-Chief: *Generaloberst* Hoepner) was brought from the northern sector of the Eastern Front via Nevel to strengthen the army group.

The *5. Panzer-Division*, which was supposed to have been shipped to Africa, came from Germany. The *Luftwaffe* also provided strong forces. The *VIII. Flieger-Korps* (aviation corps) (*General der Flieger Freiherr* von Richthofen) was also shifted back from the northern sector to the area of *Luftflotte 2* (2nd Air Force) in the center. The *II. Flak-Korps* (*Generalleutnant* Deßloch) was brought in from the southern sector of the Eastern Front.

Organization of Heeresgruppe Mitte from South to North

Heeresgruppe Mitte was organized from south to north as follows:

Armeegruppe Guderian (*Generaloberst* Guderian)
2. Armee (*Generaloberst Freiherr* von Weichs)
4. Armee (*Feldmarschall* von Kluge)
Panzergruppe 4 (*Generaloberst* Hoepner)
9. Armee (*Generaloberst* Strauss)
Panzergruppe 3 (*Generaloberst* Hoth)

As part of *Panzergruppe 4*, *SS-Division "Reich"* was initially attached to the *LVII. Panzer-Korps* (*General der Panzertruppen* Kuntzen) on 24 September 1941 and then, as of 3 October 1941, to the *XXXX. Panzer-Korps* (*General der Kavallerie* Stumme). The *2. Panzer-Division* and the familiar *10. Panzer-Division* (known from joint employment with *Panzer-Regiment 7* in Poland in 1939, the advance to Jelnja in 1941 and fighting together in the Jelnja salient) fought in that corps.

Heeresgruppe Mitte headquarters had issued an attack order on 26 September whereby the *4. Armee* with attached *Panzergruppe 4* was to attack Moscow with its *Schwerpunkt* on both sides of the Roslawl — Moscow road.

Panzergruppe Guderian, renamed *Armeegruppe Guderian*, was to turn 180 degrees from the Kiev front and move up to the Gluchow sector. As a result, it was unable to grant its divisions even a single day of rest. In guarding the right wing of the army group, *Armeegruppe Guderian* had been given the most distant attack objective. Therefore, it was to start its attack several days ahead of the rest of the army group.

In the last four weeks, while *Heeresgruppe Mitte's* offensive made no additional eastward progress, the Red Army reorganized. It positioned the following twelve armies —newly formed, reorganized or brought from the rear area — from north to south: 22nd, 29th, 30th, 19th, 16th, 20th, 24th, 43rd, 50th, 3rd, 13th and 40th Armies.

Armeegruppe Guderian set out as ordered on 30 September in thick morning fog. Even though not all the corps was at its starting positions and the right wing was initially actually unprotected, the attack rolled forward.

The veteran *XXIV. Panzer-Korps* advanced on both sides of the Sswesk —

Orel road with the *3.* and *4. Panzer-Divisionen* in the lead and surprised the enemy. The corps captured Sswesk on the next day while the *10. Infanterie-Division (mot.)* provided flank security on the right.

The *XXXXVII. Panzer-Korps* also advanced rapidly north of Sswesk and into the Karatschew area west of Orel with its *17.* and *18. Panzer-Divisionen*.

In two days these two corps achieved an incredible success. They had broken through the Soviet front and penetrated 130 kilometers. And then they ran out of fuel. Despite this, they had secured the right wing of *Heeresgruppe Mitte*. (paraphrased from Werner Haupt, *Heeresgruppe Mitte*", pp. 86-87. Bad Nauheim: Podzun-Pallas-Verlag, 1968.)

Sub-Section h)

Breaking Through the Desna Position 2 - 4 October 1941

During the night of 1/2 October, when Operation Typhoon (*Unternehmen "Taifun"*) began, the leaders and commanders of the units read Hitler's order of the day:

The final decisive battle of this year will strike the enemy a destructive blow...With it we will free the *Reich* and all of Europe for all time from the danger that has loomed as a terror over the continent ever since the time of the Huns and, later, the advancing Mongol hordes...

Therefore, the German people will be even closer to you in the coming weeks than ever before!

The Commander-in-Chief of *Panzergruppe 4, Generaloberst* Hoepner, issued the following order of the day on 2 October:

Order of the Day

2 October is the birthday of the immortal *Generalfeldmarschall*...von Hindenburg.

He was the first one to win great victories over the Russians and, in so doing, prevent their invasion of the *Reich*.

On his birthday we begin a decisive engagement with the last great Russian group of forces. Let our motto for the *Panzergruppe* on 2 October 1941 be: "Hindenburg — Forward — Victory!"

/signed/ Hoepner

Werner Haupt wrote the following regarding the start of Operation "Typhoon"

The offensive against Moscow began on 2 October in sunny fall weather. Once again, as on the first day, the bomber squadrons of *Luftflotte 2* flew ahead and cleared the way, which the artillery batteries had already softened up. The formations were fairly well filled out with men and materiel — and the German soldier still felt superior to his Russian opponent. (Werner Haupt, *Heeresgruppe Mitte"*, p. 88. Bad Nauheim: Podzun-Pallas-Verlag, 1968.)

Panzergruppe 4 launched the attack at 0530 hours. Within two hours its corps had built bridgeheads on the east bank of the Desna.

The *XXXX. Panzer-Korps* forced the enemy back. By evening *Generalmajor* Fischer's *10. Panzer-Division* was already 30 kilometers past the Desna River and had broken open the Soviet front. There were no more cohesive Russian formations facing it.

At 1730 hours *SS-Division "Reich"* received orders from *Panzergruppe 4*. Starting on 3 October from Kritschew, it was to proceed to the Pokinitscha — Pigorje — Malaja Koschkina — Ladischino (east of Roslawl) area. After arriving there the division would be attached to the *XXXX. Panzer-Korps*. Combat engineers were to be integrated toward the front of the column of march.

On 3 October, starting at 0600 hours, the division set out for the area east of Roslawl in the following order of march: *SS-Kradschützen-Bataillon "Reich"*, *SS-Aufklärungs-Abteilung "Reich"*, *SS-Panzer-Jäger-Abteilung "Reich"*, *SS-Pionier-Bataillon "Reich"*, *SS-Flak-Abteilung "Reich"*, elements of *SS-Artillerie-Regiment "Reich"*, *SS-Infanterie-Regiment "Deutschland"*, *SS-Infanterie-Regiment "Der Führer"*, *SS-Infanterie-Regiment 11*, divisional medical services and divisional supply services.

Upon reaching the designated area, the division was attached to the *XXXX. Panzer-Korps* (*General der Kavallerie* Stumme).

The *10.* and *2. Panzer-Divisionen* crossed the Bolwa River during the evening of 3 October.

The last elements of the division reached their billeting area in the early morning hours of 4 October. *SS-Division "Reich"* followed the *10. Panzer-Division*, and its leading elements reached the Desna. After assuming tactical formations, they closed up along the route of advance and awaited further orders.

The route of advance led via Kassizy (23 kilometers southeast of Roslawl), Prigory, Gromaschowo, Pawloskaja and then over a bridge two kilometers northeast of Schtschipan. The combat organization of the division was: *SS-Pionier-Bataillon "Reich"*, *SS-Aufklärungs-Abteilung "Reich"*, *SS-Kradschützen-Bataillon "Reich"*, division command group, march serial *SS-Infanterie-Regiment "Deutschland"*, march serial Blume (*SS-Flak-Abteilung "Reich"*), march serial *SS-Infanterie-Regiment "Der Führer"* and march serial *SS-Infanterie-Regiment 11*.

On 5 October the *10. Panzer-Division* advanced 40 kilometers and captured Juchnow.

SS-Division "Reich" moved forward to Bolwa. Elements of the division reached Makroje behind the *10. Panzer-Division*. The last elements of the division crossed the Desna.

The route of advance continued over the Desna bridge (2 kilometers northeast of Schtschipan), then via Buda, Bolijschtschaja Lutna — Murajewka and Makroje.

The *2. Armee*, adjoining on the right, finally gained freedom of movement, which the attack on Brjansk by the *17. Panzer-Division* made evident.

The Brjansk Pocket is Formed

The Soviet 43rd and 50th Armies fell back to the west. The infantry divisions of the *2. Armee* followed the enemy closely. On the following day they reached the Brjansk — Roslawl road. With that, the Brjansk pocket began to close.

The *XXXX. Panzer-Korps* directed the *2.* and *10. Panzer-Divisionen* north from Juchnow toward Gshatsk. At that point, however, *OKH* intervened and demanded that the pocket was not to be closed there but, according to a *Führer* order, at Wjasma. Thereupon *Panzergruppe 4* turned to the northwest to encircle the enemy in the Wjasma area. For the *10. Panzer-Division*, the attack objective was Wjasma and, for the *2. Panzer-Division*, the area to its south.

6 October 1941

SS-Division "Reich" rejoined the fighting on 6 October.

> The division's mission is to pass through Juchnow and then turn north. It is to proceed on its own and with an open right flank to the area between Gshatsk and Wjasma. It has a simultaneous dual mission: on the one hand, screen from there to the east and northeast against enemy relief attacks and, on the other hand, be prepared for possible employment north of Wjasma — oriented west — to close the Wjasma pocket.

SS-Aufklärungs-Abteilung 2 and *SS-Kradschützen-Bataillon "Reich"* proceeded at the head of the division. The reconnaissance battalion was assigned the mission of proceeding to Jegorje Kuleschi and reconnoitering from there to the line: Shelonja — Mjeshettschino — road to Gshatsk — railroad line to Wjasma.

SS-Kradschützen-Bataillon was to scout a route for the division as far as the highway at Spasskoje.

The reinforced *SS-Infanterie-Regiment "Deutschland"* marched the entire day. At 1115 hours it had a skirmish at Schatjescha, where weak enemy motorized forces were crossing the Wora River to the east at several places.

SS-Aufklärungs-Abteilung "Reich" ran into enemy resistance at 1330 hours

After the fighting at Jelnja the men of *SS-Division "Reich"* help the Russians bring in the harvest during a brief period of rest.

Farewell visit of the commanding general of the *XXXXVI. Panzer-Korps*, *General der Panzertruppen* von Vietinghoff-Scheel, seen with the commander of *SS-Division "Reich"*, *SS-Gruppenführer und Generalleutnant der Waffen-SS* Hausser. *SS-Division "Reich"* was attached to the *XXXXVI. Panzer-Korps* from the beginning of the Russian campaign until the end of the fighting at Jelnja.

Left: *Generaloberst* Guderian, commander-in-chief of *Panzergruppe 2* on a visit to the front.

Right: The commanding general of the *XXIV. Panzer-Korps, General der Panzertruppen* Geyr von Schweppenburg. *SS-Division "Reich"* was attached to the *XXIV. Panzer-Korps* during the battle of Kiew.

Grenadiers of *SS-Division "Reich"* — Assault troop leader with his men.

The People of the Ukraine. **Above**: Ukrainian women in traditional costume. **Below**: "Recreation" in a Ukrainian village.

Right: Ukrainian miller. **Left**: Peasant woman with child.

Right: *SS-Sturmbannführer Hansmann*, commander of the *II./SS-Infanterie-Regiment "Deutschland"*. **Left:** *Generaloberst* Guderian talking with the division adjutant, *SS-Hauptsturmführer* Kröger.

Opposite page, left: *SS-Sturmbannführer* Schill and Harzer, *SS-Hauptsturmführer* Rentrop and *SS-Sturmbannführer* Tietz, Lingner and Barnert (from left to right). **Opposite page, right**: *SS-Sturmbannführer* Klingenberg, commander of *SS-Kradschützen-Bataillon "Reich"*. **Right**: *SS-Hauptsturmführer* Rentrop, *SS-Flak-Abteilung "Reich"*, led an assault troop in a bold *coup de main* that captured the important Desna railroad bridge and prevented its demolition.

Opposite page: *Stukas* smash enemy resistance on both sides of the Desna. **Above**: *SS-Aufklärungs-Abteilung "Reich"* with armored cars and motorcyclists on foot crossing the bridge at Makoschin to advance to the south. **Below**: The *5./SS-Infanterie-Regiment "Der Führer"* with two *Sturmgeschütze* in an immediate counterattack at Priluki.

Above: How the successful immediate counterattack ended for the Russians. **Below**: A *Fieseler Storch* liason/observation aircraft of the division landing.

Above: Laying out air-recognition panels at the division command post. **Below**: Shot-down Russian night-harassment aircraft.

at Sacharowo and was pinned on Hill 186.8. At 1725 hours the reinforced *III./SS-Infanterie-Regiment "Deutschland"* attacked the hill from Sacharowoas as the advance-guard battalion.

After a brief fight, , the enemy was forced out of their positions with supporting fire from the reconnaissance battalion and fell back to the north. The engagement evidently involved a strong Russian rear guard with several guns. After the enemy fell back, the motorcycle battalion advanced to Jegorje Kuleschi, captured the road and railroad bridge there and, as darkness fell, built a bridgehead on both sides of the route of advance.

The advance guard of *SS-Infanterie-Regiment "Deutschland"* reached its objective of the day — Iwanowskaja — at 1945 hours and screened to the east and west. The division command post was at Krapiwka.

During the day isolated low-level enemy air attacks and bombing of *SS-Infanterie-Regiment "Deutschland"* caused slight casualties.

Werner Haupt wrote the following regarding the general situation of the *4. Armee*:

> The *10. Panzer-Division* advanced directly toward Wjasma from the south. It entered the city on 6 October.
>
> The divisions of the *4. Armee* followed close behind the armored divisions leading the advance. On the third day of the attack the army was already behind the Russian front east of Jelnja! At that point the enemy abandoned the fight. At that point the *IX. Armee-Korps*, which had been attacking frontally and taking quite a battering, was able to take the offensive. The *292. Infanterie-Division* (*Generalmajor* Lucht) captured Jelnja on 6 October (which was also the day of the first snowfall).
>
> The Wjasma pocket and the Brjansk pocket gradually burnt themselves out...At the same time *SS-Division "Reich"* set out from Juchnow and advanced irresistibly northward to Gshatsk. (Werner Haupt, *"Heeresgruppe Mitte"*, p. 91. Bad Nauheim: Podzun-Pallas-Verlag, 1968.)

With that, *SS-Division "Reich"* was far to the rear of the Russian Jelnja front. During July and August it had fought for weeks along with the *10. Panzer-Division* and *Infanterie-Regiment "Großdeutschland"* in a murderous defense of the Jelnja salient. Only a few weeks later it was south of Gshatsk behind the Jelnja front and moving to block the Smolensk — Moscow highway. Who would have believed at that time that within a relatively short period, all of the Russian forces in the central sector would have been broken through, split up and encircled and there was no course left for them but to lay down their arms?

A warning order of the division for 7 October included, among other things:

> 1.) ...Up to this point new enemy forces have not been identified coming from the east. The enemy was retreating in strength along the Wjasma — Gshatsk highway on 6 October.

2.) The division intends to advance north on the road and block the two roads coming from west and southwest as well as the railroad line at Gshatsk.

3.) Coordinating instructions:

a) *SS-Kradschützen-Bataillon "Reich"* is to secure the road and railroad bridge at Jegerje — Kaluschi, reconnoiter east of the route of advance to the right flank and be prepared to be committed forward on a new mission on 7 October.

b) *SS-Aufklärungs-Abteilung "Reich"*...is to continue reconnaissance and screen the right flank. *Schwerpunkt* of the reconnaissance: Area around Gshatsk.

c) *SS-Infanterie-Regiment "Deutschland"*...is to mop up the terrain gained during the night on both sides of the route of advance after mines have been cleared by the reinforced *16. (Pionier)/SS-Infanterie-Regiment "Deutschland"*. This work is to be accomplished as rapidly as possible so that the leading elements can start the advance via the bridge at Jegerje — Kuleschi to Gshatsk at 0800 hours.

It is essential to capture and secure the two bridges at Szawinkin and Schatjescha. Every effort should be made during the advance so that, as soon as strong enemy resistance appears on the road and after the enemy has been pinned frontally, a wide flanking movement is made — preferably to the east — outflanking the enemy and going over to pursuit with encirclement...

7 October 1941

At 0800 hours the commander of the division was at the command post of *SS-Infanterie-Regiment "Deutschland"* and altered its mission orders. After the regiment reached the first objective of the attack — Worja River crossing north of Upolosa — it was to turn to the northwest via Tubitschino and Kamjenka and move towards Wyrubowo with the mission of blocking the highway at Welitschowo to both the west and east.

SS-Aufklärungs-Abteilung "Reich" and *SS-Kradschützen-Bataillon "Reich"*, which had advanced past the advance-guard battalion of *SS-Infanterie-Regiment "Deutschland"* during some portions of the advance, ran into enemy forces north of the Worja River. The enemy forces rapidly fell back. Enemy resistance, however, strengthened at Tubitschino and Scharapewo, where it was broken with *Sturmgeschütze*.

At 1215 hours an enemy motorized column consisting of about 300 trucks was spotted on the road from Tschaly to Tupitschino. The column was attacked by the reconnaissance battalion on the right and the *II./SS-Infanterie-Regiment "Deutschland"* on the left of the route of advance. The column, however, fell back to the north as soon as it was attacked.

The division was informed at 0810 hours that employment to the west toward Wjasma would probably follow on 8 October.

At 1420 hours the hills 1.5 kilometers northwest of Scharaponowa were captured by the *II./SS-Infanterie-Regiment "Deutschland"* with *Sturmgeschütze*.

At that point the following order arrived at *XXXX. Panzer-Korps* from *Panzergruppe 4*: "*SS-Division "Reich"* is to capture Gshatsk as soon as possible in preparation for continuation of the attack on Moscow. Diversion of forces from this division for the Wjasma pocket is not desired."

At 1550 hours the *II./SS-Infanterie-Regiment "Deutschland"* captured Michejewa. The enemy fell back to the north. Accordingly, the *II./SS-Infanterie-Regiment "Deutschland"* was turned to the northwest to Sloboda Potowkaja, which it reached at 1645 hours. It then screened to the west. The bridge there was in very poor condition and required repairs by a company of combat engineers. They were immediately brought forward.

At 1730 hours the *I./SS-Infanterie-Regiment "Deutschland"* set out as the new advance guard. It continued the advance to the north in motor march and reached Kamjonka. At the same time *SS-Aufklärungs-Abteilung "Reich"* arrived at Mischejewa and captured it with the help of *Sturmgeschütze. Sturmgeschütz "Ziethen"* was damaged by a hit and was immobilized.

All of the routes that were scouted by the *1./SS-Aufklärungs-Abteilung "Reich"* and the *15./SS-Infanterie-Regiment "Deutschland"* were in very poor condition and could only be used in dry weather. Therefore, the *I./SS-Infanterie-Regiment "Deutschland"* set out at 1950 hours on foot to Kamjenka, which was captured by about 2300 hours. That day *SS-Infanterie-Regiment "Deutschland"* lost two dead and 18 wounded, including two officers. Eight heavy machine guns, one tank (20 ton), two guns (one of which was a 21-cm mortar) and two heavy mortars were captured and 184 prisoners (including four officers) were taken on that day.

A member of the *3./SS-Infanterie-Regiment "Deutschland"* wrote the following in his diary for 7 October 1941:

> We got going again early in the morning. Our column stopped frequently. Isolated Russians, some with vehicles, were in the area. They did not recognize us as enemy until too late and swung around. We bagged several vehicles. Sidecar motorcycles chased fleeing vehicles and stopped them. We nabbed several Russian trucks. One battalion in front of us was already fighting. You could tell by the noise of fighting and the burning villages ahead of us. In the evening we dismounted and continued about ten more kilometers on foot to a built-up area, where we halted. We took a great many prisoners who were wandering around in the area without any leadership.

In the evening the following radio traffic from the *XXXX. Panzer-Korps* arrived at the division: "*SS-Division "Reich"* is to capture Gshatsk as a prerequisite for the operation to the east and, at the same time, cover the rear of the *XXXX. Panzer-Korps*."

The Wjasma Pocket is Closed (Overall Situation)

The *9. Armee* (with attached *Panzergruppe 3* (Hoth)), which was the friendly forces on the left, had made the great swing to the southeast on 4

October. The *7. Panzer-Division* attacked from the northwest to the highway at Wjasma, occupied a 15-kilometer stretch of the road and established contact with the *10. Panzer-Division* in Wjasma. With that, the great pocket at Wjasma had also been closed. It was the second one after the Briansk pocket. Elements of the Soviet 16th, 19th, 20th and 32nd Armies were encircled between Jarzewo and Wjasma.

The *OKH* believed its planning had been confirmed by that great success. On 7 October 1941 it ordered: "*4. Armee* is to immediately advance against and over the Kaluga — Moshaisk line with attached *Panzergruppe 4* attacking along the Wjasma — Moscow highway."

Sub-Section i)

Advance via Gshatsk: 8 - 13 October 1941

The mission for *SS-Division "Reich"* — the capture of Gshatsk — was a significant prerequisite for the continued German advance toward Moscow.

In the first hours of morning, *SS-Infanterie-Regiment "Deutschland"* received the order to advance on the old route of advance from Juchnow to Gshatsk so as to reach the Smolensk — Moscow highway as rapidly as possible.

The *I./SS-Infanterie-Regiment "Deutschland"* was ordered to turn around in Kamjoka and follow the regiment in a motorized march.

The *III./SS-Infanterie-Regiment "Deutschland"* moved forward dismounted on the route of advance in order to close up with *SS-Aufklärungs-Abteilung "Reich"*, which was held up in an attack north of Maschina. The infantry battalion was to attack left of the road. The *II./SS-Infanterie-Regiment "Deutschland"* followed in a motorized march.

At 0730 hours the reconnaissance battalion reported a heavy Russian attack in regimental size. The *II./SS-Infanterie-Regiment "Deutschland"* then dismounted. It initially attacked with the reinforced *6./SS-Infanterie-Regiment "Deutschland"* via Skaljatino into the enemy's right flank. The main body of the battalion attacked the enemy at Pitrjajka after swinging to the left. It reached Pitrjajka at 0845 hours. After a short pause, it continued the attack.

The *III./SS-Infanterie-Regiment "Deutschland"*, after dismounting north of Strica, attacked and reached the hill at Petrjajka where it then got bogged down. After the artillery had gone into position, the attack was renewed at 1030 hours with the reconnaissance battalion on the right and the *III./SS-Infanterie-Regiment "Deutschland"* on the left of the road. The objective of the regiment's attack was Pokroff.

At 1040 hours the *II./SS-Infanterie-Regiment "Deutschland"* reached the high ground west of Waschki. At that time a battalion-sized enemy force fell back before the *III./SS-Infanterie-Regiment "Deutschland"*.

At 1115 hours the *II./SS-Infanterie-Regiment "Deutschland"* reached the southern outskirts of Pokroff and, by 1200 hours, pushed the attack through to the northern outskirts.

During that fighting the *Sturmgeschütz "Prinz Eugen"* was knocked out by a hit from an antiaircraft gun. *SS-Hauptsturmführer* Günster, the gunner and the driver were killed. The loader was only slightly wounded and brought the report to the *II./SS-Infanterie-Regiment "Deutschland"*. The death of the commander of the assault -gun battery was a serious loss for the division.

The enemy was unable to take any more firm stands since *SS-Infanterie-Regiment "Deutschland"* stayed right on his heels. The enemy had no artillery, but did have strong antiaircraft guns that he had skillfully built into sectors of his defense. The Russian antiaircraft guns were a big nuisance and presented an extremely serious danger to the *Sturmgeschütze*.

The second attack objective for the regiment was Nikolskoje. At 1305 hours the bridge north of Ssonesna was reached and *SS-Infanterie-Regiment "Deutschland"* continued the advance toward Ssiwzowa. Since the enemy fell back and was massing on the route of the advance, the *III./SS-Artillerie-Regiment "Reich"* was brought forward to engage the enemy from open firing positions. The regiment also continued to move forward along the route of advance.

Petelina was captured at 1335 hours. Strong enemy units and approximately two batteries of artillery fell back into the woods east of Nikolskoje. The *III./SS-Artillerie-Regiment "Reich"* fired from open firing positions with two batteries and pinned the enemy down in the open in front of the woods. *Stukas* returning from sorties also strafed the enemy.

At 1430 hours the *II./SS-Infanterie-Regiment "Deutschland"* fought its way to the southern outskirts of Nikolskoje and had it firmly under control by 1545 hours.

Since the previous mission of the *I./SS-Infanterie-Regiment "Deutschland"* had been overtaken by events, the battalion was brought forward to the route of advance . At 1630 hours, in spite of the onset of snow squalls, the battalion set out in motor march to reach the Smolensk — Moscow highway. About 500 meters north of Alexijewa, *Sturmgeschütz "Schill"*, which was in the lead, was knocked out by antiaircraft gun fire. *SS-Untersturmführer* Kneissl's crew were wounded but were able to get away.

The *III./SS-Infanterie-Regiment "Deutschland"*, which had mounted up again after vehicles were brought forward, followed behind the *I./SS-Infanterie-Regiment "Deutschland"*. At 1930 hours the *III./SS-Infanterie-Regiment "Deutschland"* reported that it had reached the major east-west highway (presumably the main supply route) and blocked it in both directions.

At 2010 hours the following report arrived from the *I./SS-Infanterie-Regiment "Deutschland"*:

According to local inhabitants, (we have gone) three kilometers past the highway. At present, (we are receiving) heavy resistance from antiaircraft guns or tanks on the road. We have identified infantry screening the road with light machine guns right and left of the road every 200 meters.

The *I./SS-Infanterie-Regiment "Deutschland"* had crossed the highway to the north in the snow squalls without realizing it. The *III./SS-Infanterie-Regiment "Deutschland"* took over blocking the road.

At 2025 hours the *I./SS-Infanterie-Regiment "Deutschland"* radioed the regiment:

According to interrogation of local inhabitants and contrary to the maps, the highway runs 200 meters south of Swerschkowo. Reconnoitering to railroad north of Swerschkowo.

The main bodies of the *I./* and *III./SS-Infanterie-Regiment "Deutschland"* spent the night in Swerschkowo; the *II./SS-Infanterie-Regiment "Deutschland"* and the staff of the regiment remained in Alexejewka.

On 8 October *SS-Infanterie-Regiment "Deutschland"* captured seven antiaircraft guns, five trucks, one light tank and 23 machine guns. It also took 335 prisoners. Its own losses were:

Killed: 11 noncommissioned officers and enlisted personnel
Wounded: 5 officers and 42 noncommissioned officers and enlisted personnel
Missing: 2 enlisted men.

For the *Sturmgeschütz* battery, 8 October was a day of particularly heavy fighting. It was successful but with heavy losses. The *Sturmgeschütz* battery described the day in its war diary as follows:

The Commander of the *Sturmgeschütz* Battery is Killed

SS-Infanterie-Regiment "Deutschland" continued its advance northward with the mission of reaching the Smolensk — Moscow highway as rapidly as possible.

Sturmgeschütz "Prinz Eugen", with *SS-Hauptsturmführer* Günster, and *Sturmgeschütz "Derfflinger"*, with *SS-Unterscharführer* Wittowitz, were employed with the *II./SS-Infanterie-Regiment "Deutschland"*. *Sturmgeschütz "Schill"*, with *SS-Untersturmführer* Kneissl, and *Sturmgeschütz "Blücher"*, with *SS-Unterscharführer* Schulz, were with the *III./SS-Infanterie-Regiment "Deutschland"*.

At 0900 hours the *II./SS-Infanterie-Regiment "Deutschland"* attacked at Slobodka. The Russians fell back. *Sturmgeschütz "Prinz Eugen"* was hit by a round from an antitank gun during the pursuit. The hit shattered the driver's periscope and the panoramic gun sight. The assault gun had to halt. The damage was corrected in one hour, during which the attack continued. Kneissl's platoon advanced along the road with the *III./SS-Infanterie-Regiment "Deutschland"*. Infantry targets were engaged with submachine-gun fire as they appeared.

Sturmgeschütz "Prinz-Eugen" rejoined the lead elements on the left of the route of advance at Nishnjaja-Petrjajka. Two well-camouflaged antiaircraft guns were spotted and immediately knocked out with several rounds. At the same time, the *"Prinz Eugen"* was fired on from the right by two antiaircraft guns. Before the assault gun could open fire, a direct hit penetrated the armor near the driver's periscope. *SS-Hauptsturmführer* Günster, the gunner, *SS-Sturmmann* Bückle, and the driver, *SS-Sturmmann* Lindenbach, were killed. The loader, *SS-Sturmmann* Paprocki, immediately left the assault gun with minor injuries and reported the death of his comrades at the battalion command post.

Sturmgeschütz "Derfflinger" got stuck in marshy ground.

In the meantime, *SS-Untersturmführer* Kneissl arrived with the *"Schill"* and knocked out the Russian guns (7.62-cm antiaircraft) with several direct hits. The pursuit of the fleeing Russians was renewed. Guns and columns were fired on. The *"Schill"* towed the *"Derfflinger"* out of the swampy ground.

The two assault guns rejoined the advance guard of the *I./SS-Infanterie-Regiment "Deutschland"* at Nikolskoje, and the pursuit of the Russians continued. The *"Blücher"* destroyed two antiaircraft guns close to Slobodka. Heavy snow squalls set in at 1700 hours. The *"Schill"* took the lead with mounted infantry. About 500 meters north of Alexejewa the *"Schill"* stopped to clean its optics. At that point a Russian truck and a gun were spotted at the edge of the woods across from it. They were immediately engaged. Suddenly, the *"Schill"* took antiaircraft gunfire from the left. *SS-Untersturmführer* Kneissl was wounded in the leg. The assault gun was unable to turn. A second round struck the hull. Driver Müller received a flesh wound in the back. Smoke grenades were launched. The crew bailed out. As *SS-Untersturmführer* Kneissl was dismounting as the last of the crew, a round hit the transmission. The *"Blücher"*, which was approaching, immediately knocked out the antiaircraft guns and followed the lead group. The crew of the *"Schill"* went back to the dressing station.

The sun went down and it snowed as the *Sturmgeschütz* battery bore its three fallen comrades, including its commander, to the grave. The graves were at the outskirts of Tupitschina by a row of trees. *SS-Obersturmführer* Telkamp spoke the eulogy.

Since enemy units continually attempted to break out of the Wjasma pocket to the east through the thin security lines or between the widely spaced German columns, it was nearly impossible to send supplies along the Juchnow — Gshatsk road.

The mission for *SS-Division "Reich"* from the *XXXX. Panzer-Korps* for 9 October stated:

SS-Division "Reich" is to capture Gshatsk, screen to the east and reconnoiter further to the east. It is to establish contact on the highway with the *10. Panzer-Division* in Wjasma.

9 October 1941

During the morning, *SS-Infanterie-Regiment "Deutschland"* prepared to attack Gshatsk on both sides of the route of advance with the reinforced *I./SS-Infanterie-Regiment "Deutschland"* on the right of the road and the reinforced *III./SS-Infanterie-Regiment "Deutschland"* to the left.

First attack objective: Railroad embankment.

The *II./SS-Infanterie-Regiment "Deutschland"* established security at the highway. The attack was supported by the *III./SS-Infanterie-Regiment "Deutschland"* and a battery of the *IV./SS-Artillerie-Regiment "Reich"*.

At 1015 hours a powerful combat patrol led by *SS-Untersturmführer* Cyraks reached the southern outskirts of Gshatsk. It had swung around via Petrosowa — Hochlowa and had succeeded in getting behind the enemy unnoticed. The patrol captured three Russian personnel carriers. The enemy lost 20 killed. Three guns that were hitched to trucks were prevented from going into position. They withdrew to the east.

At 1030 hours the *I./SS-Infanterie-Regiment "Deutschland"* attacked from the assembly position and, in a fast-moving advance, reached the edge of the woods one kilometer south of the railroad line. It surprised the enemy, who was in the process of occupying his prepared positions in the woods. Low-flying Russian aircraft attacked without causing any damage.

In the woods, fighting developed that was particularly costly for the *2./SS-Infanterie-Regiment "Deutschland"*. The enemy attempted to eject the Germans who had penetrated his positions in three immediate counterattacks.

The right wing of the *I./SS-Infanterie-Regiment "Deutschland"* enveloped the enemy in a rapid advance and destroyed him (about 70 Russians killed). *Sturmgeschütz "Blücher"* knocked out one gun, and several field fortifications were overrun just outside of Gshatsk.

Without further delay and without encountering great enemy resistance, the battalion crossed the railroad embankment and entered Gshatsk. It cleared the right-hand sector of the city and screened to the north and east. On the north outskirts of the city the *"Blücher"* opened fire on the fleeing columns.

The *III./SS-Infanterie-Regiment "Deutschland"* also made good forward progress in its advance. At 1115 hours it reached the southern outskirts of Gshatsk. By 1300 hours the city was solidly in German hands.

The route of advance was temporarily blocked 1.5 kilometers south of Gshatsk because isolated vehicles had been surprised by enemy forces (up to 80 men). The terrain was mopped up and the dispersed enemy either destroyed or captured.

In the wooded areas southwest of Gshatsk and along the railroad line the fight frequently continued. Individual enemy tanks often appeared. There were no signs of a coordinated enemy effort, however.

In addition to a substantial haul of captured weapons and equipment, *SS-Infanterie-Regiment "Deutschland"* brought in 465 prisoners.

The losses on 9 October were 11 noncommissioned officers and enlisted personnel killed and 1 officer and 27 noncommissioned officers and enlisted personnel wounded.

SS-Sturmmann L. Hümmer of the *3./SS-Infanterie-Regiment "Deutschland"* wrote of the day in his diary as follows:

The Capture of Gshatsk

We renewed the attack early in rain and snow squalls. We advanced under heavy enemy fire. Low-flying Russian aircraft strafed us without doing any damage. We reached our objective of Gshatsk. We captured the city and established security in all directions.

In a cafeteria-like room in a big building there was a big, clean kettle full of food — rice with meat — that had just been cooked for the Russian soldiers. They had evacuated Gshatsk just before lunch. Someone immediately passed out the plates that were on a shelf and, in the blink of an eye, the entire company shared a midday meal that the Russians had cooked for us!

The local population was very friendly and the dwellings well furnished.

A patrol — the 9th squad — was sent to reconnoiter whether the next villages were clear of the enemy. It determined that the Russians were falling back everywhere in company-sized elements. We crossed a river on a long wooden bridge and continued to the next village, mostly through woods.

Often there were numerous fleeing Russians around us. At one point the patrol had to hide in a thicket when a strong party of Russian soldiers passed only a few meters away.

All the Russian units were retreating. They did not stop in the next village either; they continued to fall back. After completing its mission the patrol headed back. The night passed quietly.

On that day *SS-Infanterie-Regiment "Der Führer"* also rejoined the fighting.

After the *16. (Pionier)/SS-Infanterie-Regiment "Der Führer"* had restored the bridge over the Oka River at Juchnow, *SS-Infanterie-Regiment "Der Führer"* set out to continue the attack north along the Smolensk — Moscow highway alongside *SS-Infanterie-Regiment "Deutschland"*. It employed the *II./SS-Infanterie-Regiment "Der Führer"* on the right and the *I./SS-Infanterie-Regiment "Der Führer"* on the left with the *III./SS-Infanterie-Regiment "Der Führer"* bringing up the rear.

Strong groups of the enemy who repeatedly attempted to cross the route of advance to the east were thrown back in heavy fighting. The Russians offered particularly heavy resistance in a built-up area south of the highway and defended with the courage of desperation. The *II./SS-Infanterie-Regiment "Der Führer"* was pinned down in an open field while attacking Mostschanowa. *SS-Obersturmführer* Holzer, commander of the *7./SS-Infanterie-Regiment "Der Führer"*, took the initiative and inspired the men of his company to attack. They penetrated into the village. Soon it was in German hands.

In the afternoon, after breaking stubborn resistance, the regiment reached and crossed the highway. Initially the regiment went over to the defensive. It oriented to the northeast, since the enemy at Sloboda was attacking from the east with strong forces and armor. The attack was repulsed and the main body of the enemy forced to turn to the east. Individual tanks were destroyed by assault guns.

The war diary of the *Sturmgeschütz* battery reported its employment with *SS-Infanterie-Regiment "Der Führer"* as follows on 9 October:

Keeping Cool is Everything

Sturmgeschütz "Lützow" set out at 0500 hours in the morning with the *II./SS-Infanterie-Regiment "Der Führer"* to Moltschanowa. The Russians fought stubbornly outside the village. The *"Lützow"* pushed on into the village with the *6./SS-Infanterie-Regiment "Der Führer"*. The Russians were forced back and even enemy positions behind the village were captured.

The attack continued to Snoski. After a short firefight, the Russians fled from the first field fortifications. Suddenly, two heavy Russian tanks appeared on the hill. The *"Lützow"* fired on the first one. Several rounds knocked the turret off the tank — it was done for. The second tank came from the side at the same time and tried to ram the *"Lützow"*. An enemy antitank gun had also opened fire on *"Lützow"*. At that critical moment, the main gun jammed. While clearing the blockage, *SS-Unterscharführer* Waller and *SS-Mann* Roßbauer were slightly wounded by fragments. At the last moment the gun was ready to fire. The oncoming Russian tank, which had come dangerously close, was set on fire by a round in the engine compartment. The antitank gun that was firing from the left was silenced with a direct hit.

A number of our infantry lay wounded in the first trench line. In spite of heavy enemy fire, the *"Lützow"* moved forward and took several wounded comrades on board. After the wounded had been brought back, the assault gun headed forward again to bring back the remaining wounded. The *Sturmgeschütz* stopped two hundred meters from the Russian positions. It had run out of fuel. In spite of heavy enemy fire, the driver, *SS-Mann* Roßbauer, climbed out and brought two cans of gasoline from the rear. After refueling, the *Sturmgeschütz* moved back to Moltschanowa.

At 1830 hours the *II./SS-Infanterie-Regiment "Deutschland"* received from the division the mission of attacking the flank of the enemy facing *SS-Infanterie-Regiment "Der Führer"* via Ssamoty. Contact was established with *SS-Infanterie-Regiment "Der Führer"*. The attack on Ssamoty, where the left wing of *SS-Infanterie-Regiment "Der Führer"* was located, was to start at 2000 hours. However, the night attack did not take place due to the unclear enemy situation.

Kradschützen Advance West on the Highway

SS-Kradschützen-Bataillon "Reich" also reached the highway on 9 October. It received the mission of establishing contact to the west with the *10. Panzer-Division*. There was heavy traffic headed east on the highway. The road was immediately blocked with *Pak* and machine guns. Two fast-driving Russian trucks packed with standing Russian soldiers were knocked out, blocking the highway. The vehicles following them could go no farther, but neither could they go back since the *Pak* had shifted their fire to the rear to the next bend in the road. Then the machine guns began their song of death. The Russians were so surprised that they hardly thought of serious resistance. A few made their way free through the vegetation, but the majority were captured.

The motorcycle companies then continued their advance to the west. Along the way the battalion ran into small groups of Russians who were overpowered. One such group of Russians consisted of nothing but cadets of an officer's school. They fought stubbornly and with extreme bravery. The last of them were killed with hand grenades.

At 1600 hours *SS-Kradschützen-Bataillon "Reich"* ran into extremely strong enemy resistance at Pissoschna-Wilitschawo. It lasted until 0500 hours the next morning.

The *XXXX. Panzer-Korps* war diary contains the following entry for 9 October:

> While the defensive front of the *XXXX. Panzer-Korps* was prepared to block the encircled enemy, *SS-Division "Reich"* launched an unstoppable attack on Gshatsk, capturing it at 1230 hours.
>
> At 1630 hours, *SS-Division "Reich"* ran into strong enemy forces in the Ssloboda area as it continued its advance, including 28 heavy and 6 light tanks.
>
> *SS-Kradschützen-Bataillon "Reich"*, which had the mission of establishing contact with the *10. Panzer-Division* on the highway, ran into enemy forces south of Welitschowo.

During the days of heavy fighting, the division's medical services particularly distinguished themselves. During the march from Juchnow to Gshatsk, the *1. SS-Sanitäts-Kompanie "Reich"* (medical company) was bombed, suffering significant losses. As a result, it was not functional for a short period of time. Therefore, the *2. SS-Sanitäts-Kompanie "Reich"*, which was intended to have some rest, had to jump in.

Because of the continued existence of the Wjasma pocket to the west, the route was not yet open for evacuating wounded to the rear. Because the route to the south around the pocket was too long and was also unsafe due to scattered enemy units, an unusually large number of wounded were collected in the area south of Gshatsk, where they awaited evacuation.

It was in an extremely unfavorable place. In addition, the electric equipment — the Edison generators — were inoperational. Operations were impossible without light. Something had to be improvised. Beeswax was collected and made into candles that provided light. Men were then positioned in the corners of the operating tent with torches. Operations were then performed by the light of that makeshift illumination.

Several times during the day the division command group with the commander of the division and operations officer were attacked by Russian fighter planes. However, in spite of numerous hits on the individual vehicles, no one was injured. During these days, at least in the area in which the division was fighting, the Russians clearly controlled the skies.

The translator for the commander of the division, Dr. Windisch M.D., was constantly at the divisional commander's side. He contributed this information:

The Division Command Group

The command group of the division consisted of the *KFZ 15* with the division commander, *SS-Obergruppenführer* Hausser, the operations officer, *SS-Obersturmbannführer* Ostendorff, myself (*SS-Hauptsturmführer Dr.* Windisch) and the driver, *SS-Hauptscharführer* Schmidt. Also with us were the vehicle of the adjutant, *SS-Hauptsturmführer* Kröger, and the radio vehicle and the messenger echelon. The command group was at the most forward command posts in many decisive attacks.

How often we must have spent the decisive minutes or even hours at the command post of the attacking regiment, battalion or company. Many times we crawled or crept up to the most forward foxholes because the division commander wanted a better view of the terrain and the enemy positions. Prisoners were then interrogated, captured maps studied and important decisions made.

I was regularly given special tasks, such as interrogating prisoners at the various units and looking for and finding Russian artillery maps. Those were excellent maps; of the best quality and accuracy. I found most of them in abandoned trains vehicles, particularly the special-purpose vehicles of the Russian field artillery. Interrogation of prisoners was often not very productive. The poor devils did not know much anyway, especially when it dealt with military matters. But, at least, sometimes one learned something important, especially from noncommissioned officers and officers. Also, many a general told me interesting things. I always made sure that the prisoners, whenever possible, were fed and housed.

10 October 1941

SS-Kradschützen-Bataillon "Reich" did not get any rest during the night of 9/10 October.

The Night in Osstaschkowa

The *5. (schwere)/SS-Kradschützen-Bataillon "Reich"* was quartered in the evening in Osstaschkowa, a little village directly south of the highway. Security was posted. At about 0100 hours the battalion was attacked by strong forces. Two Russian light tanks, which moved through the middle of the village several times at high speed, were finally destroyed when they overran ramp obstacles that the combat-engineer platoon had set up. The Russian attack, which lasted almost until morning, was repulsed with heavy losses for the enemy.

In addition to the two tanks, 12 Russian vehicles, including a self-propelled antiaircraft gun, several machine guns and many submachine guns and rifles were captured. The heavy attack was repulsed in the gray light of dawn. Eighty-three Russian dead were counted in the village and north of it on the highway. The *5. (schwere)/SS-Kradschützen-Bataillon "Reich"* lost eight killed, including *SS-Standartenoberjunker* (officer candidate) Meier of the infantry-gun platoon, who had just joined the company. There were also several wounded. The combat-engineer platoon had borne the main burden of the fighting. It was employed as infantry, while the infantry-gun platoon and the *Pak* platoon provided outstanding close-range supporting fire. Every man was an infantryman that night.

The enemy also attacked the other motorcycle companies at 0200 hours with heavy fire and shouts of "Urrahh!". They were also repulsed. Early in the morning the men of the *2./* and *4./SS-Kradschützen-Bataillon "Reich"* were more than a little surprised to find the roadside ditches on both sides of the highway full of Russians creeping toward them. An attempt through an interpreter to persuade the Russians to surrender failed. The Russians were either eliminated or chased off with the help of a heavy mortar and a machine gun.

Then, however, one saw a picture that illustrated the stubbornness of the enemy. About 3-4 kilometers to the west was a road intersection on a small piece of high ground where a north-south road crossed the highway. It was open to good observation. Silhouetted on that road was an immense Russian column of several hundred vehicles moving north. The vehicles were packed full of Russian soldiers attempting to escape north from the pocket. Unfortunately, the column was beyond the range of the battalion's weapons. The enemy facing the motorcycle battalion had clearly attempted to break through to the north and then, later, covered the withdrawal of the Russian column to the north. When the column had vanished in the distance, the enemy facing the motorcycle battalion surrendered and the battalion took several hundred prisoners.

During the course of the morning, the motorcycle battalion was pulled back to Szimjeschkina where it screened to the north, west and south until 11 October. It had to repulse several more night attacks there, some with individual tanks.

The division attack order for 10 October (excerpts):

1.) From 6 - 8 October the reinforced *SS-Infanterie-Regiment "Deutschland"*, *SS-Aufklärungs-Abteilung "Reich"* and *SS-Kradschützen-Bataillon "Reich"* have smashed strong enemy forces and captured numerous weapons and much equipment through untiring attacks against enemy forces that attempted to resist the advance from Juchnow to Gshatsk.

On 9 October *SS-Infanterie-Regiment "Deutschland"* captured Gshatsk in a hasty attack and screened the city to the east, north and west.

SS-Infanterie-Regiment "Der Führer" captured the terrain on both sides of Filissowa while oriented north. It attacked against numerically superior enemy forces that had armor. The regiment then held the position against strong enemy counter-attacks.

SS-Kradschützen-Bataillon "Reich" advanced on the highway from Swerschkowa toward Wjasma and encountered enemy forces in improved positions at Pessotschna.

The light *Flak* batteries and the *Sturmgeschütz* battery have decisively supported all these attacks.

2.) The enemy, who fell back before our attacks with inferior forces, was reinforced with new forces on 9 October. Several infantry battalions and strong armored formations concentrated in the Budjewo area. Those forces attacked to the southwest in the afternoon of 9 October. Additional attacks can be expected on 10 October.

3.) *SS-Division "Reich"*, which has the mission of capturing the Gshatsk area and holding it as the basis for continuing the operation, is to attack and destroy the enemy in the Budjewo area on 10 October.

4.) ...

5.) *SS-Infanterie-Regiment "Der Führer"* is to attack enemy forces on the high ground west of Ssloboda from the previous limit of advance at 0800 hours. It is to capture the high ground with its *Schwerpunkt* on the left wing. The *2./SS-Flak-Abteilung "Reich"* remains attached to the regiment for that attack.

6.) *SS-Infanterie-Regiment "Deutschland"* is to attack the enemy at Ssamoty at 0800 hours with the *II./SS-Infanterie-Regiment "Deutschland"*. It is to move in conjunction with the *I./SS-Infanterie-Regiment "Der Führer"*, making it possible for the latter to capture Ssamoty.

After Ssamoty is captured the battalion is to halt.

The *I./SS Regiment "Deutschland"* is to move to the railroad line south of Baryschew via Sswaschkowa by 0800 and attack Budjewo via Weselewa.

The *II./SS-Infanterie-Regiment "Deutschland"*, after completion of its first mission, is to move to the northeast bank of the Aljoschnja River at Petrezowa and follow the attack of the *I./SS-Infanterie-Regiment "Deutschland"*.

The *III./SS-Infanterie-Regiment "Deutschland"*, to which the *III./Artillerie-Regiment "Reich"* is attached, is to secure Gshatsk and screen to the east, north and west. It is to clear the city itself of troops and vehicles.

7.) *SS-Aufklärungs-Abteilung "Reich"* is to reconnoiter south and north of the highway as far as the railroad line. Its *Schwerpunkt* lies between the division and the Worja River.

The east - west road north of the railroad line is to be observed.

The main body of the battalion is to advance into the area east of Wetza during the course of the two regiments' attack, so that enemy forces withdrawing to the east along the highway can be taken under fire with all available weapons.

...

19.) Coordinating Instructions

After the attacks of the two infantry regiments have had their effect it then becomes necessary to prevent the enemy from withdrawing in other directions than to the east on the highway. At the start of enemy movement to the rear, the infantry regiments are to follow the enemy beyond the specified objectives of the attack, but only so far as to prevent an orderly retreat.

Enemy units withdrawing on the highway are to be destroyed by fire from all available heavy weapons, particularly by artillery and, later, by *SS-Aufklärungs-Abteilung "Reich"*, which will be brought forward east of Wetza.

All units must attempt to completely destroy the enemy.

/signed/ Hausser

It was clear from all the reports that the enemy resistance and forces in the area east of Gshatsk were strengthening rapidly. Clearly the intent was to regain the strategically important area around Gshatsk by any means.

An advance by the *3./SS-Infanterie-Regiment "Deutschland"* within the framework of the regimental attack discovered and occupied large-scale Russian positions with improved bunkers, blockhouses with stoves and a large underground field bakery. Large amounts of freshly baked bread, which were most welcome to the men of the *I./SS-Infanterie-Regiment "Deutschland"*, were in all the bunkers. The stoves and ovens were still hot. It was thus discovered that the Gshatsk area was also a major supply point of the Russians. They had lost that as well.

The attack by *SS-Infanterie-Regiment "Der Führer"* started according to plan. The leading elements were attacking the high ground east of Kobylkina at 0945.

The enemy, however, did not stand and fight, but fell back before the regiments' attack. The division therefore reached the Ssloboda — Frolowka (*SS-Infanterie-Regiment "Der Führer"*) — Gshatsk (*SS-Infanterie-Regiment "Deutschland"*) line and went over to the defensive.

The *II./SS-Infanterie-Regiment "Deutschland"*, which was sent to the northern wing of *SS-Infanterie-Regiment "Der Führer"* in the evening of 9 October on a relief attack along the highway, reached Kobylkino in a bold attack behind the enemy during the night. In the course of the morning it had to repulse a strong Russian counterattack with numerous tanks.

The division command post was located in Ssnoski. The enemy continually strengthened his forces in the area but did not take a stand on 10 October. He was clearly preparing for a new attack with strong forces. The division, accordingly, temporarily went over to the defensive during the evening of 11 October so as to hold the strategically important Gshatsk area.

The division order of 10 October for the defense on 11 October included the following:

1.) ...

During an enemy counterattack with numerous tanks, the battalion commander of the *II./SS-Infanterie-Regiment "Deutschland"*, *SS-Hauptsturmführer* Stadler, personally brought a beginning rearward movement of the battalion to a halt. In so doing he was wounded.

2.) The enemy east of the division is falling back before the attack of *SS-Infanterie-Regiment "Der Führer"* and apparently concentrating his forces north of Wetzna. New enemy forces consisting of motorized infantry with artillery and some tanks are approaching Gshatsk from the east on the road north of the railroad line.

West and south of Gshatsk are no more than dispersed units, individual batteries and tanks, which are attempting to escape to the east.

3.) *SS-Division "Reich"* is to go over to the defensive in the previous limit of advance and defend with its *Schwerpunkt* to the east. Elements are oriented west.

4.) The main line of resistance: High ground west of Ssloboda — southwest bank of the Aljoschnja Reiver — Stolbowo — Bulytschowa — Potitschnaja — western outskirts of Gshatsk — Koschina —Bratki estate.

5.) Sectors:

Right: *SS-Infanterie-Regiment "Der Führer"* to railroad line Gshatsk to the east (inclusive).

To its left: *SS-Infanterie-Regiment "Deutschland"* to Koschina (exclusive).

To its left: *SS-Pionier-Bataillon "Reich"*.

...

Loss figures for 10 October are only available for *SS-Infanterie-Regiment "Deutschland"*:

Killed: 28 noncommissioned officers and enlisted personnel
Wounded: 3 officers and 78 noncommissioned officers and enlisted personnel
Missing: 6 enlisted personnel.

In the war diary of the *XXXX. Panzer-Korps* the entry for 11 October includes the following:

On 10 October *SS-Division "Reich"* launched a major attack from the Nikolskoje area to the northwest, which had been outflanked by the Russian 18th Tank Brigade. One *SS-Infanterie-Regiment* lost 500 men in the operation. (Translator's Note: The 500 figure is believed to be a typographical error in the original German edition, since none of the information provided so far would indicate such catastrophic losses for any given regiment.)

11 October 1941

During the night of 10/11 October the enemy situation changed fundamentally, however.

Reconnaissance during the night revealed that about 20 tanks were at Wetzna and truck-mounted infantry were being brought east. The enemy was digging in south of Hp. Drownino on both sides of the highway for a kilometer to both the north and south of the road. Battered enemy units were apparently being brought back into that position. In addition, a motorized infantry battalion was brought up there from the east.

Based on this altered picture of the enemy situation, the *XXXX. Panzer-Korps* immediately reorganized its forces. The defense order was overcome by events and the division received the following mission from the corps:

SS-Division "Reich" is to pursue the beaten enemy toward Moscow on 11 October.

First intermediate objective: Moshaisk.

The reinforced *Panzer-Regiment 7* of the *10. Panzer-Division* is to follow behind *SS-Division "Reich"*, initially as far as Gshatsk.

Additional forces will be continually sent forward as they become disengaged from the pocket front.

Werner Haupt wrote the following concerning the changed situation:

The *XXXX. Panzer-Korps* (*General der Kavallerie* Stumme) was slowly closing up to the east after clearing the Wjasma pocket. The first division to be freed up, *SS-Division "Reich"* (*SS-Obergruppenführer* Hausser), had captured Gshatsk and was continuing to advance to the east. Six days passed before the *2.*, *5.*, and *10. Panzer-Divisionen* were able to follow.

SS-Division "Reich" stood alone against two Russian armies! (Werner Haupt, *Heeresgruppe Mitte*, p. 97. Bad Nauheim: Podzun-Pallas-Verlag, 1968.)

At 1000 hours *SS-Division "Reich"* crossed the former main line of resistance with two attack spearheads:

The right-hand attack group — *SS-Infanterie-Regiment "Der Führer"*, commanded by *SS-Obersturmbannführer* Kumm — consisted of:

SS-Infanterie-Regiment "Der Führer"
Artillerie-Gruppe Hecht: *II./Artillerie-Regiment 61* and *I./SS-Artillerie-Regiment "Reich"*
Panzer-Jäger-Abteilung "Reich" (minus one company)
2./SS-Flak-Abteilung "Reich"
1 company from *SS-Pionier-Bataillon "Reich"*
1 8.8-cm *Flak*
1 medical company.

Attack group *SS-Infanterie-Regiment "Der Führer"* attacked on both sides of the highway to the east.

The left-hand attack group — *SS-Infanterie-Regiment "Deutschland"*, commanded by *SS-Oberführer* Bittrich — consisted of:

SS-Infanterie-Regiment "Deutschland"
SS-Artillerie-Regiment "Reich" (minus the *I./SS-Artillerie-Regiment "Reich")*
1 *Panzer-Jäger* company
1 *Flak* battery
1 company from *SS-Pionier-Bataillon "Reich"*
1 medical company.

Attack group *SS-Infanterie-Regiment "Deutschland"* attacked along the Gshatsk — Staraja — Drowino — Moshaisk road in order to divert the enemy from attack group *SS-Infanterie-Regiment "Der Führer"*.

After breaking the enemy resistance, both attack groups were to advance toward Moshaisk with strong mounted units.

A Russian Armored Train Attacks

Before the attack had even begun, a report reached the *I./SS-Infanterie-Regiment "Der Führer"*, which was to attack left of the highway, that a Russian armored train was coming from the Jelnja (II) area. (Jelnja II as distinguished from the Jelnja of the hotly contested Jelnja salient.)

Shortly thereafter the train was spotted as it was slowly approaching Gshatsk. The armored train was immediately engaged by *Sturmgeschütz "Lützow"*, which was with the *I./SS-Infanterie-Regiment "Der Führer"*, and also by attack group *SS-Infanterie-Regiment "Deutschland"*. Since the railroad line had already been blown up southeast of Gshatsk, demolition parties were immediately sent out from the *16./SS-Infanterie-Regiment "Deutschland"* and the *3./SS-Pionier-Bataillon "Reich"* to blow up the railroad tracks at the Holesniki stop and block the armored train's return route.

Sturmgeschütz "Lützow" moved toward the armored train and immediately opened fire. Round after round struck the locomotive, the armored turrets and the quad machine guns. The armored train slowly backed up while delivering heavy fire.

The elements of *SS-Artillerie-Regiment "Reich"* that were attached to *SS-Infanterie-Regiment "Deutschland"* went into open firing positions east of Iwashkowo and fired on the train at a range of 1,500 meters. The *4./SS-Artillerie-Regiment "Reich"* advanced to within 400 meters of the train. The salvos were right on. The train came to a stop with hits to the locomotive, but it still maintained heavy fire. By 1200 hours the armored train was totally out of action and the crew fled.

The *I./SS-Infanterie-Regiment "Der Führer"*, advanced through Woinowa and Kurjanowa to the east, but bad road conditions brought the advance to a standstill. The *Sturmgeschütze* and ammunition carriers had to spend the entire night pulling out vehicles that were bogged down. While this battalion was held up, the *II./* and *III./SS-Infanterie-Regiment "Der Führer"* were also held fast by heavy fighting outside a patch of woods on both sides of the highway. The enemy, a master of camouflage, could not be identified. He kept up extremely heavy fire on both battalions from numerous machine guns.

The Russian artillery began to register its fire. In spite of the employment of all the heavy weapons attached to *SS-Infanterie-Regiment "Der Führer"* against the wood line, it was impossible to silence the enemy.

The division received unexpected help.

Gruppe Hauenstein — the reinforced *Panzer-Regiment 7* of the *10. Panzer-Division* (reinforced with *Kradschützen-Bataillon 10* and one self-propelled artillery battalion*)* — had been brought forward in the meantime from the Wjasma pocket front. Around 1300 hours it reached the highway/road intersection four kilometers south of Gshatsk. By corps order, it was initially attached to *SS-Division "Reich"*. The *I./Panzer-Regiment 7* was directed to support attack group *SS-Infanterie-Regiment "Der Führer"*. The *II./Panzer-Regiment 7* was directed to support attack group *SS-Infanterie-Regiment "Deutschland"*.

While *SS-Infanterie-Regiment "Der Führer"* was still bogged down under extremely heavy fire from Russian artillery and machine guns, the commander of the *I./Panzer-Regiment 7* reported to the command post of *SS-Infanterie-Regiment "Der Führer"*. He had 70 tanks available to launch an attack along with the regiment's grenadiers. Seldom had there been more joy at the sight of these trusted comrades-in-arms from the fighting in the Jelnja salient than at that moment.

The tanks deployed north of the road. They rolled forward toward the strongly held wood line and took it under fire. A few moments later, approximately 30 Russian tanks emerged from the woods in a counterattack. The tanks had been the weapons used to provide the steady machine-gun fire that had kept everyone pinned down. A dramatic armored engagement developed which ended within half an hour in a complete success for the German tanks. Ten Russian tanks were left in flames. The others withdrew as fast as they could. Three friendly tanks had run over mines and become disabled. One Russian antitank gun was then knocked out as well.

The *III./SS-Infanterie-Regiment "Der Führer"* then mounted on the tanks and immediately continued the advance eastward with them. It was able to break through Russian field fortifications during the night.

The *I./Panzer-Regiment 7* formed a hedgehog position in Chalopowa. The *III./SS-Infanterie-Regiment "Der Führer"* closed up on foot. Together, the two units posted security for the night. During the midday hours of that day, *General der Kavallerie* Stumme visited the division command post.

The assault of attack group *SS-Infanterie-Regiment "Deutschland"* made good initial progress at 1000 hours. The *I./SS-Infanterie-Regiment "Deutschland"* reached Stolbowo and Sujewa and engaged field fortifications. During the advance, *Sturmgeschütz "Blücher"* disposed of an armored car and two Russian medium tanks.

Friendly Artillery against Russian Armor

The *"Blücher"* advanced with mounted infantry through the woods toward Staraja at the head of *SS-Infanterie-Regiment "Deutschland"*. As it was negotiating the woods, a Russian tank suddenly appeared ahead. The *"Blücher"* immediately opened fire. One after another, its armor-piercing rounds struck the Russian tank but failed to penetrate. The tank turned away, but a second and third tank came over the high ground. At that point, a *Pak* came up and opened fire but without any effect. In the meantime, the *"Blücher"* had fired off all its ammunition but remained to offer moral support.

Then the German artillery joined the fight with armor-piercing rounds. One Russian tank was set afire. The crew climbed out of the other tank and fled. It was later determined that one of the tanks had been immobilized by fire from the *"Blücher"*, which had damaged the enemy's track.

At 1100 hours the *I./* and *III./SS-Infanterie-Regiment "Deutschland"* reached Staraya and negotiated it without enemy contact.

The *II./SS-Infanterie-Regiment "Deutschland"* was brought forward to Iwaschkowo in motor march. It continued to advance but ran into catastrophic road conditions and later its vehicles bogged down hopelessly at Palenjewa.

Around 1320 hours Paleninowa was captured. At 1430 hours the *I./* and *III./SS-Infanterie-Regiment "Deutschland"* reached the high ground east of Kurjanowa just as five Russian tanks (T 34's) attacked from the woods five kilometers to the east. They were repulsed.

A heavy gun of the artillery knocked out one T 34 as it was turning. The

Russian tanks then fired from the woods and kept the open area to their front under fire.

Assault troops of the *III./SS-Infanterie-Regiment "Deutschland"* worked their way through the woods to the Russian tanks. They succeeded in knocking out three of the T 34's.

At 1730 hours additional Russian tanks advanced from the woods. The guns of *SS-Artillerie-Regiment "Reich"* were in open firing positions. They destroyed three more T 34's at a range of 300 meters.

***

At 1800 hours the commander of the *II./Panzer-Regiment 7* of the *10. Panzer-Division* reported to the command post of *SS-Infanterie-Regiment "Deutschland"*. The tank battalion had reached Staraya by 1800 hours and secured there during the night.

According to statements of prisoners, the enemy had 29 heavy and 40-50 light tanks available in the sector. The armor consisted of factory-new tanks that had never been in action before.

During the night, *SS-Infanterie-Regiment "Deutschland"* held the positions at the limit of the day's advance. In the morning it intended to continue the advance through the woods to the east with the *II./Panzer-Regiment 7*.

On 11 October, attack group *SS-Infanterie-Regiment "Deutschland"* captured or destroyed 14 tanks (of which six were destroyed by artillery), one armored car, one gun, one antitank gun, and three trucks. One armored train was destroyed.

Six noncommissioned officers and enlisted personnel were killed. One officer and 22 noncommissioned officers and enlisted personnel were wounded.

The war diary of the *XXXX. Panzer-Korps* stated:

> *SS-Division "Reich"* reached the line Kzutiny — Kuzjanowa in its attack against enemy forces in the line Iwniki — Drowino. The opposing enemy had armor. The terrain was mined in areas.

While the *14. Infanterie-Division (mot.)* and the *36. Infanterie-Division (mot.)* received the mission of continuing the advance to the northeast toward Kalinin, *SS-Division "Reich"* was radioed the following mission from the *XXXX. Panzer-Korps* by radio for 12 October:

> *SS-Division "Reich"*, with the units of the *10. Panzer-Division* that are attached for the attack, is to break through the Moscow defensive position and take possession of Moshaisk.
>
> Reinforced *Panzer-Regiment 7* that is temporarily attached to *SS-Division "Reich"* is to revert to the command of its division upon arrival of the division commander.

For purposes of unified command and control of the conduct of the fighting during the capture of Moshaisk, the *10. Panzer-Division* will be attached to *SS-Division "Reich"*.

In addition, a courier brought the division a written document based on the experiences of the *3. Infanterie-Division (mot.)* for the attack of *SS-Division "Reich"* through the Moscow defensive position.

Here is another first-hand account from the command post of *SS-Division "Reich"* in Ssnoski south of Gshatsk during the morning of that day. The command post was near some thick woods. The division interpreter, *SS-Hauptsturmführer Dr.* Windisch, wrote:

"Russians on the Right!"

Early in the morning the vehicles of the individual sections of the division staff formed up to follow the units that had set out along the "old mail route" through Gshatsk toward Borodino.

Shortly before the departure someone shouted: "Russians on the right!"

Everyone immediately went into position or dove for cover. Through my binoculars, I just as quickly identified the supposed Russians as Latvians. They came right out of the thick woods with three antiaircraft guns. I immediately ran to the commander (*SS-Obergruppenführer* Hausser) to tell him. He wanted to know why I was so sure. I quickly explained to him that, as a Baltic German, I had served my compulsory military service in the Latvian army in 1930. Therefore I immediately recognized the typical blue caps, the color of the Latvian artillerist.

Since the Latvians also held off and showed no intentions of attacking, I raced over to them with my sidecar-motorcycle and spoke to them in Latvian, whereupon they broke out in shouts of joy. The whys and wherefores were quickly explained. They had the mission of securing the main Smolensk Moscow highway with their antiaircraft guns against enemy aircraft — therefore, against ours.

"We have taken pains, however, not to hit your airplanes!" they assured me. They requested they be able to continue the fight on our side against the Russians, since the Latvians had never been friends with the Bolsheviks. I presented their requests to the commander. Unfortunately, nothing came of it. At that time we were not yet ready for that. I felt sorry for the poor Latvian soldiers who now had to walk the bitter road to captivity.

A few years later there would be two Latvian divisions in the *Waffen-SS*. Who would have guessed at that time that such a thing would ever happen!

Heavy Fighting in the Approaches to the Moscow Defensive Position

12 October 1941

During the course of the morning *SS-Infanterie-Regiment "Der Führer"* renewed the attack. As noon approached, the *I./Panzer-Regiment 7* advanced behind the regiment.

According to aerial reconnaissance, strong enemy positions and antitank ditches had been identified at Starjowka. They were bypassed by going west of Starjowka. Then the regiment, along with the *I./Panzer-Regiment 7,* broke into the field fortifications and destroyed the enemy. With that, one important intermediate position of the Moscow defensive position had been captured.

While the tank battalion and elements of *SS-Infanterie-Regiment "Der Führer"* attacked and captured Starjowka, the *1./Panzer-Regiment* 7 and elements of the *4./SS-Infanterie-Regiment "Der Führer"* pursued the enemy on the highway. Taking advantage of a *Stuka* attack, the reinforced company made it to the Jelenka sector, destroying enemy armor, antiaircraft and antitank guns along the way. Several bridges were blown up behind the aggressively advancing company, so the battalion was unable to follow on the highway. It had to swing out to the north and then back to the south to regain the highway.

In the sector of *SS-Infanterie-Regiment "Deutschland"* the tanks of the *II./Panzer-Regiment 7* rolled into the assembly position and began the attack at 0530. The *I./* and *III./SS-Infanterie-Regiment "Deutschland"* closed up to the advance. The *II./SS-Infanterie-Regiment "Deutschland"* was to follow in motor march. The edge of the woods east of Kurjanowka was still held by Russian infantry. Strong enemy armored forces were in the woods. The forest trails were extremely bad. Even the tanks had trouble moving forward.

Soon after crossing the front line and advancing through small but dense patches of woods, the leading tank companies knocked out the first enemy armor. The *III./SS-Infanterie-Regiment "Deutschland"* reached Shulewo at 0730 hours and continued to advance. By 0800 hours friendly tanks had already knocked out 27 Russian tanks and armored engagements were constantly in progress along the route of advance.

At 0830 hours enemy infantry was forced out of the western outskirts of Durykino. At 1030 hours a bridgehead was built over the Konopljowka River, thus attaining the division's designated objective. An ongoing armored engagement developed throughout the entire morning that soon drew in the entire *II./Panzer-Regiment 7,* as well as all approaching enemy armor. In spite of this, the advance progressed well and the men of the *III./SS-Infanterie-Regiment "Deutschland"* followed close behind the tanks. During the individual phases of combat 41 Soviet tanks were knocked out and four friendly tanks were lost. The advance reached the day's objective, Drownino, at 1130 hours. The command post of *SS-Infanterie-Regiment "Deutschland"* was located at the edge of town. Flanking artillery fire came down on the bridgehead from the south.

The *II./Panzer-Regiment 7* then crossed the Konopljowka Creek east of Drownino. It established security at Twerdiki on the high ground on the far side of town. The battalion, however, took fire from antitank guns from the wooded areas east of the town and artillery from a wooded area south of the highway. The latter was soon silenced by *SS-Artillerie-Regiment "Reich"*.

SS-Infanterie-Regiment "Deutschland" reported to the division its intention of continuing the advance to Kaluzkowa or to Papowka and requested a decision from the division.

At 1240 hours, the division radioed: "Attack objective: Papowka. *SS-Infanterie-Regiment "Der Führer"* has been informed."

At 1300 hours Russian aircraft dropped aerial torpedoes, which caused no damage but demonstrated the significance of the Moscow defensive position for the enemy. At 1330 hours the reinforced *SS-Infanterie-Regiment "Deutschland"* set out for the new attack objective. The *II./Panzer-Regiment 7* again set out with the regiment. Soon, however, the armor turned to the southeast. However, because of a shortage of fuel, the tanks had to halt their advance.

At 1510 hours Papowka was reached without encountering enemy resistance and contact was established on the highway with *SS-Infanterie-Regiment "Der Führer"*. The *II./Panzer-Regiment 7* quartered itself in Papowka and formed a hedgehog position for the night. *SS-Infanterie-Regiment "Deutschland"* also spent the night in the area of its farthest advance.

On 12 October 1941 the *II./Panzer-Regiment 7* and *SS-Infanterie-Regiment "Deutschland"* accounted for 41 enemy tanks (destroyed), one infantry gun, onc antitank gun, 27 trucks and 115 prisoners.

At 2045 hours the Regiment was radioed the following mission from the division for 13 October:

> *SS-Infanterie-Regiment "Deutschland"* is to advance with armor from the limit of the previous advance along the Gshatsk — Moshaisk road and reach Kolozkoje. It is to reconnoiter the enemy position from there.

The regiment lost one killed and ten wounded.

The command post of *SS-Division "Reich"* was in Atemoskowa.

The war diary of the *XXXX. Panzer-Korps* included, among other entries for 12 October, the following:

> At 0800 hours in the morning, *SS-Division "Reich"* and the armored brigade (sic!) of the *10. Panzer-Division* moved out after preparing the bridge at Krutizy. In combat with strong enemy forces, it reached the line Papowka — Lapunscha during the course of the day. The tanks of the *10. Panzer-Division* advanced to five kilometers west of Jelnja (II). The *10. Panzer-Division* has destroyed a total of 56 Russian tanks, including ten T 34's, since 11 October.

The capture of the most important intermediate position in the Moscow defensive position was accomplished on that day.

Penetration of the Moscow Defensive Position

13 October 1941

At 0630 hours *SS-Infanterie-Regiment "Deutschland"*, reinforced with the *II./Panzer-Regiment 7*, set out via Papugicha on the road at Grigarowa and from there along the route of advance to Kolozkoje.

The men of the *III./SS-Infanterie-Regiment "Deutschland"* and the regiment's command group mounted the tanks of the *II./Panzer-Regiment 7* at Grigorowka. The *I./*and *II./SS-Infanterie-Regiment "Deutschland"* followed on foot, since the wheeled vehicles of the regiment had to turn around the day before at Kurjakowo due to the bad road conditions. Only tracked vehicles could get through. The regiment's motor vehicles, including the *13./, 14./, 15./* and *16./SS-Infanterie-Regiment "Deutschland"*, had to advance via Gshatsk to get to the regiment. They followed behind *SS-Infanterie-Regiment "Der Führer"* on the main highway.

Kolozkoje was reached at 0930 hours after encountering no more than light enemy resistance. Security was set up to the east. The *9./SS-Infanterie-Regiment "Deutschland"*, together with the reinforced 3rd platoon of the *5./Panzer-Regiment 7*, was sent out to reconnoiter the system of enemy positions near Rogatschewo.

The platoon leader of the tank platoon, *Oberleutnant* Lohaus, related his experiences in the after-action report that follows:

After-Action Report on the Reconnaissance Conducted by the Reinforced 3rd Platoon of the *5./Panzer-Regiment 7* and the *9./SS-Infanterie-Regiment "Deutschland"* on 13 October 1941

The combined-arms reconnaissance group had the mission of determining whether the railroad line at Kolotsch and the streambed to its south was negotiable and at what position the tank battalion could best attack through the system of positions. Approach route: Kolozkoje, Akinschino, Golobino, Kolotsch train stop and Rogatschewo.

The *SS* (the *9./SS-Infanterie-Regiment "Deutschland"*) mounted our tanks and moved with us via Akinschino, in which we could not identify any enemy resistance, to Golobino, where we received the first rifle fire. The *SS* men dismounted and advanced into Golubino, where a hastily established field fortification was identified. Together with the *SS* men, we worked our way as far forward as Golubino. From there we had a good view of the system of positions, which was heavily wooded and extended south of the Kolotsch sector.

We observed through binoculars how the enemy was still working on his positions without the faintest idea we were there. He was digging trenches and in the process of building new bunkers. The system of positions extended, for the most part, halfway up the slope in an arc from the northeast to the southwest as far as Rogatschewo and from there to the southwest toward Jelnja (II).

We reached the train stopping point at Kolotsch. The 3rd Platoon of *Panzer-Regiment 7* went into position and covered the advance of the *SS* company into the streambed south of Kolotsch. The *SS* made good forward progress and the 3rd Platoon of *Panzer-Regiment 7* advanced with three *Panzer III's* on the Kolotsch — Rogatschewo road into the streambed.

When the first tank was 50 meters from the bridge, the bridge went up in the air. There was another demolition 75 meters south of the bridge — the last crossing over the antitank ditch. The enemy fire increased as we looked for a crossing point over the creek with the *SS*. The two *Panzer IV's*, which were in position on some high ground were able to suppress that fire, however. Four enemy bunkers were destroyed in a short time.

In the meantime, under cover of the tanks' gunfire, the *SS* had approached the enemy system of positions through the streambed and the antitank ditch.

The 3rd Tank Platoon leader, *Oberleutnant* Lohaus, and his section leader, *Oberfeldwebel* Scholz, climbed out of their tanks, approached the streambed under cover and, after a long search, located a crossing. On the far side of the stream there was still the antitank ditch, which they reached on foot. It was about eight meters wide and four meters deep.

In the meantime, the *SS* had already advanced as far as the houses in Rogatschewo, where they were then pinned down by steadily increasing enemy fire. The left wing of the company hung back even more, since the high ground to the left was heavily wooded and a bunker, which had initially remained silent, opened fire. A *Panzer IV* that had gone into position was fired on by that bunker, taking two hits. The bunker was put out of action by the concentrated fire of the two *Panzer IV's*.

The place that offered the best chance for crossing the antitank ditch was the site where the demolition had earlier been observed. The demolition had not been a complete success. At that point the ditch was only half as deep as elsewhere and could be filled up with tree trunks that were lying nearby, making a crossing possible.

By that time the *I./SS-Infanterie-Regiment "Deutschland"* had arrived and was attacking Rogatschewo. The command relationship of our reinforced platoon was not entirely clear. Finally, I received an order from the commander of *SS-Division "Reich"* to proceed with the *I./SS-Infanterie-Regiment "Deutschland"* to Rogatschewo — Jelnja (II).

I set out with my platoon. I had just crossed the antitank ditch, which the *SS* had made passable, with my tanks when I received a radio message that, by order of the corps, I was to return to my company and battalion. I turned around and returned via Kolotsch, Golobino and Akinschino to Kolozkoje, where I rejoined my company. (*Oberst a. D.* Walter Straub, *Geschichte des Panzerregiments 7*, ?. Unpublished manuscript.)

Under the initial covering fire of the tanks, which were unable to follow because of the antitank obstacles, the *9./SS-Infanterie-Regiment "Deutschland"*, reinforced with a heavy machine-gun platoon from the *12./SS-Infanterie-Regiment "Deutschland"*, attacked the enemy. Utilizing the element of surprise, it captured the field fortifications 150 meters northwest of Rogatschewo.

With that, the *9./SS-Infanterie-Regiment "Deutschland"* was the first to penetrate the Moscow defense position, although its original mission had only been to determine the exact extent of the Russian system of positions and how they were fortified.

A Time for SS-Infanterie-Regiment "Deutschland" to Shine

When the commander of the regiment, *SS-Oberführer* Bittrich, learned of the success of the *9./SS-Infanterie-Regiment "Deutschland"*, he decided to advance with the entire regiment. With the battalions echeloned behind each other, they would move through the breach that had been created unexpectedly and broaden the penetration.

At 1322 hours he reported his intention to the division, which answered by radio at 1430 hours:

> Approved. Advance past Jelnja (II) to the north. *SS-Infanterie-Regiment "Der Führer"* will join you in the attack.

In the meantime, *SS-Infanterie-Regiment "Deutschland"*, set out for the decisive attack via Golowino. Its battalions moved out in numerical order. As of 1600 hours, *Gruppe Hauenstein* — the reinforced *Panzer-Regiment 7* — was ordered back to the *10. Panzer-Division* and proceeded to the highway. *Panzer-Regiment 7* headed back on the highway to the west to a staging area in the Ssloboda area. Accordingly, the breakthrough into the Moscow defensive position took place as a pure infantry operation. Initially, it had no heavy infantry-weapon support or armor.

The war diary of the *XXXX. Panzer-Korps* includes in its entries for 13 October:

> *SS-Division "Reich"* is to reconnoiter along the highway and south of it. The attack is to be launched on 14 October based on the results of the reconnaissance. *Nebel-Regiment 54* from *Arko 128* (the corps artillery) is attached to *SS-Division "Reich"*.
>
> At 1400 hours the operations officer of *SS-Division "Reich"* telephoned. He stated that the reconnaissance which had been ordered had located a weak place in the Jelnja (II) position near Kolozkoje. As a result, *SS-Division "Reich"* was attacking at that position at 1530 hours to build a bridgehead east of there.

The commanding general informed the operations officer of the *10. Panzer-Division*, in the absence of its commander, of the following:

> *SS-Division "Reich"* is attacking the Jelnja (II) position at 1530 hours. Therefore, a new directive: Instead of a northward enveloping attack with the armor, it will advance onward through the breach created by *SS-Division "Reich"*. The *10. Panzer-Division* will effect the necessary coordination.

***

Under covering fire from a battery that was quickly brought into position,

SS-Infanterie-Regiment "Deutschland" broke into the Moscow defense position. The breakthrough was successful. The enemy was totally surprised. A continuous antitank ditch with wire obstacles was quickly crossed. At 1612 hours *SS-Infanterie-Regiment "Deutschland"* reported to the division: "We have broken through the forward positions and reached the village area three kilometers northeast of Jelnja."

The *I./SS-Infanterie-Regiment "Deutschland"* had attacked into the site where the *9./SS-Infanterie-Regiment "Deutschland"*, led by *SS-Obersturmführer* Tost, had penetrated. The battalion extended the penetration to the southern outskirts of Rogatschewo. At the same time, the *II./SS-Infanterie-Regiment "Deutschland"* combed through the wood line east of Rogatschewo from the Kolotsch train stop. The *III./SS-Infanterie-Regiment "Deutschland"* followed behind the *I./SS-Infanterie-Regiment "Deutschland"*.

The *II./Panzer-Regiment 7,* which had previously been directed to support *SS-Infanterie-Regiment "Deutschland"*, was removed from its attachment to the division and called back to the *10. Panzer-Division*. Upon crossing the enemy main line of resistance, the tank platoon that had supported the *9./SS-Infanterie-Regiment "Deutschland"* and, initially, been employed by the commander of *SS-Division "Reich"* to support the penetration, was ordered back by the corps (see after-action report above).

Because of these incomprehensible measures, the regiment radioed the division at 1640 hours:

> Pass on to corps headquarters: Infantry has broken through without heavy weapons. Order withdrawing armor is irresponsible.
>
> /signed/ Bittrich

SS-Hauptsturmführer Dr. Windisch of the division command echelon reported on the above attack:

Three Generals Observe the Fight for the Moscow Defensive Position

In the afternoon we stood beside the main road in the protection of the woods and observed the enemy, who was racing about with tanks. One battery of 8.8-cm *Flak* went into position and fired on the Russian armor. One could clearly see the tracers and follow their gently curved trajectory, as they struck the armor — and ricocheted off. Our grenadiers of *SS-Infanterie-Regiment "Deutschland"* had penetrated into the enemy system of positions north of the main road. They fought their way through in bitter, costly fighting.

While that was going on, a firefight began of an intensity that I had not yet experienced. Under the concealment of trees and bushes, we stood with three generals on the high ground and tensely watched the movements of both friendly and hostile troops. We had the commanding general of the *XXXX. Panzer-Korps, General der Kavallerie* Stumme, our division commander, *SS-Obergruppenführer* Hausser and an Army artillery general.

Suddenly, I heard the characteristic sound of the Russian rocket launchers, the so-called Stalin organs. That was certainly meant for us, for everyone suddenly vanished into foxholes. Since I had not dug one for myself, I could not vanish without a trace. So I simply dived behind a tree and experienced the horribly beautiful spectacle of the bursting rockets as they impacted. The smell of the powder smoke and the gloomy black-red-violet light from the tulip-shaped shell bursts were something I shall never forget.

The entire area, the whole atmosphere, was filled with the explosions of the impacting rounds. Suddenly, all Hell also broke loose behind us. I did not, in fact, know what was happening and ran to my friend Mix, the division intelligence officer, who was under cover not far from me. He laughed and answered my question: "Our *Nebelwerfer*!"

That ear-shattering racket had to have been heard to be believed. It mixed with the crash of the incoming Russian rounds. It whistled, thundered, hissed and roared with the discharges and impacts of artillery, machine guns, mortars and *Nebelwerfer*. The effect of the latter on the enemy must have been dreadful. The fighting lasted throughout the entire night. I interrogated prisoners. They were in a state of severe shock, distraught and happy to have come through it alive. In their opinion, the effect of our rocket launchers had a decisive influence on the outcome of the fighting...

At 1730 hours, as darkness fell, the *I./SS-Infanterie-Regiment "Deutschland"* attacked through the woods 500 meters southeast of Rogatschewo. The attack made good forward progress and ran into strong enemy resistance 400 meters northwest of Jelnja (II). The *II./SS-Infanterie-Regiment "Deutschland"* was employed screening the regiment's left flank. The *III./SS-Infanterie-Regiment "Deutschland"* was held in reserve in the woods 500 meters southeast of Rogatschewo. The *9./SS-Artillerie-Regiment "Reich"* supported the regiment's attack.

Around 2300 hours the leading elements were two kilometers northwest of Jelnja (II).

At 2300 hours the following radio message arrived at *SS-Infanterie-Regiment "Deutschland"* from the division:

Special praise from the commanding general for *SS-Infanterie-Regiment "Deutschland"*. Seek contact with the left wing of *SS-Infanterie-Regiment "Der Führer"*. Armored support is probable.

SS-Infanterie-Regiment "Deutschland" captured 2 tanks, 11 heavy machine guns, 5 guns, 3 antitank guns, 4 heavy mortars and took 205 prisoners on 13 October.

The war diary of the *XXXX. Panzer-Korps* contains the following entry for the day:

At 1630 hours the report arrived that *SS-Infanterie-Regiment "Deutschland"* had broken through the position and that the leading elements of *SS-Division "Reich"* were already at Woronina, three kilometers east of Koletzkoje.

SS-Infanterie-Regiment "Deutschland" has advanced southward toward Jelnja (II) and had strong enemy resistance facing it in the evening.

By the time darkness fell, fighting had extended the penetration to a depth of 500 meters and a breadth of one kilometer.

Night Attack by SS-Infanterie-Regiment "Der Führer"

The situation of the reinforced *SS-Infanterie-Regiment "Der Führer"*, the division's right attack group, had developed as follows on 13 October:

The attack continued along the highway. The *III./SS-Infanterie-Regiment "Der Führer"* again rode mounted on the tanks of the *10. Panzer-Division*, while the *I./* and *II./SS-Infanterie-Regiment "Der Führer"* followed on their own vehicles. The attack group advanced through Klemjatina and Rykatschowa, reaching the Moscow defense position by afternoon.

Continued progress demanded detailed reconnaissance and staging. The position to be attacked was in rolling terrain that rose to the east from the lowlands near a stream. The position had a depth of more than two kilometers. Five obstacles protected it from armor: The streambed, a "dragon's tooth" obstacle, an antitank ditch, "hedgehogs" and herringbone trenches. Within the position were continuous trenches. It was heavily wired and had concrete bunkers and fighting positions. Tanks had been dug in so that only the turrets were exposed. It only became clear during the course of the ensuing fighting that 50 built-in flamethrowers secured the highway bridges and that, on the far side of the position, additional armor was positioned in the edge of the woods that gave the enemy excellent artillery observation positions.

The leading armored element halted on a woods-covered ridge on both sides of the highway. The *III./SS-Infanterie-Regiment "Der Führer"* and the *II./SS-Infanterie-Regiment "Der Führer"*, which soon arrived, immediately reconnoitered through the woods and brought back initial reports of the extent of the enemy system of positions. The regiment's command post was brought forward to the hill about 500 meters from the start of the enemy position. Late in the afternoon the commander of the division arrived and ordered reconnaissance. The forces were to be staged for an attack to take place early on 14 October. The reconnaissance had already been dispatched. The battalion and company commanders personally went forward to reconnoiter favorable possibilities to penetrate the enemy positions. The companies waited in well-concealed positions in the woods. The *II./SS-Infanterie-Regiment "Der Führer"* was to the right of the highway, the *III./SS-Infanterie-Regiment "Der Führer"* to the left. The *I./SS-Infanterie-Regiment "Der Führer"* was about three kilometers to the rear. The enemy fired heavy harassing fire into the assembly area.

Late in the evening the division commander showed up again on the hill and informed the commander of the regiment that *SS-Infanterie-Regiment "Deutschland"*, the friendly forces on the regiment's left, had succeeded in a surprise penetration of the Moscow defense position. He ordered *SS-*

Infanterie-Regiment "Der Führer" to attack during that night.

The reconnaissance revealed that the possibilities for breaking through the position were more favorable north of the highway, in the sector of the *III./SS-Infanterie-Regiment "Der Führer"*, than to the south of the highway. The commander of the regiment, *SS-Obersturmbannführer* Kumm, therefore brought up the *I./SS-Infanterie-Regiment "Der Führer"* and staged it to the left of the *III./SS-Infanterie-Regiment "Der Führer"*. He ordered the attached *Artilleriegruppe Hecht*, consisting of the *II./Artillerie-Regiment 61* and the *I./SS-Artillerie-Regiment "Reich"*, to also go into position to the left of the highway with forward observers with the *I./* and *III./SS-Infanterie-Regiment "Der Führer"*. While these two battalions were to carry out the attack, the *II./SS-Infanterie-Regiment "Der Führer"* was to screen on both sides of the highway and provide supporting fire for the attack. The regiment then launched its attack during the night.

It broke into the system of positions. In bitter, hand-to-hand fighting conducted almost exclusively with hand-held weapons, the two battalions' assault troops penetrated the enemy positions. Facing them was an elite Russian formation — the Siberian 32nd Rifle Division. The assault troops fought their way forward from one section of trench to the next. During the night of October 13/14 they broke through nearly the entire depth of the position in a narrow wedge.

Contact was established with *SS-Infanterie-Regiment "Deutschland"*. By 2015 hours the *I./SS-Infanterie-Regiment "Der Führer"* was northwest of Jelnja (II). At 2315 hours corps order No. 6 telephonically reached *SS-Division "Reich"* at Kandassowa with the following mission for 14 October:

> *SS-Division "Reich"* is to complete breaking through the Moscow defense position. As first objective, it is to advance to the line: Fomino — Artemki — Utizy — Semenowskoje — Kolotscha River south of Borodino. It is to clear those enemy units that have not been attacked out of the positions between Karshen and Borodino. As soon as the combat elements of the *10. Panzer-Division* have been brought forward, it is to renew its attack, advancing via Bol. Sokolowo and Moshaisk and then continues the attack to Rusa.

Sub-Section k)

Breaking Through the Moscow Defense Position: 14 -26 October 1941

14 October 1941

During the night of 13/14 October, *SS-Infanterie-Regimenter "Deutschland"* and *"Der Führer"*, were able to broaden the penetration in heavy, costly fighting, often hand-to-hand. By morning, they had broadened the penetration point to three kilometers.

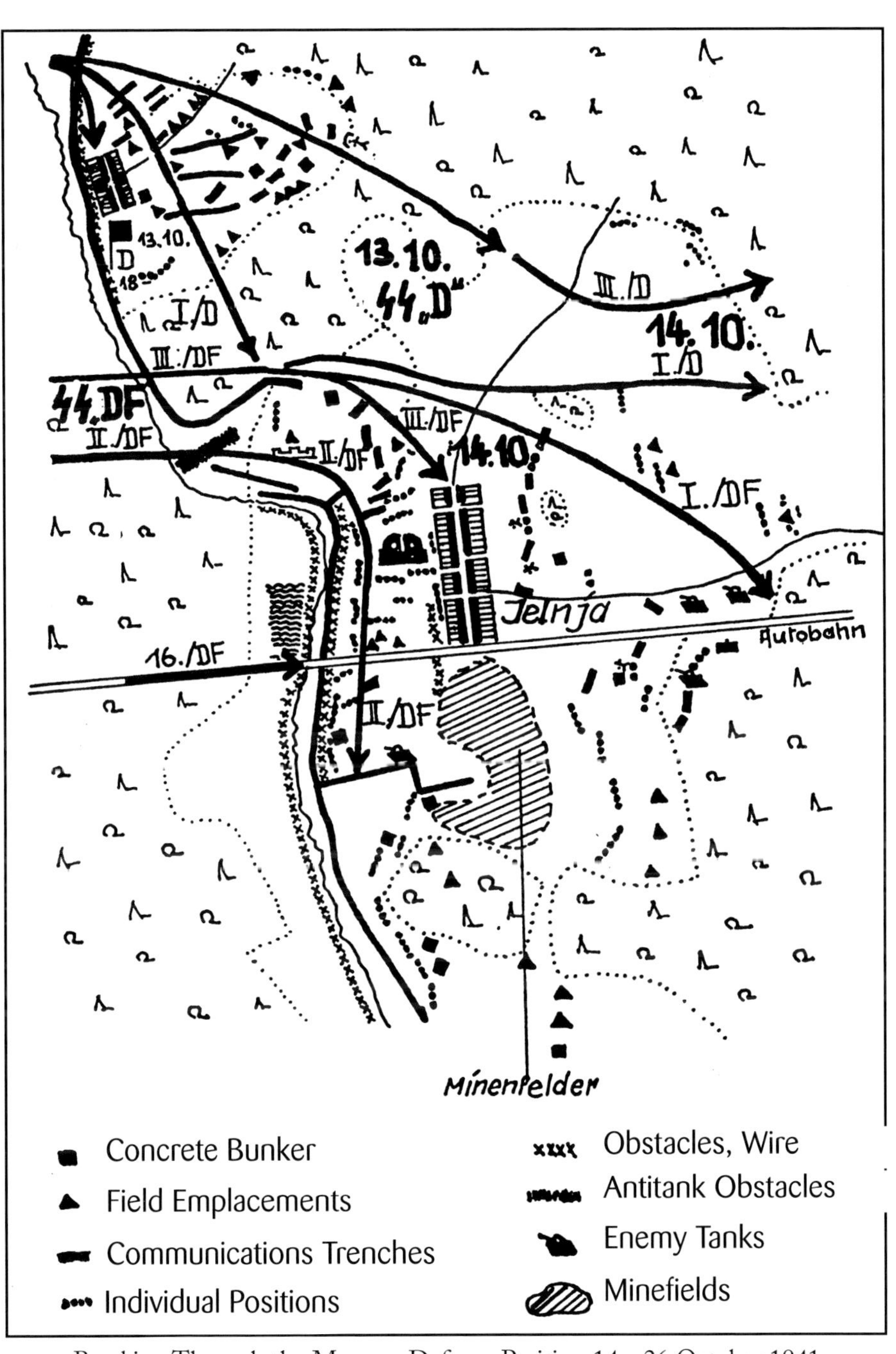

Breaking Through the Moscow Defense Position 14 - 26 October 1941

During the morning of 14 October, the *II./SS-Infanterie-Regiment "Der Führer"* was brought forward with the mission of rolling up the enemy system of positions to the south past the highway. That would clear the road for the *10. Panzer-Division*, which was standing by to move out. *Sturmgeschütz "Blücher"*, which was employed with the *II./SS-Infanterie-Regiment "Der Führer"*, supported the battalion's fight. The *"Blücher"* immobilized one of the new Russian 32-ton KV 2 tanks by damaging its tracks.

The left-hand attack group, *SS-Infanterie-Regiment "Deutschland"*, employed all three battalions in the forward line with the *I./SS-Infanterie-Regiment "Deutschland"* on the right, the *II./SS-Infanterie-Regiment "Deutschland"* in the center and the *II./SS-Infanterie-Regiment "Deutschland"* on the left. The regiment's final attack objective was the edge of the woods three kilometers east of Jelnja (II) and Artemki. All three battalions reached the specified attack objectives by 1115 hours. The enemy fell back to the east.

While this fighting was still in progress, the combat engineers of the *16./SS-Infanterie-Regiment "Der Führer"* advanced along the highway. They searched the highway bridges with mine detectors, disarmed the mines and removed the demolition charges under heavy enemy fire. At least 50 built-in flamethrowers were captured on the highway before the Russians could use them.

Prisoner statements confirmed that the hard-fighting enemy was the Siberian 32nd Rifle Division, consisting of the 17th, 113th and 302nd Rifle Regiments. It had been brought in from the Japanese front. This division came from Vladivostock and had been reinforced with two new armored brigades with T 34 and KV 2 tanks. The Siberians were big, strong men in long coats with fur caps and felt boots. They were extravagantly equipped with antiaircraft and antitank guns and, above all, the *"Ratsch-Bumm"* — the dangerous 7.62-cm multi-purpose guns. They were stolid. They knew no such thing as panic. They killed and let themselves be killed. It was a terrible fight...

The Soviet medium T 34's appeared for the first time at Borodino in organic formations. Since the friendly 8.8-cm *Flak* were not always on the spot, the men had to knock out the T 34's with concentrated charges. Many times the fighting balanced on a razor's edge...

Paul Carell wrote the following:

All of the army artillery that was available in the *Panzergruppe* sector had been concentrated under the unified command of the corps artillery — *Arko 128* — and its commander, *Oberst* Weidling, so as to smash open a breach in the Soviet defensive front for the grenadiers of the *Waffen-SS* in their death-defying assault. First, however, the built-in flamethrowers with their electric fuses had to be disabled. Then came the minefields. The wire obstacles. Bunkers.

The experienced assault troops ran under the defensive fire of the massed antiaircraft and antitank guns and mortars. Immediate counterattacks by Russian tanks were repulsed in close-in fighting. All Hell broke loose.

Soviet low-flying aircraft hissed above their heads. Friendly fighters of the *VIII. Flieger-Korps* swept through the broken clouds in the smoke-filled heavens. The dressing stations filled up...

Tankers lay in rows in their black uniforms — the grenadiers in their torn-up field blouses — the men of the *Waffen-SS* in their spotted camouflage jackets. Dead. Severely wounded. Burned. Stunned. Eyes filled with rage — on both sides. There was no longer any mercy.

And then the trenches and bunker lines of the Siberians were torn open at one spot. The two infantry regiments (sic!) of *SS-Division "Reich"*, *SS-Infanterie-Regiment "Deutschland"* and *SS-Infanterie-Regiment "Der Führer"*, attacked. There was no time for firing. Spades and rifle-butts were the weapons of choice. The Siberian batteries were captured from behind. Gun crews defended themselves behind the firing positions of the antiaircraft and antitank guns and machine guns, where they were cut down in hand-to-hand fighting. The motorized rifle regiments of the *10. Panzer-Division* fought exactly the same kind of fight. They fought on the very battlefield where Napoleon had stood 130 years before and they stormed the stubbornly defended historical fortifications of Semenowskoje. The Siberians defended in vain. (Paul Carell, *Unternehmen Barbarossa*, pp. 125-126. Frankfurt am Main / Berlin (West): Verlag Ullstein GmbH, 1963)

The Division Commander Severely Wounded!

On that day *SS-Division "Reich"* suffered a particularly heavy blow in addition to its other heavy losses. About 300 meters in front of the command post of *SS-Infanterie-Regiment "Der Führer"*, the commander of the division, *SS-Obergruppenführer* Hausser, who was revered by all, received a severe facial wound to his right eye. It came from a round fired by a tank as he personally reconnoitered the highway bridge.

SS-Hauptsturmführer Dr. Windisch, the physician and interpreter who was accompanying the division commander, wrote the following:

Early in the morning on 14 October we (division command group) were up front again. We left the motor vehicles behind and continued on foot, always trying to stay concealed along the wood line. Combat engineers were busy with a highway bridge and we approached to see how the work was coming along. Rounds from enemy tanks struck here and there repeatedly...Suddenly, the commander stopped and clutched at his right eye. We were frozen with horror. We ran to him immediately to be of assistance. He was severely wounded in the right half of his face and in the eye...After an emergency dressing had been applied he was brought to the *1. SS-Sanitäts-Kompanie*. After surgical care he was flown on from there with a *Fieseler Storch*...We were seriously concerned about his wounds. His subsequent absence was painfully felt by all of us. It was he who had truly stamped the entire division with his personality.

The bad news ran through the entire division like wildfire. Every officer, noncommissioned officer and man was deeply shaken. It was to be the last day that "Papa Hausser", as he was known to all, would lead his so frequently proven *SS-Division "Reich"*. Even though his old division repeatedly served under him when he became the commanding general of the *SS-Panzer-Korps*, the 7. *Armee* and *Heeresgruppe "G"*, *SS-Division "Reich"* had forever lost its former commander. The hearts and unconditional allegiance of his men were forever his. He was a tremendous military professional and a forceful military personality. He was respected by all of the senior commands that dealt with him. It was a black day for the division!

If, in the continued course of the war, *SS-Division "Reich"* repeatedly proved itself anew after unheard of blood-lettings and evidenced its right to an outstanding military reputation through the very end, it was more than a little thanks to the outstanding foundation laid by *SS-Obergruppenführer und General der Waffen-SS* Hausser.

SS-Oberführer Bittrich, the commander of *SS-Infanterie-Regiment "Deutschland"*, assumed command of the division. *SS-Standartenführer* Jürgen Wagner, heretofore commander of *SS-Infanterie-Regiment 11*, assumed Bittrich's former command. Wagner, in turn, was replaced as commander of *SS-Infanterie-Regiment 11* by *SS-Obersturmbannführer* Schmidhuber.

By evening of this bloody day of major fighting the first Moscow defense position had been torn open across the highway and was in friendly hands to a breadth of four kilometers.

This decisive day was outlined in the war diary of the *XXXX. Panzer-Korps* as follows:

By the morning of 14 October *SS-Division "Reich"* had advanced as far as the line: western outskirts of Jelnja (II) — eastern outskirts of Rogatschewo. It faced stronger forces which frequently attacked with armor during the course of the morning. By engaging the enemy armor with attached heavy *Flak* and by destroying pockets of resistance, the division was able to continue the attack forward so that *SS-Infanterie-Regiment "Deutschland"* reached the line Artemki — Utizy at 1400 hours. The Russians fell back to the east from Utizy.

SS-Infanterie-Regiment "Der Führer" was employed to the east of Jelnja (II) over the highway to the southeast to clear up the wooded ridges south of the highway.

Unfortunately, prior reconnaissance indicated that it would be impossible to bring up the tank brigade of the *10. Panzer-Division*, since the terrain north of the highway appeared unsuitable for armor. Passage along the highway was also impossible since there was still a Russian-occupied bunker at Jelnja (II) behind the forward limit of advance. That bunker kept up fire on the road and prevented improvement of the seriously damaged road.

The war diary of *Panzer-Regiment 7* included the following for 14 October 1941:

According to directives from corps (*XXXX. Panzer-Korps*), the regiment was initially to protect the *SS* from enemy armor and defeat the various enemy attacks with immediate counterattacks.

At 0330 hours the regiment moved out on the highway to the east in the following order of march: *I./Panzer-Regiment 7*, regimental staff, *II./Panzer-Regiment 7*. At Nowo Wassiljewka it was halted with the order to stage south of the highway.

During that period *SS-Division "Reich"* attacked the Jelenka sector, which the enemy stubbornly defended with a newly introduced Siberian division. The enemy also had light and medium tanks with him. *Panzer-Regiment 7*, however, did not need to get involved. Moving back at 1600 hours, the regiment's staff and the *I./Panzer-Regiment 7* spent the night in Ranin Fjodorowskoje and the *II./Panzer-Regiment 7* in the Chwaschtschjowka area.

While breaking through the first Moscow defense position, *SS-Division "Reich"* captured the following: 21 guns, 14 antitank guns, 92 heavy machine guns, 10 heavy mortars, 14 tanks, 65 flamethrowers, 2 trucks, 1 staff car, 1 armored car and 1 combat-engineer equipment site. Eight hundred fifty-nine prisoners were brought in.

Paul Carell wrote the following in *Unternehmen Barbarossa*: "The Siberian 32nd Rifle Division died on the hills of Borodino. When that happened, the great barrier of the first Moscow defense position on the highway to Moscow was broken." (Paul Carell, *Unternehmen Barbarossa*, p. 126. Frankfurt am Main / Berlin (West): Verlag Ullstein GmbH, 1963)

At 1930 hours the *XXXX. Panzer-Korps* sent out the following missions for 15 October to its attached formations:

The *10. Panzer-Division* is to cross the combat-outpost line of *SS-Division "Reich"* as early as possible on 15 October in pursuit. Advance past Moshaisk to the south, if possible, its first attack objective is the Kubinka area. It is to report the time it moves out.

SS-Division "Reich" is tp clear the enemy out behind the forward limit of advance that has been reached in the Karshen (inclusive) sector of the front as far as Borodino. It is then to follow directly behind the combat elements of the *10. Panzer-Division* and capture Moshaisk and the bridge over the Moskwa directly north of Moshaisk.

The additional forward movement of the division via Rusa or behind the *10. Panzer-Division* depends on the results of route reconnaissance. For that purpose, route reconnaissance patrols are to be sent out at an appropriate time with the forward elements of the *10. Panzer-Division* to scout the Moshaisk — Rusa and Dorochowa — Rusa roads.

For both divisions it is essential to gain ground to the east as rapidly as possible.

The division order for 15 October 1941 read in part:

1.) *SS-Division "Reich"*, supported by *Panzer-Regiment 7*, reached the Moscow defense position in a rapid advance on 13 October 1941. Along with the tanks of *Panzer-Regiment 7*, the division destroyed a very large number of enemy tanks. This success was mentioned in the *Wehrmacht* Report on 13 October 1941.

After locating a weak point in the enemy defense position, *SS-Infanterie-Regiment "Deutschland"* attacked immediately on 13 October and penetrated the position. In hard fighting against stubbornly defending enemy forces, the penetration was widened into a breakthrough by that regiment and *SS-Infanterie-Regiment "Der*

Führer". The breakthrough was particularly difficult in the sector of *SS-Infanterie-Regiment "Der Führer"*. While struggling for that success, *SS-Infanterie-Regiment "Der Führer"* was unable to bring field kitchens forward for several days and had no warm food in the cold weather.

2.) The enemy facing the division is strong in infantry but relatively weak in artillery. He is fighting with numerous individual tanks.

3.) Taking advantage of the movement along the highway by the *10. Panzer-Division*, *SS-Division "Reich"* is to advance on 15 October along the highway to the east, capture and secure the specified attack objective, Artemki, and hold the line Artemki — Utizy. On 16 October, moving out behind the *10. Panzer-Division*, the division will attack Rusa...

15 October 1941

With the *XXXX. Panzer-Korps* on the right — with *SS-Division "Reich"* and the *10. Panzer-Division* on the right — and the *XXXXVI. Panzer-Korps* on the left, both corps were then to attack toward Moshaisk — Moscow. There were still 100 kilometers to Moscow. Wheeled vehicles could barely move. Supplies still did not arrive. The main supply route was blocked with immobilized columns. The highway was blocked. A battle had begun with the weather and the roads.

During the night the Russians brought up substantial reinforcements. Artemki was strongly held and secured by two improved field fortifications. The Russians fired on the highway and the woods on both sides of the highway west of Artemki with heavy artillery, causing serious losses to *SS-Division "Reich"*. The Russians also employed multiple-rocket launchers (Stalin organs). Snamenskoje, Judinki and Fomina were still held by the enemy, thus threatening the right flank of *SS-Division "Reich"*. In addition, aerial reconnaissance identified ten batteries of Russian antiaircraft guns in the Tschebunowo — Moshaisk area along the highway.

These reports caused the corps decision to have the *10. Panzer-Division* advance through the combat outposts of *SS-Division "Reich"* to be overcome by events. As a result, both divisions received the following new mission early on the following morning:

Artemki is to be captured under unified command of the commander of the *10. Panzer-Division* by *SS-Division "Reich"* and tanks of the *10. Panzer-Division*. To that end, *SS-Infanterie-Regiment "Deutschland"* is to attack after a systematic artillery preparation. It is to be supported by tanks that are kept "on a short rein".

However, neither of those two missions for the *10. Panzer-Division* and *SS-Division "Reich"* could be carried out. It became increasingly clear that only the first Moscow defense position had been breached on 13 and 14 October. While it was the strongest blocking position, additional defensive positions organized in considerable depth lay ahead.

The *10. Panzer-Division* reported to the corps that the terrain east of Jelnja (II) with its numerous north-south stream courses offered the enemy repeated opportunities for renewed defense, making a rapid advance or a breakthrough with armor impossible. The motorized rifle brigade of the *10. Panzer-Division*, which had been employed on the Wjasma pocket front, had not yet arrived. Therefore, the division was not fully equipped for the mission of advancing on Moshaisk along the highway.

The *10. Panzer-Division* therefore proposed that it attack via Utizy and Borodino toward Tatarin and leave *SS-Division "Reich"* to capture Artemki.

The corps accepted that recommendation and, to ensure unified artillery preparation, attached the corps artillery to *SS-Division "Reich"* in a direct-support role. *SS-Division "Reich"* was to begin its attack at 1100 hours.

At 1230 hours the operations officer of *SS-Division "Reich"*, *SS-Obersturmbannführer* Ostendorff, reported to the corps that the Russians on the right flank were too strong for the attack on Artemki to succeed. It would be necessary to first eliminate the threat to the flank. During the course of the morning the enemy repeatedly counterattacked the division's combat-outpost line in battalion strength and units also attacked Rogatschewo from the northeast.

Elements of *SS-Infanterie-Regiment "Deutschland"* were pulled out of Utizy with the mission of forcing the enemy east of Rogatschewo back to the railroad line north of the town.

In the sector of *SS-Infanterie-Regiment "Der Führer"*, the *I./* and *III./SS-Infanterie-Regiment "Der Führer"* had advanced during the night of 14/15 October farther to the east via Artemki. They had gone over to the defense at the edge of some woods several kilometers west of Borodino. In the meantime, the *II./SS-Infanterie-Regiment "Der Führer"* mopped up the first Moscow defense position farther to the south. The way was clear for the tanks of the *10. Panzer-Division*.

The unpublished history of *Panzer-Regiment 7* includes the following:

Panzer-Regiment 7 reached Jelnja (II) in the morning and turned north from there with the mission of advancing via Utizy, Borodino and Tatarinowa to attack Moshaisk from the west. The regiment assembled for the attack in the woods south of Utizy, where the front line of *SS-Division "Reich"* ran. The *I./Panzer-Regiment 7* then advanced through the enemy field fortifications at Utizy toward Borodino. With that, the tanks of the Württemberg regiment stood on historic ground. On 7 September 1812, other soldiers from Württemberg had fought and won a victory on that same ground for Napoleon.

In the second wave, the *II./Panzer-Regiment 7* advanced rapidly in close cooperation with the *SS* infantry to the foot of the wooded hills of Utizy. A monument to Napoleon stood there. Elements of the *II./Panzer-Regiment 7* and *SS* infantry mopped up the strongly improved and fortified position. Miserable road conditions prevented the infantry from moving up, so the attack had to be stopped. Nevertheless, the *1./Panzer-Regiment 7* captured Borodino, knocked out several Russian tanks in the process, and cut the Smolensk — Moscow railroad line. The *I./Panzer-Regiment 7* then screened from Borodino to the east and south. The *II./Panzer-Regiment 7* secured it to the north and west. One *SS* company was integrated into the positions to provide security for the tanks. (Walter Straub, *Geschichte des Panzer-Regiment 7.* Unpublished manuscript)

Snow and light frost made the roads practically impassible for wheeled vehicles. The fighting became increasingly difficult. Winter had arrived earlier than anticipated.

The two infantry regiments, *SS-Infanterie-Regiment "Deutschland"* and *SS-Infanterie-Regiment "Der Führer"*, suffered extraordinarily high losses. Arriving replacements only partially filled the existing gaps.

The enemy armor that had appeared in such great numbers the day before had vanished. In the evening the situation was:

SS-Division "Reich" screened to the east in the line: High ground north of Fomino — eastern wood line east of Jelnja (II) — eastern outskirts of Utizy. Additional combat outposts to the south were in the woods south of the highway. Outposts to the north were west of Utizy and, to the northeast, in Rogatschewo.

The main body of the *10. Panzer-Division* was in the area of Utizy and southwest of it. During the night, the main body of the motorized rifle brigade of the *10. Panzer-Division* reached the area east of Gshatsk.

As they had done earlier, Russian heavy artillery fired on the woods west of Artemki and multiple-rocket launchers (Stalin organs) plastered the positions.

The commander of *SS-Aufklärungs-Abteilung "Reich"*, *SS-Hauptsturmführer* Mühlenkamp, was wounded. *SS-Hauptsturmführer* Kment, who had been the commander of the *1./SS-Kradschützen-Bataillon "Reich"*, assumed command of the reconnaissance battalion. *SS-Hauptsturmführer* Weidinger took over his company.

It did not become known until evening, but early in the morning the alarm had been given at the main dressing station of *SS-Infanterie-Regiment "Deutschland"*. Word passed from mouth-to-mouth: "The Russians have broken through!" Mortar fire was already landing on the main dressing station. Everyone who could move made his way to the main dressing station of *SS-Infanterie-Regiment "Der Führer"*. The remaining wounded were loaded in haste. Fortunately, they made it to the main dressing station of *SS-Infanterie-Regiment "Der Führer"*. They were followed by Russian fire. The journey continued from there on trucks in a snowstorm to the *SS* hospital in Gshatsk.

16 October 1941

The Russian counterattack that had been expected as a result of statements by prisoners did not take place, except for a weak attack in company strength without artillery preparation. This attack, which came in the early hours of morning, was repulsed.

The mission of the *XXXX. Panzer-Korps* for 16 October read:

The corps is to carry out the planned attack via Utizy to Tatarin and then on to Moshaisk. It is to turn elements from Tatarin to the west to roll up the enemy position to Borodino.

SS-Division "Reich" is to broaden the breakthrough to the north and south so that flanking action against the highway is eliminated and the enemy still on the division's flanks is destroyed. The forward limit of advance is to be held.

SS-Infanterie-Regiment "Der Führer", to which the *II./SS-Infanterie-Regiment 11* was attached as of 0600 hours, was reorganized so that elements of the regiment oriented east along its limit of advance. The main body of the regiment was staged by 0800 hours to attack southward. The mission read:

Those positions located in the wooded area southeast of Jelnja (II) and west of those woods are to be captured and rolled up as far as the line: Snamenskoje — Judinki — southeast corner of the woods.

At 1100 hours the regiment was attacking Snamenskoje. The enemy's combat power had not been broken by breaking through the first Moscow defense position. After a planned artillery preparation directed by the corps artillery, *SS-Infanterie-Regiment "Der Führer"* succeeded in capturing Snamenskoje, Judinki and Fomino. There was heavy fighting in attacks against individual sectors. It also cleared the wooded terrain south of the highway. The Russians continued to hold Artemki with strong forces.

In spite of the increasing snowfall, the enemy employed greater numbers of ground-attack aircraft, an indicator of how much he had at stake. The weather deteriorated daily. Strong snow squalls alternated with rain; light frost at night and thaws during the day. The roads and countryside turned to sticky mud.

Losses had reached a level where the fighting could only be conducted by employing the last reserves. The companies had an average fighting strength of 35 men organized in two platoons, each consisting of two extremely weak squads. Nevertheless, the regiment reached every assigned attack objective, but at the cost of unspeakable pains and strain, according to the personal notes of the commander of *SS-Infanterie-Regiment "Der Führer"*, *Obersturmbannführer* Otto Kumm.

During the night of 15/16 October, *SS-Infanterie-Regiment "Deutschland"* reorganized its battalions so that the *II./SS-Infanterie-Regiment "Deutschland"* took over security for the regiment to the east. The *I./* and *III./SS-Infanterie-*

Regiment "Deutschland" were pulled out in the gray light of morning to roll up enemy positions north of the railroad line.

The commander of the regiment of *Schützen-Brigade 10* commandeered one platoon of antiaircraft machine guns, one platoon of *Flak* and the *Sturmgeschütz "Blücher"* as support against the Russian field fortifications. Those forces had been moving forward as directed on their way to the *I./SS-Infanterie-Regiment "Deutschland"* at Jelnja (II). The *"Blücher"* moved forward and opened fire on the built-up area and the positions in front of it, destroying an antitank gun in the process. The group then proceeded to the *I./SS-Infanterie-Regiment "Deutschland"*. On the way, the assault gun threw a track, which eliminated it from employment for the day.

Starting at 0800 hours, the *I./SS-Infanterie-Regiment "Deutschland"* cleared the woods east of Rogatschewo and attacked Fomino. Farther east, the motorized rifle brigade of the *10. Panzer-Division* advanced via Jelnja (II) to Schewardino.

At 1100 hours the *III./SS-Infanterie-Regiment "Deutschland"* set out as infantry support for the armored attack on the Borodino railroad station. By 1330 hours it had reached the edge of the woods east of Woronina. Farther south, the motorized rifle brigade was tied up until evening in a heavy firefight. As a result, the *III./SS-Infanterie-Regiment "Deutschland"* was halted and employed to secure the railroad embankment. The *III./SS-Infanterie-Regiment "Deutschland"* took heavy flanking fire from the hills southeast of Fomino and suffered heavy losses.

In light of the mission for the coming day, the *I./SS-Infanterie-Regiment "Deutschland"* was pulled back to the Kolotsch railroad station. Some elements moved to Borodino and combat outposts were left behind at the railroad.

SS-Kradschützen-Bataillon "Reich" was brought forward during the day on the highway with the mission of pushing through from the south so as to give both regiments some breathing space.

Weak elements of the *10. Panzer-Division* advanced during the day as far as the stream five kilometers west of Moshaisk. Since it had been determined that Semenewskoje and Schewardino were still strongly held by the enemy in the rear of the division, the main body of the *10. Panzer-Division* was pulled back in the evening to Tatarin, where it formed a hedgehog defense. The motorized riflemen of the *10. Panzer-Division* captured Schewardino in an attack during the evening.

The highway was totally blocked with vehicles. Pothole after pothole, deep craters…two to three thousand vehicles were stuck fast just in the section of highway between Gshatsk and Moshaisk.

***

Regarding that fighting, the *Wehrmacht* Report for 16 October 1941 stated:

In the east there is already fighting at several places on the outermost line of defenses of the Soviet capital about 100 kilometers outside of Moscow.

The vital cities of Kaluga and Kalinin, 160 kilometers to the southwest and northwest of Moscow, have been in our hands for some time.

The missions of the *XXXX. Panzer-Korps* for 17 October read:

The *10. Panzer-Division* is to mop up the enemy in the area between Schewardino and Tatarin. The main body is to proceed with the attack on Moshaisk as soon as possible.

SS-Division "Reich" is to attack on and south of the highway to the east with its main effort south of the highway. Advancing in phases, it is to advance as far as the area of the road intersection six kilometers southwest of Moshaisk.

Boundary between SS-Division "*Reich*" and the 10. Panzer-Division:

Highway as far as Jelnja (II) (to be used by both divisions) — route from Jelnja (II) to Utizy (for the *10. Panzer-Division*) — St. Borodino — southern outskirts of Nowossurino.

The *7. Infanterie-Division*, which is attached to the *XXXX. Panzer-Korps* effective immediately, is to capture Wereja and continue to advance to the Schelkowka road intersection.

17 October 1941

According to a division intelligence report, the enemy situation had developed as follows:

After the first German offensive, the enemy organized his forces on his entire western front into southern, central and northern groups. The battle of encirclement east of Kiev decisively weakened the southern group. The major portion of the central group was destroyed in the Brjansk and Wjasma pockets. The northern group suffered serious losses as a result of the German advance south of Lake Ilmen. Formations from the central group were withdrawn and employed in the north to strengthen the northern group. Attacks by that group in the Wolchow sector attempted to relieve the Leningrad army.

The enemy initially had no organized reserves to withstand the German advance east of Gshatsk. He succeeded in gaining time, however, and bringing in the 32nd Rifle Division from his northern front for the defensive positions at Jelnja (II). That was the division's opponent when it broke through the first Moscow defense position.

Belonging to that division are the 52nd Howitzer Regiment and the 133rd Light Artillery Regiment (already committed). According to statements by prisoners, an additional artillery regiment (154th?) has been brought in. Also facing the division are: Elements of the 36th Motorcycle Regiment and a march regiment that had closed up to the 32nd Division with battalions VIII, IX and X . The arrival of a large number of tanks of the 18th and 19th Tank Brigades is expected. The enemy has employed the 367th Anti-Tank Regiment for antitank defense. The fighting power of the forces in the system of positions is good.

According to statements by prisoners and captured papers, field fortifications and concrete bunkers must be expected on both sides of the highway east of Artemki.

In summary: The enemy has been forced to bring in strong forces from other frontal sectors in order to defend the Moscow defense position at Jelnja (II). After the recent defeats in the south and at Brjansk and Wjasma, he can no longer hold off the German attack on Moscow with the forces he has left.

According to the division order for 17 October, the enemy on both flanks of the site of the divisional breakthrough had been successfully attacked and forced back. In the north the fighting was still in progress. Strong enemy forces still faced the front in Artemki. New enemy forces with armor were being brought in from the east.

After bringing up the main body of *SS-Infanterie-Regiment "Deutschland"* from the northern flank as well as *SS-Kradschützen-Bataillon "Reich"*, the division staged for an attack in the woods east of Jelnja (II) in the morning of 17 October. It was intended to attack at 1000 hours to the east. The *Schwerpunkt* would be south of the highway.

The elements of the division that had fought to clear the southern flank remained there and screened it against enemy counterattacks.

SS-Infanterie-Regiment "Der Führer" (minus the *II./SS-Infanterie-Regiment "Der Führer"*) assembled for the attack in the woods west and northwest of Fomino, while screening toward Artemki. *SS-Kradschützen-Bataillon "Reich"* was then attached to the regiment after its arrival in the early morning hours. The attack was to be deeply echeloned with *SS-Kradschützen-Bataillon "Reich"* at the front. The motorcycle battalion had been employed blocking the highway Gshatsk — Wjasma— west of Gshatsk until that point. The attack was to proceed via Fomino (built-up area) to one kilometer east of Fomino and then to Siwkowka.

After the attack of *SS-Infanterie-Regiment "Deutschland"* freed up the *I./* and *III./SS-Infanterie-Regiment "Der Führer"* from the front, they were to assemble in the security zones. They would then close up to *SS-Kradschützen-Bataillon "Reich"*.

SS-Aufklärungs-Abteilung "Reich" had the mission of advancing to Michailowskoje with its main body. It would reconnoiter to the right flank and its front as far as the line Protwa River — Borisowo — southern outskirts of Moshaisk.

The *Gruppe Schmidthuber* — the reinforced *II./SS-Infanterie-Regiment 11* and the *II./SS-Infanterie-Regiment "Der Führer* — was to screen in its previous positions and reconnoiter to the south and southeast.

Two artillery battalions were directed to support *SS-Kradschützen-Bataillon "Reich"*.

After a planned artillery preparation, the division launched the attack south of the highway at 0730 hours with the reinforced *SS-Kradschützen-Bataillon "Reich"* (one assault gun, one antiaircraft machine-gun platoon and one *Pak* platoon). For the entire day, the division fought its way farther forward to the east. The enemy was weaker than expected.

SS-Infanterie-Regiment "Deutschland" on the left was to capture Artemki from the north. Its attack was scheduled for later.

The situation changed in the morning in the sector of the *10. Panzer-Division* to the extent that the Russians attacked in the rear of the division in an enveloping movement from the north. Weak forces advanced from the woods east of Golobino. That made an immediate advance on Moshaisk impossible and called for the immediate clearing of the terrain in the rear of the *10. Panzer-Division.*

In the early gray dawn, the enemy attacked all three battalions of *SS-Infanterie-Regiment "Deutschland"*, so the intended attack to the east had to be postponed. The enemy continued to hold the field fortifications north of the railroad line, where he could threaten the highway from the north if the regiment withdrew.

Nevertheless, the order telephonically arrived at 1200 hours that the *I./* and *III./SS-Infanterie-Regiment "Deutschland"* were to pull out. The regiment (minus) was to assemble at the edge of the woods west of Artemki — Utizy for an attack to the east.

At 1525 hours Russian aircraft delivered a low-level attack with bombs and strafing on the woods and along the wood line. An ammunition vehicle was hit and burned up. There were no other losses.

At 1630 hours the *III./SS-Infanterie-Regiment "Deutschland"* attacked Artemki via the edge of the woods and through an antitank ditch. The *I./SS-Infanterie-Regiment "Deutschland"* had orders to follow, echeloned to the left rear. At 1700 hours the enemy had not yet discovered the approach. When the advance was only 400 meters from Artemki, nine *Stukas* attacked Artemki. It was a complete surprise to friendly forces, to whom the attack had not been announced. In the blink of an eye, the friendly forward line was marked by orange smoke and flare signals.

Taking immediate advantage of that terrific support, the *III./SS-Infanterie-Regiment "Deutschland"* advanced into Artemki and took over 200 prisoners. The aerial attack had killed many Russians.

At 2000 hours the *III./* and *I./SS-Infanterie-Regiment "Deutschland"* took control of Artemki, while the *II./SS-Infanterie-Regiment "Deutschland"* remained in foxholes at the edge of the woods. When this happened, the stubbornly defended center of strong enemy resistance in the center of the first Moscow defense position, which had prevented the division's advance for so long, was finally eliminated. Captured in Artemki were two tanks (knocked out by the *II./SS-Infanterie-Regiment "Deutschland"*), three heavy antiaircraft guns and numerous machine guns. The number of prisoners rose to 240.

The heavy, bitter fighting of the last few days began to yield results.

SS-Infanterie-Regiment "Der Führer" captured Siwkoka with the attached motorcycle battalion. As evening drew near, *Sturmgeschütze "Ziethen"* fired on a retreating enemy column. Heavy fire from Russian antiaircraft guns prevented a continued advance. As darkness fell the attack was halted in Siwkowa.

The corps commanders were briefed on the continued conduct of the operation against Moscow at a meeting with the commanding general of *Panzergruppe 4* on 17 October. The discussion ran as follows:

> *Panzergruppe 4* will cut Moscow off from the west, north and northeast. Moscow itself is not to be entered, by order of the *Führer*. The beltway is the limit of advance.
>
> Friendly forces on the right: *4. Armee*. Friendly forces on the left: *9. Armee*. In addition to the *XXXX. Panzer-Korps*, the *XXXXVI. Panzer-Korps* and the *VIII. Armee-Korps* are attached to *Panzergruppe 4*.
>
> *XXXX. Panzer-Korps* will advance against the west and northwest front of Moscow. It is essential that mobile forces cross to the north bank of the Moskwa River. The corps has the initial mission of capturing Wereja and Moshaisk.

Regarding the enemy situation, *Generaloberst* Hoepner stated:

> The Russians no longer have an army and, therefore, cannot continue to conduct operations. They have, however, brought in the Manchurian 32nd Division, a thoroughly effective formation, and four newly formed armored brigades. In Moscow itself they will have police and security formations. Those, however, will not be able to be employed outside of Moscow.

The missions of the *XXXX. Panzer-Korps* for 18 October read:

> The *10. Panzer-Division*, massing its forces, is to attack Moshaisk from the Tatarin area.
>
> *SS-Division "Reich"* is to advance with its main body south of the highway. It is to advance as far as the Akssjenjewo — Moshaisk road, turn to the northeast and advance on both sides of the named road via road intersection 197.1 to Moshaisk.

Assault on the Highway Intersection Southwest of Moshaisk

18 October 1941

Early in the morning the reinforced *SS-Kradschützen-Bataillon "Reich"* set out within the framework of *SS-Infanterie-Regiment "Der Führer"* to the north to the highway. It then continued along the highway to attack the road intersection south of Moshaisk. Thanks to favorable weather conditions, the *Luftwaffe* played a particularly successful role in the early morning as it attacked enemy armor and artillery positions at Kokarino, and antiaircraft positions near the road intersection southwest of Moshaisk and Wereja.

Several antiaircraft guns and vehicles were captured on the highway.

The *Luftwaffe* provided outstanding support for the division during these difficult days.

Sturmgeschütz "Ziethen", which was advancing with the leading elements, had to cross a weak bridge that collapsed under its weight. The *"Ziethen"* fell about four meters, but was then hauled out by the *"Yorck"*.

As the advance continued, approaching Russian armor was fired on and forced to turn away. While the *"Ziethen"* continued to fire on the Russian tanks, the *"Yorck"* opened fire on an ammunition column, setting five vehicles on fire. After a brief halt in Tschebunowa, the advance continued six kilometers farther east along the highway. The lead infantry elements rode on the two *Sturmgeschütze*. Two kilometers farther, the leading elements took heavy fire from both right and left. The *Kradschützen* immediately took cover and the *"Ziethen"* fired on and destroyed one of the 7.62-cm antiaircraft guns that was doing the firing.

In order to identify additional targets, the vehicle commander of the *"Ziethen"*, *SS-Oberscharführer* Engelputzeder, opened the hatch for a moment and observed with binoculars. In that moment a bullet from a sniper in a tree killed him. The *"Ziethen"* moved back with its dead commander to evacuate his remains.

The attacking spearhead of the motorcycle battalion was held up for a long time by no more than a few riflemen in foxholes and snipers in trees until the snipers in the trees were eliminated by spraying the crowns of the trees with machine-gun fire. The riflemen in the foxholes in the midst of the woods had a restricted field of fire. They were enveloped by several squads of the *3./SS-Kradschützen-Bataillon "Reich"*. They held their positions to the death.

After the *"Ziethen"* moved back to the front with a new commander, the two *Sturmgeschütze* engaged retreating Russian columns.

A difficult woodland fight developed shortly outside the road intersection southwest of Moshaisk (western intersection). After the *3./SS-Kradschützen-Bataillon "Reich"* launched a northward enveloping attack in the woods, the *1./* and *2./SS-Kradschützen-Bataillon "Reich"* succeeded in storming and holding the intersection itself after costly and bitter hand-to-hand fighting.

The *3./SS-Kradschützen-Bataillon "Reich"* sent out a patrol led by *SS-Oberscharführer* Kloskowski to Moshaisk. The patrol brought back important information that contributed to the rapid capture of the city. Russian artillery and multiple-rocket launchers laid down concentrated fire on the wooded area west of the road intersection. It seemed that all Hell had broken loose — but it was too late. The vital road intersection was already in German hands and was immediately secured. Before darkness fell Russian tanks were fired on at long range and forced to turn away. The two assault guns stayed to secure the highway that night while the *Kradschützen* provided security for them.

The Capture of Moshaisk

SS-Infanterie-Regiment "Deutschland" launched its attack at 0800 hours with the *I./SS-Infanterie-Regiment "Deutschland"* to the right of the highway and the *III./SS-Infanterie-Regiment "Deutschland"* to the left of it. The *II./SS-Infanterie-Regiment "Deutschland"* followed behind the latter battalion. While still en route to the *III./SS-Infanterie-Regiment "Deutschland"* at Kromino, two *Sturmgeschütze* — the *"Lützow"* and *"Blücher"* — opened fire on Russian tanks. The Russian tanks did not reply, they withdrew instead.

Initially, the regiment encountered only limited enemy resistance. One antiaircraft battery was surprised while tearing down and was shot to pieces. Four heavy antiaircraft guns and prime movers were left on the highway. All of the highway bridges had been blown up.

At 1145 hours the division commander, *SS-Oberführer* Bittrich, who was with the leading elements of the regiment, turned the two leading battalions to the northeast with the mission of initially reaching Sobolki and securing there. The *II./SS-Infanterie-Regiment "Deutschland"* was brought up to Sokolowo and advanced toward Nowossurjino, which was reached at 1300 hours without any enemy contact.

For the capture of Moshaisk, *SS-Infanterie-Regiment "Deutschland"* attacked the southern part of the city from the southwest while the *10. Panzer-Division* attacked the northern part from the northwest.

Combat reconnaissance was sent from Sokolowo. The two battalions received the mission from the commander of the regiment, *SS-Standartenführer* Wagner, that they were to advance via Nowosurjino to the section of the city of Moshaisk that was south of the railroad and to secure the high ground east of the city to the east and south.

At that point it was uncertain whether the *10. Panzer-Division*, which was attacking the northern sector of the city, had already reached its objective.

At 1400 hours the commanding general of *Panzergruppe 4*, *Generaloberst* Hoepner, showed up at the regiment's command post in Sobolki and was briefed on the situation.

At 1500 hours the *III./* and *I./SS-Infanterie-Regiment "Deutschland"* set out from Nowossurjino to Moshaisk, which they reached. The *"Blücher"* destroyed one gun and one antiaircraft gun en route, while the *"Lützow"* destroyed an antitank gun. Individual Soviet tanks also appeared in Moshaisk, two of which were destroyed. It was obvious the enemy placed a high priority on holding the highway/road intersections southwest and south of Moshaisk. At the same time, he clearly no longer had enough forces available to simultaneously defend the city of Moshaisk.

At 1600 hours the commanding general of the *XXXX. Panzer-Korps*, Stumme, and the division commander arrived at the regiment's command post. That was a sign of the importance and significance attached to the capture of Moshaisk and reaching and crossing the Moskwa River.

Motorized infantry accompanied *Panzer-Regiment 7* in its attack on Moshaisk. After they had traversed the woods west of Kukarino, the *II./Panzer-Regiment 7* received orders at 1430 hours to capture Moshaisk in conjunction with the motorized infantry. It was then to screen to the east from the eastern portion of the city of Tschertanowo.

The *II./Panzer-Regiment 7* bypassed an antitank ditch at Hill 211 by swinging around to the northeast. Coming from the northwest, it reached a major road and Moshaisk without enemy contact. During the advance the tank battalion was informed by the regiment that elements of *SS-Division "Reich"* were approaching the city from the south. Pushing on through, the battalion reached Tschertanowo, where the leading company knocked out five out of eight approaching Russian tanks.

During the night, the *I./* and *III./SS-Infanterie-Regiment "Deutschland"* established contact with *Schützenbrigade 89 (10. Panzer-Division)* in Janskaja (the southern part of Moshaisk) and screened to the south and east.

As a result, *SS-Division "Reich"* and the *10. Panzer-Division* had taken the important city of Moshaisk and were 100 kilometers from Moscow!

The *II./SS-Infanterie-Regiment "Deutschland"* remained in Nowossurjino. During its advance to Moshaisk, *SS-Infanterie-Regiment "Deutschland"* had captured four heavy antiaircraft guns with prime movers and taken 94 prisoners.

The regiment's signals platoon picked up the following Russian radio message: "The *SS* is attacking along the highway. We are suffering heavy losses in men and materiel. Urgently request armor and antiaircraft support."

SS-Infanterie-Regiment "Deutschland" reported to the division that it had heavy losses of men due to the incessant physical and mental overloads during the recent days of major fighting roughly coinciding with breaking through the first Moscow defense position. Along with the heavy losses in killed and wounded, these were men who were totally exhausted and had been pushed to the extreme limits of their physical and psychological capabilities. The attack in muddy terrain covered with slush — covering many kilometers to Moshaisk while carrying heavy weapons, ammunition and equipment on their shoulders — had exhausted the last reserves of the men's strength. It would be impossible to demand more of troops than had been demanded of the men of *SS-Division "Reich"*. Demands they had freely accepted.

At 1800 hours Moshaisk was firmly in German hands. The combat outposts of the two divisions were at the eastern outskirts of the city. The enemy was placing harassing fire on the city from the northeast.

As a result of the success that had been achieved, the corps sent the following missions to the divisions:

The *10. Panzer-Division* is to advance through Schelkowska to Rusa in order to continue the advance from there to Swenigorod. The road via Moshaisk — Otjakowo — Michailowskoje — highway and the old post road are at its disposal.

SS-Division "Reich" is to mop up the highway to Michailowskoje.

The *5. Panzer-Division* is to advance via Moshaisk to Wjedjenskoje.

The corps artillery will move out on 19 October with the main body of the army-level artillery to the *10. Panzer-Division.*

Move out as soon as possible. Report departure times.

19 October 1941

Paul Carell wrote the following regarding the capture of Moshaisk:

Panic in Moscow — "The Germans are Coming!"

Moshaisk fell on 19 October 1941. Moshaisk! That was at the gates of Moscow. Only a hundred kilometers on the highway. And the Moshaisk highway led right to the Soviet capital. "Moshaisk has fallen," was heard in the streets of Moscow. "Moshaisk has fallen. The *Germanjetzki* are coming."

The chimneys of the Kremlin poured out smoke as if it were -30 degrees Celsius (-22 degrees Fahrenheit). The secret archives that could not be evacuated were being burned. The Muscovites were stunned. Only fourteen days ago they had been infused with confidence in victory when they were told of America's promises of aid.

On 2 October Churchill's representative, Lord Beaverbrook, and Roosevelt's agent, Harriman, had signed the protocol regarding the Anglo-American supply of weapons. Although the United States was still neutral and not in the war, it was proclaimed that the three great powers were resolved to work together to attain victory over the German archenemy of all nations. For the first ten months, starting on 1 October, the following were promised and supplied:

3,000 aircraft — 2,000 more than the *Luftwaffe* had in service on 30 September on the Eastern Front.

4,000 tanks — three times as many as all three *Panzergruppen* had available on 30 September.

30,000 motor vehicles.

But was that all coming too late? Had Hitler again won the race against the western powers, just as he had won it once before in 1939 in the Kremlin?...

...On 15 October at 1250 hours Foreign Minister Molotow received the American ambassador Steinhardt and informed him that the regime, except for Stalin, was leaving Moscow. The diplomatic corps would be evacuated to Kuybischew, 850 kilometers east of Moscow. Each person could bring only as much luggage as he could personally carry.

As word of that spread through the city and, what was more, news spread that Lenin's coffin had been transported from the mausoleum on Red Square, panic broke out: “The Germans are coming!” (Paul Carell, *Unternehmen Barbarossa*, pp. 126-127. Frankfurt am Main / Berlin (West): Verlag Ullstein GmbH, 1963.)

During the night of 19 October the following series of alarming radio messages from the *10. Panzer-Division* reached the corps:

The division staff and other staffs have been involved in heavy fighting since 2200 hours. Heavy losses. Staff temporarily incapable of moving…

Division staff still involved in fighting. Artillery fire from the north..

Firefight still in progress, including 2 - 3 enemy tanks!…

Heavy losses in Nowaja-Derewnja and with the reconnaissance battalion, which has been attacked in Kriwuschimo, where it has repulsed attacks by armor. Mopping up still in progress…

At 0840 hours the *10. Panzer-Division* stated that the mission of attacking farther to the east was impossible as long as the enemy to the north had not been attacked.

The area in the rear of the *10. Panzer-Division* was mopped up and, in the course of the day, contact was established with *SS-Division “Reich”*. The Russians who had penetrated with weak units into Moshaisk were again thrown out and the eastern outskirts of the city were secured.

Numerous strong enemy forces were still on the northern and southern flanks of the *XXXX. Panzer-Korps*. However, the only place that they attempted to break through to the east was in the north in the sector of the *10. Panzer-Division*. Some of the enemy on the southern flank of *SS-Division “Reich”* remained in their positions and some units attempted to withdraw to the east.

Reinforced *SS-Kradschützen-Bataillon “Reich”* launched an attack to the east on the highway toward the road intersection south of Moshaisk (the east crossing) and Jasenow. Heavy underbrush made the attack very difficult and several Russian tanks and antitank guns joined in the fight. The enemy put up a stubborn defense. *Sturmgeschütz “Yorck”* knocked out a 24-ton tank and two antitank guns while engaging the field fortifications. The *“Ziethen”* came under heavy fire from the left from an antiaircraft gun while it was engaging an antitank gun, which it knocked out. The hull of the assault gun was penetrated. The crew was forced to bail out and take cover. The *“Ziethen”* was later able to move back under its own power.

Within *SS-Kradschützen-Bataillon “Reich”*, the commander, *SS-Sturmbannführer* Klingenberg, was slightly wounded, but remained with his unit. The battalion adjutant, *SS-Obersturmführer* André, was killed and the commander of the *2./SS-Kradschützen-Bataillon “Reich”*, *SS-Obersturmführer* Wagner, was wounded.

SS-Infanterie-Regiment “Deutschland” received orders during the night to attack the point of woods south of Kolatschewo as far as the highway. It was to advance via Kolatschewo. The attack was intended to roll up the enemy in his positions from the flank, thus relieving the pressure on *SS-Infanterie-Regiment "Der Führer"*.

A second battalion was to attack the eastern road intersection and establish a hedgehog position there. After mopping up the positions facing *SS-Infanterie-Regiment "Der Führer"* and regrouping, the attack was to continue along the highway to Michailowskoje.

The *II./SS-Infanterie-Regiment "Deutschland"* — minus the *1./SS-Infanterie-Regiment "Deutschland"*, which was detailed as security for the division staff) and with the attached *16.(Pionier)/SS-Infanterie-Regiment "Deutschland"* — took over the screening mission from the other two battalions.

The *III./SS-Infanterie-Regiment "Deutschland"* launched its attack on the field fortifications facing *SS-Infanterie-Regiment "Der Führer"* at 0700 hours, while the *I./SS-Infanterie-Regiment "Deutschland"* attacked the road intersection. Both battalions received heavy enemy fire from heavy weapons from the southern outskirts of Jamskaja.

At 0800 hours the *I./SS-Infanterie-Regiment "Deutschland"* captured Hill 230 after an intense firefight and remained there under heavy enemy fire for the time being. The attack of the *III./SS-Infanterie-Regiment "Deutschland"* stalled in heavy enemy fire at the southern outskirts of Jamskaja. At the same time Jamskaja was under heavy fire from enemy artillery and multiple-rocket launchers.

Russian infantry was able to advance along the railroad embankment as far as the edge of the built-up area at the boundary between the *II./SS-Infanterie-Regiment "Deutschland"* and the *10. Panzer-Division*. The immediate counterattack by the *7./SS-Infanterie-Regiment "Deutschland"* forced the enemy — two companies strong — back and resulted in the capture of more than 50 prisoners.

At 0955 hours a combat patrol of the *III./SS-Infanterie-Regiment "Deutschland"* advanced into Kolatschewo. At 1000 hours *SS-Kradschützen-Bataillon "Reich"* was able to find and advance its attack into a soft spot in the enemy defenses. At 1100 hours the battalion reached the east edge of the woods 1,200 meters west of the road intersection. The *III./SS-Infanterie-Regiment "Deutschland"* was then turned to the east to join *SS-Kradschützen-Bataillon "Reich"* in attacking the road intersection.

Eight Russian tanks probed the deep flanks of the *I./SS-Infanterie-Regiment "Deutschland"*. Three of the tanks were knocked out. The battalion screened the regiment's left flank from Hill 230 to the east.

The enemy suffered heavy losses from the concentrated fire of all weapons as the main body of the battalion advanced into the deep flank of the enemy forces that were falling back before *SS-Infanterie-Regiment "Der Führer"*. At

1210 hours an energetic advance by the *III./SS-Infanterie-Regiment "Deutschland"* reached the road intersection, which the battalion then secured to the north and east. The battalion also established contact with *SS-Infanterie-Regiment "Der Führer"* and *SS-Kradschützen-Bataillon "Reich"*.

At 1400 hours the following order went out to all elements of the division:

> *SS-Division "Reich" is to* secure and holds the previous limit of advance, reconnoiter to its front and on the right flank and close up with the main body in the area east of Artemki.

With that the men of the division were finally granted at least a brief period of quiet. The reconnaissance sent out farther eastward did not make any contact with the enemy.

Most of the vehicles of both divisions were stuck fast and it was necessary to close them up. In addition, the troops needed a day of rest after the hard fighting, so the corps chose not to continue the attack on 20 October. The divisions received the mission to improve the current combat-outpost lines and prepare for a systematic attack on 21 October by sending out combat and zone reconnaissance.

On that day the commander-in-chief of *Heeresgruppe Mitte*, *Generalfeldmarschall* von Bock, issued his appreciation of the conclusion of the double-battle of Wjasma – Brjansk in the form of an order-of-the-day. *SS-Division "Reich"* participated in that operation through its advance via Juchnow to Gshatsk and through the advance of *SS-Kradschützen-Bataillon "Reich"* to the west on the Gshatsk — Wjasma highway, which it then blocked in the direction of Wjasma. *Generalfeldmarschall* von Bock's order read:

Order of the Day

The battle of Wjasma and Brjansk collapsed the Russian front with its many successive lines of fortifications. In heavy fighting with the numerically superior enemy, eight Russian armies with 73 rifle, 73 cavalry and 13 armored divisions and brigades, along with strong army artillery were eliminated.

Enemy losses included: 673,098 prisoners, 1,277 tanks, 4,378 guns, 1,009 antiaircraft and antitank guns, 87 airplanes and vast amounts of military equipment.

You have come through this heavy fighting with honor. In so doing, you have brought about the greatest feat of arms of the campaign!

I offer my special thanks and recognition to all the commands and formations that have taken part in this success, both in and behind the front.

/signed/ von Bock
Generalfeldmarschall

***

The division sent its "Report on the operations from 10 - 20 October 1941" to the *SS* Main Office in Berlin. The report outlined the attack east of Gshatsk and the penetration of the Moscow defense position. In addition to other matters, the report closed with the following:

The forces have been attacking without let-up since 6 October 1941. Great successes have been attained in spite of terrible road conditions and the worst weather imaginable (snowstorms, glare ice, thaws) and, oftentimes, without opportunity to bring vehicles, particularly field kitchens, forward.

The forces are now at the end of their capabilities: Officers, men and vehicles. Intestinal diseases, stomach diseases, frostbite and a general condition of weakness are setting in. Uniforms and equipment must be repaired and maintained.

A period of several days rest with the opportunity to bring the men into heated quarters is required to accomplish the minimal preparations for continuation of the attack.

Addendum: According to directives that have just arrived, the division is to set out on 23 October 1941 to continue the advance to the east behind the *10. Panzer-Division.*

***

The commanding general of the *XXXX. Panzer-Korps* prepared a comprehensive report to *Panzergruppe 4* that, yet again, brought out the decisive part played by *SS-Division "Reich"* in breaking through the Moscow defense position. The report states as follows:

The Beginning of the Battles to Encircle Moscow and the Capture of Moshaisk

The mission of capturing Moshaisk was assigned when the *XXXX. Panzer-Korps* was still employed in the pocket battle of Wjasma. For that purpose all forces that were freed up were withdrawn from the front and sent to *SS-Division "Reich"* at Gshatsk. A reinforced tank regiment of the *10. Panzer-Division* was set in movement to *SS-Division "Reich"* in spite of serious concerns by *Panzergruppe 4*. That measure worked out quite well. As a result of receiving the armored support, *SS-Division "Reich* was able to reach the Moscow defense position after costly fighting with enemy armor southeast of Gshatsk and rapidly breaking enemy resistance east of the city.

On 13 October the first discussion regarding carrying out the mission took place with the division commanders of the *10. Panzer-Division* and *SS-Division "Reich"*. The *10. Panzer-Division* left no more than Bülow's motorized infantry brigade at Wjasma so that it could reassume command of the elements of the *10. Panzer-Division* that had been attached to *SS-Division "Reich"* up to that point. *General der Waffen-SS* Hausser was not yet able to give a final estimate regarding the position at Jelnja (II) west of Moshaisk. However, he passed on his impression that the position was well built and strongly held.

I decided to have the *10. Panzer-Division* outflank Moshaisk — if possible via Porjetsche or Bultschewo — in order to capture the city from the north or northeast. It could be assumed that the Moscow defense position was not as strongly held at Karatscharowo or Gorsztowo and that the direction of attack was favorable from there for the capture of Moshaisk.

I therefore ordered an immediate route reconnaissance of both routes by the *10. Panzer-Division*. *SS-Division "Reich"* was to conduct zone reconnaissance on both sides of the highway and zone reconnaissance of the routes south of the highway so that, if necessary, that division would be able to attack with its *Schwerpunkt* south of the highway. My own reconnaissance of the position at Jelnja (II) showed that the position made good use of the terrain and would be difficult to capture frontally if the troops holding the position were suitably led and had sufficient supporting weapons. Not a shot was fired. About 200 Russians proceeded, fully exposed, into their positions. Apparently, they had been ordered to occupy their positions.

SS-Division "Reich" approached the position with both regiments deployed abreast. During that movement, however, the route north of the road (the post road) turned out to be so bad that heavy weapons could not be brought forward with the troops. It was only possible for prime movers to get through. I decided to prepare a deliberate attack to the front with *SS-Division "Reich"*. I wanted to concentrate the artillery in the expectation that the enemy might have an adequate number of infantry but lacked adequate heavy weapons and artillery. Deserters indicated that morale was poor.

In accord with that decision, appropriate orders were to be issued when *SS-Infanterie-Regiment "Deutschland"* reported it had broken through the position north of the highway at Rogatschewo and captured Doronino. On its own initiative, *SS-Division "Reich"* then ordered an immediate attack by *SS-Infanterie-Regiment "Der Führer"* on both sides of the highway to capture Jelnja (II) so that *SS-Infanterie-Regiment "Deutschland"* would not be left hanging in the air.

That fundamentally changed the situation. It had become clear that the position was not strongly held at every point, at least to a depth of several kilometers.

That encouraged the belief that an attack in the morning would be able to break through the position, even with deliberate attack planning preparations. If that was correct, it seemed that the wide outflanking movement of the *10. Panzer-Division* was no longer necessary. A breakthrough in depth could lead more rapidly and surely to the objective. In addition, the zone reconnaissance to Porjetsche had only progressed as far as eight kilometers from Gshatsk and found the route to be bottomless mud.

I therefore decided to stage the *10. Panzer-Division* behind *SS-Division "Reich"*. It could then either use its armor to get an infantry attack that had bogged down moving again or, if that was not necessary, then it could pass through the infantry of *SS-Division "Reich"* and move onto Moshaisk as soon as the system of positions had been penetrated by the infantry of *SS-Division "Reich"*, thus clearing the way for the armored division. A corresponding limit of advance was established in the enemy's rear area.

The attack the following morning proved that this decision was correct.

The main effort was with *SS-Infanterie-Regiment "Deutschland"*, which advanced from the northwest to the southeast, while *SS-Infanterie-Regiment "Der Führer"* advanced to its front. That day, in spite of enemy armored attacks — a Russian armored brigade had, in the meantime, been reported — the attack reached the far edge of the woods west of Artemki. It was, however, only late in the day that the attack reached the antitank ditches and steel-hedgehog obstacles, since the numerous stubbornly defended flanking bunkers prevented an approach. The combat engineers were not able to finish bridging over the ditches so that armor and vehicles could cross until the following morning.

Although *SS-Division "Reich"* had not fully reached the specified line for the passage of the *10. Panzer-Division* — Fomino — Artemki — Utizy — I nevertheless decided to have the *10. Panzer-Division* pass through it the next day and capture Moshaisk from the south. In the meantime, its motorized infantry brigade had closed up. I would leave *SS-Division "Reich"* to mop up the infantry position along the highway and both sides of it. *SS-Division "Reich"* would then continue to advance to the east behind the *10. Panzer-Division* on the highway and the post road.

***

Before the start of the movement, the *10. Panzer-Division* requested unified command on the battlefield. That meant that those elements of *SS-Division "Reich"* that were not involved in mopping up the position and were facing the enemy would be attached to the *10. Panzer-Division.* I indicated my approval and issued corresponding orders to *SS-Division "Reich"*. After a short time, the commander of the *10. Panzer-Division* requested permission to leave the highway and post road and turn his division via Utizy — Borodino railroad station to the northeast so that, after reaching the Borodino — Moshaisk road, he could capture the city from the northwest. He believed he would run into too many difficulties on the highway due to mines, antitank guns and destroyed bridges and thus lose much time. That deployment was desirable and I had already planned it. Only bad weather conditions and extremely bad roads had prevented me from ordering it.

Those objections of mine were partially invalidated by the division commander, since his zone reconnaissance indicated the negotiability of the route. I called his attention to the unconditional necessity of clearing his left flank before turning toward Moshaisk. He had already included that in his plan and felt that it would neither be difficult nor time consuming to accomplish with an armored advance with infantry forces. After verbal discussion I gave my approval to that deployment in the expectation that it would eliminate the otherwise unavoidable friction between the divisions on the highway and post road. It would also allow, if necessary, an attack on Moshaisk from two sides. That seemed all the more desirable to me since, according to statements by prisoners and aerial photographs, Moshaisk had been fortified and was intended to be held. That would later be confirmed.

For *SS-Division "Reich"* it proved that mopping up was particularly necessary to the south. Strong enemy resistance in depth along the highway could force the main effort of that division. It soon turned out that the enemy intelligence estimate was incorrect. The information provided by *Panzergruppe 4*, that the enemy had only occupied positions extending a few hundred meters on both sides of the major road, while the other positions were unoccupied, also proved false. The Russian 32nd Infantry Division, an armored brigade and various other units had occupied the entire position, which they stubbornly defended. With that, the bitter struggle to widen the breakthrough and resume the operation against Moscow began.

Very bad road conditions did the rest. The *10. Panzer-Division*, whose tanks reached the Tatarin area relatively quickly, could only clear the way to the northeast one step at a time with infantry and artillery. Heavy fighting with the bunker crews in the depth of the position drew the fighting out for several days. The fighting by *SS-Division "Reich"* to broaden the breakthrough toward Judinki also proved difficult.

The second day of the attack was dominated by snowstorms that rendered forward movement nearly impossible. An attempt by the tanks of the *10. Panzer-Division* to advance alone from Tatarin to Moshaisk miscarried. A deliberate attack would be required there as well and would first call for mopping up the western flank to a greater extent than had been accomplished to date. It was repeatedly proven in the course of the fighting that lasted for days that it was extremely difficult to advance along the highway itself.

Therefore the main effort of *SS-Division "Reich"* was shifted to the south so that it would be possible with a later turn to the north to roll up the positions of the enemy along the highway by attacking him in the rear. That was a complete success.

The situation of the *10. Panzer-Division* proved particularly difficult. The division was only partially successful in clearing up its west flank. In its rear, at Borodino — Gorki, the enemy remained in his positions. Nevertheless, it was not possible to wait until that enemy was completely eliminated. Time pressed. The enemy kept bringing new reinforcements forward.

SS-Division "Reich" made good forward progress on the fourth day of the attack. It drew near to the road leading southwest from Moshaisk, thus gaining a favorable direction of attack to the northeast against the city. Clearing up the extensive wooded area in the rear and flanks of the division would have to be left for a later time.

The *7. Infanterie-Division*, coming from the south, was attached to the corps. The difficulties of the two motorized divisions in advancing gave rise to doubts about the imminence of capturing Moshaisk. On the other hand, the situation demanded that Moshaisk be in our hands as the jump-off point for continued operations. I therefore resolved, in spite of serious reservations, not to bring that division forward to the northeast on the road from Wereja. Instead, I would have it turn directly to the north to help in the capture of Moshaisk.

As it turned out, *SS-Division "Reich"* was able to penetrate into Moshaisk surprisingly quickly and link up there with the *10. Panzer-Division* while the *7. Infanterie-Division* was still far spread out to the south.

A serious crisis that developed on 19 October, when the enemy attacked Moshaisk and the intersection to its south with strong forces from the east, was resolved thanks to the stubborn defense put up by *SS-Division "Reich"*. The enemy failed to achieve his ordered objective, recapturing Moshaisk under any circumstances. Moshaisk remained firmly in our hands.

20 October 1941

The night of 19/20 October was a quiet night with no enemy action for the corps. It had snowed.

After a strong artillery preparation, *SS-Kradschützen-Bataillon "Reich"* attacked the east intersection on the highway south of Moshaisk. An engagement developed in which *Sturmgeschütz "Prinz Eugen"* knocked out a Russian self-propelled gun in a duel. During the fighting the *3./SS-Kradschützen-Bataillon "Reich"*, previously in reserve, was brought forward to good effect. The fighting was decided after contact was established with *SS-Infanterie-*

Regiment "Deutschland", which attacked south through the woods from the north. The eastern intersection was captured and security established to the east. The advance reached Lytkino.

The old post road, the improved road toward Moscow, the highway to Moscow and the Smolensk — Moscow railroad line all met at that important intersection.

The Russian positions were well constructed and cleverly laid out. *SS-Kradschützen-Bataillon "Reich"* captured several tanks, some of which had been knocked out by 8.8-cm *Flak* and *Sturmgeschütze*, and several antitank and antiaircraft guns, some of them self-propelled. The battalion probed farther to the east. It was intended for it to establish contact with the reconnaissance battalion of the *7. Infanterie-Division* at Borisowo. A strong enemy presence in Borisowo and at the Mshut River, however, rendered that impossible.

The reconnaissance that the division sent out reported that the wooded terrain southeast of the road intersection at Jasewo was clear of the enemy. The Russians were generally quiet, though they laid down intermittent harassing fire on Moshaisk and the road intersection south of it. As a result, it was not yet possible to shift the traffic, particularly the northward movement of the *5. Panzer-Division*, through the eastern intersection. The consequence was substantial traffic jams resulting from the bottomless mud conditions of the so-called "main roads".

The massive traffic jams prevented the vehicles with cleaning materials and changes of underwear for the resting infantry regiments from being brought up. That rendered an orderly and complete refitting impossible.

In spite of repeated replenishment of *SS-Infanterie-Regiment "Deutschland"* with replacement officers, noncommissioned officers and enlisted men since the beginning of the campaign in Russia, the following combat strengths were reported to the division as of 20 October 1941:

Unit	Officers	Platoon Leaders	Combat Strength	Remarks
1./SS-IR "D"	—	*2 Unterführer*[1]	37	only one platoon
2./SS-IR "D"	*1*	*1 Unterscharführer*	67	
3./SS-IR "D"	*1*[2]	1 NCO	27	company consists of a single platoon
4./SS-IR "D"	*2*	*2 Unterscharführer*	98	
5./SS-IR "D"	*1*	*1 Unterscharführer*	60	only two platoon
6./SS-IR "D"	*1*	*2 Unterscharführer*	58	only two platoons
7./SS-IR "D"	*1*	*1 Oberjunker* *2 Unterscharführer*	85	
8./SS-IR "D"	—	*3 Oberscharführer*	94	1 MG PLT disbanded
9./SS-IR "D"	—	*3 Unterscharführer*		70
10./SS-IR "D"	—	*3 Unterscharführer*		65

11./SS-IR "D"	*1*	*1 Unterscharführer*	47
12./SS-IR "D"	*1*	*4 Oberscharführer*	98

[1] Noncommissioned officers [2] Officer candidate

***

The divisions received the following missions for 21 October:

The *10. Panzer-Division* is to attack on both sides of the old post road and, after reaching the area east of Puschkino, also on both sides of the highway. The objective of the attack is the Dorochowo area.

SS-Division "Reich" is to attack on both sides of the highway to the east. After Puschkino is captured it is to halt its advance to the east temporarily. In addition, it is to mop up the area south of the highway. It is essential to establish contact with the reconnaissance battalion of the *7. Infanterie-Division* at Borisowo. A sufficiently strong force is to be employed to accomplish this mission.

21 October 1941

SS-Infanterie-Regiment "Deutschland" was to attack north of the highway with Michailowskoje as its first attack objective and Puschkino as its second attack objective.

When the *I./* and *III./SS-Infanterie-Regiment "Deutschland"* arrived in the staging area the enemy laid down several salvos from his multiple-rocket launchers on the route of advance. No significant damage resulted. The attack that started at 0715 hours soon reached the northwest outskirts of Otjakowo, which was clear of the enemy.

At 0810 hours a strong Russian attack from the southeast and east, consisting of two battalions supported by armor and artillery, hit *SS-Kradschützen-Bataillon "Reich"*, which was securing the eastern road intersection. The right wing of *SS-Infanterie-Regiment "Deutschland"* with the *16./SS-Infanterie-Regiment "Deutschland"*, along with the *9./* and *11./SS-Infanterie-Regiment "Deutschland"*, which had just been employed, was also involved. The left wing of *SS-Infanterie-Regiment "Der Führer"* with the *I./SS-Infanterie-Regiment "Deutschland"* was also hit. All three formations had to go over to the defensive. *Sturmgeschütz "Prinz Eugen"* supported the defensive effort. The firing positions of the *2./SS-Artillerie-Regiment "Reich"* were also endangered. After half an hour of extremely hard defensive fighting, in which individual guns had to engage in direct fire, the attack was repulsed.

The enemy had brought in the 82nd Motorized Rifle Division — a Soviet elite formation from Mongolia — to regain the vital highway/road intersection.

***

Paul Carell wrote the following regarding this defensive fighting:

When *Hauptmann* Kandusch, a liaison officer serving with the intelligence officer of the *XXXX. Panzer-Korps,* reported to *General* Stumme, there were tears in his eyes. The 18- and 20-year-old youths had hurled back two Soviet battalions in hand-to-hand combat with spades, hand grenades and bayonets. Many of the young *SS* men had been killed. And all of them were barefoot in their boots — at -15 degrees Celsius (5 degrees Fahrenheit)! (Paul Carell, *Unternehmen Barbarossa*, ?. Frankfurt am Main / Berlin (West): Verlag Ullstein GmbH, 1963.)

(Ten days of wading through mud, slush and rain had "dissolved" the men's socks and no supplies had made it forward.)

The *II./SS-Infanterie-Regiment "Deutschland"* on the regiment's left flank had moved out in the meantime and made good forward progress without any enemy contact. Michailowskoje was captured around 1500 hours, during which *"Lützow"* knocked out two enemy tanks. The battalion remained in Michailowskoje and secured it while the *I./SS-Infanterie-Regiment "Deutschland"* and two *Sturmgeschütze* moved on against Gratschewo.

The *III./SS-Infanterie-Regiment "Deutschland"* continued its attack to the day's objective of Puschkino, during which *"Blücher"* knocked out a 15-cm gun and engaged fleeing enemy columns. After heavy fighting west of the village, Puschkino was captured around 1620 hours. In the process the battalion came upon an enemy artillery column and captured five guns with tractors.

The *I./SS-Infanterie-Regiment "Deutschland"* captured Gratschewo around 1645 hours, destroying four enemy tanks.

That day *SS-Infanterie-Regiment "Deutschland"* captured 7 tanks, 22 motor vehicles, 10 guns with tractors and ammunition, 6 light and heavy machine guns, 3 heavy mortars and 1 prime mover. It also took in 80 prisoners.

The division's attack advanced so well on the left wing that by 1500 hours the corps could already send traffic to the front via the road intersection at Jasewo. Traffic returning from the front was directed via the road intersection southwest of Moshaisk

SS-Infanterie-Regiment "Der Führer" advanced as directed on the division's right wing with *"Prinz Eugen"* to the south and attacked Borisowo. The attached *SS-Kradschützen-Bataillon "Reich"* and the *I./SS-Infanterie-Regiment "Der Führer"* continued to screen the east road intersection, which was important for subsequent operations, to the east and southeast.

The large town of Borisowo, not far south of the highway, was located on a long ridge that was naturally protected to the north and south by a broad stream valley. It looked like a fortress. The reconnaissance battalion of the *7. Infanterie-Division* had captured Borisowo from the south but was forced to give it up again in heavy fighting. As a result, the march route north was temporarily blocked for the *7. Infanterie-Division.*

The enemy had constructed good positions at the outskirts of Borisowo and was supported by artillery fire coming from the east. With the *III./SS-Infanterie-Regiment "Der Führer"* on the right and the *II./SS-Infanterie-Regiment "Der Führer"* on the left, the regiment attacked from its staging area in the morning. The companies were pinned down, however, in the low ground of the stream valley by flanking fire and were unable to move so much as a step forward.

The *II./SS-Artillery Regiment "Reich"* under *SS-Sturmbannführer* Wunder supported the attack. He rapidly identified the hotspots of the enemy defense and concentrated the fire of all the guns on them. In this fashion one strongpoint after another was shot to pieces. The concentrated fire of the entire battalion was then directed on the enemy who was moving in Borisowo and rendered him combat ineffective. Utilizing that artillery fire, the companies advanced into Borisowo with effective support from *Sturmgeschütz "Prinz Eugen"* and then established contact with the reconnaissance battalion of the *7. Infanterie-Division* south of Borisowo. However, the Russians continued to put up determined resistance in the built-up area and had to be rooted out in bitter house-to-house fighting.

The *10. Panzer-Division* launched its attack in the morning on both sides of the old post road. The enemy was forced back relatively quickly. Rylkowo, Schkolowo and Alexandrowo were captured during the morning.

During a meeting of the chief of staff of the *XXXX. Panzer-Korps* at *Panzergruppe 4*, the chief of staff discovered the higher headquarters' intention to have the *XXXX. Panzer-Korps* assume the northern sector during the encirclement of Moscow.

In the evening the corps radioed to *Panzergruppe 4* that the highway between Jelnja (II) and Kromino was in a state of complete disintegration, giving rise to serious concern. Rapid employment of all available construction forces at that spot was required.

The missions the corps gave the two divisions for 22 October stated:

The *10. Panzer-Division* is to continue to attack and capture the road intersection at Dorochowo.

SS-Division "Reich" is to finally establish contact with *Aufklärungs-Abteilung 7* by continuing its attack at Borisowo. It is to assume responsibility for securing traffic on the road from the Prodwa River crossing at Borisowo (inclusive) to the road intersection at Jasewo.

In addition, it is to mop up the area south of the highway.

The enemy that has been identified at Korowino and Bigajlowo is to be observed and destroyed by fire.

22 October 1941

The cold increased from one day to the next.

In the morning the *10. Panzer-Division* initially continued the attack with ground elements from Modenowo to the east. After restoring a bridge east of Modenowo, it again advanced with armor and, advancing along the old post road, reached the western outskirts of Schelkowka by evening. The enemy there put up a stubborn defense, which led to a decision against making a night attack.

SS-Infanterie-Regiment "Der Führer mopped up Borisowo and took firm possession of the place. The bridge over the Prodwa River south of Borisowo had been blown up. The security mission that had been given to the division the previous evening was cancelled. Enemy forces south of the highway were dispersed by a *Stuka* attack in the morning and mopped up by *SS-Division "Reich". SS-Infanterie-Regiment "Der Führer"* established contact with the *7. Infanterie-Division* at Mitinka and Slatoustowo.

SS-Infanterie-Regiment "Deutschland" established contact with the *7. Infanterie-Division* and the *10. Panzer-Division.* Combat patrols were sent out to reconnoiter and clear the enemy out of surrounding villages. The enemy was active in the air.

SS-Infanterie-Regiment 11 is Disbanded

During the course of the day, *SS-Infanterie-Regiment 11*, which had fought courageously and repeatedly proven itself since the beginning of the Russian campaign, was disbanded by order of the division. ("Division Order for Reorganizing the Infantry effective 22 October 1941")

In order to restore the combat effectiveness of *SS-Infanterie-Regimenter "Deutschland"* and *"Der Führer"*, most of the officers, noncommissioned officers and enlisted men of *SS-Infanterie-Regiment 11* were transferred to the other two infantry regiments. The reassignment was to last until the division was refitted after the campaign. Twenty noncommissioned officers and three hundred enlisted personnel were assigned to *SS-Infanterie-Regiment "Deutschland"* and forty-seven noncommissioned officers and four hundred enlisted personnel were assigned to *SS-Infanterie-Regiment "Der Führer"*.

In order to allow the possibility of rebuilding *SS-Infanterie-Regiment 11*, the core of the staffs of the regiment, the battalions and the companies remained extant. They were combined under command of *SS-Obersturmbannführer* Schmidhuber and quartered in Moshaisk.

The motor vehicles of *SS-Infanterie-Regiment 11* were inspected by the motor vehicle technical officer to determine which vehicles were good for no more than being scrapped to insure a small stock of replacement parts.

With that, *SS-Infanterie-Regiment 11* practically ceased to exist. It must be said at this point that it was never reconstituted. Nevertheless, the achievements and sacrifices of that regiment, which was formed and made ready for the front by the former commander of *SS-Aufklärungs-Abteilung "Reich"*, *SS-Obersturmbannführer Dr.* Wim Brandt, are not forgotten.

The estimates that the corps had devoted to the question of continuing the operations, particularly regarding the choice of routes of movement, concluded that under the existing weather conditions the only route suitable for two-way traffic was the highway. The Russians fought, just as we did, along the highway, and substantial new enemy resistance could be expected at the bottleneck between the lakes at Kubinka. Accordingly, the *XXXX. Panzer-Korps* decided that the advance would continue from Schelkowka via Rusa to the north. That would possibly avoid continued heavy losses, especially in light of a report of improvement in the weather. It would also position it for assuming the northern sector in the ring of encirclement around Moscow

The *10. Panzer-Division* received the mission for 23 October of closing up with its main body at Dorochowo and capturing the bridge over the Moskwa River at Staraya Rusa with an advance guard. It was then to stand by to advance to the north. *SS-Division "Reich"* received the mission of assembling in the Borisowo — Lininka — Puschkino — Rylkowo— Jamskaja — Nowoßurjino — Sobolki — Jeol - Ponferki area in order to regroup for new employment. It was to take over security to the northwest and west in the line: Bridge over the Moskwa (northwest of Moshaisk) — Nowaja Derewnja — Kukarino — Nowossurjino. It was to position a battalion in the western part of Moshaisk. Finally, it was also to mop up the area south of the highway.

23 October 1941

The division was not committed. The main body enjoyed a period of quiet. It regrouped and repaired and maintained weapons and equipment. The commander of the division, *SS-Brigadeführer und Generalmajor der Waffen-SS* Bittrich, released an order of the day:

Division Order of the Day

SS-Division "Reich" has attacked from 6 - 21 October 1941 with hardly a break. We advanced from Juchnow north to Gshatsk with two open flanks. We advanced past the eastern edge of the Wjasma pocket. In so doing, strong enemy forces were defeated or eliminated and, in a bold advance, the division reached its objective: The Smolensk — Moscow highway. At the same time army divisions attacked from the west and recaptured the Jelnja positions east of Potschinok, which the division had defended in weeks of defensive fighting. With that, "our dead of Jelnja were avenged", as it was put in a corps order of the *XXXXVI. Panzer-Korps*.

Without pause for rest, the division then pushed on and advanced along and north of the highway to the east. Thanks to the speed of that advance and the readiness of officers and men to give their utmost, the enemy was prevented from an orderly concentration in and behind his Moscow defense position. Bottomless roads, snowstorms and biting frost presented just as little hindrance to the division as the determined counterattacks of the numerically far superior enemy. That portion of the fighting proved itself equal to the previous accomplishments of the division. Great was the success. All elements of the division share equally in it.

We salute our fallen comrades. Their deaths shall not have been in vain.

We honor our wounded. They have earned our best wishes. The commander of the assault-gun battery, *SS-Hauptsturmführer* Günster, died as one of the bravest. Our division commander, *SS-Obergruppenführer* Hausser, was severely wounded in the forward-most lines. He has sent his best wishes to the division for its future operations.

For the next phase of our battle we will again have to stand our ground. I know I can rely on you. We will again defeat the Red Army wherever we encounter it. We will help destroy Bolshevism so that Germany can live.

Hail to the *Führer*!

/signed/ Bittrich
SS-Brigadeführer

***

The *Wehrmacht* Report for 23 October included the following:

In spite of severe weather conditions, the outermost defenses of the Soviet capital have been broken through on a broad front from the southwest and west in the last few days.

The spearheads of our attack have fought their way in some places to within 60 kilometers of Moscow...!

24 October 1941

The situation remained quiet for the division. The division surgeon, *SS-Oberführer Dr.* Dermietzel, reported personnel losses of the division to the *SS* Main Office in Berlin:

Personnel Losses of *SS-Division "Reich"* (Russian Campaign)

Aggregate table based on daily reports of personnel losses: (+) = losses of officers.

	Killed	Wounded	Missing	Sick
Brest - Jelnja 22 JUN - 31 AUG 41	889 (+32)	2793 (+124)	100 (+2)	
Nowgorod - Severskji - Priluki 1-19 SEP 41	213 (+12)	942 (+47)	7	

Romny 20-30 SEP 41	104 (+5)	392 (+13)	10	
Gshatsk - Moshaisk 6-23 OCT 1941	392 (+15)	1130 (+40)	30	
	1598 (+64)	5257 (+224)	147 (+2)	747

Total losses of personnel: 8039

/signed/ Dermietzel
SS-Oberführer und Divisionsarzt

This loss report bears the note: "Has been presented to the *Führer*" (signed Schulze, *SS-Hauptsturmführer*)

***

The sobering figures show what heavy losses in killed, wounded and ill the division had to bear during the first five months of the Russian campaign.

At 1130 hours the *10. Panzer-Division* had advanced as far as the Moskwa River at Staraya Rusa. The bridge had been blown. There were only weak enemy forces with artillery on the north bank, and they soon fell back.

After reconnoitering a ford, the tanks continued the advance to Rusa, where they were received with Molotow cocktails and fire from antitank guns. The tanks therefore halted for the evening at the southeastern outskirts of Rusa.

***

The division reported the following totals for material captured and destroyed from the start of the Russian campaign until 23 October 1941:

	(1) Until close of fighting at Jelnja Salient	(2) Ops east of Kiew	(3) Ops at Romny	(4) Until 23 OCT 41	Total
Guns	23	314	23	134	494
Antitank guns	21	24	3	30	78
Heavy MG's	92	51	24	234	401
Heavy mortars	49	51	10	32	142
Tanks	116	17	39	116	288*
Flamethrowers				65	65
Aircraft				45	45

*) 61 tanks were knocked out by attached armed forces formations.

In addition, four armored trains and numerous individual handheld weapons, ammunition dumps, vehicles and medical equipment were captured or destroyed. All of the materiel was either destroyed or captured from the enemy in the course of fighting. The division never captured any materiel after the conclusion of the battle of encirclement.

25 October 1941

During the night the Russians increased their artillery fire on Schelkowka. *Pionier-Bataillon 49* repaired the bridge over the Moskwa River by 0300 hours. This insured the continued advance of the *10. Panzer-Division.*

During the early morning hours the tanks and motorized infantry of the *10. Panzer-Division* moved out. At 0630 hours Rusa was in German hands. At 1000 hours the leading units had crossed the Serna River west of Dubrowo. The bridge was intact.

Enemy resistance strengthened anew in front of the *7. Infanterie-Division.* Russian tanks went into action on the highway, and there was harassing fire from artillery and multiple-rocket launchers.

In spite of the extremely bad terrain conditions, the *10. Panzer-Division* was able to advance to Marjina by evening.

Increasing rainfall made movements ever more torturous. An endless column of stuck vehicles stretched more than 50 kilometers along the highway between Gshatsk and Moshaisk. Often two or three columns were side-by-side and stuck to the axles. Some vehicles had sunk up to the radiators in the mud. Whereas the prime movers had been able to help pull the vehicles out of the mud earlier, even the half-tracked vehicles were hopelessly bogged down now. Everyone eagerly awaited the frost that would again make the ground and roads passable.

A combat patrol of the *III./SS-Infanterie-Regiment "Der Führer"* brought in two giant elk, a joyously welcomed addition to the meager "menu" for the men.

***

The missions of the corps for 26 October stated:

The *10. Panzer-Division* is to resume the attack on Nowo-Petrowskoje. After reaching the attack objective it is to turn toward Istra while employing strong units to screen the Denkowo sector to the west.

SS-Division "Reich" is to follow close behind the *10. Panzer-Division* with its reconnaissance battalion. That battalion is to cross the railroad bridge at Schelkowka at 0700 hours to the north. On reaching the fork in the road one kilometer southwest of Podporina, it is to reconnoiter along the Podporina — Onufrijewo — Istra road. It is essential to receive reports on the condition of the roads and the enemy situation for later advance by *SS-Division "Reich"*.

The main body of the division is to move out over the railroad bridge at Schelkowka to the north at 1300 hours. It is to follow the army-level artillery that is proceeding behind the *10. Panzer-Division* as far as possible toward Rusa. Those elements that have heretofore been staged south of the highway are — aside from *SS-Infanterie-Regiment "Der Führer"* — to be brought north of the old post road via Moshaisk or the connecting route to Schalikowa by 1300 hours.

SS-Infanterie-Regiment "Der Führer" is to stand by until the route of advance becomes free.

The Mud Season Begins

26 October 1941

According to the division order for the advance, the division was to move out behind the *10. Panzer-Division* via Rusa toward Istra. The first elements were to move on 26 October, while the main body would move on 27 October.

The four march serials were to stand by to move out as called forward:

March serial Klingenberg: reinforced *SS-Aufklärungs-Abteilung "Reich"*
March serial Weiß: Division staff + *SS-Nachrichten-Abteilung "Reich"*
March serial Wagner: Reinforced *SS-Infanterie-Regiment "Deutschland"*
March serial Kumm: Reinforced *SS-Infanterie-Regiment "Der Führer"*

***

However, this day marked the onset of persistent downpours that rendered all routes practically impassable for wheeled vehicles. By order of the division, *SS-Infanterie-Regiment "Deutschland"* had to make Michailowskoje and Gratschewo available for infantry units of the *7. Infanterie-Division.*

Starting at the old post road, the vehicles of the *I./SS-Infanterie-Regiment "Deutschland"* remained hopelessly stuck in the mud while moving to Schokolowa. The troops reached the new billeting area on foot. The vehicles had to be towed to the railroad embankment by artillery prime movers in the days that followed.

In the meantime, the Russians attacked in the afternoon. They employed armor north of the old post road. They captured Trutanowka, forced units of the *7. Infanterie-Division* back through Boltino and continued their advance as far as Dorochowo.

Aside from the enemy artillery fire, it was impossible for the division to continue its advance that day because of the traffic jam and the bottomless roads. The situation became even more critical in the evening with the enemy counterattack. Russian armor broke through and fired into the battery positions of *schwere Mörser-Abteilung 637* (heavy howitzer) at Kusolewo. *SS-Division "Reich"* was thereupon ordered to keep one battalion on alert in its billeting area. The *II./SS-Infanterie-Regiment "Deutschland"* was designated as the alert battalion.

The *10. Panzer-Division*, which had advanced to Marjiana in spite of the difficult road conditions, closed up with its main body in the area north of Rusa by 1000 hours. The division reported early in the morning that a continued advance at that time was impossible due to the bottomless road conditions.

The commanding general personally went forward and convinced himself of this fact. The corps then gave up the idea of continuing the advance to Nowo-Petrowskoje, since any forward movement by a powerful formation was impossible due to the mud. An advance with smaller elements would lead to a splitting up the forces.

This signaled the start of the dreaded autumn mud season. The mud season brought the combat troops to a state of near total immobility and rendered it practically impossible to bring forward the urgently needed supplies.

The combat elements of *SS-Division "Reich"* that were urgently needed to support the *10. Panzer-Division* had to remain inactive in the Moshaisk area, where they were stuck fast in the mud. For the time being there was no way they could move forward.

During the course of the morning, the Russians attacked Ssloboda — Lyskowa with armor. The attack was repulsed.

The motorized infantry regiments and combat engineers of the *10. Panzer-Division* were immediately detailed to improve the roads. Approximately five kilometers of corduroy road had to be built.

SS-Aufklärungs-Abteilung "Reich" remained stuck in the muck east of Podporina. The intended advance of the battalion via Podporina — Onufrijewo — Istra was impossible.

The *II./SS-Infanterie-Regiment "Deutschland"* was instructed to establish contact with the *267. Infanterie-Division* (*VII. Armee-Korps*) in Schelkowa so as to be on call in the event that the Russians continued their attacks.

The *10. Panzer-Division* formed a hedgehog defense at Marjina and Lyskowo. *SS-Division "Reich"*, however, waited for an opportunity to start moving again, in spite of the mud and the traffic jams.

Achievements of the Supply Services of SS-Division "*Reich*"

The German advance on Moscow was brought to a halt for two weeks by the onset of the mud season and by the temporary exhaustion of the attack capabilities of the German troops. At this point it is appropriate to consider the men of the supply services of *SS-Division "Reich"*, who have often received only marginal recognition. However, it was thanks to their superb achievements that the prerequisites were provided for the advance of the combat troops so near the gates of Moscow. They were the commanders, officers, noncommissioned officers and enlisted men of the division's logistics troops.

At the start of the Eastern Campaign, the division's logistics officer, *SS-Hauptsturmführer* Kunstmann, attended a conference at the army of general staff officers of the divisions. It was made clear to all participants that the capacity of the supply services would be exhausted by the time the attack had progressed 600 kilometers. From that point on, a smooth continuation of the advance would depend on conversion of the railroad from the Russian broad gauge to standard gauge and on "the improvisational abilities of the logistics officers". It was essential that captured goods such as fuels and foodstuffs be distributed to the forces in a logical manner.

The logistics officer with his staff and supply services personnel operated accordingly.

Meeting the division's logistical requirements in the fighting that had already taken place and that was impending represented a masterpiece of achievement, without which the impressive combat performance of the division would have been inconceivable.

While the division was engaged in extremely heavy defensive fighting in the Jelnja salient against an enemy that outnumbered it five times over, the division's supply route for the supply columns stretched for 450 kilometers. If one considers the fact that the Smolensk — Moscow main supply route was not yet open and all of the supply traffic between Orscha and Jelnja had to follow the southern road — which was already congested with advancing infantry divisions — it is hardly surprising that there was a shortage of ammunition at times at Jelnja.

It was not until the strategic significance of the Jelnja salient was realized and the army granted right-of-way priority to the logistics troops of *SS-Division "Reich"* and issued corresponding orders to the military police employed on the road, that the logistical situation suddenly improved.

The logistics liaison officer of the division at the time, *SS-Obersturmführer* Fritz Steinbeck, indicated in his notes that he was on the main supply route to Orscha day and night during those weeks. He had to bring the right-of-way priority orders from the army to the most congested stretches of roads so that the division columns could move forward past the advancing infantry divisions or pass through on their return trips to Orscha. The officer's car was soon known to the military police posted at the bottlenecks and bridges so that they had already started clearing the so-called "roads" as soon as they saw him appear.

On every supply trip a number of vehicles were left behind along the way due to mechanical problems caused by the catastrophic condition of the roads or as a result of heat and dust or as victims of enemy ambushes. The men of the supply columns were at the steering wheels day and night and had long since been driven to the limits of their endurance. That is why it sometimes happened that entire columns failed to start moving after a long halt because the drivers had all fallen into the deep sleep of total exhaustion.

The fact that the supply of the *4. Armee* and *Panzergruppen 2* and *3* required 22 supply trains daily, of which only 14 actually arrived, coupled with the 450-kilometer route that the supply convoys had to drive gives a rough picture of the state of the logistical situation at that time. It also gives an idea of the stupendous achievements of the division supply services in dealing with that situation.

The situation was similar on the advance from Roslawl via Juchnow to Gshatsk. The division sealed off the Wjasma pocket to the east. Russian elements continually attempted to break through the thin lines to the east. Under these circumstances, it was impossible to transport supplies over the Juchnow — Gshatsk road.

The greatest difficulties had to be overcome during the autumn mud season from the end of October to mid-November, when columns often sank axle-deep in the mud. It was only through individual initiative by officers, noncommissioned officers and men, through their constant improvisation and inventive workarounds and thanks to their ceaseless concern for maintaining contact with the combat troops that the vital supplies could be delivered.

The most important workaround in accomplishing this was the use of *Panje* wagons with the undemanding, tough little *Panje* horses. Whole supply columns were made up of them. During the winter months of snow and ice, *Panje* horses drew sleds. *Panje* wagons and *Panje* sleds also proved outstanding in transport of the wounded. (*Panje* was the term the troops use in referring to the wiry and small Russian horses and the crude but rugged diminutive wagons and sleds used by the local peasants.)

Keeping the division supplied during the rapid advance through vast expanses was especially difficult, particularly when the forces were rapidly shifted from one employment to another, as was the case with *SS-Division "Reich"*.

Special recognition is due to the drivers of the fuel and ammunition vehicles. They were frequently left entirely to their own resources during rapid breakthroughs. They usually had to drive through unsecured areas to rear-area supply bases in order to fetch urgently needed fuel and ammunition for the combat elements at the front. The loss of one such vehicle could have serious effects on the fighting. What good would it do for the soldiers to have great fighting morale if they received no more ammunition, functioning weapons, fuel or rations?

In addition, as partisan activity increased, with ambushes, blown bridges and mined supply routes, the columns were usually entirely dependent on themselves. Many times the men had to pick up their own carbines and machine guns to defend themselves.

Who can fail to think at this point of the medical care and the evacuation of the wounded by the military doctors and their medical personnel? This frequently took place under extremely difficult conditions and in primitive circumstances. One must think of the ambulance platoons and the medical personnel at the dressing stations and field hospitals. During days of major fighting the doctors and their men operated and cared for the wounded with hardly a break and to the point of physical exhaustion.

Recognition must also be given here to the accomplishments of the division chief of supply services, the weapons and vehicle repair personnel, the bakery company and the butchery platoon. The field post office must not be overlooked. Constant changes in command relationships considerably complicated its work. It had to react quickly and be flexible in order to maintain the postal connection with the homeland. Everyone who was there knows what an influence letters from home had on the mood and spirit of the forces.

The achievements of the division supply services were made easier by the fact that the commanders and officers of the combat elements and the supply services had known each other since the peacetime days of the *SS-Verfügungstruppe*. Pressing logistical questions could oftentimes be worked out in conversation between old friends in very unconventional and non-bureaucratic fashion without raising a fuss.

Every member of the divisional supply services can take pride in those great and decisive achievements. This chapter should forever preserve their memory. Without them the widely recognized and historical overall achievements of *SS-Division "Reich"* would not have been possible.

The Situation on the Russian Side

Oleg Penkowskij wrote the following regarding the situation at this time:

> ...In October the Germans broke through our lines of defense east of Smolensk and Briansk, encircled six or seven of our armies in pockets and captured about half a million prisoners. That left the way open to Moscow.
>
> General Zhukov was brought from Leningrad in all haste. He assumed command of the West Front. (Author's Note: That corresponded to commander-in-chief of *Heeresgruppe Mitte*) At the same time, Major General Artemjew, commander of the Moscow Military District, was made responsible for the direct defense of the capital. Artemjew was a NKVD general. (Author's note: NKVD = People's Commissariat of the Interior = "Secret Police") Initially he commanded an NKVD division in Moscow. He then became commander-in-chief of the military district in 1941. At that time, most of the commanding generals that Stalin posted to the various positions of the Moscow defense front came from the NKVD. Artemjew's political commissar was Konstantin Fjodorowitsch Telegin. The local-area commander for Moscow was General Sinilow and the local-area commander for the Kremlin was General Siridonow. Commanders-in-chief of the armies, such as Ivan Iwanowitsch Maslennikow and Chomenko, were also NKVD generals. Later, all of those commanding generals gave the impression that they had been active generals of the Red Army, but only one of them, Chomenko, proved himself as a good troop leader. Nevertheless, Maslennikow later became commander-in-chief of a front.

In any case, it is a fact that all those NKVD generals received commands from Stalin in the Moscow area in 1941. During the great panic that gripped the city from 16 to 19 October they proved extremely valuable to Stalin. At that time the party leadership, the NKVD and various military commands had already started to flee to the east. Everywhere the bonds of discipline loosened. The government declared the city to be in a state of siege and mobilized the populace to dig trenches and build fortifications. In addition, "volunteer divisions" were raised from the citizenry and a "people's defense" was organized. Untrained and inadequately armed, they were thrown into the battle against the attacking German forces to gain time for Zhukov to reorganize his burnt-out formations...(Oleg Penkowskij, *Geheime Aufzeichnungen*,)

Sub-Section I)

Defensive Fighting West of Moscow: 27 October – 16 November 1941

For the time being any further massed attack on Moscow was out of the question.

SS-Division "Reich" was ordered to move to the area north of Rusa to organize for defense.

During the morning, Russian forces that had penetrated with armor north of Dorochowo during the night launched a massed attack on a narrow front. They advanced between the highway and the old post road. Schelkowka and Doroshowo were under heavy fire from enemy artillery and multiple-rocket launchers, so an advance of the divisional formations was not possible.

The Russian advance on Schelkowka was particularly unpleasant for the corps since the entire supply traffic had to be rerouted through the Schelkowka road intersection because of the impassability of the Rusa — Woroizowo — Moshaisk road. The fuel situation was extraordinarily precarious.

After the road intersection was reported to have been cleared of enemy at 0730 hours, the first squads of *SS-Kradschützen-Bataillon "Reich"* passed Schelkowka with relatively minor losses and were able to reach the area designated in the orders. Many of the following march serials of the division were still stuck fast in the mud and waiting for fuel.

While reinforced *Panzer-Regiment 7* was attacked by enemy forces at Skirminowa employing artillery, multiple-rocket launchers, bombers and low-level attack planes, and only had enough fuel for a ten kilometer radius of action, the remainder of the *10. Panzer-Division* was employed building the corduroy road.

At 2130 hours the *XXXX. Panzer-Korps* received a request by telegram from the *VII. Armee-Korps* for attachment of a reinforced battalion of *SS-Division "Reich"* as a mobile reserve. *General* Stumme promised immediate assistance in case of need, but reserved to himself the decision as to the time

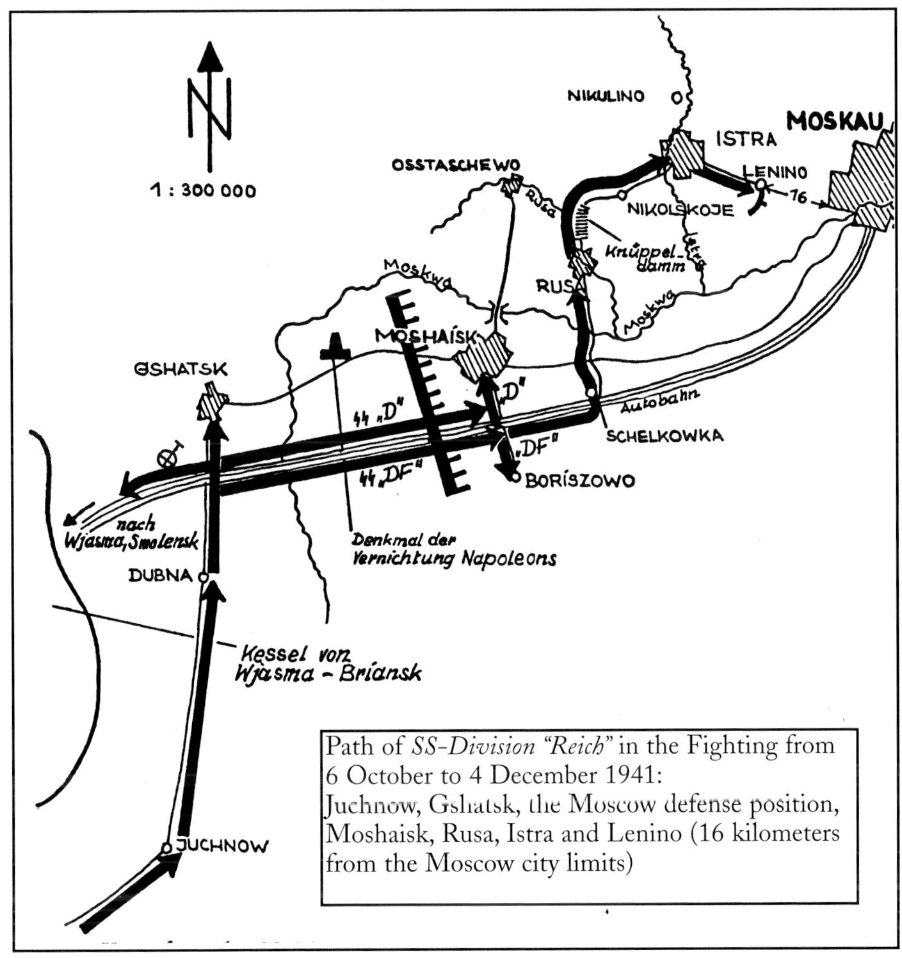

Path of *SS-Division "Reich"* in the Fighting from 6 October to 4 December 1941: Juchnow, Gshatsk, the Moscow defense position, Moshaisk, Rusa, Istra and Lenino (16 kilometers from the Moscow city limits)

of release of the battalion in order to prevent premature splitting up of *SS-Division "Reich"*.

The division received orders to send the strongest possible elements in small groups through Schelkowka during the night and in the early morning hours.

On 28 October, in spite of great difficulties and heavy artillery fire, the combat engineers, the antitank troops, the signals battalion and the division staff were able to pass through Schelkowka. *SS-Pionier-Bataillon "Reich"* constructed a military bridge over the Moskwa River.

Since the Russians had forced their way forward during the morning to the edge of the woods directly east of the road at Kusowlewo and raked the road with machine-gun and rifle fire, the main body of the division could no longer move out toward Rusa.

It was not until nightfall that the main body of the division (with *SS-*

Infanterie-Regiment "Deutschland" in the lead) started its movement to the new billeting and security area northwest of Rusa. It moved in spite of harassing artillery fire on the Schelkowka — Staraja Rusa road. It was able to reach the billeting area without losses. The division received orders to mop up the woods on both sides of Tobolowa south of the Serna River and to occupy the built-up area with strong elements.

The *XXXX. Panzer-Korps* gave the following report regarding prisoners and captured materiel during the preceding fighting to *Panzergruppe 4*:

After the end of the Wjasma pocket battle and during the period from 12 to 25 October, the *XXXX. Panzer-Korps* — with the *10. Panzer-Division, SS-Division "Reich"* and the periodically attached *7. Infanterie-Division* — advanced via Gshatsk — Moshaisk in the attack on Moscow. It reached the area east of Schelkowka and northeast of Rusa.

The outcome of the fighting, which was quite intense at times, particularly at the strongly fortified Jelnja (II) position, was:

19,634 prisoners were captured.

Weapons and equipment captured: 237 guns, 7 rocket launchers, 177 antitank and infantry guns, 616 motor vehicles and 57 antiaircraft guns.

Destroyed: 199 tanks and armored cars, 65 flamethrowers, 1 armored train and 15 aircraft (shot down).

***

Panzergruppe 4 reiterated its previous orders:

The *Panzergruppe* is to defeat the enemy before Moscow. The supply situation makes it impossible to plan a time-phased attack. However, the Russian manner of fighting and the advancing time of year demand that every division advance aggressively as soon as it has what it needs to fight and move.

The *XXXX. Panzer-Korps* is to attack the enemy at Nowo-Petrowskoje. In conjunction with the *XXXXVI. Panzer-Korps* and the *V. Armee-Korps* it is to destroy the enemy and then accelerate its advance over the Istra River to the east. It is to block the roads leading from Moscow to Klin and Dmitrow.

***

To the right of the *XXXX. Panzer-Korps* the *VII. Armee-Korps* was in the old line at Schelkowka.

To the left was the *XXXXVI. Panzer-Korps* with the *2. Panzer-Division* in the area south of Wolokolamsk, the *11. Panzer-Division* in the Achtschewino — Bultschewo area and the *5. Panzer-Division* in the area north of Moshaisk.

In the coming attack *SS-Division "Reich"* was to be employed to the northeast. As a result, zone reconnaissance had to be conducted in that area. The objective for *SS-Division "Reich"* and the *10. Panzer-Division* was Istra. The armies the Russians lacked, armies that had been smashed in the great

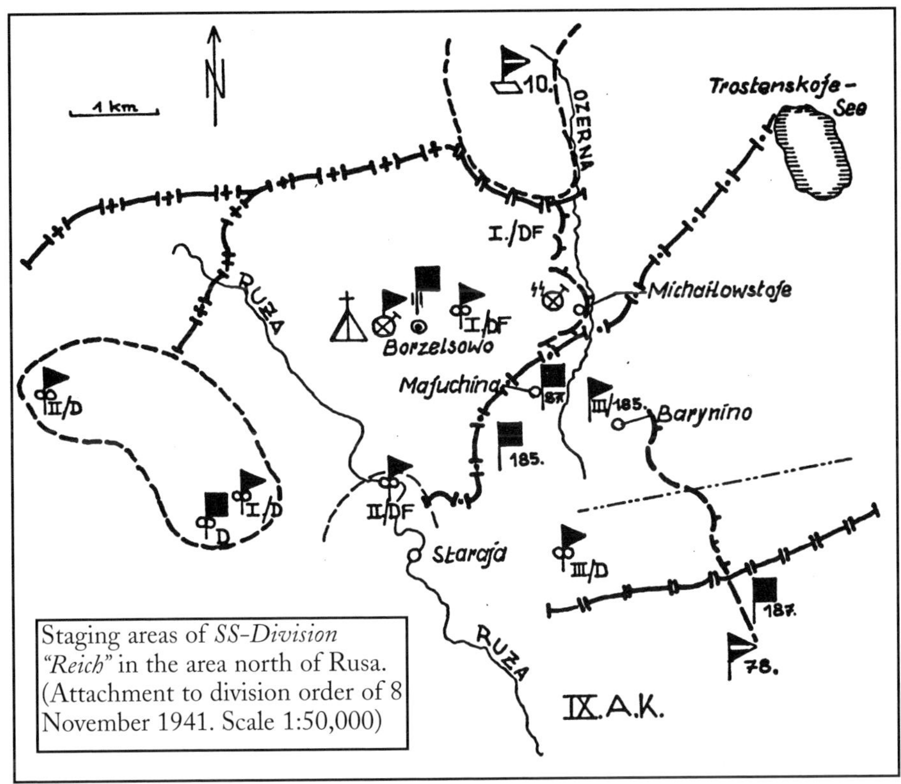

Staging areas of *SS-Division "Reich"* in the area north of Rusa. (Attachment to division order of 8 November 1941. Scale 1:50,000)

pocket battles, were replaced by "General Mud" and "General Winter". These would keep Moscow safe from German hands.

In the disastrous weather and road conditions, the villages played an important role for the German soldier, who was almost at the end of his strength. Accordingly, the corps issued orders against the needless firing into and burning down of villages, since the forces urgently needed them for billets. Since the supply of rations was not assured, it was necessary to live off the land. The special-purpose rations and emergency rations were only to be used by order of the division.

The division command post was in Timoschino. On 31 October division reconnaissance identified weak enemy security forces at the river crossing six kilometers northeast of Dubrowo. According to statements by prisoners, a new Russian tank brigade was concentrated in the area south and southeast of Lake Trostenskoje.

After *SS-Infanterie-Regiment 11* was disbanded, *SS-Division "Reich"* consisted of only two infantry regiments as of 1 November 1941.

SS-Obersturmbannführer Kumm, the commander of *SS-Infanterie-Regiment "Der Führer"* at the time, described the situation on 1 November in his notes as follows:

When the rain let up a bit at the beginning of November and a light frost occurred, *SS-Infanterie-Regiment "Der Führer"* moved via the Schapalowka road intersection from the highway north to the Rusa area. Some of the Schapalowka — Rusa road was the main line of resistance. Vehicles had to traverse it at high speed under heavy enemy artillery fire.

Weak elements of the *10. Panzer-Division* had chewed their way past Rusa through a wooded area. The deep mud of the woodland road had been made passable by a corduroy road. Day and night the Russians attempted to cut off the spearhead of the *10. Panzer-Division* by attacking from the east while, at the same time, they pinned it down with concentrated fire, especially from several batteries of multiple-rocket launchers (Stalin organs). The frost set in and snow had been falling for days.

The so-called highway between Gshatsk and Moshaisk was in such condition that, for the most part, it could no longer even be referred to as a road. The potholes reached a depth of 1.5 - 2 meters. The entire road was covered with a .5 - .75-meter layer of mud. Vehicles not only sank to the axles, most of them were stuck in mud up to the chassis. The "highway" was, therefore, closed as of 2 November to all traffic with the exception of the transport of wounded and vehicles with special permission of the *Panzergruppe* or the *252. Infanterie-Division.*

After lasting frost hardened the ground again, vehicles could again drive. But the icy east wind, filled with fine crystals of snow, covered vehicles and weapons with a thin sheet of ice. — "The war crept into the impoverished huts of the villages..."

***

General Stumme's situation report for 4 November included, among other things:

1.) The Russians stubbornly defend the outskirts of Moscow under pressure from commissars and officers. They bring in new armor and troop units for that purpose, thus possessing stronger defensive forces and weapons than previously assumed. All in all, the enemy has probably gone over to the defense. Nevertheless, offensive operations must continually be expected from the divisions that have just been brought in. Local attacks can be expected from the forces that were previously here...

2.) The offensive capabilities of our infantry have been weakened...Accordingly, attacks can only break through when infantry forces are massed, and strong artillery and concentrated heavy infantry weapons are orchestrated together at the *Schwerpunkt.*

The artillery must propel the infantry forward.

Assistance from armor and *Stukas* continues to be decisively important for the infantry.

3.) At present the *XXXX. Panzer-Korps* is advancing with the *10. Panzer-Division* in the lead and *SS-Division "Reich"* behind it on the Rusa — Skirminowa road. In accordance with its mission, it will reach the Istra — Wolokolamsk road in the Petrowskoje area by attacking and then advance to Istra...

***

During the night of 6/7 November *SS-Kradschützen-Bataillon "Reich"* relieved the security forces of the *II./Infanterie-Regiment 86* at Michalewskoje on Oserna Creek. On its first day there, the battalion came under heavy fire from artillery and multiple-rocket launchers.

The *III./SS-Infanterie-Regiment "Deutschland"*, reinforced with one *Pak* platoon and a platoon of light infantry guns, was attached to the *87. Infanterie-Division* since *Infanterie-Regiment 185* was no longer strong enough to meet the enveloping enemy attacks. The onset of frost and the arrival of limited fuel supplies made limited movement possible.

In the evening of 6 November the order went out to the divisions to defend until offensive operations resumed.

The *10. Panzer-Division* took over the defense of the Oserna sector and held open the Skirminowa bridgehead for the continuation of the attack. Elements of *SS-Division "Reich"* had the mission of securing the eastern flank on the Oserna in the Michailowskoje — Gorodischtsche sector. The main body of the division was staged in the Staraja Rusa area so that a later attack east of the Oserna River toward Borodenka would be possible.

SS-Oberstgruppenführer und Generaloberst der Waffen-SS Paul Hausser continued to follow the progress and the fighting of his old division with great interest after he was wounded. He wrote the following in his personal notes regarding the "big picture" for the new offensive against Moscow:

> The highest level of command decided on 7 November in favor of the continuation of the offensive — for a 'Flight to the Front'.
>
> Again the plan called for an envelopment from two sides. *Panzergruppe 2* (Guderian) was to advance from Tula to Kolomna on the right wing. The *4. Armee* and *Panzergruppe 4* were to advance against the western and northwestern outskirts of Moscow. The *9. Armee* and *Panzergruppe 3* were to advance to the Volga — Moskwa canal on the left wing.
>
> A written memorandum from the chief of the army general staff to the chiefs of staff of the army groups and armies justified the decision: "The expected onset of cold weather would, for a short time, make operations possible that would gain favorable prerequisites for the conduct of fighting in the winter and in the beginning of 1942."

Fighting on the "Corduroy Road"

7 November 1941

During the night *SS-Kradschützen-Bataillon "Reich"*, with an attached platoon of the *2./SS-Flak-Abteilung "Reich"*, relieved the *10. Panzer-Division* at Michailowskoje. Fedschina was captured in the fighting. However, heavy artillery fire forced its evacuation that evening.

After combing the woods south of Lyskow and turning to the east, the division's combat outposts followed the line Michailowskoje — west of Fedschina — woods north of Fedschina. Only some elements of the *10. Panzer-Division* were able to advance through the woods to the north, since the Russians had again penetrated there at midday, presumably from the northeast, and blocked the route of advance. Therefore *SS-Division "Reich"* received the mission in the evening to again comb and clear out the wooded terrain on both sides of the corduroy road as far as the northern edge of the woods. The *10. Panzer-Division* was to establish direct contact with *SS-Division "Reich's"* security elements at the division boundary and prevent renewed enemy infiltration into the woods from the northeast.

SS-Infanterie-Regiment "Der Führer" in Staraja received the mission of clearing the corduroy road of enemy and screening it to the east and south. According to information provided by the *10. Panzer-Division*, the enemy forces involved were weak. As a result, only the *I./SS-Infanterie-Regiment "Der Führer"*, reinforced with *Sturmgeschütze "Lützow"* and *"Blücher"*, one platoon of the *2./SS-Flak-Abteilung "Reich"* and a regimental heavy mortar platoon, was initially employed. The two assault guns were not employed at first because of the marshy terrain.

The *I./SS-Infanterie-Regiment "Der Führer"* suffered heavy losses in attacking in the thick woods. However, it was able to capture and occupy a small rise about 500 meters south of the corduroy road.

During the night of 7/8 November a thaw set in. The unpaved roads, particularly the stretch south of Lyskowo, rapidly became impassable for wheeled vehicles. The planned link-up with the *10. Panzer-Division* to the front was, therefore, only possible with weak elements. This also did not take into consideration the fact that the enemy had established himself firmly in the woods south of Lyskowo east of the route of advance and kept the corduroy road under mortar fire. The *I./SS-Infanterie-Regiment "Der Führer"* was no more successful in clearing out the three-kilometer long woods on 8 and 9 November, since the terrain was covered with brushy undergrowth that blocked all observation and the single-lane traffic on the corduroy road initially prevented heavy weapons from being brought forward.

Since it was not possible to employ mortars in the wooded terrain, the *XXX. Panzer-Korps* made flamethrower fuel available to *SS-Division "Reich"* for the attack on 10 November.

At 1245 hours on 9 November the *III./SS-Infanterie-Regiment "Deutschland"*, which had been attached to the *87. Infanterie-Division*, reported to its parent regiment that the enemy had attacked in the course of the day with four tanks and infantry. The attack had been repulsed. Friendly losses amounted to two dead and two wounded.

On 10 November enemy units were even able to cross the corduroy road to the north and keep it under fire from both sides. The *III./* and the *II./SS-*

Infanterie-Regiment "Der Führer" were then sent forward and employed to secure the corduroy road. Every advance into the woods to the southeast, however, was linked with substantial losses. The *3./SS-Infanterie-Regiment "Der Führer"* under *SS-Obersturmführer* Lex suffered heavy losses there.

As a result of well-placed German artillery fire and under pressure from the assault troops of *SS-Infanterie-Regiment "Der Führer"*, the Russians finally fell back farther to the east. But they still held onto field fortifications in the woods west of Gorodischtsche. They stubbornly defended their positions in the woods. It was impossible to take prisoners, since the Russians fought to the death in hand-to-hand fighting.

The *III./SS-Infanterie-Regiment "Deutschland"* — still attached to the *87. Infanterie-Division* — reported strong enemy reconnaissance activity in the gray light of dawn and that a Russian airplane had dropped incendiaries on several villages with the apparent intention of destroying them with fire, thus eliminating shelter for the German troops.

In the morning hours of 11 November strong Russian combat patrols infiltrated through the thin security lines of *SS-Infanterie-Regiment "Der Führer"* as far as the corduroy road. Using three antitank guns at the northern edge of the woods at Lyskowo, they blocked the route of advance.

The *9./SS-Infanterie-Regiment "Der Führer"* attacked in the afternoon with three *Sturmgeschütze*: the *"Blücher"*, *"Lützow"* and *"Prinz Eugen"*. They forced the Russians back to their positions east of the route of advance. The assault guns engaged enemy field fortifications, during which the *"Blücher"* got stuck in the marshy ground. The *"Lützow"* then dropped out with clutch problems. By late afternoon the route of advance was again free. Traffic, however, remained stop-and-go due to several damaged stretches where vehicles got hung up. Intermittent enemy artillery fire harassed Skirminowa and the high ground to its south.

The *III./SS-Infanterie-Regiment "Deutschland"* was relieved from attachment and returned from the *87. Infanterie-Division* to its parent regiment. It reoccupied its former billeting area in Iwonina.

On 12 November the *6./SS-Infanterie-Regiment "Der Führer"* attacked at 0700 hours with strong assault troops supported by heavy smoke and the *Sturmgeschütze "Prinz Eugen"* and *"Yorck"* to clear out the woods southeast of Lyskowo. The company initially broke through the Russian field fortifications but was then brought to a standstill when it came under heavy fire from enemy forces dug into a well-concealed woodland position. The *"Prinz Eugen"* was able to destroy one gun in thickly wooded terrain.

While that was happening, however, the *"Prinz Eugen"* came under fire from a second Russian gun and was hit in the front and on the side. The *"Yorck"* also took a direct hit on the left drive sprocket. In spite of this, the *"Prinz Eugen"* was able to destroy the Russian gun before it pulled back.

During the course of the morning and after heavy fire from artillery and multiple-rocket launchers, the enemy facing the *10. Panzer-Division* attacked Skirminowa from the north and northeast with strong forces — at least a regiment employing numerous tanks. The commander of *Panzer-Regiment 7* was killed in the fighting.

At 1340 hours the *10. Panzer-Division* reported to the corps:

Armored engagements east of Skirminowka. Skirminowka is untenable unless the *SS* attacks tomorrow and the entire corps attacks the day after tomorrow. When is the attack intended?

Although Skirminowka could be held, the enemy recaptured Marjina with the help of 19 T 34's and took the high ground northwest of Skirminowka with T 34 and 52-ton tanks. The *10. Panzer-Division* suffered heavy losses. With approval from the corps, it therefore decided to evacuate Skirminowka during the night of 12/13 November and to pull the forces employed there back into a narrow bridgehead.

The command post of *SS-Infanterie-Regiment "Der Führer"* was moved forward through the woods to Litkino. There it was located directly behind the advanced units of the *10. Panzer-Division*. Snowfall increased considerably and the nights were marked by heavy frost.

***

Werner Haupt described the larger situation on 12 November in *Heeresgruppe Mitte:*

On 12 November the chief of the general staff, Halder, personally ordered *Heeresgruppe Mitte* to continue to remain on the offensive. He was at the army group headquarters at Orscha. *Generalfeldmarschall* von Bock was of the same opinion. He set the operational objective as reaching the Moskwa River in Moscow and the Volga canal.

OKH, however, went even further: *Generaloberst* Halder ordered that the *2. Panzer-Armee*, which had only 50 tanks operational on that day (out of 600!), was to advance to Gorki! That was 400 kilometers beyond Moscow! — An impossibility that could only be heard without comment and with much shaking of heads...

...Of the daily requirement for 32 trainloads of supplies, only 20 trains arrived on a good day in Smolensk. The thermometer continued to fall.

As a result, the army group was significantly weakened. *Luftflotte 2* received orders from *OKW* to transfer immediately to Italy. The German-Italian forces in North Africa had taken a substantial beating and needed active *Luftwaffe* support if North Africa were to be held. (Werner Haupt, *Heeresgruppe Mitte*, p. 100. Bad Nauheim: Podzun-Pallas-Verlag, 1963.)

***

Collection for *Winterhilfswerk* (Winter Aid)

On the margins of the fighting, bizarre as it may sound, the division troops collected contributions for the *Winterhilfswerk* (Winter Aid). The excerpt that follows from the regimental order of *SS-Infanterie-Regiment "Deutschland"* for 13 October 1941 serves as an example of the results of the collection. It is preserved in the regiment's war diary:

1.) The collection for the *Winterhilfswerk* concert has given the regiment reason for pride.

A total of 140,959.20 *RM* (= *Reichsmark*, the German currency of the time) were collected.

Special commendation goes to the *II./SS-Infanterie-Regiment "Deutschland"*, which contributed 44,280 *RM*...

The other elements of the division had similarly high results. The combined results for *SS-Division "Reich"* produced 862,785.93 *RM*.

Helmut Günther, a motorcycle messenger with *SS-Kradschützen-Bataillon "Reich"* at the time, wrote about it in his book:

...So what were we meant to do with all that mammon? Matches, string, spark-plugs and Hindenberg lights were far more important! There were neither bars nor shops out here where we could spend our money. For us it served as no more than chips for card games. When it was gone, you were out of the game. So it was no great achievement for the *"Winterhilfswerk"* to collect undreamed of amounts from our division. We contributed to the fight against hunger and cold! What a joke! Who froze the most in the infernal winter of 1941/1942?

The newspaper at home proclaimed:

"*SS* division contributes 862,785.93 *RM*!

Berlin, 1 March. A *SS* division has contributed 862,785.93 *RM* for the *Kriegswinterhilfswerk*. That sum was contributed solely from the frontline units of a *SS* division that is engaged in the most difficult fighting against the Bolshevik enemy. In addition to fighting for *Führer* and *Reich*, over and above their bravery and death-defying courage, these *SS* men have also provided an example with their contribution that will be received in the homeland with deepest feelings of amazement for the generosity and bearing of those troops."

That certainly sounds good, doesn't it?...(Helmut Günther, *Heiße Motoren — Kalte Füße*, p. 190. Neckargemünd: Kurt-Vowinckel-Verlag, 1963.)

***

Those were the men of *SS-Division "Reich"*! With a flippant matter-of-factness and a certain understandable sarcasm they dismissed the fantastic amounts contributed, although it was clear to everyone that the military pay that was accruing did ultimately have some benefit in the event of being transferred back to Germany as a result of wounds or on the next home leave, if he lived that long.

***

As of 13 November the *II./SS-Infanterie-Regiment "Deutschland"* was designated as the division's operational reserve and was to remain on alert status in its billeting area so that it could be employed within an hour's notice to reinforce the *10. Panzer-Division.*

At daybreak the *16. (Pionier)/SS-Infanterie-Regiment "Deutschland"* repaired the bridge at Iwonina so that a reinforced battalion could roll over it without difficulty.

***

The "Division Order for Reorganization for Defense (effective 12 November 1941)" that was issued on 13 November included the following:

1.) …

2.) The *IX. Armee-Korps* is to defend its present positions.

Boundaries between the *IX. Armee-Korps* and *SS-Division "Reich"* remain unchanged.

The *10. Panzer-Division* has closed up to the north.

The boundary between the *10. Panzer-Division* and *SS-Division "Reich"*: Northern outskirts of Lyskowo — Point 215.3 — 3 kilometers southwest of Nikolskoje.

The *5. Panzer-Division is to* close up with the *10. Panzer-Division* from the southwest.

The boundary between *SS-Division "Reich"* and the *5. Panzer-Division*: Tschurino (*SS-Division "Reich"*) — Tschernowo (*SS-Division "Reich"*) — northern outskirts of Lyskowo.

3.) *SS-Division "Reich"* is to defend with elements employed on the west bank of the Oserna River and maintain standing reconnaissance patrols on the east bank to provide information for the upcoming attack.

4.) The following elements are committed:

a) Reinforced *SS-Kradschützen-Bataillon "Reich"* between the right division boundary and the line: Southern edge of the clearing in the woods at the corduroy road three kilometers northeast of Starejo — northern outskirts of Fetschino — southern outskirts of Gorodischtsche.

b) Reinforced *SS-Infanterie-Regiment "Der Führer"* from there to the northern division boundary.

The main line of resistance specified in orders on 12 November is to be held. *SS-Infanterie-Regiment "Der Führer"* is to conduct zone reconnaissance to the north for employment of the *III./SS-Infanterie-Regiment "Der Führer"* in the flank of the enemy in the event of an enemy attack on Poprowskoje.

5.) to 7.) …

8.) The narrow area available to the division for defense and the significant concentration of units, not all of which belong to the division, call for comprehensive measures...

9.) to 10.) ...

11.) Division command post: Jelniki, 3 kilometers northwest of Wolkow...

***

Based on the changes in the situation for the *XXXX. Panzer-Korps* resulting from the 12 November attack, the *5. Panzer-Division* was not attached to the corps. Instead, the *XXXXVI. Panzer-Korps* was inserted between the *XXXX. Panzer-Korps* and the *V. Armee-Korps.*

On 14 November *SS-Division "Reich"* conducted particularly successful combat patrols, in the course of which the commander of the *2./SS-Kradschützen-Bataillon, SS-Hauptsturmführer* Köhler, particularly distinguished himself. Forty automatic rifles, a quad machine gun and eight heavy machine guns were captured or destroyed.

The commanding general, *General* Stumme, commended all who took part in the combat patrols in a corps order of the day.

In the evening the enemy artillery and multiple-rocket launcher fire let up.

All of the enemy's attacks were repulsed with heavy losses to him. In the corps sector 11 enemy tanks were knocked out. Another was put out of action when it ran over a mine.

As a result of supply difficulties a general shortage of clothing, rations and field post deliveries developed.

The operations officer of the *XXXX. Panzer-Korps* brought the following points to the attention of *Panzergruppe 4* on the occasion of submitting a recommendation for the further course of the attack:

> The *10. Panzer-Division* no longer has any adequate offensive power. Therefore, its attack on the high ground at Skirminowa can only take place after the attack of the *5. Panzer-Division* has taken place at Roshdestweno.
>
> *SS-Division "Reich"* is to move out in the morning of D-Day so that all of the army-level artillery can offer initial support. The *10. Panzer-Division* will move out echeloned somewhat to the rear, since it must await the advance of the *5. Panzer-Division.*

The commanding general of the *Panzergruppe* and his chief of staff indicated their agreement with the recommendation.

On 15 November combat patrols of *SS-Division "Reich"* determined that the enemy position north of Fetschina was unoccupied. The village, however, was still held by the enemy. The *I./* and *II./SS-Infanterie-Regiment "Deutschland"* and the *II./SS-Infanterie-Regiment "Der Führer"* moved into the staging areas.

(Ernst Streng, at that time a *SS-Unterscharführer* and a squad leader in the

2./SS-Infanterie-Regiment "Deutschland", made entries in his diary concerning the heavy fighting that will be described shortly. His notes will be incorporated sporadically to add a little "local color". The author has chosen the respective section headings.)

***

For 15 November, Ernst Streng wrote the following:

It was only in the last few November days that the German forces were again issued the minimal supplies that make it possible to carry on with the planned operations.

Advance to the Staging Area

The morning of 15 November had arrived. The winter sun spread its pale light over the snow-covered land along the Moskwa. We had already loaded our personal gear and weapons on the squad vehicles. An icy east wind swept through the valley of the Moskwa and over the hills. Fine snow accumulated in the hollows where the wind did not reach it.

It was a day like all the others that had gone before, and many more like it are yet to come. Or is it even colder at 20 below (-4 degrees Fahrenheit) when the wind blows like this?...

...Our drivers have worked on the trucks since daybreak. They dragged wood over and built a fire under the engine block to preheat the engine oil, the only way to start the diesel engine. They later unscrewed the air filter so that hot air from a burning bunch of cotton waste could be sucked through the intake manifold. As a last resort, one vehicle after another had to be towed to get them properly started in the abominable cold.

While I climbed into the cab with Weindl, the leading vehicles were already moving along an ice-covered street through the village down to the river. The road then led over the fields, through the woods past isolated villages where German forces prepared to set out to the front.

Visibility was poor. The windows were iced over. Wooden poles marked the snow-covered route over the treeless hills and valleys. The columns spread far apart. The sidecar-motorcycle riders moving in the column continually got stuck in the heaped snowdrifts. By the time we came along, the icy wind had already drifted over the tracks where the column had passed only moments before, so we had to depend on our luck in following the road. I could barely stay in the cab because of the cold. Snow drifted into the farthest reaches of the vehicle through cracks and the open window. My men were wrapped tight under thick layers of blankets and tarpaulins on the benches in back.

I stamped my frozen feet on the floor, beat my hands on my knees and continued to freeze.

Early in the afternoon we stopped at the edge of some woods in which our regiment was to assemble for the attack tomorrow. Our artillery rumbled up front.

***

Unterscharführer Streng continued:

Combat Patrols

Our first platoon was designated as combat patrol for the regiment (*SS-Infanterie-Regiment "Deutschland"*). We pulled freshly washed jerseys over our uniforms as replacements for the missing camouflage blouses. Up front, in the village, at a snowy slope where the staff of the forces employed there had set up in some sheds, we reported to the regiment's command post. On both sides of a broad hollow were widely scattered artillery, *Nebelwerfer* and *Flak* positions. They laid down harassing fire on the Russian positions at irregular intervals. *Sturmgeschütze*, armored cars and radio vehicles clustered around the huts. From his observation post an artillery forward observer pointed out the way that was marked on our maps. He called our attention to identified enemy positions and gave us a lot of valuable information.

The mission: Advance to the Russian positions and reconnoiter the situation and enemy strength.

Swinging well out to the right on the reverse slope, we later advanced on the left of the road over the frozen farm fields. They finally gave way in sloping meadows to the wooded low ground of the Moskwa riverbank. Carefully looking around, Stefan and his squad crossed over the frozen river. We followed. As quietly as possible, we moved along into the Russian lines, keeping down on the ground and taking advantage of every bush and dip in the ground for cover. If only we knew where the Russians were hiding. Damn! One of us stepped on a twig that snapped — loudly.

Above, on the hill, the near edge of the woods to the left gave a broad view of a long village that stretched over the high ground. The Russian gun and infantry positions showed up clearly, rising above the pure white of the snow on the forward slope. We continued on Russian footpaths that wound through the brush. We cut a black telephone cable. Then we stood before a clearing in the woods. Stopping from time to time, I lay down on the ground and listened. A path led on through the woods. Flitting from tree trunk to tree trunk, we continued along the path.

Suddenly, as if they had grown out of the ground, two Russians stood three meters in front of us. They were just as surprised as we were. They turned around on the spot and ran off through the woods. At that very second, submachine guns chattered and rifle shots cracked, sending long echoes rolling through the winter woodland.

Clearly we had run into the repair troop working its way along the telephone cable we had cut. Therefore, Russians must also be behind us. Not a good thing — now we had certainly drawn their attention to us. That left no alternative but to turn around and, as quickly as possible, return by the same route to the Moskwa. Surprisingly, either the Russians did not see us, or they did not feel confident in taking on a strong German patrol.

In any case, we all got away from the Russians and back across the ice of the Moskwa completely unharmed. When we made our report we were told that the attack had been postponed by half a day. For us that meant two cold winter nights in the open.

Later, when we returned to the company, I immediately started to dig in with the entire squad. Starting out with a narrow depression in the ground, we dug out a deep right-angle trench in the slope. We covered the bottom and the top with brush. In the corner we made a fireplace with a chimney. That way, at least, the wind could no longer get at us. Unfortunately, the chimney did not work quite the way we had intended. By the next morning I was suffering more from the smoke than from the cold.

The Turning Point of the Campaign Looms

SS-Oberstgruppenführer und Generaloberst der Waffen-SS Paul Hausser made the following critical remarks in his personal notes regarding the time period between the defensive fighting and the resumption of the attack on Moscow:

Should the offensive be resumed after the new outbreak of cold weather or should a defense be constructed in the previous limit of advance? Resupply was becoming more and more difficult. Also, the open flank to *Panzergruppe 2* (Guderian) caused concern from a tactical perspective.

Generalfeldmarschall von Bock was in favor of resuming the offensive. Hitler saw the objective as being east of Moscow, roughly in the line: Tambow — Rybinsk (!).

Reconnaissance and preparation of positions to the rear was forbidden.

Initially, the units had to close up, bring up the artillery and secure materiel and supplies. The railroad stretches had not yet been changed to German gauge. Transport by motor vehicles was the only option for supply.

As a result, the next objective was only the Moskwa — Volga canal.

***

Alexander Werth wrote in his work on that period:

The Russians had learned from the fighting to date. A new housecleaning was carried out. Incapable officers were removed. Those who had proven themselves were employed in decisive places. Cooperation with the commissars became more realistic. Effective 7 August 1941, Stalin was the supreme commander.

In mid-October the danger of a German breakthrough from Wolololamsk to Istra was apparent. It led to a panic in Moscow and partial evacuation of the populace. Worker battalions were formed. However, the arrival of reinforcements from Siberia and central Asia had a calming effect.

The effect of the mud season on the attacker was not fully recognized since it was much less noticeable in the streets of Moscow and the suburbs.

On the anniversary of the revolution (6 November) Stalin gave a speech that was a mixture of pessimism and self-confidence, but the "fatherland" note had its effect. "Stalin's nationalism had conquered Lenin's internationalism." As a result, the panic was overcome on the Russian side. (Alexander Werth, *Der Krieg in Rußland 1941-45*, p. ?. Munich: Droemersche Verlaganstalt, ?)

***

After the date for the start of the attack had been postponed by a day,

Operations Order No. 12 for the resumption of the attack on Moscow arrived at the division from the *XXXX. Panzer-Korps* during the afternoon of 16 November. The order stated, in part:

1.) …

2.) The *XXXX. Panzer-Korps* (*SS-Division "Reich"* on the right, *10. Panzer-Division* on the left) is to break through the enemy positions on 18 November and attack via the area around and south of Bely as far as the Istra — Nowopetrowskoje (Cholojamicha — Jadrimino) road. It then is to capture Istra either by advancing along the road or by envelopment from the north.

The *5. Panzer-Division* is to attack on the left of the *10. Panzer-Division* on 18 November. It is to advance with its right wing from Iwoilowo via Gorki to Roshestwenskoye. Advancing on both sides of the road, it is to capture Petrowskoje. From there, depending on how the situation develops, it is to advance against either the south or the north end of the Istra Reservoir (north of Istra).

***

On 16 November the commanding general of the *XXXX. Panzer-Korps, General der Panzertruppen* Stumme, addressed the attached troops in an order of the day. It read:

Order of the Day

As a result of the change in the weather that brought rain and mud, we have been forced against our will to stop our advance after the pocket battle of Wjasma and breaking through the Moscow defensive position.

You have provided the prerequisites for resumption of the operation by your untiring work in the worst weather. For that you have my thanks and praise.

The enemy has made good use of the time provided by our forced halt and has attempted to bring our advance to an permanent halt by attacking. Thanks to your courageous determination and your stubborn defense in winter cold and unfavorable circumstances, his attacks have failed.

Now we are again going for the enemy's throat. We shall finally throw the enemy to the ground and reach our objective of Moscow. It is no longer very far.

/signed/ Stumme
General der Panzertruppen

16 November 1941

In the sector of *SS-Division "Reich"* the Russians increased their artillery fire and fired on the area south and southeast of Staraja Rusa. As noon approached, strong enemy forces attacked the division's positions from Gorodischtsche. By evening, the enemy attack was repulsed with heavy losses to him. In places, the attack had come to within 150 meters of the positions .

Reconnaissance that had been sent forward to screen the southern flank of the division as far as the sector of the friendly forces on the right determined that the enemy had attacked the newly inserted *252. Infanterie-Division* of the *IX. Armee-Korps* and occupied Wajuchina. The enemy was still advancing to the west late in the afternoon. Statements by prisoners confirmed that the enemy objective was to interdict the route of advance west of the Oserna Creek.

SS-Aufklärungs-Abteilung "Reich" was immediately set in march to the area southeast of Staraja to protect the southern flank. In addition, one battalion of *SS-Infanterie-Regiment "Deutschland"* was alerted to stand by as local reserve.

In accordance with its orders, *SS-Infanterie-Regiment "Deutschland"* reached the wooded terrain west of Lyskowka during the day by moving via Lenikow, Kotipzowa, Bujnino, Borsezewo and Matwejkowo. It billeted there and remained at the disposal of the division.

Sub-Section m)

Capture of Istra and Ssolnetschnogorsk: 17 November - 4 December 1941

17 November 1941

During the night of 17 November, the battalions and units of *SS-Infanterie-Regimenter "Deutschland"* and *"Der Führer"* which had not yet been employed made their way to their assembly areas.

Before dawn had broken, the enemy renewed his attacks on the boundary between *SS-Infanterie-Regiment "Der Führer"* and *SS-Kradschützen-Bataillon "Reich"* with armor carrying mounted infantry. Several tanks succeeded in breaking through.

Starting at 0630 hours, the enemy artillery fire increased and kept up until evening. The positions at Michailowskoje were singled out and kept under fire from heavy artillery. At times 50 impacts per minute were counted.

An enemy attack from Fetschina with nine tanks was repulsed at 1530 hours. Five tanks were knocked out.

The attack of the *252. Infanterie-Division*, the friendly forces to the right of the corps, to mop up the area that had been lost to the previous day's Russian advance, got no farther than the eastern outskirts of Wajuchina. Although the enemy fell back to the woods east of Wajuchina, he still held on to the southwest corner of those woods.

Based on what was happening on the right, the possibility remained of a threat to the southern flank of *SS-Division "Reich"*. Accordingly, the *XXXX. Panzer-Korps* concluded that an attack on 18 November by *SS-Division*

"Reich" would not be possible.

The attack progressed well for the friendly forces on the left. The intended jump-off position for the *5. Panzer-Division* for 18 November was the limit of previous advance in the line Gorodischtsche — Lyshki — Ivoilow. The *XXXX. Panzer-Korps* joined the attack of the *5. Panzer-Division* on 18 November with the *10. Panzer-Division*. All of the army-level artillery was directed to support their attack.

The situation dictated that *SS-Division "Reich"* would not be able to start its attack until 19 November.

On 17 November, the commander-in-chief of *Panzergruppe 4*, *Generaloberst* Hoepner, released the following order of the day to the units that had been attached for the impending attack:

Order of the Day

The time of waiting is past. We can attack again. The last Russian defense before Moscow has been defeated. We must bring the heart of the Bolshevik resistance to a standstill in order to end the campaign for this year.

The *Panzergruppe* has the good fortune to be able to conduct the decisive attack. Therefore we must concentrate all our strength, all of our fighting spirit and indomitable will for the merciless destruction of the enemy.

Stir up the troops! Inspire them with your spirit! Show them the objective that will bring them a glorious conclusion to the heavy fighting and the promise of well-earned rest! Lead them energetically and with confidence in victory! May the God of War grant you good fortune!

/signed/ Hoepner
Generaloberst

DISTRIBUTION: Down to battalions, separate battalion and separate commanders

(*Oberst a. D.* Straub, *Geschichte des Panzerregiments 7*, p. ?. Unpublished mimeograph.)]

18 November 1941

Due to the postponement of the division's attack by a day, the troops were exposed to the bitter cold for an additional day. Although it remained relatively quiet in the division's sector during the morning, strong enemy artillery fire suddenly opened up on the sector of *SS-Kradschützen-Bataillon "Reich"* around noon.

At 1300 hours the enemy — the 3rd battalion of the Russian 258th Rifle-Division — attacked from Fetschina and was repulsed. The attack was repeated two more times, at 1430 hours and 1530 hours. Both times the enemy came within hand-grenade range but was repulsed in concentrated fire of artillery and heavy infantry weapons. According to statements by prisoners, the attacking Russian battalion was completely fresh and in action for the first time. At 1300 hours *Kampfgruppe Chevallerie* of the *10. Panzer-Division* launched an attack at Roshdestweno and, by late afternoon, reached the western outskirts of Skirminowa.

19 November 1941

At 0715 hours *SS-Division "Reich"* attacked.

While *SS-Kradschützen-Bataillon "Reich"* initially remained in its previous positions, the reinforced infantry regiments attacked with *SS-Infanterie-Regiment "Der Führer"* on the right (with the motorcycle battalion adjoining on the right) and *SS-Infanterie-Regiment "Deutschland"* on the left.

The Fight for Gorodischtsche

SS-Infanterie-Regiment "Der Führer", which had assembled for the attack with the *II./SS-Infanterie-Regiment "Der Führer"* on the right and the *III./SS-Infanterie-Regiment "Der Führer"* on the left, was given the mission of attacking to the southeast through the woods and capturing Gorodischtsche on the far side. In the gray light of dawn it launched the attack but ran into extraordinarily heavy resistance.

A reconnaissance patrol of the *2./SS-Aufklärungs-Abteilung "Reich"* was the first element to encounter the enemy in the sector of the *III./SS-Infanterie-Regiment "Der Führer"*. A forward passage of lines of the battalion was accomplished when the battalion attacked.

The Siberian 78th Rifle Division, superbly equipped, defended the woods from excellent positions. It fought hard and with stubborn determination.

After the failure of the first attack, an attempt was made to smash the enemy in his positions in the woods with fire from one light and one heavy *Nebelwerfer* battalion. However, even after that inferno of fire, the subsequent attack by the *I./* and *III./SS-Infanterie-Regiment "Der Führer"* was repulsed. The effect of the *Nebelwerfer* fire in the woods was less than expected.

The only remaining possibility for the commander of the regiment, *SS-Obersturmbannführer* Kumm, was to send the *II./SS-Infanterie-Regiment "Der Führer"* around the woods to the north and make an enveloping attack on Gorodischtsche. The battalion penetrated into the built-up area, where heavy house-to-house fighting developed. Every house had to be cleared out individually. The *III./SS-Infanterie-Regiment "Der Führer"* was employed to eliminate the flanking fire from the woods east of Gorodischtsche. During the course of the day it rolled up the woodland positions in heavy fighting.

During the afternoon, Russian immediate counterattacks on Gorodischtsche from the southeast, which were repulsed, made it clear that the enemy had no intention of evacuating. Two Russian battalions still held the west bank.

By evening the *II./SS-Infanterie-Regiment "Der Führer"* had chewed its way into the center of Gorodischtsche in hard house-to-house fighting. The *I./SS-Infanterie-Regiment "Der Führer"* also renewed its attack, reaching the east outskirts of Fetschina. The enemy still held on in the point of woods north of Fetschina. An immediate counterattack in the size of two battalions from the Pawelkowo area was repulsed in the evening.

The Fight for Ssloboda

SS-Infanterie-Regiment "Deutschland" attacked at 0600 hours. It succeeded in surprising the enemy and forcing a crossing of the Oserna River. The first objective of the attack was Ssloboda.

The *I./SS-Infanterie-Regiment "Deutschland"* was employed on the right; the *II./SS-Infanterie-Regiment "Deutschland"* on the left.

The *II./SS-Infanterie-Regiment "Deutschland"* was supported by the *Sturmgeschütze "Blücher"* and *"Lützow"*. After crossing the Oserna, it swung to the north in order to attack Ssloboda from the south in accordance with its orders. It surprised the enemy strongpoint on the high ground 600 meters south of Ssloboda. Only at that moment did the Russians in Ssloboda become aware of the German attack from the south. In a rapid assault, the *II./SS-Infanterie-Regiment "Deutschland"* was able to approach the southern outskirts of Ssloboda, where its attack bogged down in stubborn infantry fighting. The Russians had created strong fighting positions by excavating under all of the houses in the built-up area.

Russian antitank and machine-gun fire blocked the only available crossing of the Oserna west of Ssloboda, so no heavy weapons were available. Therefore, the only way to get at the Russians in their fortified houses was through tough hand-to-hand fighting.

After restaging, the *II./SS-Infanterie-Regiment "Deutschland"* made a second attack on Ssloboda with support from artillery and *Nebelwerfer* and the two *Sturmgeschütze*.

***

SS-Unterscharführer Streng of the *2./SS-Infanterie-Regiment "Deutschland"* that adjoined on the right, observed the fighting of the *II./SS-Infanterie-Regiment "Deutschland"* as follows:

> Two kilometers to our left a long, extended village stretched over an open ridge. Our 2nd Battalion had been submerged there in a hurricane of fire as it attacked. Since early dawn it had vainly charged the Russian positions on the forward slope.
>
> There was a faint rumble and howl from the distance. Then a wide, fiery comet-tail swept overhead. *Nebelwerfer*! Tongues of fire leaped in the air! Like glowing masses, the weight of countless explosions covered the Russian positions on the left outskirts of the village. The German shell bursts danced among the huts like giant will 'o the wisps. Swirling clouds of smoke and dust enveloped the dark hill. Numerous

machine guns joined in with their sharp staccato. The *II./SS-Infanterie-Regiment "Deutschland"* launched its attack for the second time under the curtain of German artillery fire. Strings of pearls marked the trajectories of rounds from the light *Flak* as they joined the fight.

***

However, this attack, too, achieved no success. In extremely hard house-to-house fighting, the *II./SS-Infanterie-Regiment "Deutschland"* chewed its way to the northern half of the village by noon, but the advance stopped there.

At 1600 hours the leader of the *Sturmgeschütz* platoon, *SS-Untersturmführer* Kneissl, decided to cross over the frozen Oserna to the west bank and attack Ssloboda from the west. The assault guns broke through the ice but were able to make it to the west bank. At 1630 hours they attacked Ssloboda. Within a short time they eliminated the Russian antitank and machine guns that had blocked the stream crossing until then and made their way into the village.

At long last the heavy weapons, especially the 2-cm *Flak*, could be brought into Ssloboda from the west. Thanks to this decisive flank attack, the sticking point of the assault had been overcome. However, in spite of the superiority of friendly fire, the enemy still did not give up the fight. Each building had to be set ablaze by gunfire over the enemy's heads before resistance was broken. As darkness fell, Ssloboda was finally firmly in the hands of the *II./SS-Infanterie-Regiment "Deutschland"*. The enemy had fought to the death in his positions without surrendering, providing an impressive example on the other side of steadfastness and for the concept of "defense".

However, friendly losses were also high. The *II./SS-Infanterie-Regiment "Deutschland"* lost 138 dead and wounded on that day. This amounted to almost half of its combat strength.

The *I./* and *III./SS-Infanterie-Regiment "Deutschland"* made good initial progress advancing south of Ssloboda until they came up against heavy resistance from the Siberians at the edge of the woods west of Nikolskoje. That brought them to a standstill.

***

SS-Unterscharführer Streng sketched the following horrifying scene:

The Siberians Give No Quarter

After an hour, our third platoon (of the *2./SS-Infanterie-Regiment "Deutschland"*) returned with bloody heads. End result: Two killed, five wounded...Then I saw one of the severely wounded creeping over the snow-covered field in front of us. In his pain and need he had erred somewhat in direction and was now creeping directly toward the Russian position. A long trail of blood was visible in the snow. Meter by meter he crept along on his elbows, dragging his limp body behind him. I jumped up and waved him to me with my arms to divert him from his path to destruction. He heard us shout, lifted his head from the snow, and I could clearly see through the

The divisional artillery

Top: Another view of the divisional artillery in action. **Below**: 8-wheeled radio armored car. **Opposite page**: The handiwork of *SS-Aufklärungs-Abteilung* "*Reich*"

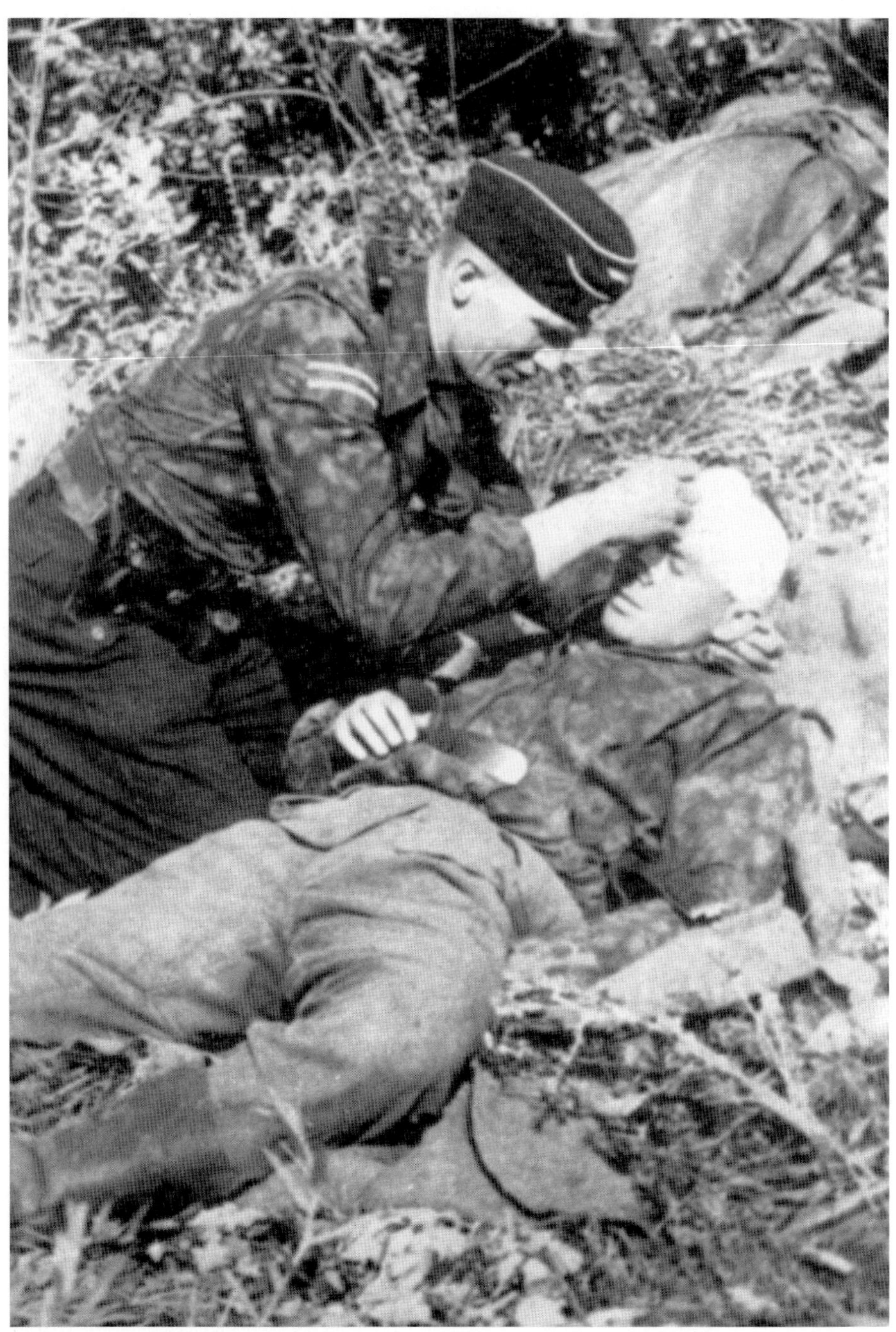

Care of the wounded...

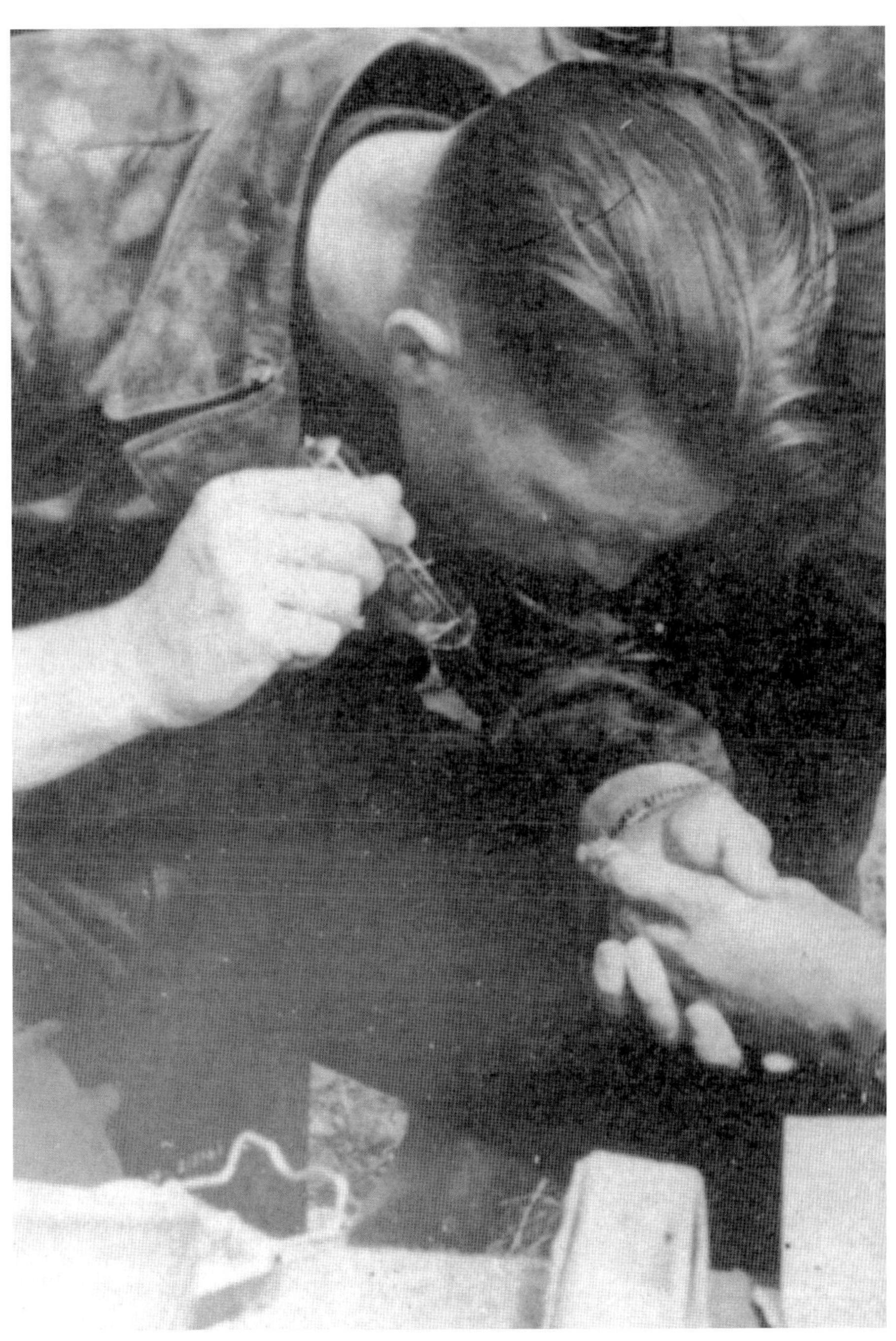

...in this case by crews of armored vehicles

Opposite page: Soldiers' graves along the route of advance. **Above:** The *10. Panzer-Division* and grenadiers of *SS-Division "Reich"* after breaking through the Moscow defense position

Wilhelm Bittrich

SS-Obergruppenführer und General der Waffen-SS

Born: 26 February 1894 in Wernigerode

Died: 19 April 1979 in Wolfratshausen

1914 - 18: Service in World War I. Iron crosses, First and Second Class; by war's end *Leutnant* and pilot.

1919 - 23: Member of a *Freikorps* in the east;

1923: Transferred to the *Reichswehr* and detached to Russia for pilot training;

1934: Entered *SS-Verfügungstruppe* (Hamburg);

1938: On formation of *SS-Standarte "Der Führer"* the *II./SS-Standarte "Deutschland"* under *SS-Sturmbannführer* Bittrich was transferred to Vienna and redesignated as the *I./SS-Standarte "Der Führer"*.

Polish campaign 1939: *SS-Standartenführer* in *"Leibstandarte SS-Adolf Hitler"*.

End of 1940: Named commander of *SS-Infanterie-Regiment "Deutschland"*

Russian campaign, 1941: Knight's Cross for breaking through Moscow defense position;

14 October 1941: After *SS-Obergruppenführer* Hausser was wounded, assumed command of *SS-Division "Reich"*;

1942: Division commander of *SS-Kavallerie-Division "Florian Geyer"* during its activation

1943: Division commander of *SS-Panzer-Grenadier-Division "Hohenstaufen"* in France at its formation; Employed in March 1944 west of Tarnopol.

Invasion front, 1944: After *SS-Obergruppenführer* Hausser was appointed commander-in-chief of the *7. Armee*, Bittrich succeeded Hausser as commanding general of the *II. SS-Panzer-Korps*

21 August 1944: The breakout of the encircled *7. Armee* from the Falaise pocket was made possible by the advance of his corps from the east to the high ground north of Chambois. For that he was awarded the Oakleaves to the Knight's Cross.

17 September 1944: Successful defense against the English airborne operation in the Arnhem — Nymwegen area by elements of the *II. SS-Panzer-Korps*.

Battle of Ardennes, 1944/45: Advance by *II. SS-Panzer-Korps* with the *2. SS-Panzer-Division "Das Reich"* and the *9. SS-Panzer-Division "Hohenstaufen"* to Grandmenil.

1945: Employment of *II. SS-Panzer-Korps* in Hungary between Lake Balaton and Lake Velence under his command; and fighting withdrawal to Vienna.

6 May 1945: Awarded Swords to the Knight's Cross.

After the capitulation, *SS-Obergruppenführer* Bittrich was turned over to the French by the Americans. In France he was tried and sentenced in June 1953 to pro forma sentence of time served. He was then released to Germany. After the death of *SS-Oberstgruppenführer* Hausser, *SS-Obergruppenführer* Bittrich was the senior officer of the *Waffen-SS* and honorary president of the federal association of former *Waffen-SS* soldiers until his death in 1979.

Above: Artillery struggles forward through deep snow. **Below**: Defense in the Istra position.

Above: The cathedral of Istra. **Left**: The commanding general of the *XXXX. Panzer-Korps*, *General der Kavallerie* Georg Stumme. During the Moscow offensive *SS-Division "Reich"* was attached to his corps from 2 October to 13 December 1941. **Opposite page, top**: Fires rage in the city of Istra. **Opposite page, bottom**: Crossing the Moskva River in a rubber boat, winter 1941.

Opposite page: left: Covered with snow. **Opposite page, right**: The last position before Moscow. **Above**: Retreat to the Istra position. **Left**: Before the retreat.

binoculars how his face lit up when he saw us. With renewed willpower he continued to creep up the gentle slope on his elbows, his lower body dragging lifelessly through the snow.

All of us had leaped up, regardless of the threatening danger, and yelled to him to stop. But the more we yelled and waved, the faster he crawled to certain death. Then he was only 15 meters from the hostile group of brush, then 10 meters, 9 meters...ping...ping. His elbows buckled. His corpse lay, lifeless, in the snow. He had been felled by round to the head 30 meters before our eyes — and there was nothing we could do! We could have screamed with rage. The Siberians gave no quarter even to an obviously defenseless, severely wounded enemy in his life-or-death need.

Our rounds hammered into the brush. Ricochets and tracers zipped back and forth over the ground. Hand grenades detonated with blue balls of smoke. Four machine guns hammered away. It hissed, burst and crashed. The first and fourth squads crept forward, attempting to advance along the hedge that approached the position. Again they looked into rage-distorted Mongol faces and those, in turn, stared black, cold-blooded and serious. Three, four, five comrades fell in the snow, shot through the head. The others made their way back and threw themselves down beside our own machine-gun positions.

Here and there we heard the wounded cry for help as they writhed in the snow with the agony of their wounds.

The resistance put up by the Mongol foe was of a stubbornness and fanaticism such as we had rarely experienced. The Siberians were dug into circular foxholes so that we could only work our way close to them with heavy losses. They threw hand grenades, fired from their holes and ducked back beneath the earth. They defended like devils — until we received orders to halt the attack.

***

The strain on the men was unspeakable. From early in the morning until late at night they lay in the snow and icy wind with hardly a break. Never before had they known what physical pain bitter cold could cause, pains that were often almost unbearable — yet they had to be borne.

In the early morning hours of 19 November the division intercepted a radio message:

We can no longer hold against the pressure of the *SS* fascists. We are falling back to the line designated in orders. (War diary of *SS-Kradschützen-Bataillon "Reich"*, entry for 19 November 1941)

The message did not appear to apply to all the enemy facing the corps sector, however.

The following Teletype arrived at the corps from the commanding general of *Panzergruppe 4*, *Generaloberst* Hoepner:

Russian radio traffic makes a withdrawal seem likely. Pass on to troops: Indefatigable pursuit! Avoid losses! Shorten the campaign!

***

Compared with the previous day, Russian artillery was strikingly weak. It was probable that the enemy had withdrawn the bulk of his artillery, but still held the old sector with strong rear guards.

The division received the following missions for continuing the attack on 20 November:

The *XXXX. Panzer-Korps is to* capitalize on today's success by attacking on 20 November through and south of Bely as far as the Istra — Nowo Petrowskoje road.

The *10. Panzer-Division* is to capture Bely and be prepared to continue the advance to the major road between Jadromino (inclusive) and Duplewo (south).

SS-Division "Reich" is to mop up the northern sector of the Oserna bend. It is to open the crossing at Nikolskoje by employing elements north of the Oserna. It then is to advance via Budjkowo to the Istra — Nowo Petrowskoje road on both sides of Cholyjanicha.

The division is to screen against enemy units remaining in the southern sector of the Oserna bend and in the bridgehead west of Gorodischtsche with the weakest forces possible.

For the purpose of opening the crossing at Nikolskoje, one tank company of the *10. Panzer-Division* is temporarily attached to the division. It is to stage in Bulanina. After completion of this mission. The tank company is to revert to the *10. Panzer-Division.*

***

Personnel Losses of the Division

On 19 November *SS-Division "Reich"* reported the following losses to higher headquarters:

	Killed		Wounded		Missing	
	O /	NCO/EM	O /	NCO/EM	O /	NCO/EM
22 June - 18 Nov 1941	78	1,575	202	5,175	2	154
19 Nov 1941	4	74	4	126	—	—
Total losses since 22 June 1941	82	1,649	206	5,301	2	154

20 November 1941

The combat reconnaissance sent out during the night determined that the enemy facing the division had not withdrawn.

During the early morning hours *SS-Infanterie-Regiment "Der Führer"* repulsed a new enemy attack in approximately battalion size against Gorodischtsche from Pawelkowo. At 1130 hours the *II./SS-Infanterie-Regiment "Der Führer"*, reinforced with *Sturmgeschütze "Yorck"* and *"Prinz*

Eugen", again attacked Gorodischtsche. This attack finally succeeded. After heavy house-to-house fighting the regiment had control of the village by evening. The last enemy resistance in the woods had been crushed.

The fighting counted as the heaviest and most costly which the division had experienced up to that time.

In heavy fighting the division cleared the enemy out of the southwest portion of the Oserna bend. After a last desperate, immediate counterattack in the late afternoon, the weak Russian remnants fell back through the woods east of Gorodischtsche.

Capturing the Nikolskoje Narrows

Reconnaissance by *SS-Infanterie-Regiment "Deutschland"* determined that heavy enemy columns filled the Glinki — Nikolskoje road. Extensive enemy mining was found in Borodenka.

At 1100 hours *SS-Infanterie-Regiment "Deutschland"* moved out with the *I./* and *III./SS-Infanterie-Regiment "Deutschland"* to Borodenka to assemble there for the attack. *Sturmgeschütze "Blücher"* and *"Lützow"* were attached.

The *II./SS-Infanterie-Regiment "Deutschland"* was pulled out of Ssloboda and assembled at the point of the woods 1,200 meters southwest of Nikolskoje for the attack on that village.

The plans for the mining of Nikolskoje were found in an abandoned bunker in Borodenka. The narrows east of Nikolskoje were particularly heavily mined. The enemy had emplaced more than 3,000 mines in the Nikolskoje area, which were cleared by the *16. (Pionier)/SS-Infanterie-Regiment "Deutschland"* and elements of *SS-Pionier-Bataillon "Reich"* with the help of those plans.

The start time of the attack on Nikolskoje, which had originally been set for 1400 hours, was moved up to 1245 hours since reconnaissance had found only weak enemy forces there.

Without significant opposition, the *I./* and *III./SS-Infanterie-Regiment "Deutschland"* passed through the lanes that had been cleared through the minefield. At 1400 hours they took possession of the Oserna crossing (narrow point in the marshland) east of Nikolskoje. The enemy had evacuated the village. On the high ground outside of Nikolskoje field fortifications were identified at a range of about 1,200 meters. The *Sturmgeschütze* fired on the positions while the infantry continued to advance.

The bridge at the Oserna crossing had been blown. The causeway, which was several hundred meters long, had been prepared for demolition. The combat engineers immediately removed the demolition charges. Since the ice would not bear the weight of heavy weapons, they had to be left behind. The *I./* and *III./SS-Infanterie-Regiment "Deutschland"* occupied Warwarina and

Gorodischtsche and established security there.

The combat engineers had to work without a break until the next morning clearing mines. In spite of maximum exertion by all available manpower, construction of the bridge and an approach to the causeway were probably also going to require the next day.

The *II./SS-Infanterie-Regiment "Deutschland"* remained in Nikolskoje for the time being and screened to the south. Since the attack made good progress on the entire corps front and the enemy had withdrawn during the night from the sector of *SS-Kradschützen-Bataillon "Reich"*, the battalion was pulled out of the positions at 0500 hours in the morning. By evening it had reached Gorodischtsche north of Lake Troszjenskoje, proceeding along the left flank of the *10. Panzer-Division* via Manoschina. The battalion established contact with the *I./* and *III./SS-Infanterie-Regiment "Deutschland"* and established combat outposts with them.

***

The war diary of the *XXXX. Panzer-Korps* for 20 November 1941 states:

The Siberian 78th Rifle Division, which had been badly battered in that fighting — only remnants of the 40th and 258th Rifle Regiments were able to escape to the east — was the toughest opponent that *SS-Division "Reich"* had yet met at any time in the eastern campaign. Very well armed and equipped, every single man fought to the death. The fact that 812 dead Russians were counted in and around Gorodischtsche alone bears witness to the intensity of the fighting. So brutal an opponent could only be met with equal measures.

In the following Teletype *Generaloberst* Hoepner emphatically referred again to that fact:

"In the evening the enemy was able to capture a village in the sector of the *V. Armee-Korps* in which there were about 30 wounded German soldiers. After a brief interrogation, the bestial enemy shot all the wounded. This type of treatment is typical of the Bolsheviks and is a mockery of all of international law. I desire that this incident be made known to every German soldier of the *Panzertruppe*. Mercy toward such an enemy is out of place. [Such an enemy] must be mercilessly destroyed. Every German soldier is fighting for his life.

***

The *10. Panzer-Division* fought for and captured the exit from the woods east of Bulanino. At 1120 hours it captured Bely and broke through the enemy position at the Molodilnja sector that same evening. In spite of a counterattack by a Russian battalion with seven T 34's, Rubzowo was captured in night fighting.

The mission for *SS-Division "Reich"*, to advance to the Istra — Nowo Petrowskoje road, remained unchanged for the following day.

21 November 1941

At 0900 hours *SS-Kradschützen-Bataillon "Reich"* set out ahead of *SS-Infanterie-Regiment "Deutschland"* on the woods road to Budjikowa. Road conditions were miserable. The *1./SS-Kradschützen-Bataillon "Reich"* became involved in heavy woodland fighting. The *4./SS-Kradschützen-Bataillon "Reich"* was employed to protect the flank of its sister company.

***

SS-Unterscharführer Streng (*2./SS-Infanterie-Regiment "Deutschland")* wrote about the fighting:

> As our First Battalion (*I./SS-Infanterie-Regiment "Deutschland")* advanced over the white fields as local reserve for the attack, the bloody harvest of the heavy woodland fighting staggered back toward us. *Kradschützen* with arm and chest wounds, blood-soaked bandages wrapped around their heads. *Sankas* (= *Sanitätskrankenkraftwagen* = ambulances) and motorcycles recovered the bloody bundles of humanity and brought them to the village

***

The *SS-Kradschützen* advanced from Budikowa via Kolonja and Tompa to Jadromino, where contact was established with the *10. Panzer-Division*. The tankers had already captured Jadromino.

SS-Infanterie-Regiment "Deutschland", which was following *SS-Kradschützen-Bataillon "Reich"* in the sequence *III./, I./,* and *II./SS-Infanterie-Regiment "Deutschland"*, reached Budikowa at 1300 hours. The regiment then proceeded to Lisina while *SS-Kradschützen-Bataillon "Reich"* turned off to the northeast with the mission of initially proceeding to Tschassowaja.

Because strong enemy resistance was expected in the Molodilnja sector, strong reconnaissance was to check out the possibilities of establishing a bridgehead.

The *III./* and *I./SS-Infanterie-Regiment "Deutschland"* were employed to the front with the remaining battalion following. After the armored combat patrols of *SS-Aufklärungs-Abteilung "Reich"* identified enemy horse-drawn columns approaching the flank of *SS-Infanterie-Regiment "Deutschland"* from Schibanowa in the afternoon, the *II./SS-Infanterie-Regiment "Deutschland"* was echeloned to the right rear behind the *III./SS-Infanterie-Regiment "Deutschland"*.

In Lisina, the *III. SS-Infanterie-Regiment "Deutschland"* was sent against Troiza with the *Sturmgeschütze "Prinz Eugen"* and *"Derfflinger"*. The enemy had established himself in good field fortifications. Within an hour the positions were taken. By evening, Troiza was captured while the *I./SS-Infanterie-Regiment "Deutschland"* attacked Wassiliewskaja.

***

SS-Unterscharführer Streng wrote:

The Capture of a Village

In Troiza we swung off to the right and advanced through the woods. Somewhere not far away a Russian tractor chugged around in the woods. This time we were hard on the Russians' heels. After two kilometers my squad and I advanced out of the wood line. A hundred meters farther a village (Wassiliewskaja) huddled on the descending slope. As we got closer I saw brown-clad figures break out of the huts and the wood line, turn to the rear and dash away down the steep slope with long jumps. Then a cry burst from our throats — sure of victory and inspiring! Suddenly, all the Russians ran down the slope. Swinging out wide, my squad and I ran to the village. There I saw a bunch of Russians fleeing up the other slope and into the underbrush. In a wild dash, we leaped down the slope, hard on the heels of the fleeing Russians. Then my squad and I were called back from above. The battalion assembled in the village.

***

The *III./SS-Infanterie-Regiment "Deutschland"* attacked an enemy motorized column, which fell back from the southwest to the northeast and went over to the defensive. The enemy column suffered heavy losses. As darkness fell, it moved back toward Weretenki.

During the night the *III./SS-Infanterie-Regiment "Deutschland"* established security at Troiza, the *I./SS-Infanterie-Regiment "Deutschland"* at Wassilewskaja and at the intersection one kilometer southwest of Wassilewskaja and the *II./SS-Infanterie-Regiment "Deutschland"* at Lisina. The regiment's command post and the division forward command post were also at Lisina.

That day *SS-Infanterie-Regiment "Der Führer"* initially followed *SS-Infanterie-Regiment "Deutschland"*.

The *XXXX. Panzer-Korps* was to continue the attack to capture Istra on the next day. With regard to this attack, the division received the following mission from the corps for 22 November 1941:

SS-Division "Reich" is to capture Cholujanicha. It then is to attack across the line Shilkino — St. Cholschtschewiki far enough to the east so that it will be possible for the division to turn via Cholschtschewiki to Dedeschino. It is to promptly establish a bridgehead over the Magluscha at Dedeschino.

The *10. Panzer-Division* is to gain a crossing over the Magluscha in the Dedeschino (exclusive) — Filatowo (inclusive) sector and advance via Jefimonowo to the Istra. It is essential to establish a bridgehead over the Istra before the enemy has time to occupy the east bank of the Istra.

Boundaries:

Between the *IX. Armee-Korps* and *SS-Division "Reich"*: Istra River.

Between *SS-Division "Reich"* and *10. Panzer-Division*: Cholujanicha (*SS*) — Bukarewo (*10.*) — Jefimonowo (*10.*) — Andrejewskoje (*10.*).

The corps artillery will be attached to *SS-Division "Reich"* on request to assure unified control of the employment of artillery.

22 November 1941

The reconnaissance sent out by the *I./SS-Infanterie-Regiment "Deutschland"* during the night and in the early morning hours determined that Weretenki was clear of the enemy. At 0800 hours the *I./SS-Infanterie-Regiment "Deutschland"* moved out against Weretenki with the mission of sending strong reconnaissance to Cholujanicha and the major road Istra — Wolokolamsk. This reconnaissance identified strong enemy forces occupying Cholujanicha and field fortifications on the road on both sides of Cholujanicha.

At 1030 hours the *II./* and *III./SS-Infanterie-Regiment "Deutschland"* were brought forward to Weretenki and assembled on both sides of the village for the attack.

While the *I./* and *II./SS-Infanterie-Regiment "Deutschland"* were to launch a frontal attack on Cholujanicha, the *III./SS-Infanterie-Regiment "Deutschland"* was to advance through the woods southeast of Cholujanicha. It was to eject the enemy from the field fortifications and woods positions at the road and one kilometer east of Cholujanicha. Following that, it was to turn to the northwest and attack Cholujanicha.

A heavy Russian artillery barrage that included some large-caliber fire struck the assembly area causing serious losses. The *1./SS-Infanterie-Regiment "Deutschland"* alone lost eight killed, while the *2./SS-Infanterie-Regiment "Deutschland"* suffered three killed. Both companies lost a large number wounded. The *III./SS-Infanterie-Regiment "Deutschland"* became involved in heavy woodland fighting and only made slow forward progress. The thick underbrush prevented heavy weapons from being brought forward.

In spite of artillery and *Nebelwerfer* support the two battalions were unable to advance. The *Sturmgeschütze "Prinz Eugen"* and *"Yorck"* destroyed one 7.62-cm antiaircraft gun, three antitank guns and one field gun. The enemy put up a stubborn defense that included armor. After an additional *Nebelwerfer* salvo from two battalions on the field fortifications at the southwest edge of Cholujanicha, the enemy fell back into the wooded terrain to the east, thus running into the flank of the attacking *III./SS-Infanterie-Regiment "Deutschland"*. Intense hand-to-hand fighting resulted during which a battalion-sized enemy was partly destroyed and partially forced back to his previous positions.

At 1600 hour the attack of the *I./SS-Infanterie-Regiment "Deutschland"* gained ground and succeeded in penetrating into Cholujanicha. As darkness fell the enemy moved back to the northeast.

During the afternoon, the commander of *SS-Infanterie-Regiment "Deutschland"*, *SS-Standartenführer* Jürgen Wagner, was wounded by a shell fragment while at the regiment's command post in Weretenki. During the attack, the division commander, *SS-Brigadeführer* Bittrich, led the regiment. After the attack was completed, the commander of the *III./SS-Infanterie-Regiment "Deutschland"*, *SS-Sturmbannführer* Schulz, assumed command of the regiment. *SS-Hauptsturmführer* Kröger, the division adjutant, assumed command of the *III./SS-Infanterie-Regiment "Deutschland"*.

SS-Infanterie-Regiment "Deutschland" lost the following on 22 November 1941:

Killed: 4 officers and 43 noncommissioned officers and enlisted personnel
Wounded: 3 officers and 114 noncommissioned officers and enlisted personnel
Missing: 1 noncommissioned officer/enlisted personnel.

SS-Infanterie-Regiment "Deutschland" captured or destroyed the following on 22 November 1941: 2 guns (7.62 cm), 6 heavy machine guns, 1 light mortar, 1 heavy antiaircraft gun, 4 heavy antitank guns, 2 gun limbers, 1 ammunition vehicle and 2 chests of "Molotov cocktails".

***

The war diary of the *XXXX. Panzer-Korps* stated the following for 22 November 1941:

SS-Division "Reich" attacked Cholujanicha with *SS-Infanterie-Regiment "Deutschland"*. The *I./* and *II./SS-Infanterie-Regiment "Deutschland"*, which attacked the built-up area, became involved in heavy house-to-house fighting. The *III./SS-Infanterie-Regiment "Deutschland"*, which captured the woodland positions to the southeast in heavy fighting, advanced from there to Cholujanicha. In the evening, in spite of extremely heavy fighting — in part against a unit of the Siberian regiment — Cholujanicha was captured. The heavy fighting in the woodland position southeast of Cholujanicha is only comprehensible if one personally inspected the Russian positions. The enemy had constructed machine-gun positions, foxholes with dugouts and numerous earthen bunkers in a position facing Cholujanicha. The positions had a depth of 500 meters.

Smoking out those woodland positions, in which every foxhole was well camouflaged, could only be accomplished in hand-to-hand combat, since employment of mortars and *Pak* was practically impossible in the thick woods.

The fighting was complicated by the following circumstance: The *II./SS-Infanterie-Regiment "Deutschland"*, which rolled up the positions from the south from the woods east of Weretenki, was surprised by a hasty Russian relief attack of about 400 men that advanced from Cholujanicha to the east.

Every single foxhole and machine-gun position had to be taken in hand-to-hand fighting. The Russians were well supplied with materials for hand-to-hand fighting such as hand grenades and "Molotov cocktails". By evening the battlefield was covered with innumerable Russian dead.

The *III./SS-Infanterie-Regiment "Deutschland"* lost more than 40 dead and 80 wounded in that fighting.

One company that had advanced to Shilkino reported four occupied enemy positions. It established security at the edge of the woods west of Shilkino.

***

Paul Carell reported on the fighting in that sector as well:

The *XXXX.* and *XXXXVI. Panzer-Korps* of *Panzergruppe 4* had to capture village after village, one patch of woods after another, from the Siberians. The advance guards and *Kampfgruppen* of the *5.* and *10. Panzer-Divisionen* as well as *SS-Division "Reich"* worked their way, one step at a time, through the terrain, often over open, windswept fields and through deep, snowbound woods. (Paul Carell, *Unternehmen Barbarossa*, p. 159 ff. Frankfurt am Main / Berlin (West): Verlag Ullstein GmbH, 1963.)

***

The American historian, George H. Stein, noted *Waffen-SS* casualties as follows:

Characteristically, *Waffen-SS* losses were proportionally much higher than those of the Army. SS-Division "*Reich*", for example, had lost 60 per cent of its combat strength by mid-November, including 40 per cent of its officers; yet it spearheaded a major attack on Moscow, achieving one of the deepest penetrations of the offensive. During the course of the Russian winter counteroffensive, *SS-Division "Reich"* — like all the *Waffen-SS* units on the Eastern Front — attempted to obey Hitler's "no withdrawal" order to the letter and hence suffered even greater losses. (George H. Stein, *Geschichte der Waffen-SS*, p. 151. Düsseldorf: Droste-Verlag, 1967.)

23 November 1941

As a result of the weak combat strength and the cold — and also to provide the exhausted men an occasional chance to warm up and a few moments of recuperation — the division henceforth conducted the attack by *Kampfgruppen*, alternating *SS-Infanterie-Regiment "Deutschland"* and *SS-Infanterie-Regiment "Der Führer"*.

As a result, *SS-Infanterie-Regiment "Der Führer"* attacked at 0930 hours as ordered with the *II./* and *III./SS-Infanterie-Regiment "Der Führer"*. They passed through the combat outposts of *SS-Infanterie-Regiment "Deutschland"*. The regiment crossed the old post road and the Wolokolamsk — Moscow railroad embankment with the mission of capturing Gorki, establishing a bridgehead over the Magluscha Creek and capturing Glebowo.

Since the *I./SS-Infanterie-Regiment "Der Führer"* was screening adjacent to the *III./SS-Infanterie-Regiment "Deutschland"* and a relief-in-place would have caused too large a displacement, the *II./SS-Infanterie-Regiment "Deutschland"* was attached to *SS-Infanterie-Regiment "Der Führer"* for the attack and the *I./SS-Infanterie-Regiment "Der Führer"* was attached to *SS-Infanterie-Regiment "Deutschland"*. Those elements remained in the security sector of the previous evening.

In advancing to the northeast, *SS-Infanterie-Regiment "Der Führer "* reached Gorki, which was only held by weak enemy forces. The enemy had apparently fallen back over Magluscha Creek to Glebowo. *Sturmgeschütze "Yorck"* and *"Lützow"* supported the infantry advance over the creek, although they were not able to cross it themselves.

With their support, however, *Kampfgruppe "Der Führer"* established a bridgehead over Magluscha Creek and, late in the afternoon, captured Glebowo. The bridgehead position there was favorable, since the eastern bank was considerably elevated and the enemy farther east still held Brusilowo, which was in a hollow.

Kampfgruppe "Deutschland" screened the right flank of the division to the southeast from the road southeast of Cholujanicha, the railroad 1.5 kilometers northeast of Cholujanicha and one kilometer south of Gorki.

The friendly forces on the left, the *10. Panzer-Division,* also established a bridgehead on 23 November over the Magluscha at Kursakowo — Markowo.

***

With the establishment of the two bridgeheads, the *XXXX. Panzer-Korps* had established the prerequisites for continuing the attack on Istra.

***

At 2300 hours the division received the following corps order:

Excerpt from the *Panzergruppe 4* order: *Panzergruppe 4* is to attack with all its forces so as to totally destroy the enemy north of the Moskwa. By rapidly pursuing and maintaining pressure, the enemy is to be prevented from establishing new positions! The *Schwerpunkt* for *Gruppe Geyr* is clearly at Istra. Istra is to be captured by envelopment from the south and north.

Addition from *XXXX. Panzer-Korps*: It is essential for the *XXXX. Panzer-Korps* to gain a crossing over the Istra north of the city of Istra and capture the city as rapidly as possible. This is to occur regardless of the progress of the *XXXXVI. Panzer-Korps.*

/signed/ Stumme

24 November 1941

At 0200 hours during the night of 24 November, *SS-Aufklärungs-Abteilung "Reich"* and *SS-Kradschützen-Bataillon "Reich"* took over the combat outposts of *SS-Infanterie-Regiment "Deutschland"*.

The *I./* and *III./SS-Infanterie-Regiment "Deutschland"* were brought forward directly behind *SS-Infanterie-Regiment "Der Führer"*, and the *II./SS-Infanterie-Regiment "Deutschland"*, which had been attached to *SS-Infanterie-Regiment "Der Führer"*, was returned to its parent regiment's control.

After assembling south and east of Bukarewo, *SS-Infanterie-Regiment "Deutschland"* moved out of the bridgehead. It passed through the lines of *SS-Infanterie-Regiment "Der Führer"* with the *II./SS-Infanterie-Regiment "Deutschland"* on the right (via Senkino) and the *I./SS-Infanterie-Regiment "Deutschland"* on the left (through the woods east of Bukarewo). The *III./SS-Infanterie-Regiment "Deutschland"* followed the *II./SS-Infanterie-Regiment "Deutschland"*.

Since Senkino was held by no more than weak enemy forces, the *I./* and *III./SS-Infanterie-Regiment "Deutschland"* were redirected.

The *I./SS-Infanterie-Regiment "Deutschland"* was brought forward past and to the south of Jefimonowo with the mission of reaching the point of woods south of Babkino, where it was to establish security and scout possible crossing sites over the Istra.

The *III./SS-Infanterie-Regiment "Deutschland"* was committed to attack Jefimonowo, which was taken at 1400 hours after breaking weak enemy resistance.

The *I./SS-Infanterie-Regiment "Deutschland"* determined by reconnaissance that Babkino was clear of the enemy. However, it was not possible to cross the Istra there.

The *II./SS-Infanterie-Regiment "Deutschland"*, advancing from the north via Bukarewo, reached the corner of the woods on the hill 500 meters east of the town. While doing this, *Sturmgeschütz "Blücher"* knocked out an antitank gun. Field fortifications were engaged and Kutschi was taken under fire from the newly gained position. The *"Lützow"* destroyed one gun in the process.

In spite of locally stubborn resistance, the north bank of the Magluscha had been taken. With it was the jump-off position for the advance on the city of Istra.

Staging for the Attack on Istra

The *XXXX. Panzer-Korps* order for 25 November read, in part:

The *XXXX. Panzer-Korps* is to capture Istra on 25 November.

I expect that the divisions are aware of the decisive significance of this attack and will employ all their strength in attaining this objective.

The *10. Panzer-Division* is to attack in its sector across the Istra as far as the Sokoljniki area without waiting for the advance of the *5. Panzer-Division*. It is to turn there to the southwest and continue the attack on Istra. It is essential to cut the enemy's retreat routes to the northeast and east early on.

SS-Division "Reich" is to cover the southern flank of the *10. Panzer-Division* by advancing a regimentally sized element via Senkino to Nikulino. An attack on Istra from the west is to be simulated by advancing strong combat patrols to Istra. Any favorable opportunities for penetrating into the city of Istra as a result of the feint are to be utilized. The main body of the division is to follow from Senkino via Jefimonowo close behind the combat elements of the *10. Panzer-Division* onto the east bank of the Istra. It is to attack south from the Maksimowka area. The weakest possible forces are to be left facing the enemy position at Cholschtschewiki. Attacks by combat patrols are to pin the enemy and pursue the withdrawing enemy.

/signed/ Stumme

***

The "Division Order for Continuation of the Attack on 15 November 1941" included the following regarding the overall conduct of the attack on Istra within the framework of *Panzergruppe 4*:

While the *IX. Armee-Korps* (to the right of *SS-Division "Reich"*) attacks Istra from the line Petrowskoye — Davidowskoje — Kotowo from the south and south-east, the *XXXX. Panzer-Korps* is to advance to the river Istra north of the city of Istra. It establishes a bridgehead on the east bank in order to attack the city of Istra from the north by turning south from the bridgehead.

Accordingly, the *10. Panzer-Division* (left of *SS-Division "Reich"*) is to advance to Babkino via Sholesnikowo and continue its attack from the northeast after reaching the Sokoljniki area.

Regarding the conduct of the fighting by the division, the above division order stated:

3.) *SS-Division "Reich"* is to continue the attack on 25 November from the bridgehead at Glebowo to the east. It is to reach Senjikino and advance from there to Babkino with the main body adjacent to the *10. Panzer-Division*. Elements are to attack from Senjikino through the wooded area northwest of Istra. In the area of Hill 186.5 they are to deceive the enemy regarding the movement of the main force with heavy weapons fire and active patrol activity supported by artillery.

Elements of the division are to deceive the enemy regarding the direction of the attack with continuous patrol and combat-patrol activity opposite the field fortifications and south of the Petrowskoje — Istra road.

SS-Infanterie-Regiment "Deutschland" is to stage behind the combat outposts at Bukarewo, in such a way that it can attack at 0800 hours to the east. First attack objective: Semjkino. From there the attack will continue via Jefimonowo to Babkino.

SS-Infanterie-Regiment "Der Führer" is to screen the right flank of the attacking *SS-Infanterie-Regiment "Deutschland"* by following and forming various points of main concentration in securing the southern flank.

SS-Kradschützen-Bataillon "Reich" is to relieve *SS-Infanterie-Regiment "Deutschland"* with its main body and its combat outposts. Elements are to relieve the *I./SS-Infanterie-Regiment "Der Führer"*.

SS-Aufklärungs-Abteilung "Reich" is to screen against the enemy positions and reconnoiters on the right flank of the division between *SS-Kradschützen-Bataillon "Reich"* and the *252. Infanterie-Division* (division adjoining on the right).

***

Panzergruppe 4 praised the fighting of the *XXXX. Panzer-Korps* in the following Teletype:

The corps is now on its own! Forward! Capture Istra! And on to Brechowo. The divisions have fought superbly.

/signed/ Hoepner

***

The attachment of the *XXXX. Panzer-Korps* to the *IX. Armee-Korps* ended on that day.

The Attack on Istra

25 November 1941

The *10. Panzer-Division* captured Shelesnikowo in a bold attack during the night of 25 November. After breaking strong resistance, the *Kampfgruppe* continued its advance in the early morning hours. It dislodged the enemy, captured Busharowo and established a bridgehead east of Busharowo across the Istra. In so doing, it was able to capture the bridge intact.

The enemy appeared to be surprised by the *10. Panzer-Division's* outflanking maneuver to the northeast. Some of the Russians in Busharowo were caught in their underwear. The positions north of Busharowo were effectively unoccupied.

SS-Infanterie-Regiment "Deutschland" attacked. The east bank of the Istra was reported to be lightly held. Crossing points along the Istra were not initially identified.

Around 1350 hours the *III./SS-Infanterie-Regiment "Deutschland"* reached Jefimonowo. The *I./SS-Infanterie-Regiment "Deutschland"* was, at that time, advancing through woods 800 meters south of Jefimonowo.

Establishing a Bridgehead over the Istra

During the advance of the *II./SS-Infanterie-Regiment "Deutschland"*, the following new order arrived for the assault-gun platoon of *SS-Untersturmführer* Burmeister: "Advance to the Istra and capture the Istra bridge!"

At that same time, *SS-Infanterie-Regiment "Der Führer"* sent its *15. (Kradschützen)/SS-Infanterie-Regiment "Der Führer"* to reconnoiter toward Istra.

***

The war diary of *SS-Sturmgeschütz-Batterie "Reich"* and an after-action report from *SS-Infanterie-Regiment "Der Führer"* on 25 November 1941 describe the fighting involved in establishing a bridgehead over the Istra

River:

An armored car of *SS-Aufklärungs-Abteilung "Reich"* and *Sturmgeschütze* with mounted infantry of the *II./SS-Infanterie-Regiment "Deutschland"* moved out. The leading element received rifle fire at Nikulino. Istra, with its great cathedral surrounded by a thick wall, was located on the hill on the far bank. Well-constructed field fortifications were identified close to the city. While the Russians at the edge of the woods fled, great masses of Russians came out of Istra and the cathedral. They were attempting to get to the field fortifications.

The assault guns opened fire. The Russians ran around in total disorder, a sign that the attack came as a surprise. Fleeing columns that attempted to reach the bridge were engaged. Russians fled from the field fortifications on our side of the Istra over the provisional bridge to the left of the demolished big bridge (600 meters south of Nikulino).

Since there was danger that the provisional bridge would also be blown up, the *Sturmgeschütze "Prinz Eugen"* and *"Yorck"* moved right up to it.

Strong infantry fire from the windows of the cathedral and the loopholes in the wall covered the bridge. *SS-Sturmmann* Purbs took a quick look out of the hatch of his assault gun for orientation and was mortally wounded.

While the assault guns shelled the area around the cathedral, the *15./SS-Infanterie-Regiment "Der Führer"*, led by *SS-Obersturmführer* Wolkersdorfer, overran the enemy positions on the west bank in a rapid, surprise advance and pushed on among the fleeing Russians over the bridge. Wires leading to the demolition charges that had been installed were cut. The company immediately built a small bridgehead.

The Russians succeeded in bringing an antitank gun into position and opened fire on the *"Prinz Eugen"*. However, none of the six hits penetrated. The antitank gun was identified and destroyed with a direct hit. The *"Yorck"* moved back a bit and the dead man was offloaded. The two *Sturmgeschütze* alternated in proving security at the Istra until the following morning.

***

The small bridgehead of the *15./SS-Infanterie-Regiment "Der Führer"* was under heavy enemy fire from the Istra bastion, as the fortress-like complex of buildings was called in the maps.

After the surprise establishment of this bridgehead, the *II./SS-Infanterie-Regiment "Deutschland"*, under *SS-Sturmbannführer* Hansmann, was employed to expand it. For the fighting at the Istra, the battalion was attached to *SS-Infanterie-Regiment "Der Führer"*.

***

Istra was a medium-large city that began about 500 meters beyond the bridge and extended widely over a ridge east of it. The small Istra River flowed in a half circle around the west side of the city. The cathedral of Istra — also referred to as a citadel, a bastion or a museum bastion — was a complex of six large church-like buildings, the mightiest of which was the beautiful old cathedral itself. The cathedral complex was built on a ridgeline of the hill that projected to the west as far as the river. The entire complex was surrounded by a thick five-meter high wall. A lofty causeway led from the vehicular bridge to the edge of the city.

The Russians had organized their defense in well-constructed positions on the rim of the hill. From there they commanded the broad snow-covered plain between their positions and the river with machine-gun fire. The cathedral was particularly suitable as a defensive fortress and was strongly held. In addition, the enemy was supported by substantial artillery fire.

The brave comrades of the *10. Panzer-Division* forced the enemy from the north into the city. The division had been decimated. It had only 28 operational tanks, four weak infantry battalions and ten guns at its disposal. This was all that was left of that proud armored division.

Storming the Citadel of Istra

As darkness fell on 25 November, the *III./SS-Infanterie-Regiment "Der Führer"* was brought forward over the Istra bridge and the regiment's forward command post was set up in a small building east of it.

During the night, the *9./SS-Infanterie-Regiment "Der Führer"*, led by *SS-Obersturmführer* Schober, achieved a major success. In a daredevil advance, the company broke into the city with a "Hurrah". In bitter night fighting, the company established a firm foothold; it was followed by additional elements of the *III./SS-Infanterie-Regiment "Der Führer"*. That same night the entire complex of the citadel of Istra was captured in extremely hard fighting.

SS-Infanterie-Regiment "Deutschland", together with the assault guns of Kneissl's platoon, captured Jefimonowo whereupon the Russians withdrew. The *III./SS-Infanterie-Regiment "Deutschland"* immediately attacked Maksimowka east of the Istra River. The assault guns were unable to follow the infantry across the Istra, however, since the bridge had been blown. The *"Blücher"* engaged a Russian battery that was firing and forced it to change position. Nevertheless, Maksimowka could not be captured that night.

The *I./SS-Infanterie-Regiment "Deutschland"* was halted in Nikulino to screen the left flank of *SS-Infanterie-Regiment "Der Führer"*. The *II./SS-Infanterie-Regiment "Deutschland"* advanced over the bridge that evening, but was then held up in heavy enemy defensive fire from the citadel.

SS-Kradschützen-Bataillon "Reich" mopped up the wooded area west of Cholschtschewiki. When that was completed, it pursued the enemy falling back to Istra. During those operations a patrol of the *2./SS-Kradschützen-Bataillon "Reich"* led by *SS-Standartenoberjunker* (officer candidate) Heise was wiped out behind enemy lines.

Disruption of the field telephone connections between the *XXXX.*

Panzer-Korps and the *10. Panzer-Division* and *SS-Division "Reich"* prevented the former from receiving a clear picture that evening regarding the situation. The situation around and in Istra was uncertain to the corps.

The City of Istra in Friendly Hands

26 November 1941

The telephone connection was finally restored at midnight of 25/26 November. The operations officer of *SS-Division "Reich"*, *SS-Obersturmbannführer* Ostendorff, orientated the corps chief of staff as follows:

The bastion is in friendly hands. The *III./SS-Infanterie-Regiment "Deutschland"* crossed the Istra and, as darkness fell, was advancing on the city. Istra, itself, is on fire. Reconnaissance that was sent out did not encounter any enemy.

***

Up to this point the division itself had also had no clear overall picture of the developing success. It only really became clear during the second half of the night and was achieved through intense night fighting.

***

A small but unforgettable experience from the citadel of Istra was recounted by a member of the *III./SS-Infanterie-Regiment "Der Führer"* in the December issue of the 1966 edition of *"Der Freiwillige"* (page 8) under the title *"Die Zitadelle"*. Unfortunately, the author's name remains unknown:

That was a Time for Singing…in the Citadel of Istra...

…They blew the doors off with concentrated charges. The blood trails left by the defenders led from courtyard to courtyard. Then the shouts, the orders and the noise of the last fighting died down. The tramping sound of the marching men of the last companies to arrive echoed from the arched entry. That night the men would get some sleep. After four days of ceaseless attack their sleep would be leaden and deep. The air in the areas in which they would find quarters for the night was icy, so wood would have to be provided to burn in the fireplaces in the walls.

And, again, there was someone there who took the opportunity to put a joyous face on a bad situation. He struck a quick chord on a piano that had been dragged out of some corner. Three others who were nearby stepped over and joined him in a rousing song. A new song and the pianist picked up the accompaniment. Someone shoved over a stool for him. Already there were ten men gathered around the piano, picking up the beat with stomping feet. The song surged and clear voices, filled with joy, carried to the corridors beyond. Then there was a clatter and the thunder of hobnailed boots as men from other floors filled the room and, then, the corridors too. Soon the entire citadel seemed to be a single chorus of ringing voices.

The men had four days of unrelenting attack behind them; nights, often with only a few hours of sleep, and, right up to that moment when they had smashed the last resistance of the defenders, their efforts had been superhuman. And now they sang! Among them were wounded, with bandaged arms and heads, and they sang. The wild, joyous songs soared, tender and dreamy, filled with the nostalgia of linden trees, the peace of moors, the forests, mountains and rivers of home, the Weser and the Rhine, and of the North Sea waves. Hardly had one song come to an end when the next began, and the new one drew no less applause than the one that had just ended. When the rapid rhythm of dance songs throbbed, the men beat time with their feet.

The hour was late when the *Spieß* finally called for quiet. But when the piano fell silent, voices continued in song. Some of the men still didn't seem sated and wanted to sing what filled their hearts. They got four hours of sleep. The march was to resume at six bells in the morning...

***

The *10. Panzer-Division* had captured Maksimowka. Its intention was to continue its advance on Istra from the north.

At the corps, the surprising capture of the citadel and the rapid penetration into the city raised the question of whether to continue to employ the *10. Panzer-Division* at Istra or to continue the advance to the east with it alone.

On the basis of favorable reports from *SS-Division "Reich"* that raised hopes that the division would be able to capture Istra without support, the *10. Panzer-Division* was given the mission of advancing via Andrejewskoje and Sokolniki in order to prepare there for continuing the attack to the east. If necessary, elements of the *10. Panzer-Division* were to advance to Istra on order from the corps.

***

SS-Division "Reich" received the following mission:

SS-Division "Reich" is to mop up Istra and the road east of Cholschtschewiki. It is to send elements to the high ground east of Aleksino in a timely manner.

Since, however, this mission was more than the weak forces of the division could accomplish in the expansive city with the enemy situation still uncertain, the division radioed the corps at 0630 hours:

The citadel is firmly in friendly hands. The houses on the northeastern outskirts have been under attack since 0600 hours. Area to the east and at Nikulino is held by the enemy. Situation in the city still unclear. Employment of the *10. Panzer-Division* required.

At 0700 hours the corps combat-engineer battalion set out from Cholschtschewiki to Istra along with *SS-Kradschützen-Bataillon "Reich"*. The road had been blown up east of Cholschtschewiki. The woods on both sides of the road were mined.

At 0750 hours the *10. Panzer-Division* received orders from the corps:

Set out immediately to Istra. Capture Istra!

***

As morning broke on a cold, hazy day at 20 degrees below zero (-13 degrees Fahrenheit), *SS-Infanterie-Regiment "Der Führer"* found itself in a difficult situation. The attack of the *III./SS-Infanterie-Regiment "Der Führer"* had come to a standstill in the citadel. An attack by the *I./* and *II./SS-Infanterie-Regiment "Der Führer"* to extend the bridgehead had been repulsed by concentrated fire from Russian machine guns. During the night, the enemy had reoccupied his field fortifications.

The *Sturmgeschütze* engaged the field fortifications, eliminating one anti-tank gun. The Russians attacked again with artillery support. The battalions were unable to gain any ground as a result. The bridge, however, was still held. The assault guns advanced over the bridge at least ten times through enemy fire to bring back wounded.

The regiment's command post was in a bad position and under heavy artillery fire. The commander of the regiment, *SS-Obersturmbannführer* Kumm, therefore moved his command post to the *III./SS-Infanterie-Regiment "Der Führer"*, which moved out from the citadel at noon to continue the attack on the city.

At the same time, *Kampfgruppe Oberstleutnant Mauß* (the reinforced *Schützen-Regiment 69* of the *10. Panzer-Division*) entered the fighting for the city from the north.

***

Paul Carell wrote the following concerning the fighting at the outskirts of Istra:

> Klingenberg's *SS-Kradschützen-Bataillon "Reich"* had to clear the wooded obstacle and bunker barrier that was defended by units of the infamous Siberian 78th Rifle Division on the Wolokolamsk — Moscow highway directly west of Istra. That division was known for the fact that its men neither took prisoners nor allowed themselves to be taken prisoner.
>
> Bunker after bunker had to be captured in hand-to-hand fighting with hand grenades and spades. Klingenberg's *SS-Kradschützen* fought with bravado, and many of the young men of the *Waffen-SS* paid with their lives… (Paul Carell, *Unternehmen Barbarossa,* p. 160. Frankfurt am Main / Berlin (West): Verlag Ullstein GmbH, 1963.)

***

The *I./* and *III./SS-Infanterie-Regiment "Deutschland"* launched their attack at noon and made good forward progress.

As dusk fell, the field fortifications on the east bank of the Istra were rolled up and the attack was aggressively driven forward into the city. Enemy units fell back to the west to the Istra River, apparently surprised by the *10. Panzer-Division* attack from the north.

In aggressive urban fighting, the battalions advanced to the southern outskirts of the city. Enemy elements that had remained hidden or were falling back from the west renewed the fighting to the rear. Street by street, the city had to be combed again in fighting that lasted until midnight.

As elements of *SS-Division "Reich"* and the *10. Panzer-Division* penetrated into the western and northern portions of the city at 1700 and 1730 hours after long and heavy fighting, the following order from the corps was telephonically passed on at 1800 hours:

Northern sector of Istra is for the *10. Panzer-Division*; southern sector for *SS-Division "Reich"*. Boundary: Church — Kaschino road.

At 1900 hours *SS-Division "Reich"* was able to report to the corps: "Istra has been captured."

***

Paul Carell wrote the following concerning the fighting for Istra:

Located in a bend of the river in front of Istra, the citadel commanded the western approaches to the city. *SS-Division "Reich"* captured the citadel by surprise. *SS-Infanterie-Regimenter "Deutschland"* and *"Der Führer"*, supported by *SS-Artillerie-Regiment "Reich"*, broke in from the south and infiltrated into the fortified streets. Neither Hitler's nor Stalin's guards yielded an inch. The Siberians had to fall back. Istra, the nucleus of the last Moscow defense position, was captured. (Paul Carell, *Unternehmen Barbarossa,* p. 161 ff. Frankfurt am Main / Berlin (West): Verlag Ullstein GmbH, 1963.)

***

The war diary of the *XXXX. Panzer-Korps* states the following for 26 November 1941:

At 1900 hours *SS-Division "Reich"* reported: "Istra captured." The capture of Istra had been delayed by the fact that the approach of the *10. Panzer-Division* had been considerably complicated by terrain problems, especially in the streambed north of Maksimowka as well as by mines. Just between the bridge at Michailowka and Istra, the *10. Panzer-Division* discovered 700 mines.

The forward movement of the motorcycle battalion of *SS-Division "Reich"* on the Duplewo — Istra road was also delayed for the same reason. Nineteen sites where the road had been blown up had to be bridged using field expedients, and a great number of mines had to be removed.

***

In order to take advantage of the success, the following missions for 28 November went out in the evening to the two divisions:

The divisions are to form or enlarge the bridgeheads specified in orders so that direct enemy influence on Istra is eliminated. In addition, the divisions are to close up so that that the attack can be continued toward Moscow on 28 November.

Boundary: Woskressensk (*10. Pz. Div.*) — Wyssokowo (*SS*) — road from

Wyssokowo toward Moscow (road for *SS-Division "Reich"*).

***

SS-Infanterie-Regiment "Deutschland" committed the *III./SS-Infanterie-Regiment "Deutschland"* against Polewo at midnight. The battalion captured the bridge that had been prepared for demolition and, at 0200 hours, established security at the eastern outskirts of Polewo. The *I./* and *II./SS-Infanterie-Regiment "Deutschland"* secured in Istra.

***

The "Division Order for Continuation of the Attack on 27 November 1941" stated the following (excerpts):

1.) Since the beginning of December, *SS-Division "Reich"* has smashed the main body of the Siberian 78th Division, an elite division of the Red Army. This was initially accomplished through an offensively conducted defense and, since the beginning of the attack by *Panzergruppe 4*, by advancing through the enemy positions east of the Oserna and pursuing the withdrawing enemy. After crossing the Magluscha and Istra Rivers, the division captured the citadel west of Istra and, today, the city of Istra in heavy fighting. In so doing, a critical cornerstone of the last defensive front west of Moscow has been removed. The route has been cleared for the final attack on Moscow.

The *Kradschützen* company of *SS-Infanterie-Regiment "Der Führer"* (reinforced with assault guns), the *III./SS-Infanterie-Regiment "Der Führer"* and the *II./SS-Infanterie-Regiment "Deutschland"* played a major part in building the bridgehead over the Istra and in the nighttime fight for the citadel.

I commend the entire division and, especially, those units named above, for these achievements.

2.) The main body of the enemy has evacuated the east bank of the Istra and the city during 26 November. In the evening he is falling back behind rearguards before the division's attack.

An orderly retreat by the enemy can be expected, with constant rearguard actions at the edges of woods and built-up areas and in field-expedient field fortifications.

Since breaking through the Oserna position, no new enemy formations have been identified.

The enemy will presumably go over to the defensive on the north bank of the Istra River south of the city against the attack of the *IX. Armee-Korps*, while his forces fall back on the Istra — Moscow road. They will cover the withdrawal with strong rearguards.

3.) The *XXXX. Panzer-Korps* is to attack Moscow north of the Istra with *SS-Division "Reich"* on the right and the *10. Panzer-Division* on the left.

Friendly forces on the right: *IX. Armee-Korps*; on the left: *5. Panzer-Division.*

4.) Boundaries:

Between the *252. Infanterie-Division* (*IX. Armee-Korps*) and *SS-Division "Reich"*: the Istra River.

Between *SS-Division "Reich"* and the *10. Panzer-Division*: Woskressensk (*10. Panzer-Division*) — Wyssokowo (*SS-Division "Reich"*) — road to Moscow (*SS-Division "Reich"*).

5.) *SS-Division "Reich"* is to attack from the Polewo bridgehead and advance south of the Istra — Moscow road to the east-southeast. It is to gain as much ground as possible on 27 November.

For that purpose, three *Kampfgruppen* are to be formed:

a) *Kampfgruppe Schulz* (reinforced *SS-Infanterie-Regiment "Deutschland*)

b) *Kampfgruppe Kumm* (reinforced *SS-Infanterie-Regiment "Der Führer"*)

c) *Kampfgruppe Klingenberg* (reinforced *SS-Kradschützen-Bataillon "Reich"* and *SS-Aufklärungs-Abteilung "Reich"*...)

6.) Concept of the operation:

Kampfgruppe Kumm is to attack from the Polewo bridgehead and pass through the combat outposts that *Kampfgruppe Schulz* posted during the night of 26/27 November. It is to assemble for the attack along the Polewo — Wyssokowo road.

Kampfgruppe Klingenberg is to movs out echeloned to the right rear on the route via Katschabrowo — Sannikowo to Lushuzkoje. It will screen the right flank of *Kampfgruppe Kumm* and reconnoiter south of the main road as far as the Istra River. If strong resistance develops on the main road, the *Kampfgruppe* will turn to the north to envelop while elements continue to carry out reconnaissance and screening missions on the right flank.

Kampfgruppe Schulz is to be employed on either the right or left depending on where the strongest enemy resistance develops and where the road conditions are the best. It will become the main effort at that point.

7.) To accomplish its mission, ***Kampfgruppe Kumm* is to** stage behind the Polewo bridgehead by 0800 hours so that it can attack Wyssokowo with its *Schwerpunkt* on the right. The first attack objective is Wyssokowo. The completion of the staging is to be reported to the division by 0800 hours.

Reconnaissance is to be sent out in a timely manner so that it passes through the combat-outpost lines at the woods to the east and southeast of Polewo at 0630 hours, at the latest. The patrols are, if possible, to take along backpack radio equipment to insure continuous reporting.

8.) After the Istra bridge south of the museum is ready, ***Kampfgruppe Klingenberg*** is to move out through the southern sector of the city of Istra and, if possible, reach its route of advance via Makruscha — Trussowo. The time for crossing the bridge 1.5 kilometers south of Polewo will be specified by radio. Reconnaissance is to be sent out as early as possible.

While the advanced elements of the *Kampfgruppe* will probably have to start out dismounted, the main body follows mounted initially so as to be able to rapidly pursue the enemy if the opportunity is presented.

The *252. Infanterie-Division*, which has advanced as far as the line Petrowskoje — Bunikowo with its leading elements, has been asked to maintain close contact with the right wing of *SS-Division "Reich"* in its continued advance. That contact is also to be sought from our side.

Whenever possible, the *Kampfgruppe* is to bypass strong enemy resistance. Where that is not possible and the resistance cannot be broken by the *Kampfgruppe* itself, the division must be informed of the situation as soon as possible.

9.) ***Kampfgruppe Schulz*** is to withdraw its combat outposts at the outskirts of the city of Istra and the bridgehead after *Kampfgruppe Kumm* has passed through the Polewo bridgehead. It is to reorganize its forces so that, on order of the division, it can follow one of the leading *Kampfgruppen*.

10.) **Artillery:**

Arko 128 (the corps artillery) is to execute the following missions with the attached *SS-Artillerie-Regiment "Reich"*, *Nebelwerfer-Regiment 54*, *Beobachtungs-Abteilung 36* (Observation Battalion) and the *II./Artillerie-Regiment 72*:

a) Support the initial attack of *Kampfgruppe Kumm* with strong elements from its present firing positions.

b) Forward displacement of the other elements after daybreak in the area around Istra so as to support the *Schwerpunkt* of the advancing attack.

c) The *7./SS-Artillerie-Regiment "Reich"* is attached to *Kampfgruppe Klingenberg*.

11.) **Combat Engineers:**

During the night of 26/27 November *SS-Pionier-Bataillon "Reich"* is to clear obstacles and mines in order to create a cleared corridor through Istra from the bridge north of the museum to Polewo. It is also to ensure trafficability over the streambed on the western outskirts of Polewo for all vehicles by 0730 hours.

The main body of the combat-engineer force is to be concentrated with *Kampfgruppe Kumm*. The commander of *SS-Pionier-Bataillon "Reich"* is to maintain close contact with the *Kampfgruppe*.

The *16./SS-Infanterie-Regiment "Der Führer"* is attached to the divisional combat engineer for unified command of combat-engineer forces. This is essential to ensure timely route reconnaissance so that the road is rapidly cleared of mines, other obstacles are cleared and that destroyed bridges are restored.

The combat-engineer platoons of *Kampfgruppe Klingenberg* are to be combined for unity of effort.

12.) ***SS-Panzer-Jäger-Abteilung "Reich"* is to** place one company under the operational control of *Kampfgruppe Kumm*. One platoon is to be attached to *Kampfgruppe Klingenberg* and is to be brought forward to the southern section of Istra by 0800 hours.

13.) ***Flak*:**

SS-Flak-Abteilung "Reich" is to provide one light battery to *Kampfgruppe Kumm* in direct support. One platoon is attached to *Kampfgruppe Klingenberg*. The remainder of the light battery is to go to *Kampfgruppe Schulz* and provide direct support.

Leichte Flak-Abteilung 93 is requested to provide area defense of Istra...

***

This division order for the final advance toward Moscow demonstrates classical command language and attention to detail. Even after months of attritional fighting with numerous days of major combat, the division was still just as firmly led by *SS-Brigadeführer* Bittrich, his operations officer, *SS-Obersturmbannführer* Ostendorff, the operations liaison officer, *SS-Hauptsturmführer* Albert and the operations staff as in the first days of the Russian campaign. And this was in spite of extremely primitive conditions, numerous losses and almost constant enemy action affecting the division staff. During the preceding months, the division command had also been tried to the limit in bitter fighting.

Thus, this order from the critical days outside of Moscow, is a genuine document of the classical art of command. It clearly demonstrates the hand of the first commander of the division, *SS-Obergruppenführer und General der Waffen-SS* Hausser — the great teacher, mentor and trainer of the division and, with it, of the *Waffen-SS* since 1935.

27 November 1941

The battalions of *SS-Division "Reich"* combed through the city of Istra several more times during the night of 26/27 November, pulling about four companies of Russians from the houses.

The commanding general of the *XXXX. Panzer-Korps, General der Panzertruppen* Stumme, commended the achievements of the units of *SS-Division "Reich"* that had been employed in capturing the citadel of Istra in the following order of the day:

Order of the Day (27 November 1941)

I particularly commend the officers of the *III./SS-Infanterie-Regiment "Der Führer"*, the *II./SS-Infanterie-Regiment "Deutschland"* and the motorcycle company of *SS-Infanterie-Regiment "Der Führer"* —reinforced with *Sturmgeschütze* — for the initiative and courage with which they led their troops in the capture of the museum bastion of Istra.

The same commendation goes to all the men of the formations named, who, with their guts, forward drive and outstanding courage, have played an extremely essential part in the capture of Istra.

The commander-in-chief of the *Panzergruppe, Generaloberst* Hoepner, has asked me to also pass on his own thanks and commendation.

/signed/ Stumme

***

Who were these men? Men who had repeatedly earned the highest praises from their superiors in orders of the day for their courage and their military prowess. Men who had subjected themselves to months of enervating, bloody fighting to dust, mud, rain, heat, cold, snow and wet. Men who toiled through unspeakable rigors…

SS-Unterscharführer Streng of *2./SS-Infanterie-Regiment "Deutschland"* wrote in his notes about his comrades:

> The magnificent, athletic, combat-hardened soldiers of the summer months had become emaciated by constant strain, men who were physically and spiritually exhausted. They were "fed up to the chin line." Gaunt faces with dark shadows around the eyes and a bitter turn to the mouth, unshaven for weeks; frozen faces. A staff in one hand, a rifle in the other, their thoughts increasingly dominated by a longing for rest back home. How often had their spirits risen at a sudden rumor of an impending relief for the division and transfer to Germany — a Fata Morgana that always dissolved into nothingness.
>
> If, after hours in biting frost, the men were able to crowd together into an impoverished hut, then they lay on and under the benches, on the large stove or on the cold floor and, in steel helmet and coat, quickly fell into the deep sleep of total exhaustion. They were, plain and simply, too "done in" to feel the biting and crawling of the lice on their bodies. Nevertheless, their senses remained subconsciously alert for any danger that threatened and, if needed, waked the sleepers instantaneously. There were soldiers among them who literally smelled any danger and instinctively evaded it.
>
> It was a well-known fact that our "old hands" subconsciously threaded their way through every danger as if they had some sixth sense, while the new replacements from the homeland usually had to be stricken from the company roster within a few days, killed or wounded.

The Attack on Moscow Continues

After building a bridgehead at Polewo, the division launched a pincers attack on Wyssokowo at 1500 hours with *SS-Infanterie-Regiment "Der Führer"* — *Kampfgruppe Kumm.* The attack followed an artillery barrage.

The *7./SS-Infanterie-Regiment "Der Führer"* led the rest of its battalion in the attack. It was supported by *Sturmgeschütze* under *SS-Untersturmführer* Burmeister. The Russian field fortifications were overrun. The spearhead of the attack then penetrated Wyssokowo and conducted house-to-house fighting, during which *Sturmgeschütz "Derfflinger"* knocked out an antitank gun and a field gun.

As the *"Derfflinger"* turned into a row of houses, it was suddenly face-to-face with a Russian antitank gun. Both fired at the same moment. A round penetrated through the vision slit of the *Sturmgeschütz*. The driver, *SS-Sturmmann* Arnold, was mortally wounded.

The *Kampfgruppe* sent combat outposts as far forward as the stream one kilometer east of Wyssokowo.

Kampfgruppe Klingenberg (*SS-Kradschützen-Bataillon "Reich"* and *SS-Aufklärungs-Abteilung "Reich"*) launched an attack at noon on the railroad line to Moscow southeast of Istra and south of Polewo.

Sturmgeschütze "Lützow" and *"Blücher"* advanced against Troizkij via Katschaprowo with squads of *Kradschützen* mounted on them. Troizkij was captured and fleeing Russian columns were engaged by the *Sturmgeschütze*. A number of Russian officers were captured there. The high ground east of Troizkij was occupied. *SS-Infanterie-Regiment "Deutschland"* remained in Istra on 27 November. It finished mopping up the city and posted security.

***

The *10. Panzer-Division*, the friendly forces on the left, initially had to fend off a series of attacks. In the afternoon, however, it advanced with motorcycle troops, a rifle battalion and the seven remaining tanks (out of 150!) to the east, capturing Petschkowa and Kaschino. In the evening the divisions received Operations Order No. 13 with the following missions:

The *XXXX. Panzer-Korps* is to attack on both sides of the Istra — Moscow road and advance through Pawschino.

The attack is to be conducted with *SS-Division "Reich"* on the right and the *10. Panzer-Division* on the left.

Boundaries for reconnaissance and attack:

Between the *IX. Armee-Korps* and *SS-Division "Reich"*: Course of the Istra River to the junction of the Nachabinka — Iszakowo (*IX. Armee-Korps*) — Pawschino (*XXXX. Panzer-Korps*).

Between SS-Division "*Reich*" and the 10. Panzer-Division: Istra — Moscow road (for SS-Division "*Reich*").

Between the *10. Panzer-Division* and the *XXXXVI. Panzer-Korps:* Busharowo — Eremejewo — Kosino (for the *XXXXVI. Panzer-Korps*).

For *SS-Division "Reich"* it is essential to break strong resistance on the road, primarily by envelopment from the south.

28 November 1941

While *Kampfgruppe "Der Führer"* established security in the positions that had been attained the previous evening and repulsed a surprise attack from the northeast against Wyssokowo, *SS-Infanterie-Regiment "Deutschland"* set out with its battalions from Istra to the assembly area in the woods one kilometer northwest of Wyssokowo.

The battalions lined up behind each other in the sequence *I./, III./,* and *II./SS-Infanterie-Regiment "Deutschland". Sturmgeschütze "Yorck", "Lützow"* and *"Blücher"* were staged near the railroad-crossing shack at Troizkij. The crews were awakened in the morning by incoming salvos from Russian multiple-rocket launchers. The Russians tried to break through but were beaten back.

The combat outposts of *Kampfgruppe "Der Führer"* were positioned 600 meters east of the village. Reconnaissance determined that the Manichino railroad station was held by enemy forces.

At 0900 hours the *I./SS-Infanterie-Regiment "Deutschland"* attacked Hill 204.3, via the railroad-crossing shack. The *2./SS-Infanterie-Regiment "Deutschland"* shot down a Russian reconnaissance aircraft in its staging area. The *I./SS-Infanterie-Regiment "Deutschland"* captured the weakly held Manichino railroad station after a short firefight. From there it advanced to the eastern edge of the woods east of Manichino and reorganized for attack.

At 1020 hours *SS-Infanterie-Regiment "Deutschland"* received orders by radio to attack the Pawlowskoje — Lushezkoje — Manichino complex with *SS-Kradschützen-Bataillon "Reich"*. The villages were to be attacked after an air strike. The *III./* and *II./SS-Infanterie-Regiment "Deutschland"* were committed against Pawlowskoje. The *I./SS-Infanterie-Regiment "Deutschland*, which had captured Hill 204.3 was to advance along with the other two battalions and capture Perwommaiskij.

SS-Kradschützen-Bataillon "Reich" was committed against Lusheskoje.

After preparation for the attack by *Nebelwerfer* fire and several ground-attack aircraft, *SS-Infanterie-Regiment "Deutschland"* attacked at 1400 hours. The artillery fire did not achieve its full effect, since the original time of the attack had been set at 1430 hours for the artillery. However, in consideration of the employment of air support, it had been necessary to move the time forward to 1400 hours. The enemy defended the three localities primarily from their western outskirts.

At 1515 hours Pawlowskoje was firmly in friendly hands. *SS-Kradschützen-Bataillon "Reich"*, along with three *Sturmgeschütze*, launched its attack on Lushezkoje at the same time as *SS-Infanterie-Regiment "Deutschland"* had launched its attack on Pawlowskoje. Both commenced immediately after the strike by the ground-attack aircraft on those places. The attack was rewarded with speedy success. At 1600 hours Lushezkoje was captured and an all-around defense was established.

Since the regiment was receiving flanking fire from Manichino, the *II./* and *III./SS-Infanterie-Regiment "Deutschland"* were formed up anew to take Manichino from the south. The attack from the south followed preparation by *Nebelwerfer*. The *I./SS-Infanterie-Regiment "Deutschland"* penetrated the village from the northeast at the same time.

By 1600 hours the entire complex of villages had been captured and mopped up. The *Sturmgeschütze* received orders to advance toward Sannikowo. Strongly fortified Russian field fortifications had been identified. As was later determined, they were held by a Russian machine-gun battalion. The *Sturmgeschütze* took the positions under fire, whereupon the Russians fled.

The *10. Panzer-Division* captured Darna and Aleksino. One 52-ton Russian tank and six T 34's were knocked out during the heavy fighting.

Waves of Russian aircraft bombed the city of Istra and the attacking spearheads of the two divisions throughout the day. The 3.7-cm *Flak* scored no successes against the partially armored Russian aircraft. The heavy antiaircraft batteries were, for the most part, employed in a ground-fire mode with the divisions, where they defended against Russian T-34's. The heavy *Flak* were an extraordinarily effective antitank weapon with overwhelming success.

SS-Infanterie-Regiment "Deutschland" spent the night in Istra. Thanks to luck, the battalions had moved from Istra to the east into their assembly areas so that they were spared for the most part from the inferno from the air.

***

Paul Carell wrote the following about the fighting at the time:

> That same day the Soviets began ceaseless air attacks on Istra. They were not going to let the Germans have that transportation center west of Moscow undamaged. As radio intercepts revealed, the German staffs were not to find any quarters. The onion-shaped domes of the churches collapsed. House after house fell under the Russian aerial attack. Two thousand bombs dropped on the small city and, in truth, there were no intact quarters left...
>
> Early on 28 November the *Waffen-SS* (*SS-Division "Reich"*) captured Wyssokowo and continued to advance on Moscow. The assault troops were now within a 30-kilometer ring around the Kremlin.
>
> The thermometer read -32 degrees Celsius (-26 degrees Fahrenheit). The men had to lie out in the open at night. They wore every article of clothing that they had, but it was not enough. They had no furs, no fur hats, no felt boots, no fur gloves. Toes froze, fingers turned white and stiff in the thin woolen mittens.
>
> But in all the bitterness of each difficult day there were also comforting hours and moments. In the tense, dark, unsettling nights of November and December before 1942, while the entire land congealed in bitter frost, the *Junkers* swept overhead toward Moscow and the nighttime horizon was illuminated by Soviet antiaircraft fire, that was when the Belgrade radio station was tuned in at 2200 hours and Lale Andersen's dark voice rang out, and the *Landser* listened: "Underneath the lantern, by the barracks gate...my Lili of the lamplight, my own Lili Marlene." It is hard to believe, but anyone who was before Moscow at that time and came away with their life knows and will never forget how a sentimental soldier's song brought homesick longing and tears to the eyes. (Paul Carell, *Unternehmen Barbarossa*, p. 161. Frankfurt am Main / Berlin (West): Verlag Ullstein GmbH, 1963)

***

Generaloberst Hoepner visited *SS-Division "Reich"* to gain a personal impression of the heavy fighting.

Conditions steadily worsened. Although the combat effectiveness of the enemy formations had significantly diminished, numerically they still far outnumbered the German divisions and, above all, had adequate artillery of all calibers and ammunition for their heavy weapons.

In spite of the replenishment they had received from disbanding *SS-Infanterie-Regiment 11*, the combat strength of the companies of both infantry regiments had sunk to an average of only 25 men per company.

The II./SS-Infanterie-Regiment "Der Führer" is Consolidated

At that time the *II./SS-Infanterie-Regiment "Der Führer"* had to be consolidated with the remaining battalions of the regiment. *SS-Sturmbannführer* Harmel, the commander of the battalion, was named commander of *SS-Infanterie-Regiment "Deutschland"* on 4 December 1941. The remaining personnel of the companies of the tried-and-true battalion were split up between the *I./* and *III./SS-Infanterie-Regiment "Der Führer"*.

Temporarily, the *II./SS-Infanterie-Regiment "Deutschland"* ceased to exist.

29 November 1941

SS-Kradschützen-Bataillon "Reich" received the mission of forcing weak enemy forces out of Lamanowo and, in the event that Kujunowo (Chenowo) was only weakly held by the enemy, of also capturing it.

Lamanowo (Lamnowa) was captured around 1100 hours and the attack continued through the woods against Kujonowo. The attack, however, came to a standstill in the face of well-constructed positions at the edge of the built-up area. They were positioned on the wooded slopes that rose toward the village. As a result of the unfavorable terrain, *SS-Kradschützen-Bataillon "Reich"* pulled its combat outposts back to Lamanowo in the afternoon.

At 1000 hours *SS-Infanterie-Regiment "Deutschland"* prepared to attack Krjukowo with the *II./SS-Infanterie-Regiment "Deutschland"* on the right of the road and the *III./SS-Infanterie-Regiment "Deutschland"* to its left. The *I./SS-Infanterie-Regiment "Deutschland"* staged at the Manichino road — railroad-crossing shack to attack Hill 208. The hill was occupied at 1100 hours without significant opposition.

The *II./* and *III./SS-Infanterie-Regiment "Deutschland"*, however, had to overcome stubborn resistance. The enemy defended himself in good field fortifications that were skillfully laid out. He also used houses and outbuildings in his defense. Firing ports had been knocked out of the walls just above the ground. Krjukowo was finally captured by 1600 hours with the help of *Sturmgeschütze "Blücher"*, *"Derfflinger"* and *"Lützow"*.

The commander of the *III./SS-Infanterie-Regiment "Deutschland"*, *SS-Hauptsturmführer* Kröger, was killed in that fighting. He received a head wound from a bunker at extremely short range. The bunker was taken under fire by a 5-cm antitank gun until the occupants surrendered.

Particularly unfavorable for the division was the fact that the friendly forces on the right, the *IX. Armee-Korps*, did not attack with its left wing, the *252. Infanterie-Division*. This resulted in a failure to pin the enemy on the commanding south bank of the Istra. As a result, the enemy could take the division under effective fire from the flank. The enemy even launched an attack from Shewnewo, but the attack was repulsed.

In his personal notes, *Generaloberst* Hausser wrote:

> The strength of the attack was expended against far superior defenders in positions at a temperature of -30 degrees Celsius (-22 degrees Fahrenheit).

The commander-in-chief of *Panzergruppe 4* reported the following to *Heeresgruppe Mitte* on 29 November 1941:

> The moment may very soon arrive when the enemy's superiority in the air and on the ground will force the attack to be called to a halt.

30 November 1941

Kampfgruppe Kumm (SS-Infanterie-Regiment "Der Führer") attacked the enemy positions at the railroad one kilometer west of Lenino with the *III./SS-Infanterie-Regiment "Deutschland"* and with three *Sturmgeschütze* of Burmeister's platoon. Terrain difficulties forced the *Sturmgeschütze* to move slowly as they followed the infantry. The *III./SS-Infanterie-Regiment "Deutschland"* was able to destroy a stubborn opponent in hand-to-hand fighting and capture the railroad station and the factory area north of the station by late evening. Hill 215.9 and Trucholowka were also captured. The enemy continued to hold Shewnewo.

The *10. Panzer-Division* captured Petrowsko and Turowo with tanks and motorized infantry after hard fighting. The Russians were particularly active in the air, concentrating low-level attacks with bombers and fighter planes on the spearheads of the divisions' attacks.

The III./SS-Infanterie-Regiment "Deutschland" is Consolidated

While *SS-Infanterie-Regiment "Deutschland"* established security at the limit of its previous advance it reorganized itself. The heavy losses of the previous weeks made it necessary to consolidate the *III./SS-Infanterie-Regiment "Deutschland"* with the remaining two battalions of the regiment. The remnants of those companies were incorporated in the *I./* and *II./SS-Infanterie-Regiment "Deutschland"*. Thus, the division was temporarily reduced by another battalion .

1 December 1941

The situation of the *XXXX. Panzer-Korps* worsened. The commanding general, Stumme, went to *Panzergruppe 4*. Guided by the estimates of the situation by the division commanders and based on personal impressions gained in his visits to the front, he told *Generaloberst* Hoepner the following:

The *XXXX. Panzer-Korps* with the *10. Panzer-Division* and *SS-Division "Reich"* no longer possesses the combat power to successfully continue to attack and then, later, to repulse enemy attacks in the Moscow defensive front. It is therefore unconditionally necessary that the corps be pushed out of the lines by the adjoining corps as soon as possible.

***

Werner Haupt wrote the following concerning the catastrophic conditions facing the frontline commanders:

Feldmarschall von Bock called the chief of the general staff of the Army from his headquarters in Orscha on 1 December. He implored: "The attack now appears to be without sense or objective, the more so since the time is drawing very near when the strength of the forces will be exhausted." (Werner Haupt, *Heeresgruppe Mitte*, p. 111. Bad Nauheim: Podzun-Pallas-Verlag, 1968.)

***

SS-Obergruppenführer und General der Waffen-SS Hausser wrote the following in his handwritten notes:

On 1 December *Heeresgruppe Mitte* reported to the army high command that the ordered attack could have no operational effect. Remaining before the gates of Moscow was not possible. It was necessary to occupy positions to the rear that were suitable for defense.

There was no decision.

***

SS-Division "Reich" used the day to prepare for the 2 December attack on Roshdestweno. Shewneno and Lenino were also held by the enemy.

The consolidation of the *III./SS-Infanterie-Regiment "Deutschland"* and its integration into the remaining two battalions of the regiment was carried out as ordered.

Winter Camouflage

A division order required that the steel helmets be camouflaged with chalk paste or white cloth. It also ordered that snow shirts be made or, at the very least, that white cloth be used for camouflage.

Since the *Luftwaffe* complained of the lack of identification of the forward lines, red cloths were laid out as field-expedient identification panels whenever there was a lack of swastika flags.

On 1 December German aircraft were employed with winter paint schemes. The underside was blue-white, the fuselage white with gray fields.

The wingtips remained yellow.

The Russian bombers carried new national markings consisting of the red Soviet star on a white field with blue perimeter. The troops were immediately informed of the new markings.

Immediately after occupying a built-up area, every unit had to post signs at all the entrances with the place's name so that the numerous vehicle drivers and motorcycle messengers who drove without maps could find their destinations.

***

The "Division Order for the Attack on 2 December 1941" included the following (excerpt):

1.) The enemy facing *SS-Division "Reich"* fights skillfully in defense, utilizing the rear edges of woods to reduce the effectiveness of our heavy weapons. He is adept in emplacing himself in all built-up areas. His men fight to the death in their positions.

It is therefore essential in order to reduce losses for every attack to bring up and employ whatever heavy weapons are available. For all intents and purposes, the enemy should be smashed before the infantry arrive.

2.) The ***IX. Armee-Korps*** (on the right) launched an attack on 1 December on a broad front. It reached Padikow and the western outskirts of Borikowo with its left wing by noon.

The *10. Panzer-Division* (friendly forces on the left) captured the western portion of Nefedjewo with the spearhead of its attack. After hard fighting, its right wing has taken Sseltwanicha.

3.) The ***XXXX. Panzer-Korps*** is to continue the attack on Moscow on 2 December. Friendly forces on both side are also to attack. It is to capture the terrain needed for the attack on the presumed enemy position behind the Nachabinka River.

4.) For that purpose, ***SS-Division "Reich"*** is to capture Shewnewo and Roshdestweno so that, on the following day, the attack can continue in an east-southeast direction with the *Schwerpunkt* on the right wing.

5.) …

2 December 1941

SS-Kradschützen-Bataillon "Reich" was attached to *SS-Infanterie-Regiment "Deutschland"* for the attack on Shewnewo. The regiment was to attack the enemy southwest of Hill 215.9 and fight its way to the eastern edge of the woods. *SS-Infanterie-Regiment "Der Führer"*, after completing its reorganization, was to screen the attack of *SS-Infanterie-Regiment "Deutschland"*.

SS-Kradschützen-Bataillon "Reich" launched its attack on Shewnewo late in the morning. It was to have been supported by all five *Sturmgeschütze*. However, *Sturmgeschütze "Prinz Eugen"*, *"Lützow"* and *"Blücher"* dropped out with track and engine problems on the move to the assembly area so the attack was only supported by the *"Yorck"* and *"Derfflinger"*.

Artillery and *Nebelwerfer* laid down fire on both sides of Shewnewo and the field fortifications in preparation for the attack. The enemy fought extraordinarily hard. The attack probably would not have succeeded without the two *Sturmgeschütze*. After two hours of fighting, the *SS-Kradschützen* captured Shewnewo around 1330 hours. The *"Yorck"* eliminated three mortars and one long-barreled gun during the engagement while the *"Derfflinger"* knocked out two mortars and another long-barreled gun.

Prisoner statements indicated that Shewnewo, which was a pillar of the Russian local system of positions, was to have been held unconditionally to the last man. Three Russian antiaircraft guns were positioned in outbuildings and 20 light mortars were captured in a fortified field position. In the truest sense of the word, the enemy had fought to the death in his positions.

The two *Sturmgeschütze* then moved to the *I./SS-Infanterie-Regiment "Deutschland"* to support the attack on Roshdestweno. Ground-attack aircraft and *Nebelwerfer* also prepared the way for the attack there. At 1600 hours Roshdestweno was captured after a successful *Stuka* attack.

With that, the division had reached the following line by evening: Shewnewo — eastern outskirts of Roshdestweno — Hill 215.9 — factory land northeast of the Smigari railroad station — one kilometer east of Trucholowka. The leading elements of the division were close to Lenino.

***

SS-Unterscharführer Streng of the *2./SS-Infanterie-Regiment "Deutschland"*, wrote about the soldiers' situation in his notes:

> We could only draw near to our final objective of Moscow one step at a time. It was icy cold around us — and that in miserable quarters and with insufficient rations for the combat troops. Supply difficulties constantly increased. They were the main cause of our problems. Otherwise, we would have been much closer to our objective.
>
> Nevertheless, the soldiers gained the upper hand time after time through superhuman exertions. With amazing patience they fought their way through all adversities.
>
> Many times the soldiers provided themselves with Russian coats and fur caps so they were hardly recognizable as German soldiers. There was a general lack of winter clothing. Everyone was infested with lice. Fires had to be built under the vehicle chassis so that the engines would start. The fuel was partially frozen and the engine oil became thick. There was no antifreeze to prevent the water from freezing in the cooling systems.
>
> The limited combat strength remaining in the units was further diminished by losses due to frostbite. The soldiers could no longer be given major tasks. The day was drawing near when the troops would not only be at the end of their strength but when the numerous losses due to wounding, frostbite and death would completely wipe out the fighting strength of the companies.

In addition, the automatic weapons of the squads and platoons often failed to fire in the intense cold. The bolts did not move in the machine guns. In the event of an enemy attack or counterattack that presented another mortal danger.

Those fighting, half-frozen German troops at the front stood and lay in merciless cold that sometimes sank below -45 degrees Celsius (-49 degrees Fahrenheit) in their normal uniforms, normal leather boots, without gloves, galoshes or scarves, abandoned in a merciless battle and exposed to the winter.

In complete contrast to the above, we found out daily from our Russian prisoners that they had the best that one could imagine in the way of overall winter equipment. Their thick winter uniforms were quilted throughout. They all wore felt boots, fur mittens and fur caps. In order to keep themselves from freezing, the German soldiers salvaged those valuable articles of winter clothing from the stiffly frozen dead. Preserving bodily warmth was simply an elemental necessity for survival.

Our Objective Before Us — Moscow

SS-Unterscharführer Streng continues:

I stared far into the clear, silent starry night. In that terrible cold, minutes stretched to eternity. It was still long before midnight.

Beyond the suburbs of Moscow giant illuminating rockets suddenly hung like so many stars of Venus, and tight bundles of searchlight beams searched the sky, back and forth, were extinguished, then, twitched in spectral splendor, rising and crossing to form giant bundles of rays. Between them rose the flashing string-of-pearl displays of the Russian heavy antiaircraft fire. Bursts of dark red and orange red tracers drew long strings of light across the nighttime heavens.

Moscow rumbled with loud drumming through the December night. Every night German heavy bomber formations attacked Moscow from the air, bringing death and confusion to the center of enemy power. Explosions flickered above the contours of the outlying hills as trains of bombs burst. Then, after half an hour, the night returned to its accustomed silence…

…We were quartered at night in a house where two women lived. The younger woman spoke faultless German. She worked in Moscow, returning every evening by train. She told us at length about the city of Moscow and her present life.

Moscow had opened the prisons and armed the liberated convicts. Worker brigades were formed in the factories; women and children set to digging fortifications. Fresh Siberian troops were on the way. Forces of the Red Army, marching to the front, filled the streets of Moscow…

***

The *10. Panzer-Division's* combat power was non-existent. It was no longer capable of attack. It sent a request to the corps that it be withdrawn.

***

In the evening the divisions received the following missions for the coming day:

The *10. Panzer-Division* is to establish security with strongpoints along the line Nefedewo — Turowo — Petrowsko — edge of woods north of Sseliwanicha. The Petrowo strongpoint must be held. The division is to determine whether the Nefedewo and Turowo strongpoints can be pulled back to the line Petrowsko — Nadrowraschje in the event of strong enemy pressure.

While maintaining security and conducting reconnaissance, *SS-Division "Reich"* is to turn to the east and north against the Talizy — Lenino road. It is to capture Lenino and establish contact with the *10. Panzer-Division* at Petrowsko (moving via Sseliwanicha).

The Attack on Lenino

3 December 1941

At 0900 hours the combat outposts of *SS-Infanterie-Regiment "Deutschland"* were relieved by *SS-Kradschützen-Bataillon "Reich"*. Reconnaissance reported that Selenkowo, east of the stream, was free of enemy. One motorcycle company was sent there by the division to secure the crossing for the *IX. Armee-Korps*. The company occupied Selenkowo and the field fortifications west of the built-up area.

After staging for the attack, the *I./* and *II./SS-Infanterie-Regiment "Deutschland"* launched an attack on both sides of the Roshdestweno — Lenino road. Initially, the two battalions swung west of "Pear Hill" in order to cover the right flank on the open plain below the commanding hill.

Heavy fighting developed when the two battalions came up against strong Russian field fortifications in the woods southeast of Lenino. At the same time, heavy mortar fire opened up from the east. The enormous fragmentation effect of the mortar rounds in the woods exacted heavy casualties that included serious losses of officers.

Wounded were: The commander of the regiment (*SS-Sturmbannführer* Schulz), the commander of the *I./SS-Infanterie-Regiment "Deutschland"* (*SS-Sturmbannführer* Meyer), the commander of the *II./SS-Infanterie-Regiment "Deutschland"* (*SS-Hauptsturmführer* Hansmann), the regimental liaison officer, (*SS-Obersturmführer* Balzer) and the adjutant of the *I./SS-Infanterie-Regiment "Deutschland"* (*SS-Untersturmführer* Ott).

The regimental commander and the commander of the *II./SS-Infanterie-Regiment "Deutschland"* continued to lead their units until evening.

The Russians launched two immediate counterattacks. Both, however, were repulsed with heavy losses by the *Sturmgeschütze*. The attack on Lenino made little forward progress. The fighting was too bitter at that point and the few attacking companies were too weak.

After mopping up the woods, the *Sturmgeschütze* advanced on line to a point 500 meters south of Lenino. Field fortifications and columns of vehicles were taken under fire. The *"Derfflinger"* destroyed two antitank guns and the *"Schill"* eliminated one antitank gun. As darkness fell, the *I./SS-Infanterie-Regiment "Deutschland"* succeeded in penetrating Lenino from the east.

In the meantime, *SS-Infanterie-Regiment "Der Führer"* had attacked the western part of Lenino from the south. It penetrated into the industrial sector in heavy fighting in the western part of Lenino. The enemy continued to defend the center of the town in hand-to-hand fighting.

The fighting around Lenino lasted late into the night. Initially only a portion of the town was captured. At 2300 hours the *II./SS-Infanterie-Regiment "Deutschland"* received orders to attack Lenino from the west and capture it, whatever the cost. The *Sturmgeschütze* attacked along with the *6./SS-Infanterie-Regiment "Deutschland"*, but the enemy had withdrawn in the darkness. Lenino was captured and mopped up. The companies of *SS-Infanterie-Regiment "Der Führer"* also advanced through the built-up area and on through to the railroad station.

Since heavy Russian artillery fire covered Lenino, it was again evacuated by order of the division to avoid additional heavy losses.

SS-Division "Reich" went over to the defensive in the line western outskirts of Lenino — high ground south of Lenino. The battalions were pulled back during the same night to their jump-off positions.

The Russians who immediately pushed back into Lenino were taken under fire by the heavy weapons.

***

On 3 December, on his own initiative, the commanding general of *Panzergruppe 4, Generaloberst* Hoepner, ordered a three-day halt in the attack. The attack was never resumed.

In reaching Lenino, SS-Division "Reich" reached one of the suburbs of Moscow, about 17 kilometers from the outskirts of the city.

The commander of *SS-Infanterie-Regiment "Der Führer", SS-Obersturmbannführer* Kumm, discussed this in the history of the regiment:

> The Russians threw worker militias with armored support into the fighting in counterattacks. The men of the regiment believed that they could count the number of days until they entered Moscow on the fingers of one hand. In clear, frosty weather the towers of the city could be seen without binoculars. A forward-emplaced 10-cm cannon battery fired harassing fire into the city. The attack was called to a halt at the limit of the previous advance. The battalions, the *III./SS-Infanterie-Regiment "Der Führer"* on the right, the *I./SS-Infanterie-Regiment "Der Führer"* on the left on the highway, organized for defense. (Otto Weidinger, *Kameraden bis zum Ende*, p. 101. Göttingen: Plesse-Verlag, 1962.)

The leading elements of the *1./SS-Kradschützen-Bataillon "Reich"* had reached the terminus station of the Moscow streetcar system.

SS-Obergruppenführer und General der Waffen-SS Hausser remarked in his handwritten notes:

On 3 December 1941 *Panzergruppe 4* reported to *Heeresgruppe Mitte* "that its offensive power was at its end. The reason for that was physical and mental overexertion, non-sustainable losses of unit commanders and inadequate winter equipment. A decision was due as to whether a withdrawal was required. The line that had been attained on the Svenigorod — Istra highway would be suitable for that purpose."

Without waiting for orders, *Panzergruppe 4* ordered a three-day halt in the attack.

***

The headquarters of the *4. Armee* called a halt to any continued attack and pulled back all of the forward divisions to the jump-off positions behind the Nara. A renewal of the attack appeared unlikely.

With that, the frontal attack by the 4. Armee and the 4. Panzer-Armee on Moscow finally failed.

4 December 1941

During the night the division went over to the defensive in the line designated in its orders.

At 0700 hours Lenino was shelled by Russian artillery. One hour later the Russians attacked the sector held by *SS-Kradschützen-Bataillon "Reich"* with two battalions. The motorcycle troops repulsed the attack with support from the artillery, antiaircraft machine guns and *Nebelwerfer*. The enemy sustained heavy losses. At 1000 hours the Russian attack was finally broken. About 200 dead Russians remained on the battlefield. It remained quiet in the sectors of the two regiments.

Orders came from the corps to pull the *10. Panzer-Division* out of the front.

The Departure of the 10. Panzer-Division

When the *10. Panzer-Division* was withdrawn from the front of the *XXXX. Panzer-Korps* outside of Moscow, *SS-Division "Reich"* lost its partner-in-arms and a trustworthy neighbor that had been proven in many battles fought side-by-side. During the heavy fighting in the attacks of the months gone by the two divisions had ideally complemented one another.

The exemplary combat partnership of an army armored division and the senior division of the *Waffen-SS* thus came to an end. An old comradeship linked the two divisions ever since the summer of 1939 in East Prussia. There, *Panzer-Regiment 7* (Zinten, East Prussia), together with the core elements of the later *SS-Verfügungs-Division (SS-Division "Reich")*, were molded together within the framework of the newly formed *Panzerdivision Kempf* in combined exercises and maneuvers at the Stablack Training Area.

The *SS* men and the tankers shared their first combat experience during the Polish campaign, where they advanced inexorably eastward around Warsaw to the Weichsel south of the city in a great pincers movement, thus encircling the Polish capital city from the east. An example of the superb way that the young German armored branch passed its baptism of fire.

Ever since the start of the Russian campaign the two divisions, along with *Infanterie-Regiment (mot.) "Großdeutschland"*, belonged to the *XXXXVI. Panzer-Korps.* Together they advanced eastward as the spearhead of the attack of *Heeresgruppe Mitte* to the hills east of Jelnja, where the three elite formations defied the assault of Russian forces that outnumbered them five times over. For weeks those three formations held the position in the Jelnja salient. It was the most forward position in the entire Eastern Front.

Together, the two divisions advanced eastward from the Gshatsk operational area on both sides of the highway as part of the *XXXX. Panzer-Korps.* Once again, they were the spearhead of *Heeresgruppe Mitte.* In days of unrelenting and extremely heavy fighting, the two divisions broke through the Moscow defense position and advanced close to the gates of Moscow.

The sacrifices, losses and hardships that the two divisions had borne together has already been described in detail. On the occasion of their separation, which would prove final, the men of *SS-Division "Reich"* thanked their unforgettable comrades-in-arms of the *10. Panzer-Division* for their commitment as self-sacrificing neighbors and for their unfailingly exemplary comradeship!

The *10. Panzer-Division* was later transferred to Africa where it joined the *Deutsches Afrika Korps.* It never returned to the Eastern Front.

Failure of the Moscow Offensive

From 4 December 1941 to the present day questions have not ceased regarding the reasons for the failure of the great offensive against Moscow when it was so close to its goal.

SS-Obersturmbannführer Kumm, the commander at that time of *SS-Infanterie-Regiment "Der Führer"*, assembled the questions in his notes as follows:

Was it General Winter? There is no doubt that the temperature, which at times reached -52 degrees Celsius (-62 degrees Fahrenheit) caused great difficulties for the German soldier. Vehicles and weapons were neither set up nor prepared for that.

Was it the Siberian divisions? Possessing combat power and being rested, equipped with white camouflage outfits and the best of weapons, without question those formations played an essential role, but not a decisive one. At Istra, for example, those formations also fell back before the weak companies of the regiments.

Was it the Russian road system?

Was it the planning errors of the Armed Forces High Command, the *Führerhauptquartier* and the general staff?

Had they underestimated the Red Army and failed to include in the calculations the sources of assistance, particularly all those east of Moscow?

Why was there such exceedingly inadequate equipment for imminent winter war?

Was the *Luftwaffe* incapable of disrupting and interdicting enemy supply lines to the front east of Moscow?

Was it due to the railroad network in the conquered areas? Had the locomotives been prepared for winter service? Or were there problems in resetting the tracks to the western track gauge?

Many of those arguments are certainly relevant. But there is no question that the German frontline divisions gave their best. Months of unbroken combat had sapped their strength and bled the regiments white. Losses due to frostbite, at times, exceeded the number killed and wounded.

Overall losses on the Eastern Front totaled about 750,000 soldiers up to 5 December.

The question that begs itself is whether fresh forces and, even more important, forces that were well equipped for winter combat, could have broken the last resistance before Moscow? Even against such a courageous and, in part, fanatically defending enemy? It seems quite probable.

***

Today, we know the full extent of the preparations for the Russian counteroffensive and know what forces were assembled for that purpose from the Asiatic area east of Moscow. We also clearly understand now the extent to which the American shipments of military materiel had begun to arrive. We can now state with near certainty that it was no longer possible for the German offensive against Moscow to succeed. This is true even if the spearheads of the German attack had succeeded in advancing as far as the outskirts of the city of Moscow or even in capturing the city by summoning up their last reserves of strength.

What would have happened then? Would Moscow have become the giant trap for *Heeresgruppe Mitte*? Surely the giant city would have swallowed up and tied down all of the exhausted German attacking forces, giving the Russian shock armies an even better chance to surround *Heeresgruppe Mitte*.

It is probable that the timely halting of *Panzergruppe 4* and the concomitant initial withdrawal to the Istra position and, later, to the Rusa position, already contained the kernel of success for the defensive fighting at Rshew. The success at Rshew prevented the very encirclement of *Heeresgruppe Mitte* by the Russian shock armies.

Losses of the XXXX. Panzer-Korps: 9 October - 5 December 1941

Based on the original strength figures, the losses of the two divisions — *SS-Division "Reich"* and the *10. Panzer-Division* — and the corps troops for that time period from 9 October – 5 December 1941 were:

7,582 officers, noncommissioned officers and enlisted personnel

This represented approximately 40% of the table-of-organization strength of these combat forces. (See also Paul Carell, *Unternehmen Barbarossa*, p. 171. Frankfurt am Main / Berlin (West): Ullstein Verlag GmbH, 1963)

Chapter III: On the Defense 5 December 1941 – 17 January 1942

Sub-Section n)

Defensive Fighting Outside Moscow: 5 - 21 December 1941

The Russian Counteroffensive

In his personal notes *SS-Obergruppenführer und General der Waffen-SS* Hausser writes regarding the planning of the Russian counteroffensive, as seen from the opponent's viewpoint:

> The summer and fall campaigns were a severe test, but the dreaded breakthrough to Moscow did not succeed.
>
> The Russian high command hoped to get through the rest of the year and, through comprehensive measures in the central sector, save the capital from the enemy's grasp. The main body of the forces (40%) remained close to Moscow.
>
> However, at the beginning of October the fighting around Moscow had led to serious failures for the West Front and Briansk Front (two pocket battles).

Wjasma and Gshatsk had been lost. Confusion reigned in the staffs. The most dangerous direction of the German attack was Moshaisk — Moscow. It was only the Kalinin Front in the north that was still quiet. On 10 October Timoschenko was removed. The West and Reserve Fronts fell under Zhukov's command. Kalinin fell on 14 October. A new front was formed behind the Volga as far as the reservoir. Tula held in the south. The wings were secured.

In October 20 divisions and one shock army arrived from the far east as well as from the Northwest and Southwest Fronts. They occupied the Moscow defense positions. The fortification of Moscow began. Militia, worker and women's battalions were formed. The weather also helped.

At the end of October the attack had reached the line Volga — reservoir (north of Istra) — Wolokolamsk — Oka — Aleksin — Tula — Don.

The evening reports of the Soviet Information Bureau for 25 November 1941 stressed "how hopeless the enemy's effort to capture Moscow is. Soon it will be defeated."

The West Front was reorganized.

On 27 November 1941 Pravda wrote "...the destruction of the enemy will start outside Moscow."

The Russian West Front grew stronger daily. The concentration of the Russian reserve armies was completed and kept secret. The defense of Moscow could be conducted offensively. However, initially, the plan was only to launch a frontal attack against the immediate enemy.

Only gradually did the plan develop to conduct an operational-level counterattack in the German style and envelop *Heeresgruppe Mitte* toward Smolensk.

On 30 November 1941 the military council of the West Front laid its plan for the counteroffensive in front of the high command of the Red Army. It proposed the following: Attack of the 1st Shock Army against the enemy's northern wing; attack by the forces of the Briansk Front against the southern wing. The strong West Front was to attack and pin the forces facing it; prior to that, the Kalinin Front would advance into the enemy's deep flank west of Rshew.

***

Werner Haupt also wrote about the operational planning of the Russians:

"This was to be the hour of the Red Army!"

The military leadership of the Soviet Union had planned since October how it would bring the German offensive to a final end. It had an unequaled potential for force generation at its disposal.

The industries that had been moved to Siberia began to enter production. Rigorous measures taken by political and economic administrators succeeded in evoking immense output from the people and resources of the giant realm. Moscow's agents reported that Japan would not enter the war against the USSR. Thereupon STAVKA immediately ordered that the troops of the Far East Army be sent to the West Front.

Accordingly, 30 rifle divisions, 3 cavalry divisions, 33 rifle brigades and 6 armored brigades arrived new at the front in the first days of December. During that period the German army received neither men nor weapons, neither rations nor fuel!

STAVKA reorganized the forces outside of Moscow. It formed its armies into strong battle groups that would ruthlessly attack. The plan's intentions were:

1.) Cut off the German armored wedges in the north and south outside of Moscow.
2.) Attack through the open flanks.
3.) Destroy *Heeresgruppe Mitte.*

The assault forces were to meet at Wjasma. When that occurred, all of *Heeresgruppe Mitte* would be encircled and the German army in the east catastrophically defeated. (Werner Haupt, *Heeresgruppe Mitte*, p. 109. Bad Nauheim: Podzun-Pallas-Verlag, 1968.)

***

The Russian army concentrated for the mighty counteroffensive from north to south as follows:

Kalinin Front: Four armies (22nd, 29th, 31st and 30th Armies)
West Front: One shock army (1st Shock Army) and eight armies (20th, 16th, 5th, 33rd, 43rd, 49th, 50th and 10th Armies)
Southwest Front: Three armies (3rd, 13th and 61st Armies).

***

Werner Haupt continues:

As before, the Soviet air forces remained attached to the armies. In comparison to the weak forces of the *VIII. Fliegerkorps*, the Soviet forces were far superior in the air…

…That powerful concentration was neither noticed nor expected by the Germans. It was only the officers and soldiers at the front who subconsciously perceived that "something" was brewing to the east…

***

In the evening of 4 December the intelligence officer of the *XXXX. Panzer-Korps* passed on the information that three new Russian divisions had arrived in front of the friendly forces to the left, the *XXXXVI. Panzer-Korps.* Prisoners stated that the Russians would attack the entire northern front at 0400 hours on 5 December. The divisions were informed.

5 December 1941

At midnight *Panzergruppe 4* gave notice that a cold front of –30 to -40 degrees Celsius (-22 to -40 degrees Fahrenheit) was expected. At the same time the news arrived that the Istra bridge south of the Istra Bastion had been blown up, presumably by remote control.

Starting at midnight, unusually heavy artillery fire against the friendly forces to the left of the corps could be heard.

The withdrawal and relief of the *10. Panzer-Division* by the *5. Panzer-Division* went ahead as planned.

At 0730 hours a reinforced battalion of the enemy attacked Roshdestweno in the sector of *SS-Kradschützen-Bataillon "Reich"* after artillery preparation. The attack was repulsed by noon, however, in concentrated machine-gun fire and fire from the *Sturmgeschütze*, which had gone into position at the outskirts of the built-up area. The remnants of the Russian battalion escaped into the woods to the east.

On 5 December *SS-Sturmbannführer* Harmel officially assumed command of *SS-Infanterie-Regiment "Deutschland"*. He had previously been the commander of the *II./SS-Infanterie-Regiment "Der Führer"*. *SS-Hauptsturmführer* Tost commanded the *I./SS-Infanterie-Regiment "Deutschland"* and *SS-Obersturmführer* Diercks had the *II./SS-Infanterie-Regiment "Deutschland"*.

***

At a meeting with all the chiefs of staff of the corps of *Panzergruppe 4* the combat capabilities of the individual corps was discussed. *Oberst* von Kurowski reported the following for the *XXXX. Panzer-Korps*:

> ...*SS-Division "Reich"* was still aggressive (Author's Note: It was more likely "capable of attack" than "aggressive") and had continued to carry out attacks recently. As a result of its seriously diminished combat capability, however, it was only suitable for attacks with limited objectives where it advanced with other formations on its flanks. As for defense, there were no reservations even when considering its diminished capabilities.
>
> The *10. Panzer-Division* was no longer capable of attack...

However, the situation had suddenly changed in all of the other sectors of *Heeresgruppe Mitte*.

***

Werner Haupt discussed the initial results of the Soviet counteroffensive:

> Then the Red Army struck!
>
> On the morning of 5 December its offensive broke loose. Hundreds of bombers and low-level attack planes dove on the freezing, hungry German soldiers, dropping bombs and strafing with machine-gun fire. Thousands of rounds smashed the last German shelters and guns. "Hurrah" roared forth from thousands upon thousands of Russian throats.
>
> The full weight of the attack struck the German front. The Kalinin Front advanced along its entire sector between the Waldai Hills and Kalinin in an attack to the south.

The West Front and Southwest Front followed on 6 December with 88 rifle divisions, 15 cavalry divisions and 24 armored brigades.

The temperature remained below -30 degrees Celsius (-22 degrees Fahrenheit). The Russian troops were 100% equipped for winter fighting.

The German front fell back in flight. Only the *4. Armee* initially held in its good positions behind the Nara. (Werner Haupt, *Heeresgruppe Mitte*, p. 111. Bad Nauheim: Podzun-Pallas-Verlag, 1968.)

***

It was not until 5 December that *General* Jodl gave *Heeresgruppe Mitte* the discretion to halt its attack, thus lagging far behind the actual situation at the front.

6 December 1941

At 0430 hours heavy Russian artillery and mortar fire began to fall on Roshdestweno. During the night severe cold (about -30 degrees Celsius [-22 degrees Fahrenheit]) arrived, which had a very serious effect on men and equipment.

At 0700 hours strong Russian forces attacked in the sector of *SS-Infanterie-Regiment "Deutschland"*. They advanced as far as the outskirts of the villages but were eliminated in concentrated fire. Many hundreds of dead Russians covered the field east of Roshdestweno. The Russians attacked repeatedly during the course of the day but were always repulsed.

The regiment's command post and the building housing the communications platoon received direct hits. The regiment's surgeon and the artillery liaison officer, along with two thirds of the signaleers, became casualties.

Throughout the entire day heavy artillery and mortar fire continued on Roshdestweno and the road to Snigiri.

At noon the regimental and separate battalion adjutants were directed to the division to receive instructions on conducting reconnaissance for establishing defensive positions behind the Istra.

In the sector of *SS-Kradschützen-Bataillon "Reich"*, which had been shifted somewhat to the south, the Russians again attacked during the afternoon. Artillery fire fell on Roshdestweno. It was initially light but intensified to a heavy barrage. The enemy then worked his way up to the friendly positions under cover of increasing darkness, even though forced to the ground by German *Nebelwerfer* and artillery fire. Remarkably, there was hardly a rifle shot from the Russians.

In order to illuminate the battlefield, some outbuildings were set ablaze by fire from antitank guns, making the battlefield almost as light as day. By then the enemy had worked his way extremely close and had penetrated into the village on the left in small groups. The friendly machine guns suffered numerous misfires as a result of the intense cold. The gunners' fingers were frozen numb and stiff. Fortunately, hand grenades were present in abundant quantity. They decided the fight. The enemy, creeping forward along the ground, was destroyed in hand-to-hand fighting. Those Russians who could flee, fled. Numerous dead covered the field of combat.

***

The corps war diary for 6 December 1941 reported:

> Due to the changed situation, it is the intention of *Panzergruppe 4* to halt the attack and pull the front back to a line of defense that is favorable for the winter. The intention is to pull back from the current lines starting 10 December 1941. However, preparations must also be made to pull back the lines even earlier on orders from above. It is intended to offer resistance for one more day along a line designated on the map prior to occupying the final defensive positions...
>
> The *XXXX. Panzer-Korps* has emphasized that stopping east of the Istra or maintaining a bridgehead at the Istra Bastion is out of the question...The situation at the front is unchanged. The corps is in a position where it can repulse enemy attacks and hold the present limit of advance given the current enemy situation...

7 December 1941

SS-Infanterie-Regiment "Deutschland" fended off constant Russian attacks by newly introduced forces for the entire day.

In other sectors of the division it was notably quiet, suggesting that the enemy was preparing to attack on the next day.

The *XXXX. Panzer-Korps* war diary described the situation as follows:

> Friendly forces to the right, the *IX. Armee-Korps*, informs us...that its left wing, the *252. Infanterie-Division,* can no longer hold its present position. The forces are exhausted and no longer fit for combat.
>
> Under these circumstances the situation of the *XXXX. Panzer-Korps* also appears threatened, since it is not possible to take back the previous limit of advance. At present there is only **one** bridge over the Istra River. The other one, however, is expected to be restored to service on 7 December. 1,500 wounded are still at the main dressing station in the Istra museum, including numerous seriously wounded whose removal will require some additional time.

According to Teletype orders from *Panzergruppe 4,* the intended line of defense for the *XXXX. Panzer-Korps* was to be the city of Istra — Maksimowka — Istra reservoir.

At this point, the corps informed *Panzergruppe 4* that, under no circumstances, could it take over the defense east of the Istra. It therefore recommended the line of defense be moved to the west bank of the Istra River to avoid unnecessary losses. *Panzergruppe 4* approved the recommendation.

The corps combat engineers worked on a comprehensive barrier and mining system in the area surrounding the Istra and its museum/bastion.

According to an order from *Panzergruppe 4, t*he *XXXX. Panzer-Korps* was to fall back during the night of 9/10 December to its previous at Manichino — Aleksino. During the night of 10/11 December the entire front was to be pulled back to a line of defense west of the Istra.

A difficult question in the corps' new sector and, thus, for *SS-Division "Reich"* as well, was billeting. A major portion of the villages had been destroyed in the previous fighting. In addition, partisans had smashed the windows in the houses that had not yet been destroyed.

***

The commanding general, *General* Stumme, issued the following **Memorandum to the Commanders of the Divisions and Corps Troops:**

It is more necessary than ever before for the commanders and leaders of separate formations and units to take every possible opportunity to **personally** inform their soldiers regarding the military situation and political events and give their subordinates opportunities to raise relevant questions. We want to ensure the entire corps receives the same **uniform** message.

If we have failed to take our objective of Moscow this winter — even though we approached to within artillery range of it — it is primarily due to extraordinarily bad weather conditions in the fall and the onset of winter. The enemy has found the opportunity, during the halt in operations that has been forced upon us, to bring in fresh troops from the far east. According to the orders from our *Führer* and supreme commander, we will no longer meet them in attack, but will hammer them in victorious defense until the favorable hour again calls us to attack and, in so doing, totally destroy the enemy. Our ultimate victory remains certain, if each of us does his duty to be hard on himself and be aggressive and confident of our superiority over the enemy, as the German army has constantly done to date.

If any soldier has the misfortune to fall into enemy hands, he must be clear regarding the fact that nothing he says, no matter how much he says what he believes the enemy wants to hear, can improve his lot or save him from either violent death or a slow death from hunger and cold in the far east. Unworthy and stripped of honor, such cowardly and unfavorable statements about the army and the homeland constitute betrayal of the homeland and, thus, endanger the German people in its entirety.

Many sacrifices and much effort that has often pressed us to the limits of our capabilities have been demanded of us recently. They have borne fruit. The courage and toughness of our soldiers have defeated the enemy in numerous victorious battles and fighting. The enemy losses are proof enough. We now prepare ourselves for new deeds in defense so that we can later defeat the enemy for all time.

I draw the attention of all commanders and leaders of separate units to the importance of this uniform line of thought. It is not exhaustive but contains what is most important for this hour.

/signed/ Stumme

***

The following notes from 17 December 1941 were made available by the surgeon of the *1. SS-Sanitätskompanie "Reich"*, *SS-Sturmbannführer Dr.* Roschmann. They bear witness, in a most impressive manner, to the self-sacrificing activity of the physicians and the entire medical personnel of the casualty clearing stations and aid stations of the division during those difficult days.

At the Casualty Clearing Station at Weretenki

Day and night there was no break. We also got lice from the lice-infested wounded. There were numerous severely wounded: Plenty of amputations, stomach and lung wounds, bones broken by gunshot. And, in all of that, the sad certainty that all of them had to be evacuated. They all urgently needed rest, but evacuation was not the best for them in these circumstances. That, and the uncertainty about having enough transport capacity available at the right time, occasioned a great deal of nervous strain.

There were wondrous frosty clear, star bright nights and magical scenery in the snowbound woods. But who continued to see that?

In the few minutes that were not filled with the bloody handwork, one tottered from operating and dressing room to the houses in which the wounded lay to inspect, to bandage and to seek out those who were capable of being evacuated. In the meantime reports came that even more new wounded had arrived, perhaps eight, perhaps 20.

One ate in the operating room, quickly grabbing a few bits of bread, a quick gulp of coffee during the pauses created by the necessity to remove bloody dressings, trimmed-off pieces of skin, bloody gauze pads, scraps of uniforms and amputated limbs. The break was only as long as it took until new wounded would be brought in again.

Eyes closed on their own and one slept standing. Tears flowed and eyes threatened to fall out. Legs numbed, without sensation; the horror of the bloody work sent shudders up the spine. Lice bit and, when the next wounded man was laid on the table, one concentrated on him as intensely as if he were the first one and one was fully rested. The necessary heat and the constant operation of the autoclave made the air in the operating room thick enough to cut, to say nothing of the smells and exhalations of the many men crammed in and working there. And all of that was in a Russian house that already reeked with cabbage, old bread and mouldy clothes.

The wintry cold prevented the wounded from first being taken into another room and prepared for care. The wounds were exposed by cutting off the emergency bandages and uniform and then bandaged. Often it was determined that, in addition to one wound, there were yet others, or that only the entry wound had been bandaged.

As a result of the evacuation of Istra, we were the closest clearing station to the front. The press of wounded persisted. Many times we believed we were at the end of our rope…

8 December 1941

After a quiet night the Russians followed an artillery preparation that started at 0700 hours with a time-phased attack in about regimental strength on the entire division front. They penetrated into the northern part of Roshdestweno and five tanks advanced through Lenino.

The enemy penetrated along the boundary between *SS-Kradschützen-Bataillon "Reich"* and the *16./SS-Infanterie-Regiment "Deutschland"* with his efforts.

SS-Sturmbannführer Harmel, the commander of *SS-Infanterie-Regiment "Deutschland"*, committed the last available company, the *3./SS-Infanterie-Regiment "Deutschland"* (25 men strong) with two *Sturmgeschütze*. The enemy was thrown back out. After clearing up the penetration, only the company commander and four men were left from the company.

***

The commanding general immediately went to *SS-Division "Reich"*. The tanks of the *10. Panzer-Division* that were staged in Petschkowa and Jermolino and two platoons of 5-cm *Pak* (corps reserve) were immediately set in march to Wysokowo as reinforcement. A counterattack by *SS-Infanterie-Regimenter "Deutschland"* and *"Der Führer"*, along with *SS-Kradschützen-Bataillon "Reich"* and particularly effective action by the *Sturmgeschütze*, successfully restored the situation in the entire division sector.

The enemy was held at bay during the day, which ensured the start of an orderly disengagement.

A strong enemy attack was observed in the sector of the friendly forces on the right, which the greatly weakened, bled-white and exhausted *252. Infanterie-Division* was no longer able to withstand. After a while, the sound of the fighting moved ever farther to the west.

Roshdestweno remained in friendly hands. However, the enemy constantly brought up reserves, including artillery, from Lobanowo (via Selenkowo) and from Dedowsskij to the west. He even committed artillery to the fighting in open firing positions on the hill east of Roshdestweno.

***

The war diary of the *XXXX. Panzer-Korps* continues:

> Although the situation had been rectified by noon, renewed attacks by the enemy had to be expected later in the day, during the night and on the following day…
>
> After thorough artillery preparation, the enemy renewed his attacks in the afternoon. His *Schwerpunkt* was on the right wing of *SS-Division "Reich"*. *SS-Division "Reich"* repulsed the attacks with stubborn determination. Some enemy units, however, advanced from the south over the Istra to the area southwest of Roshdestweno. Since the combat strength of *SS-Division "Reich"* had further diminished in recent days, and since the Russian advance southwest of Rosdestweno (against the friendly forces on the right) endangered the division's south flank, the division ordered the right wing (*SS-Infanterie-Regiment "Deutschland"*) to evacuate its positions starting at

2000 hours and fall back to the line: east edge of Lamanowo — Trucholowka.

***

Starting at 2100, hours the last elements of *SS-Infanterie-Regiment "Deutschland"* were withdrawn from the main line of resistance as part of the division plan. The vehicles and trains elements had already fallen back to the west.

The withdrawal from the enemy took place as directed light mortar fire fell. The regiment reached and occupied the new line of resistance at the eastern outskirts of Krjukowo.

SS-Kradschützen-Bataillon "Reich" was employed on the right, *SS-Infanterie-Regiment "Deutschland"* in the center and *SS-Infanterie-Regiment "Der Führer"* on the left in the new divisional sector.

SS-Infanterie-Regiment "Der Führer", with one battalion each from *SS-Infanterie-Regimenter "Der Führer"* and *"Deutschland"*, remained in contact with the enemy as the division's rearguard under the command of *SS-Obersturmbannführer* Kumm. The Russians immediately spotted the movement and pursued with strong forces, especially with armor.

Russian Attack on the Entire Front

The day was also a major day of combat for *SS-Sturmgeschütz-Batterie "Reich"*. Its war diary includes the following after-action report:

The *Sturmgeschütz* platoon was alerted at 0830 hours. The Russians were attacking the entire front with strong forces. In comparison with the enemy, our own line was only weakly held. The three *Sturmgeschütze* drove forward on line and went into position north of Roshdestweno. They were partially concealed by haystacks.

The first attack collapsed under fire from the *Sturmgeschütze*. Visibility was severely limited by snow squalls. The Russians also brought up heavy weapons in the meantime. An antitank company was identified approaching in march order at 1,000 meters. It was taken under fire and destroyed by the *Sturmgeschütze*.

Nevertheless, several antitank guns fired on *"Yorck"*. The *Sturmgeschütz* was hit several times, but suffered no significant damage.

While that was going on, the two other *Sturmgeschütze* held down the Russians, who were then attacking in battalion and regimental strength. The *Sturmgeschütze* were on their own. There was no longer any infantry in that sector. The expenditure of ammunition was high. The *Sturmgeschütze* took turns in moving to the rear to secure ammunition.

The enemy attempted to silence the *Sturmgeschütze* with artillery. One battery that was firing at a range of about 1,300 meters at the edge of the woods was forced by fire to relinquish its positions. Since the north flank was inadequately covered, the Russians penetrated into the northern part of Roshdestweno. That, in turn, forced the *Sturmgeschütze* to change position. Roshdestweno was then attacked from the front. A company of *SS-Infanterie-Regiment "Deutschland"* that was rushed over attacked from the south and forced the Russians out of Roshdestweno.

Soon after that the enemy attempted to break through with all means on the high ground north of Roshdestweno.

The *Sturmgeschütze* hastened to the assistance of the weak forces fighting there. At 0300 hours the enemy fell back to his jump-off positions. The *Sturmgeschütze* took up the pursuit and threw some of the Russians out of their positions. The positions on Hill 200.5 were also effectively shelled so that the enemy evacuated them. After the wood line was fired on for a short time, quiet ensued. The scene of the engagement was littered with dead and wounded Russians.

Late in the evening Roshdestweno caught fire and fell victim to the flames. The *Sturmgeschütze* fell back to Lushezkoje via Krjukowo. Wounded were brought along on the return trip and stuck vehicles were pulled out. The battery left Nikulino, moved to Dedeschino and quartered there.

***

SS-Obergruppenführer und General der Waffen-SS Paul Hausser wrote the following concerning the situation in his personal notes:

On 8 December 1941, Hitler ordered a shift to the defensive in Directive 39. He wanted the establishment of "front line boundaries that would free up forces" and the "withdrawal of the mechanized divisions" for refitting! The latter was impossible!

The army group then ordered the reconnaissance and establishment of a rear position as a "winter position" in the line Kursk — Orel — Kaluga — Rshew.

9 December 1941

The war diary of the *XXXX. Panzer-Korps* contains the following entry for 9 December 1941:

The commanding general highly commends *SS-Division "Reich"* for its exemplary behavior during these critical times through the following order of the day:

Order of the Day

With the same indomitable spirit of attack with which the victorious battles and fighting of the recent past have been fought by *SS-Division "Reich"*, you men of the *SS* achieved a defensive victory over a numerically far superior enemy on 8 December. The enemy attempted to overrun you from all sides with stubborn bitterness using all available heavy weapons. In defeating the enemy you added new laurels to your banners. This victory has special significance for the entire operation.

My thanks and highest commendation for your outstanding achievements.

We dip our banners for your brave fallen comrades and we are united in the certainty that, despite all difficulties from the weather and the concomitant extreme physical exertions and strains, we shall firmly remain where ordered. Our final victory remains certain.

Hail to our *Führer*!

/signed/ Stumme

***

The night of 9 December was strikingly quiet. The disengagement and rearward movement to the new line passed without incident. The enemy, who had lost about 1,500 men in the fighting on 8 December, appeared to have no forces available for immediate pursuit. Burning the villages denied shelter to the Russians. In addition, the numerous mines that had been laid hindered his continued attack.

The situation for the corps, however, remained tense. *SS-Division "Reich"* held nearly all of the corps sector. As a result of limited combat strength, the division could not hold its present line against a sharp pursuit or attack on the entire front. This was particularly so because most of the heavy weapons were already in the new line of defense west of the Istra or were in transit to that position.

The Russians quickly followed into the empty area even though it had been heavily mined.

During the late afternoon the Russians were already running up against the division's newly occupied positions, but they were repulsed. The Russians laid down mortar and artillery fire on the division's central sector at Krjukowo.

While the combat forces held at the front, the division and corps combat engineers mined the terrain east of the Istra. They demolished structures that offered observation positions for the enemy and for artillery fire control. The built-up areas were, for the most part, set on fire by gunfire.

As darkness fell the rearguards were able to disengage from the enemy unobserved. They fell back to the blocking positions behind the Istra in a single bound. During the previous few days, all available combat-engineer forces had constructed fighting positions and bunkers for living. By the time the forces arrived enough had been prepared so that elemental protection was provided.

***

Werner Haupt provides a glimpse into the overall situation:

Feldmarschall von Bock reported the following to the *Oberkommando des Heeres* on 9 December: The army group is no longer in a position to withstand enemy attack at any point. (Werner Haupt, *Heeresgruppe Mitte*, p. 112. Bad Nauheim: Podzun-Pallas-Verlag, 1968.)

***

Helmut Günther wrote the following concerning his experiences as a *Kradschütze* at the time:

The Retreat Order

In the afternoon of 9 December we got to see how the situation was seen "in the rear". I had something to do at the command post when the field telephone rang. *SS-Untersturmführer* Buch picked up the handset, reported and passed the handset to Klingenberg. Actually, I should have vanished, but I was curious, and I stayed. I shall never forget the moments that followed.

Buch also stared at the "Old Man," who alternately turned white and red. I slowly began to understand what was up from the short questions and answers. The "old man's" lower jaw jutted out, and he obviously had trouble forcing out the *"Jawohl"*. Then the handset crashed against the cradle.

I felt decidedly queasy — if only I were already outside!

Klingenberg stared at the situation map that was spread out before him on a wooden chest. Strike me dead if he did not actually wipe his hand across his eyes. He looked as if he were chasing off a mosquito, but where do mosquitoes come from in winter? I had known Klingenberg since France. Ever since he had taken over the battalion, we messengers had been with him almost daily. Yet I had never seen him so shaken.

So! You really want to know what was going on? He had only received a brief military order, the order to **retreat!** The capture of Moscow was no longer in the cards for that year!

For a time, not one of the men in the command post spoke a word. Everyone looked at the commander. The radio operator in the corner nervously chewed his fingernails. *SS-Untersturmführer* Schramm made a big show of taking off his glasses and fumbled around them with his handkerchief. Buch ground his teeth and absentmindedly passed his hand across his cheek...

...The paralysis that had fallen upon the entire command post when that order was passed quickly ended. Hardly a few minutes had gone by when the adjutant appeared and we received work in heaps. After we had received our orders we were out of there...(Helmut Günther, *Heiße Motoren — Kalte Füße*, p. 221. Neckargemünd: Vowinckel-Verlag, 1963.)

10 December 1941

The withdrawal movement to the Istra position west of the river began in the early morning hours.

At 0900 hours the Russians were observed to be assembling at Krjukowo for an attack. The *Sturmgeschütze* moved forward and took the enemy assembly position under fire so that, for the time being, he was unable to start the attack.

Enemy units succeeded in going around the German lines south of Lamanowa, however. Therefore, the *Sturmgeschütze* moved onto Hill 207.2 and fired on the enemy's flank. They then returned to Krjukowo and, together with the *1./SS-Infanterie-Regiment "Deutschland"*, repulsed the attacking Russians who, by then, were attacking continuously.

The division's reserve company, which had been employed with

Panzergruppe 4 up to that point, was requested to be returned to the division. It was set in march to point 206.0 south of Manichino to screen the division's south flank.

Around 1500 hours the enemy advanced in battalion strength along the Istra toward Lushki and reached the woods west of Lamanowo — Krjukowo. That placed him behind friendly lines.

The southern wing of *SS-Division "Reich"* therefore had to be pulled back to the area north of Lamanowo.

The infantry broke contact with the enemy at 1600 hours, covered by the *Sturmgeschütze*. It was bitterly cold and an intense snow squall reduced visibility.

The men of the division marched and fought during those difficult days from 8 - 10 December with icy calm, even though the great elan of the first months had evaporated and their mood had sunk to the null point. Several enemy tanks were destroyed in individual combat and every Russian attempt to break through the extremely thinly held lines was for naught.

On the Russian side, the 8th Guards Rifle Division "Panfilow" and the 1st Guards Armored Brigade fought against *SS-Division "Reich"*.

***

SS-Unterscharführer Ernst Streng of the *2./SS-Infanterie-Regiment "Deutschland"* wrote about the experiences of the withdrawal at the time:

Retrograde Movement

In the early morning hours of 10 December the remnants of the regiments and battalions marched back from the broad high ground to the city of Istra. Snow lay in the streets and ruins, fine powder snow. It had drifted together in places into entire walls. A truck had been sent to us on which all the equipment and weapons were loaded. The sky was reddened by the reflection of the fires in the night. The snow shone. It was a long, arduous march and every one was preoccupied with his own thoughts. We stumbled and slid forward and dragged ourselves through the snow...

The dark walls of the citadel of Istra loomed over the black water of the river. Gray fog and mist floated over the deep valley...

...While combat engineers and the available trains elements blasted and hacked out the new earthen bunkers of the line of resistance at the river bank and on the west slope into the meter-deep frozen earth in arduous labor, the infantry formations, exhausted by the long night march, slept in the warm huts of the village during the bright December day...

***

In order to make possible the timely construction of the Istra position on the west bank of the river, a tank company of the *10. Panzer-Division* was positioned on the wooded hills about five kilometers east of Istra with the last few tanks. They had the mission of holding off the tentatively pursuing leading elements of the enemy for as long as possible and then crossing over from the east bank.

***

In the history of *Panzer-Regiment 7* by *Oberst* Walter Straub we read:

After a heavy mortar and artillery barrage, the Russians attacked with several tanks. An 8.8-cm *Flak* that was screening along the road set one Russian 52-ton tank and two light tanks on fire. One of our own tanks was hit in the running gear and another ran over a mine. Fortunately, only one man was wounded. Both of our tanks attempted to move back. Additional Russian T 34's that arrived were driven off by the fire of our tanks so that the withdrawal movement that had been begun could proceed smoothly.

The tanks fell back as the last unit and, on their way, picked up the *SS* combat engineers. The tank company had fulfilled its mission. It crossed the Istra to the west and returned to the battalion.

With the departure of the last fighting unit of the *10. Panzer-Division*, which ended with a comradely act toward the *SS* combat engineers, SS-Division *"Reich"* became the last major combat formation left in the XXXX. Panzer-Korps.

The Istra Position

11 December 1941

The war diary of the *XXXX. Panzer-Korps* for 11 December 1941:

By midnight of 10/11 December the main body of *SS-Division "Reich"* successfully pulled back to the west bank of the Istra River. By early morning both of the Istra bridges had been blown up. Weak combat outposts remained at Polewo — Petschkowo — Jermolino. However, they fell back before the pursuing enemy to the west bank of the Istra at 1230 hours.

Friendly artillery fire scattered the approaching enemy, who pulled back into the wooded area east of Istra. Friendly artillery fire was fired exclusively on the east bank of the Istra.

Except for a few enemy patrols on skis, which were outfitted with snow shirts, no enemy could be identified in front of the new line of defense.

The difficult disengagement could be considered to have been completed successfully by the evening of 11 December. Poor visibility, snow squalls and low cloud cover made enemy air action impossible, thus preventing accurate air and ground reconnaissance. That significantly assisted the division's disengagement. However, great difficulties still had to be overcome. The great shortage of prime movers made necessary an echeloned withdrawal of almost all of the heavy weapons. Because of the persistent cold, most of the motor vehicles had to be towed away ahead of time. Clutches and transmissions were frozen. In addition, vehicles of the *10. Panzer-Division* were still on the road, significantly complicating the smooth flow of vehicles

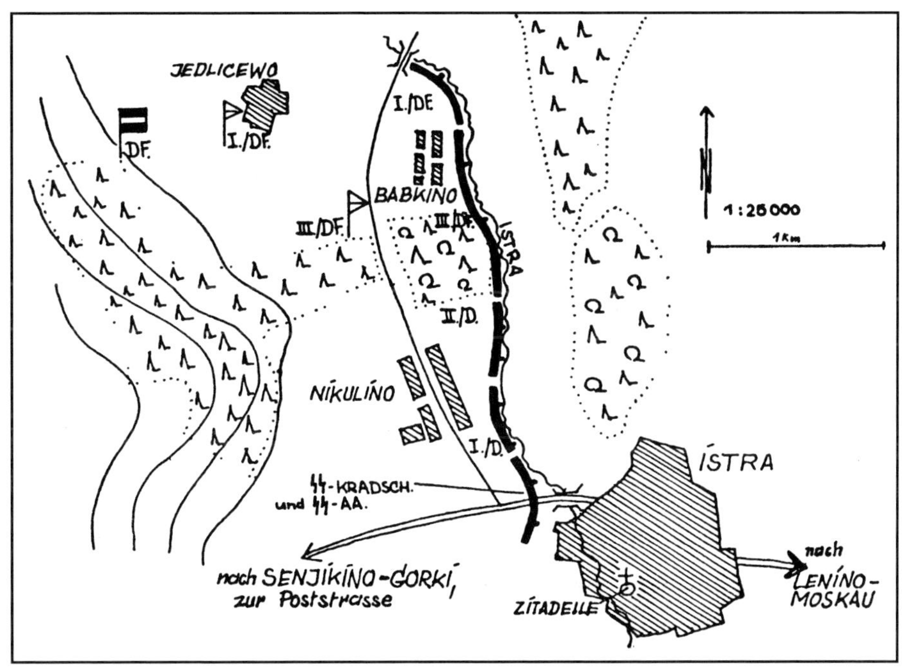

The Istra Position, 11 - 14 December 1941

of *SS-Division "Reich"*.

***

A Teletype from the commander-in-chief of the army, *Generalfeldmarschall* von Brauchitsch, arrived at the corps. The following was immediately passed on to the corps formations:

> The difficulty of the situation at the front — in battle with the enemy and nature — is fully known to me and, likewise, to our Supreme Commander. Everything is being done to bring forward troops and supplies as soon as possible to bring relief. I am personally aware of the demands I must make on the officers and forces at Germany's behest until the relief can become perceptible.
>
> My faith in the victorious spirit of the German soldier continues.
>
> The Commander in Chief:
> /signed/ von Brauchitsch

***

General Stumme and his chief of staff met with the commander of *Panzergruppe 4*, *Generaloberst* Hoepner, to discuss the situation. *General* Stumme presented the situation of the *XXXX. Panzer-Korps* to the commander of *Panzergruppe 4* as indicated in the corps war diary:

> *SS-Division "Reich"* has successfully conducted defensive fighting in recent days, exacting heavy casualties from the enemy. The fighting strength of the division has

been severely diminished by heavy losses in killed and wounded. It is, however, still in a position to successfully defend in its sector west of the Istra River for a long time.

The *Generaloberst* (Hoepner) pointed out that the central sector of the *Panzergruppe* (*SS-Division "Reich"*) was secure; the situation at Klin (*Panzergruppe 3*) and on the north wing of the *V. Armee-Korps* was extremely tense. A counterattack by the *2. Panzer-Division* could not continue due to shortage of fuel." (end of the entry in the war diary).

***

The division order for the improvement of the Istra position for that same day (11 December) ordered the sector commanders to work closely with the supporting combat engineers. The sectors were broken down as follows:

Right: *SS-Kradschützen-Bataillon "Reich"* (Klingenberg)

Center: *SS-Infanterie-Regiment "Deutschland"* (Harmel)

Left: *SS-Infanterie-Regiment "Der Führer"* (Kumm)

The order directed the improvement of the fighting and squad positions, to include the digging of tunnels, the improvement of camouflage, the installation of shields from antitank guns at machine-gun positions, the setting up of the issued stoves, the mining of the west bank of the Istra and the construction of barbed-wire obstacles after the arrival of the wire. Positions in the depth of the main defensive area were to be reconnoitered and, after completion of the above, constructed.

All of the division's vehicles that had not been able to be repaired by the maintenance personnel of the formations were to be set in march to the *4. Werkstattkompanie* (4th Maintenance Company) in Moshaisk by 12 December at the latest.

The division command post was located in Brykowo.

The following combat engineer units were directed to support the sector commanders:

With *SS-Kradschützen-Bataillon "Reich"*: *Pionier-Bataillon 48* (army)

With *SS-Infanterie-Regiment "Deutschland"*: *SS-Pionier-Bataillon "Reich"*, to which the *1./Pionier-Bataillon 752* (army) and the *1./Straßenbau-Bataillon 507* (army) (507th Road Construction Battalion) was attached.

With *SS-Infanterie-Regiment "Der Führer"*: *Panzer-Pionier-Bataillon 49 (army)*.

***

The commander of *SS-Division "Reich"* issued the following order of the day on 11 December 1941:

Order of the Day

Men of SS-Division "*Reich*"!

In three weeks of extremely heavy fighting with a stubborn enemy you have destroyed numerous enemy units in spite of the intense cold and advanced to within a few kilometers of Moscow.

Even though the attack has now been halted and we have gone into a defensive position behind the Istra, that does not represent a withdrawal in the face of enemy strength. It is far more due to the onset of a hard winter that has caused such great difficulties in combat operations that a winter position has been occupied.

The battle for the liberation of Germany and the destruction of Bolshevism goes on. In spite of all difficulties that we may yet run into we shall achieve final victory.

Hail to the *Führer*!
/signed/ Bittrich

12 December 1941

The enemy did not pursue. Everything remained quiet along the division's front.

The Istra position was to be the winter position. With respect to terrain, it was a strong sector and was to be enhanced further daily. The soldiers of the division calmly awaited the enemy, who only felt his way forward slowly and tentatively.

***

The combat-engineer units that had been employed in the position provided valuable service. The achievements of the division's combat engineers, as well as the army combat-engineer units that had supported the division during the advance on Moscow and the withdrawal to the Istra position, cannot be sufficiently praised. Their employment in constructing bridges and routes, in clearing and laying mines and, above all, in constructing positions and building bunkers in the Istra position provided decisive help to the infantry. Indeed, the combat engineers often provided the prerequisites for continuation of the battle.

They worked around the clock in icy cold, in snow squalls, ice and rain, often to the absolute limit of total physical exhaustion. Their share in the successful advance and the successful withdrawal was enormous.

***

The adjutant of *SS-Infanterie-Regiment "Deutschland"*, *SS-Obersturmbannfüher* Schuster, was wounded during a Russian low-level air attack on the regiment's command post in Senjikino. His successor was *SS-Obersturmführer* Diercks, who had been the acting commander of the *II./SS-Infanterie-Regiment "Deutschland"*.

***

A Teletype from *Panzergruppe 4* announced on 10 December that the corps headquarters of the *XXXX. Panzer-Korps* along with corps troops and artillery would be withdrawn from the central sector and held at the disposal of the *Panzergruppe* after the new defensive front had been occupied.

***

The war diary of the *XXXX. Panzer-Korps* includes in its entry for 12 December:

The operations officer of the *XXXXVI. Panzer-Korps* arrived at the corps command post to discuss the assumption of a command relationship over the forces employed in the sector of the *XXXX. Panzer-Korps...*

The chief of staff stated the following:

SS-Division "Reich", which is presently holding the sector of the *XXXX. Panzer-Korps*, had fought very well. The fighting strength was severely diminished. The heavy weapons, however, were largely in order. The division would be able to hold its defensive sector at least as long as the Istra River remained unfrozen. Regulation of the flow of water from the reservoir might possibly prevent the Istra from freezing.

Three battalions of combat engineers were employed carrying out demolitions and laying mines in the terrain leading to the line of defense. The museum bastion had been sufficiently destroyed to deny the enemy possibilities for observation. Construction of positions had progressed to the point where heated living quarters and firing ports were available for the front line. Construction of rearward positions, however, was yet to take place. The chief of staff emphasized in particular that the right flank of the division was the danger point and that, at present, the corps combat-engineer battalion was employed there constructing a blocking position.

At present the entire artillery of the corps was committed. It was intended, however, to withdraw one battalion immediately. It was also expected that the artillery of the *10. Panzer-Division* would be withdrawn very soon...

***

Within three days the Rusa position was fully prepared for defense. The friendly force to the left of *SS-Division "Reich"* was the *5. Panzer-Division*, which had first arrived in November.

The friendly forces on the right had crossed the Istra and fallen back far to the west. This completely exposed the right wing of the division. The situation on the left wing with the *5. Panzer-Division* was exactly the same.

13 December 1941

The war diary of the *XXXX. Panzer-Korps* reported the following for 13 December 1941:

SS-Division "*Reich*" leaves the XXXX. Panzer-Korps.

The commanding general commends the division's accomplishments and parts with them with the following:

Order of the Day

Today *SS-Division "Reich"* departs from the area of my command.

From the Desna via Gshatsk, Jelnja, Moshaisk, Goroditsche, Cholujanicha, Istra and Lenino you have cleared the way deep into the outer fortifications of Moscow in a continuous series of victorious engagements.

I am pleased with and proud of your deeds, which are already a part of the history of the war, but it is also with heartfelt regrets that I part from you. I know that you will remain the men on whom the *Führer* and Supreme Commander can depend in any situation, no matter how bad it may appear.

I wish continued success to this proud division, a soldier's good fortune to each and a happy homecoming after the war is successfully concluded.

Long live *Führer*, folk and fatherland!

/signed/ Stumme
General der Panzertruppen

DISTRIBUTION:

SS-Division "Reich"

to the company level.

***

SS-Division "Reich", along with the *5. Panzer-Division*, immediately came under the command of *General der Panzertruppen* von Vietinghoff's *XXXXVI. Panzer-Korps*. The division had already fought with the *XXXXVI. Panzer-Korps* from the initial portion of the Russian campaign through the defensive fighting in the Jelnja salient.

The enemy advanced most rapidly in the sector of *SS-Infanterie-Regiment "Deutschland"*. At 0800 hours it was reported that the enemy had constructed a footbridge over the Istra directly east of Nikulino, and about two squads were already on the west bank. An immediate artillery barrage laid down in barrage area C forced back or destroyed the enemy. The east bank of the Istra and the field fortifications that were available there were strongly held. Movement within friendly positions was impossible during the day.

At 1100 hours the enemy was spotted assembling to cross at the same place with rubber rafts in the strength of approximately two battalions. Outstanding artillery support with barrages from both battalions smashed that attempt.

In the evening a strong assault troop of the *16./SS-Infanterie-Regiment "Deutschland"* beat back weak enemy forces that had already reached the west bank.

SS-Kradschützen-Bataillon "Reich", which alternately relieved and was relieved by *SS-Aufklärungs-Abteilung "Reich"*, occupied its positions at noon.

Sounds of heavy fighting could be heard from the area of the friendly forces on the right. The sounds once again shifted toward the rear.

***

In spite of the difficult situation, the men of the division did not give in. The following song was sung with true gallows humor to the strains of *"Lili Marlen"* among the men of *SS-Kradschützen-Bataillon "Reich"*:

On the road from Moscow is a battalion,
It is the last bits of our division.
We once gazed at Moscow from afar,
Then had to bolt, to save our skins,
Just like Napoleon, just like Napoleon.

Auf der Straß' von Moskau zieht ein Bataillon,
es sind die letzten Reste von unsrer Division.
Wir sah'n Moskau schon von ferne stehn;
jedoch wir mußten stiften gehn,
Wie einst Napoleon, wie einst Napoleon.

14 December 1941

After the enemy had been repulsed with heavy losses in several attacks against the division's positions and those of the *5. Panzer-Division*, he advanced past both sides of the positions and outflanked the two divisions. That presented the danger of encirclement, the enemy's obvious objective.

Holding the Istra position thus proved illusory. The tragic situation that resulted was that the division had to suddenly evacuate a strong, winter-proof defensive position. It could have been held throughout the winter and successfully defended. It had been outmaneuvered by outflanking the two divisions.

After another enemy attack had been successfully repulsed with rocket-launcher support in the sector of the *I./SS-Infanterie-Regiment "Deutschland"*, the verbal warning order was issued by the division in the afternoon for all vehicles from all formations to move west. Since many vehicles were not operational, major transportation difficulties ensued.

***

The commanding general of the *XXXXVI. Panzer-Korps*, *General der Panzertruppen* von Vietinghoff, issued the following guidelines to his commanders on that day:

Guidelines for Commanders.

(Operations: Number 1409/41 (SECRET), 14 December 1941)

After months of incomparable achievements by our soldiers and unprecedented success for our corps in the Wjasma fighting against an enemy far superior in numbers and equipment, the ensuing fighting pursuit has finally come to a halt and been replaced by retrograde movements. It is necessary to explain the reason for these measures to the soldiers to prevent the formation of a false picture of the situation.

Therefore, I give the following guidelines to the commanders. Unfortunately, I am unable to assemble you for a personal discussion given the present combat situation:

1.) The reason for and objective of our operations against Soviet Russia was and is the destruction of Bolshevist armed forces. The territory gained in so doing is a bonus but is not essential.

2.) The superiority of our army, the source of our great success, lies in a war of maneuver that has found its classic expression in the great pocket battles.

The main body of the old Bolshevik army and an immense amount of materiel has been destroyed in the process.

In order to take advantage of that success, pursuit to the utmost limit of our capabilities was necessary. It found its limit at the moment when winter made a war of maneuver impossible and, simultaneously, we ran up against fresh Russian units that brought our movements to a halt against their fortified positions.

3.) Positional warfare — and its offshoot, the attack against such positions — expends combat power to a high degree without any successes comparable to those attainable in a war of maneuver. Our supreme command has made a major decision to call a halt to the war of movement.

4.) It is vitally important to totally free ourselves of all recollections of the positional warfare of the World War, in which each success, every foot of ground gained, every village won had to be defended in costly fighting.

It is better to occupy a position after a broad withdrawal that can be held throughout the winter with the smallest possible force expenditure, the greatest sparing of the troops and where refitting the divisions can proceed.

Whether that position is at the Istra or — to name an extreme example — at the Desna, is a matter of complete indifference from the overall perspective. By occupying such a position we force the enemy to pursue under conditions that are unfavorable for him. In so doing, we will gain the initiative for renewed major battles of maneuver next summer.

5.) The time of transition until occupation of the final position is difficult. It demands tough, effective, foresighted leadership, tight cohesion of the unit, the best organization of movements, unshakeable fighting spirit and iron discipline.

6.) At our level, the enemy's strong flanking advances to the Moskwa and south of the Volga reservoir north of Klin have succeeded in putting our most forward attacking elements in a difficult situation which, at present, has not yet been resolved. The bulk of our withdrawal movements depend on the outcome of the heavy fighting currently in progress there.

7.) Our corps is the only corps in the *Panzergruppe* to date that hasn't been threatened in the flanks and has held a coherent front. As a result, it forms the solid nucleus of the withdrawal movements.

I have continued confidence that the fighting spirit of the troops of my corps, which has remained at such an unusually high level and has been proven in so much intense fighting, will prove itself equally well in conditions that, as a result of the cold, are particularly difficult.

The Commanding General
/signed/ von Vietinghoff.

The above guidelines are only to be transmitted verbally and then destroyed.

***

In *SS-Division "Reich"* the above guidelines were passed on down to the battalion commanders.

15 December 1941

The westward movement of vehicles took place slowly. Many had to be towed. Badly damaged vehicles were blown up, their wrecks littering the route of withdrawal.

At 1400 hours the Division Order for the Movements from 15 - 17 December 1941 reached the units. It read, in part:

1.) The enemy facing the *XXXXVI. Panzer-Korps*, to date, exhibits only combat-patrol activity and artillery harassing fire. His attempts to cross the Istra have been thwarted so far.

Enemy penetrations have succeeded in the fronts of both adjoining corps, which has forced the front to be pulled back.

2.) The deliberate withdrawal will begin on 15 December 1941.

The *XXXXVI. Panzer-Korps,* to which *SS-Division "Reich"* has been attached since 13 December 1941, is initially organizing itself for defense behind the sectors of Oserna and Grjada.

SS-Division "Reich" is in the following sector (boundaries also apply for billeting in rear areas):

Right: Sloboda (exclusive) — Pokrowskoje — Matweizewo — Pachonjewo (including built-up areas) — Djakowo (exclusive)

Left: Schilowo — Sobowo (excluding built-up areas) — Karabusino (inclusive) — Glasowo (exclusive)

Friendly forces on the right: *IX. Armee-Korps.*

Friendly forces on the left: *5. Panzer-Division.*

3.) Three sectors are specified:

Right: *SS-Kradschützen-Bataillon "Reich"* with attached *SS-Aufklärungs-Abteilung "Reich"*

Center: *SS-Infanterie-Regiment "Deutschland"*

Left: *SS-Infanterie-Regiment "Der Führer"*

4.) General course of the main line of resistance:

Northeast outskirts of Pokrowskoje — northeast outskirts of Wert. Stjadkewo — course of the Grjada River.

...

The designated withdrawal route ordered: Choujanicha — Duplewo — Bely — Nikolskoje — Lyskowo — new main defensive area or billeting area.

The rearguard, which initially is to remain in contact with the enemy, will consist of:

1 reinforced battalion of *SS-Infanterie-Regiment "Deutschland"* (*II./SS-Infanterie-Regiment "Deutschland"*)
1 reinforced battalion of *SS-Infanterie-Regiment "Der Führer"*
1 light artillery battalion
1 *Sturmgeschütz* platoon

The commander of the rearguard is the commander of *SS-Infanterie-Regiment "Der Führer"*, *SS-Obersturmbannführer* Kumm.

***

The vehicles only flowed very slowly to the west. Serious damage to the road at Jadromino and Cholujanicha caused long stops for the vehicle columns. A steep stretch at Bely occasioned giant traffic jams. Many vehicles had to be blown up. The same picture held true near Nikolskoje. Although everyone went to extremely great pains to bring back vehicles, weapons and equipment, the state of the weather, the condition of the roads and the mechanical failure of many vehicles often made that impossible.

The withdrawal movement began around 1600 hours.

Since the withdrawal of the rearguard was set to begin at 2400 hours, the movement of the main body had to be concluded as rapidly as possible.

Around 1800 hours *SS-Aufklärungs-Abteilung "Reich"* reported from the right wing that the enemy had broken through the friendly forces on the right, a battalion of the *252. Infanterie-Division*. In order to avoid being outflanked, the reconnaissance battalion pulled back its right wing.

At 2025 hours the *II./SS-Infanterie-Regiment "Deutschland"*, as part of the rearguard, disengaged from the enemy ahead of schedule in accordance with a telephoned verbal order of the division. Around 2300 hours, it occupied the first passage position along the line: Jadromino — Lissino. *SS-Infanterie-Regiment "Deutschland"* occupied a billeting area with the reinforced *I./SS-Infanterie-Regiment "Deutschland"* and the regiment's command post in Nikolskoje.

The command section of *SS-Infanterie-Regiment "Deutschland"* joined the military police in regulating traffic in Nikolskoje. Almost every vehicle had one or two other vehicles in tow.

Since the route of retreat was the only road for the division and the open right flank occasioned a certain degree of nervousness among the drivers, a tight grip and energetic involvement by all ranks was required to prevent chaos.

During the evacuation of Dedeschino, *Sturmgeschütz "Lützow"* failed to start due to engine problems. Attempts to take it in tow proved unsuccessful and, along with one staff car and two captured trucks, it had to be blown up. During the withdrawal movement, the *"Prinz Eugen"* broke through the ice on Magluscha Creek and sank half way in. Attempts to pull it out failed and it also had to be blown up — two irreplaceable losses!

As the *4./SS-Kradschützen-Bataillon "Reich"* left the village where it had been billeted, Russian tanks moved into the other side.

The rest of the rearguard disengaged from the enemy at midnight. Continuing snowfall and black ice made the road conditions indescribably bad. Some of the vehicles remained stuck along the route of withdrawal and had to be blown up. It was hard for the men to part with their vehicles. They had represented a little bit of home for so long. The last of their personal possessions were frequently stored on them. At this point they only had what they could carry on their backs — and that belonged to the army.

SS-Obersturmführer Buch, the adjutant of *SS-Kradschützen-Bataillon "Reich"* at the time, describes a particular accomplishment in the following:

A Daring Feat

On 15 December 1941 *SS-Kradschützen-Bataillon "Reich"* withdrew from the Istra sector. The *1./SS-Kradschützen-Bataillon "Reich"* was employed on the division's right wing on the boundary with the *252. Infanterie-Division*. The company had sent the sidecar motorcycles to the rear. They could no longer be counted on mechanically. Only the reliable machines remained at the front. The ones you could rely upon to be able to withdraw without incidents. Those dependable machines were almost entirely the old *BMW R 12's*, built in 1935. They had been carefully broken in during peacetime and had been carefully maintained.

When the motorcycle battalion was pulling out, the headquarters section leader of the *1./SS-Kradschützen-Bataillon "Reich"*, *SS-Hauptscharführer* Hans Bader, came to the battalion command post. The commander hoped to hear that the company's withdrawal was proceeding as ordered. However, he discovered that, for unexplained reasons, the order had not made it to the company and the company was still in its previous position.

The only route of withdrawal for the battalion was the old post road, which approached Istra from the northwest. That road, already saturated with bomb and shell craters, had already been negotiated by T 34's.

In peacetime, Hans Bader had spent years as a motorcycle messenger in the *15. (Kradschützen)/SS-Infanterie-Regiment "Deutschland"* in Munich. At that time he had repeatedly demonstrated his mastery of the *R 12* solo *BMW* at the Bavarian country fairs and at the *Oktoberfest* by riding his motorcycle while standing, tests of driver's skills, jumping through flaming rings and the like. At that point Bader's driving skills came to his aid. The long peacetime practice and his bravery were the salvation of his company. He took a good 750 cc solo machine and raced back to his company over the icy post road with no regard for the Russians and their T 34's. He informed his company of the order to withdraw.

The company was able to make its way out of the nearly complete encirclement with no personnel losses, though they did have to abandon their motorcycles. Bader returned the same way that he had come. He raced through the startled Russians and back to the battalion. He was able to report that his company was falling back to the designated new line.

Hans Bader was awarded the German Cross in Gold for that daredevil performance. Bader was killed in action on 8 August 1944 as an *SS-Obersturmführer* and company commander at Tukkum in Latvia.

16 December 1941

As the last elements of the rearguard of *SS-Infanterie-Regiment "Der Führer"* went over to the defensive in the designated line in the gray dawn light, the other elements of the division continued the withdrawal movement in the early morning.

The echeloned withdrawal of the rearguard was again successful. Late in the morning, the *II./SS-Infanterie-Regiment "Deutschland"* as rearguard, withdrew from the second line of resistance and blocked the Oserna River in the line Grinkowo — Nikolskoje. It had the mission of blowing up the bridge at Nikolskoje after the last vehicles had crossed.

The enemy was hesitant in following the withdrawal movement. Fuel shortages gradually became evident among the division vehicles.

The division thereupon advised all commanders that every possible means must be used to bring back all vehicles, equipment and weapons.

The withdrawal movement proceeded extremely sluggishly since the prescribed route (Borodenka — Sloboda — Lyskowo — Petrowskoje) was jammed with the vehicles of three divisions: The *10. Panzer-Division*, *SS-Division "Reich"* and the *252. Infanterie-Division*.

At 2200 hours all elements of the rearguard battalion (the *II./SS-Infanterie-Regiment "Deutschland"*) had reached the second blocking position and prepared the bridge for demolition. The main route of retreat was blocked with mines by the combat engineers. A major traffic jam formed outside of Pokrowskoje as a result of a steep stretch of road.

***

SS-Obergruppenführer und General der Waffen-SS Hausser discussed the withdrawal in his personal notes:

Two orders from the *OKW* limited the movements. An order on 16 December required "fanatical resistance" and forbade major withdrawal movements.

It is probably for this reason that the words "retreat" and "withdrawal" no longer appeared in division orders. Instead, the orders referred to "falling back". In reality, however, the movements were withdrawal movements to new positions.

The Grjada Position

17 December 1941

After all operational vehicles had crossed the bridge at Nikolskoje, it was blown up at 0230 hours.

During the course of the morning, the main body of *SS-Infanterie-Regiment "Deutschland"* arrived in the Samoschkino area.

After the company commanders of the *I./SS-Infanterie-Regiment "Deutschland"* had been briefed, the battalion occupied the Grjada position in the afternoon. The defensive sector was four kilometers wide. Unfortunately, it offered good opportunities for the enemy to approach it. There were only an extremely limited number of bunkers. Those that existed were in very poor condition. The day brought particularly intense cold, which only increased the difficulties.

The enemy was soon there. Some of the enemy forces were winter units on skis that clung closely to friendly movements. Both regiments and the reinforced *SS-Kradschützen-Bataillon "Reich"* fought until darkness fell. During the night of 16/17 December the next rearward bound took place.

An enemy penetration of the corps adjoining on the right (the *IX. Armee-Korps*) threatened the right wing of *SS-Division "Reich"* and offered the enemy the possibility for envelopment. Therefore, the intention was to fall back to yet a new line of resistance with sharply pulled back right wing.

During the night of 17/18 December the following order went out to the units (excerpts):

Division Movement Order for 18 December 1941

1.) The enemy is following our movements with infantry and some armor as we fall back.

2.) The *XXXXVI. Panzer-Korps* is to continue a deliberate retreat to the southwest in order to evade envelopment resulting from the extension of the penetration east of Rusa. It is essential to bring back all guns and heavy weapons in a timely manner. The destruction of vehicles, particularly those that can no longer proceed under their own power, must be accepted, but is not to take place until the last units of infantry overtake them.

The southwest bank of the Rusa will be reached in several phases during the course of the day. The defense will be resumed on that bank and held by order of the

Führer.

3.) *SS-Division "Reich"* is to conduct the retreat as follows:

a) All vehicles not required for the fighting retreat are to be sent back immediately on the division's march route over the Rusa and to be taken to the new billeting area in accordance with paragraph...The movements are also to be continued throughout the night without a break.

b) The main body of the division is to reach the Oserna line by 0700 hours on 18 December. It is to maintain contact on the right with the *252. Infanterie-Division* (at Lyskowo) and the *5. Panzer-Division* on the left.

c) During the course of 18 December the forward combat-outpost line is to be pulled back with the left wing at Pritykino. The right wing is to be pulled back in accordance with the retrograde movements of the *252. Infanterie-Division.*

It is intended to reach the following line by 1600 hours on 18 December: Nikulniki — Jeruli — Weina — Nemirowo — Pritykino.

The objective for pulling back the right wing so radically is to have a defensible position in place in the event of an enemy breakthrough from the southeast.

4.) New boundaries for movement and defense:

To the right with the *252. Infanterie-Division*: Pokrowskoje — Nikulniki — Laschino — Borowino (villages: *SS-Division "Reich"*.)

To the left with the *5. Panzer-Division*: Schtschalkanowo (*5. Panzer-Division*) — Pritikyno — ...

Boundary separating *SS-Infanterie-Regiment "Deutschland"* on the right and *SS-Infanterie-Regiment "Der Führer"* on the left (On the Oserna): Wert — Stjadkowo (*SS-Infanterie-Regiment "Deutschland"*) — Samaschkino (*SS-Infanterie-Regiment "Deutschland"*) — Weina (*SS-Infanterie-Regiment "Der Führer"*).

5.) The regiments have to conduct the fighting in such fashion that strongpoints will be formed on the roads leading from the east and southeast. They will avoid a continuous occupation of the designated lines. Patrols are to maintain contact between those strongpoints. It is essential to be able to defend in the event of an enemy advance at any location in spite of the great width of the sector...

***

Generalfeldmarschall von Bock fell seriously ill on 17 December 1941 and had to give up his command. *Generalfeldmarschall* von Kluge assumed command of the army group. Command of the *4. Armee* passed to *General der Gebirgstruppen* Kübler.

18 December 1941

SS-Kradschützen-Bataillon "Reich" and the attached *SS-Aufklärungs-Abteilung "Reich"* were to be withdrawn in the early morning and reach Wederniki on the division's route of march. Once there, they were to come under divisional control. As a result, the *I./SS-Infanterie-Regiment*

"Deutschland" had to also assume their screening mission at Pokrowskoje in the form of strongpoints. As a result, the battalion's sector was greatly enlarged.

The enemy did not probe the division's front very hard. On the other hand, sounds of heavy fighting could be heard from the sector of the *252. Infanterie-Division* on the right.

As noon approached, the two regiments renewed their rearward movement — first *SS-Infanterie-Regiment "Deutschland"* then *"SS-Infanterie-Regiment "Der Führer"* — were to again go over to the defensive in the line designated in the orders. The rearward movement of the motor vehicles caused increasing difficulties. In order to save those vehicles that were still operational, all the vehicles that were in tow had to be destroyed.

***

At 1815 hours the following order went out to the units by radio:

The line designated in the radio traffic at 1545 hours has been overtaken by events.

Starting at 0900 hours on 19 December, the regiments are to move as far as the line 500 meters southwest and west of Weretenki. They are to move via Rupzow.

Right: *SS-Kradschützen-Bataillon "Reich"*. Center: *SS-Infanterie-Regiment "Deutschland"*. Left: *SS-Infanterie-Regiment "Der Führer"*.

19 December 1941

The enemy probed the division's combat outposts with weak forces and attacked the sector of the *I./SS-Infanterie-Regiment "Deutschland"* with a company-sized element. Thereupon the battalion fell back to and held Berjaski until the rearward moving *II./SS-Infanterie-Regiment "Deutschland"* had reached its assigned position. The latter was committed to the right of the *I./SS-Infanterie-Regiment "Deutschland"* at noon.

As evening approached, the vehicles moved out somewhat more rapidly, since all the drivers had been ruthlessly aggressive with regard to the destruction of towed motor vehicles. In addition, limited quantities of fuel arrived.

Determination of the course of the main line of resistance, which was only to be held in the form of strongpoints, was left to the discretion of the battalion commanders. This was a sign that this line of defense would only be held temporarily.

In the evening the report arrived that Hitler had relieved *Generalfeldmarschall* von Brauchitsch on 19 December and personally assumed supreme command over the Army.

The following "*Führer* Decree" arrived from Hitler's headquarters:

From: The *Führer* and Supreme Commander of the *Wehrmacht*:

To: Soldiers of the Army and the *Waffen-SS*!

The struggle for the freedom of our people approaches its high point. Decisions of worldwide significance are imminent. The mainstay of the battle is the army. As a result, I have personally taken command of the army this day. As a soldier in many battles in the World War I feel myself extremely closely united with you in our will to victory.

/signed/ Adolf Hitler

***

The previous commander-in-chief of the army, *Generalfeldmarschall* von Brauchitsch, issued the following order of the day regarding his relinquishment of the command of the army:

Order of the Day to the Army

Soldiers!

As of this day, at a time of impending extremely important decisions, the *Führer* has assumed command of the army as the mainstay of the battle. At the same time he has accepted my request of some time standing to relieve me of command of the army because of my heart condition.

Soldiers! For nearly four years, I have led the best army in the world as your commander-in-chief. Those years include a plenitude of the greatest historical events for Germany and, for the army, the greatest military successes. I look back on this time with pride and gratitude, proud of your accomplishments, grateful for your loyalty.

Great tasks have been accomplished. Great and difficult ones lie ahead.

I am convinced that you will also accomplish those. The *Führer* will lead us to victory.

Harden your will like steel, look to the future.

Everything for Germany!

/signed/ von Brauchitsch
Generalfeldmarschall

***

The change in the highest level of command of the army was met with mixed feelings among the men of the division. It was yet another example of how critical the situation had become in which the German army in the east had been forced to retreat from Moscow. On the other hand, they reacted with a certain degree of imperturbability. They knew that in such a situation events were almost exclusively dictated by the pursuing enemy and not by the German army command.

For the soldiers of the army and the *Waffen-SS* at the time it was a matter of simple survival. During the fighting retreat and the withdrawal movements every individual was engaged in an immediate struggle against the enemy who was following on foot, against the threat of capture, against hunger, cold, weariness, total physical and mental exhaustion and also against his own resignation.

For the simple soldier at the front, the change in the highest level of command at that moment had only secondary significance.

***

In the evening of 19 December the following divisional order was issued (excerpts):

Division Order
for the Defense of the Rusa Position

1.) The Russians have not succeeded in their attempt to encircle the *XXXXVI. Panzer-Korps*. In a planned withdrawal, the corps has fallen back to a bridgehead position that will be held on 19 December. On 20 December the corps is to go back across the Rusa from the bridgehead. It is to leave combat outposts on the northeast bank.

It is only thanks to the discipline and the iron will of all officers and men that the enemy was denied the success he hoped for and that the forces came through the crisis with the minimum possible losses in materiel.

The enemy is slowly following our movement. He is exerting stronger pressure on the *IX. Armee-Korps* and on the left wing of the *XXXXVI. Panzer-Korps.*

2.) The *XXXXVI. Panzer-Korps* is to hold the Rusa position.

Task organization:
Right: *SS-Division "Reich"*
Left: *5. Panzer-Division* with attached *Kampfverband Scheller.*

Friendly forces on the right: 252. Infanterie-Division (IX. Armee-Korps)

3.) Boundaries for defense and reconnaissance:

a) Between the *252. Infanterie-Division* and *SS-Division "Reich"*: Laschino (*SS-Division "Reich"*) — Schtscherbinki (*SS-Division "Reich"*) — Borowino (*SS-Division "Reich"*)

b) Between *SS-Division "Reich"* and the *5. Panzer-Division*: Slidmowo — southeast outskirts of Warakssino — Ostaschewo — Terechowa (villages for *SS-Division "Reich"*)

4.) Task organization:

Right: *SS-Kradschützen-Bataillon "Reich"* with attached *SS-Aufklärungs-Abteilung "Reich"*
Center: *SS-Infanterie-Regiment "Deutschland"*
Left: *SS-Infanterie-Regiment "Der Führer"*

5.) Main line of resistance is the Rusa. On the left wing (on the boundary with the *5. Panzer-Division*), the main line of resistance is to be extended from the knee of the bend in the river 500 meters north of Owinischtschi to the knee of the bend in the river at Warakssino, if possible. Establish contact there with the *5. Panzer-*

Division.

6.) The main defensive area is to be reconnoitered in depth as far as the Aschtscherino — Ostaschewo road and gradually improved…

The rest of the order concerned itself with establishing the command and control relationships for the divisional heavy weapons and division troops.

***

The commander of *SS-Infanterie-Regiment "Der Führer"*, *SS-Obersturmbannführer* Otto Kumm, wrote the following in his notes regarding the retreat between Istra and Rusa from 17 to 20 December 1941:

And so it went via Ssloboda — Lyskowo — Kurowa — Scherwinski to behind the Rusa. Defending against Russian attacks by day, wearisome marches through knee-deep snow in icy cold by night — thirty, thirty-five kilometers back.

***

Werner Haupt discussed Hitler's "no-retreat" order in his book:

He (Hitler) issued General Order Number 442 182/41:

"Any large-scale retreat is impermissible, since that would lead to a total loss of heavy weapons and materiel. By personal example the commanders-in-chief, formation commanders and all officers must make the forces defend their present positions with fanatical determination regardless of whether the enemy has broken through on the flanks and in the rear!"

The Soviets attacked the *4. Armee* and the *4. Panzer-Armee* head on in the area west of Moscow. The retreat of the *4. Armee* cost much blood and heavy losses. The losses came less through wounds than through frostbite. Frostbite accounted for more than 90% of all frontline losses.

The Soviet 5th, 33rd and 43rd Armies had advanced through the front of the *4. Armee* starting on 12 December and forced the front back between Juchnow and Moshaisk…(Werner Haupt, *Heeresgruppe Mitte*, p. 115. Bad Nauheim: Podzun-Pallas-Verlag, 1968.)

The Rusa Position

20 December 1941

During the night of 19/20 December the final, particularly exhausting stage was completed. During the morning the battalions reached the new main line of resistance at the Rusa in a single bound.

SS-Kradschützen-Bataillon "Reich" and the motorcycle troops of *SS-Aufklärungs-Abteilung "Reich"* under *SS-Obersturmführer* Pötschke were employed in the right sector, where they maintained contact with the *252. Infanterie-Division.* The boundary with the *252. Infanterie-Division* was in a hollow. The bled white and exhausted division had substantial problems organizing for defense. In order to support it in constructing positions, *SS-*

Kradschützen-Bataillon "Reich" provided the adjoining infantry battalion of the *252. Infanterie-Division* with its combat-engineer platoon under *SS-Obersturmführer* Wegener. The combat engineers constructed a bunker for the battalion staff and a bunker for the left-most squad of the neighboring infantry battalion.

Only a few bunkers were present in the division sector.

SS-Infanterie-Regiment "Deutschland" employed its *I./SS-Infanterie-Regiment "Deutschland"* (command post in Schukowka) on the right and its *II./SS-Infanterie-Regiment "Deutschland"* (command post in Schepujowa) on the left.

SS-Infanterie-Regiment "Der Führer" employed its *III./SS-Infanterie-Regiment "Der Führer"* on the right and its *I./SS-Infanterie-Regiment "Der Führer"* on the left.

Since a large gap still existed between *SS-Infanterie-Regiment "Deutschland"* and *SS-Infanterie-Regiment "Der Führer"*, the division ordered the former to extend its left wing and the latter to extend its right wing. As a result, the regimental boundary area was particularly threatened.

Terrain reconnaissance determined that the ice on the Rusa was 75 cm thick and armor could cross it, at least in the center of the sector.

***

The liaison officer for the divisional logistics officer at the time, *SS-Obersturmführer* Fritz Steinbeck, described the exemplary actions of a *SS-Hauptscharführer* of the supply section of the division staff:

Fuel for the *Sturmgeschütze* at the Last Minute

After the withdrawal before Moscow behind the Rusa in December 1941 *SS-Obersturmführer* Telkamp was stranded east of the Rusa because of lack of fuel. A combat-engineer *Oberleutnant* had orders to blow up the bridge over the Rusa at 0600 hours. *SS-Hauptsturmführer* Enseling of *SS-Pionier-Bataillon "Reich"* made a 16-ton prime mover available to me. A *SS-Hauptscharführer* from the supply section whose name I do not recollect brought several drums of gasoline in the pitch-black night against the flow of traffic of the retreating units filling the narrow path in the woods to the bridge.

There the fuel was transferred to jerry cans and dragged to the *Sturmgeschütze*. They were within sight of the bridge and firing in all directions from a hedgehog position. Covering each other through fire and movement, the *Sturmgeschütze* made it back to the safety of the bridge at the last minute. We all knew what four *Sturmgeschütze* meant to the division in that situation. We also know, however, how to appreciate the accomplishment of the driver and the *SS-Hauptscharführer* whose names are no longer known.

21 December 1941

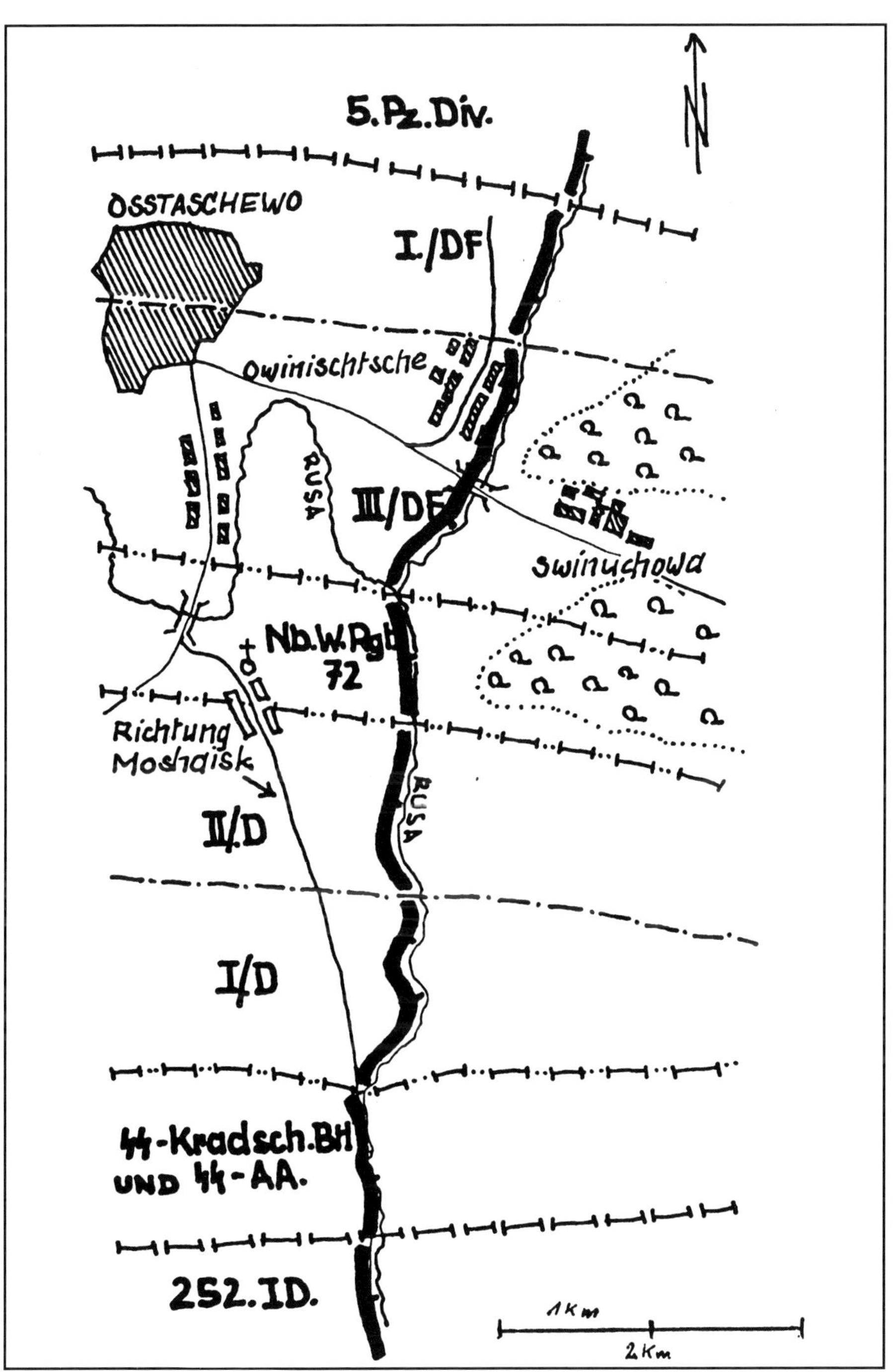

The Rusa Position, 22 - 31 December 1941
(Reconstructed and supplemented by means of a sketch of the *III./SS-Infanterie-Regiment "Der Führer"* and the war diary of the *XXXXVI. Panzer-Korps*)

In his notes, the commander of *SS-Infanterie-Regiment "Der Führer"*, *SS-Obersturmbannführer* Kumm, described his regiment's occupation of the Rusa position as the last combat element to arrive:

In the gray light of dawn of 21 December the battalions reached the Rusa. Some of the heavy infantry weapons were loaded on horse-drawn sleds. The men in their filthy snow-shirts were totally exhausted. It was a picture that would move even the hardest of men. While the commander of the regiment discussed the employment of combat outposts in the previously reconnoitered lines with the battalion commanders, the enemy was already attacking again with strong forces. Under those circumstances, the combat outposts were dispensed with and the regiment was organized for defense as quickly as possible west of the Rusa.

Aside from five or six large holes in the ground in the regiment's approximately six-kilometer-wide sector, there had been no preparations for defense. Just as the battalions were being guided into their sectors — the *III./SS-Infanterie-Regiment "Der Führer"* on the right, the *I./SS-Infanterie-Regiment "Der Führer"* on the left — the enemy broke through in the sector of the *III./SS-Infanterie-Regiment "Der Führer"*. Within half an hour the companies of the *III./SS-Infanterie-Regiment "Der Führer"* threw the enemy back in a ferocious manner with heavy losses for the Soviets.

The portents for the final winter position to be held were not at all good. In spite of the poor prospects, the men immediately began improving the positions. Where spades and pickaxes failed to penetrate the hard, frozen ground, blasting caps and *Teller* mines blew holes. Three days of indescribably exhausting labor — constantly interrupted by defense against strong enemy attacks — and the regiment was ready to defend the Rusa position.

The enemy understood that he could not break through at that location and let up in his activity. Only the hostile artillery fire increased. It disrupted supply routes and caused vehicular losses. Due to the deep snowdrifts, traffic close to the main line of resistance was only possible with *Panje* sleds. Intense cold and the dreaded snowstorms set in. In a few days the landscape was covered with deep snow. Drifts made the roads almost impassible.

So it was that the regiment approached Christmas — frozen pea soup, frozen bread, shoes and socks almost entirely in shreds, supplies highly questionable due to the shortage of winterized locomotives and huge snowdrifts on all roads and highways…

***

Nevertheless, at this point the division finally received winter clothing: Fur-lined parkas and trousers, felt boots and fur coats. Most of the additional Christmas rations that were dropped by *Luftwaffe* transport planes (*Ju 52's*) landed in enemy territory.

In the evening the division learned that the commander of the division, *SS-Brigadeführer und Generalmajor der Waffen-SS* Wilhelm Bittrich, had been awarded the Knight's Cross.

Accordingly, he issued the following order of the day on 21 December 1941:

Order of the Day

Comrades!

At this serious time I have been awarded the Knight's Cross by the *Führer* and Supreme Commander.

You must realize that I do not wear this for myself alone. I see this cross on every warrior of the division. I wear it for the dead and for you who still fight.

With heads held high we will defeat the enemy at the Rusa so that we may gain time for future operations.

I stand in reverence for the dead and for your spirit of sacrifice.

/signed/ Bittrich
SS-Brigadeführer und Generalmajor der Waffen-SS

Sub-Section o)

Defensive Fighting in the Rusa and Wolokolamsk Positions: 22 - 31 December 1941

22 December 1941

The combat outposts of the *I./SS-Infanterie-Regiment "Deutschland"* fell back before heavy enemy pressure — about two companies. Friendly artillery fire prevented the continuation of the enemy attack.

The main line of resistance and the main defensive area in the division's sector continued to be improved. Supply difficulties arose due to the great distance from the trains and drifted snow.

In the afternoon the *II./SS-Infanterie-Regiment "Deutschland"* repulsed an enemy attack with the help of an attached 8.8-cm *Flak*. Three Russian tanks were knocked out. One tank got stuck on the bank of the Istra.

23 December 1941

By order of the division, the Rusa position was reorganized:

Kampfgruppe Dietrich (infantry units of *Nebelwerfer-Regiment 72*), which had been attached to the division, was inserted between *SS-Infanterie-Regiment "Deutschland"* and *SS-Infanterie-Regiment "Der Führer"*, thus narrowing the sectors of the two regiments.

In the overall sector of the division, several enemy attacks were repulsed by artillery fire, and a small penetration was cleaned up by *SS-Kradschützen-Bataillon "Reich"*.

24 December 1941

Since enemy attacks could be expected on Christmas Eve, all Christmas celebrations were forbidden. Only chocolate and cigarettes were distributed from the "Ribbentrop Donations". For the time being, alcohol was withheld. Christmas mail did not arrive.

Replacement officers and enlisted personnel arrived at the units, about four officers and 120 men per regiment.

The commanding general and the division commander issued Christmas orders.

The commanding officers and their adjutants visited the men in the bunkers of the main line of resistance. Once the men had received a bit of rest after the long hardships, they exhibited an excellent and confident mood.

Somehow even a bit of Christmas spirit was conjured up. Traditional Christmas carols were played on a harmonica. Diminutive Christmas trees decked with silver threads and lights appeared from somewhere and all eyes were fixed on the small flames. Thoughts were far away and with the loved ones at home, and those hours were filled with longing for peace, rest and security.

The men longed to escape from the narrow path between life and death, where those young soldiers had lived for months. The sometimes almost superhuman physical and mental hardships had made them into men. If only they could get away from the inferno of privation and death, of hunger and cold, the almost constant danger of being wounded or freezing, the total exhaustion and weariness.

Apart from light artillery and mortar fire and a few salvos from multiple-rocket launchers, the enemy remained quiet.

25 December 1941

During the course of the day, an attack on Neshitino by approximately two companies was repulsed in the right portion of the division sector. At about noon, an attack on Kukischewo was defeated.

Quiet prevailed in the center of the sector. Fourteen Russian tanks appeared in front of the northern sector. They were immediately taken under effective fire by antitank weapons that went into position. None were knocked out, since some of the armor included heavy tanks (52 tons). Isolated attacks by limited numbers of infantry were repulsed. At times the northern sector was hit by artillery barrages from about 15 batteries and from multiple-rocket launchers.

An enemy assault troop of about 100 men that had penetrated into a position on the boundary with the *5. Panzer-Division* was forced back. It left about 50 dead and one radio set behind. Several bunkers were put out of action by fire from enemy antitank guns.

According to statements from prisoners, the Russians had the 518th Reserve Regiment and the 365th Armored Brigade facing the division in addition to the 37th and 49th Rifle Brigades. Facing the left wing of the division was the 1199th Infantry Regiment of the 354th Infantry Division. An artillery regiment was approaching from the southeast.

Additional work was done to improve the positions. Christmas mail finally arrived, which gave rise to some additional Christmas spirit.

26 December 1941

The front remained quiet.

Werner Haupt wrote the following regarding the overall situation

> The Christmas period of 1941 made it clear that the army group was fighting for its life. At last even *OKH* understood that. (Werner Haupt, *Heeresgruppe Mitte*, p. 117. Bad Nauheim: Podzun-Pallas-Verlag, 1968.)

Because of "unauthorized" orders, the two outstanding armored commanders, *Generaloberst* Guderian and *Generaloberst* Hoepner, had to depart at the very moment when their forces found themselves in a desperate battle.

Werner Haupt continues:

> At the time *Heeresgruppe Mitte* defended a 780-kilometer-wide front. Its six armies fought — without any air support, without heavy tanks, without supply — against sixteen Soviet armies and two cavalry corps that were superbly equipped for winter fighting. (Werner Haupt, *Heeresgruppe Mitte*, p. 117. Bad Nauheim: Podzun-Pallas-Verlag, 1968.)

From 28 - 31 December 1941 the division's entire sector remained quiet.

The commander of *SS-Infanterie-Regiment "Der Führer"* wrote in his reminiscences of the end of the year:

> Despite everything...The same confident determination everywhere to continue the fight as before, was unshaken. Everywhere was the knowledge that we were totally superior to the enemy. The enemy increasingly felt that his attacks against our sector of the front were costly and fruitless. He only continued to conduct feints with weak forces, suppress us with artillery fire. The *Schwerpunkt* of his attacks shifted to weaker sectors of the front.
>
> The year 1941 thus ended in the Rusa position with nothing unusual happening. Tribute should be paid to the outstanding service of the staff officers and the trains units at this point. In the most difficult of conditions and with total personal commitment, they supplied the line companies in a way that stretched the limits of what was possible. They also had an equal share in the tremendous accomplishments and successes...of the recent past.

These words of praise obviously applied equally well to the supply elements of the entire division.

***

So it was that the fateful year of 1941 came to an end. In the earthworks and in the deeply snow-covered villages of the Rusa position, the "celebrations" took on an introspective tone.

1942

Sub-Section p)

Defensive Fighting in the Winter Position of the 9. Armee: 1 - 17 January 1942

1 January 1942

The new year began without combat operations and the quiet at the front was interrupted only by the coupled firing of extremely heavy Russian mortars on the eastern outskirts of Schukowka, which did not result in any great damage.

The thermometer sank to -30 degrees Celsius (-22 degrees Fahrenheit). Five Russians, who had been trained in Schulgino, were captured by *SS-Infanterie-Regiment "Deutschland"*. According to their statements, 15 multiple-rocket launchers were in position there as well as 20 light tanks.

By order of the division, all vehicles that were not needed by the combat elements were set in march for the new billeting area southwest of Gshatsk. Each vehicle was allowed only such fuel as was absolutely necessary for it to reach the new area.

***

The commander-in-chief of *Panzergruppe 4* issued the following order of the day on 1 January 1942:

Order of the Day for 1 January 1942

The leadership of the corps and divisions of the *Panzergruppe* and the splendid fighting spirit of their troops have achieved enormous successes in the year now ending. The Fatherland will be eternally grateful to you for that. Every officer and combatant should take extremely great satisfaction in the knowledge of having done his best!

May the memory of our fallen heroes show us the seriousness with which we must fulfill our duty!

The New Year will demand much from each of us. May the Lord God grant us victory and personal good fortune to every individual!

/signed/ Hoepner

2 January 1942

A Siberian cold front spread over the land. The division recorded a temperature of -35 degrees Celsius (-31 degrees Fahrenheit).

Werner Haupt wrote the following concerning the situation of the army group at the beginning of 1942:

Winter closed in without mercy. Temperatures at the turn of the year ranged between -20 to -30 degrees Celsius (-4 to -22 degrees Fahrenheit). Snow lay up to a meter deep on roads, in the fields and in the thick woods. There were no longer any permanent quarters. The houses of the impoverished villages had been burned down. The soldiers had to seek makeshift protection from the icy east wind behind walls of snow. There was hardly any winter clothing. Losses due to frostbite increased at a terrifying rate and far exceeded the number of injuries from gunfire.

Nevertheless, the soldiers of the army group staggered and stamped onward. They were entirely on their own. The horses collapsed in the snow from hunger and weakness. Wherever they sank to the earth, they were covered with a thick sheet of ice in a few minutes.

The motorized units were bogged down the same as the infantry battalions. Measures that had hitherto worked to protect fuel and oil from the cold failed. Engines had to be heated before they would start. The artillery had to blow up the guns. There were no more prime movers and, if there had been, the guns could no longer fire because the breechblocks were frozen shut.

Bringing the wounded to the rear on litters and in ambulances was a constant race with death by freezing. All too often frost and cold were the victors. The shadow of Napoleon's *Grande Armée* hovered over *Heeresgruppe Mitte*, though one could hardly still refer to it as an army group...(Werner Haupt, *Heeresgruppe Mitte*, pp. 118-119. Bad Nauheim: Podzun-Pallas-Verlag, 1968.)

***

The commander of the division, *SS-Brigadeführer* Bittrich, issued the following order of the day:

Order of the Day

The *Reichsführer-SS*, who has followed the heavy fighting of *SS-Division "Reich"* during recent weeks with extreme sympathy, has written me a personal letter expressing his special commendation for the exemplary conduct of the division. He thanks all officers, noncommissioned officers and enlisted personnel for their singular accomplishments.

/signed/ Bittrich

3 January 1942

SS-Hauptsturmführer Tychsen assumed command of the division reserves in Borodino. *SS-Sturmbannführer* Schulz assumed command of the *III./SS-Infanterie-Regiment "Der Führer"*.

The temperature continued to plunge and reached -37 degrees Celsius (-34.5 degrees Fahrenheit).

Due to the shortage of firewood, friendly forces in the army-group sector repeatedly cut down telephone poles from the field telephone system or cut out sections of wire to use in wiring lights, thus destroying important field telephone connections.

The commander-in-chief of the army group therefore forbade any sawing down of telegraph poles and any misappropriation of wire and post material for any purpose other than communications. The order closed with:

I consider the destruction of telephone poles as premeditated destruction of war materials and a premeditated endangerment of the combat power of the *Wehrmacht*. According to Section 1 of the...supplement to the penal code for protection of the defensive capability of the German people of 25 November 1939...such an act can be punished with death.

All soldiers of the army group are to be informed of this order immediately.

/signed/ von Kluge
Generalfeldmarschall

***

Conditions remained quiet on the defensive front. The division commander visited *SS-Infanterie-Regiment "Deutschland"* and the men of the *II./SS-Infanterie-Regiment "Deutschland"* in their bunkers.

***

The following changes took place in *SS-Kradschützen-Bataillon "Reich"*:

All of the motor vehicles of the battalion were loaded for shipment to Germany for repairs and maintenance. The drivers joined the line companies. Whatever was left of the *2./* and *4./SS-Kradschützen-Bataillon "Reich"* was consolidated as the *2. Kompanie* (*SS-Hauptsturmführer* Grünwalder).

Right: Smolensk 1941 **Below**: "Put to a different use."

This page: The "Stalin Organ" — Russian multiple-rocket launcher — with ammunition

Matthias Kleinheisterkamp

SS-Obergruppenführer und General der Waffen-SS

Born: 22 June 1893 in Elberfeld.

First World War, 1914 - 1918: Front-line soldier, severely wounded, Iron Crosses, First and Second Class.

1918 - 1920: *Freikorps* in the east.

1921: *Reichswehr*. Entered the 100,000-man army. Final rank/position: *Hauptmann* and company commander

1934: *SS-Verfügungstruppe* and *Waffen-SS*. Transferred to *SS-Verfügungstruppe*; initially training officer with *SS-Verfügungstruppe* in Hamburg.

1935: Tactics instructor at the newly opened *SS-Junkerschule Braunschweig* under *SS-Oberführer* Paul Hausser.

Effective summer of 1936: Staff officer with *SS-Brigadeführer* Hausser who had been named the inspector general of the *SS-Verfügungstruppe* in Berlin.

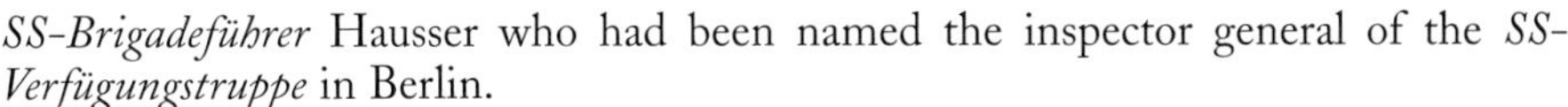

Spring of 1938: Transferred to staff of *SS-Standarte "Deutschland"* in Munich under *SS-Standartenführer* Steiner.

October 1938: Appointed to command the *III./SS-Standarte "Deutschland"*.

Polish Campaign, 1939: Commander of one of the three *Kampfgruppen* in *Panzerdivsion Kempf* (Army + *SS Verfügungstruppe*). First member of the division to receive the Iron Crosses, First and Second Class for outstanding leadership and personal bravery.

Western Campaign, 1940: Renewed proof of ability as commander of the *III./SS-Infanterie-Regiment "Deutschland"* (*coup de main* at Vlissingen /Holland). 3 July 1941: Transferred to *SS-Division "Totenkopf"* and appointment to command *SS-"Totenkopf" Regiment 3*.

Russian Campaign: Continued proof of ability as regimental commander; after wounding of division commander, *SS-Gruppenführer* Eicke, assumed temporary command of *SS-Division "Totenkopf"*. 9 November 1941: Promoted to *SS-Brigadeführer*.

9 January 1942: Designated commander of *SS-Division "Reich"* in the midst of the heavy winter fighting in the Rusa position in Russia; for renewed proof of ability and outstanding command of the division in the winter fighting at Sytschewka and Rshew he received the Knight's Cross.

Later, after promotion to *SS-Gruppenführer*, assumed command of *SS-Division "Nord"* in Finland, which he commanded until fall of 1944. He formed a friendly relationship with *General* Dietl.

Effective the fall of 1944 he was the commanding general of the *XI. Armee-Korps*. On 9 May 1945 *SS-Obergruppenführer* Kleinheisterkamp received the Oakleaves to the Knight's Cross.

SS-Obergruppenführer Kleinheisterkamp has been missing since the end of the war. (He is believed to have committed suicide in the Halbe Pocket on 2 May 1945 to avoid capture by the Soviets.)

Opposite page, top: Temporary defensive position during the retreat. **Opposite page, bottom**: Tanks of the *10. Panzer-Division* with grenadiers of *SS-Division "Reich"* during the advance. **Above**: Ski company (the *15./SS-Infanterie-Regiment "Deutschland"*) with *Kampfgruppe SS-Division "Reich"*, 1942. **Below:** *SS-Sturmbannführer* Ehrath, commander of the *I./SS-Infanterie-Regiment "Deutschland"*, with his staff before the winter fighting at Rshew.

Above: Military cemetery and memorial of *SS-Infanterie-Regiment "Deutschland"* in Kashino near Rshew. **Below**: Fighting at Rshew, February 1942. *General der Panzertruppen* Model visits *SS-Division "Reich"* with the *Fieseler Storch*.

Above: *SS-Standartenführer* Ostendorff, operations officer of *SS-Division "Reich"* and eventual commander of *Kampfgruppe "SS-Reich"*, discusses the situation with *General der Panzertruppen* Model. **Below**: Work and worry start early in the morning. New reports arrive at the regiment's command post in Beli Kolodes in February 1943 — *SS-Obersturmbannführer* Heinz Harmel

Opposite page, left: *SS-Standartenführer Ostendorff*, commander of *Kampfgruppe "SS-Reich"*. **Opposite page, right**: *SS-Obersturmbannführer* Otto Kumm, commander of *SS-Infanterie-Regiment "Der Führer"*, after the fighting at Rshew, 1942. **Right**: Battalion command post of the *I./SS-Infanterie-Regiment "Deutschland"* in the winter of 1941/42. **Above**: Standard of *SS-Infanterie-Regiment "Deutschland"* in Aschewo.

Opposite page, top: Command post of *SS-Infanterie-Regiment "Deutschland"* in Aschewo. From right to left: *SS-Obersturmführer* Elfering, *SS-Hauptsturmführer* Weiß, *SS-Obersturmführer* Kryp and *SS-Obersturmführer* Buch. **Opposite page, bottom**: Hotly contested Aschewo. **Above**: Medical section of *SS-Kradschützen-Bataillon "Das Reich"* with *SS-Hauptsturmführer Dr.* Rueff. **Below**: "Dumbbell Woods", end of March 1942. Collection point for the dead in the southern portion of the woods.

Kampfgruppe Tychsen was formed from *SS-Kradschützen-Bataillon "Reich"* and *SS-Aufklärungs-Abteilung "Reich"*.

***

On 7 January *Sturmgeschütz "Seydlitz"*, which had been sent back to Germany with serious damage from Romny, was returned overhauled to the battalion. It was greeted with joy.

Throughout the division's sector, all the roads had to be cleared of snow every day.

The Russian command, however, prepared for new operations.

Situation and Intent on the Russian Side

Werner Haupt wrote about Russian intentions at the time as follows:

The high command of the Red Army gave its armies and fronts the new objectives for the second phase of the offensive on 7 January 1942:

The Briansk Front, which had recaptured 1100 localities by then and had completely smashed the right wing of *Heeresgruppe Mitte* in a bold attack, was advancing on Orel.

The West Front received orders to advance against Juchnow and, in coordination with the Kalinin Front, encircle the German formations (Author's Note: Including *SS-Division "Reich"*) in the Moshaisk — Gshatsk — Wjasma area.

The Kalinin Front was to attack Rshew with the 29th and 31st Armies. The 30th and 39th Armies were to advance past Rshew to the west against Sytschewka, while the 22nd Army was to cut the Rshew — Welikije Luki railroad line.

The Northwest Front on the extreme right wing had the mission to separate *Heeresgruppe Mitte* from *Heeresgruppe Nord* with the newly formed 3rd and 4th Shock Armies. The front would operate offensively against Cholm, Welikije Luki, Toropetz and Welish.

On 2 January *Feldmarschall* von Kluge, the commander-in-chief of the army group, requested a rapid pullback of the armies after the Soviet penetrations and breakthroughs at Malojaroslawez and Staritza became evident. However, the *OKH* took the position that the existing gaps had to be plugged before any consideration could be given to evacuating positions. (Werner Haupt, *Heeresgruppe Mitte*, p. 119. Bad Nauheim: Podzun-Pallas-Verlag, 1968.)

It was hardly possible to talk about a front at the army group at the time.

Change in Command of SS-Division "Reich"

On 8 January 1942 the division commander, *SS-Brigadeführer und Generalmajor der Waffen-SS* Bittrich, was transferred. *SS-Brigadeführer und Generalmajor der Waffen-SS* Kleinheisterkamp assumed command of *SS-Division "Reich"* in his place.

Since *SS-Obergruppenführer* Hausser was wounded, Bittrich had led the men of the division in outstanding fashion during a particularly difficult stage of the winter campaign in Russia. He had led them to the gates of Moscow and then in the fighting retreats and defensive fighting in the Istra and Rusa positions that had so sapped the division's strength. On his departure, the outgoing division commander released the following order of the day:

Order of the Day

My Comrades!

The order of the *Reichsführer* calls me from your side to new assignments.

That means departing from the battle-proven division, from my old regiment *"Deutschland"* and from all of you who have, under my command, fulfilled your duty as soldiers to the point of self-sacrifice. The old and the new fame of the division is the fame of each of you, but it is also the fame of the brave whom Russia's soil now covers. You have advanced from victory to victory and have withstood the hardest tests in a difficult period.

I know that you will give to the new commander, *SS-Brigadeführer* Kleinheisterkamp, the same obedience and the same unbreakable loyalty that you gave to me.

With pride and a grateful heart I depart from you. The shared experience of incomparable victories and the extremely bitter fighting in this decisive campaign unite us past this parting.

The unshakeable fighting spirit and unconditional willingness to sacrifice of the *Waffen-SS* unites us. Wherever the *Führer* may send us, we vow:

Our entire strength, our life for Germany's freedom!

/signed/ Bittrich

(Taken from appendix 229 of the war diary of *SS-Infanterie-Regiment "Deutschland"* for 8 January 1942)

***

On 9 January the division issued the warning order for evacuation of the Rusa position on D-Day, which would be announced 24 hours prior to execution.

For the soldiers, who had thought of their defensive sector as secure as it ever was, it came as a complete surprise. The war diary of *SS-Infanterie-Regiment "Deutschland"* for 9 January 1942 expressed the following:

> It seemed incomprehensible to the regiment how this position could be evacuated. However, it was attributed to great reversals at other places on the front that made it necessary to pull the Rusa front back.

Given the situation of *Heeresgruppe Mitte* outlined above, there was in fact no other option except evacuation of the Rusa position.

The division prepared the following warning order for the withdrawal (excerpts):

Warning Order for Pulling Back to a Rearward Position

1.) The Rusa position is likely to be evacuated in the next few days. After falling back to several blocking positions, the main line of resistance is to be pulled back to the "G" Position in order to shorten the front and, in so doing, release forces…

The order then specified the boundaries to the adjoining divisions and the boundaries between divisional formations during the withdrawal, at blocking positions along lines "A" – "F" and the final main line of resistance. The individual lines were each to be held one day, except that line "D" was tentatively to be held for two days.

Three resistance-groups (*Widerstandsgruppen*) were formed:

a) ***Widerstandsgruppe Tychsen,*** composed of *SS-Kradschützen-Bataillon "Reich", SS-Aufklärungs-Abteilung "Reich"* and the division reserve.

b) ***Widerstandsgruppe Harmel***, composed of *SS-Infanterie-Regiment "Deutschland"*

c) ***Widerstandsgruppe Kumm*** composed of *SS-Infanterie-Regiment "Der Führer"*

The resistance groups were directly subordinated to the division. On falling back from Line "B", *Gruppe Dietrich* was to go directly back behind the new main line of resistance. Additional orders were to follow.

Regarding the conduct of fighting, the warning order stated the following in paragraph 9:

One reinforced battalion will be employed in each sector along the designated lines. The battalions are to leapfrog back in a *single* bound to the line beyond the one occupied by the other battalion.

...Lines "B" and "C", as well as "E" and "F" are to be occupied with strongpoints in the built-up areas. The *Schwerpunkt* is on the withdrawal route and other traveled routes. Areas with deep snow cover are to be screened by patrols on skis…

(Taken from appendix 231 of the war diary of *SS-Infanterie-Regiment "Deutschland"* for 9 January 1942)

The division command post was to be located in Chotanki until D+2 and in Galyschkino until D+5.

On 10 January 1942 the quiet on the defensive front was interrupted by an enemy assault troop with approximately 25-30 men. It attempted to advance against the left sector of the *II./SS-Infanterie-Regiment "Deutschland"*. It was wiped out by infantry fire.

***

On 11 January 1942 the new division commander issued the following order of the day:

Order of the Day

SS men of the proud *SS-Division "Reich"*!

I have assumed command of the division as of 9 January 1942. I am fully aware of the honor granted to me as an old member of the division in commanding you through the winter months.

Your deeds, your devotion to duty, your professional demeanor and your discipline are exemplary in the history of the *Waffen-SS* and the Army. I am firm in the conviction that under my command you will also continue to commit your entire strength in maintaining and securing the successes that have been won.

It is a pleasure to pass on to you the heartfelt greetings and best wishes of your division commander, *SS-Obergruppenführer* Hausser, who may soon return to you.

In grateful respect we remember our dead and wounded comrades.

We shall do our duty in love and loyalty to our people and to our best comrade, our *Führer*

Sieg Heil!
/signed/ Kleinheisterkamp

(Taken from appendix 230 of the war diary of *SS-Infanterie-Regiment "Deutschland"* for 11 January 1942)

***

The commander of *SS-Kradschützen-Bataillon "Reich"*, *SS-Sturmbannführer* Heinz Klingenberg, known for his *coup de main* that resulted in the capture of Belgrade, fell ill from dysentery and was ordered to return to Germany to complete his recovery. He never again returned to the division.

After his convalescence, he was transferred to the *SS-Junkerschule Tölz* (officer candidate school at Bad Tölz). He was active there for the next few years as instructor in tactics, class advisor, and commandant of the training program for Germanic volunteers. In April 1944 he assumed command of *SS-Junkerschule Tölz*. In January 1945, as a *SS-Standartenführer*, he assumed command of the *17. SS-Panzer-Grenadier-Division "Götz von Berlichingen"*. He was killed in the defensive fighting in the west on 22 March 1945 in the front lines at Herxheim.)

After disbanding the division reserve, *SS-Hauptsturmführer* Tychsen assumed command of *SS-Kradschützen-Bataillon "Reich"*. *Kompanie Burfeind*, which was formed from personnel from *SS-Panzer-Jäger-Abteilung "Reich"*, went from the division reserve to become the *4./SS-Kradschützen-Bataillon "Reich"*.

***

Paul Carell wrote the following about the deteriorating situation of *Heeresgruppe Mitte*:

After the breakthrough at Toropez (Author's note: The outermost Russian pincer arm around *Heeresgruppe Mitte*) there was no longer any continuous German front in the 125-kilometer stretch between Welikije Luki and Rshew. That was the bitterest, most dangerous hour for *Heeresgruppe Mitte* since 6 December 1941.

Three Soviet armies — with Jeremenko's 4th Shock Army far ahead with its four rifle divisions, two rifle brigades and three ski battalions — reached for the great victory. Stalin had promised them it would result in the destruction of *Heeresgruppe Mitte* and, with that, the turning point in the war. (Paul Carell, *Unternehmen Barbarossa*, p. 321. Frankfurt am Main / Berlin (West): Verlag Ullstein GmbH, 1963.)

The Russian armies, however, did not attain their objective of cutting the Minsk — Smolensk — Moscow highway, the spinal cord of *Heeresgruppe Mitte*, even though the airfield at Smolensk was under Russian artillery fire.

The Russian leadership had underestimated its enemy and overestimated its own strength. Carell continues:

As a result, the most dangerous advance of the Russian winter offensive against *Heeresgruppe Mitte* — into the rear of the *9. Armee* — had failed. The outermost arm of the Russian pincers that was to advance deep behind the German front had been broken.

Catastrophe, however, still threatened north and south of the highway at Rshew and at Suchinitschi. The inner pincer arms of the Red offensive directly endangered the units fighting at the front of the *9.* and *4. Armeen.*

Above all else, Rshew was the objective of the Soviet attack. The Russians wanted to capture that cornerstone of the German central front no matter what it cost. If they were to succeed in that, then the *9. Armee* would be in danger of being outflanked and encircled.

When enemy tanks suddenly rolled past the front door of an army command post and the front was only one kilometer away, then a catastrophe was imminent. Late in the afternoon of 12 January 1942 such a catastrophe looked the *9. Armee* squarely in the eye. (Paul Carell, *Unternehmen Barbarossa*, pp. 322-323. Frankfurt am Main / Berlin (West): Verlag Ullstein GmbH, 1963.)

***

The sector facing *SS-Division "Reich"* remained quiet. On 14 January 1942 the division issued an order expanding the Rusa sector (excerpts):

Division Order for Expanding the Rusa Sector

1.) The enemy facing *SS-Division "Reich"* has dug in. He is strong in artillery but suffers from an ammunition shortage.

2.) The sector of *SS-Division "Reich"* has been expanded in the north to the northern outskirts of Kusminskoje — southern outskirts of Sepelewo — northern outskirts of Lukino — south outskirts of Lupunowo.

3.) Reinforced *SS-Aufklärungs-Abteilung "Reich"* is to be withdrawn from the right wing to occupy the new sector.

> The division reserve is to be disbanded. In accordance with separate orders, one company is to be attached to *SS-Kradschützen-Bataillon "Reich"* and two companies are to be attached to *SS-Aufklärungs-Abteilung "Reich"*.
>
> The southernmost part of the newly added sector is to be assumed by *SS-Infanterie-Regiment "Der Führer"*.
>
> . . .

***

That order, however, had already been overtaken by events on 15 January 1942.

Werner Haupt wrote about that day:

> On 15 January the *Oberkommando des Heeres* had ordered a general retreat to the line: Rshew — Gshatsk — Juchnow. That was intended to preserve at least some continuity to the front. (Werner Haupt, *Heeresgruppe Mitte*, p. 122. Bad Nauheim: Podzun-Pallas-Verlag, 1968.)

***

With that withdrawal to a considerably shortened front, *SS-Division "Reich"* was freed up for new and difficult missions. No one, however, knew what employment faced the division. Everyone could feel that time was pressing.

***

On 16 January 1942, at 0400 hours, the division telephonically passed on the following order (excerpts):

> Division Order for Falling Back in a Single Movement
> to the Area West of Gshatsk
>
> *SS-Division "Reich"* is to fall back in a single movement to the area west of Gshatsk: Sjask (inclusive) as far as Gshatsk (exclusive). The movement is to begin on 16 January at nightfall.

With that, *SS-Division "Reich"* departed from the command of the *4. Armee*. Initially, it was directly attached to the *9. Armee*.

For the infantry, intermediate quarters en route were specified in orders while the motorized elements were to reach the new billeting area in a single move.

With the fall of darkness the troops of *SS-Division "Reich"* withdrew from the Rusa position. It remained quiet in front of the division's sector. The forces marched toward the rear throughout the entire night on the designated road in extreme cold. This time, however, they were not followed by the enemy.

After a short period of rest on 17 January from 0500 to 0930 hours, the march continued until the day's objective had been reached by about 1600 hours.

By 1700 hours the division had already radioed the following order to *SS-Infanterie-Regiment "Deutschland"*:

All available motor vehicles are to be ready to move out by 1200 hours on 18 January.

The regimental liaison officer was then sent to the trains elements and motor-vehicle echelons, which were quartered 20 kilometers southwest of Gshatsk. They were to immediately unload all available and operational motor vehicles, stage and move to the regiment's new command post that was still being reconnoitered in Gshatsk.

At 2045 hours the following order was radioed from the division to *SS-Infanterie-Regiment "Deutschland"* (southern portion of Gshatsk):

All unloaded vehicles, including those of the trains units, are to be employed in shuttle service to transport personnel. The greatest possible speed and sparing of the soldiers are required.

***

The division command post was located in Brylowo.

On 17 January *General der Panzertruppen* Model assumed command of the *9. Armee* after the previous commander-in-chief, *Generaloberst* Strauß, was relieved of his position for health reasons.

***

SS-Oberstgruppenführer und Generaloberst der Waffen-SS Hausser quoted from Carl Wagener in his personal notes regarding that phase of the war:

Rarely has a retreat been conducted more poorly than the retreat from Moscow.

That it succeeded is primarily thanks to the performance of the soldiers. It verges on a miracle.

The supreme command did everything in its power to complicate it and make it all but impossible.

Once it was clear to everyone that the attack on Moscow had failed, a major decision had to be reached and the forces pulled back to a line that could be held in winter.

The purpose of a retreat is to disengage from the enemy. That form of combat — and retreat is a form of combat, not a disaster, flight or disgrace — should serve to break off the fighting and, in so doing, retain the initiative, independent of the will of the enemy. (Carl Wagener, *Moskau 1941 — der Angriff auf die russische Hauptstadt*, p. ? ?: ?,?)

***

On 18 January 1942 the elements of the division remained in the area they had reached.

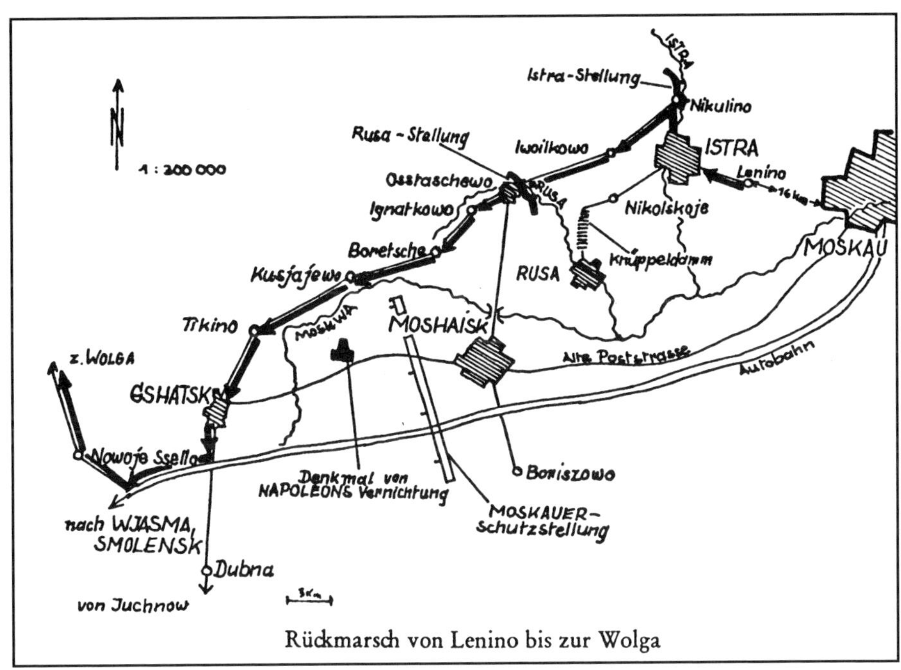

Rückmarsch von Lenino bis zur Wolga

Withdrawal from Lenino to the Volga

The emptying of the motor vehicles that were with the trains and the concentration of those columns — about 30 vehicles — took up the entire day. As a result of snowdrifts and one-way traffic, the empty column did not get to the command post of *SS-Infanterie-Regiment "Deutschland"* in Gshatsk until 2400 hours.

***

A short division order that went out to the units on 18 January read as follows:

By order of the *Oberkommando des Heeres SS-Division "Reich"* is to stage on 17/18 January 1942 in the Spassk — Cholm — Gshatsk (exclusive) — Nowo Sselo area.

All formations quartered there must, by order of the *OKH*, free up as much space as may be required for the additional billeting requirements of *SS-Division "Reich"* in that area.

FOR THE COMMANDER:

Operations Officer

/signed/ Ostendorff

SS-Obersturmbannführer

(Taken from appendix 239 of the war diary of *SS-Infanterie-Regiment "Deutschland"* for 18 January 1942)

This order made it clear that the *Oberkommando des Heeres* had taken a direct hand in the impending employment of *SS-Division "Reich"*.

***

The particular significance of this employment also was evident in the additional order issued the same day:

Special Directives for Organization in the New Billeting Area

1.) The following billeting areas are changed with respect to the previously designated ones:

a) *SS-Infanterie-Regiment "Deutschland"*: Dubrowka (west of Spassk) — Schubenka — Ssachina — Odnurowka area

b) *SS-Infanterie-Regiment "Der Führer"*: Nowo Sselo-Dubrowka (2 kilometers southwest of Basskakowo) — Ilino area.

An authorization for freeing up billets for the division's forces is being sent to the formations in the attachments. Permission is granted to occupy additional built-up areas adjacent to the areas designated in the order.

The roads from the billets to the Gshatsk — Spassk through route are to be kept clear at all times.

2.) The units are to conduct clothing exchange and foot care by 20 January. Thorough washing!

3.) All vehicles available for transporting personnel are to be kept ready for continued movement.

4.) All additional men who are fit for service with the combat elements are to be pulled out of the trains elements.

5.) All commanders are responsible for speedy and thorough completion of the measures ordered.

6.) Continuation of the movement is expected on 21 January.

7.) to 8.) …

9.) Division command post (command section and logistics section): Brylowo (18 kilometers west of Gshatsk).

(Taken from appendix 240 of the war diary of *SS-Infanterie-Regiment "Deutschland"* for 18 January 1942)

There was a peculiar tension in the air. Everybody knew that decisive fighting was impending.

***

The division commander, *SS-Brigadeführer* Kleinheisterkamp, passed on directives for the conduct of operations (excerpts):

Directives for the Conduct of Operations

In the impending attack, the success of the first day is decisive for the course of the entire operation. If it succeeds in giving the enemy a feeling of inferiority on the first day and our own troops regain the unequivocal feeling of superiority, then the decision will take place within a few days...

...It is essential that every officer, noncommissioned officer and enlisted man is fully aware that the impending attack is decisively important for the entire future course of the eastern campaign, because we are the first to go over to the attack from either the defense or a withdrawal. Every last man must know this to his inner core.

/signed/ Kleinheisterkamp

A great, decisive battle was clearly impending.

Chapter IV: The Winter Fighting at Rshew 19 January to 20 February 1942

Overview of the Development of the Situation

How had the general situation of *Heeresgruppe Mitte* developed since the start of the New Year?

This overview is necessary in order to understand and appreciate the significance of this decisive winter battle.

The start of the New Year of the war in 1942 had brought about the partial destruction of *Heeresgruppe Mitte*. This was partially a result of the superiority in manpower and materiel of the Red Army, which was outstandingly equipped for the winter war, and partially due to the merciless Siberian cold (at Lake Ilmen the temperatures dropped as low as -50 degrees Celsius [-58 degrees Fahrenheit].

The forces of *Heeresgruppe Mitte*, which had come within 16 kilometers of Moscow in December, fought their way back to the west at the height of the Russian winter under unspeakable conditions.

Hitler's strict order — "Defend every place that has been occupied at any price" — and the combat superiority of the German soldiers eventually led to the formation of a firm front.

Werner Haupt wrote:

> From the German side, it must be said here that the strict *Führer* order — "Hold at any price" — in that terrible situation of the *Heeresgruppe* and at the inhumanly cold temperatures was correct. An unorganized retreat through ice and snow would have led to the dissolution of the army group within a few days. In addition, the will of the simple soldier to survive must not be forgotten. That also contributed immensely to the stabilization of the front. (Werner Haupt, *Heeresgruppe Mitte*, p. 123. Bad Nauheim: Podzun-Pallas-Verlag, 1968.)

After conducting a fighting retreat, the *9. Armee* under *Generaloberst* Strauß had forced its way to the point of exhaustion from the Kalinin area as far as the Gshatsk — Rshew line. However, the closely pursuing enemy redoubled his efforts to smash the German front. The positions of the bled-white infantry and armored corps were stretched to the breaking point. The Soviets repeatedly tried to eliminate those lines by employing armor and ground-attack aircraft.

Their first objective was the city of Rshew, the cornerstone of the entire German defensive front in the central sector, the actual center of strength and supplies of *Heeresgruppe Mitte*. Four Russian armies — the 29th, 30th, 31st and 1st Shock Armies — concentrically attacked Rshew from the north, northeast and east. The loss of that city, however, would have meant the collapse of the Gshatsk — Rshew position that Hitler had ordered. Further, it probably would have sealed the fate of *Heeresgruppe Mitte*.

The first enemy frontal attack against the northeast corner of Rshew, which was held by the *VI. Armee-Korps*, failed. At that point, the Russians reorganized their forces.

Enemy Breakthrough West of Rshew

On 4 January 1942 the enemy attacked the front of the *256. Infanterie-Division* (*XXIII. Armee-Korps*) from the north with massively superior forces. He intended to bypass Rshew to the west, advance to the south and capture the city by envelopment from the southwest. This offensive led on that same day to a deep penetration that split off the *XXIII. Armee-Korps* from the *IX. Armee*. On 5 January a gap of 15 kilometers already yawned between the flanking divisions (the *206. Infanterie-Division* and the *256. Infanterie-Division*).

The Soviet divisions advanced over the Volga in spite of the heroic defense of the *XXIII. Armee-Korps* and the courageous actions of the *VIII. Flieger-Korps*. By evening the leading Russian units were in an area eight kilometers west and southwest of Rshew.

The situation was threatening as never before. For the first time in the campaign the army group fought for its very life. The danger for Rshew had mounted to extreme levels.

Then an additional *Führer* order arrived:

"Rshew is to be held at any price!"

The situation could only be cleaned up by a German counterattack with the initial objective of fending off the immediate threat to Rshew. It could then close the gap in the front and prevent a subsequent influx of strong enemy forces.

An attack to the west with four hastily assembled weak battalions of the *VI. Armee-Korps* along the road to Mol. Tud on 6 January failed. A supplemental attack from the west to the east on 7 January in a heavy snowstorm by *SS-Brigade Fegelein* also failed. That brigade had been brought up in forced marches. Both attacks were doomed to failure after initial successes because the enemy had already become too strong in the gap in the front.

Fortunately, the enemy frittered away his forces at that decisive moment so that the west front at Rshew could be assembled in great haste.

Every separate battalion, regular battalion and company that could be spared was then thrown into the new position. In spite of snow squalls and intense frost, the indefatigable *Luftwaffe* continued to play a decisive role in preventing the enemy from rapidly utilizing his previous successes. In addition, battalions arriving in Orscha and Smolensk were brought forward to Rshew by air. Additional reinforcements flowed in daily to the movement control center at Rshew from the combing out operations directed by the headquarters of the *9. Armee.*

The Soviets, however, increased their strength daily. The 39th Army in its entirety had broken the German front to the south — with armor, infantry and sled columns. The enemy was then in the process of shoving additional divisions and two cavalry corps into the gap.

To oppose this, the *9. Armee* could only pull two infantry regiments out of the former lines and set these weak formations against the overwhelmingly superior enemy. The heavy snow drifts and the Siberian cold front that arrived on 8 January not only caused an appalling rise in the casualties due to frostbite but also interfered with any rapid movements.

On 9 January 1942 the great offensive of Jeremenko's army in the Waldai Hills broke loose against the left wing of the cut-off *XXIII. Armee-Korps.* The situation in the Ostaschkow area became more critical from hour to hour, and the enemy threatened to inundate the widely stretched and thinly held German front. The army group repeatedly ordered counterattacks, but the *9. Armee* was simply not in a position to carry them out. The arrival of the *1. Panzer-Division*, the newly attached *SS-Division "Reich"* and additional infantry formations had been delayed. These units first had to be relieved in their previous positions, which then had to be taken over by adjoining formations.

Heavy attacks against the right wing of the *VI. Armee-Korps* had to be regarded as a precursor of an impending concentric offensive against Rshew.

The command of the *9. Armee* clearly understood that the situation could only be saved by repeating the attack to close the gap in the front but with substantially stronger forces.

The renewed attack was initially to be launched toward to the west from the Rshew area no earlier than 15 January. It was to be conducted with the *1. Panzer-Division*, which had to be relieved and pulled out of its present positions, and two infantry regiments.

The situation, however, rapidly worsened. On 11 January a strong enemy group was already 20 kilometers northwest of Sytschewka. It threatened the vital Sytschewka — Rshew railroad line as well as the transport and supply center of Sytschewka itself.

The *1. Panzer-Division*, which was approaching its assembly position, was diverted at the last minute to Sytschewka. After a night march it arrived there at the moment when the enemy was already fighting at the railroad station. Fortunately, the enemy was "enjoying life to the full" in the Sytschewka supply dumps with the marvelous things found there, including special rations for aviators and tank drivers. The Russian soldiers were particularly enjoying the French cognac that was stored there.

An immediate attack by a reinforced motorcycle company destroyed the enemy that constituted the most life-threatening danger to the *9. Armee*. Together with the somewhat later arriving *SS-Division "Reich"*, the Sytschewka area was cleared of the enemy.

***

Werner Haupt wrote the following concerning the change of command of the *9. Armee*:

> As the situation appeared to reach its most dangerous point, Hitler relieved the former commander-in-chief of the army, *Generaloberst* Strauß, and placed the conduct of the fighting around Rshew in the hands of the still relatively unknown *General der Panzertruppen* Model. (Author's Note: In the pocket battle of Kiev, Model had commanded the *3. Panzer-Division*, which had advanced to the south as the spearhead of the northern pincer arm. On 14 September it had made contact with the *16. Panzer-Division*, which was advancing from the south, thus closing the Kiev pocket.)
>
> When the general arrived at the army command post he was asked, "What reserves are you bringing us, *Herr General*?"
>
> His answer: "Me!"
>
> With Model's assumption of command the headcount of the army may not have

changed, but its strength to hold out certainly did! The diminutive general was, at once, everywhere and nowhere. It was as if his appearance alone strengthened his troops and weakened those of the enemy. From then on the name Model became something of terror for any Soviet commander!

General Model immediately moved to develop the plan of attack described above with his own special energy and personal bravery that approached the irrational. On 18 January the order was issued to the divisions. The attack to close the gap in the front was set for 21 January. (Werner Haupt, *Heeresgruppe Mitte*, ?. Bad Nauheim: Podzun-Pallas-Verlag, 1968.)

Sub-Section q)

Offensive Operations Northwest of Sytschewka: 19 January - 7 February 1942

20 January 1942

The command post of *SS-Infanterie-Regiment "Deutschland"* was moved to Bogdanowo at 0600 hours. The commander of the regiment, *SS-Sturmbannführer* Harmel, established contact with the *1. Panzer-Division* from there.

The *I./SS-Infanterie-Regiment "Deutschland"*, the regiment's communications platoon, one platoon each of the *13./* and *14./SS-Infanterie-Regiment "Deutschland"* and half of the *II./SS-Infanterie-Regiment "Deutschland"* moved separately in a motor march to the assembly area at Bogdanowo.

The rest of the regiment moved by train on orders from the division. Not enough empty vehicles were available for a motor march. It was brought forward via Sytschewka to the assembly area.

The units that had been loaded on motor vehicles arrived at the assembly area in a shuttle operation during the course of the afternoon and evening.

The *1. Panzer-Division* screened to the west and northwest with weak forces in the general line Rshew — Sytschewka — Loszmina River. The villages to the west and northwest of that line were still in friendly hands at this point.

SS-Infanterie-Regiment "Deutschland" assembled according to regimental order on 20 January 1942 in the Bogdanowo — Krjukowo — Schkrjukowo (8 kilometers north-northwest of Sytschewka) area for a later attack toward the northwest.

The elements were staged as follows:

- *I./SS-Infanterie-Regiment "Deutschland"* with the *13.* and *14./SS-Infanterie-Regiment "Deutschland"*, regimental staff and communications platoon in Bogdanowo

II./SS-Infanterie-Regiment "Deutschland" in Krjukowo

15./ and *16./SS-Infanterie-Regiment "Deutschland"* in Schrjukowo

Adjoining units:

On the right: Elements of the *1. Panzer-Division*

On the left: *Kampfgruppe Tychsen* (*SS-Kradschützen-Bataillon "Reich"* and *SS-Aufklärungs-Abteilung "Reich"*)

March route to the assembly area: Tessowo, Nowo Dugino, Koporicha, Sytschewka, Krjukowo. All elements unloaded at Krjukowo.

Sturmgeschütz "Seydlitz" was brought forward to the *I./SS-Infanterie-Regiment "Deutschland"* at Bogdanowo.

***

At 1800 hours the following order was issued (excerpt):

Division Order for the Attack on 21 January 1941
(1:50,000 Sytschewka Map)

1.) During the last few days the **enemy** has attacked the *1. Panzer-Division*, which is defending the Rshew — Wjasma stretch of railroad between Wasusa Creek (18 kilometers north of Sytschewka) and Koslowo (4 kilometers southwest of Sytschewka). The attacks, carried out by several divisions with strong infantry elements, were repulsed. The division has built a bridgehead around Sytschewka to the northwest.

2.) ***Gruppe Sytschewka*** (*1. Panzer-Division*, *SS-Division "Reich"*, *Luftwaffe* formations under *Oberst* Biermann, *Gruppe Wosskressenskoje* under *Oberstleutnant* Decker) under command of the commander of the *1. Panzer-Division* is to launch a counterattack to the northwest in the morning of 21 January in order to take the enemy advancing to the south in the flank. It is to defeat him and, in coordination with the *VI. Armee-Korps*, seal the gap west of Rshew.

3. ***SS-Division "Reich"*** is to assemble during the night of 20/21 January in the area north of Sytschewka so that it can attack at first light on 21 January to the northwest on the right of the *1. Panzer-Division*.

4.) a) **Assembly areas:**

SS-Infanterie-Regiment ***"Deutschland"***: Borodino and Pomelnizuj
Gruppe Tychsen: Sucharewo — Stepankowo

b) **Boundaries:**

Between *SS-Division "Reich"* and *1. Panzer-Division*: Eastern outskirts of Wolkowo — western outskirts of Karabanowo — western outskirts of Borschtshewka — northeastern outskirts of Sswerkuschino — southwestern outskirts of Gussewo — northeastern outskirts of Jablonzewo

Between *SS-Infanterie-Regiment "Deutschland"* and *Gruppe Tychsen*: Southern outskirts of Bogdanowo — southern outskirts of Tararujkino

— northern outskirts of Poswasje — Hill 204.1 (one kilometer east of Maximowo)

...

Attack Objective on 21 January for *SS-Infanterie-Regiment "Deutschland"*: Sewlotschok. This is to be strongly secured.

Attack objective for *Gruppe Tychsen*: Maximowo

...

Of decisive importance for the smooth functioning of the attack is route reconnaissance of the roads. If necessary, routes must be cleared of snow in order to allow heavy weapons to be brought up.

Each *Kampfgruppe* is to equip one company for clearing snow and have it stand by for that purpose.

If the troops are in open terrain at nightfall, they are to be pulled back into built-up areas. Key terrain to the front is to be held by combat outposts with hourly relief.

Concentration of all available weapons and timely coordination of artillery support — if necessary through division — must be accomplished so that the infantry, on entering a built-up area, can capture it in the shortest possible time. In addition to losses caused by enemy fire, exposure in open terrain under the present weather conditions brings losses due to severe frostbite. That must be avoided.

5.) - 6.) ...

7.) **Artillery**:

All of the artillery of *Gruppe Sytschewka* is to be under the command of *Artillerie-Regiment 73, Oberstleutnant* Holste.

SS-Division "Reich" is to be supported by *Gruppe Eichberger* (*9./SS-Artillerie-Regiment "Reich"* and the *11./Artillerie-Regiment 109*).

8.) ...

9.) *SS-Infanterie-Regiment* ***"Der Führer"*** is to be brought forward on 21 January to the Kudinowka — Drostowo area. The main body of the regiment to be staged there at the disposal of the headquarters of the *9. Armee*. A reinforced battalion is to be transported to Rshew and attached to the *VI. Armee-Korps*. The battalion commander to proceed ahead of his battalion to the corps command post in Rshew...

10.) ***SS-Pionier-Bataillon "Reich"*** is to be transported to Sytschewka on 21 January. Arrival is to be reported to the division.

11.) *VIII. Flieger-Korps* is to support the division's attack.

12.) ...

13.) An agent employed as a Russian pilot will drop reports in small bags (annotated map sectors and sketches). The bags are weighted with a steel nut and provided with rags to serve as small flags. They are to be passed on to the division immediately.

14.) …

15.) The division command post: Sytschewka

/signed/ Kleinheisterkamp

***

Initially, the intention of the *9. Armee* was to stabilize the situation around Sytschewka. It would then secure the Rshew — Sytschewka — Wjasma railroad line as a vital supply line, attack the Soviet 29th and 39 Armies in the flanks and, finally, seal the area of the breakthrough at Solomino by attacking from the west and east.

"Attack, regain the initiative and dictate the course of action to the enemy." This was the fundamental principle of *General* Model.

21 January 1942

At 0600 hours the entire *Gruppe Sytschewka* began the counterattack to the northwest. It was -45 degrees Celsius (-49 degrees Fahrenheit).

Although not all elements of *SS-Infanterie-Regiment "Deutschland"* had arrived by 0500 hours, the commander of the regiment decided to start the attack as ordered at 0600 hours. The *I./SS-Infanterie-Regiment "Deutschland"* set out from Tararujkino to attack Charino. The *1./SS-Infanterie-Regiment "Deutschland"* broke weak enemy resistance in Charino and took possession of the place at 0900 hours.

Sturmgeschütz "Seydlitz" had to pull back after the first round was fired because the extreme cold had so thickened the fluid in the hydraulic recoil mechanism that the gun could not be fired. The *I./SS-Infanterie-Regiment "Deutschland"* attacked Tarkino from Charino with the *1./ SS-Infanterie-Regiment "Deutschland"* in the lead. It captured the village after a short fight in the built-up area. A 7.62-cm gun was captured. Shortly thereafter the *7./SS-Infanterie-Regiment "Deutschland"* also arrived in Tarkino, having arrived via Pomelnizy.

While the *3./SS-Infanterie-Regiment "Deutschland"* remained in Tarkino, the *1./* and *7./SS-Infanterie-Regiment "Deutschland"* set out to attack Ssewlotscheck. They encountered four enemy light tanks at the southeast outskirts of the village. Since the meter-high snow prevented bringing up heavy weapons, the tanks could not be effectively engaged. They turned away toward Maximowo. The companies captured Ssewlotscheck after a short fight within the built-up area and immediately secured to all sides.

The regiment's command post moved at 0915 hours to Charino. The companies established hedgehog positions for the night in the three villages that had been captured. Twenty prisoners were taken during the fighting. The radio traffic between *SS-Infanterie-Regiment "Deutschland"* and the division ended with the comment: "The morale of the troops is excellent."

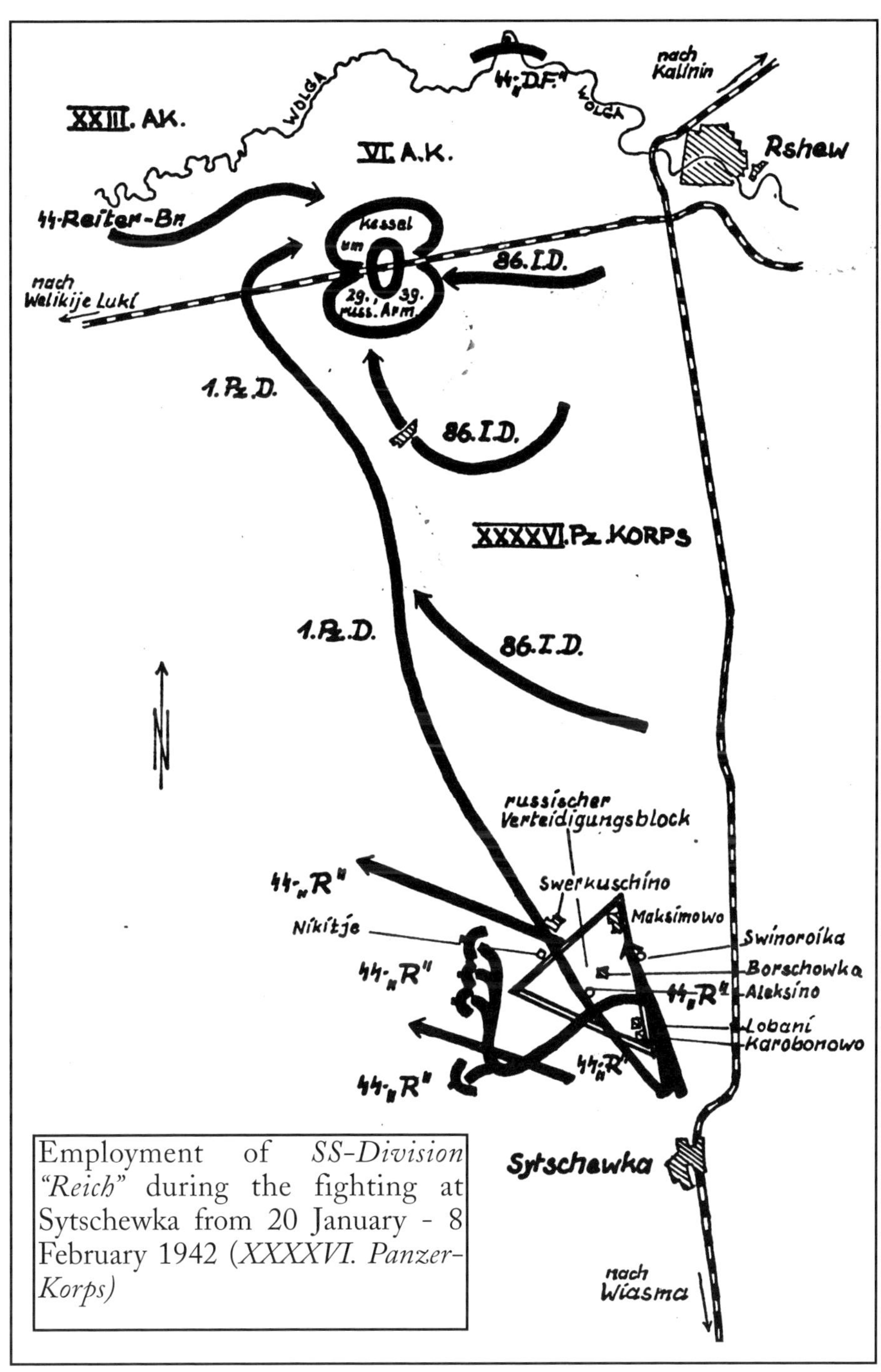

Employment of *SS-Division "Reich"* during the fighting at Sytschewka from 20 January - 8 February 1942 (*XXXXVI. Panzer-Korps*)

***

By order of the division, the *5./SS-Infanterie-Regiment "Deutschland"* was attached to *SS-Aufklärungs-Abteilung "Reich"*.

A Black Day for SS-Kradschützen-Bataillon "Reich"

The attack was substantially more difficult and costly for *Gruppe Tychsen*.

SS-Kradschützen-Bataillon "Reich" launched its attack against Pisino. At 0730 hours the *1./SS-Kradschützen-Bataillon "Reich"* broke into the southern portion of the village from the east, while the *4./SS-Kradschützen-Bataillon "Reich"* approached from the south in a pincers attack. The village was held by a Russian battalion. When the *1./SS-Kradschützen-Bataillon "Reich"* had nearly gained firm possession of the northern portion of the village and the *4./SS-Kradschützen-Bataillon "Reich"* had penetrated to the center of the village in hard close-quarters fighting, a Russian regiment joined the fighting. It had approached from the northwest and forced both companies back.

The commander of the *1./SS-Kradschützen-Bataillon "Reich"*, *SS-Hauptsturmführer* Ortmann, and 30 men of his company were killed. Many others, including the leader of the company headquarters section, *SS-Hauptscharführer* Hans Bader, were seriously wounded. *SS-Standartenoberjunker* (officer candidate) Rasel was also among the fallen.

Eighteen men under *SS-Standartenoberjunker* Müller were able to establish a firm position in an outbuilding and repulse numerous Russian attacks. The *2./* and *3./SS-Kradschützen-Bataillon "Reich" Kompanien*, under *SS-Hauptsturmführer* Grünwalder, had lost contact with the *1./SS-Kradschützen-Bataillon "Reich"* and were then brought up by *SS-Hauptsturmführer* Tychsen personally. Attacking from the south, they fought their way via the badly battered *4. SS-Kradschützen-Bataillon "Reich"*.

The acting commander of the *3./SS-Kradschützen-Bataillon "Reich"*, *SS-Untersturmführer* Möller, was killed, as was *SS-Standartenoberjunker* Buchmann (of the *2./ SS-Kradschützen-Bataillon "Reich"*). More officers were put out of action, some of them severely wounded. They included: *SS-Untersturmführer* Pawelka (*3./SS-Kradschützen-Bataillon "Reich"*), *SS-Standartenoberjunker* Quendler (*2./SS-Kradschützen-Bataillon "Reich"*) and *SS-Standartenoberjunker* Köhler (*4./SS-Kradschützen-Bataillon "Reich"*). The attack ground to a standstill.

At 1000 hours five light tanks of the *1. Panzer-Division* rolled in from the south from the direction of Systschewka. On the way they eliminated Russians who had threatened the battalion from the south. Some of these Russians had penetrated the village from the south during the fighting and were taken prisoner. The tanks joined the fighting, renewing its forward progress. In another hour the rest of the village had been captured. A large number of sleds were captured on which the numerous wounded could be transported to Sytschewka. The assistant battalion surgeon, *SS-Untersturmführer Dr.* Grünwalder, had accompanied the attack and set up a dressing station in the southern part of the village.

After the fighting, 450 dead Russians were counted in and around Pisino. Of the battalion's 450 officers, noncommissioned officers and enlisted personnel, four officers and almost 70 noncommissioned officers and enlisted personnel had been killed. Five officers and about 170 noncommissioned officers and enlisted personnel had been wounded. The losses mounted and the condition of the wounded deteriorated because the temperature ranged between - 45 and - 48 degrees Celsius [-49 and -54 degrees Fahrenheit], causing additional casualties due to freezing.

This meant that the total losses due to death and wounding in *SS-Kradschützen-Bataillon "Reich"* amounted to at least 250 men.

After that extremely costly fighting *SS-Kradschützen-Bataillon "Reich"* could no longer proceed with the attack that had been ordered against Karabonowo (west of Pisino).

At 1200 hours the division commander, *SS-Brigadeführer* Kleinheisterkamp, was at the battalion to form his own picture of the situation. The battalion was in the process of organizing itself. It was attempting to determine its casualties and its new combat strength. The dead Germans and Russians could scarcely be distinguished from each other. Therefore, it was not immediately possible for the division commander to get a picture of the extent of friendly losses. Accordingly, he initially required *SS-Hauptsturmführer* Tychsen to carry on the attack, but then rescinded the order when, as he walked through the village, he became convinced of the magnitude of the actual losses.

The working relationship with the *1. Panzer-Division* was outstanding, as was the timely involvement of that division's five light tanks in Pisino. They helped master a serious crisis for *SS-Kradschützen-Bataillon "Reich"*. The help was gratefully received by the men of the battalion.

Oberstleutnant i. G. Rolf Stoves wrote about the fighting in his history of the division:

> ...The cooperation with formations of the *Waffen-SS* proved to be outstanding. For the first time since Dunkirk, they were attached to the division in a larger than regimental framework. The division was happy that it could rely on such comrades who fought shoulder to shoulder with its men in that difficult situation. (Rolf Stoves, *Geschichte der 1. Panzer-Division*, ?. Bad Nauheim: Podzun-Pallas-Verlag, 1961.)

***

During the course of the day, *SS-Aufklärungs-Abteilung "Reich"* captured Swinoroika and secured in all directions.

A memorandum of the *XXXXVI. Panzer-Korps* states, in part:

On 20 January 1942 *SS-Division "Reich"*, which had suffered severe attrition during the previous fighting before Moscow, took over a portion of the sector of the western ring around Szytschewka that had been pushed forward by the *1. Panzer-Division*. It exacted substantial losses from the enemy in repeated heavy defensive fighting.

In addition to their combat missions, both divisions overcame the difficulties caused by the ever diminishing motorization of the units through field-expedient organization of ski and sled formations. However, the losses in the previous fighting and due to frostbite were painfully apparent in those units as well. (*XXXXVI. Panzer-Korps, Die Winterschlacht von Szytschewka 25.1.42 -12.2.42*, p. 2. Unpublished memorandum)

22 January 1942

SS-Kradschützen-Bataillon "Reich" secured and reorganized after the heavy bloody fighting of the previous day in Pisino.

At 0600 hours a Russian battalion coming from the northeast broke into the northern portion of the village by surprise. Hand grenades exploded in the billets. The platoon leader of the attached *Panzer-Jäger* platoon was seriously wounded. The Russians were thrown out of the village again in hand-to-hand combat. They withdrew to the west to Karabonowo.

Bloody Fighting by SS-Infanterie-Regiment "Deutschland"

SS-Infanterie-Regiment "Deutschland" had the mission of attacking and capturing Karabonowo. The attack, which would be carried out by the *II./SS-Infanterie-Regiment "Deutschland"*, was to be supported by all the heavy weapons of the regiment, by *Kampfgruppe Tychsen* and also by four tanks of *Panzer-Kompanie Albrecht* (*1. Panzer-Division*).

In the gray light of dawn, the *II./SS-Infanterie-Regiment "Deutschland"*, under *SS-Hauptsturmführer* Jobst, arrived from the north to mount the attack on Karabonowo. As morning approached, the temperature was measured at -51 degrees Celsius (-60 degrees Fahrenheit). The oil in the machine guns was frozen and they would not fire.

The staging for the attack was completed at 0600, but catastrophic snowdrifts prevented the tanks from arriving. As a result, heavy infantry guns initially provided the preparation. The attack was launched from the northern outskirts of Pisino by the *7./SS-Infanterie-Regiment "Deutschland"*. Tank support was still not available.

The company made only slow forward progress against strong enemy resistance. In the end, it was pinned down in the open just before reaching Karabonowo. The snow-covered open expanse of terrain provided no cover. Whatever moved was fired upon.

Those who had not been wounded sought cover behind the dead. Since they had to lie in the open in the Siberian cold, those at the front died from the cold in a short period of time while facing the enemy. A constant flow of wounded arrived at the dressing station of *SS-Kradschützen-Bataillon "Reich"* in Pisino. Only those who had not advanced too far were able to break contact with the enemy when the attack was called off. Even the tanks, which had arrived in the meantime, were unable to get the attack moving forward, even though they took part in the firefight.

The *7./SS-Infanterie-Regiment "Deutschland"* was methodically shot to pieces in the northern portion of Karabonowo by superior enemy forces.

The *2./SS-Infanterie-Regiment "Deutschland"*, which launched its attack on the southern section of Karabonowo from Pisino, got to within 80 - 100 meters of the village and then stalled in heavy machine-gun, antitank-gun and heavy fire. It was impossible to establish contact between the *2./* and *7./SS-Infanterie-Regiment "Deutschland"*.

The *2./SS-Infanterie-Regiment "Deutschland"* also suffered heavy losses since it was pinned down in plain sight of the enemy in deep snow on an open field. All platoon and squad leaders were killed or wounded. The company commander, *SS-Obersturmführer* Hallwachs, was also wounded. Nevertheless, he continued to command the company until noon. Every attempt to renew the attack stalled due to the enemy's heavy defensive fire.

At 1030 hours the four tanks of the *1. Panzer-Division* set out from Pisino to get the attack of the *2./SS-Infanterie-Regiment "Deutschland"* moving. It was still pinned down in the open field.

Thereupon the already greatly weakened *2./SS-Infanterie-Regiment "Deutschland"* started a third attempt against Karabonowo. One tank received a direct hit on its turret when it was 80 meters from the village. In spite of the armored support, the attack only gained a few meters of ground. It then bogged down again in the face of the enemy's defensive fire when it was 50 meters from the edge of the built-up area. The battalion commander, *SS-Hauptsturmführer* Jobst, was also wounded in the attempt.

In a courageous move, the tanks advanced under heavy enemy defensive fire right up to the village and fired on strong points of resistance at the edge of the built-up area. In spite of everything, it proved impossible to capture Karabonowo.

At 1130 hours the *II./SS-Infanterie-Regiment "Deutschland"* broke contact with the enemy after all the wounded had been retrieved. It was covered again by the fire of the splendid comrades in the tanks and an artillery barrage. The battalion fell back to Pisino and occupied security positions there. Two officers and 75 noncommissioned officers and enlisted personnel were killed in the futile attack. Sixty noncommissioned officers and enlisted personnel were wounded. Thirty dead from the *7./SS-Infanterie-Regiment "Deutschland"* were in a hollow 20-50 meters from the Russian snow positions.

The fallen were later buried in a mass grave at the edge of Sytschewka beside those of *SS-Kradschützen-Bataillon "Reich"*.

The *1./* and *2./SS-Kradschützen-Bataillon "Reich"* were combined into a single company.

Plugging the Gap

On that day the *VI. Armee-Korps* attacked as the main effort to the northwest against the point of the Soviet breakthrough.

On the same day, the *XXIII. Armee-Korps*, which had been cut off near Olenino, attacked from the west with the *206. Infanterie-Division*, *SS-Kavallerie-Brigade Fegelein* and *Sturmgeschütz-Abteilung 189* and fought its way eastward toward the formations of the *VI. Armee-Korps*.

The Russians were suddenly faced with men of *SS-Kampfgruppe Zehender* — cavalrymen employed as infantry — as well as the assault guns of *Sturmgeschütz-Abteilung 189*.

The German double attacks against the point of the Soviet breakthrough succeeded in closing the gap between Nikolskoje and Solomino. The German forces had been strained to the utmost,

The *VIII. Flieger-Korps* under *General der Flieger* Wolfram von Richthofen suppressed the Soviet antiaircraft and artillery positions in the area of the breakthrough. Heavy howitzers smashed the Soviet antitank gun positions.

Employment of SS-Infanterie-Regiment "Der Führer"

While *SS-Division "Reich"* and the *1. Panzer-Division* were engaged in heavy fighting in the Sytschewka area, *SS-Infanterie-Regiment "Der Führer"* was detached from the division's command and control and was temporarily, directly attached to the headquarters of the *9. Armee* headquarters for separate employment at another location.

As the last unit pulled out of the Rusa position, the regiment marched all day on foot via Gshatsk to Spassk. It entrained there and was transported by rail to Sytschewka.

The commander of the regiment moved ahead by staff car for a briefing at the command post of *SS-Division "Reich"*. He reported his impressions of the trip to the division:

> My drive was about 120 kilometers long and followed behind the front lines. I encountered an almost unbelievable disparity between the combat units of all branches of the *Wehrmacht* and supply units, rations units, maintenance elements and construction units. While approximately 50-100 men per kilometer fought at the front — including staffs and heavy weapons — thanks to the overcrowding of all the villages and collective farms that we drove through, I could hardly find a little spot for

myself and my driver to rest. Everything was filled to bursting with rear-area units. With that disparity between combat and combat-service-support elements, the front could not possibly be held for long.

***

In a discussion at the command post of *SS-Division "Reich"* at which *General* Model was personally present, the *General* declared: "The *Führer* has expressly ordered that a *SS-Regiment* is to be employed in closing the point of the breakthrough northwest of Rshew."

He ordered the commander of *SS-Division "Reich"* to attach a regiment to the *VI. Armee-Korps* in Rshew. It was to be used to help close the gap in the front west of Rshew and for the subsequent defense of the old breakthrough position at the Volga.

SS-Infanterie-Regiment "Der Führer" was the only regiment which could be considered for the mission since it had not yet been committed. It was thus detached from the division and attached to the *VI. Armee-Korps*. The destination of the railroad transports that were on the way was immediately changed to Rshew.

SS-Infanterie-Regiment "Der Führer" was hastily inserted at the Volga, exactly at the position where the Soviet 29th Army had moved across the frozen river.

"Hold no matter what!" was Model's personal order to Kumm. "Under all circumstances," the *General* repeated for emphasis.

Kumm saluted: "Jawohl, Herr General!"

Would he be able to hold that decisive position with only one regiment?

The limited combat power gave reason for concern — two battalions, heavy weapons, staffs and communications personnel — all together 650 men! The *I./*and *III./SS-Infanterie-Regiment "Der Führer"* at that time still had two companies and the remnants of a machine gun company. The *13./SS-Infanterie-Regiment "Der Führer"* had a light and a heavy infantry-gun platoon, and the *14./SS-Infanterie-Regiment "Der Führer"* was outfitted with two platoons of antitank guns (3.7 cm). The personnel of *15./* and *16./SS-Infanterie-Regiment "Der Führer"* had already been consolidated among the regiment, as had the proven *II./SS-Infanterie-Regiment "Der Führer"*.

The commander of the regiment drove ahead and reported to the *VI. Armee-Korps*.

The Rshew Area of Operations

23 January 1942

The two-sided attack from east and west to close the point of the breakthrough succeeded, though it demanded maximum effort. The spearheads of the attack of the *XXIII. Armee-Korps* and *Gruppe Recke* of the *VI. Armee-Korps* made contact at 1245 hours.

The *XXIII. Armee-Korps* again had contact with the *9. Armee*, even if only over a narrow land bridge. The two Soviet routes through the snow across the Volga were blocked and the corps of the 29th and 39th Armies that had broken through were cut off from their rear areas and any supplies.

This was Model's hour. He had regained the initiative on the battlefield between Sytschewka and the Volga and he had no intention of losing it again. His first action was to reinforce the land bridge that had been won between the *VI.* and *XXIII. Armee-Korps* — with *SS-Infanterie-Regiment "Der Führer"*. The Russians, naturally, were exerting all their strength to break the barrier and reestablish connection with their nine divisions that had broken through. That had to be prevented.

At the orders conference of the *VI. Armee-Korps* on 23 January the commander of the regiment, *SS-Obersturmbannführer* Kumm, was given the mission as part of *Gruppe Recke* of closing the existing gap by attacking. *Gruppe Recke* would then hold the positions attained under any circumstances and organize for defense. The rail transports of the regiment continued to roll toward Rshew. The men repeatedly had to fight to clear the rail line between Sytschewka and Rshew from enemy before they could continue their journey — and this cost time.

The Sytschewka Area of Operations (SS-Division "Reich")

During the night of 22/23 January an enemy company infiltrated from the woods southeast of Philippowo (west of Pomelnizy) and another company from Alexino (south of Swinoroika and Charino) through the area of operations of *SS-Infanterie-Regiment "Deutschland"*. They moved south to Borodino and took possession of the village.

To regain Borodino a company of combat engineers, a tank company (Albrecht) and *Kompanie Intorf* (remnants of *II./SS-Infanterie-Regiment "Deutschland"*) set out at 0930 hours from the south, southeast and west. The main body advanced along the railroad line to Borodino. The attack succeeded. At 1000 hours Borodino was again firmly in friendly hands.

The remnants of the enemy (about 100 men) initially attempted to fall back to the northwest. They received defensive fire from the German combat outposts at Pomelnizy and turned away to the southwest. There they ran into the concentrated fire of the defenses of Charino and the Pedwjasje strongpoint. In addition, they were fired on by a 15-cm gun belonging to the artillery and a light infantry gun in an open firing position. The remnants of the enemy were completely wiped out south of Sswinoroika by *SS-Aufklärungs-Abteilung "Reich"*.

Several Russian attacks were successfully repulsed by the *I./SS-Infanterie-Regiment "Deutschland"* at Ssewlotschek.

At 0800 hours *SS-Aufklärungs-Abteilung "Reich"* reported enemy attacks from the north, south and east. Some of them were supported by armor. However, they were repulsed.

In the morning the Russians attacked the trains elements of *SS-Kradschützen-Bataillon "Reich"* that were quartered north of Sytschewka. Led by *SS-Hauptscharführer* Mittermaier, the men of the trains elements forced the enemy back in an immediate counterattack, during which Mittermaier was severely wounded. There were additional losses in dead and wounded.

***

The commander of *Gruppe Sytschewka*, *Generalmajor* Krüger (*1. Panzer-Division*), issued the following order of the day:

Order of the Day

The commander-in-chief of *Heeresgruppe Mitte* has specially commended the officers and men of *Gruppe Sytschewka* for their outstanding performance.

Thanks to the aggressiveness of the attack, it has been possible to draw so many of the enemy's forces here and against the troops fighting in Sytschewka that the prerequisites were established for the attack of the *VI. Armee-Korps* and the *XXIII. Armee-Korps* to succeed in such a surprisingly successful manner.

Because *Gruppe Sytschewka* successfully engaged five enemy divisions by its constant attacks, the gap between the *VI.* and *XXIII. Armee-Korps* was sealed in two days of fighting.

I am pleased to be able to pass that commendation on to the officers and soldiers of the combat forces that have fought together in *Gruppe Sytschewka*. We shall continue to perform our duty in the same manner until the enemy, who has now been cut off from his base of supplies, is destroyed. Any weak point of the enemy and every opportunity for attack are to be utilized.

This commendation is to be made known to all formations.

/signed/ Krüger

(Taken from appendix 251 of the war diary of *SS-Infanterie-Regiment "Deutschland"* for 23 January 1942)

24 January 1942

During the night there was intense enemy patrol activity in the division's combat sector.

At 0745 hours the *I./SS-Infanterie-Regiment "Deutschland"* in Ssewlotschek was attacked from the northeast, north and northwest by a Russian battalion. The attack was, however, repulsed after heavy fighting. The weapons attached to the *I ./SS-Infanterie-Regiment "Deutschland"* — artillery, *Sturmgeschütze* and 2-cm *Flak*— played a substantial role in that success.

Stukas attacked enemy-occupied Maximowo from 1215 hours to 1230 hours.

The situation in the Sytschewka area of operations was marked by Russian attacks from all sides on the division's individual strongpoints. During the attacks various villages to the rear of the German forces changed hands at times and the situation in general was up in the air.

The Rshew Combat Sector (SS-Infanterie-Regiment "Der Führer")

The *VI. Armee-Korps* intended to start the attack on 24 January with forces assembled behind its left wing. It assigned *SS-Infanterie-Regiment "Der Führer"*, which had been attached to the *256. Infanterie-Division*, the mission of attacking from the limit of the previous advance to the northwest at dawn on 26 January. It was to reach the Volga knee northwest of Rshew and go over to the defensive on both sides of the river, where it was to orient northeast in a sector about 6 kilometers wide. At the same time other forces were to defend to the southwest against the enemy who had been cut off in the German rear area as a result of the *SS* regiment's attack.

At the last minute the greatly delayed transports of *SS-Infanterie-Regiment "Der Führer* arrived during the night of 24/25 January in Rshew.

25 January 1942

In the early morning the battalion and regimental units were moved forward to Spas Mitkowo. Without a pause, *SS-Infanterie-Regiment "Der Führer"* launched its attack at 0900 hours. The enemy offered no significant resistance. During the course of the morning the attack reached the Volga. The attack moved forward smoothly with the *I./SS-Infanterie-Regiment "Der Führer"* (*SS-Sturmbannführer* Ehrath) on the left and the *III./SS-Infanterie-Regiment "Der Führer"* (*SS-Hauptsturmführer* Schulz) on the right. The attack continued through the line attained the previous evening by *Infanterie-Regiment 471* at the Volga knee and onward from Noshkino toward the northwest. The mission was to mop up the woods west of Timonzewo and advance to the line Kolubakino — Klepenino. Any opportunity to capture Solomino in conjunction with the *Sturmgeschütz* attack was to be used.

The hip-deep snow in the so-called "Scenery" Woods and on the steep slopes of the deeply frozen Volga made it difficult for the men.

At 1200 hours the *III./SS-Infanterie-Regiment "Der Führer"* reported the capture of Klepenino.

In the sector of the *I./SS-Infanterie-Regiment "Der Führer"*, *SS-Oberscharführer* K. Mayer, the battalion liaison officer, worked his way forward through the so-called "Assembly Area" Woods on his own initiative. He then reconnoitered to Solomino. The village was clear of the enemy. In accordance with the mission, the *2./SS-Infanterie-Regiment "Der Führer"* occupied the village and organized there for defense. Security was pushed forward to Pajkowo. As a result of these actions, the gap was sealed.

After darkness fell the commander of the regiment established the main line of resistance with the two battalion commanders. The sector was about 6.5 kilometers wide and was oriented north-northeast. It was bisected by the Volga. The river itself was frozen solid enough for crossing, but the steep banks on both sides were about 30 meters high. The newly gained main line of resistance ran on both sides of the Volga. The *I./SS-Infanterie-Regiment "Der Führer"* was committed on the left, west of the Volga, and the *III./SS-Infanterie-Regiment "Der Führer"* established itself on the right, east of the river.

From this point on, the weak *III./SS-Infanterie-Regiment "Der Führer"* had to hold the sector originally designated for the entire regiment. *SS-Hauptsturmführer* Schulz set up his command post in Klepenino. *SS-Hauptsturmführer* Ehrath (*I./SS-Infanterie-Regiment "Der Führer"*) moved his command post to Lebsino.

The regimental command post was located at Noshkino. During the night the temperature dropped to -40 degrees Celsius (-40 degrees Fahrenheit) under a clear, starry night with an icy wind.

After reaching the designated main line of resistance, the companies immediately set to work blasting foxholes in the deeply frozen snow by using blasting caps and mines. Machine-gun and rifle positions were laid out at intervals of one to two hundred meters. As a result, the front line was thinly occupied. The defensive position had no depth. The regiment had no reserves available.

The frozen Volga was able to bear the weight of heavy tanks. The village of Klepenino, consisting of about thirty houses, was on the right bank of the Volga in the sector of the *III./SS-Infanterie-Regiment "Der Führer"*. Adjoining to the right was a broad, gently undulating snow-covered expanse of open terrain. At a distance of about 80 meters from the main line of resistance, which followed the northern outskirts of the village, was the start of a wooded area that led back to the northeast. Another patch of woods was located about 600 meters behind the battalion.

The positions of the *I./SS-Infanterie-Regiment "Der Führer"* were somewhat more favorable. The main line of resistance ran about 200 meters north of a patch of woods and had a good field of fire and extensive observation into the terrain in front of the lines.

The attack of *SS-Infanterie-Regiment "Der Führer"* had clearly come at a favorable time in which the Russian 29th and 39th Armies had broken completely through the gap in the German front but the Russian command did not yet have new forces available north of the point of the breakthrough. The enemy was apparently in the process of reorganizing or bringing up new units, which would certainly not be long in coming.

The Sytschewka Combat Sector (SS-Division "Reich")

On 25 January 1942 the *XXXXVI. Panzer-Korps* under *General der Panzertruppen* von Vietinghoff took over command of the formations involved in heavy defensive fighting around and west of Sytschewka. These included the *1. Panzer-Division*, *SS-Division "Reich"* and elements of *Infanterie-Regiment 409* and the *III./Infanterie-Regiment 314*.

***

In a special order of *SS-Division "Reich"* on 25 January the following changes in the combat organization were ordered:

1.) The *II./SS-Infanterie-Regiment "Deutschland"* is temporarily disbanded. The *5./ - 7./SS-Infanterie-Regiment "Deutschland"* are consolidated into a single rifle company.

2.) The *8./SS-Infanterie-Regiment "Deutschland"* is consolidated with the *4./SS-Infanterie-Regiment "Deutschland"*...

3.) ...

4.) The *15./SS-Infanterie-Regiment "Deutschland"* is attached to the *1./SS-Infanterie-Regiment "Deutschland"*.

5.) ...

6.) The infantry forces, with the exception of *SS-Infanterie-Regiment "Der Führer"*, are combined into *Kampfgruppe Harmel*. The *Kampfgruppe* consists of

Staff, signals platoon, *13./, 14./, 16./SS-Infanterie-Regiment "Deutschland"*.

Gruppe Tost (*I./SS-Infanterie-Regiment "Deutschland"*)

Gruppe Tychsen (reinforced *SS-Kradschützen-Bataillon "Reich"*)

Gruppe Kment (reinforced *SS-Aufklärungs-Abteilung "Reich"*)

/signed/ Kleinheisterkamp

(Taken from appendix 253 of the war diary of *SS-Infanterie-Regiment "Deutschland"* for 25 January 1942)

***

The **Division Order for Defense North of Sytschewka** for 25 January 1942 (excerpts):

1.) The enemy was attacked by *Gruppe Sytschewka* on 21 and 22 January 1942.

The bridgehead northwest of Sytschewka was significantly extended by the capture of several villages. The enemy suffered extremely heavy losses in men and materiel.

The enemy's *Schwerpunkt* has shifted since 23 January to the north wing. The Russians are attacking *Gruppe Sytschewka*, which has gone over to the defensive, with strong forces, especially our right wing. Numerous attacks by day and by night have been repulsed with heavy losses to the enemy.

2.) *SS-Division "Reich"*, minus *SS-Infanterie-Regiment "Der Führer"* and attached since 1200 hours on 25 January to the *XXXXVI. Panzer-Korps*, is to defend in the line marking the limit of the advance and secure the Sytschewka — Rshew stretch of railroad against acts of sabotage in the event of an enemy breakthrough. Attached to the division are the *II./Infanterie-Regiment 309* and the *2./* and *5./Infanterie-Regiment 309*.

3.) Improvement of the defense:

The occupied villages are to be improved for all-around defense by reinforcing houses and outbuildings. Positions are to be established immediately using the houses.

Strongpoints (huts that can be heated, camouflaged with snow, with snow positions on both sides of the huts) are to be constructed along the patrol routes between the built-up areas.

It is essential that enemy breakthrough attempts are spotted in a timely manner and can be suppressed long enough so that reserves for immediate counterattacks can be brought up...

(Taken from appendix 253 of the war diary of *SS-Infanterie-Regiment "Deutschland"* for 25 January 1942)

***

A Russian company-sized attack in the sector of the *I./SS-Infanterie-Regiment "Deutschland"* was repulsed.

The Rshew Combat Sector (SS-Infanterie-Regiment "Der Führer")

26 January 1942

Reconnaissance by the *III./SS-Infanterie-Regiment "Der Führer"* revealed that the woods directly in front of the main line of resistance were held by the enemy.

No enemy had been identified facing the sector of the *I./SS-Infanterie-Regiment "Der Führer"* on the near bank of the Volga. *SS-Hauptsturmführer* Ehrath had mines laid on the former Russian route of advance in and around Pajkowo to enhance security. Combat outposts were established in the built-up area and toward Krutiki.

SS-Obersturmbannführer Kumm briefed the friendly forces situation to the commander-in-chief of the *9. Armee* during the latter's visit to the regi-

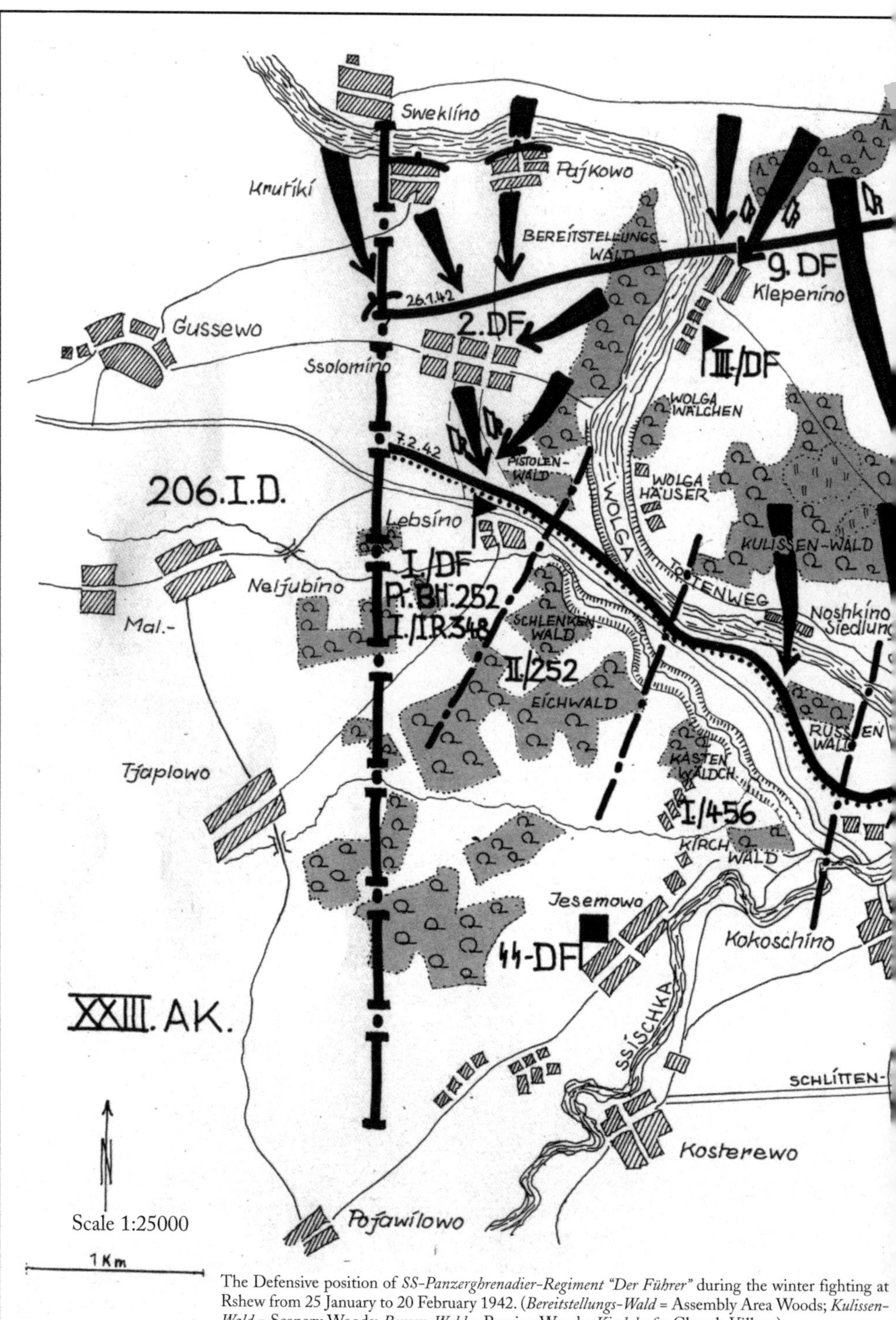

The Defensive position of *SS-Panzerghrenadier-Regiment "Der Führer"* during the winter fighting at Rshew from 25 January to 20 February 1942. (*Bereitstellungs-Wald* = Assembly Area Woods; *Kulissen-Wald* = Scenery Woods; *Russen-Wald* = Russian Woods; *Kirchdorf* = Church Village)

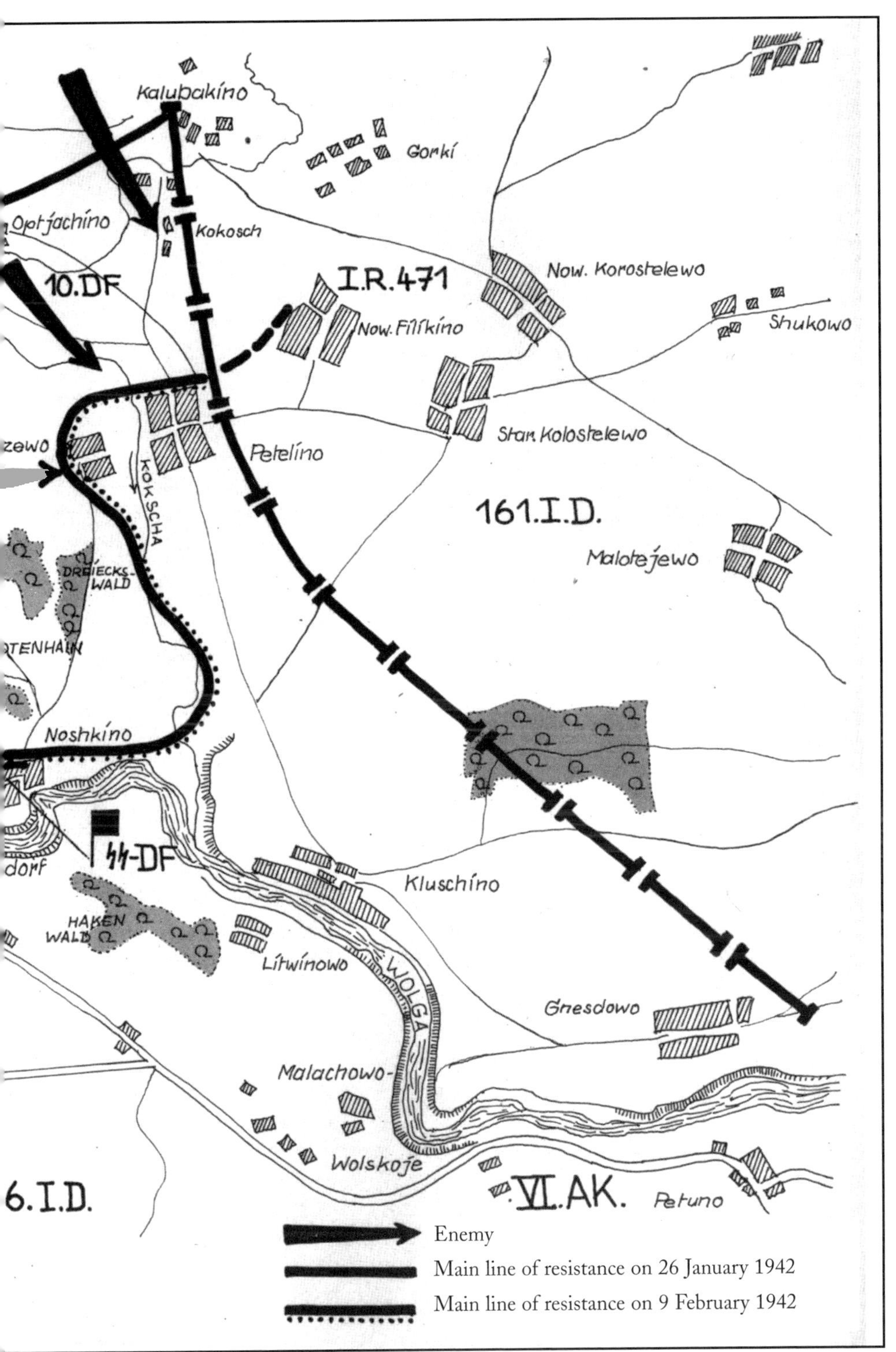
Kalubakino
Gorki
Optjachino
Kokosch
10.DF
I.R.471
Now. Korostelewo
Now. Filikino
Shukowo
Stan. Kolostelewo
Petelino
KOKSCHA
161.I.D.
Malotejewo
DREIECKS-
WALD
Noshkino
SS-DF
Kluschino
HAKEN
WALD
Litwinowo
WOLGA
Gresdowo
Malachowo
Wolskoje
6.I.D.
VI.AK.
Petuno
Enemy
Main line of resistance on 26 January 1942
Main line of resistance on 9 February 1942

ment's command post in Noshkino.

In order to improve it own main line of resistance, the *III./SS-Infanterie-Regiment "Der Führer"* wished to advance its positions to the edge of the woods north of Point 203.6. *General* Recke, the commander of the artillery group, was in full agreement with this recommendation, especially since the woods on the knoll represented a significant threat to the main line of resistance. The friendly forces on the right of the *III./SS-Infanterie-Regiment "Deutschland", Infanterie-Regiment 471*, promised support in the form of a strong assault troop.

The commander of the regiment agreed to the attack, which was carried out with artillery support.

In the assault, however, the attacking troops were surprised to encounter well constructed and strongly held enemy positions, the old Russian Volga positions from back in the fall! In spite of extreme effort, it was not possible to eliminate these positions and the situation became increasingly critical.

The commander of the *III./SS-Infanterie-Regiment "Der Führer", SS-Hauptsturmführer* Schulz, personally lead the attack. He directed the withdrawal of the assault troops back to the main line of resistance. In so doing he set an example and died a soldier's death, a particularly difficult and tragic loss in this critical situation.

SS-Hauptsturmführer Bollert, who had been commanding the *10./SS-Infanterie-Regiment "Der Führer"*, assumed command of the battalion. The pursuing enemy was repulsed with artillery and fire from the heavy machine guns of the *12./SS-Infanterie-Regiment "Der Führer"*.

During the morning, assault troops from the *I./SS-Infanterie-Regiment "Der Führer"* made a surprise attack over the Volga and penetrated into Sweklino. The enemy was eliminated and, after the assault troops withdrew, the small village was left unusable as a strongpoint.

27 January 1942

A glance at the situation of the *9. Armee* gives the following picture:

The *VI. Armee-Korps*, employed to the northwest, and the *XXIII. Armee-Korps*, which had been split up, had exerted every last effort in extremely strenuous fighting to form a weak blocking position, a tenuous "bridge" for the German formations. It was a weak barrier against the units of the Red Army that had broken through — the 29th and 39th Armies as well as the 11th Cavalry Corps — and their lines of communications. However, the Russian forces that had broken through were in no way beaten — to the contrary. They had achieved an operational breakthrough with nine rifle divisions and three to four cavalry divisions. Following the German example, they wanted to complete a large pocket battle that would destroy *Heeresgruppe Mitte*.

The Mission for SS-Infanterie-Regiment "Der Führer"

The weak "barrier" at the site of the breakthrough on the Volga therefore had to be strengthened and held under any circumstances against the Russian formations that were following the earlier ones to the south.

This was the mission that *SS-Infanterie-Regiment "Der Führer"* — along with all of the army and *Waffen-SS* formations that would be attached to it in the course of the coming defensive fighting — was given. Here at the former site of the breakthrough by the two Russian armies, was the actual center of gravity of the great fight — certainly an unenviable mission for the regiment.

Therefore it was no surprise that, day after day, the commander-in-chief of the *9. Armee*, *General* Model, personally appeared at the command post of *SS-Infanterie-Regiment "Der Führer"* in order to discuss the situation with the commander of the regiment, *SS-Obersturmbannführer* Kumm, and consider all requisite measures. He usually came by motor vehicle. One time he landed on the frozen Volga with a *Fieseler Storch* and once he came on horseback.

It was said of him that he spent one hour a day at the situation map but could be found with the troops at all the sectors of the front for ten hours. Carell wrote: "Wherever he appeared he worked like a generator that recharged the drained energies of the commanders."

On 27 January Model arrived at noon at the command post of *SS-Infanterie-Regiment "Der Führer"* in Noskino. He held a commanders' conference there to discuss the future conduct of the fighting. Present were the commanding generals of the *VI.* and *XXIII. Armee-Korps*. The commanders of the *161.* and *206. Infanterie-Divisionen* were also brought in. The main theme was securing the boundary between the two corps.

During the discussion, a report arrived from the *I./SS-Infanterie-Regiment "Der Führer"*: "The enemy is attacking on this side of the Volga from the northwest toward Solomino with strong forces, about 1,000 men."

The enemy had broken through in the adjoining sector to the left. Immediate countermeasures were instituted, which did not affect the regiment.

During the night of 26/27 January several enemy advances were repulsed in front of the regiment's sector. In the gray light of dawn the enemy launched a futile attack on Timonzewo.

At 0830 hours the *III./SS-Infanterie-Regiment "Der Führer"* reported strong enemy concentrations in front of Klepenino. The enemy continually reinforced his forces until 1030 hours. The first appearance of enemy armor in front of the battalion was reported.

The companies and heavy weapons remained in a constant state of maximum alert. However, the penetrating cold made everything difficult.

Nevertheless, all weapons were carefully maintained in a state of combat readiness — for their readiness was the only guarantee for surviving the next enemy attack. An icy wind sweeping over the Volga repeatedly caused all pathways and snow positions to be snowed over in a short period of time.

The Sytschewka Area of Operations (SS-Division "Reich")

On 27 January replacement manpower arrived from the replacement battalion. *SS-Kradschützen-Bataillon "Reich"*, for example, received 80 replacements.

***

At 1900 hours the following order went out to the division (excerpt):

Division Order for Continuation of the Attack on 28 January 1942

1.) After learning of the complete encirclement of his forces, the **enemy** facing the *XXXXVI. Panzer-Korps* has apparently not come to any decision to how to continue the fighting. He has gone over to the defensive and presumably waits for relief from the north.

2.) The ***XXXXVI. Panzer-Korps*** is to continue the attack to destroy the encircled enemy forces west and northwest of Sytschewka on 28 January. Initially it is to attack to the west with the *86. Infanterie-Division* and to the northwest with *SS-Division "Reich"* and the reinforced *1. Panzer-Division.*

Boundary between *SS-Division "Reich"* and the *1. Panzer-Division* remains unchanged.

The ***1. Panzer-Division***, in conjunction with *SS-Division "Reich"*, is to capture the group of houses south of Karabonowo.

3.) On 28 January ***SS-Division "Reich"*** (with the attached tank company) initially is to capture Lubany (one kilometer northwest of Karabanowo) and then Karabonowo. It is to establish strongpoints in both villages and positions itself there so it can continue the attack against Lentewo and Borschtschewka on 29 January

4.) **Concept of the operation:**

SS-Sturmbannführer Harmel is to command the attack. One tank company of *Panzer-Regiment 7* is to be attached to *Kampfgruppe Harmel* and will be brought forward in a timely manner in accordance with later verbal instructions.

As of 0600 hours on 28 January, the command post of *Kampfgruppe Harmel* is to be located at the fork in the road 1.5 kilometers north of Pujsino.

One reinforced company of *Gruppe Kment* and the tank company will be brought up from the northeast by 0745 hours about 400 meters from the northeastern outskirts of Lubany. They can exploit the *Stuka* attack (last bombs at 0745 hours) for the advance into the built-up area at that time. After the capture of Lubany, the infantry is to rapidly organize itself into strongpoints.

The main body of *Gruppe Kment* is to prevent the attack from being outflanked from Lentewo by concentrated fire of all heavy infantry weapons and units of artillery on Lentewo.

Artillery will additionally screen Aleksino and Rshawino with fire, preventing outflanking from there.

Infantry elements are to prevent an enemy attack from Lentewo against the flank of the attacking forces.

The attack on Karabonowo is to follow completed staging of the armor at 1015 hours. It is to exploit an additional bombing attack on Karabonowo. A reinforced company of *Gruppe Tychsen* is to lead the attack with support from artillery and all available heavy infantry weapons from Pujsino. At the same time the tank company is to attack the rear of the positions at Karabanowo from Lubany. Last bombs on Karabonowo at 1015 hours.

Also starting at 1015 hours, the *1. Panzer-Division* will attack the village one kilometer south of Karabonowo from the south.

> It is essential that the staging of infantry and armor be carried out so that immediate advantage can be taken of the bombing attacks and that all heavy infantry weapons and artillery are concentrated up to the time of the infantry assault on the built-up areas.

5.) – 6.) …

7.) ***SS-Pionier-Bataillon "Reich"*** is to improve the strongpoints according to verbal instructions. The engineer main effort is the improvement of the villages captured on 28 January (in conjunction with *Kampfgruppe Harmel*). The commander of *SS-Pionier-Bataillon "Reich"* is responsible.

8.) – 11.) …

12.) Division command post: Sytschewka.

/signed/ Kleinheisterkamp

Supplement: Russian intelligence reveals that partisan groups have tapped into German field-telephone cables and listen in on important command conversations. Attention is again directed to the need for strictest use of signal security by officers in tactical conversations.

(Taken from appendix 255 of the war diary of *SS-Infanterie-Regiment "Deutschland"* for 27 January 1942)

Formation of the Pocket

28 January 1942

All elements of the *XXXXVI. Panzer-Korps* started the attack at 0600 hours in heavy snow squalls and icy wind. They attacked from the previously held area to the west and northwest. Their mission was to reduce the developing pocket and bring the encircled Russian formations closer to destruction.

Kampfgruppe Harmel had the mission of capturing Lubany and

Karabonowo. For this purpose *Panzer-Kompanie Albrecht* (*1. Panzer-Division*) was attached to the *Kampfgruppe*.

After a *Stuka* attack on Lubany, the reinforced *Kompanie Damsch* that had assembled southeast of Swinoroika near point 202.2 launched its attack on the village together with *Panzer-Kompanie Albrecht*. Shortly after the tanks moved out a retrograde movement of strong enemy forces from Karabanowo to Lubany was spotted. Thereupon the 11 tanks of *Panzer-Kompanie Albrecht* moved out with great *elan*. Temporarily separating themselves from the infantry, they attacked the enemy movement in the flank and fired into the surprised enemy with all weapons. The tanks were the first to reach Lubany. Enemy troops organizing for defense were taken under effective fire and some were eliminated. The rest were driven off.

After the tanks had advanced through the village, some of the tanks brought the infantry company forward to mop up Lubany. The infantry had only made slow progress advancing through the deep snow. At 0810 hours the village had been cleared of enemy and was firmly in friendly hands.

Then, at 0830 hours, *Kompanie Grünwalder*, which had assembled in Pisino, advanced against the northern outskirts of Karabanowo. The company was superbly supported by the flanking fire of the eleven tanks. After the infantry company had nearly reached Karabanowo, the tanks advanced to the west of Lubany and attacked Karabanowo from the rear. They hit the enemy, who was already falling back, one more time with destructive fire from all barrels. The tanks and infantry linked up in the center of the village.

At 0945 hours Karabanowo was reported as having been thoroughly mopped up and occupied by friendly troops.

In his memorandum regarding the departure of *Panzer-Kompanie Albrecht* from his *Kampfgruppe*, *SS-Sturmbannführer* Harmel concluded with:

> It gives me extraordinary pleasure once again to be able to confirm in these three engagements that the working relationship between infantry and armor has been outstanding and, as a result, outstandingly successful.
>
> The armor has not only provided moral support to the infantry, it has also given effective supporting fire. The armor and infantry have mutually inspired each other with their fighting spirit and dash and superbly complemented each other with their weapons. The outstanding assistance provided by *Panzer-Kompanie Albrecht* has spared the regiment heavy losses.
>
> In the name of *SS-Infanterie-Regiment "Deutschland"* I wish *Panzer-Kompanie Albrecht* continued fortune in war and complete success.
>
> /signed/ Harmel
> *SS-Sturmbannführer* and Regimental Commander

***

At 1430 hours *Kampfgruppe Kment* (*SS-Aufklärungs-Abteilung "Reich"*) launched its assault-troop operation against Lestjewo. At 1600 hours Lestjewo was captured. A counterattack by two reinforced enemy battalions from Alexino and Borschtschewka was repulsed.

Patrol activity during the night within *Kampfgruppe Harmel* was specified by orders. At 2000 hours the division notified the units by field telephone that the attack on Maximowo would probably be carried out on 29 January.

On 28 January *SS-Division "Reich"* passed the following on to all units:

Führer Decree

Soldiers of the *9. Armee* !

The gap in your front northwest of Rshew has been sealed.

The enemy that penetrated there has been cut off from his rearward lines of communications as a result. If you continue to perform your duty in such fashion in the coming days, a large number of Russian divisions will be destroyed.

I thank all of you who, in your comradely devotion to duty, came from the adjoining fronts to attack the site of the breakthrough. I am grateful that, in spite of the severe rigors of the winter, your aggressive spirit could not be broken. I know, my soldiers, what that means. My grateful commendation therefore goes to you, soldiers of the *9. Armee*.

/signed/ Adolf Hitler

(Taken from appendix 260 of the war diary of *SS-Infanterie-Regiment "Deutschland"* for 28 January 1942. Operations diary number 12/42g)

***

In the meantime, the combat elements of *Kampfgruppe Harmel* "converted" from motorized vehicles to horse-drawn sleds. Only a portion of the trains units remained motorized.

The complement of horses for the individual units:

SS-Infanterie-Regiment "Deutschland": 20 horses
3./SS-Pionier-Bataillon "Reich": 30 horses
SS-Kradschützen-Bataillon "Reich": 80 horses
SS-Aufklärungs-Abteilung "Reich": 34 horses

***

In the war diary of *SS-Sturmgeschütz-Batterie "Reich"* is the following entry for 28 January 1942:

The Last Assault Gun — Lost

At 1230 hours the *"Seydlitz"* was ordered to *SS-Aufklärungs-Abteilung "Reich"* at Swinoroika. A mounted combat patrol was launched from there in the direction of Lentewa. Three hundred meters outside of Lentewa a bunker was identified and engaged, whereupon the occupants fled. After that, an antitank gun in an outbuilding could be destroyed. During that time, the village was attacked by *Stukas*. The infantry, supported by the *"Seydlitz"*, advanced after the *Stuka* attack.

After a short distance the crew heard a powerful detonation. The *Sturmgeschütz* was lifted. The crew bailed out. The assault gun had run over two or three mines. The hull had been torn open. Oil began to burn. Attempts to extinguish the fire proved impossible. The crew moved back. The assault gun burned. The ammunition detonated. The *"Seydlitz"* was completely ripped apart. The last assault gun of the division has been destroyed.

As a result, *SS-Division "Reich"* lost the last example of a unique weapon. Their outstanding support of the grenadiers of the division since the beginning of the Russian campaign enabled, to a considerable degree, its great successes and the avoidance of high losses.

Paul Carell wrote how the enemy evaluated the *Sturmgeschütze*: "Kambulin (Author's note: a Russian lieutenant) was severely wounded, then froze to death. Shortly before his death he wrote the final entry in his diary: 'The German assault guns are a deadly weapon, which we have no means to combat.'" (Paul Carell, *Unternehmen Barbarossa*, p. 331. Frankfurt am Main / Berlin (West): Ullstein Verlag GmbH, 1663. That is but one account among many in his book concerning the effectiveness of the *Sturmgeschütze*.)

The Rshew Combat Sector (SS-Infanterie-Regiment "Der Führer)

On 28 January heavy snow fell starting at 0200 hours. During the night attacking enemy were repulsed by the companies at Klepenino and Opjachtino. Those attacks continued throughout most of the day. The enemy did not stop them until 1700 hours. One T 34 was knocked out.

General Model was right at the command post of *SS-Infanterie-Regiment "Der Führer"* when the men of the *I./SS-Infanterie-Regiment "Der Führer"* brought in a captured Russian who stated that he was a radio operator on the staff of the Russian 30th Army — a decided rarity since such people knew more than many commanders.

He made the following statement in the presence of the commander-in-chief:

> The formations of the entire 30th Army are lined up, one behind the other, on the road from Kalinin via Wissokoje to the Volga knee: Seven rifle divisions and six armored brigades. They have the mission of continuing the attack of the 29th Army, which has broken through. The start of the attack has been set for tomorrow morning.

He then named the sequence and designations of the individual divisions, regiments and brigades. The breakthrough to relieve the encircled armies was to be forced at any cost.

Model left the command post in a concerned state of mind. He parted from the commander of the regiment with the words, "Kumm, I am relying on you!" Laughing, he added: "But it may also be that Ivan has fooled us."

Start of the Russian Offensive

29 January 1942

The Russian army radio operator had not played any tricks. The offensive of the Soviet 30th Army began in the morning, and exactly at the spot where the 29th Army had broken through before. Traces of the 29th Army's movement were still recognizable as two broad routes on both sides of the Volga. The enemy attacked at that spot without let-up for three weeks, day and night.

He (the Russian) made a tactical error, but a typical Russian error. He did not concentrate all his forces for a great breakthrough. He neglected to form a main effort. He threw battalion after battalion, then regiment after regiment and, finally, brigade after brigade into the fight. (Paul Carell, *Unternehmen Barbarossa*, p. 333. Frankfurt am Main / Berlin (West): Verlag Ullstein GmbH, 1963.)

***

The regimental commander at that time, *SS-Obersturmbannführer* Kumm, wrote the following regarding that fighting in his notes:

The men of the regiment held their positions against all attacks. What every one of them accomplished in the way of heroism during those days far eclipsed any previous action! Every attack was repulsed with fearful losses to the enemy, often in hand-to-hand fighting with hand grenades and bayonets. The enemy dead piled up into walls before the positions of the companies.

The most frightening thing, however, were the attacks by enemy armor.

***

Two antitank platoons of *Panzer-Jäger-Abteilung 561* of the army took over the antitank defense in the sector of the *III./SS-Infanterie-Regiment "Der Führer"*. Their action was decisive to the success of the defense. In addition, however, the brave grenadiers were able to repulse additional armored attacks with mines, Molotov cocktails and concentrated charges.

And there was no end in sight to the enemy assaults. Nevertheless, *SS-Infanterie-Regiment "Der Führer"* and the attached army units held their positions in this decisive sector of the front.

The crisis in which the *9. Armee* found itself continued to intensify as leading elements of the enemy that had broken through on 29 January reached the highway west of Wjasma. The enemy then sometimes blocked the highway for entire days. However, intercepted radio conversations of the cut-off enemy revealed that he was also suffering severe shortages of fuel and rations, although he received considerable quantities of ammunition by air-drops at night.

The Sytschewka Combat Sector (SS-Division "Reich")

On 29 January there was no combat activity in the sector of *Kampfgruppe Harmel.* The day was used by all elements to improve and fortify the villages and positions and for clearing roads and the like.

***

At 2345 hours the following order went out to all units:

Division Order for Continuation of the Attack on 30 January 1942

1.) On 28 January ***Kampfgruppe* Harmel**, supported by all the heavy weapons and one tank company, captured several villages. Together with the attack group of the *1. Panzer-Division*, it defeated the focal point of the enemy defense northwest of Sytschewka.

On 29 January the *86. Infanterie-Division* and the *1. Panzer-Division* gained considerable ground in successful attacks on both wings of the corps.

The enemy continues to stubbornly defend every built-up area and conducts a fighting withdrawal to the west.

2.) The ***XXXXVI. Panzer-Korps*** is to continue the concentric attack on Sereda on 30 January.

Attack objectives:

86. Infanterie-Division: Sereda
SS-Division "Reich": Swerkuschino
Reinforced *1. Panzer-Division*: Nikite

3.) ***SS-Division "Reich"*** initially is to capture Borschtschewka, simultaneously with the advance of the *1. Panzer-Division* against Aleksino. From there it is to support the attack of the *1. Panzer-Division* on Nikite with heavy weapons and then captures Maximowa. The division is to be prepared to advance to and capture Swerkuschino, after the capture of Maximowo.

. . .

30 January 1942

After the artillery barrage and subsequent *Stuka* attack on Maximowo, *Kampfgruppe Tost* attacked from Swineroika with the *2./SS-Infanterie-Regiment "Deutschland"*.

Taking advantage of the second artillery barrage and the *Stuka* attack, the *2./* and *3./SS-Infanterie-Regiment "Deutschland"* penetrated the village. The *2./SS-Infanterie-Regiment "Deutschland"* attacked from the south and advanced rapidly, quickly reaching the southern outskirts of the village. After brief but heavy house-to-house fighting, the center of Maximowo was reached.

The *3./SS-Infanterie-Regiment "Deutschland"*, after breaking enemy resistance at point 204.9, attacked the enemy from the north and mopped up the northern portion of the village. The two companies then met in the center of town. At 1615 hours Maximowo and point 204.9 were firmly in friendly hands.

After reaching Maximowo from the east, the *I./SS-Infanterie-Regiment "Deutschland"* pushed rapidly on through the village to the west to Perejesdnaja. It occupied the village and set up all-around security.

Kampfgruppe Tychsen moved via Charina and Takina to Ssewlotschek and staged there.

The situation remained quiet for *Kampfgruppe Kment.*

The Rshew Combat Sector (SS-Infanterie-Regiment "Der Führer")

The heavy defensive fighting continued in the sector of *SS-Infanterie-Regiment "Der Führer"*. The temperature again sank to -46 degrees Celsius (-49 degrees Fahrenheit) in a heavy storm with drifting snow. The enemy's aerial resupply operation for the encircled Soviet divisions in the pocket continued throughout the night.

At 0845 hours the *III./SS-Infanterie-Regiment "Der Führer"* reported an enemy attack on the right wing against Kokosch. The *I./SS-Infanterie-Regiment "Der Führer"* made a similar report from Solomino. The combat outposts still remained in Pajkowo.

The enemy attacked with infantry and armor between Kokosch and Klepenino. The *III./SS-Infanterie-Regiment "Der Führer"* reported at 1035 hours that it had knocked out seven enemy tanks. Renewed strong enemy concentrations were observed in the woods near point 203.6. Six enemy tanks with about two companies of infantry reinforced the Russian forces that were already in those woods.

At 1145 hours two Soviet tanks and about 40 Red soldiers were in the point of woods about 700 meters west of Timonzewo. They fired on the positions of the *III./SS-Infanterie-Regiment "Der Führer"* from the rear. A company of the combat-engineer battalion of the *256. Infanterie-Division* was to be committed against that enemy.

Reports of high losses for the battalions arrived at the command post of *SS-Infanterie-Regiment "Der Führer"*. Some of the companies had a "trench strength" of only 20-30 men. The same situation held for the brave comrades of *Infanterie-Regiment 167*. The enemy continued to launch massed attacks until 1545 hours. Eleven of the twenty-four Soviet tanks that had attacked up to that point were eliminated.

In general, the regiment's sector could be held. It was only east of Klepenino that Russian tanks were able to overrun three machine-gun positions, destroying the weapons and putting the crews out of action.

The enemy infiltrated through that gap into the woods west of Timonzewo but was forced back out in an immediate counterattack.

Around 1800 hours heavy hand-to-hand fighting was in progress against an enemy group that had penetrated with tanks into the eastern part of Klepenino. The enemy infantry may not have been of the highest fighting quality, but the fighting men of the *III./SS-Infanterie-Regiment "Der Führer"* still had a difficult time holding their own against the enemy masses.

The overall situation of the *VI. Armee-Korps* was extremely tense.

At 1930 hours *General* Model ordered a halt to the intended attack against the enemy pocket behind the lines of the northern defensive front, in which *SS-Infanterie-Regiment "Der Führer"* also fought.

For 31 January the staff of *Infanterie-Regiment 471* was assembled with the *I./Infanterie-Regiment 471* and four *Sturmgeschütze* and attached to *SS-Infanterie-Regiment "Der Führer"* for a counterattack to clean up the penetration in the sector of the *III./SS-Infanterie-Regiment "Der Führer"*.

The bitter fighting continued until 2200 hours. In Klepenino the *9./SS-Infanterie-Regiment "Der Führer"* defended with a total of 30 men. The staff of the *III./SS-Infanterie-Regiment "Der Führer"* and the remnants of the *10./SS-Infanterie-Regiment "Der Führer"* fought desperately in Optjachino and Timonzewo. Since the positions in between had been eliminated, the Russians could infiltrate freely into the so-called "Scenery" Woods between Timonzewo and Klepenino. In Klepenino itself the *9./SS-Infanterie-Regiment "Der Führer"* struggled doggedly with the enemy in intense hand-to-hand combat. The combatants were almost at the end of their strength.

31 January 1942

The winter storms persisted with a temperature of -14 degrees Celsius (7 degrees Fahrenheit) and substantial snowdrifts. The enemy attacked Opjachtino (*10./SS-Infanterie-Regiment "Der Führer")* and the small group that remained of the *9./SS-Infanterie-Regiment "Der Führer"* in Klepenino without letup. Apparently, the Russians had not yet detected the wide gap in the front.

During the night a weak company of combat engineers of the *256. Infanterie-Division* proved unable to throw the enemy out of the part of the village of Klepenino that it held.

At 0900 hours the *I./SS-Infanterie-Regiment "Der Führer"* reported that it had repulsed an enemy attack in the size of approximately two companies. Another two enemy tanks were destroyed in Klepenino.

The counterattack that had been set for 0930 hours by the *I./Infanterie-Regiment 471* — reinforced with two companies of the *256. Infanterie-Division* and assault guns of the *2./Sturmgeschütz-Abteilung 189* — was postponed until 1110 hours. The time needed for staging the attack had been underestimated.

A single company of *Infanterie-Regiment 471* and the *1./Infanterie-Regiment 456* attacked together with four *Sturmgeschütze*. An engagement immediately developed between the assault guns and the Russian tanks. Three Soviet tanks were knocked out. The rest of the enemy armor and the infantry fell back to the woods near Point 203.6.

Together with the *1./Infanterie-Regiment 456*, the men of the *10./SS-Infanterie-Regiment "Der Führer"* occupied the positions between Klepenino and Optjachino. They were decisively supported by the assault guns.

By 1330 hours the situation had been stabilized. The Soviet tanks dared to fire no more than a few quick rounds from the thickets of the woods. They immediately vanished when the hidden *Sturmgeschütze* opened fire.

The Sytschewka Combat Sector (SS-Division "Reich")

Within the framework of the *XXXXVI. Panzer-Korps*, *SS-Division "Reich"* carried on the attack to the north on 31 January 1941 with Swerkuschino as its objective.

***

The attack was planned in three phases:

Phase 1: Simultaneous with the advance of the *1. Panzer-Division* (friendly forces on the left) on Alexino, attack on Borschtschewka.

Phase 2: Attack on Maksimowka and Persdnaja.

Phase 3: Advance on Swerkuschino.

After *Kampfgruppen Kment* and *Tychsen* assembled for the attack, *Kampfgruppe Kment* launched the attack at 0830 hours, following ten minutes of intensely concentrated fire preparation by artillery and all of the heavy weapons. The attack was successful. Borschewka was in friendly hands at 0945 hours.

At 1345 hours *Kampfgruppe Tost* had completed assembly for the attack. Its assembly was reinforced with strong supporting fire from *Kampfgruppe Tychsen* on the northern outskirts of Ssewlotschek.

At 1400 hours the attack on Sswerkuschino began with strong artillery support. Sswerkuschino was captured by 1530 hours with tanks of the *1. Panzer-Division*, which attacked from the south.

***

A memorandum prepared by the *XXXXVI. Panzer-Korps* discusses this aspect of the fighting:

Under the same weather conditions and continually worsening snowdrifts, the successful attacks continued against the enemy, who continued his stubborn defense. Elements of the *VIII. Flieger-Korps,* under extremely unfavorable weather conditions, continued to support the ground fighting with particular success.

In spite of furious enemy counterattacks, the *1. Panzer-Division* and *SS-Division "Reich"* captured the Karabonowo — Rshawinje — Nikitje — Maxsimowo defensive network in an extremely difficult, hard-fought attack. (*XXXXVI. Panzer-Korps, Die Winterschlacht von Sytschewka (25.1 — 12.2. 1942),* p. 4. Unpublished)

1 February 1942

Werner Haupt wrote about the overall situation of *Heeresgruppe Mitte* at the time:

At the end of January it became evident that the German army fronts had stabilized. The Soviets called a halt to their offensive between Kalinin and Kursk.

The Kalinin and Briansk Fronts, which had advanced far to the west, had to overcome supply problems that could not be resolved with the available means and forces. (Werner Haupt, *Heeresgruppe Mitte,* p. 123. Bad Nauheim: Podzun-Pallas-Verlag, 1968.)

The Sytschewka Combat Sector (SS-Division "Reich")

On 1 February Sereda was captured by the reinforced *1. Panzer-Division* and the *86. Infanterie-Division.*

The attacks that had been conducted, particularly toward the northwest from Sytschewka against Sereda by *SS-Division "Reich"* and the *1. Panzer-Division,* necessarily resulted in an increasingly long and open west flank for the corps. *SS-Division "Reich"* (hitherto to the right of the *1. Panzer-Division*) was shifted behind and past the left flank of the *1. Panzer-Division* to protect that flank.

After the enemy positions directly west of Sytschewka had been broken through and after the enemy's extraordinarily high manpower losses, to which fields of corpses beyond any yet seen even in the east bore witness, the enemy's power of resistance noticeably decreased. Even an apparently disciplined concentration of the weakened remnants of individual divisions under unified command could not prevent the enemy from increasingly falling back to the west. Nevertheless, the enemy had not yet been overthrown and continued to offer senseless local resistance. (*XXXXVI. Panzer-Korps, Die Winterschlacht von Sytschewka (25.1 — 12.2. 1942),* p. ?. Unpublished)

***

The **Division Order for Assuming the Security Mission West and Southwest of Sytschewka** issued on 1 February 1942 stated (excerpts):

1.) *SS-Division "Reich"* reached its attack objective on 31 January with *Kampfgruppe Harmel* and support from all heavy weapons, thereby achieving a great success in spite of the extremely difficult weather conditions.

SS-Infanterie-Regiment "Der Führer", which remains attached to the *VI. Armee-Korps,* has repulsed extremely heavy Russian attacks in the last few days and destroyed a large number of heavy tanks. The enemy continues to fight while falling back to the west and northwest.

2.) The XXXXVI. Panzer-Korps is to continue to attack in the previous direction with the *86. Infanterie-Division* and the *1. Panzer-Division*.

3.) *SS-Division "Reich"* is to be pulled out of its previous combat sector on 1 February 1942 and assume the flank-guard mission for the left flank of the corps...

...The division is to maintain contact on the right with the *1. Panzer-Division*, which is attacking to the northwest. It is later to move the security line further west through offensive operations...

...

8.) *Sicherungsgruppe* Sytschewka (security group) under *Oberst* Hempel and the *I./Artillerie-Regiment 620* are attached to the division...

SS-Sturmgeschütz-Batterie "Reich" is Disbanded

Effective 1 February 1942 *SS-Sturmgeschütz-Batterie "Reich"* was temporarily deactivated after the loss of its last *Sturmgeschütz*. Thirty-two noncommissioned officers and enlisted personnel were transferred as infantry to *SS-Infanterie-Regiment "Der Führer"*. The first cadre personnel — which then comprised all of the *5./SS-Infanterie-Regiment "Der Führer"* — had already gone ahead from that unit.

The remaining members of the battery were in Pewnaja. On 3 February 1942, 14 noncommissioned officers and enlisted personnel left from there for an armored course at Vienna. The rest of the battery was moved to Wjasma on 7 March. On 9 March they then entrained for Prague.

With these actions, the unique weapons system of the division temporarily ceased to exist. It will surface again later when recformed as an assault-gun battalion, where its achievements will be specially recognized.

The Rshew Combat Sector (SS-Infanterie-Regiment "Der Führer")

During the night there were occasional enemy artillery barrages mixed with salvos from Stalin organs. Soviet reconnaissance probes were repulsed. The *I./SS-Infanterie-Regiment "Der Führer"* had to withdraw its combat outposts in Krutiki and Pajkowo to strengthen the force in Solomino. Snowfall and light frost interfered with all movements. In general, uncanny quiet prevailed in front of the main line of resistance. During the evening hours the enemy was observed clearing mines that had been laid outside of and in Krutiki. Work crews were seen clearing snow from the Krutiki — Pajkowo route. Those were preparations for a new attack!

***

The commander of *SS-Infanterie-Regiment "Der Führer"*, *SS-Obersturmbannführer* Kumm, released the following order of the day on 1

February 1942:

Order of the Day

Men!

In many days of extremely heavy fighting the regiment has held a critical sector of the front and caused extremely heavy losses to the enemy.

The enemy's intention of breaking through our sector with four rifle divisions, one armored brigade and innumerable heavy weapons to relieve his divisions that have been cut off to the south has foundered.

The commander-in-chief of the *9. Armee*, *General der Panzertruppen* Model, has reported your determination and success to the *Führerhauptquartier*, naming the regiment. Take pride in what you have accomplished.

The enemy will continue to attack. However, I am firm in the conviction and the trust that you will also continue to fight just as courageously. This is the most difficult test that we have been faced with and we will pass it together.

All of you have earned my thanks and commendation. I have been directed to express the special thanks of the commander-in-chief of the *9. Armee* to you.

/signed/ Kumm
SS-Obersturmbannführer

2 February 1942

During the night, at 0100 hours, the enemy started to feel his way forward to Solomino. At 0850 hours, combat outposts of the *I./SS-Infanterie-Regiment "Der Führer"* identified strong enemy concentrations at the Volga near Pajkowo. At the same time the *III./SS-Infanterie-Regiment "Der Führer"* reported enemy assembling north of Optjachino. All available friendly artillery was employed against these forces.

At 1215 hours, the *III./SS-Infanterie-Regiment "Der Führer"* reported heavy enemy attacks on Klepenino, along with substantially stronger infantry forces than previously employed. One of three T 34's was knocked out. Well-placed friendly artillery fire was unable to stop the Russian infantry. The enemy again penetrated into the houses on the northern outskirts of Klepenino.

What was left of the *9./SS-Infanterie-Regiment "Der Führer"*, supported by men of the *3./Pionier-Bataillon 356*, forced the Russians back out. In the center of the sector, between Klepenino and Optjachino, the vastly superior enemy forces overpowered the *1./Infanterie-Regiment 256*. That gave the enemy renewed access to the "Scenery" Woods. Enemy artillery fire continually interrupted field-telephone connections, particularly between Klepenino and the regiment's command post in Noshkino. Accordingly, no report of the situation of the *1./Infanterie-regiment 256* got through. The immediate counterattack was unsuccessful.

It could only be a question of time before the powerful enemy assault would wipe out the *III./SS-Infanterie-Regiment "Der Führer"*.

On this day *SS-Artillerie-Regiment "Reich"* released 200 artillerymen to *SS-Infanterie-Regiment "Der Führer"* to serve as infantry. The desperate nature of the situation of the *9. Armee*, and especially that of *SS-Infanterie-Regiment "Der Führer"*, is best illustrated by the fact that these specialists were employed as infantry, as was previously the case with the *Sturmgeschütz* crews. Personnel with experience at the front were desperately needed as reinforcements and were thrown into the raging defensive fighting as infantry.

The Sytschewka Combat Sector (SS-Division "Reich")

During the course of the day (2 February), *Kampfgruppe Harmel* occupied its security sector to secure the left flank of the *XXXXVI. Panzer-Korps* after completing its shift to the left flank. The forces were arrayed as follows:

Kampfgruppe Tost (*SS-Infanterie-Regiment "Deutschland"*): Pokrowskoje area
Kampfgruppe Tychsen (*SS-Kradschützen-Bataillon "Reich"*): Borosowka, Plotki and Bol Ossinowka area
Kampfgruppe Kment (*SS-Aufklärungs-Abteilung "Reich"*): Kaposstino — Likono — Kaurowo — Toroptschino.

There was no combat activity in the security area of the *Kampfgruppe*.

The Rshcw Combat Area (SS-Infanterie-Regiment "Der Führer")

3 February 1942

Bitter fighting continued during the night in the entire sector. In spite of repeated friendly advances, it was not possible to regain the field positions between Klepenino and Optjachino.

The commander of the regiment, *SS-Obersturmbannführer* Kumm, personally went to the *256. Infanterie-Division* and *VI. Armee-Korps* and urgently called attention to the dangerous situation in his sector.

In the Klepenino area two antitank platoons of *Panzerjäger-Abteilung 561* (with 5-cm guns) had been attached to the regiment and in position for some time. Under the resolute leadership of *Leutnant* Petermann the splendid *Panzerjäger* decisively supported the fighting of the grenadiers of the *9./SS-Infanterie-Regiment "Der Führer"* and the combat engineers of the *3./Pionier-Bataillon 256* with their 13 guns. These guns had knocked out 20 T 34's by 3 February.

A tank overran and crushed one *Pak* near the command post of the *III./SS-Infanterie-Regiment "Der Führer"*. One gun received three different crews in a short period of time. The gun was snowed in over the axles and the burnt-out enemy tanks in front of the position significantly reduced its field of fire. No prime mover could move forward into the heavy enemy fire to bring ammunition or allow a change of position. In the end, the grenadiers and combat engineers were on their own, making death-defying attacks on the rolling steel monsters with mines, Molotov cocktails and concentrated charges.

During the course of the morning the enemy redoubled his efforts to achieve a breakthrough.

The End of the 10./SS-Infanterie-Regiment "Der Führer"

A Russian armada of 30-40 T 34's moved forward in the open facing the positions of the *10./SS-Infanterie-Regiment "Der Führer"* in the Optjachino sector. Three or four tanks faced every machine-gun position and foxhole, firing with all weapons at a range of 30-40 meters into the company positions. The Soviet gunners systematically knocked out machine-gun nest after machine-gun nest, foxhole after foxhole. The hurricane of fire lasted half an hour.

Paul Carell described the end of the *10./SS-Infanterie-Regiment "Der Führer"*:

> ...thirty minutes long. Then they moved back into the woods. Silence and sparkling, clear cold lay over the open area. Two hours later, one man crawled out of the shot-up positions of the company to the battalion command post. He was *SS-Rottenführer* Wagner. Seriously wounded, with frozen hands, he attempted to stand up for the battalion commander to make his report. But he collapsed and reported as he lay there: "*Hauptsturmführer!* I am the last man of the company! All the others are dead!"
>
> He died. And then there was no one left from the *10. Kompanie*...(Paul Carell, *Unternehmen Barbarossa*, p. ?. Frankfurt am Main / Berlin (West): Verlag Ullstein GmbH, 1963)

The Front is Torn Apart

This left a yawning gap of more than a thousand meters in the regiment's main line of resistance. There were no more reserves available to seal the gap. In response to the urgent appeal of the regimental commander to the *VI. Armee-Korps*, an alarm company with a strength of 120 men was sent to the regiment to seal the gap. It was composed of drivers, cooks, cobblers and tailors and led by paymasters. There was no doubt they were all honorable men and soldiers, but they were totally inexperienced in combat, particularly in the exceptional conditions of the murderous fight in bitter cold that demanded the utmost from even the old, experienced frontline soldiers.

With a heavy heart *SS-Obersturmbannführer* Kumm entrusted this unit with the mission of sealing the gap and reoccupying the positions of the *10./SS-Infanterie-Regiment "Der Führer"*. The regiment expected new enemy attacks in the coming night, which would be directed against the open sector of the front.

The alarm company reoccupied the positions of the *10./SS-Infanterie-Regiment "Der Führer"*. Scarcely had it occupied the positions when, after a mortar barrage, the Soviets attacked with cries of "Urrah!" The inexperienced men lost their nerve, abandoned their positions and were shot down to a man on the open area as they moved back. Too much had been demanded of them.

The corps had no other reserves to send to the regiment.

4 February 1942

The enemy was then free to advance through the broad gap during the night. Starting at 0230 hours, Red soldiers attacked Klepenino and east of the village with bitter rage and strong artillery support. They put everything they had into achieving the decisive breakthrough. Despite a desperate defense, the enemy was able to break through at first light into the "Scenery Woods" south of Klepenino. The combat engineers and construction troops employed there preparing blocking positions were surprised at their work, overrun and dispersed.

In the early morning hours the enemy was at the southern edge of the "Scenery Woods" with strong infantry and armored forces, about 50 meters from the regiment's command post.

As a precaution, approximately eight houses had been prepared for defense. Deep holes were dug in the floors and firing ports established in the lower timbers. Every man of the regiment's staff — adjutant, officers, radio operators, messengers and drivers — was then committed to hold that sector of the front.

For three solid days the enemy attacked from the woods and shot the houses to bits with tanks. Nevertheless, all of the massed attacks that were so vigorously driven forward were repulsed with bloody losses for the enemy.

The soul of the resistance was the regiment's adjutant, *SS-Hauptsturmführer* Holzer. He acted in the same manner that he had earlier, when he was commander of first the *7./* and then the *11./SS-Infanterie-Regiment "Der Führer"*. He ran from man to man, repeatedly inspiring each with renewed defensive willpower.

Carell also wrote regarding this phase of the fighting:

> ...It was no phrase, but terrible reality in the most literal sense when the reports stated: "The dead lay in great heaps outside of Klepenino... (Paul Carell, *Unternehmen Barbarossa*, p. ?. Frankfurt am Main / Berlin (West): Verlag Ullstein GmbH, 1963)

***

What was left of the *I./Infanterie-Regiment 456* was committed against the enemy which had broken through. The battalion had also been badly battered. It was to attack along the Volga to the northwest with one company and towards Timonzewo with the other. An enemy company-sized attack on Timonzewo from the "Scenery Woods" landed in the midst of friendly preparations for the attack.

The situation for the friendly forces was totally unclear. On the north side of the "Scenery Woods" the right-hand company of *Infanterie-Regiment 456* suffered heavy losses. Nevertheless, the commander of the company and twelve grenadiers reached Timonzewo. The company on the left reached the north side of the "Scenery Woods" along the Noshkino — Klepenino road. At 1430 hours, it attempted with great bravado to force the enemy back so it could then advance to Klepenino. This, however, proved unsuccessful since that company was attacked from out of the wood line.

At 1630 hours, *SS-Infanterie-Regiment "Der Führer"* sent a strong combat patrol in a generally northward direction to determine where the enemy had firmly established himself.

Throughout the entire day the enemy fired for effect on the regiment's sector. The field-telephone cables to the battalions and to the division were cut. It was only by a messenger arrived from the combat patrol that *SS-Obersturmbannführer* Kumm learned that the enemy had established himself firmly at the northern edge of the "Scenery Woods", east of the Noshkino — Klepenino road.

Three enemy tanks were put out of action in Klepenino during the course of the day.

The commander of the regiment again urgently requested that the corps change the unbearable situation by committing reserves. The situation report had the result that the chief of staff of the *VI. Armee-Korps* showed up at the command post of *SS-Infanterie-Regiment "Der Führer"* to personally inform himself of the situation. Half an hour there convinced him…

That same evening a regimentally sized formation — a *Regimentsgruppe*—under the commander of *Infanterie-Regiment 167* was set in march. It comprised the *I./Infanterie-Regiment 456* (two companies), one company of *Infanterie-Regiment 167*, the reassembled *3./Pionier-Bataillon 256* and three assault guns of the *2./Sturmgeschütz-Abteilung 189*. It was given the mission at midnight of forcing the enemy back out of the "Scenery Woods" and over the main line of resistance, of establishing a new main line of resistance and sealing the gap by closing up with the *9./SS-Infanterie-Regiment "Der Führer"* on the right.

5 February 1942

At 0045 hours the commander of *SS-Infanterie-Regiment "Der Führer"* ordered assault detachments to simultaneously attack from both Optjachino and Klepenino. They were to force the enemy out of the positions between the two villages. The attack from Klepenino never got started, but the attack from Optjachino captured and occupied several field fortifications. During the attack the enemy was observed bringing approximately three companies in from the north to reinforce his forces in the "Scenery Woods". Reconnaissance from the regiment's command post determined that the enemy at the south side of the "Scenery Woods" intended to establish himself facing Noshkino. The main body of the enemy, however, was at the northeast wood line and was oriented towards Timonzewo.

Elements of the Soviet 363rd, 359th, 371st and 375th Rifle Divisions had already been identified facing the regiment's sector from Solomino through Klepenino, Optjachino and Timonzewo as far as Petelino. They had been supported in their attacks to date by the 21st and 58th Armored Brigades. New forces of the Soviet 1229th, 1198th and 1245th Rifle Regiments were located in the southern part of the "Scenery Woods" outside of Noshkino.

6 February 1942

The attack of the *Regimentsgruppe* under the commander of *Infanterie-Regiment 167*, which began in the first gray light of dawn, was under an unlucky star. The companies had barely entered the woods when they were forced back out by an enemy counterattack in which they suffered heavy losses. Any successful repetition of the attack by the seriously thinned-out companies was out of the question. The commander of *Infanterie-Regiment 167* was recalled to the corps and what was left of the *Regimentsgruppe* was attached to *SS-Infanterie-Regiment "Der Führer"*. These companies were employed along the Volga from Klepenino southward to the command post of *SS-Infanterie-Regiment "Der Führer"* in order to prevent the enemy from crossing the Volga in the rear of the *I./SS-Infanterie-Regiment "Der Führer"*.

The 2./SS-Infanterie-Regiment "Der Führer" Fights to the Last Man

While these events were taking place, the *I./SS-Infanterie-Regiment "Der Führer"* and what was left of the *III./SS-Infanterie-Regiment "Der Führer"* were under constant frontal attack from the "Assembly Area Woods" east and northeast of Solomino. As a result, the enemy was able to penetrate the positions of the severely weakened *2./SS-Infanterie-Regiment "Der Führer"*. It defended to the last man; not one man returned. In spite of that, the dangerous attack was repulsed at 1630 hours under the defensive fire of the grenadiers and the concentrated barrages of friendly artillery. The last reserves had to be called in.

Additional staging areas for 300 Red soldiers with armor were reported in Pajkowo by the *I./SS-Infanterie-Regiment "Der Führer"*.

***

SS-Obersturmbannführer Kumm pointed out to the *256. Infanterie-Division* and the *VI. Armee-Korps* the alarming and almost hopeless situation of his own troops and the men entrusted to him from other units.

Finally, the corps sent the regiment strong reinforcements in the form of *Aufklärungs-Abteilung 256*. Led by the outstanding *Major* Mummert, the battalion was attached to the regiment. The battalion took over the positions of the regiment's staff so that, at least temporarily, a continuous main line of resistance existed.

At 1015 hours, the reconnaissance battalion captured the "Church Village" west of the Volga and, by 1200 hours, the village was mopped up — a decided help in an almost hopeless situation.

At 1710 hours, a strongpoint of *Aufklärungs-Abteilung 256* in the "Russian Woods" northwest of the "Church Village" was attacked and eliminated.

At 1900 hours, ten Soviet tanks with infantry support attacked the *I./SS-Infanterie-Regiment "Der Führer"* in Solomino. According to statements by prisoners, there were four companies of 200 men each and two penal companies of 150 men each in the "Scenery" Woods.

The heavy fighting lasted until 2150 hours. At that time the enemy tanks that had broken into the main line of resistance finally withdrew. At 2245 hours *Aufklärungs-Abteilung 256* reported that the "Russian Woods" were once again free of enemy.

According to the evening report in the war diary of the *VI. Armee-Korps* on 6 February 1942, *Kampfgruppe "Der Führer"* had the following infantry fighting strength:

SS-Infanterie-Regiment "Der Führer": 226 men
(friendly forces to the right: *Infanterie-Regiment 167* with 821 men)
Aufklärungs-Abteilung 256: 150 men
Pionier-Bataillon 256: 68 men
Panzer-Jäger-Abteilung 561: 52 men

Total: 496 men

The complement of crew-served weapons of the reinforced *SS-Infanterie-Regiment "Der Führer"*, including all attached units, was given as follows:

3.7-cm *Pak*: 8 guns
5-cm *Pak*: 3 guns
Light infantry guns: 4 guns
Heavy infantry guns: 1 gun
2-cm *Flak*: 3 guns

The Sytschewka Combat Sector (SS-Division "Reich")

In the sector of *SS-Division "Reich"* the individual *Kampfgruppen* secured the long open west flank of the *XXXXVI. Panzer-Korps* on 3 and 4 February against the densely wooded terrain west of Sytschewka. No combat activities, however, took place.

SS-Infanterie-Regiment "Deutschland" formed a ski company.

Since Sytschewka had been repeatedly bombarded during the preceding night, all the motor vehicles of *SS-Infanterie-Regiment "Deutschland"* were pulled out and ordered to a new staging area.

In the sector of *SS-Kradschützen-Bataillon "Reich"* a strong combat patrol of the combat-engineer platoon of the *5./SS-Kradschützen-Bataillon "Reich"* was sent out from Chochlowka to a village west of the security line. The non-commissioned officer and ten men never returned. It was assumed it ran into an enemy trap. The patrol was reported missing. Its fate continues to remain unknown.

On 5 February conditions also remained quiet on the front of *SS-Division "Reich"*. The trains elements of the *3./SS-Kradschützen-Bataillon "Reich"* were hit during a nightly bombing of Sytschewka, resulting in four dead and three wounded.

The Battle of the Pocket

In the evening of 5 February the *9. Armee* ordered the destruction of the encircled enemy. As a result, the main burden of the attack fell once again on the formations of the *XXXXVI. Panzer-Korps*. The *VI. Armee-Korps* (*256. Infanterie-Division*) and the *XXIII. Armee-Korps* (*206. Infanterie-Division*) initially had to hold the wall of the pocket. *SS-Infanterie-Regiment "Der Führer"* remained in the sector of the *256. Infanterie-Division*.

During the pocket battle the division continued to secure the increasingly long west flank of the *XXXXVI. Panzer-Korps*. The previous security line of the division was extended accordingly on 6 and 7 February.

***

With regard to the flank-guard mission, the division order for 6 February (1500 hours) included the following (excerpts):

1.) *XXXXVI. Panzer-Korps* joined hands on the Rshew — Welikiluki railroad stretch at Tschertolino (2 kilometers west of Rshew) on 5 February with the *SS-Reiterbrigade* that was coming from the northwest. As a result, the enemy formations that had broken through west of Rshew have been encircled and will be destroyed by concentric attack.

The enemy forces west of the *XXXXVI. Panzer-Korps* are falling back to the west.

2.) ***SS-Division "Reich"* is to** extend the previous security line to the north to the

Sswerkuschino — Katerjuschki road (exclusive of road) by 1800 hours on 6 February.

The security line is to be extended again by 1200 hours on 7 February along the road to Katerjuschki (inclusive). Contact there will be with the *1. Panzer-Division*...

In closing, the security sectors were specified for the individual *Kampfgruppen*.

The Rshew Combat Sector (SS-Infanterie-Regiment "Der Führer")

7 February 1942

The enemy attacked Solomino and Klepenino with armored support starting at 0430 hours. Soon there were no more *Pak* able to fire in Solomino.

At 0610 hours the *I./SS-Infanterie-Regiment "Der Führer"* reported that six enemy tanks had been spotted advancing on Lebsino. At 0730 hours six T 34's were in the western part of Solomino with about 300 Red soldiers. At the same time the enemy increased pressure on the units of *Aufklärungs-Abteilung 256* in the "Church" Village. That seriously endangered the lines of communication for the *III./SS-Infanterie-Regiment "Der Führer"* and *Infanterie-Regiment 471* that were located in Klepenino.

At 0900 hours the *I./SS-Infanterie-Regiment "Der Führer"* reported that the situation had been restored in Solomino. The assault guns of the *2./Sturmgeschütz-Abteilung 189*, led by *Oberleutnant* von Malachowski, again came to the aid of the hard-pressed men, including the combat engineers of *Pionier-Bataillon 256*. The aggressive assault gunners knocked out five enemy tanks.

A massed enemy attack followed heavy bombing of Timonzewo. By 0800 hours the attack had been repulsed by what was left of the *III./SS-Infanterie-Regiment "Der Führer"* along with elements of *Infanterie-Regiment 167*.

At 1400 hours Solomino was again in enemy hands. In the opinion of the *256. Infanterie-Division*, which the *VI. Armee-Korps* did not disagree with, the *I./SS-Infanterie-Regiment "Der Führer"* and the combat engineers of *Pionier-Bataillon 256* could no longer recapture the village. In order to strengthen the main line of resistance, *Pionier-Bataillon 251* was committed to hold Lebsino.

The *I./SS-Infanterie-Regiment "Der Führer"* attempted to form a new defensive line about 300 meters south of Solomino with only two light machine guns.

In Klepenino the remnants of the *III./SS-Infanterie-Regiment "Der Führer"* desperately tried to stem the Russian tide. It had been days since the wounded could be transported to the rear. *Sturmgeschütze* brought forward urgently needed ammunition.

***

The war diary of the *256. Infanterie-Division* contains the following entry for 7 February 1942:

> ...*SS*-Woods ("Scenery Woods"), in which strong enemy forces have infiltrated, cannot be regained. The following defensive line is recommended: Petelino — Timonzewo — Koksch Creek — Noshkino — Volga bank — Lebsino...

***

After discussion with the commanding general, the chief of staff of the *VI. Armee-Korps*, *Oberst* Degen, approved this new main line of resistance.

During the afternoon the remnants of the *III./SS-Infanterie-Regiment "Der Führer"* evacuated the northern portion of Klepenino. Fourteen men and twenty-eight wounded still held the southern portion of the ruined village.

Under these circumstances, the commander of *SS-Infanterie-Regiment "Der Führer"* decided to evacuate Klepenino with the exception of a single shot-up house. He would temporarily attach the last fourteen men of the *III./SS-Infanterie-Regiment "Der Führer"* to the *I./SS-Infanterie-Regiment "Der Führer"* and pull the positions of the *I./SS-Infanterie-Regiment "Der Führer"* even with the battalion command post.

The regiment's command post was moved to a little village west of the Volga, directly behind the *I./SS-Infanterie-Regiment "Der Führer"*. Although it remained within range of enemy artillery and mortar fire, it was no longer directly in the main line of resistance.

The Russians continued to attack without a break. Their artillery fire increased from one day to the next.

Aufklärungs-Abteilung 256 received orders to mop up the "Russian Woods" just northwest of the "Church Village".

In the evening of 7 February, *SS-Infanterie-Regiment "Der Führer"* received 120 replacements. By express order of the corps they were to be inserted into the new main line of resistance immediately.

At the same time, *SS-Obersturmbannführer* Kumm received news that the staff of *SS-Infanterie-Regiment "Deutschland"* and the *I./SS-Infanterie-Regiment "Deutschland"* would entrain in Sytschewka and should arrive in Rshew by 2000 hours. These elements of *SS-Division "Reich"* were to be brought forward by truck. they had the mission of occupying the main line of resistance between Timonzewo and Noshkino.

***

The war diary of the *VI. Armee-Korps* states the following on 7 February 1942:

> ...The staff of the regiment and the *I./SS-Infanterie-Regiment "Deutschland"* have, by current standards, a very high combat strength (590 men) and are superbly equipped with weapons and equipment. The employment of those elements will pro-

vide substantial strengthening of the front that has been stretched to bursting, if it can still be accomplished before the front breaks down completely…

The Sytschewka Combat Sector (SS-Division "Reich")

8 February 1942

Statements by prisoners and deserters attest to the toughness of the already encountered and expected opposition. According to those statements, the pocket includes the operations section of the 29th Army, including the artillery commander of the Kalinin Front, several high officers and, ostensibly, the brigade commissar belonging to the war council and, in the wooded area of Jersowo alone, 50 high officers and commissars…(*XXXXVI. Panzer-Korps, Die Winterschlacht von Sytschewka (25.1 — 12.2. 1942)*, p. 8. Unpublished)

***

Regardless of the danger posed by additional significant stripping of the west flank of the *XXXXVI. Panzer-Korps*, the command echelon of *SS-Infanterie-Regiment "Deutschland"* and *Kampfgruppe Tost* (*I./SS-Infanterie-Regiment "Deutschland"*) were pulled out by order of the *9. Armee* during the morning of 8 February. In the afternoon, they were loaded on a transport train that was standing by at the north railroad station in Sytschewka and sent to reinforce the increasingly exposed northern front of the *VI. Armee-Korps*.

These units were brought in rapid transport to the area west of Rshew to assist the threatened *256. Infanterie-Division*. These forces were then attached to the *VI. Armee-Korps*.

The *13./*, *14./*, and *16./SS-Infanterie-Regiment "Deutschland"* as well as the *15./SS-Infanterie-Regiment "Deutschland"*, which had been reorganized into a ski company, remained for the time being in their previous positions and were attached to *Kampfgruppe Drechsler*.

The Rshew Combat Sector (SS-Infanterie-Regiment "Der Führer")

During the night of 7/8 February hazy, snowy weather prevailed with light frost and strong, gusting winds.

The withdrawal of the remnants of the *III./SS-Infanterie-Regiment "Der Führer"* was successfully completed during the nighttime hours, including recovery of all the wounded, who could then receive proper medical care. The last nine men of the *III./SS-Infanterie-Regiment "Der Führer"* were employed with the *I./SS-Infanterie-Regiment "Der Führer"* in Lebsino.

The front flared up again at 0500 hours. Two Soviet battalions with four tanks attacked Lebsino. Several waves of Red soldiers without armor attacked Noshkino.

By 0800 hours, all of the attacks had been repulsed, though at a cost of heavy casualties and expenditure of weapons. Two light field howitzers and four 3.7-cm *Pak* were overrun and crushed by tanks in Lebsino. Three Soviet tanks were added to the array of wrecks.

At 1230 hours the enemy advanced via Kokosch to the east of Optjachino. At approximately 2045 friendly forces evacuated Kokosch.

Since a Russian breakthrough could be expected at any moment due to the diminishing combat strength that had stretched the front to the limit, the friendly forces to the left of the regiment received orders to be prepared to be committed in the Noshkino — Lebsino sector. Those forces — regimental elements, the *I./Infanterie-Regiment 348* and the *II./Infanterie -Regiment 252* all under *Oberst* Wuth — maintained close contact with *SS-Obersturmbannführer* Kumm, who had moved his command post to Jessemowo.

Sub-Section r)

Defensive Fighting in the Bend of the Volga West of Rshew: 9 - 20 February 1942

9 February 1942

During the night, the train with the *I./SS-Infanterie-Regiment "Deutschland"* and the command echelon of *SS-Infanterie-Regiment "Deutschland"* with *SS-Sturmbannführer* Harmel arrived in Rshew. The elements were initially quartered in the north part of the city. Guides and quarters were made available by the garrison commander (*VI. Armee-Korps*).

The city lay under scattered artillery fire. During the day the companies of the *I./SS-Infanterie-Regiment "Deutschland"* were brought forward in shuttle movement by a motor-vehicle column of the *VI. Armee-Korps*. They advanced via Kowalowo (2 kilometers west of Rshew), Grischino and Petunowo to the Luschino — Petelino area and were committed between *SS-Infanterie-Regiment "Der Führer"* (left) and *Infanterie-Regiment 167* (right). The battalion command post of the *I./SS-Infanterie-Regiment "Deutschland"* was in Petelino. The command post of *SS-Infanterie-Regiment "Deutschland"* was in Petunowo.

There was light frost with snowfall. How had the day begun?

***

Starting at 0500 hours and after an intense fire preparation, the enemy attacked Lebsino extremely aggressively. At the same time he increased pressure on the entire sector of *SS-Infanterie-Regiment "Der Führer"*.

***

At 0805 hours, the operations officer of the *256. Infanterie-Division*, *Major* von Warburg, reported the following to the *VI. Armee-Korps*:

1.) Starting at 0500 hours the Russians have engaged in an extremely strong attack from the northwest and north against Lebsino. At the moment they are about 200 meters in front of the main line of resistance.

2.) One T 34 has been knocked out and another tank is still loose in the area.

3.) Three assault guns are proceeding to Lebsino.

4.) *Oberst* Wuth has established contact with *SS-Obersturmbannführer* Kumm.

5.) 107 prisoners were taken last night southwest of Lebsino.

***

General der Panzertruppen Model, who was present at the command post of the *256. Infanterie-Division* at 1245 hours, ordered that all of the divisional artillery of the *251. Infanterie-Division* was to support the defensive fighting of the *256. Infanterie-Division* in front of the threatened sector of reinforced *SS-Infanterie-Regiment "Der Führer"*.

The fighting continued with undiminished intensity into the afternoon hours.

***

At 1315 hours the *VI. Armee-Korps* radioed the *256. Infanterie-Division*:

1.) Lebsino is to be held under all circumstances.

2.) The *II./Infanterie-Regiment 252* is immediately attached to the *256. Infanterie-Division* for employment at Lebsino.

3.) Arranged by express order of the commander-in-chief of the *9. Armee*.

Major von Warburg replied that the *256. Infanterie-Division*, including the remaining units of *SS-Infanterie-Regiment "Der Führer"* and the other attached elements, would not be in a position to hold out much longer.

The enemy attempted to break through and relieve the encircled Russian formations in the area northwest of Sytschewka at any price. He committed unimaginable amounts of materiel and masses of infantry to do that. Up to that point, however, all his attacks foundered on the defensive spirit of the German soldiers.

Once again, the almost impossible took place: By 1700 hours all enemy attacks had been repulsed and the main line of resistance was firmly in the defender's hands. The unbroken destructive fire by the enemy artillery exacted high losses in dead and wounded, however.

Pionier-Bataillon 251 radioed *SS-Obersturmbannführer* Kumm from Lebsino:

I./SS-Infanterie-Regiment "Der Führer": 21 men with two machine guns

III./SS-Infanterie-Regiment "Der Führer": 20 men with no machine guns,

1./ and *3./Pionier-Bataillon 251*: 25 men and 2 machine guns as well as 4 3.7-cm *Pak*, 2 5-cm *Pak* and one 8.8-cm *Flak* (without crew).

At 1800 hours the operations officer of the *256. Infanterie-Division* radioed *VI. Armee-Korps*:

The *I./SS-Infanterie-Regiment "Der Führer"* will be withdrawn, if possible, and brought up to a new combat strength of 200 men with the remnants of the *III./SS-Infanterie-Regiment "Deutschland"*. The latter will be relieved by units of *Infanterie-Regiment 167* at Optjachtino and brought forward. It will initially remain behind the left wing of the division in Tjapolowo as reserve.

It is intended for those men, who have stood for eight days in heroic defensive fighting, to get a chance to rest for one or two days. It is intended to reorganize them.

In the meantime, the *II./Infanterie -Regiment 252* had occupied the main line of resistance southeast of Lebsino with its weak companies. With that, the remaining units of the *I./* and *III./SS-Infanterie-Regiment "Der Führer"* were pulled out of the defenses. *SS-Obersturmbannführer* Kumm and his staff remained in command of the former sector.

At the same time an artillery group of the *251. Infanterie-Division* — the *II./Artillerie-Regiment 251* with three light batteries and one heavy battery — was directed to provide direct support to *SS-Obersturmbannführer* Kumm.

The new organization of the defensive front — *SS-Obersturmbannführer* Kumm and the staff of *SS-Infanterie-Regiment "Der Führer"* in command — controlled the following formations after the withdrawal of the combat elements of *SS-Infanterie-Regiment "Der Führer"*,:

I./Infanterie-Regiment 456 : From the "Church Village" (exclusive) to the Volga knee
II./Infanterie-Regiment 252 : From the Volga knee to Lebsino (exclusive)
Pionier-Bataillon 251: Lebsino (inclusive) with contact with right wing of the *205. Infanterie-Division*
Aufklärungs-Abteilung 256: in Noshkino (*Major* Mummert).

***

Panzer-Jäger-Abteilung 561 reported the following to the *VI. Armee-Korps* via the command post of *SS-Infanterie-Regiment "Der Führer"*:

Six tanks of the new T 60 type were positively identified on 3, 4 and 5 February at Klepenino. All of the tanks were penetrated and set on fire at ranges between 30 and 200 meters. Enemy losses from 21 January to 9 February 1942: 1 KV 1 tank; 16 T 34's; 3 medium tanks; 2 tanks of unidentified type; 6 T 60's; 2 Russian antitank guns; and, 1 7.62-cm gun.

10 February 1942

By order of the *9. Armee*, *SS-Division "Reich"* and all its elements left the command sector of the *XXXXVI. Panzer-Korps* in the Sytschewka area of operations and was transferred to the threatened north front of the *VI. Armee-Korps*.

It was intended to insert the division in command of the front formerly held by *SS-Infanterie-Regiment "Der Führer"*. The friendly forces on the right would be the *256. Infanterie-Division* and the friendly forces on the left the *206. Infanterie-Division*.

In the meantime *SS-Infanterie-Regiment "Deutschland"* had taken over the Petelino — Timonzewo — Noshkino (exclusive) sector with the *I./SS-Infanterie-Regiment "Deutschland"*. The regimental command post was in Petuno. Shortly after establishing its positions, it repulsed an intense enemy attack on Timonzewo.

At 1100 hours the Red soldiers again attacked the main line of resistance at Noshkino, where the equally seriously weakened forces of *Aufklärungs-Abteilung 256* and its brave commander steadfastly and grimly defended their positions and repulsed all attacks.

The Soviets repeatedly attacked Lebsino until 1510 hours. Four more enemy tanks were destroyed. However, the veteran combat engineers and the valiant grenadiers of the *II./Infanterie-Regiment 252* had a difficult time holding their own against that assault.

(All the war diary files of *SS-Infanterie-Regiment "Deutschland"* for the period from 10 February to 19 March 1942 were lost as a result of a direct hit on the command post of the regiment and the ensuing fire.)

***

The American historian, George H. Stein, wrote the following about the casualties of the division during that period:

> ...as of 10 February 1942, the division had lost a total of 10,690 men (not including officers). While *SS-Division "Reich"* was the hardest hit of all the *SS* divisions, the others also suffered heavy casualties. Before long all of Himmler's reserves were required merely to keep the field units of the *Waffen SS* capable of conducting operations. (George H. Stein, *Geschichte der Waffen-SS*, p. 168. Düsseldorf: Droste-Verlag, 1968.)

11 February 1942

The remaining elements of *SS-Kradschützen-Bataillon "Reich"* were relieved in the Sytschewka area of operations and were to be transferred by rail to the Rshew area of operations as the last formation of the division.

SS-Division "Reich" established its command post one kilometer northeast of Trosstina.

In the Focal Point of the Defensive Fighting

Since the early morning hours the defensive sector commanded by the commander of *SS-Infanterie-Regiment "Der Führer"* was unmistakably the focal point of the defense.

The enemy was finally able to force the combat engineers of *Pionier-Bataillon 251* and the severely thinned-out companies of the *II./Infanterie-regiment 252* out of Lebsino and the positions east of the village.

The alerted grenadiers of the *I./SS-Infanterie-Regiment "Der Führer"* — everything that remained of the regiment as well as the regiment's replacements had been combined in this battalion— forced the enemy back in an immediate counterattack. The fighting was extraordinarily bitter and the biting cold made it difficult for both friend and foe.

The *I./SS-Infanterie-Regiment "Der Führer"* was able to hold the ruins that had been Lebsino until 1315 hours. Then a Russian assault force supported by armor again penetrated the built-up area.

At about the same time, the enemy attacked Noshkino with two rifle regiments. The entire main line of resistance was then enveloped in a hurricane of bombs, shells and fire. It appeared that all the previous efforts had been in vain. With the courage of desperation, the *I./SS-Infanterie-Regiment "Der Führer"* launched yet another counterattack by order of *SS-Obersturmbannführer* Kumm. In fact it was able to force the enemy back out of Lebsino by 1345 hours. Since early morning the bitter fight had raged for that god-forsaken place on the Volga. Another five enemy tanks were burning. But the friendly losses were also barely able to be endured.

Oberstleutnant von Recum, commander of the *II./Infanterie-Regiment 459* of the *251. Infanterie-Division* in the Rshew area of operations, gave this account regarding the defensive fighting at Rshew:

> The commander of *Infanterie-Regiment 459*, *Oberst* Fisher, told me at the time about the heavy fighting in that sector. Neighboring friendly forces, all that was left of a company of the *Waffen-SS*, literally defended with heavy machine guns to the last man.

This winter battle was a struggle for life and death of almost apocalyptic proportions that was fought with a bitterness hardly seen in any previous engagement. There seemed no alternative possible but to win or die. The unusually high number of dead on both sides is shocking proof of this. In no previous operations were so many entire companies of *SS-Division "Reich"* and the combat formations of the army wiped out to the last man by death, wounds and freezing as here in the memorable and decisive winter battle of Rshew.

The small "Church Village" where the Ssichka joins the Volga was also the scene of bitter fighting. The unshakeable comrades of *Aufklärungs-*

Abteilung 256 fought there for its possession. It was, indeed, captured by the Red soldiers for a short time, but the group of houses were reported clear of the enemy at 1400 hours after a successful immediate counterattack by *Major* Mummert's reconnaissance soldiers.

In the course of the day *SS-Kradschützen-Bataillon "Reich"* was moved by rail from Sytschewka to Rshew, where it detrained and was immediately set in march for the front.

At 1500 hours the staff of *SS-Division "Reich"* arrived on the battlefield with the first elements of the motorcycle battalion. The staff was briefed at Montscharowa by the *256. Infanterie-Division.*

By 2050 hours the situation at Lebsino had so intensified that the *II./Infanterie-Regiment 252* was totally burnt out and the *I./SS-Infanterie-Regiment "Dr Führer"* and what was left of *Pionier-Bataillon 251* were simply overtaxed by the defense of the sector.

By order of the *256. Infanterie-Division*, the *I./Infanterie-Regiment 348* was sent to *SS-Infanterie-Regiment "Der Führer"* and attached to it. *SS-Obersturmbannführer* Kumm was informed by radio that *SS-Division "Reich"* would assume command of the Petelino — Lebsino sector at 2400 hours on 12 February.

12 February 1942

During the night the enemy attacked Lebsino in heavy falling snow. He had reinforced his attacking forces with the 24th Ski Brigade. At the same time, the Soviets attacked Noshkino and the "Church Village" with the 21st Armored Brigade. Newly identified was the Soviet 174th Rifle Division. All the attacks were repulsed and the entire sector remained relatively quiet until 0730 hours. Only at the "Church Village" did the enemy continue to feel his way forward.

At 1810 hours the *256. Infanterie-Division* reported the following fighting (trench) strength to the *VI. Armee-Korps* concerning the defensive sector of *SS-Infanterie-Regiment "Der Führer"* (about 4.5 kilometers wide):

1.) **Lebsino sector:**

Pionier-Bataillon 251 and the *II./Infanterie-Regiment 252* — a total of 100 men.

I./SS-Infanterie-Regiment "Der Führer": 130 men

2.) **Sector southwest of Lebsino:**

I./Infanterie-Regiment 456: 250 men

3.) **Noshkino — "Church Village" Sector:**

Aufklärungs-Abteilung 256: 150 Men

Total fighting strength: 630 men

An order arrived from the *VI. Armee-Korps* at the division command post in Abramowo that *SS-Kradschützen-Bataillon "Reich"* was attached to *Infanterie-Regiment 348* under *Oberst* Wuth and that, in turn, to the command of *SS-Obersturmbannführer* Kumm until *SS-Division "Reich"* took over command at 2400 hours. *SS-Kradschützen-Bataillon "Reich"* was to assemble in the Jessemowo — Pojawilowo area.

The commander of *schwere Artillerie-Abteilung 848* was appointed artillery commander for the sector of *SS-Division "Reich"* and was directed to report to the commander of the division, *SS-Brigadeführer* Kleinheisterkamp. By division order, the *II./, III./* and *IV./Artillerie-Regiment 251* were directed to support *SS-Infanterie-Regiment "Der Führer"*. The *III./Artillerie-Regiment 256* was assigned the sector of *SS-Infanterie-Regiment "Deutschland"* (*SS-Sturmbannführer* Harmel).

At 1230 hours the enemy continued his attack on Noshkino, which cost him heavy casualties. Around 1500 hours strong enemy forces advanced against Lebsino and the "Church Village". Uninterrupted Soviet attacks throughout the entire sector of the regiment began at 1730 hours. The Soviet 359th Rifle Division attacked Lebsino and the Soviet 371st and 171st Rifle Divisions advanced against Noshkino. In addition, 40 tanks of the Soviet 70th Armored Brigade rolled forward against the German positions.

At 1810 hours heavy snow squalls set in. The greatly superior Red forces penetrated into Noshkino. The small band of survivors from *Aufklärungs-Abteilung 256* fought to total exhaustion. Every soldier in the entire regimental sector put in an almost superhuman performance.

At 1915 hours new enemy staging areas were identified north of Noshkino. The enemy then also attacked the defensive positions of the *I./SS-Infanterie-Regiment "Deutschland"* in Timonzewo.

At 1940 hours the enemy advanced from the "Russian" Woods against the *I./Infanterie-Regiment 456*, which was holding there. The Russians achieved limited penetrations of the lines.

SS-Hauptsturmführer Tychsen Badly Wounded

SS-Kradschützen-Bataillon "Reich" under *SS-Hauptsturmführer* Tychsen was brought forward into the threatened sector. It was to clean up the situation in the "Russian" Woods by attacking the following day. *SS-Hauptsturmführer* Tychsen reported for this purpose to the command post of *SS-Infanterie-Regiment "Der Führer"*, to which the battalion had been attached. During terrain reconnaissance that afternoon, *SS-Hauptsturmführer* Tychsen, accompanied only by a messenger, was severely wounded in the chin by a shell fragment. His adjutant, *SS-Obersturmführer* Buch, immediately brought him to the hospital in Sytschewka in the vehicle. *SS-*

Hauptsturmführer Weiß, a company commander in *SS-Aufklärungs-Abteilung "Reich"*, went to the front with the same vehicle. By division order, he assumed temporary command of *SS-Kradschützen-Bataillon "Reich"*.

At 2000 hours the Russians attacked with the 174th and 348th Rifle Divisions in the sector of *SS-Infanterie-Regiment "Deutschland"*. The enemy had discovered a gap in positions of the friendly forces to the right and was able to break into the main line of resistance. One company of the *I./SS-Infanterie-Regiment "Deutschland"* was quickly dispatched to the *256. Infanterie-Division*, where it was to clean up the penetration at Now. Filikino with an immediate counterattack and restore the former main line of resistance. At 2045 hours *SS-Sturmbannführer* Harmel was able to report the stabilization of the situation in his own sector to the division, though heavy enemy fire from all weapons continued to fall on the friendly positions.

***

At 2000 hours *SS-Division "Reich"* received the following order from the headquarters of the *VI. Armee-Korps* (Order *200/42* — SECRET):

1.) Headquarters *SS-Division "Reich"* is to assume the Petelino — Lebsino sector at 2400 hours on 12 February and defend it. The sector is to be strengthened in strongpoint fashion.

2.) Upon assumption of command authority, the following are to become or remain attached to *SS-Division "Reich"*:

a) All elements of *SS-Infanterie-Regimenter "Der Führer"* and *"Deutschland"* employed in the sector.

b) *II./Infanterie-Regiment 396* (as previously task organized)

c) *I./Infanterie-Regiment 456* (as previously task organized)

d) *I./Infanterie-Regiment 348* (as previously task organized)

e) The 5-cm *Pak* of *Panzer-Jäger-Abteilung 561*

f) The *Sturmgeschütze* of *Sturmgeschütz-Abteilung 189*

3.) *SS-Kradschützen-Bataillon "Reich"* is available as of 13 February and is to be guided into the sector by *Infanterie-Regiment 348*.

4.) By 15 February the remaining elements of *Aufklärungs-Abteilung 256*, *Pionier-Bataillon 251*, *Pionier-Bataillon 256* and *Infanterie-Regiment 471* are to be pulled out of the line.

5.) *SS-Division "Reich"* will have the following artillery attached as of the time it assumes command:

Staff of *schwere Artillerie-Abteilung 848* (at the same time artillery commander)

III./Artillerie-Regiment 256 with *6./Artillerie-Regiment 39, 8./Artillerie-Regiment 241* and *8./Artillerie-Regiment 210*

IV./Artillerie-Regiment 241 with *2./* and *3./Artillerie-Regiment 120* and *5./Artillerie-Regiment 201*

II./Artillerie-Regiment 251 with *4./*, *6./* and *11./Artillerie-Regiment 251*

III./Artillerie-Regiment 251 with *7./* and *9./Artillerie-Regiment 251.*

As a result, 10 different army units were attached to *SS-Division "Reich"* in the focal point of the defensive front, including three infantry and four artillery battalions (with a total of 11 firing batteries).

13 February 1942

SS-Division "Reich" assumed command in the designated defensive sector at precisely 2400 hours.

During the nighttime hours the enemy repeatedly attacked Noshkino and the "Church Village". By summoning up every last available force, the attacks were repulsed.

At 0730 hours *SS-Infanterie-Regiment "Deutschland"* reported that the company that had been committed at Now. Filikino had cleaned up the situation there and returned to the regiment.

At 1100 hours the Soviets again attempted to break into Lebsino. They were supported by four tanks. The weak remnants of *Pionier-Bataillon 251* and the *I./SS-Infanterie-Regiment "Der Führer"* repulsed that attack. Three tanks were left in flames.

SS-Infanterie-Regiment "Der Führer" reported the following combat strengths to the division:

	O	NCO	EM
I./SS-IR "Der Führer"	—	2	12
III./SS-IR "Der Führer"	1	5	17
13./SS-IR "Der Führer"	1	3	22
14./SS-IR "Der Führer"	—	1	2
15./SS-IR "Der Führer"	—	3	2
16./SS-IR "Der Führer"	1	1	—
Signals Platoon	1	3	13
Regimental Staff	4	6	12
Totals	8	24	80

The enemy also renewed his attacks at Timonzewo. The company of *SS-Infanterie-Regiment "Deutschland"* that was committed there had a fighting strength of 30 men.

By 1930 hours *SS-Kradschützen-Bataillon "Reich"*, under *SS-Hauptsturmführer* Grünwälder, cleaned up the situation in a rapid attack and, more importantly, sealed the point of penetration. However, the attempt to continue the attack to force the Soviets back out of the "Russian Woods"

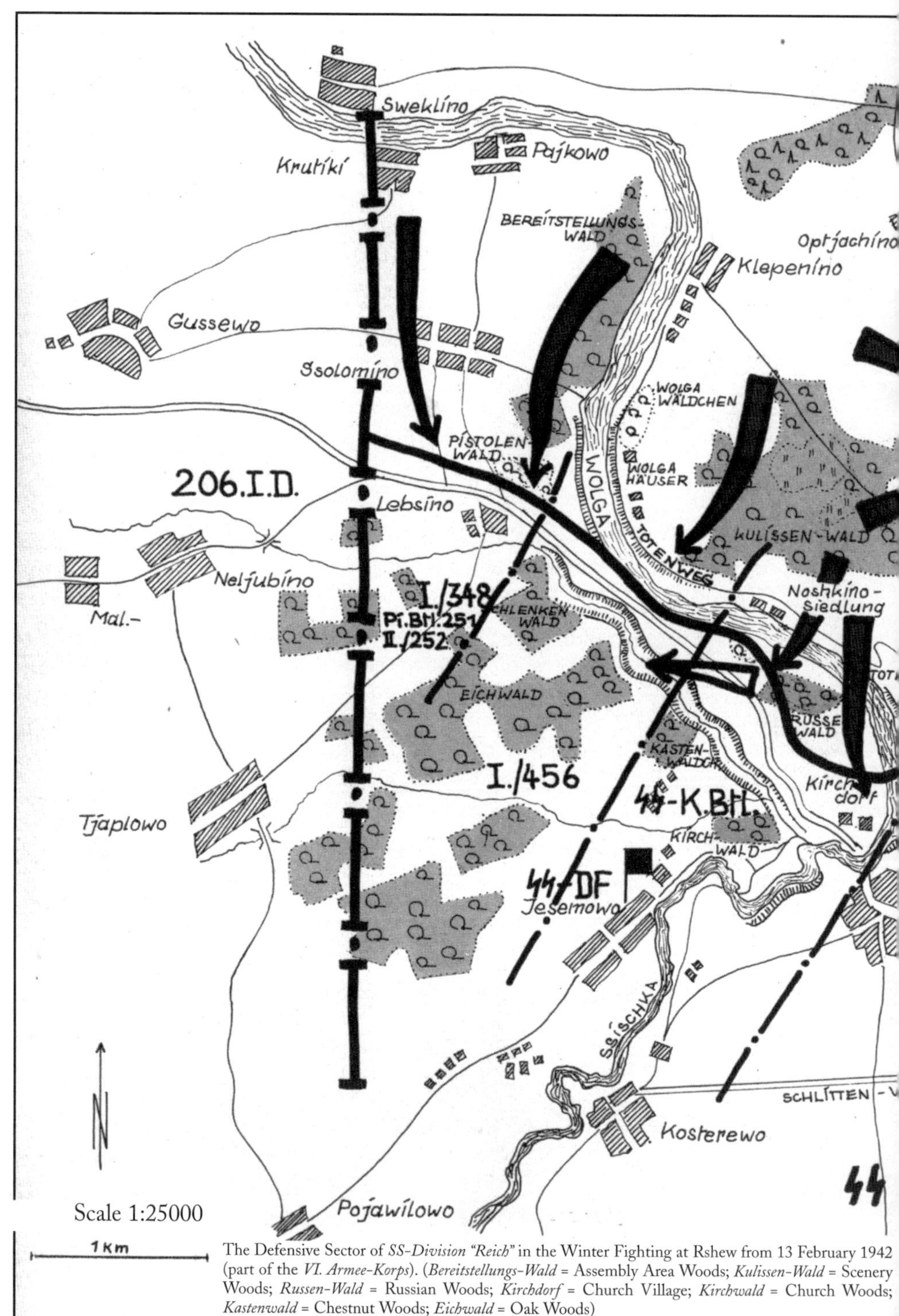

The Defensive Sector of *SS-Division "Reich"* in the Winter Fighting at Rshew from 13 February 1942 (part of the *VI. Armee-Korps*). (*Bereitstellungs-Wald* = Assembly Area Woods; *Kulissen-Wald* = Scenery Woods; *Russen-Wald* = Russian Woods; *Kirchdorf* = Church Village; *Kirchwald* = Church Woods; *Kastenwald* = Chestnut Woods; *Eichwald* = Oak Woods)

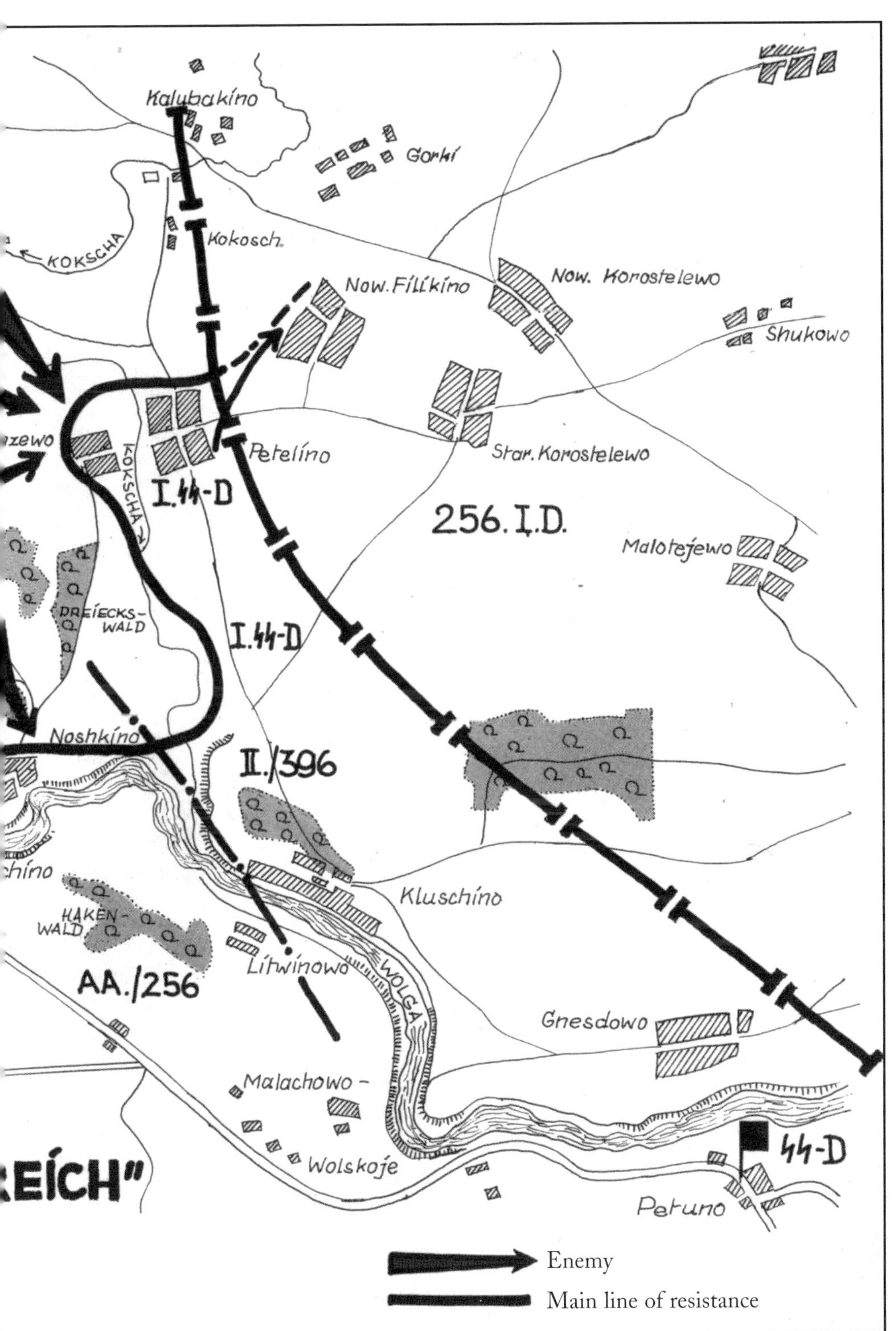

Kalubakino
Gorki
Kokosch.
KOKSCHA
Now. Filikino
Now. Korostelewo
Shukowo
Petelino
Star. Korostelewo
I. ϟϟ-D
KOKSCHA
256. I.D.
Malotejewo
DREIECKS-WALD
I. ϟϟ-D
Noshkino
II./396
Kluschino
HAKEN-WALD
AA./256
Litwinowo
WOLGA
Gnesdowo
Malachowo
Wolskoje
ϟϟ-D
Petuno
Enemy
Main line of resistance

foundered with heavy losses due to the massive firepower of the Russian defense. *SS-Untersturmführer* Müller, *2./SS-Kradschützen-Bataillon "Reich"*, was killed, and *SS-Untersturmführer* Böckmann was wounded in the attempt. The total losses of the battalion came to 85 dead and wounded.

***

SS-Obersturmführer Buch, the adjutant at the time of *SS-Kradschützen-Bataillon "Reich"*, gave his impression of the fighting in his personal notes:

Our System of Defense

When we returned to the battalion on 13 February, the attack against the "Russian Woods" failed with substantial losses. The battalion organized for the defense with the *2./SS-Kradschützen-Bataillon "Reich"* on the right. The company was commanded by Grünwälder, who was killed during that time period. The *3./SS-Kradschützen-Bataillon "Reich"* was in the center and, at the focal point of the fighting on the left, was the *4./SS-Kradschützen-Bataillon "Reich"* under *SS-Obersturmführer* Burfeind. The *5./SS-Kradschützen-Bataillon "Reich"* under *SS-Hauptsturmführer* Hoffman was still intact, particularly the infantry-gun platoon (*SS-Untersturmführer* Bär) and the mortar platoon. Practically nothing was left of the combat-engineer platoon and the *Pak* platoon was also gone. The communications section was still intact. There was contact on the right between the *2./SS-Kradschützen-Bataillon "Reich"* and *Aufklärungs-Abteilung* 256 of *Major* Mummert. On the left were army units.

Since the front was very thinly held, everything depended on the heavy weapons. We were in snow bunkers and under heavy artillery fire all day long. The *2./SS-Kradschützen-Bataillon "Reich"* suffered the most from that. Although it was relatively quiet at night, the battalion command post tensely focused its attention on what was going on with the *4./SS-Kradschützen-Bataillon "Reich"* during the day.

With stolid regularity the same events were repeated hourly: Generally one Russian company — but never more than a battalion — would advance from the steep bank of the Volga. It came through the "Russian Woods" and attempted to overrun the *4./SS-Kradschützen-Bataillon "Reich"* by moving through an approximately ten-meter-wide stretch of vegetation. During the pauses, the company was under heavy artillery fire, as was the entire battalion.

Whenever the firing stopped, the sentries looked over the cover. The Russians came. The sentries alerted *SS-Obersturmführer* Burfeind. Machine guns, submachine guns and hand grenades forced the enemy to take cover. In the meantime, Burfeind called down an artillery barrage. Infantry guns and mortars had registered precisely on the stretch of vegetation. The friendly artillery fire could not be brought in close enough since the barrels of the overworked guns had been so worn down that a dispersion of 300 meters had to be calculated from individual guns. As soon as the Russian attack collapsed, the enemy artillery resumed and the "game" began all over again.

Fortunately we had enough ammunition. At that time 600 rounds a day were fired by each infantry gun and heavy mortar — it must be said it was a masterful accomplishment for the ammunition logistics personnel. One heavy mortar had a burst barrel.

In that heavy defensive fighting between Lebsino and Jessemowo in the Volga bend the battalion suffered such heavy losses that the companies were worn down to only a few men.

At the same time, our attention was directed to the north to the adjoining sector. Again and again the enemy attacked with T 34's. Whenever things flared up there, the assault guns of *Sturmgeschütz-Abteilung 189* under *Oberleutnant* von Malachowski moved past us. Initially, there were five *Sturmgeschütze*. Then there were less and less. They were magnificent men, those *Sturmgeschütz* cannoneers. Each time they moved back after repulsing an attack they called out their "kills" to us, for example, "Six T 34's!" or "Only three T 34's this time!"

***

The enemy had found such well-constructed positions in the "Russian Woods" that there was no getting him out of them. However, the enemy was suppressed with fire from a 21-cm heavy howitzer that fired a round into the patch of woods every 4-7 minutes. The "Church Village", a small rise with a church and a few houses, changed hands about ten times during the course of this time period. In the end, however, it remained firmly in the hands of *Aufklärungs-Abteilung 256*.

14 February 1942

In spite of heavy snow squalls, the Soviet Air Force bombed the division's positions from Petelino — Lebsino with about 20 Il 2 bombers and attacked the entire front with tanks and infantry. A penetration by several T 34's at Lebsino was cleaned up by the assault guns of *Sturmgeschütz-Abteilung 189*.

At 1250 hours the operations officer of *SS-Division "Reich"*, *SS-Obersturmbannführer* Ostendorff, checked out the situation with *SS-Obersturmbannführer* Kumm in Jessemowo. He gained the following impression:

The enemy was attacking to the south and west from the "Russian Woods". Local penetrations were immediately cleaned up by the *SS* motorcycle troops. The withdrawal of *Aufklärungs-Abteilung 256* and the *I./Infanterie-Regiment 459* had to be postponed, since the situation at Noshkino would otherwise be questionable. *Pionier-Bataillon 251* could be withdrawn and, at the same time, the *I./Infanterie-Regiment 456*, which had a fighting strength of 2 officers, 2 noncommissioned officers and 17 enlisted personnel. At the time, *SS-Kradschützen-Bataillon "Reich"* still had a fighting strength of ten officers, 24 noncommissioned officers and 200 enlisted personnel, thus constituting a strong support for the defense of the entire sector.

After the meeting, *SS-Obersturmbannführer* Ostendorff briefed the *VI. Armee-Korps*. Its chief of staff gave permission for the *I./Infanterie-Regiment 459* and *Aufklärungs-Abteilung 256* to remain in the division sector for the time being.

15 February 1942

During the morning hours massed enemy forces pressed against the entire defensive sector between Noshkino and Lebsino. Several enemy advances were also reported in the sector of the *I./SS-Infanterie-Regiment "Deutschland"* at Timonzewo, but all were repulsed.

Around 1100 hours the Soviets massed their attacks and the *I./SS-Infanterie-Regiment "Deutschland"* reported knocking out its third enemy tank of the day.

Two battalions and eight T 34's achieved a penetration at Lebsino. As a precaution, the *I./Infanterie-Regiment 348* had occupied a blocking position southeast of the village, because the Soviets shoved tanks and infantry into Lebsino with the obvious intention of extending the penetration and finally forcing a breakthrough to the south.

After seven tanks had been knocked out by *Sturmgeschütze* and burned out, the pressure let up for the moment. The entire battlefield was covered with knocked-out wrecks and burnt-out Soviet tanks.

At 1245 hours the enemy bogged down outside Noshkino after an unsuccessful attack.

At 1530 hours *SS-Division "Reich"* reported to the corps that the attack that had been launched by the *I./Infanterie-Regiment 348* on Lebsino had failed. Holding the position with the available forces appeared pointless since the enemy was putting up a stubborn defense and continually bringing in fresh forces. In addition, friendly losses were frighteningly high.

Around 1525 hours the Russians achieved a penetration at Noshkino and the "Church Village" after another heavy attack from the "Russian Woods". They then advanced from there farther to the west to the "Box" Woods and the "Oak Woods".

In the early afternoon, the commander of the *III./Infanterie-Regiment 396* reported to *SS-Obersturmbannführer* Kumm. This battalion had also experienced extremely difficult and strenuous days of fighting with heavy losses behind it. It had a fighting strength of 130 grenadiers.

The *VI. Armee-Korps* fully appreciated the tense situation that had been strained to the breaking point in the sector. Accordingly, the *251. Infanterie-Division* was ordered to relieve the *I./Infanterie-Regiment 451* from its current sector as soon as possible and have it establish contact with *SS-Obersturmbannführer* Kumm.

According to the reports that arrived by 1700 hours, two *Sturmgeschütze*, one 8.8-cm *Flak* and one 5-cm *Pak* had been lost in the failed morning attack of the *I./Infanterie-Regiment 348* on Lebsino — an irreplaceable loss of valuable weapons at this high point of the crisis, along with heavy friendly losses in killed and wounded.

The Russians hesitantly felt their way forward one more time to Noshkino around 1900 hours but were repulsed. It almost seemed as if the enemy was also gradually reaching the end of his strength in men and materiel at this point.

In the evening the ski company (*15./SS-Infanterie-Regiment "Deutschland"*) under command of *SS-Untersturmführer* Hannes Schulzer, was committed in the sector of *SS-Kradschützen-Bataillon "Reich"*.

At 2030 hours *SS-Division "Reich"* reported to the *VI. Armee-Korps* that the attack on Lebsino would be carried out with the newly introduced units and led by *SS-Obersturmbannführer* Kumm. The attack would be supported with a *Stuka* attack scheduled for 0830 hours.

A *Panzer III* joined the remaining two *Sturmgeschütze* of the indefatigable *Sturmgeschütz-Abteilung 189*.

Not counting the newly introduced units, *SS-Obersturmbannführer* Kumm reported the following combat strengths in the Noshkino — Lebsino sector to the division:

	Officers	NCOs	EM
Staff of *SS-IR "Der Führer"*	4	4	25
13./SS-IR "Der Führer"	—	6	9
Aufklärungs-Abteilung 256	3	3	27
I./Infanterie-Regiment 471	3	11	42
Heavy Weapons	2	11	36
SS-Krad.-Btl. "Reich"	6	10	95
Heavy Weapons	3	4	35
I./Infanterie-Regiment 459	6	25	135
Totals	27	74	404

16 February 1942

During the course of the morning *General der Panzertruppen* Model met with *SS-Obersturmbannführer* Kumm in Jessemowo and was briefed in detail. The commander-in-chief was visibly impressed by the unvarnished situation report and promised speedy help from frontal sectors that were less threatened at the moment.

SS-Obersturmbannführer Kumm received the unmistakable order one more time that the front must be held unconditionally so as to avoid endangering the impending success of the friendly attack groups against the enemy encircled in the area northwest of Sytschewka — the Soviet divisions that had broken through to the south.

At 1010 hours Kumm reported to the division that the *Stuka* attack had been extraordinarily successful, bringing perceptible relief to the friendly troops. Unfortunately, the planned attack on Lebsino with the *III./Infanterie-Regiment 396* and the *I./Infanterie-Regiment 451* was not carried out since the *Sturmgeschütze* had gotten stuck in deep snow. Even by early afternoon the assault guns had not been shoveled free. As a result, the planned attack had to be postponed to the following day. Thus, for the time being, the *Stuka* attack had been wasted.

At 2020 hours the *VI. Armee-Korps* radioed *SS-Division "Reich"* that Lebsino must be recaptured without exception on the following day. The corps expected that this relatively quiet day would be followed by renewed strong enemy attacks on 17 February.

The commander-in-chief of the *9. Armee* expressly ordered that all means be employed on 17 February to defeat the encircled enemy forces in the Sytschewka pocket. It was hoped that this would also mean a letup in the Soviet attacks on the sector of *SS-Division "Reich"* and the entire northern front of the *VI. Armee-Korps*.

At 2100 hours *SS-Division "Reich"* received the following radio message to pass on to *SS-Obersturmbannführer* Kumm and to the *VI. Armee-Korps*:

> ...Glasgen's battalion of the *6. Panzer-Division* is to relieve *SS-Pionier-Bataillon "Reich"* and the *14./SS-Infanterie-Regiment "Deutschland"* in the flank-guard positions west of Sytschewka. Those units are to be transported in rapid transport via Rshew to the headquarters of *SS-Division "Reich"*. They are to return to division control.

Day of Decision

17 February 1942

A decisively fateful day dawned. Red soldiers penetrated the "Church Village" by surprise at 0540 hours.

At 0600 hours *SS-Obersturmbannführer* Ostendorff (division operations officer) reported to the *VI. Armee-Korps* that two groups, each with about six Soviet tanks and accompanied by infantry, had broken through the main line of resistance. One of those groups pushed via the "Church Village" and Woods toward Jessemowo. The other group pushed south toward Brodnikowo.

A speedy response was required. As a result, the two *Sturmgeschütze* intended for the attack were set in march against the enemy group at the "Church" Village, where the *SS-Kradschützen* were defending against the superior enemy with the courage of desperation.

The enemy tanks that had broken through toward Brodnikowo were pinned by the artillery of the rapidly alerted *1. Panzer-Division* and destroyed after a short firefight.

The counterattack planned against Lebsino, however, had to be temporarily postponed due to the critical development of this situation.

The operations officer of *SS-Division "Reich"* reported to the corps at 0910 hours that the counterattack of *SS-Kradschützen-Bataillon "Reich"* was in progress with all available means and forces and that the attack on Lebsino was set for 1300 hours. An additional *Stuka* attack would be necessary for that.

In the meantime, the *SS* motorcycle troops and the indomitable cannoneers of the two assault guns of *Sturmgeschütz-Abteilung 189* had penetrated the "Church Village" in an aggressive attack. However, both of the overworked *Sturmgeschütze* became non-operational with mechanical problems at midday — a tragic occurrence. The Russians had barricaded themselves in the church in the center of the small village. Four exploding enemy tanks attested to the stubborn persistence of the friendly counterattack.

Due to the loss of both *Sturmgeschütze* the division again had to postpone the planned attack on Lebsino until 1530 hours.

The SS-Kradschützen Hold the Front – and are Bled White

At 1245 hours the enemy renewed his attack in the "Church Village" after staging and introducing new forces. He attacked the paper-thin line of the *SS-Kradschützen* with great force. By 1330 hours the Russian penetration in the main line of resistance had been extended to the "Russian Woods". However, the Red soldiers also suddenly seemed to run out of strength for a continued breakthrough at that point, and the motorcycle troop were once more able to stabilize the situation in this sector of the front. Unfortunately, the losses in killed and wounded for *SS-Kradschützen-Bataillon "Reich"* were extraordinarily high. The commander of the *2./SS-Kradschützen-Bataillon "Reich"*, *SS-Hauptsturmführer* Grünwälder, was killed in the heavy fighting. *SS-Obersturmführer* Hackerodt took his place. The fighting strength of the battalion amounted to 70 men. Remaining were:

3./SS-Kradschützen-Bataillon "Reich": *SS-Hauptsturmführer* Sayda and 17 men

4./SS-Kradschützen-Bataillon "Reich": *SS-Obersturmführer* Burfeind and one *SS-Oberscharführer*

5./SS-Kradschützen-Bataillon "Reich": *SS-Hauptsurmführer* Hoffman, *SS-Untersturmführer* Bär and three men of the infantry-gun platoon.

The heavy and seesaw fighting raged from early until late in the evening. The Russians clearly wanted once more to throw all available forces into the fighting and put everything on a single card in order to tip the scales and break through to the south to relieve what was left of the Russian 29th and 39th Armies.

Once again the fate of the *9. Armee* hung by a silk thread. The defensive front at this critical point of the battle had been torn asunder one more time. Summoning the last reserves of strength, the men of the army and the *Waffen-SS* joined in hurling themselves into the breach to plug the impending Red breakthrough.

With the last bit of their strength, the motorcycle troops were able to seal the penetration of the enemy infantry and separate them from their tanks. At 1400 hours the two *Sturmgeschütze* were withdrawn from the "Church Village" after their mechanical problems had been fixed. They immediately rolled to the assembly area of the *III./Infanterie-Regiment 396* and the *I./Infanterie-Regiment 451* for the planned attack on Lebsino.

After a daredevil attack by *Ju 87's* that bombed and made strafing runs, *SS-Division "Reich"* was able to report to the corps at 1710 hours that elements of both battalions had again advanced into Lebsino.

The Soviets, however, did not let up. At 1830 hours *SS-Obersturmbannführer* Kumm had to report that a Russian counterattack with seven tanks and 200 Red soldiers had forced the weak friendly force of 60 riflemen in Lebsino back out of the village. There were additional heavy friendly losses.

At 1850 hours *SS-Division "Reich"* received orders from the corps whereby all of *Infanterie-Regiment 451* was to be hastily inserted into the threatened sector between Lebsino and Noshkino to strengthen the main line of resistance.

The Turning Point of the Fighting

The day marked the turning point — and the scales of fortune finally inclined toward the German side, as if fate could no longer deny success to those who were ready for the ultimate sacrifice and had surpassed themselves.

Here we can best let the official report of the headquarters of the *9. Armee* do the talking. In its after-action report on the fighting, it states:

> The enemy, compressed into an ever-shrinking area, fought with fanatical determination under the leadership of his commissars and officers. Deserters stated that the enemy had been inoculated with the expectation that "*General* Model has all prisoners shot." Even the most enticing leaflets that were dropped over the pocket in great numbers could not bring the enemy to surrender. The enemy forces located to the west of the pocket attempted in repeated massed attacks to open the pocket from the southwest, suffering extraordinarily high losses in killed and wounded in every attempt, especially outside of Stupino.
>
> The 17th of February was the climax of the pocket battle. In extremely hard fighting it was possible to wrest the last villages from the enemy on the inner front of the pocket. At the same time on the northern front, the enemy gathered himself up in a last great attempt to break the German "bridge" and free his encircled divisions.

In mass attacks that eclipsed everything that had been seen up to that point, he assaulted the exhausted German defensive front with great expenditure of artillery and aircraft, throwing in all that was left of his armor in massed advances. Wave followed wave in the attack. Six tanks broke through far to the south, but the infantry following them was stopped in heroic fighting.

The tension was almost palpable. It appeared that success in the fighting that had been attained with unspeakable exertion and extreme sacrifice would still be lost in the final hour. The army group was already recommending against continuing the attack on the pocket; it was suggesting, instead, that a major portion of the forces engaged there be thrown into the northern front. But the soldiers and the leadership withstood that final and most difficult test of their nerve.

The commander-in-chief personally and with all possible speed alerted the affected units and set them against the tanks that had broken through. Those had already rolled through into the rear of the *1. Panzer-Division*, which was fighting oriented into pocket. The Russian tanks, however, were stopped before they could reach the pocket, and five of them were destroyed by artillery fire. With that the worst danger was eliminated and success in the fighting assured. (*9. Armee*, After-Action Report entitled: *"Die Winterschlacht von Rshew*, p. 8.)

***

With that the attack of the exhausted divisions of the Soviet 30th Army against the northern front of the *VI. Armee-Korps* became senseless, and it was only a question of time before the Soviet command clearly recognized it. — It became clear very quickly.

***

In the war diary of the *VI. Armee-Korps* stands the entry:

...17 February was one of the most crisis-filled days and, in fact, it only hung by a hair whether the front that had been held with all sorts of field-expedient means and extreme efforts by command and troops would be torn open...

Late in the afternoon *SS-Obersturmbannführer* Kumm received a call from his division commander, *SS-Brigadeführer* Kleinheisterkamp. The contents of the telephone conversation represented the conclusion of the battle that had so ravenously consumed manpower. It signified the richly deserved praise for the extraordinarily high and painful sacrifice, for the thousands of physical and mental hardships suffered in the weeks gone by of almost ceaseless fighting against a vastly superior enemy.

The division commander informed him the enemy in the Sytschewka pocket had been destroyed. *SS-Infanterie-Regiment "Der Führer"* would be withdrawn from the front on the next day. Finally, he informed Kumm that he had been awarded the Knight's Cross in recognition of the regiment's outstanding achievements.

Oftentimes victory and defeat are just two sides of the same coin!

What nobody had previously dared to hope for became reality in one fell swoop: Victory in battle, the end of the fighting for the regiment and the highest decoration for the commander and the troops.

The senselessness of continued attacks very soon became clear to the Soviet command. Almost as if by magic, the fighting and fire of all weapons died down.

The results of the sudden change began to show on the German side. The corps order at 1850 hours stated that it was planned for the *251. Infanterie-Division* to relieve *SS-Division "Reich"* on 18 February. The artillery was reorganized in accordance with that intended change, but the *Schwerpunkt* remained as before: On the left wing of the division, where *SS-Infanterie-Regiment "Der Führer"* and its attached units had stood their ground.

18 February 1942

After isolated weak enemy advances, all of which were repulsed, the Soviet attacks on the division's front suddenly ceased.

SS-Kradschützen-Bataillon "Reich" was relieved by two battalions of *Infanterie-Regiment 451*. At the time it was relieved it had a combat strength of only 30 men.

At 0930 hours a counterattack of the *II./* and *III./Infanterie-Regiment 451* against the "Church Village" bogged down in heavy Russian defensive fire.

At 1400 hours *SS-Division "Reich"* turned over command of the sector to the headquarters of the *251. Infanterie-Division.*

At 2015 hours a radio message arrived from the headquarters of the *9. Armee* stating that the enemy in the pocket had been destroyed for the most part and *SS-Division "Reich"* and its formations and units were to assemble west of Rshew.

Late in the afternoon the *VI. Armee-Korps* radioed:

Infanterie-Regiment 255 is to be attached to the *251. Infanterie-Division* as of 19 February in order to relieve *SS-Infanterie-Regiment "Deutschland"*, including the *II./Infanterie-Regiment 396*, in the Petelino — Noshkino sector during the night of 19/20 February.

SS-Division "Reich" is to assemble its elements in the area west of Rshew and refit them.

The division is to remain in the Santalowo — Greschikowo — Kowalewo — Chorochewo area as army reserve until further notice.

SS-Pionier-Bataillon "Reich" is to initially remain with the 251. Infanterie-Division and is to be attached to it.

SS-Division "Reich" is to be attached to the *XXXXVI. Panzer-Korps* in the designated refitting area.

***

On 18 February 1942 the commander-in-chief of the *9. Armee*, *General der Panzertruppen* Model, issued the following order of the day at the conclusion of the fighting:

Order of the Day

Soldiers of the *9. Armee!*

My proven warriors of the Eastern Front!

After sealing the gap west of Rshew, the *9. Armee* has now smashed the enemy armies that had broken through in weeks of heavy fighting and destroyed the greater part of another army, in spite of strong countermeasures and relief attempts from the north and the southwest.

Every officer and man of the army has his share in this successful feat of arms! Had it not been for the indestructible defensive shield to the east and north, it would not have been possible for the sharp sword of our counterattack to destroy the enemy. The exemplary involvement of all leaders in the mission of our army and the battle-proven cooperation of all arms, especially the *Luftwaffe*, were indispensable prerequisites for this success.

Your devotion to duty as officers and warriors in the frontlines and in the logistics arena has proven anew that we are superior to the weapons and soldiers of Soviet Russia in spite of the persistent harshness of the Russian winter.

The *Führer* has awarded me the Oak Leaves to the Knight's Cross. I shall bear it in grateful pride in you, soldiers of the *9. Armee* — in particular for those of your ranks who have given their lives for our mission — and as a visible symbol of all of your military actions.

Your actions as warriors in the battles of this winter war of 1941/1942 — which will enter the history of our greater German people as a famous feat of arms — give us all firm confidence that we shall successfully deal with every enemy, every situation and every mission that the *Führer* may assign us in the future with that same martial spirit that has only now come to full fruition.

/signed/ Model
General der Panzertruppen

19 February 1942

During the course of the day *Kampfgruppe Harmel* (*SS-Infanterie-Regiment "Deutschland"*) prepared to be relieved by *Infanterie-Regiment 255*. Additional elements of the *251. Infanterie-Division* arrived in Jessemowo. Their commanders were briefed there on the sector by *SS-Obersturmbannführer* Kumm.

The battle handoff was carried out during the afternoon. At its conclusion, *SS-Obersturmbannführer* Kumm and what was left of his *SS-Infanterie-Regiment "Der Führer"* marched to the division command post and reported back to *SS-Brigadeführer* Kleinheisterkamp.

The commander-in-chief of the *9. Armee* was also present.

Paul Carell described the meeting:

...When *SS-Obersturmbannführer* Kumm reported...to the command post of his division, Model was already there.

He said: "I know what your regiment has had to go through, Kumm, but I have to ask the question: How strong is it now?"

Kumm pointed toward the window with his hand and answered: "*Herr General*, my regiment has formed up outside!"

Model looked out. Outside were thirty-five men...(Paul Carell, *Unternehmen Barbarossa*, p. ?. Frankfurt am Main / Berlin (West): Verlag Ullstein GmbH, 1963)

The combat power of the regiment had been totally used up.

***

The commanding general of the *VI. Armee-Korps*, Bieler, had the following entry made in the corps war diary at the conclusion of the fighting in that sector:

With the conclusion of the fighting the heroism of the troops must be acknowledged here one more time. Day and night, in extreme cold and under conditions of severe deprivation, they repulsed unceasing attacks that the enemy continually fed with new forces. It was a decisive place for the army and for *Heeresgruppe Mitte* of the army in the east.

Not only did the enemy commit eight divisions to the battle — one after another in a narrow area— he also committed strong armored formations with the newest tanks, masses of artillery of every caliber and strong formations of his air force in all weather conditions in order to realize his plan.

Oftentimes, as a result of our own heavy losses and the lack of reserves, the situation was balanced on a razor's edge, but it was mastered again and again by the leadership and the soldiers.

The deeds of every individual soldier who stood in the hell holes of Klepenino, of Ssolomino, Lebsino, Noshkino, the "Church Village" and of Timonzewo were heroic deeds beyond all praise. They shall forever have their place in the history of the German army of the east.

***

Otto Weidinger wrote about the fighting in the regimental history:

During those weeks the enemy lost approximately 15,000 killed in the division's sector. The total number of enemy wounded is inestimable. Thanks to the exact knowledge of the unit designations of the Soviet regiments, it was possible to determine the losses of the individual Russian battalions and regiments. Those determinations were confirmed repeatedly by the daily statements of prisoners. The commander of the regiment considers himself justified on those grounds in standing by that extraordinarily high number of enemy losses. During the same time more 70 enemy tanks were knocked out in the regiment's sector. That number does not include tanks that broke through and then were destroyed by other units.

However, the regiment also suffered heavy losses and casualties. Of the 650 men committed at the start of the fighting, 150 soldiers were killed and a far larger number put out of action with wounds or freezing injuries...

...During that fighting seven army battalions and separate battalions in succession were attached to the regiment. Their share in the defensive success must be highly rated.

Based on the recommendation of the commander of *SS-Infanterie-Regiment "Der Führer"*, the commander of *Aufklärungs-Abteilung 256*, *Major* Mummert, was awarded the Knight's Cross for the heroic fighting and performance of his men and for his own outstanding service in the defense of the regiment's sector.

Particular commendation is also due for the outstanding support...(of the battery commander of the *5./Artillerie-Regiment 256*, *Oberleutnant* Tiesemeyer)...to the regiment. During the entire time period that officer directed the fire of his guns from the frontlines. Every enemy concentration, every enemy attack was successfully combated and, by order of the commander of the (artillery) regiment, the entire ammunition allotment of the battalion was made available to that battery...

Special recognition is also due to one army assault-gun battery...(the *2./Sturmgeschütz-Abteilung 189*, commanded by *Oberleutnant* von Malachowski)...The cannoneers brought tangible relief to the men of the regiment in many enemy advances, sometimes with only the last remaining operational *Sturmgeschütz*.

The men of *SS-Sturmgeschütz-Batterie "Reich"* fought courageously as infantrymen as part of the regiment. After the battery had lost its last *Sturmgeschütz* on 28 January 1942, a total of 32 noncommissioned officers and men were transferred to the regiment on 1 February 1942. (Otto Kumm, *Kameraden bis zum Ende*, 2nd edition, pp. 109-111. Preußisches Oldendorf: Verlag K.W. Schütz KG, 1978.)

The "Miracle on the Volga"

SS-Oberstgruppenführer und Generaloberst der Waffen-SS Hausser wrote in his personal notes with regard to the winter fighting:

On 19 February the battle was decided. The main body of the Russian 29th Army and a large part of the 39th Army were destroyed.

As a result, the enemy who had started out with great hopes and prospects for success suffered his first setback in the sector of the *9. Armee*. It was from German troops fighting during a retreat and with an inverted front — a small miracle on the Volga! (paraphrased from Wagener)

That success was a turning point in the winter fighting. The troops had had to hold out in all the rigors of the Russian winter and the shortages of supplies.

That winter was significantly colder than the notorious winter of 1812 with its retreat from Moscow over the Beresina.

Our weapons and engines were not set up for those cold temperatures. Decisive for supporting the forces were the living quarters. Security and fighting, however, mostly took place outdoors. Winter-mobile formations and ski units were improvised. Rivers and marshland were universally trafficable. Winter clothing was scarce.

The commander-in-chief of the *9. Armee, General* Model, particularly commended the performance of *SS-Division "Reich"*. He had a major share in the success due to his personal involvement — mostly in a *Fieseler Storch.*

***

The "Miracle on the Volga" was no accident. It would have been unthinkable without the brilliant performance of the German command with its unequaled skill in improvisation and ever-new field expedients. Those skills reached their supreme expression in the fascinating command personality of Model. The "Miracle" would never have been possible without the courage, the self-sacrifice, the toughness and the will to survive of the German soldiers.

***

The commander of *SS-Division "Reich"*, *SS-Brigadeführer* Mathias Kleinheisterkamp, was awarded the Knight's Cross on 31 March 1942 for the decisive combat performance of the division in the winter fighting at Rshew.

20 February 1942

The after-action report of the headquarters of the *9. Armee* concerning the fighting concludes with the following:

On 20 February the winter fighting at Rshew came to an end. It marked a turning point in the winter fighting on the Eastern Front. For the first time German superiority was proven again in attack.

What the German soldier achieved in those four weeks of unbroken fighting in the depths of winter against superior enemy forces will enter German history as a heroic epic. It was a three-fold fight: Against the enemy, against the elements and against shortages of supplies. During that fighting the soldiers lived from hand to mouth. There were no stocks of rations. Reduced rations for man and horse were the rule. Only by complete exploitation of supply columns and trains elements could the most necessary supplies be brought forward in the nick of time. Half of the allotted supply trains did not arrive during that time period. It was only due to the performance of the indefatigable supply sections and their forces that even this amount of supplies made it to this sector.

The heroism of the German soldiers overcame all of those deficiencies. The numbers speak for themselves:

The main body of two Russian armies was defeated or destroyed.

In terms of specifics: Six enemy rifle divisions were destroyed and four rendered ineffective. Nine more, along with five armored brigades, were badly battered.

In addition there were 4,833 prisoners, 26,647 Russian dead, 187 destroyed or captured tanks, 343 guns, 265 antitank guns, 7 antiaircraft guns, 1,148 mortars and machine guns and hundreds of motor vehicles, sleds and other equipment.

Over and above that, the formations of the *VIII. Fliegerkorps* shot down 51 aircraft and destroyed 17 more on the ground in that fighting. In addition, they destroyed four tanks, two batteries, 28 guns, more than 300 motor vehicles and just as many horse-drawn vehicles and more than 200 sleds.

That decisive success had to be paid for with the blood of German soldiers. The high losses bear witness to the highest devotion to duty. They were especially heavy in the following formations: the *86. Infanterie-Division, SS-Division "Reich"* (particularly in *SS-Infanterie-Regiment "Der Führer"* and *SS-Kradschützen-Bataillon "Reich"*), the *256. Infanterie-Division* (particularly *Infanterie-Regiment 456*), the *251. Infanterie-Division* (particularly *Infanterie-Regimenter 459* and *471*) and in *SS-Brigade Fegelein*.

Finally, the formations on the eastern front of the army also contributed to the victorious outcome of the winter fighting. In anxious, difficult weeks they not only held the eastern front (of the army group) but additionally stripped their own sectors extensively and sent every last man who could be spared to the Rshew front. (*9. Armee*, After-Action Report entitled: *"Die Winterschlacht von Rshew*, p. ?.)

***

In summary, it can be said that the "Winter Battle of Rshew" was without precedent and without parallel in the history of the war. The event was, up to that time, unique. An exhausted army group was retreating in the depths of winter and staring its destruction in the face at the hands of a new enemy offensive with newly introduced formations and new materiel. The enemy had attained an operational breakthrough and, with it, almost succeeded in his first large battle of encirclement. The dying army group, however, pulled itself together. Thanks to a unique combined performance by leadership and men it turned its own encirclement into a deadly pocket for the enemy in a dazzling combination of blocking maneuvers and a pocket battle — and all the while retreating and with an inverted front!

The success of the battle not only signified the survival of *Heeresgruppe Mitte* but went far beyond it. In the final analysis, it decided the entire continuation of the campaign in Russia.

This battle also illustrated *one* thing: even in the most hopeless situation a fascinating, dynamic command personality such as that of *General der Panzertruppen* Model can change the outcome of a battle.

With the conclusion of the fighting, *SS-Infanterie-Regiment "Der Führer"* wrapped up the most difficult combat operation of its history to that point. It had completed the mission assigned by the commander-in-chief of the *9. Armee* at extremely great sacrifice. It had sealed off the site of the breakthrough and prevented the Russian 30th Army from breaking through and relieving the encircled Russian armies.

The regiment had been completely bled white and devastated in that murderous defensive fighting. It had practically ceased to exist. It was extremely unlikely that this battle-tested regiment that had proven itself in so many engagements would ever regain its old combat power.

***

And yet, the unlikely happened!

A Commander Fights for his Regiment

(From a report by the commander of the regiment at that time, Otto Kumm, regarding his effort to reconstitute his regiment.)

February 1942. The battle of Rshew — for the regiment the hardest defensive battle to date — was over. The regiment was relieved in its positions by an army division. The commander of the regiment, Otto Kumm, marched with what was left of the regiment to the division command post. There he was decorated with the Knight's Cross by the commander-in-chief of the *9. Armee*, *General der Panzertruppen* Model. Model had requested that for him at the climax of the fighting — a recognition of the performance of the entire regiment.

The commander-in-chief handed Kumm a bottle of wine and asked: "Do you have any other wish?"

Kumm answered: "I would like to reconstitute the regiment in Germany."

"That is impossible," the commander-in-chief said. "I will get you the requisite replacements as quickly as possible so that you can be operational in short order. How many men does the regiment still have?"

"Please look outside, *Herr General*. The regiment has assembled out there — 35 men."

"That is something else again, but I cannot give you permission. Neither can the army group. What I propose to you is that tomorrow morning you fly to the *Reichsführer*. Perhaps he can help you."

The following day the commander of the regiment flew to Rastenberg with the express permission of the commander-in-chief and reported first to the *Reichsführer-SS*. After a brief greeting, Himmler asked what brought him. The commander of the regiment outlined the condition of his regiment and requested permission to reconstitute it at a training area in Germany.

"That is entirely out of the question!" Himmler reacted, incensed. "In the present situation at the Eastern Front we cannot expect the *Führer* to withdraw a regiment from the front. I will immediately give you 100 officers and 1,000 men. In three weeks you can reconstitute the regiment in an area near the front."

"*Reichsführer*, 100 officers and 1,000 men are hardly a regiment, let alone *SS-Infanterie-Regiment "Der Führer"*. For that one requires basic training and professional development and carrying on a tradition won in heavy fighting. For what you intend you must find someone else — I cannot do it."

Himmler became quiet. "I will go with you for supper in the *Führerhauptquartier* and will introduce you to the *Führer*. You must see whether you can speak with him yourself."

There were about 30 generals and officers and several politicians waiting in the dining room of the *Führerhauptquartier* for the arrival of the *Führer*. Hitler entered the room accompanied by Himmler. The *Reichsführer* waved Kumm over and introduced him to Hitler. Hitler laid his arm on Kumm's shoulder and led him to sit to his right at the table. Initially Hitler outlined to him in his unique fashion the actions of the regiment: The breakthrough of the Grebbe line, the Jelnja salient, the pocket battle of Kiev, the breakthrough of the Moscow defensive position and then — the defensive battle of Rshew. It was astounding how much he knew about everything. He then congratulated the commander on his outstanding regiment.

"And how is the regiment presently doing?"

Kumm answered: "That is why I am here, *mein Führer*. We have come through the battle of Rshew with 35 men and I would like to reconstitute the regiment on a training area."

Hitler replied spontaneously: "Of course! Immediately! I shall make sure that you will be fully resupplied with personnel and materiel. However, you must be operational again in three months."

Kumm had something else he wanted to say. "If I receive permission to get back all of the wounded and convalescing men of the regiment we will be operational again in three months.

Hitler then immediately assigned the *Reichsführer* the mission — right at the dinner table — of immediately ordering the rest of the regiment back to Germany, specifying a training area for the reconstitution and attending to the immediate replacement of soldiers and weapons.

That evening, the regimental commander dispatched a Teletype ordering the return of the regiment to the homeland. With a joyful heart, he then was able to go to Klagenfurt for a brief leave. Initially, the soldiers would receive a well-earned leave and, in mid-March 1942, assemble at the Fallingbostel Training Area on the Lüneberger Heath.

About 400 men of the old regiment could be brought together from *SS-Ersatz-Bataillon "Der Führer"* at Stralsund and from various hospitals. With that experienced old cadre and about 3,000 recruits the regiment looked forward to its reconstitution and the restoration of its old combat power.

Chapter V:
Defensive Fighting in the Volga Bend:
25 February – 10 June 1942

Kampfgruppe "SS-Reich" – 1942
(Kampfgruppe Ostendorff)

On 20 February 1942 *SS-Division "Reich"* assembled its remaining formations in the area west of Rshew for a brief refitting near the front. On 21 February it was again attached to the *XXXXVI. Panzer-Korps*. It remained as army reserve in the Santalowo — Greschnikowo — Kowalewo — Chorochewo area until 24 February.

The division commander, *SS-Brigadeführer* Kleinheisterkamp, was recalled at that time and *SS-Standartenführer* Ostendorff, formerly the operations officer of *SS-Division "Reich"*, assumed command of what remained of the division, which was redesignated *SS-Kampfgruppe "Reich"*.

Since the war diaries of *SS-Division "Reich"* have been lost and because the war diary of *SS-Infanterie-Regiment "Deutschland"* for the period from 10 February to 19 March 1942 was destroyed, records for this time period are very meager. Therefore, no details can be reported. However, we can follow the path of *Kampfgruppe "SS-Reich"* in outline form through a variety of sources. First, there is a comprehensive after-action report of the *XXXXVI. Panzer-Korps* with the title *"Abwehrschlacht im Wolgabogen"* ("Defensive Fighting in the Volga Bend") that was prepared by the corps intelligence officer and dated 15 April 1942. There is also the corps war diary for the period. Finally, we have the diary entries of *SS-Obersturmführer* Hermann Buch, who was adjutant of *SS-Kradschützen-Bataillon "Reich"* at that time.

From 20 to 28 February 1942 *SS-Kradschützen-Bataillon "Reich"* was refitted and reorganized. The replacements came from what remained of *SS-Infanterie-Regiment "Der Führer"*, from the commander of the division supply services, the divisional medical elements and, in addition, 200 men from Germany who arrived on 28 February. The refitting took place in Rshew, which was occasionally under fire from long-range Russian artillery. Several times it was bombed by enemy aircraft.

Sub-Section s)

Offensive Operations Along the Rail Line Rshew – Olenino – Ossugo: 25 February - 13 March 1942

After the termination of the Russian attack in the Rshew area of operations due to the destruction of the encircled Russian 29th Army and formations of the Russian 39th Army the enemy, bled white and exhausted, appeared to have given up on his intentions to break through. The greatest danger for the *9. Armee* had been eliminated.

***

Werner Haupt wrote about the operations that followed the Rshew fighting:

> The crisis for *Heeresgruppe Mitte* was not, however, mastered by that (the victory at Rshew). On 16 February the high command of the Red Army ordered the "Kalinin Front" and the "West Front" to reopen the offensive to finally destroy the German armies between Juchnow and Rshew. Both army groups received two guards corps, ten rifle divisions, two airborne brigades and four air regiments. The first objective of those forces was to reinforce the Russian 33rd Army and 1st Guards Cavalry Corps, which had broken through at Juchnow. (Werner Haupt, *Heeresgruppe Mitte*, p. 130. Bad Nauheim: Podzun-Pallas-Verlag, 1968.)

***

In the after-action report of the *XXXXVI. Panzer-Korps* the situation is described as follows:

> The German command utilized the abatement of the assault in the north to extend the front southwest of Rshew. At the end of March the *XXXXVI. Panzer-Korps* (to which *Kampfgruppe "SS-Reich"* was attached) began the destruction of the enemy whose main body was located in the Ossugo Valley. Oriented to the south, the corps attained rapid and sweeping success in the Sawido area.
>
> Increasingly deteriorating weather conditions complicated the offensive operation. Heavy snowdrifts crippled the formations' mobility. An icy snowstorm rapidly set in with winds of 11-12 meters/second (25-27 mph), quickly pushing the already excessively overworked troops to the limits of their capabilities. Frostbite and exhaustion took on terrifying dimensions. More and more of the horses, their resistance already reduced by lack of fodder, collapsed and died. The most vital supplies for the combat troops became increasingly scarce.

***

On 1 March 1942 *Kampfgruppe "SS-Reich"* prepared for movement and, on 2 March, was transferred westward by rail to the area east of Olenin.

At 2000 hours on that same day the *Kampfgruppe* received orders to take over the west wing of the *XXXXVI. Panzer-Korps.*

From 2 to 10 March *Kampfgruppe "SS-Reich"* was employed in the area of operations southeast of Olenin. The *Kampfgruppe* was able to recapture the church village of Sawidowo.

Kampfgruppe "SS-Reich" was again in continuous action. The *Kampfgruppe* consisted primarily of the *I./SS-Infanterie-Regiment "Deutschland"* under *SS-Hauptsturmführer* Tost, the remaining elements of *SS-Aufklärungs-Abteilung "Reich"* under *SS-Hauptsturmführer* Pötschke and *SS-Kradschützen-Bataillon "Reich"* under *SS-Hauptsturmführer* Weiß.

During this period of time 30 villages were captured in night attacks with minimal friendly losses. The companies worked their way up to the villages in the night. When the horn signal for the attack was blown, they broke into the villages with a "*Hurrah!*" and captured one or two more villages each night. As a result, the attack objective was attained by dawn. The stubborn Russian daytime counterattacks were repulsed with heavy losses for the enemy.

Herbert Thomson, a member of the *13./SS-Infanterie-Regiment "Deutschland"*, wrote about these operations:

> Offensive and defensive operations alternated in the Olenin area. The strong Russian pressure on Olenin and on the Olenin — Rshew rail connection made it difficult for us to operate, allowing us no rest by night or by day. The fighting there was not only for villages. Oftentimes it was for individual houses and, if necessary, for a single cellar. Cold and hunger were our constant companions. The infantry guns were moved by manpower. The villages in which we were employed at that time were Swinino, Nicolino, Kaminzy, Komissarewo, Wysowocho, Pany, Ustinka and Gorki (eight kilometers from Olenin).

***

On 5 March the enemy broke through to the north at Stubenki via the Olenin — Rshew railroad. They moved toward the *Kampfgruppe* staff. An immediate counterattack by the division messengers under *SS-Obersturmführer* Elfering, however, forced them back.

***

The entry for 5 March 1942 in the war diary of the *XXXXVI. Panzer-Korps* reads:

> In the sector of *Kampfgruppe "SS-Reich"* the village one kilometer south of Potachowa and a strongpoint two kilometers southeast of it were captured. Increased enemy artillery activity has caused heavy losses. The *I./SS-Infanterie-Regiment "Deutschland"* attacked at 1915 hours and captured Wjasowacha and the village 800 meters west of Grischina.

***

On 6 March 1942 *SS-Kradschützen-Bataillon "Reich"* linked up with elements of *SS-Kavallerie-Brigade Fegelein* in Alexino.

The war diary of the *XXXXVI. Panzer-Korps* continues with the following entries:

7 March 1942: *Kampfgruppe "SS-Reich"* captured the village 2.3 kilometers northeast of Grischina in the dawn after fighting!

9 March 1942: *Kampfgruppe "SS-Reich"* forced a breakthrough in the enemy line of bunkers east and northeast of Grischina during the night. During the early morning hours eight villages were captured and occupied after overcoming strong resistance. The enemy fell back to the southeast.

10 March 1942: *Kampfgruppe "SS-Reich"* utilized the nighttime attack successes to advance to the line Ustinka — Odrumaja in the eastern sector of the division. Six villages were occupied.

***

The corps after-action report for this time period reads:

In the meantime the enemy brought new and numerically strong replacements to his bled-white formations on the north front during the period from 7 to 10 March 1942. On 12 March 1942 he initiated a new attempt to break through to the south from Frolow in the Volga bend at the boundary between the *VI.* and *XXIII. Armee-Korps*. Thanks to the losses occasioned by the piercing cold and the exhausting sentry and security duties in field-expedient positions, the superior enemy forces achieved a large penetration the first day. Favored by a snowstorm that lashed against the German lines the Russian forces were able to extend the penetration to the southwest and south in the days that followed. The situation became increasingly critical, especially since the railroad line and road from Rshew to Olenin — the lifeline of the formations positioned west of Rshew — was seriously endangered by that penetration.

In order to interdict that dangerous penetration on the boundary and then restore the main line of resistance, the commander-in-chief of the *9. Armee* assigned the *XXXXVI. Panzer-Korps,* commanded by *General der Panzertruppen* von Vietinghoff, to assume command of the penetration sector on 15 March 1942. The corps had previously been employed in the southern sector. Facing an enemy advancing on a 15-kilometer front with nearly five divisions were the *206.* and *251. Infanterie-Divisionen*, which had already been seriously weakened in the previous fighting…

To strengthen the increasingly critical defense, the veteran *SS-Division "Reich"*, which had been reduced to a *Kampfgruppe* in the previous ceaseless fighting, was brought up as soon as possible.

***

Between 10 and 13 March 1942 *Kampfgruppe "SS-Reich"* received orders to proceed from the previous area of operations at Wjasowacha — Bredowacha — Sheltawez — Grischino via Olenin and Kalowka to the Truschkowo area. The *Kampfgruppe* was to attack the enemy which had built a bridgehead across the Volga there and was attempting to extend it by advancing to the southwest. The *Kampfgruppe* was to restore the old main line of resistance.

From 10 to 18 March 1942 *Kampfgruppe "SS-Reich"* proceeded in a strenuous march under its commander, the newly promoted *SS-Standartenführer* Ostendorff. The *Kampfgruppe* moved from its previous area of operations to reach its new area of operations in the Volga bend. Extraordinarily heavy snowfall not only had to be cleared in front of the extended march order but also in the middle of the column, which sank almost out of sight in the snow, so that the sleds could get through. Meter-high walls of snow towered on both sides of the Olenin — Ashewo road. The road was cluttered with the cadavers of horses.

Kampfgruppe "SS-Reich" was also hard hit by the loss of the undemanding and loyal *Panje* horses which had, for quite some time, converted the *Kampfgruppe* to a horse-drawn unit after most of the motor-horsepower had surrendered to the conditions of the Russian winter. By 28 January 1942 *SS-Division "Reich"* had a complement of 164 horses.

Around 13 March the sun broke through and nighttime temperature again reached -40 degrees Celsius (-40 degrees Fahrenheit). By 17 March the route of advance was again near the front and under enemy fire. The *Kampfgruppe* reported 25 cases of frostbite to the corps in just one company.

Kampfgruppe "SS-Reich" in the Focal Point of the Fighting

The corps after-action report continues:

In strenuous and exhausting marches, *Kampfgruppe "SS-Reich"* fought its way through meter-deep snowdrifts to the site of the penetration. There it was committed between the *206.* and *251. Infanterie-Divisionen* in the focal point of the fighting.

Initially, the formations of the corps had to prevent an extension of the enemy penetration to the south. A defensive front had to be established by intensive improvement of field-expedient positions. To do that, *Gebirgs-Pionier-Bataillon 85* (85th Mountain Combat Engineer Battalion) was committed north of Jagodino. It was the last reserve from the corps troops.

In response to a request to the army headquarters, further reinforcements were sent to the corps defensive front in long and difficult marches. These included: *Infanterie-Regiment 548* of the *328. Infanterie-Division*, the *III./Infanterie-Regiment 77* of the *26. Infanterie-Division*, a snowshoe company of the *86. Infanterie-Division*, one tank company each from the *1.* and *7. Panzer-Divisionen*, one *Sturmgeschütz* battery, the *II./Nebelwerfer-Regiment 51* and the *3. (Mörser)/Artillerie-Regiment 816*. At the time that the corps took over the sector, *Infanterie-Regiment 11* and *Infanterie-Regiment 167* were also employed in defense of the breakthrough site.

The corps artillery, which had been directed toward the south, turned in its positions to face north. In an attempt to make good of some of the increasing losses, pressing requests were made for the accelerated arrival of promised personnel replacements.

Sub-Section t)

Defensive Fighting in the Volga Bend West of Rshew: 17 March - 8 April 1942

The *XXXXVI. Panzer-Korps* continues in its after-action report:

While the defensive front was reinforced with those forces on a daily basis, a total of 20 enemy attacks — usually battalion-sized — were repulsed during the period from 16 to 19 March 1942 in heavy fighting.

The *Schwerpunkt* of those attacks, which were executed with fresh forces, was primarily in the Tarutino area (*Kampfgruppe "SS-Reich"*).

According to a captured Russian division order, the Russians were continuing in their intention of breaking through and advancing to the southwest in order to join the forces that were south of the Rshew — Olenin railroad line and, thus, finally closing the ring around Rshew.

The enemy also repeatedly attacked the right-hand sector of the corps front in the sector of the *251. Infanterie-Division*. Aerial reconnaissance explained the source of the indefatigable enemy advance that did not let up in spite of unusually heavy losses: The enemy constantly brought fresh forces forward toward the site of the breakthrough in long columns.

In order to improve the fighting spirit of the replacements, most of whom were of an older generation, and inspire them to perform as best they could, two of the seven rifle divisions employed facing and in the penetration sector were awarded the Soviet honorific of "Guards Division". Enemy reinforcements were also identified south of the Rshew — Olenin railroad line. The enemy was able to cut the railroad in several locations as a result of isolated advances by combat patrols and assault troops.

As in previous fighting in the hard winter, the thoughts and intentions of the German command and soldiers were again directed toward the possibility of an effective and destructive counterattack.

Accordingly, the *206. Infanterie-Division* and the *Kampfgruppe* of *SS-Division "Reich"* (Author's Note: The latter following assembly for the attack in Linikowo and Ashewo) attacked the enemy in the woods west of Reshetalowo after a particularly effective *Stuka* attack by formations of the *VIII. Flieger-Korps*. They advanced into the southern portion of the woods.

On 18 March 1942 the *Stuka* formations provided palpable relief to their comrades of the army in their heavy fighting as a result of destructive attacks on the enemy assembly positions in "Pear" Woods.

***

Herbert Thomson (*13./SS-Infanterie-Regiment "Deutschland"*) wrote the following on 19 March 1942:

At 0600 hours Russian low-level aircraft attacked Linikowo. A direct hit by a bomb on the company command post of the *13./SS-Infanterie-Regiment*

"Deutschland" killed the company commander, *SS-Obersturmführer* Jerusel, and a *SS-Standartenjunker*. *SS-Obersturmführer* Ristau, formerly with the *I./Artillerie-Regiment "Reich"*, assumed command of the *13./SS-Infanterie-Regiment "Deutschland"*.

***

The *XXXXVI. Panzer-Korps* continues in its after-action report:

The corps issued orders for the decisive attack to completely clear up the enemy penetration in the Tarutino area to take place on 20 March.

The attack plan employed the *251. Infanterie-Division* from the east and *Kampfgruppe "SS-Reich"* from the west to cut through the spearhead of the enemy wedge advancing to the south in the line Usowo — Tschernowo — Ashewo and destroy the enemy in the resulting pocket.

The *206. Infanterie-Division* received the mission of advancing from the west toward Pogorelki. It was to eliminate a flank threat from the northwest to *Kampfgruppe "SS-Reich"* with concentrated fire of all its weapons.

In accordance with that plan, the formations of the corps launched the counterattack in the early hours of 20 March 1942.

Bloody Attack by the SS-Kradschützen

20 March 1942

The *3./SS-Kradschützen-Bataillon "Reich"* set out at 0100 hours as spearhead of the attack on Dorogino. At the same time, the Russians attacked from the woods directly east of Kondrakowo and Gontschuki. Friendly artillery fired a barrage against that attack.

The company bogged down in heavy enemy defensive fire a hundred meters from Dorogino. The company commander, *SS-Hauptsturmführer* Sayda, was shot in the stomach and severely wounded. *SS-Obersturmführer* Buch assumed command of the company. Friendly artillery could no longer fire on the western wood line of Dorogino for fear of endangering its own troops. The *2./SS-Kradschützen-Bataillon "Reich"* was brought forward and also committed.

Dorogino was captured by 0300 hours. The houses formed a ring around a broad village square. Houses on the eastern outskirts of the village were on fire and blocked observation.

The Russians launched an immediate counterattack from "Hind-Leg Woods" with several T 34's before the village was firmly in friendly hands. The Russians recaptured the eastern portion of the village, forcing the *3./SS-Kradschützen-Bataillon "Reich"* back into its northwest section. The *2./SS-Kradschützen-Bataillon "Reich"* reached the western section of Dorogino and, with the other company, was just able to contain the enemy, which continued to attack with superior forces. The company received the mission of forcing back the enemy who continued to attack from the east and southeast. The

2./SS-Kradschützen-Bataillon "Reich" launched an immediate counterattack and again reached the eastern edge of Dorogino by 0510 hours.

Extremely strong enemy snow positions were located at the western wood line of "Hind-Leg Woods". At 0623 hours the commander of *SS-Kradschützen-Bataillon "Reich"*, *SS-Hauptsturmführer* Weiß, reported: "The enemy is attacking Dorogino from 'Hind-Leg Woods' with tanks and infantry."

At 0630 hours the enemy made a low-level air attack on the command post of *SS-Infanterie-Regiment "Deutschland"* in Sajzewo with six bombs but did no damage. At 0705 hours enemy tanks and infantry were in the center of Dorogino and the *SS-Kradschützen* were involved in intense hand-to-hand combat with the Russian infantry.

At 0730 hours *Stukas* intervened in the critical situation and eliminated the Russian tanks at the center of the village square. The *Stukas* were attacked by Russian fighter planes and aerial combat ensued. Shortly thereafter, a platoon of friendly *Panzer III*'s arrived as support. With their help the *2./* and *3./SS-Kradschützen-Bataillon "Reich"* succeeded in forcing the enemy out of the village and destroying him on the open snow-covered terrain.

Friendly losses in this fighting, however, were extraordinarily high. The *3./SS-Kradschützen-Bataillon "Reich"* lost 40 out of 90 men and 15 of its 19 noncommissioned officers. The losses in the *2./SS-Kradschützen-Bataillon "Reich"* were similar.

Starting at daybreak, constant enemy air attacks struck Ashewo where the command post of the *Kampfgruppe* was located.

The motorcycle troops again attacked "Hind-Leg Woods", which was under fire from friendly artillery. They were supported by four tanks and two *Sturmgeschütze*.

At 0850 hours the battalion headquarters received orders to send the *1./SS-Infanterie-Regiment "Deutschland"* forward as soon as *SS-Kradschützen-Bataillon "Reich"* reached the western edge of "Hind-Leg" Woods. The main body of the motorcycle troops entered "Hind-Leg Woods" at 0855 hours.

While the *I./SS-Infanterie-Regiment "Deutschland"* in Panowo rapidly set out to Dorogino, the ski company was brought forward to Ashewo. At 0900 hours the enemy fell back in large numbers from Kischkino to Pogorelski.

At 0912 hours the commander of the *1./SS-Infanterie-Regiment "Deutschland"* received the order to move as "fast as possible with his reinforced company to 'Hind-Leg Woods'. Mount tanks and capture Kischkino with the tanks!"

At 0920 hours *SS-Kradschützen-Bataillon "Reich"* reported: "The enemy is pulling out of Panowo via the southern part of 'Hind-Leg Woods' to Tschernowo." At that point *Panzer-Kompanie Hummel* and the ski company were immediately attached to *SS-Infanterie-Regiment "Deutschland"*. The reinforced regiment was given the following mission: "Advance immediately via Dorogino to the south. Clean up 'Y' Woods and take Panowo. Prevent the enemy from falling back to the east and northeast!"

At 1000 hours 10 *Stukas* escorted by eight fighters attacked Kischkino.

At 1016 hours the *1./SS-Infanterie-Regiment "Deutschland"* and the attached assault-gun battery received the order: "Immediately advance on Kischkino with *Panzerkompanie von Orloff*." Around 1030 hours Russian aircraft again attacked the command post of *SS-Infanterie-Regiment "Deutschland"*, dropping four bombs. The result was several wounded in the artillery position at Sajzewo.

Around 1345 hours all the reports that had arrived by then yielded the following picture of the fighting:

The infantry of the *1./SS-Infanterie-Regiment "Deutschland"* was unable to accompany the attack into Kischkino with the attached assault guns until the tanks penetrated into the village. Whenever the infantry exited the eastern wood line, it received heavy flanking fire from the direction of "Boot Woods", Point 215.7 and the wooded area south and north of Kischkino, which forced it to ground. *Panzer-Kompanie von Orloff* destroyed three 52-ton enemy tanks, one T 34 and two light tanks in Kischkino. However, it lost two assault guns and 3 Skoda tanks in the armored engagement. After *Panzer-Kompanie von Orloff* pulled back out of Kischkino, the *1./SS-Infanterie-Regiment "Deutschland"* fell back to the east edge of "Hind-Leg Woods".

The *I./SS-Infanterie-Regiment "Deutschland"*, which had moved out from Dorogino, also received flanking fire from the woods north of Kischkino and was unable to leave "Hind-Leg Woods". It remained at the northern and eastern edges of "Hind-Leg Woods" and reinforced the combat outposts of *SS-Kradschützen-Bataillon "Reich"*. A Russian attack on "Boot Woods" was repulsed.

The losses of *SS-Kradschützen-Bataillon "Reich"* that day were so high that there were no longer sufficient forces available for screening the northern part of "Hind-Leg Woods" and Dorogino. The main body of the *I./SS-Infanterie-Regiment "Deutschland"* had to assume that mission. The *2./* and *3./SS-Kradschützen-Bataillon "Reich"* sank to half of their fighting strength in a single day. The *3./SS-Kradschützen-Bataillon "Reich"*, for example, consisted of the company commander, one *SS-Oberscharführer*, two *SS-Unterscharführer* and 50 men. The losses of the *2./SS-Kradschützen-Bataillon "Reich"* were similar. More than 200 wounded were cared for at the dressing station that day. Employment at the enemy *Schwerpunkt* to the south demanded sacrifices.

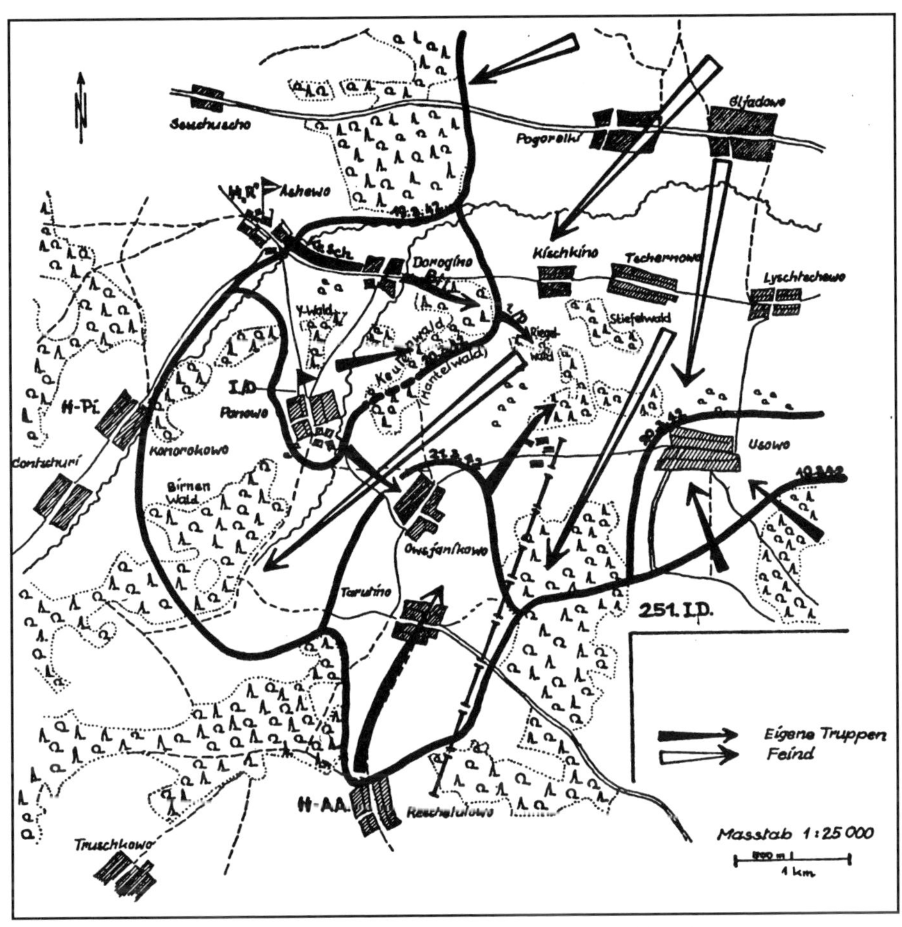

The Area of the Soviet Penetration in the Volga Bend

Panowo Captured and Held

Panzer-Kompanie Hummel and the *Schi-Kompanie/SS-Infanterie-Regiment "Deutschland"* captured Panowo. The majority of the enemy forces were eliminated. The tank company was given the mission of establishing all-round security at Panowo. *Schi-Kompanie/SS-Infanterie-Regiment "Deutschland"* augmented the security and established contact patrols to Point 230.5 in the southern portion of "Hind-Leg Woods" and to *SS-Pionier-Bataillon "Reich"* at Kondrakowo.

At 1430 hours Russian aircraft attacked Ashewo. A direct hit on the forward command post of *SS-Infanterie-Regiment "Deutschland"* severely wounded two doctors. One tank officer and most of the men of the regiment's signals platoon who were established in the house were killed.

At 1530 hours *Panzer-Kompanie Hummel* reported:

Strong enemy attack (1-1/2 companies) from "Pear Woods" with one tank. Unable to continue holding Panowo with available weak forces. Commander of the ski company has been wounded. Elements in "Hind-Leg Woods"; elements attempting to maintain contact with Kondrakowo. Two tanks out of action.

The tank company was ordered to hold Panowo under all circumstances. Elements of *SS-Pionier-Bataillon "Reich"* were to arrive at any moment in Panowo. At 1730 hours the ski company was reinforced with the *2./SS-Infanterie-Regiment "Deutschland"*. The enemy held the woods southwest of Panowo with strong forces. After the combat engineers arrived, *SS-Hauptsturmführer* Boden of *SS-Pionier-Bataillon "Reich"* assumed command in Panowo.

At 2030 hours a ski squad consisting of eight men had not yet returned from the southern part of "Hind-Leg Woods" and had to be considered lost. At the same time, the enemy again attacked the southwestern outskirts of Panowo from "Pear Woods". Enemy armor was identified in "Boot Woods".

The *II./Infanterie-Regiment 413* was attached to *SS-Infanterie-Regiment "Deutschland"*, effective immediately. The battalion commander checked in by telephone.

The regiment's adjutant, *SS-Obersturmführer* Diercks, arrived in Panowo at the location of the ski company at 2255 hours and assumed command of the company in place of the wounded company commander, *SS-Untersturmführer* Schreiber. The mission for the coming day: "Work forward to the southern part of 'Hind-Leg Woods' while it is still dark. Then mop up the wooded area."

The *XXXXVI. Panzer-Korps* continues in its after-action report:

While the units of *Kampfgruppe "SS-Reich"* were able to capture Dorogino from the west in extremely hard fighting with the support of a few tanks and enter Kischkino before noon, the *251. Infanterie-Division* ran into particularly strong enemy resistance outside of Usowo. Those formations initially bogged down at the outskirts of the village with considerable friendly losses.

The *206. Infanterie-Division* also initially advanced into Pogorelki with the help of a few tanks. However, after losing five tanks, it had to give up the ground it had gained to avoid unnecessary losses. Similarly...*Kampfgruppe "SS-Reich"*...was unable to continue to remain in Kischkino, but captured Panowo. There it repulsed strong enemy counterattacks with heavy losses for the enemy.

In spite of tough enemy resistance, the *251. Infanterie-Division* was able to proudly report another success on that significant day: By concentrating all its forces, the enemy was forced out of Usowo, a particularly strong and improved bastion of the enemy position, in stubborn fighting.

Thus, on the first day of the attack, the enemy lost critical strongpoints in his breakthrough position with heavy losses. Even though the intended sealing off was not completely accomplished, the basis for the final clearing had been established.

By conservative estimate the enemy lost 1,700 dead on 20 March. In addition, 13 tanks, 3 guns, 14 antitank guns, 6 mortars, 3 antitank rifles and 34 machine guns were captured and 80 prisoners brought in. The formations of the *VIII. Flieger-Korps* again played a decisive role in this success, causing substantial losses to the enemy, primarily through *Stuka* attacks. Even though friendly losses were substantial, the forces involved could look back with ample pride on the successes attained.

21 March 1942

The attack was resumed before daybreak. At 0550 hours Tarutino was captured in spite of strong enemy resistance.

During the night the ski company repulsed enemy attacks from the southwest and north. The woods west of the "Y Woods" were held by the enemy. A *Stuka* attack on Owsjanikowo had good effect and the village was captured at 0850 hours.

SS-Kradschützen-Bataillon "Reich" reported that the southern portion of "Hind-Leg Woods" was clear of the enemy.

At 0920 hours the *I./SS-Infanterie-Regiment "Deutschland"* received the mission of screening the southern portion of "Hind-Leg Woods" to the south and north.

At 0935 hours the commander of *SS-Pionier-Bataillon "Reich"*, *SS-Sturmbannführer* Tietz, received orders to mop up "Pear Woods" after a *Stuka* attack at 1000 hours.

Attack on "Boot" Woods

Around 1230 hours *Kampfgruppe "SS-Reich"* issued the following attack order:

Kampfgruppe "SS-Reich" is to capture "Boot Woods" on 21 March 1942. *Angriffsgruppe Harmel* (attack group), with the reinforced ski company, is to move out from Owsjanikowo.

The *I./SS-Infanterie-Regiment "Deutschland"* is to support the attack by fire. A reinforced platoon is to advance toward "Barrier Woods" west of Point 215.7 and capture it. An additional platoon is to be prepared to screen.

The *I./SS-Infanterie-Regiment "Deutschland"* is to advance with attacking units to Point 215.7 and set up a hedgehog defense there. Contact is to be immediately established with the ski company.

Last *Stuka* attack at 1310 hours.

1310-1313 hours artillery fire mission by all artillery. Additional support through artillery forward observers and friendly heavy weapons. The tanks of *Panzer-Kompanie Hummel* in Dorogino are to move forward along the route to support the attack. They are to be attached to the *I./SS-Infanterie-Regiment "Deutschland"*.

After a slight delay, the *Stukas* attacked "Boot Woods" from 1315 to 1335 hours. The barrage from all available artillery followed at 1338 hours.

At 1415 hours the *I./SS-Infanterie-Regiment "Deutschland"* reported that the commander of *1./SS-Infanterie-Regiment "Deutschland"*, *SS-Untersturmführer* Berger, had been wounded. *SS-Untersturmführer* Pohl, the battalion adjutant, had assumed command of the company. The command tank of *Panzer-Kompanie Hummel* was knocked out in an enemy artillery barrage on Dorogino at 1445 hours. The remainder of the company was ordered back to Truschkowo.

The attack on "Pear Woods" and "Gunsight Woods" did not get moving. The assault troop of the *I./SS-Infanterie-Regiment "Deutschland"*, which had set out as ordered, was shot to pieces.

During the course of the afternoon an additional battalion of *Infanterie-Regiment 413* was to be brought up and relieve the elements of the *I./SS-Infanterie-Regiment "Deutschland"* between the northern part of "Hind-Leg Woods" and the woods north of Dorogino.

At 1810 hours the assistant operations officer of the *Kampfgruppe*, *SS-Hauptsturmführer* Lingner, informed *SS-Infanterie-Regiment "Deutschland"* of the following:

> The ski company has boxed its way through "Boot Woods" to Hill 215.7 and formed a hedgehog position there since it is surrounded. The regiment's adjutant, *Obersturmführer* Diercks, who is leading the company, has been seriously wounded.

It was intended for *SS-Infanterie-Regiment "Deutschland"* to free the ski company with an attack on "Boot Woods" in the dark. Artillery support prepared for the attack during the late afternoon. The attack was to begin at 1935 hours after an (additional) artillery strike, after elements of the *II./Infanterie-Regiment 413* had assumed the sector of the *I./SS-Infanterie-Regiment "Deutschland"* at 1840 hours.

At 2025 hours the operations officer of the *Kampfgruppe* passed on the following information to *SS-Infanterie-Regiment "Deutschland"*: "The ski company is at Point 215.7, the northeast corner of 'Boot Woods'. *Obersturmführer* Diercks has been recovered in Owsjanikowo."

Around 2055 hours the *I./SS-Infanterie-Regiment "Deutschland"* bogged down outside of "Boot Woods" in heavy enemy fire coming from Kischkino, snow positions south of Kischkino along the stream bed, the western edge of "Brick Woods" and positions south of "Barrier Woods". Artillery support was impossible due to a shortage of ammunition.

In the meantime, the ski company had returned from "Boot Woods" to Owsjanikowo with a mortar squad and a heavy machine-gun squad. There were five noncommissioned officers and 26 enlisted men. Lost were two killed and six wounded.

At 2130 hours the *I./SS-Infanterie-Regiment "Deutschland"* broke contact with the enemy as ordered and occupied its former positions at the eastern edge of "Hind-Leg Woods". By 2250 hours 50 men had returned. All the wounded were recovered. The dead could not be recovered.

The *2./SS-Kradschützen-Bataillon "Reich"* carried on with the attack to the east during the course of the day, while the *3./SS-Kradschützen-Bataillon "Reich"* continued to defend Dorogino. The Russians brought 7.62-cm guns into position on the hills at Pogorelki. During the next two days those guns destroyed the last houses in Dorogino, so that the motorcycle troops had to "*bivouac*" in the cellars of the burnt-out houses. On that day 65 wounded were cared for in the dressing station.

***

The *XXXXVI. Panzer-Korps* continues in its after-action report:

On 21 March the attack was continued. *Kampfgruppe "SS-Reich"* captured Tarutino in the morning after overcoming strong enemy resistance. Then, in conjunction with the *251. Infanterie-Division*, Owsjanikowo was taken. The enemy suffered serious losses and lost a substantial amount of weapons and equipment. In spite of that, the enemy's fighting power was not broken. The continued advances of *Kampfgruppe "SS-Reich"* to the north ran into extremely strong Russian opposition from "Boot Woods". The Russians launched repeated battalion-sized counterattacks against Usowo from there.

The advance of *Kampfgruppe "SS-Reich"* cut off strong groups of the enemy in "Pear Woods" (west of Tarutino). It was not possible to complete the destruction of that enemy on this day, but preparations for so doing were largely completed. All in all, this day was also particularly successful. The enemy lost about 1,300 killed. Two tanks, two guns, five antitank guns, four antitank rifles, one mortar, and six machine guns were destroyed and 135 prisoners taken.

While the main burden of the defensive and offensive fighting fell in the immediate sector of the penetration upon *Kampfgruppe "SS-Reich"* and the *251. Infanterie-Division*, the enemy facing the sector held by the eastward-oriented *206. Infanterie-Division* initially remained inactive. However, increasing artillery fire made it clear that the enemy was steadily reinforcing his artillery. For the time being, the bulk of the guns were still northeast of the Volga. The continued employment of the friendly observation battery led increasingly to the conclusion that the enemy had more than 90 guns facing the site of the penetration and continually brought batteries forward over the Volga to the southwest. His intentions to continue the attack could find no better confirmation.

22 March 1942

Shortly after midnight the *2./SS-Infanterie-Regiment "Deutschland"* reported back. Losses: one dead and six wounded.

At 0550 hours the Russians moved from "Pear Woods" toward "Boot Woods". At 0715 hours *Stukas* and close-support aircraft attacked Kischkino, Tschernowo, "Barrier Woods" and "Boot Woods".

At 1030 hours the regiment's surgeon, *SS-Haupsturmführer Dr.* Hauk, reported a direct hit on the dressing station which killed a medic, severely wounded the assistant surgeon and slightly wounded the regiment's surgeon. Three sleds for transporting wounded were lost.

After the wounding of the regiment's adjutant, *SS-Obersturmführer* Diercks, the regiment's liaison officer, *SS-Untersturmführer* Le Coq, served as acting adjutant for the regiment.

The regimental adjutant of the Russian 922nd Rifle Regiment was captured in "Pear Woods".

At 1430 hours the command post of *SS-Infanterie-Regiment "Deutschland"* in Sajzewo was shaken so severely by a bombing attack that all the windows and all telephone connections were broken. Eight heavy bombs fell around the command post. The telephone connections were restored within twenty minutes.

Schwerpunkt on Both Sides of the Front – "Boot Woods"

The *I./SS-Infanterie-Regiment "Deutschland"* was to be relieved in the evening by elements of *SS-Aufklärungs-Abteilung "Reich"*. At 1530 hours it received the following warning order from *SS-Standartenführer* Ostendorff:

Reinforced *I./SS-Infanterie-Regiment "Deutschland"*, supported by *Sturmgeschütz-Batterie von Malachowski* and *Panzer-Kompanie Hummel*, is to attack "Boot Woods" on 23 March 1942. It is to advance to the northwest from the area southwest of Usowo in coordination with elements of the *251. Infanterie-Division*. It is to advance through the woods and eliminates the enemy forces in position in and west of "Boot Woods".

Elements of *SS-Infanterie-Regiment "Deutschland"* and *SS-Kradschützen-Bataillon "Reich"* in "Hind-Leg" Woods are to launch a frontal attack to the east as soon as the attack of the main body of the *I./SS-Infanterie-Regiment "Deutschland"* takes effect in the rear of the enemy positions. When the enemy withdraws from Kischkino, the attack is to follows into the village and capture it.

III./Infanterie-Regiment 11 is to establish contact in Kischkino after it has been captured and advance the main line of resistance from Kischkino to Point 208.6.

/signed/ Ostendorff

***

The commander of the regiment, *SS-Sturmbannführer* Harmel, asked the commander of the *Kampfgruppe* to postpone the attack 24 hours because of the condition of his men.

At 2035 hours Ostendorff informed the regimental commander that the corps had given permission to postpone the attack by 24 hours. The relief of the *I./SS-Infanterie-Regiment "Deutschland"* was completed at 2315 hours.

23 March 1942

The *3./SS-Kradschützen-Bataillon "Reich"* was relieved by units of *Infanterie-Regiment 40* in Dorogino and committed between the *1./SS-Infanterie-Regiment "Deutschland"* and the *2./SS-Kradschützen-Bataillon "Reich"* in the east edge of the "neck" of "Dumbbell Woods" (also called "Hind-Leg Woods"). Elements of *Infanterie-Regiment 40* were committed in the north part of "Hind-Leg Woods".

At 0955 hours *SS-Sturmbannführer* Harmel, the acting adjutant and the signals officer (*SS-Untersturmführer* Wilfling) rode on a tank of *Panzer-Kompanie Hummel* to Reschetalowo to the command post of *SS-Aufklärungs-Abteilung "Reich"*. A meeting took place there regarding the next morning's attack. In attendance were the commander of *Kampfgruppe "SS-Reich"*, the commander of the *I./SS-Infanterie-Regiment "Deutschland"* and the commander of *SS-Aufklärungs-Abteilung "Reich"*.

At 1530 hours Harmel went to Tarutino with the commander of the *I./SS-Infanterie-Regiment "Deutschland"* and to the wooded terrain east of Owsjanikowo for terrain reconnaissance. *Schi-Kompanie/SS-Infanterie-Regiment "Deutschland"* was attached to *SS-Aufklärungs-Abteilung "Reich"* and received the mission of reconnoitering the southern edge of "Boot Woods". It was determined by telephone that the friendly forces on the right, *Infanterie-Regiment 167*, had not yet been briefed by the *251. Infanterie-Division* regarding the intended attack.

At 1730 hours four close-air support aircraft attacked "Boot Woods". At 2050 hours the commander of the regiment learned from the *Kampfgruppe* that *Stuka* support would not be available the next morning. Given the exhausted condition of the forces at the time, an attack was no longer possible without the concentrated support of all weapons, above all that of the *Luftwaffe*. *SS-Sturmbannführer* Harmel reported that without *Stukas* an attack on "Boot Woods" could only take place with extremely heavy losses. He proposed that the attack again be postponed by 24 hours.

His opinion was confirmed by the reconnaissance results at 2110 hours, whereby the ski-company patrol received heavy fire from all weapons from "Boot Woods" and "Gunsight Woods", causing losses. The corps again gave permission at 2135 hours for the attack to be postponed another 24 hours.

After entire weeks of hardship and fighting, the men of the *Kampfgruppe* suffered particularly in these operations from the fact that the snow thawed during the day and soaked their felt boots with water which then, during the night, froze again in the low temperatures. This gave rise to frostbite, the more so since some of the men lacked adequate winter experience. The transition period provided new problems. Many men had only come out in winter as replacements from Germany. Others had been with rear-area units until the end of February and therefore also lacked winter experience at the frontlines. From 20 March to 3 April the men never removed their uniforms and could not wash themselves. The best they could do was rub themselves with snow. Naturally, every one of them had lice, and the plague of lice became increasingly unpleasant. In addition to that, men of all ranks were physically and mentally exhausted. The condition of the troops should always be compared to the disinterested accounts, reports and orders in the war diaries and, in most cases, is far less evident than it should be.

24 March 1942

All incoming reports pointed to ongoing enemy reinforcement. There were troop movements toward Kischkino — northern point of "Boot Woods" and continued march columns south from Pogorelki and from Lyschtschewo to Tschernowo. That strengthened the impression that the enemy was concentrating for an attack. Friendly intentions, accordingly, were to organize for defense, let the enemy run up against the defense and then eliminate him.

At 1250 hours the commander of *SS-Infanterie-Regiment "Deutschland"* requested clarification from the *Kampfgruppe* of command and control relationships in the event of an attack and in the event of defense.

New snowdrifts on the supply routes complicated anew the supply problem. The commander of the *I./SS-Infanterie-Regiment "Deutschland"*, *SS-Hauptsturmführer* Tost, reported at 1910 hours that "Boot Woods" was very strongly held and that the enemy there had small campfires. Based on that situation, two *Stuka* attacks on "Boot Woods" would be unconditionally required as support for a possible attack. The attack order was not issued.

At 2345 hours *SS-Standartenführer* Ostendorff informed the regiment:

> According to statements by prisoners, the Russians have been ordered to recapture their old position by 27 March.
>
> The attack by *Kampfgruppe "SS-Reich"* will not take place in the morning since the *Stukas* have called off their attack due to bad weather.

During the course of the day the *3./SS-Kradschützen-Bataillon "Reich"* was relieved in Dorogino by elements of *Infanterie-Regiment 11* and moved to the middle section of "Dumbbell Woods". The *2./SS-Kradschützen-Bataillon "Reich"* was in the southern part and a battalion of *Infanterie-Regiment 11* in the northern part of the woods.

***

The *XXXXVI. Panzer-Korps* continues in its after-action report:

> During the period from 22-24 March combat activities were limited to ongoing mopping up of the captured patches of woods and defense against repeated, but generally weaker enemy attacks. While clearing just "Pear Woods" alone (east of Gonschuki), *Gebirgs-Pionier-Bataillon 85* and elements of the *206. Infanterie-Division* counted 280 Russian dead.

Georg Keppler

SS-Obergruppenführer und General der Waffen-SS

Born: 7 May 1894 in Mainz. Father: *Oberst a. D.* Otto Keppler. Schooled in Humanities. Associate degree in 1913.

Died: 16 June 1966 in Hamburg.

February 1913: *Fahnenjunker* (officer candidate) in *Füsilier-Regiment 73* (Hanover)

October 1913 - May 1914: *Fähnrich* (officer candidate) at the Glogau military school;

19 June 1914: Promoted to *Leutnant* (regular army) in *Füsilier-Regiment 73*.

First World War: Western Front. 29 August 1914: Severely wounded at St. Quentin; volunteered to return to the field, both Eastern and Western Front. 1917: *Oberleutnant*and regimental adjutant. Iron Crosses, First and Second Class, and other awards for bravery.

1918 - beginning 1920: Demobilized in Hanover.

Beginning 1920 - July 1926: *Schutzpolizei* (municipal police), Hanover as adjutant. July 1925 to July 1926: precinct commander. 1920: Advanced promotion to *Polizei-Hauptmann*.

July 1926 - beginning of July 1935: State police in Thuringia as a district commander. 1 July 1931: *Polizei-Major* and commander of the police districts of Jena and Gotha.

Begining 1935 - October 1935: Taken into the reestablished army as a *Major*. Voluntarily discharged and entered *SS-Verfügungstruppe* as commander of *I./SS-Standarte "Deutschland"* in Munich.

October 1935 - March 1938: Battalion commander in Munich. March 1938: March into Austria.

April 1938 - July 1941: Commander of *SS-Standarte "Der Führer"* in Vienna. March into Sudetenland and Czechoslovakia (Prague: Guard Regiment). Western Campaign. Knight's Cross. Eastern campaign to Dnjepr.

July - September 1941: Commander *SS-Totenkopf Division* in the northern sector of the Eastern Front.

September 1941 - June 1942: Under medical treatment (meningitis).

June 1942 - beginning of 1943: Commander of *SS-Division "Das Reich"*. Assumed command at Rshew. Reorganization at Fallingbostel and in France. Charkow. Meningitis relapse.

Summer 1943 - August 1944: Commander-in-chief of the *Waffen-SS* in Bohemia and Moravia and then in Hungary.

August 1944 - January 1945: Commanding general of the *I. SS-Panzer-Korps* during the invasion in the west and of the *III. SS-Panzer-Korps* in Kurland.

8 February - 26 April 1945: Commanding general of the *XVIII. SS-Armee-Korps* in the southern sector of the Western Front.

May 1945 - April 1948: Prisoner of war and interned by Americans.

April 1948 - December 1952: Work at home and town clerk in Upper Bavaria.

January 1953 - beginning of 1961: Salesman and then chief administrator in Hamburg. Pensioned in 1961. Died in 1966.

Above: *SPW* command vehicle during the fighting. **Below**: *Panzergrenadiere* dismount.

The new weapons of the division. **Above:** The tank battalion. **Below:** *Panzer III's*

Above: The *Tiger* **Below:** Advance to Moshaisk **Opposite page, top**: *Porsche-Schwimmwagen* entering the water during an exercise **Opposite page, bottom**: The commanding general of the *SS-Panzer-Korps* (right) with his chief of staff, *SS-Standartenführer* Ostendorff.

Above: An exercise in France. From left to right: *SS-Standartenführer* Ostendorff, *SS-Obergruppenführer* Hausser, *SS-Gruppenführer* Keppler and *SS-Hauptsturmführer* Weiß. **Below**: A sporting event during an organizational day for the *I./schnelles SS-Schützen-Regiment "Langemarck"*. From left to right: *SS-Hauptsturmführer* Walter Kniep, *SS-Standartenführer "Käpt'n"* Schuldt (regimental commander) and *SS-Sturmbannführer* Fick (battalion commander).

Reception of the Italian commanding general Olearo by *SS-Obergruppenführer* Hausser on the occasion of the relief of German troops by Italian forces on the Mediterranean coast in the Toulon area.

Opposite page: The French fleet scuttles itself in the harbor of Toulon on 27 November 1943 during the *coup de main*. **Above:** Between the Donez and Dnjepr in the winter of 1942/43. **Below:** Eight-wheel armored car in "winter dress".

The penetration at Tarutino was carried out by a Red rifle division. Three additional rifle divisions followed echeloned behind it in the second wave, while one other rifle division west of Pogorelki had the mission of conducting a pinning attack against the *206. Infanterie-Division*. An additional rifle division, reinforced with a motorized rifle regiment, closed up to the north.

Facing the *251. Infanterie-Division* as far as the Volga knee south of Bachmutowo were two rifle divisions.

According to aerial reconnaissance and friendly observation, those enemy formations with a strength of from seven to eight rifle divisions — reinforced with tanks employed individually and more than one and a half armored brigades — continually received new reinforcement. Newly arriving tanks were repeatedly identified. Enemy artillery fire increased daily. A renewed enemy attack was imminent at the site of the old penetration.

Later statements from prisoners confirmed the correctness of that presumption. According to those statements, the enemy had brought from the Urals two new armored brigades during the period of 26-27 March. Those formations had only been formed in February. They were immediately committed.

New Russian Offensive

25 March 1942

Around 0200 hours continuous enemy attacks with strong armored support in surprising concentration suddenly struck the entire front of the site of the penetration on a width of ten kilometers. After a barrage from multiple-rocket launchers on the southern part of "Dumbbell Woods" ("Hind-Leg Woods") the enemy attacked at 0207 hours in the sector of *SS-Kradschützen-Bataillon "SS-Reich"*, but was repulsed until 0245 hours.

By order of the *Kampfgruppe* five tanks had to be set in march immediately to Suchuscha to *Infanterie-Regiment 11*, where the Russians had attacked the Kischkino — Dorogino road.

In the sector of the friendly forces to the right, *Infanterie-Regiment 167*, the enemy attacked Usowo.

By 1040 hours the enemy had captured Dorogino and Point 208.6, as well as the northern part of "Dumbbell Woods" ("Hind-Leg Woods"). *SS-Sturmbannführer* Harmel immediately had to assume command in the left sector, where the Russians attacked with 25 T 34's. Enemy infantry accompanied the attack on sleds towed by the Russian tanks. Four T 34's were knocked out.

The *1./SS-Infanterie-Regiment "Deutschland"* blocked against the Russian-occupied north section of "Hind-Leg Woods" ("Dumbbell Woods"). The *2./SS-Infanterie-Regiment "Deutschland"* was immediately set in march to Truschkowo by the battalion commander, and *SS-Sturmbannführer* Harmel went with *Panzer-Kompanie Hummel* from Reschatelowo to Truschkowo. En route the tanks overtook the *2./SS-Infanterie-Regiment "Deutschland"*. Since speed was of the essence, the infantry climbed onto the tanks. Upon arriving in Truschkowo, the *2./SS-Infanterie-Regiment "Deutschland"* was ordered to screen "Y Woods" to the east.

After a meeting with *Infanterie-Regiment 11*, *Panzer-Kompanie Hummel* was ordered to advance to Ashewo. The commander of *SS-Infanterie-Regiment "Deutschland"* proceeded on foot from Truschkino to Sajzewo.

At 1400 hours *Stukas* effectively attacked Dorogino, with the result that the Russians evacuated the village with two tanks and infantry. German and Russian tanks engaged each other at the western outskirts of the village.

At 1610 hours the wounded commander of the *5./SS-Infanterie-Regiment "Deutschland"*, *SS-Obersturmführer* Mentel, reported at the regimental command post:

> Taking advantage of cover provided by a depression, the Russians attacked at 0500 hours with tanks towing sleds carrying infantry. As a result, the *5./SS-Infanterie-Regiment "Deutschland"* was unable to successfully engage. Since the heavy weapons had been dug in, they could not be pulled out. They fired until the tanks were upon them and either rolled right over them or put the crews out of action. Because of that, two 2-cm *Flak*, one light infantry gun and two 3.7-cm *Pak* were lost.

***

During the firefight at Dorogino five Russian tanks were knocked out. One friendly tank was destroyed.

At 1755 hours the following formations were attached to the forces under the commander of *SS-Infanterie-Regiment "Deutschland"*: *III./Infanterie-Regiment 301*; *III./Infanterie-Regiment 11*; *SS-Pionier-Bataillon "Reich"*; *Panzer-Kompanie Hummel*; *Panzer-Kompanie von Orloff*; *2./SS-Infanterie-Regiment "Deutschland"*; what was left of the *1./* and *5./SS-Infanterie-Regiment "Deutschland"*; elements of the *4./SS-Infanterie-Regiment "Deutschland"*.

This group launched an immediate counterattack on Dorogino. At 1800 hours heavy enemy artillery fire was placed on the village. The friendly infantry was unable to follow the tanks in the heavy enemy fire, so the tanks had to return to Dorogino.

The *III./Infanterie-Regiment 301* and *SS-Pionier-Bataillon "Reich"* received orders to occupy positions around the village and block the route to Panowo and the area west of Dorogino Creek.

At 1935 hours *SS-Sturmbannführer* Tietz, the commander of *SS-Pionier-Bataillon "Reich"*, reported:

> Dorogino is again in friendly hands as of 1830 hours. New main line of resistance: Southern wood line north of Dorogino — northwest outskirts of Dorogino — southwest outskirts of Dorogino and south wood line of upper "Hind-Leg Woods"

— eastern wood line of lower "Hind-Leg Woods".

***

A direct hit on the battalion command post of *SS-Kradschützen-Bataillon "Reich"* killed the adjutant, Schütze. The battalion surgeon, *Hauptsturmführer Dr.* Ruef was wounded.

***

The *XXXXVI. Panzer-Korps* continues in its after-action report:

The enemy attacked the main line of resistance in aggressive advances with strong artillery support, particularly in the Usowo, Owsjanikowo and Dorogino areas. He achieved small penetrations; in addition to other places, and captured Dorogino and the northern part of "Dumbbell Woods". Fierce fighting also raged in the afternoon in the same places.

A powerful counterattack by *Kampfgruppe "SS-Reich"*, supported by a few tanks, succeeded by evening in stubborn fighting in recapturing Dorogino. It cleaned up most of the other small penetrations as well. By the time darkness fell, the old main line of resistance — with the exception of the northern part of "Dumbbell Woods" — was firmly in friendly hands in spite of operations that involved heavy losses for the superior enemy forces,.

A total of 11 enemy tanks were knocked out on 25 March. Of those, the courageous *Kampfgruppe "SS-Reich"*, led by *SS-Standartenführer* Ostendorff, knocked out seven tanks. That formation also had to carry the main burden of the infantry fighting on that day and, in spite of that, decisively forced the superior enemy back in powerful immediate counterattacks.

26 March 1942

At 0230 hours the battalion reported that the commander of the *2./SS-Infanterie-Regiment "Deutschland"*, *SS-Obersturmführer* Diecke, had been killed.

The seven enemy tanks that had been reported destroyed the previous day were knocked out in the sector of the *I./SS-Infanterie-Regiment "Deutschland"*.

At 0740 hours *Stukas* attacked the northern "Hind-Leg Woods", Kischkino and "Boot Woods".

At 0930 hours the enemy, escorted by two tanks, attacked Dorogino from the northern part of "Hind-Leg Woods" through the streambed. The positions of the *2./SS-Pionier-Bataillon "Reich"* were engaged by the tanks.

At 0955 hours Dorogino was again occupied by Russians, approximately 100-men strong. *Panzer-Kompanie Hummel* was ordered at that point to move to Ashewo. The *I./SS-Infanterie-Regiment "Deutschland"* held two companies ready for an immediate counterattack. Harmel went to Ashewo to form a picture of the situation.

***

At 1030 hours the commander of the *I./SS-Infanterie-Regiment "Deutschland"*, *SS-Hauptsturmführer* Tost, was severely wounded by a shell fragment. The regimental surgeon, *SS-Hauptsturmführer Dr.* Hauk, immediately went to the dressing station but could only report at 1115 hours that *SS-Hauptsturmführer* Tost had just died.

The death of this young commander was a heavy loss for all of *Kampfgruppe "SS-Reich"*. He had proven himself so outstandingly throughout the entire summer and winter operations in 1941/42. As a company commander at that time, he had led his *1./SS-Infanterie-Regiment "Deutschland"* brilliantly in breaking through the Moscow defensive position

***

At 1140 hours eight Russian tanks were in the Dorogino area. In order to recapture the village, artillery fired on Dorogino at 1255 hours, followed by *Panzer-Kompanie Hummel* attacking the village. At 1340 hours Dorogino was back in friendly hands. The tank company (with an assault troop of the *2./SS-Infanterie-Regiment "Deutschland"*) and the *III./Infanterie-Regiment 301* had then jointly eliminated the enemy in the village. The positions at the eastern outskirts of Dorogino were improved.

***

Herbert Thomson of the *14./SS-Infanterie-Regiment "Deutschland"* wrote in his personal notes:

> Around 0630 hours came the daily visit by the T 34's and thirty minutes of fire from all weapons. A few hours later Russian infantry attacked Dorogino with armored support. We had to pull out of the positions in the village. When that happened my second platoon in Panowo had to really keep our eyes on the ball so as not to be cut off. The two villages were 800-1,000 meters apart. At 1300 hours 10 *Stukas* attacked Dorogino and a immediate counterattack restored the situation.
>
> What we had to go through during those weeks in that little sector in the way of fighting and strain cannot be put into words. We were, at that time, the small remnants of *SS-Division "Reich"*.

***

Statements from Russian prisoners placed the 916th and 922nd Rifle Regiments of the 250th Rifle Division and the 81st Tank Brigade facing *Kampfgruppe "SS-Reich"*. These enemy formations were also seriously weakened.

In the evening report the situation in Dorogino could be reported as cleaned up. The northern part of "Hind-Leg Woods", however, remained occupied by the enemy.

***

The *XXXXVI. Panzer-Korps* continues in its after-action report:

On 26 March the enemy continued his aggressive attacks with undiminished force. Again and yet again, with all means and at any price, he attempted to achieve his great objective before the onset of the mud season. But on that day as well, his numerous attacks — again carried out with strong armored support — brought no success to the Reds. With the loss of four tanks, the Russians had to call a halt to their attacks for that day.

27 March 1942

During the night the enemy was noticeably quiet. There was only minimal artillery fire on the friendly positions.

A *Stuka* attack came as preparation for the attack of the *II./Infanterie-Regiment 53* on the northern part of "Hind-Leg Woods".

During the morning hours, a T 34 tank was knocked out east of Dorogino by a 5-cm *Pak*. Another tank was destroyed east of the woods north of Dorogino by an 8.8-cm *Flak*.

At 0830 hours four T 34's with mounted infantry attacked toward Owsjanikowo from "Boot Woods". They were knocked out at 0840 hours by the long-barreled tanks that had been attached to *SS-Aufklärungs-Abteilung "Reich"*. The attack of the Russian infantry bogged down in friendly artillery and infantry fire.

At 0955 hours *Stukas* attacked the north wood line of "Hind-Leg Woods". That was followed by an artillery barrage. However, the *II./Infanterie-Regiment 53* was unable to utilize that for its attack because the battalion's preparations had been delayed. When the battalion had completed assembling for the attack, the artillery fire mission was repeated 40 minutes later. The *II./Infanterie-Regiment 53* launched its attack and, by 1300 hours, had advanced about 400 meters.

All the heavy weapons of the *Kampfgruppe* joined in support of the attack on the northern part of "Hind-Leg Woods". Around 1450 hours the *II./Infanterie-Regiment 53*, which attacked under the command and control of the *14. Infanterie-Division (mot.)*, reached the northern part of "Hind-Leg Woods". At 2020 hours the northwest corner of "Hind-Leg Woods" was also in friendly hands.

***

The *XXXXVI. Panzer-Korps* provides the following additional information in its after-action report:

On 27 March the position in the northern part of "Dumbbell Woods" ("Hind-Leg Woods") that had been lost on 25 March was recaptured in fierce hand-to-hand fighting by the *14. Infanterie-Division (mot.)* that had been reinforced for the attack. The massed attacks of the Reds that were executed with stubborn determination that day again collapsed in front of the German lines. This time the enemy paid a price of eight tanks.

A few resolute warriors who had made it through the extreme rigors of this winter sat in the German positions. They knew that the time was no longer far away when the German soldier would again be the attacker. In order to secure jump-off positions for that time, those tough winter warriors had to hold out and repeatedly repulse the massed attacks of superior Red forces. Again and again they had to allow the enemy armor to roll forward to extremely short range, where they could then be destroyed by death-defying gun crews or courageous lone fighters in single combat.

28 March 1942

During the course of the night the northern part of "Hind-Leg Woods" ("Dumbbell Woods") was mopped up, in which the *1./SS-Infanterie-Regiment "Deutschland"* and the *3./SS-Kradschützen-Bataillon "Reich"* took part. The latter was able to "collect" 30 German machine guns that had fallen into enemy hands in the Russian offensive on 25 March. These provided a valuable supplement and reinforcement of the friendly weapons complement.

The command post of *SS-Infanterie-Regiment "Deutschland"* was to be moved to "Pear Woods". The commander of the *2./SS-Infanterie-Regiment "Deutschland"*, *SS-Obersturmführer* Rossberger, was directed to conduct reconnaissance. He reported, however, that a movement there would be impossible since the five available bunkers were overflowing with dead Russian soldiers.

Prisoners of the Russian 376th Rifle Regiment of the 220th Rifle Division were brought in. They were trains drivers who had been brought forward to combat units because of heavy losses.

Kampfgruppe "SS-Reich" was expected to again take over the left-hand sector (southern wood line of northern section of "Hind-Leg Woods" — southern wood line north of Dorogino) on 30 March since *Infanterie-Regiment 53* was participating in an attack to the north.

29 March 1942

The enemy again attacked the northern part of "Hind-Leg Woods". At 1610 hours the enemy attacked from the southwest part of "Boot Woods" toward Owsjanikowo. However, the attack was repulsed by the *2./SS-Kradschützen-Bataillon "Reich"* from the southern part of "Hind-Leg Woods".

At 1650 hours an enemy battery was engaged and silenced through counter-artillery fire with the help of an artillery spotter plane.

Orders remained unchanged for the *Kampfgruppe* to assume the left-hand sector by 2300 hours on 30 March. Fire from multiple-rocket launchers fell in the evening on the hollow east of Ashewo. In the first half of the night bombs were repeatedly dropped on Sajzewo and its surroundings.

***

The war diary of the *XXXXVI. Panzer-Korps* includes the following entry for 29 March 1942:

> Heavy enemy artillery and tank fire caused a total of approximately 1,000 casualties in *Kampfgruppe "SS-Reich"* during the period from 18-28 March 1942.

The bled-white motorcycle battalion was relieved by units of *SS-Infanterie-Regiment "Deutschland"* after additional losses by armored attack, artillery fire and frostbite.

***

The *XXXXVI. Panzer-Korps* provides the following additional information in its after-action report concerning the events of 28 and 29 March 1942:

> On the days that immediately followed, the enemy attacks concentrated primarily in the sector of the *14. Infanterie-Division (mot.)* on "Dumbbell Woods" east of Dorogino. The situation remained critical there, since the deeply snowbound terrain particularly complicated bringing forward antitank weapons. In spite of heavy casualties, enemy infantry worked its way ever closer to friendly positions. It was protected by several tanks. The attacks could be repulsed in their entirety and irreplaceable losses inflicted on the enemy, however, due to the outstanding support provided by formations of the *VIII. Flieger-Korps.*

30 March 1942

After a quiet night, four enemy tanks with mounted infantry appeared at the eastern wood line of "Hind-Leg Woods" at 0710 hours. The infantry were eliminated by friendly forces on the left. The tanks continued to maneuver and moved in front of the northeast wood line of "Hind-Leg Woods" and fired on the positions of the *II./Infanterie-Regiment 53.*

At 0830 hours *SS-Aufklärungs-Abteilung "Reich"* reported:

> Enemy attack by five T 34's and about 100 infantry on Usowo from the southeast corner of "Boot Woods". Three tanks already knocked out.

***

Two tanks attacked Owsjanikowo at 1400 hours. One of them was put out of action by a Molotov cocktail.

The number of tanks attacking Usowo in the sector of the *251. Infanterie-Division* had risen to twelve, seven of which had been knocked out.

A *Kampfgruppe* order directed various regroupings. In the evening the relief of several units of *SS-Kradschützen-Bataillon "Reich"* was completed.

***

The *XXXXVI. Panzer-Korps* provides the following additional information in its after-action report:

> But not even the repeated bloody blows dealt (the enemy) deterred him from his

intentions. During the morning of 30 March, he launched yet another concentrated offensive on a broad front in the position of the penetration after a long, powerful artillery preparation. After resolute defense against that powerful assault, he continued to pick at that same place in stubborn local attacks during the afternoon. Those also met with no success. Eighteen tanks were destroyed — That desperate assault also failed in the final analysis.

With these operations the Russian offensive was finally defeated.

***

On 1 April 1942 what was left of *SS-Kradschützen Bataillon "Reich"* was concentrated in the *1./SS-Kradschützen-Bataillon "Reich"* under *SS-Obersturmführer* Hackerodt as part of the internal reorganization. It, along with what was left of *SS-Aufklärungs-Abteilung "Reich"* under *SS-Hauptsturmführer* Pötschke, were consolidated into a single battalion and attached to *SS-Infanterie-Regiment "Deutschland"*.

In the course of the day preparations were made for the relief of the *I./SS-Infanterie-Regiment "Deutschland"* by *Infanterie-Regiment 53*, which was completed during the night by 0100 hours. The command post of the regiment was in Sajzewo. The *Kampfgruppe* issued an order of the day (not available).

On 2 April 1942 Putoschka — Wolowo — Teljatjewo were established as a billeting area for the *I./SS-Infanterie-Regiment "Deutschland"* after reconnaissance of the area. The command post of the regiment was moved to Kaschkino. The command post of the *Kampfgruppe* was located in Meschkowo.

Reorganization of Kampfgruppe "SS-Reich"

In accordance with the recommendation of the commander of *SS-Infanterie-Regiment "Deutschland"*, *SS-Sturmbannführer* Harmel, the *Kampfgruppe* was reorganized as follows:

The staff of *SS-Infanterie-Regiment "Deutschland"* was moved to the Bergen Training Area for reorganization.

The commander of the regiment assumed command of the *I./SS-Infanterie-Regiment "Deutschland"*.

What was left of the *1./SS-Infanterie-Regiment "Deutschland"* was consolidated with the *2./SS-Infanterie-Regiment "Deutschland"*, thereby filling out that company.

The *1./SS-Kradschützen-Bataillon "Reich"*, under *SS-Obersturmführer* Hackerodt, replaced the 1./*SS-Infanterie-Regiment "Deutschland"*.

Schi-Kompanie/SS-Infanterie-Regiment "Deutschland" was distributed among the elements of *SS-Aufklärungs-Abteilung "Reich"*. *SS-Untersturmführer* Schreiber, the commander of the ski company, was transferred to the *I./SS-*

Infanterie-Regiment "Deutschland" as adjutant.

The *5. (schwere)/SS-Infanterie-Regiment "Deutschland"* was split up among the *13./* and *14./SS-Infanterie-Regiment "Deutschland"* and *SS-Flak-Abteilung "Reich"*.

Cadre personnel of the units that had been split up were ordered to Germany for reconstitution.

At 2110 hours the assistant operations officer of the *Kampfgruppe, SS-Hauptsturmführer* Lingner, announced that a company of army replacements was in Sidorowo (near Sytschewka) and that it would be assigned to the *Kampfgruppe*. It remained in its previous assembly area and was trained there by *SS-Obersturmführer* Drechsler (*SS-Aufklärungs-Abteilung "Reich"*) and four noncommissioned officers of the *Kampfgruppe*. *SS-Infanterie-Regiment "Deutschland"* had to detail two instructors and one truck for that purpose.

The relief of *SS-Pionier-Bataillon "Reich"* by *Infanterie-Regiment 53* could not yet take place because an enemy attack was in progress in the evening. The enemy, a company-sized element with five tanks, was repulsed during the night. The relief of *SS-Pionier-Bataillon "Reich"* was completed by 0120 hours.

As a result of these regroupings, *Kampfgruppe Harmel* was dissolved. The reorganization of the regiment and preparation for the departure of the cadre personnel followed.

At last the men could get some rest and recover physically and mentally. After a long time without maintenance, weapons, equipment and clothing could be put in order again.

During the ensuing mud period, *SS-Infanterie-Regiment "Deutschland"* and *SS-Aufkläruns-Abteilung "Reich"* took turns in manning their assigned sectors. On the fourth evening *SS-Infanterie-Regiment "Deutschland"* relieved *SS-Aufklärungs-Abteilung "Reich"* for the first time. The reconnaissance battalion was placed under the command of *SS-Hauptsturmführer* Pötschke.

SS-Hauptsturmführer Brühne was made the acting commander of the *I./SS-Infanterie-Regiment "Deutschland"*. On 4 April 1942 the freed-up cadre of *SS-Aufklärungs-Abteilung "Reich"* moved out for entraining for Germany.

5 April 1942

The enemy felt his way forward with tanks. It was assumed there were additional tanks in "Boot Woods". A *Stuka* attack from 1230 hours to 1245 hours dropped its bombs so close to the positions of the *I./SS-Infanterie-Regiment "Deutschland"* that two men were wounded by fragments.

The commander of *SS-Infanterie-Regiment "Deutschland"* awarded decorations to the men of the regimental staff who were leaving for Germany and said farewell to them.

Local Enemy Attacks Continue

6 April 1942

The enemy appeared to be staging in "Boot Woods". A Russian deserter reported to the *3./SS-Infanterie-Regiment "Deutschland"* that the 132nd Special Brigade, which consisted of three battalions of motorized infantry and a possible mixed artillery regiment, had arrived on 5 April in "Boot Woods". It had been moved from Moscow to Rshew by rail.

At 1700 hours two small enemy attacks from the southern part of "Boot Woods" on the sector of the *I./SS-Infanterie-Regiment "Deutschland"* were repulsed by final protective fires. Enemy aircraft were active in the entire sector. Two bombs fell in Reshetalowo beside the battalion command post and dressing station, in which two men were wounded by fragments. One of the two sentries on the road was killed.

7 April 1942

An enemy attack of around 200 men that was launched from "Boot Woods" on Owsjanikowo around noon bogged down in friendly protective fires.

The *I./SS-Infanterie-Regiment "Deutschland"* reported at 1320 hours:

> The enemy attacked to the south from "Boot Woods" with two tanks and mounted infantry. Directly in front of the positions of the *3./SS-Infanterie-Regiment "Deutschland"* the tanks turned to the east and advanced toward the extreme right wing of the company, overrunning one machine-gun position. The gunner and assistant gunner were killed, pistols in hand, in hand-to-hand fighting. The other men were seriously wounded or killed.

At the same time about 120 Russians attacked the positions of the *251. Infanterie-Division* located southwest of Usowo from the southeast corner of "Boot Woods". This attack was repulsed by artillery fire.

The commander of the *3./SS-Infanterie-Regiment "Deutschland"*, *SS-Untersturmführer* Pohl, cleaned up the penetration on the right wing of the company with one platoon in a immediate counterattack with artillery support. A prisoner confirmed the arrival of the 132nd Special Brigade. In the evening, there was complete quiet in the sector of the *Kampfgruppe*.

The Fighting Dies Down

The Eighth of April 1942 was another day without combat activity. The *XXXXVI. Panzer-Korps* provides the following additional information in the conclusion of its after-action report:

> The first slight signs of approaching spring brought the stubbornly fighting German soldiers certainty that even the ongoing heavy attacks of the Red Army would no longer reach the objective the Russians had set for themselves at the cost of

senseless expenditure of bleeding masses of humanity during the winter of 1941/42.

The German lines held.

The forces of the corps could look with pride upon the accomplishments and successes in the unforgettably hard defensive fighting in the Volga bend.

During the period from 15 March to 9 April, 193 enemy attacks, 94 of which were supported by armor, were successfully repulsed in the sector of the corps.

During that fighting the enemy lost: 76 armored fighting vehicles; 9 guns; 103 machine guns; and, a great amount of other weapons and military equipment.

In addition, German troops brought in 890 prisoners. To the extent that a count was possible or carried out, a conservative estimate on the battlefield yielded a figure of 9,300 dead Russians.

***

The commanding general of the *XXXXVI. Panzer-Korps*, von Vietinghoff, wrote an introduction to the corps after-action report that has been repeatedly cited. It is quoted here to complete this section of the fighting. It read:

The last great test during the unforgettable winter campaign of 1941/42 had been passed.

Once again the forces under my command held out against the onslaught that the Red Army hoped would be decisive. Through indomitable devotion to duty and incomparably tough fighting, they exacted irreplaceable losses from the enemy and, in so doing, established the prerequisites for the coming continuation of the history-making struggle of our people.

The following report is dedicated in thanks and recognition for the accomplishments achieved in that fighting.

/signed/ von Vietinghoff

Corps Command Post, 15 April 1942
Intelligence Section, No. 800/42

Sub-Section u)

Defensive Operations in the Olenino – Nelidowo Sector: 9 April - 10 June 1942

Werner Haupt described the situation in the central sector of the Eastern Front at the time:

After the spring sun began to shine at the end of March and the snow started to melt and the land was transformed into swamp and morass, the soldiers of the army group held their positions against every enemy attack just as firmly as before.

In April 1942 the fighting on the Eastern Front began to "mark time." Nowhere did the Red Army achieve another penetration into the German main line of resistance. The fighting behind the front against the encircled Soviet formations continued on grimly. (Werner Haupt, *Heeresgruppe Mitte*, p. 131. Bad Nauheim: Podzun-Pallas-Verlag, 1968)

***

The situation at the front had quieted down. Changing temperatures brought on the mud season. The roads softened up completely. Motor vehicles could not drive. Forward progress was arduous, even on foot. Resupply with ammunition and rations were naturally made more difficult.

As had been true during all of the fall and winter months, the supply services of *Kampfgruppe "SS-Reich"*, under the leadership of the division logistics officer, *SS-Hauptsturmführer* Kunstmann, put in an unequalled performance. This was also true of entire medical corps in caring for the wounded and their evacuation. Without this, the long months of offensive and defensive operations would have been unthinkable. That was especially true of the ammunition and rations drivers as well. The weapons and motor vehicle maintenance services also worked to the limit of their capabilities to maintain the combat power of the troops. Without their unstinting commitment, all combat power would have dissipated.

As already mentioned, the commander of *SS-Division "Reich"*, Matthias Kleinheisterkamp, was awarded the Knight's Cross on 31 March 1942 for outstanding leadership of the division during the winter battle of Rshew and for the magnificent performance of the entire division. In the meantime, he had been transferred to another assignment.

With the exception of small reconnaissance probes, the enemy called a halt to his attacks.

Friendly reconnaissance and patrol operations were also carried out. On 26 April 1942 the *2./* and *3./SS-Infanterie-Regiment "Deutschland"* each sent out a combat patrol. The patrols penetrated 200 meters into "Boot Woods", blew up nine bunkers and brought back one prisoner.

On 10 May two combat patrols of the *1./* and *2./SS-Infanterie-Regiment "Deutschland"* — each consisting of two squads and one heavy machine gun squad — advanced into "Boot Woods" with artillery support. Their mission was to take prisoners and determine enemy strength. Results: two prisoners; one light and one heavy machine gun destroyed; six bunkers and two fighting positions blown up. The enemy lost about 15 killed and wounded. The patrols suffered one seriously and two slightly wounded personnel.

The *I./SS-Infanterie-Regiment "Deutschland"* and *SS-Aufklärungs-Abteilung "Reich"* relieved each other every week. During the month of May 1942 the quiet at the front was only broken by artillery harassing fire, patrols and combat patrols from both sides.

Generaloberst Model is Seriously Wounded

On a flight with a *Fieseler Storch, Generaloberst* Model, the commander-in-chief of the *9. Armee*, ran into machine-gun fire from encircled enemy forces on 23 May 1942. With his last strength, the bleeding pilot brought his airplane with the seriously wounded commander-in-chief into Belij. It was only possible to save Model's life with a blood transfusion. *General der Panzertruppen* von Vietinghoff assumed acting command of the army.

The fighting with the encircled enemy forces south of the bend in the Volga began to die out at the end of May.

***

Despite the lessening of combat activity, *SS-Infanterie-Regiment "Deutschland"* sent a strong combat patrol on a successful operation into "Boot Woods" on 30 May. The war diary of *SS-Infanterie-Regiment "Deutschland"* for 30 May 1942 contains the following entry describing the last operation of *Kampfgruppe "SS-Reich"* in Russia in 1942:

30 May 1942: Day passed quietly.

1700 hours: Artillery fire from the combined batteries opened up on "Boot Woods" for the combat-patrol operation. The enemy was kept under fire until 2150 hours by alternating fire from battalions, batteries and individual guns.

1800 hours: Briefing on combat patrol operation. The combat-patrol consisted of: 1 rifle platoon from the *1./SS-Infanterie-Regiment "Deutschland"*; 1 heavy machine-gun squad from the *4./SS-Infanterie-Regiment "Deutschland"*; 5 demolition sections (1:4); 2 flamethrowers.

2150 hours to 2200 hours: Engagement of all heavy weapons on "Boot Woods".

2218 hours: Combat patrol makes contact with enemy

2225 hours: Combat patrol enters "Boot" Woods".

2230 hours: Combat patrol reaches specified objective. Russian immediate counterattack collapses in fire from the combat patrol and flamethrowers.

2240 hours: Friendly artillery fire employed on northern part of "Boot Woods" (boot shaft).

2245 hours: Combat patrol falls back. Russians pursue closely.

2308 hours: Combat patrol reports back.

Friendly losses: 1 man of *1./SS-Infanterie-Regiment "Deutschland"* and 2 combat engineers with minor wounds; 1 combat engineer severely wounded.

Captured: 1 light machine gun; 1 antitank rifle. The rifles were destroyed. 1 man captured. 25 enemy dead

Destroyed: 31 bunkers; 10 machine-gun positions; 4 rifle positions.

During the operation there was Russian harassing fire on friendly positions and Eshetalowo.

***

In conclusion, Werner Haupt wrote the following regarding the last section of that fighting:

> The fighting with the encircled forces of Lieutenant General Below died down at the end of May 1942. Repeated concentric attacks forced the Soviets closer together. Nevertheless, large elements of the 1st Guards Cavalry Corps and the 4th Airborne Brigade, including Lieutenant General Below, broke through to the south on 9 June. The *7. Infanterie-Division*, which was supposed to interdict the Soviets at Kirow, was overrun.
>
> In spite of that, the last danger for *Heeresgruppe Mitte* had finally been dispelled. The army group could orient again to the east and north. (Werner Haupt, *Heeresgruppe Mitte*, p. 132. Bad Nauheim: Podzun-Pallas-Verlag, 1968)

Conclusion of the Operations of Kampfgruppe *"SS-Reich"*

On 1 June 1942 *Kampfgruppe "SS-Reich"* was relieved by *Infanterie-Regiment 53*.

At 2400 hours the last of the heavy weapons was pulled out. The companies marched to the *bivouac* areas that had been designated in orders. With that the most difficult and fiercest action of *SS-Division "Reich"* in the 1941/42 eastern campaign and the first winter in Russia came to an end.

The losses of the division were shockingly high and distressing. But the words of the American historian, George H. Stein, in his *The Waffen-SS: Hitler's Elite Guard at War*, are valid: Elite units are never judged by the extent of their losses.

The depiction of the operations in the first half of the Russian campaign shows that *SS-Division "Reich"* was never spared by the army in the murderous struggle on the Eastern Front. Likewise, it never spared itself.

For months on end at the spearhead of the assault wedge of *Heeresgruppe Mitte* directed at Moscow, the division was shifted from one point of major concentration to another and from one defensive hotspot to the next until it had been totally expended and burnt out. The military reputation that the division earned for itself in the east was indeed bought with extraordinarily high and painful losses.

The men of *SS-Division "Reich"* honestly shared with their army brethren the oftentimes almost superhuman exertions of that campaign in summer, during the mud seasons and in the rigors of the "Siberian" winter with its innumerable bloody attacks. They bore their share of the arduous marches through viscous mud, pouring rain and crisp cold; the wounds, frostbite and hunger and the constant mental overload along with their comrades of the German army in the east.

What was left of *Kampfgruppe "SS-Reich"* entrained in the Rshew area at the beginning of June 1942 for transfer to Germany for reconstitution.

The newly designated commander of *SS-Division "Reich", SS-Gruppenführer* Keppler, arrived in the Rshew area of operations during the relief of the *Kampfgruppe* from the front. He had received another assignment during the summer of 1941 and left his command of *SS-Infanterie-Regiment "Der Führer*. Once in Rshew, he issued his first orders for the movement of the *Kampfgruppe* to Germany.

The movement proceeded via Smolensk, Witebsk, Latvia and Lithuania to Germany. The leading elements of the *Kampfgruppe* arrived at the Fallingbostel Training Area on the Lüneburger Heath on 10 June 1942 after being routed through Berlin. From there all members of the *Kampfgruppe* departed for a well-earned 14-day leave. After they returned from leave the reorganization and restructuring of the division into a *Panzer-Grenadier-Division* began.

What Did It All Mean

After the conclusion of this first great phase of the Russian campaign, unavoidable questions arise regarding the sense of this immense sacrifice of the division and, at the same time, of the entire German army in the east. These questions were raised to a far greater extent after the collapse of the *Reich* in 1945 by German soldiers who had fought at the front and by the German people.

Had the gigantic sacrifices and rigors, the mighty pocket battles, the costly advance to the gates of Moscow been anything other than completely fruitless and senseless?

Generalfeldmarschall von Manstein called the victorious campaigns and pocket battles "Lost Victories".

At this point we will quote from an historical evaluation of that fateful struggle against the Soviet Union and its place in European history at the conclusion of the murderous winter campaign of 1941/42. It was written by one of the highest-ranking soldiers of the former German armed forces, *Generaloberst* Lothar Rendulic

Generaloberst Rendulic was the last commander-in-chief of *Heeresgruppe Süd*. After the war, he became a military historian. The general, who had also been a member of the Imperial and Royal Austro-Hungarian Army, wrote a chapter in his autobiographical account of 50 years of Austrian and German history concerning that topic. It is repeated here.

Significance of the Russian Campaign

It was a major unpleasant surprise for the German command when, at the very start of the war, the Russians met our 135 divisions with more than 200, our 3,000 tanks with 10,000 and our 2,000 aircraft with 6,000. From that superiority we were soon convinced that the attack on Russia took place at the last moment that offered any possibility that superior leadership could bring about a successful outcome.

At the time, of course, I was unable to correctly evaluate the extremely significant position of the war with Russia in its geopolitical setting. The evaluation of that war only became possible after it ended. But even then the search must move beyond the superficial but so categorical judgements and penetrate the propaganda that clouds the issue. Nevertheless, I shall even now present the facts upon which an evaluation of this war must be based, because the later events of the war will be seen with different eyes than when it is viewed through narrow propaganda and the postwar military historical writing that follows that line. Its adherents assert that the war against Russia was hopeless and, therefore, unnecessary. However, a careful examination of all the facts and contexts show that even the loss of that war in no way diminish its great significance for Europe.

We shall go back to the time immediately preceding the war with Poland, to the year 1939. At that time the armed forces of France were quite weak. England had six divisions that were not ready for employment. The United States may have had a strong air force, but its ground troops were practically non-existent. Russia, on the other hand, was arming at full speed. Russia kept its armament so secret that neither the western powers nor Germany were aware of its full extent. If the war had not interrupted the process, Russia would have nearly doubled the arsenal we encountered in 1941 by 1943. No power in the world could then have prevented Russia from setting up a Communist regime in all of Europe. After the war Stalin provided a few examples in achieving that goal of Russian politics.

Germany's war with Russia led to the fact that...in 1941 their most valuable formations were wiped out and, in the hard offensive and defensive fighting of the years that followed, the new forces that were continually created were repeatedly badly battered until, by the end of the war, the Russians were totally exhausted.

(When I commanded *Heeresgruppe Süd* in Austria in 1945 and evacuated Vienna in hopes of sparing fighting there, two Russian army groups faced my front. They were incapable of continued fighting. Companies that were only nine-men strong, commanded by cooks and clerks, were nothing unusual.)

Russia was so weakened that it could not carry out its wide-ranging political plans after the war. At the same time, the western powers that had been rudely shaken awake by Germany's rearmament and conduct of war were then actually superior to the Russians. That meant that the rearmament of the western powers that had been directed against Germany was also the first step against the Russian danger. However, it turned out that the western powers, in spite of their superiority, were themselves unready to successfully counter the expansionist intentions of the Russians in Europe, even though those intentions were sharply reduced from prewar plans.

Therefore, I believe that I am not far from the truth when I assert that the rearmament of the German *Reich* in its awakening effect on the west — and especially Germany's war against Russia — saved western culture. It seems to be an irony of fate that the western powers, even without being aware of it, did everything they could to prevent that salvation. Granted, the German *Reich* may have pursued other objectives alongside the main goal of the war against Communism. That, however, is irrelevant to the geo-historical significance of its struggle. In that struggle the German *Reich* sacrificed itself — a veritable deed for western culture that was worthy of Arnold von Winkelried himself.

Such is the significance of our struggle! In that spring of 1942 we were far removed from recognizing that other, deeper significance of our actions. Today, however, I know that we did not fight in vain. (*Generaloberst a. D. Dr.* Lothar Rendulic, *Soldat in stürzenden Reichen* (Soldier in Collapsing Empires), pp. 286-288. Munich: Damm Verlag, 1965)

Reconstitution of SS-Division "Reich" and its Restructuring as a SS-Panzer-Grenadier-Division
Reconstitution and Reorganization of SS-Infanterie-Regiment "Der Führer"

The reconstitution of *SS-Infanterie-Regiment "Der Führer"* began in mid-March 1942. At the same time it was restructured as a *Panzer-Grenadier-Regiment* at the Fallingbostel Training Area under markedly favorable circumstances. The regiment was permitted to recall all returning convalescents from the training and replacement battalion at Stralsund and all sick and wounded officers, to the extent that they would be fit for field service in the next three months. As a result, about 400 officers, noncommissioned officers and men arrived in a short time, all of whom had experienced at least a portion of the fighting with the regiment and therefore formed the basis upon which the newly organized companies and battalions could be built.

In rapid succession transports arrived with young recruits; in all, about 3,000 men averaging 18-20 years old. What was still lacking in the way of officers was assigned to the regiment, some with, but most without, experience at the front.

The men who had been detailed to officer training courses shortly before the war returned to the regiment as *Standartenoberjunker* (officer candidates) from officer academies at Braunschweig and Bad Tölz.

In accordance with tried-and-true methods, noncommissioned-officer-candidate companies were immediately formed. The particularly critical gaps in the noncommissioned officer corps could be filled in the foreseeable future as a result.

The issuance of weapons and equipment was slow. Weapons training did not suffer, however. A particular bottleneck was the issuance of motor vehicles. Apart from the few old motor vehicles that had been brought along from the east, the regiment had nothing available. The training of vehicle drivers necessarily suffered from that shortage and, consequently, training as a motorized force initially came to a halt.

Battalion command positions:

*I./*SS-Infanterie-Regiment *"Der Führer"*: *SS-Hauptsturmführer* Opificius

II./SS-Infanterie-Regiment "Der Führer": *SS-Hauptsturmführer* Stadler

III./SS-Infanterie-Regiment "Der Führer": *SS-Hauptsturmführer* Horn.

SS-Hauptsturmführer Holzer continued as regimental adjutant.

All were veteran, thoroughly proven officers of the regiment. All of the companies of the regiment were provided with good commanders and platoon leaders. Unfortunately, a third of them lacked experience at the front.

At the beginning of April what was left of the division started arriving platoon by platoon at the training area. *Kampfgruppe "SS-Reich"* remained in action in the Volga bend until 1 June 1942. The first elements of the *Kampfgruppe* arrived on 10 June 1942.

Sub-Section v)

Employment in Germany: 15 April – 27 July 1942

All members of the *Kampfgruppe* returned from leave in the second half of June 1942. As a result, the reorganization and restructuring to a *Panzer-Grenadier-Division* could finally take place under the same favorable personnel provisions that had been bestowed on *SS-Infanterie-Regiment "Der Führer"*.

The new commander of the division, *SS-Gruppenführer* Georg Keppler, was a guarantor that the division would carry on its traditions in the spirit of its first commander, *SS-Obergruppenführer* Hausser. Before leaving the division, he had been a former commander of the *I./SS-Infanterie-Regiment "Deutschland"* and, later, the commander of *SS-Infanterie-Regiment "Der Führer"*.

SS-Infanterie-Regiment "Deutschland" continued to be commanded by *SS-Obergruppenführer* Heinz Harmel, the veteran *Kampfgruppe* commander. *SS-Infanterie-Regiment "Der Führer"* likewise continued to be commanded by *SS-Obersturmbannführer* Kumm, who had proven himself in the defensive fighting at Rshew.

SS-Sturmgeschütz-Batterie "Reich" Deactivated

A special division order on 4 May 1942 announced the deactivation of *SS-Sturmgeschütz-Batterie "Reich"*. (Although the battery was disbanded in the field earlier in the year due to the loss of its last assault gun, the measure had been intended as temporary. The following order was intended to be permanent in nature).

Special Division Order

The assault-gun battery of *SS-Division "Reich"* is deactivated, effective 30 April 1942.

The personnel will be transferred by special orders to *SS-Panzer-Abteilung 2, SS-Panzerjäger-Abteilung 2* and *SS-Artillerie-Regiment 2.*

Deactivation results from the reorganization of *SS-Division "Reich"* ordered by the *Führer.*

The entire division remembers with pride and gratitude the glorious operations of its assault-gun battery.

Under the command of its first battery commander, *SS-Hauptsturmführer* Günster, who fought as an exemplary *SS* officer and died at the head of his battery, and of his successor, *SS-Obersturmführer* Telkamp, the assault-gun battery was garnered a worthy page in the book of the division history.

In its many victorious engagements and skirmishes, it has been the trailbreaker and protective escort of the infantry.

Our fallen comrades of the assault-gun battery and those severely wounded in hospitals deserve our remembrance.

In their spirit and with new weapons, may we continue forward for the *Führer* and the German people.

/signed/ Keppler
SS-Gruppenführer und Generalleutnant
der Waffen-SS

No one in the division could understand why that unique weapon no longer belonged to the division. At that time it was not yet known that it would be formed again in the strength of a battalion a half year later.

Redesignation

In the course of the month of May the designation *SS-Division "Reich"* was changed by order of the *Reichsführer-SS* to *SS-Division "Das Reich".*

Even though the restructuring to an *SS-Panzer-Grenadier-Division* began at the same time as the reconstitution of the division, the designation of the division was not changed to *SS-Panzer-Grenadier-Division "Das Reich"* until November.

Reorganization

The reorganization to a *Panzer-Grenadier-Division* entailed the formation of a tank battalion with three tank companies (equipped with *Panzer III's and Panzer IV's*). The tank battalion was formed at the Fallingbostel Training Area by *SS-Sturmbannführer* von Reitzenstein. It consisted primarily of former members of *SS-Infanterie-Regiment "Deutschland".*

In addition, one infantry battalion of the division, the *III./SS-Infanterie-Regiment "Der Führer"*, was reorganized as a *Schützenpanzerwagen-Bataillon* (armored personnel carrier battalion). This battalion was primarily intended for joint employment with the tank battalion.

The *2./SS-Aufklärungs-Abteilung "Das Reich"* under *SS-Hauptsturmführer* Kämpfe received the same equipment, further strengthening the combat power of the divisional reconnaissance battalion.

As a unique feature, the division received a "*schnelles Schützen-Regiment*" (fast motorized rifle regiment) that consisted of a regimental staff and two motorized rifle battalions equipped with the new Porsche *Schwimmwagen* (amphibious *Volkswagen*) instead of sidecar motorcycles. The regiment was organized on 22 April 1942 at Fallingbostel and, at the same time, incorporated into the division.

The commander of the regiment was *SS-Obersturmbannführer* Schuldt, the former commander of *SS-Infanterie-Regiment 4 "Langemarck"*. The regiment had received that honorific for its self-sacrificing service in the winter of 1941/42 in Russia. By order of the *Führer*, the name was to be passed on to the newly formed regiment, whose full designation was *schnelles SS-Schützen-Regiment "Langemarck"*.

The former *SS-Kradschützen-Bataillon "Reich"* became the *I./schnelles SS-Schützen-Regiment "Langemarck"*. The *II./schnelles SS-Schützen-Regiment "Langemarck"* was formed from the former *SS-Infanterie-Regiment 4 "Langemarck"* and initially commanded by *SS-Hauptsturmführer* Harzer.

Before the end of June 1942, *SS-Hauptsturmführer* Tychsen, returning from convalescence, assumed command of the *II./schnelles SS-Schützen-Regiment "Langemarck"*. *SS-Hauptsturmführer* Harzer went to the division staff in preparation for attendance at the war academy. The issuance of the *Schwimmwagen* and the reorganization of the units took place on 1 June 1942.

The First of August 1942 was set as the date the division was to be entirely ready for deployment.

Formation of the First SS Corps Headquarters

In accordance with orders, the first *SS-Generalokommando* (*SS* corps headquarters) was formed at the Bergen Training Area on 28 May 1942. The first commanding general of the *Waffen-SS* was *SS-Obergruppenführer und General der Waffen-SS* Paul Hausser. His chief of staff was *SS-Standartenführer* Ostendorff, his former operations officer and the man who had also proven himself as commander of *Kampfgruppe "SS-Reich"* in Russia in 1942.

SS-Infanterie-Regiment "Der Führer" Moved to France

Since the possibility of an Allied invasion was a real threat in France, *SS-Infanterie-Regiment "Der Führer"* was moved to northwestern France (in the Le Mans area) at the beginning of June 1942. It was the first division formation ordered there. In France it was allocated to the commander-in-chief in the west and attached to the *7. Armee* under *Generaloberst* Dollmann as its operational reserve.

At the last minute the regiment received its full allotment of motor vehicles. The *I./* and *II./SS-Infanterie-Regiment "Der Führer"* again received personnel transport trucks (3-ton *Opel Blitz* trucks). The *III./SS-Infanterie-Regiment "Der Führer"* became the armored battalion from that point on and received 3-ton *Schützenpanzerwagen (SPW)*. The regimental units were also very well equipped. The vehicles provided were precisely in accord with the tables of organization and the issuance allocations of the army.

The regiment was initially billeted in the Mayenne area, northwest of Le Mans. On the day of arrival in the new billeting area, a considerably more intensive training program began than had been the case at the training area. It was particularly thanks to the chief of the general staff of the Commander-in-Chief in the West, *General* Zeitzler, that the regiment received a generous allotment of fuel and ammunition. The addition of such a complete and well-proven regiment was a most welcome reinforcement to the operational reserve in the event of an Allied invasion.

This provided the prerequisites for intensifying the formation training that was still in its initial stages. Particular emphasis was placed on combat firing exercises and platoon, company and battalion exercises with live ammunition. It was thus possible to accustom the young replacements in a short time to the oppressive effect of a firefight. Led by experienced officers and noncommissioned officers, the men worked their way to within a few meters of the enemy positions and bunkers, which were still under fire by friendly machine guns, mortars and infantry guns, in order to then break into them with live hand grenades.

The *Panzergrenadiere* of the *III. (gep.)/SS-Infanterie-Regiment "Der Führer"* and the *SPW* company of *SS-Aufklärungs-Abteilung "Das Reich"* had to move through friendly rifle and machine gun fire in their *SPW*.

Sub-Section w)

Occupation Forces in France:
25 July - 21 November 1942

At the end of July 1942 the entire division was transferred from the Fallingbostel Training Area to northwestern France. The division staff was in Le Mans.

Training exercises were then continued in conjunction with the *Panzer III's* and *IV's* of the new tank battalion and with artillery. The training was realistic and close to combat conditions. The companies learned to work their way forward to the forward limit of artillery fire in the knowledge that the artillery crews knew their great responsibility as well as the men manning the heavy infantry weapons. No rounds impacted on friendly ranks. Whoever allowed a friendly tank to roll right over him while he was in a foxhole — and the tank then remained on top of the foxhole —would also calmly await an enemy tank in a combat situation.

One concern was the poor nutritional condition of the young replacements from whom the forced pace of the training demanded a lot physically. In spite of standing regulations to the contrary, many a piece of beef, pork or veal found its way into the company field kitchens. It was a joy to see how the extra food did the trick. Anyone who was going to go back into action in a short time needed strength and reserves of strength.

At that time there was a company commander course in the division. Men were sent from all the units of the *Waffen-SS* in order to capitalize on the rich combat experience gained in the winter campaign of 1941/42 that was provided by the combat-experienced and proven commander of *SS-Infanterie-Regiment "Der Führer"*, *SS-Obersturmbannführer* Kumm. This was a special recognition for the division.

The weeks passed at a breathtaking pace. The men were also put back in top-notch physical condition by track and field events and games. This was also relaxing. Battalion and regimental athletic meets also brought top performances in a broad range of sports.

Ongoing inspections by the division commander and the commanding general, *SS-Obergruppenführer* Hausser, who again had his old division in his command — the corps headquarters had, in the meantime, been transferred to Paris — kept the command current regarding the continuous progress in the division's readiness for deployment.

For example, the training of *schnelles SS-Schützen-Regiment "Langemarck"* at the Coetquidan Training Area in Bretagne ended with a regimental training exercise in establishing a bridgehead over a river by the new *Schwimmwagen* companies. On hand was the commander-in-chief of the *7. Armee*, *Generaloberst* Dollmann, the commanding general of the *SS-Panzer-Korps* and the division commander. *SS-Standartenführer* Schuldt led the exercise. The deployability of the new Porsche *Schwimmwagen* was impressively demonstrated. The *Schwimmwagen* had been developed over a considerable period of time by the Porsche firm in Zuffenhausen and tested in close cooperation with the *SS* motorcycle replacement and training battalion in Ellwangen / Jagst.

With the help of the *Schwimmwagen*, the motorcycle troops — renamed *schnelle Schützen* (fast riflemen) — were even more mobile. In the future, water would form no obstacle. After switching to all-wheel drive and lowering the boat propeller mounted on the rear, the vehicle could continue its progress in the water. It could move at a speed of 12 kilometers/hour (7.2 mph) in the water. An obvious prerequisite was that the *Schwimmwagen* would not lose its amphibious capability from bullet or shrapnel holes while deployed.

The exercise under observation was a forced river crossing with *Schwimmwagen* on a broad front with fire support from heavy weapons. It was very impressive how the *Schwimmwagen* advanced from cover to the bank of the river. Then, without a halt at the bank, they took to the water on a broad front, crossed the river, climbed the other bank onto dry land and immediately went into action.

On 12 August 1942 the division came under command of the *SS-Panzer-Korps*.

On 27 August 1942 the logistics officer of the division, *SS-Hauptsturmführer* Fred Jantsch, was killed in a motor-vehicle accident on the return trip from a map exercise in Bordeaux. His successor was *SS-Hauptsturmführer* Steinbeck.

The overall training of the division reached a level in France that could be compared without reservation with its outstanding prewar status. In addition, there was the extremely significant factor of the rich experience at the front among officers and noncommissioned officers.

The division was again completely ready for deployment at the end of August. On 1 October, by order of the *7. Armee,* the division was moved to the area south of St. Lô. A few days later, *SS-Infanterie-Regiment "Der Führer"* transferred to the Villers-Bocage area. The division, however, remained attached to the *SS-Panzer-Korps*. The immediate primary task was to conduct reconnaissance of possible employment sites and practice countering an enemy invasion.

Was it indeed a trick of fate that, two years later, *SS-Division "Das Reich"* would actually be engaged in a bitter struggle with the Allied invasion forces in that exact area?

Schnelles SS-Schützen-Regiment "Langemarck" is Deactivated and SS-Panzer-Regiment 2 "Das Reich" is Activated

Yet another change in the combat organization of the division made it necessary that *schnelles SS-Schützen-Regiment "Langemarck"* be deactivated. The regiment was deactivated immediately after it had been moved. The regimental staff was transferred to the staff of the newly forming *SS-Panzer-Regiment 2 "Das Reich"* under command of *Oberst* Vahl, who had been detailed from the army to the *Waffen-SS* on 19 October 1942 and assigned the mission of organizing the tank regiment.

The *II./schnelles SS-Schützen-Regiment "Langemarck"* under *SS-Sturmbannführer* Tychsen was converted to the *II./SS-Panzer-Regiment "Das Reich"* and reequipped.

The *I./schnelles SS-Schützen-Regiment "Langemarck"* under *SS-Sturmbannführer* Jakob Fick, was made a divisional formation. Initially, it remained as the *I./schnelles SS-Schützen-Regiment "Langemarck"* but was later redesignated as *SS-Kradschützen-Bataillon 2 "Das Reich"*.

At a later date the *"Legion Flandern"* was formed from Flemish volunteers. The battalion-sized formation was later expanded to a brigade. For geographical reasons the Flemish people were linked to Langemarck. After the First World War the Flemish populace voluntarily cared for the graves of the German students who had been killed at Langemarck. Accordingly, the honorific was given to the brigade to carry on the tradition.

Formation of SS-Sturmgeschütz-Abteilung 2 "Das Reich"

Effective 14 October 1942 the division activated an assault-gun battalion. The battalion consisted of a battalion headquarters and three batteries with seven assault guns each. *SS-Hauptsturmführer* Walter Kniep was named battalion commander. His adjutant was *SS-Obersturmführer* Köhler. The batteries were commanded by *SS-Obersturmführer* Telkamp (*1./SS-Sturmgeschütz-Abteilung 2 "Das Reich"*), *SS-Obersturmführer* Krag (*2./SS-Sturmgeschütz-Abteilung 2 "Das Reich"*) and *SS-Obersturmführer* Kepp (*3./SS-Sturmgeschütz-Abteilung 2 "Das Reich"*). The battalion surgeon was *Obersturmführer Dr.* Sedlatschek.

All of the men who had been transferred to other units were brought back to the battalion.

The tradition of *SS-Sturmgeschütz-Batterie* "Reich" — a battery that had proven itself many times over in the East — had been restored. The battery's disbanding had been deeply regretted by all the veteran East Front fighters because it was a unique weapons system to which the Russians had no equal counter.

In the course of 1942 the face of *SS-Division "Das Reich"* changed its appearance several times as a result of reorganization and restructuring. Although it had been organized as a *Panzer-Grenadier-Division* since the start of the reconstitution at Fallingbostel, it continued to bear its old designation as *SS-Division (mot.) "Das Reich"* until 9 November 1942.

Redesignation

The official gazette of the *Waffen-SS* announced the following on 1 December 1942:

> By order of the *Führer SS-Division (mot.) "Das Reich"* bears the following designation effective 9 November 1942:
>
> **SS-Panzer-Grenadier-Division "Das Reich"**

(For tables of organizations see the appendices.)

The establishment of a three-battalion *SS-Panzer-Regiment* — two of which were already formed — exceeded the tables of organization for a *Panzer-Grenadier-Division*. In effect, it signaled the conversion to a future *Panzer-Division*. However, the final reorganization as an actual *Panzer-*

Division was not to begin until January 1944 after the division was pulled out of frontline commitment for the second time in the East. It is therefore difficult to pinpoint an exact table of organization for the division at that time, since the transformation was made fluid by several reorganizations and restructurings.

Sub-Section x)

Occupation Troops in France: 21-28 November 1942

The occupation of the rest of France was the natural and logical military reaction of the German command to the Anglo-American surprise occupation of North Africa, since the French Mediterranean coast, which was otherwise defenseless, would have been surrendered without a fight to an Anglo-American invasion from the Mediterranean area.

On 11 November 1942 the *7. Armee* issued the following order to the *SS-Panzer-Korps*:

1.) The Anglo-American surprise attack on North Africa makes it necessary to institute measures for the protection of all French territory.

2.) Along with measures outside continental France, German and Italian forces will march into the unoccupied territory to protect French interests. The entry of German troops is at the request of and in agreement with the French regime in order to protect France from further Anglo-American surprise attacks.

The occupation of the unoccupied area proceeded without a hitch on 11 and 12 November.

The *SS-Panzer-Korps* with *SS-Panzer-Grenadier-Division "Das Reich"*, *SS-Panzer-Grenadier-Division "Leibstandarte SS Adolf Hitler"* and operational elements of *Panzer-Brigade 100* were not yet committed. However, they were staged in a heightened state of readiness with their tracked elements already loaded on trains.

The Toulon fortified area was initially left unoccupied in the occupation of the French Mediterranean coast. The President of the German Army Control Inspectorate, *Generalleutnant Freiherr* von Neubronn, had special orders to determine the intentions of the fortress commander. After this was done, additional orders were to be issued by the Commander-in-Chief in the West. Those reports apparently made clear the necessity of capturing the fortress and naval harbor of Toulon by a *coup de main.*

Sub-Section y)

Coup de Main at Toulon: 27 November 1942

On 22 November 1942, the *I./schnelles Schützen-Regiment "Langemarck"* of *SS-Panzer-Grenadier-Division "Das Reich"* was attached directly to the *SS-Panzer-Korps* and moved by motor march to Brigoles (north of Toulon).

The newly formed headquarters of the *SS-Panzer-Korps* was employed for the first time by the Commander-in-Chief in the West. A rapid occupation of Toulon had become necessary. This was to be the dress rehearsal for the corps headquarters.

On 20 November 1942 the commanding general, *SS-Obergruppenführer* Hausser, received the mission from the Commander-in-Chief in the West, to capture the fortress and naval harbor of Toulon in a *coup de main*. The *7. Panzer-Division*, which was transported in from the Perpignan area, was attached along with numerous additional units of the army, navy, *Luftwaffe* and the *Waffen-SS*.

Contact with the German naval representative, *Kapitän zur See* Hoffman, and with the armistice commission representative, *Admiral* Wever, indicated that the fortress and naval harbor of Toulon was comprised of at least six coastal batteries, six heavy antiaircraft batteries and a great number of light antiaircraft batteries extending along 20 kilometers of fortified front. In addition, there were approximately 20,000 naval soldiers (including the fleet).

It had to be considered at the outset that there would be resistance, a departure of the fleet or a destruction of the fleet, particularly in light of the personal views of the commander of the fleet, *Admiral* de Laborde. This became of particular concern after the actions of the French North African fleet.

There were only seven days between the time that the mission was assigned and the time that it was to be carried out.

During the night of 24/25 November the news came that *Admiral* Darlan had called on the French fleet to depart for Dakar. The danger existed that the fleet might set sail. The Commander-in-Chief in the West ordered that the operation be executed on 27 November.

Corp order No. 1 of 25 November 1942 stated (excerpts):

1.) The corps headquarters with attached units has the mission of capturing the naval and land fortress of Toulon in a *coup de main* in order to prevent the escape of the French fleet.

In so doing the garrisons on land and crews on ships are initially to be disarmed and interned.

2.) For that purpose the reinforced *7. Panzer-Division* will be employed in three *Kampfgruppen*...(the first two *Kampfgruppen* are deleted here. The third Kampfgruppe came from *SS-Panzer-Grenadier-Division "Das Reich"* and its mission follows)

3) **Command:** *SS-Sturmbannführer* Fick

Forces: reinforced motorcycle battalion of *SS-Panzer-Grenadier-Division "Das Reich"*

Mission: Capture of the le Mourillon arsenal area, the radio station to its north and the forts on the south coast between le Mourillon and le Pradet...It is essential to capture Fort Lamargue (location of the Toulon commander-in-chief), the barracks in the northern part of le Mourillon and the southern point of the arsenal area...For details, see map. For timing see paragraph 9.

4.) to 5.) ...

6.) A special detail (from the corps signals battalion) is attached to reinforced *SS-Kradschützen-Bataillon "Das Reich"* to take over the French radio station.

7.) to 8.) ...

9.) **Time phasing**:

Execution of the *coup de main*: D-Day (D-Day will be specified verbally by a liaison officer.)

The *Kampfgruppen are to* reach the following points by 0330 hours on D-Day:

Kampfgruppe 1: ...

Kampfgruppe 2: ...

Kampfgruppe 3: Western outskirts of Valette. Point of departure: See map.

At 0400 hours all *Kampfgruppen* are to cross these points without further orders and carry out the assigned missions...

***

About 800 marines and 1,500 soldiers of the coastal artillery were directed to support the *7. Panzer-Division* in occupying the ships and coastal batteries.

***

The adjutant of *SS-Kradschützen-Bataillon "Das Reich"* at that time, *SS-Obersturmführer* Buch, wrote the following concerning the battalion's employment in the *coup de main* at Toulon:

D-Day was 27 November 1942

The march in was ordered for 0400 hours. At 0300 hours we were five kilometers northeast of Toulon. The *Gendarmerie* sentries were arrested. At 0400 hours sharp we set off. Twenty minutes later the headquarters fort of Toulon, Lamargue (*2./SS-*

Kradschützen-Abteilung "Das Reich"), and the commander, *Admiral* Marquis, were in our hands. We got him out of his bed. Then we captured the radio station (*1./SS-Kradschützen-Abteilung "Das Reich"*), the arsenal (ditto), the Negro barracks, a submarine base and the *Grosse Tour* outer works. We finished by capturing the Cap Brun (*3./SS-Kradschützen-Abteilung "Das Reich"*) and Marguerite (*4./SS-Kradschützen-Abteilung "Das Reich"*) forts, including the naval school. The only resistance was light resistance at the radio station. By 0700 hours everything was in our hands. Only two submarines were able to get under steam.

At the arsenal I ran into a French machine-gun position while riding in a side-car motorcycle to the *1./SS-Kradschützen-Abteilung "Das Reich"*. Apparently, we were mistaken for English and fired on. My driver, *SS-Rottenführer* Schraml, was shot in the stomach and died. The leader of the signals section, *SS-Oberscharführer* Hund, was shot in the elbow, and a shot grazed my chest. We were the only casualties that day.

***

That same day the headquarters of the *SS-Panzer-Korps* dispatched the following teletype to its next higher headquarters, *Armeegruppe Felber*:

The *coup de main* at Toulon proceeded according to plan on 27 November 1942. Surprise was complete everywhere. Weak resistance at isolated points was quickly crushed. The French fleet was prepared for scuttling. Scuttling began immediately after penetration of the harbor area. In some cases, our own people were already on board. Toulon was in our hands by 0850 hours.

Battleship Strasbourg went aground. Four destroyers still afloat. Due to extensive fires on several cruisers and explosion of ammunition, an exact determination is not possible at this time. Some of the guns of the coastal and antiaircraft batteries were blown up. An exact overview is still lacking. Friendly losses very limited. Numbers to follow.

Headquarters, SS-Panzer-Korps

***

The actual course of the *coup de main* at Toulon was outlined as follows in the corps after-action report:

...At 0400 hours the three assault groups crossed a line of departure about two kilometers outside the fortress area.

At 0530 hours the *Luftwaffe* started mining the entrance to the harbor. The operation was favored by a night of bright moonlight. There was resistance in isolated spots but, because of the successful surprise, it was limited and quickly crushed. It was possible to get onto a number of the warships by surprise and prevent resistance.

The flagship, *Strasbourg*, offered resistance and prevented approach to the ship by gunfire.

Shortly thereafter there were a large number of detonations on most of the ships. The fleet had prepared for destruction of the ships and they went aground.

At 0850 hours the fortress of Toulon and most of the ships were in friendly hands. Disarming the French navy could be carried out. Only the commander of the fleet, *Admiral* de Laborde, refused to leave the flagship with his staff, although the crew had already left the ship. He told an officer who came to him under a flag of truce that he would not leave the ship without orders from *Maréchal* Pétain. Thereupon an attempt was made to establish a telephone connection between *Maréchal* Pétain and the commander of the fleet. The attempt was not successful.

Maréchal Pétain's order to disembark immediately was brought over under a flag of truce. He refused to carry out the order and remained with his staff on the deserted ship that was aground. That behavior forced his removal by force and his placement under house arrest. (After-action report of the *SS-Panzer-Korps*, *Bericht über den Handstreich auf Toulon*. Taken from the corps war diary, operations section, war-diary 718g, appendix 175*)*

***

The following vessels were scuttled by their crews in the harbor of Toulon:

The flagship "Strasbourg", three heavy cruisers, two cruisers, two light cruisers, 18 torpedo-boat destroyers, 15 torpedo boats, 18 submarines, one armored ship (school ship), one aircraft carrier and a large number of dispatch boats and patrol boats. (*Admiral* Auphan and Jacques Mordal, *"La Marine Française"*, p. 312. ?: Hachette, ?)

***

On 27 November the commanding general of the *SS-Panzer-Korps* released the following order of the day:

Corps Order of the Day

The Commander-in-Chief in the West has offered his fullest commendation to the officers and forces for the successful completion of the *coup de main* at Toulon.

I fully and completely join in that commendation and offer my thanks to officers and men.

In spite of extremely short preparation time and difficult circumstances, the assigned mission was completed through exemplary cooperation of the army, navy , *Luftwaffe* and *Waffen-SS*.

It is with particular pleasure that I note that formations that have already fought shoulder to shoulder in the East have also proven themselves today.

/signed/ Hausser

***

By order of the Commander-in-Chief in the West, the *SS-Panzer-Korps* assumed coastal defense of the Toulon area in conjunction with the *335. Infanterie-Division* until further notice. The sector boundaries with the Italian forces had to be determined.

In conclusion it can be said that the destruction of the scuttling of the

French fleet had to be reckoned with from the beginning, since it did not wish to fall into the hands of either the English or the Germans. Anti-English sentiment had always been extremely strong in the French Navy. It only intensified when, on 3 July 1940, immediately after the close of the French campaign by French capitulation, English warships surprised and ruthlessly fired on and sank units of the French fleet at Mers-el-Kebir, a harbor in the Gulf of Oran. The English wanted to prevent them from falling into German hands. In the French Navy, hatred for the English was at least as great as for the Germans.

There was, thus, an internal conflict in the French navy between *Maréchal* Pétain and his regime, on the one side, and de Gaulle — Darlan on the other side. It could only be resolved by scuttling the fleet, as was the case at Toulon.

Therefore, we cannot deny the French navy our respect for its behavior in the fortress and the naval harbor of Toulon. It had conducted itself precisely the same way the German navy had done in the Bay of Scapa Flow in similar circumstances on 21 June 1919 after it had been turned over to England. It went down before English eyes with war flags flying.

That respect was also expressed by the fact that French naval officers were held in house arrest and permitted to keep their sidearms by order of the commanding general, *SS-Obergruppenführer* Hausser.

Sub-Section z)

Occupation Troops in France: 28 November 1942 – 15 January 1943

At the beginning of December 1942, *SS-Panzer-Grenadier-Division "Das Reich"* was transferred again, this time to the area south of Rennes.

For a long time it seemed that the division, along with *SS-Panzer-Grenadier-Division "Leibstandarte SS Adolf Hitler"* and *SS-Panzer-Grenadier-Division "Totenkopf"*, was slated for employment as part of the *SS-Panzer-Korps* with the *Deutsches Afrika Korps* in North Africa. In accordance with directives received, the soldiers were checked for suitability for service in the tropics. An order directing preparations for tropical employment —inoculations against tropical diseases and issuance of tropical clothing — had already been received. The degree to which those measures were carried out for operational security purposes and the veiling of German intentions remains an open question.

For the division, the quiet time of intensive training ended with the movement to the Rennes area. The desperately struggling Eastern Front was calling — everyone could feel it — and the division actually waited daily for the call to new employment.

On 7 December 1942 the demobilization of the French navy and army units was concluded. The *SS-Panzer-Korps* was relieved by the Italian XXII

Army Corps under General Olearo. *SS-Kradschützen-Bataillon 2 "Das Reich"* was relieved in its sector by the Italian *"Lupi di Toscana"* Division.

After the conclusion of the occupation of Toulon and after the *I./schnelles SS-Schützen-Regiment "Langemarck"* and units of the *10. Panzer-Division* — old comrades-in-arms from Poland and Russia — were pulled out, the headquarters of the *SS-Panzer-Korps* assumed command of the coastal sector: St. Mandrier peninsula — Toulon — Cap Plane. The *7. Panzer Division* was on the left and the Italian *"Piave"* Division on the right (under Brigadier General Tabellini). Both formations were attached to the *SS-Panzer-Korps*.

In mid-December 1942 the *I./schnelles SS-Schützen-Regiment "Langemarck"* returned to the division by high-speed transport after its relief by the Italians. It was able to celebrate Christmas in the Rennes area.

***

SS-Oberstgruppenführer und Generaloberst der Waffen-SS Hausser wrote the following concerning the overall situation at the time:

> Was it already necessary to figure on the invasion here in the west after the failed English landing attempt at Dieppe? That was improbable. On the other hand, the situation in the east had become extraordinarily critical since mid-November.

***

On 30 December 1942 a *Führer* order arrived directing that the entire corps — therefore also *SS-Panzer-Grenadier-Division "Das Reich"* — was to immediately prepare for employment in the east. With that it became clear that the next objective of the division would be the Eastern Front as part of the *SS-Panzer-Korps*. The dream of employment with the *Deutsches Afrika Korps* was over.

1943
The Campaign Against Russia
Part III: 31 January - 18 February 1943

1943 was marked by the Allied demand for "unconditional surrender" that was adopted on 23 January in Casablanca and by "Stalingrad". The employment of the first *SS-Panzer-Korps*, later redesignated the *II. SS-Panzer-Korps*, occurred in the Kharkov area in the shadow of these events. The corps, under commanding general *SS-Obergruppenführer* Hausser and his chief of staff, *SS-Standartenführer* Ostendorf, consisted of *SS-Panzer-Grenadier-Division "Leibstandarte SS Adolf Hitler"*, *SS-Panzer-Grenadier-Division "Das Reich"* and *SS-Panzer-Grenadier-Division "Totenkopf"*. That indicated a significant turning point in the development of the *Waffen-SS*. For the first time, the three longest-serving divisions of the *Waffen-SS* were employed under the command of an *SS* corps headquarters.

As a result, *SS-Panzer-Grenadier-Division "Das Reich"* was again under the command of its first division commander, Hausser, who had returned from convalescence for his serious wounds.

What had happened to the situation on the Eastern Front in the meantime?

The Soviet Winter Offensive 1942/43

The after-action report of the *SS-Panzer-Korps* offers the following overview:

In November 1942 the most powerful offensive that the Soviet leadership had mounted so far in the war began in the great bend of the Don. That offensive was notable from the beginning for the following:

— The enemy had assembled men and equipment, particularly armor, beyond anything that had taken place before.

— The offensive was on a large scale and planned according to German command principles.

— Success or failure in achieving its operational objectives could be decisive for the outcome of the war.

The following precisely timed stages of the Soviet offensive could be distinguished; each followed the other like clockwork:

— Breakthrough on the Don at Serafimowitsch; simultaneous breakthrough at Krassnoarmeisk south of Stalingrad. As a result, two Rumanian armies were defeated. Within a short period of time the *6. Armee* in Stalingrad was completely encircled and cut off.

— Attack of the two army groups assembled west and northwest of Stalingrad to the west.

— Attack by the Southern Front on both sides of the Don toward Rostow and the southern Donez region. That in itself threatened to separate the German armies in the Caucasus from their lines of communications via Rostow. (After-action report of the *SS-Panzer-Korps*, *"SS-Panzer-Korps in der Schlacht zwischen Donez und Dnjepr"*, ?. Unpublished report.)

***

SS-Obergruppenführer und General der Waffen-SS Hausser wrote the following in his personal notes:

Heeresgruppe Don — forced away from Stalingrad — was threatened with double envelopment in the direction of Rostow — disastrous to *Heeresgruppe A* in the Caucasus, the friendly force on the right.

To its north, the Russian attack front had broadened in mid-January until it also faced *Heeresgruppe B* — namely, facing the Hungarian 2nd Army and the German *2. Armee.*

The Soviet command sought to force a decision that winter by cutting off the two southern German army groups at the Sea of Azov.

***

The after-action report of the *SS-Panzer-Korps* continues:

The Southwest Front advanced in the area between the Stalingrad — Morosowsk railroad line and the Kantemirowka — Starobelsk line with the northern Donez as its objective. That attack group threatened the rear and flank of the Italian and Hungarian armies northwest of the location of the first breakthrough on the Don. In light of that threat, both armies abandoned their established positions without offering any significant resistance. In the final analysis, their withdrawal verged on flight. The Russian Southwest Front crossed the Don northwest of Stalingrad.

After the Southern Front had reached the lower Donez and the Southwest Front the Oskol, the southern wing of the Woronesh Front initiated its attack to the west.

The northern and southern flanks of the sectors of the *VII.* and *XIII. Armee-Korps* were then attacked in pincers fashion. Their sector had been left projecting far to the east by the withdrawal of the Hungarian army to the south. After the two attack groups joined at Kastornoje, the two German corps were encircled.

Following that, the entire Woronesch Front advanced to the west. The hastily formed position on the Tim was then penetrated in the *2. Panzer-Armee* sector. Kursk, Lgoff and Rylsk were captured in the course of the ensuing attacks to the west.

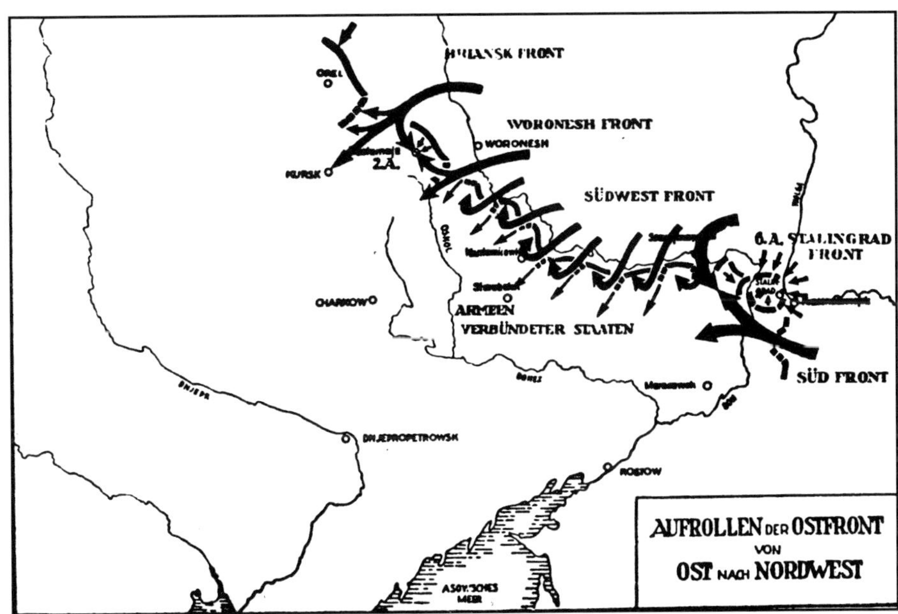

The Soviet 1942/43 Winter Offensive in the area of *Heeresgruppe Don*
Rolling up the Eastern Front from East to Northwest.

After the Woronesh Front broke through at Kursk, the Briansk Front then attacked.

The southern wing advanced from the Liwny area against the right wing of the *2. Panzer-Armee*, which was in the midst of withdrawing. The northern wing advanced from the area northeast of Orel against Orel.

The operational objective and the rhythm of the Russian winter offensive were obvious. (See the map.)

The attacks of the individual Russian Fronts followed in a time-phased sequence such that each Russian Front rolled up and broke out a portion of the German defensive front, which extended in a generally northwest direction.

The operation ran as planned from Stalingrad as far as Orel. The expected results ensued almost automatically, at least in the case of the Italian 8th Army and the Hungarian 2nd Army. More than 500 kilometers of the German front was torn apart between Slawiansk and the area north of Kursk. The armies of two Soviet fronts marched inexorably to the west.

***

SS-Obergruppenführer und General der Waffen-SS Hausser continues in his personal notes:

To the south, isolated formations, some under *Korps Kramer*, fought their way back to the Oskol alongside police formations and the *298.* and *320. Infanterie-Divisionen.*

As initial reinforcement *Infanterie-Division (mot.) "Großdeutschland"* arrived at *Heeresgruppe B* (*Freiherr* von Weichs) in the Bjelgorod area from *Heeresgruppe Mitte.*

At the strategic level, the German situation in Africa had also developed in a threatening fashion.

***

The after-action report of the *SS-Panzer-Korps* continues:

The operational objective, the collapse of the German Eastern Front, appeared to have been attained in the southern sector.

The Russian command designated the Dnjepr as its new attack objective. It paid no heed to the exhausted troops, the growing supply problems or the casualties and equipment losses suffered during the course of the attack. It concerned itself little with the fact that only some of the artillery accompanied the rapid advance. Nor did it matter that almost all of the rifle formations had been filled out with forcibly inducted civilians rather than trained infantrymen. Hardly any use was being made of artillery at the moment and untrained and poorly armed civilians were enough to subsist on.

The loss of five German and allied armies gave rise to a massive numerical superiority of the Red Armies. In the continued progress of the operations, mass was to triumph over the vastly inferior defenders.

It would, however, prove decisive that the Soviet command failed to recognize the culmination point of its offensive. That was reached at the Donez. Logistics and the ground organization of the air force failed in the unavoidable difficulties of a winter campaign over great distances. Combat power was crippled after offensive operations of several hundred kilometers.

As a result, the superiority of the German leadership and forces was able to wrest a decision in favor of friendly arms in spite of great numerical inferiority.

***

SS-Obergruppenführer und General der Waffen-SS Hausser continues in his personal notes:

Outlining the mission of *an individual division* therefore complicates the *overview of the bigger picture.*

The purpose of this work shall, therefore, be broadened in this section. The employment of the corps will provide the framework in which the events happening to the division will be embedded.

***

It goes without saying that the author desires to follow the wishes of our deceased mentor. He will outline the employment of the *SS-Panzer-Korps* since the facts themselves lend themselves to such a treatment. The fighting of the *SS-Panzer-Korps* between the Donez and Dnjepr represented a total effort by the three *SS-Panzer-Grenadier-Divisionen.* The success would not have been possible for any single division or without the command accomplishments of the corps headquarters under his leadership.

Movement of the SS-Panzer-Korps to the Eastern Front

The order for the movement of the *SS-Panzer-Korps* to the Eastern Front arrived in the first days of the new year. Transportation began on 9 January 1943.

The commanding general, *SS-Obergruppenführer* Hausser, and his chief of staff, Ostendorff, preceded the corps. While Hausser conferred in Berlin with the *SS* Main Office, *SS-Standartenführer* Ostendorff established contact with *General* Zeitzler of the Germany Army High Command. Ostendorff knew Zeitzler from the time in the west when Zeitzler was chief of the general staff of the Commander-in-Chief in the West. Following this they continued by air via Kiev and Taganrog to Woroschilowgrad, where they reported to *Generalfeldmarschall* von Manstein and *Armee-Abteilung Fretter-Pico,* to which the corps would be attached temporarily. They then flew on to Kharkov. On 26 January, the corps was attached to *Heeresgruppe B* under *Generaloberst* von Weichs (chief of staff: von Sodenstern).

In the meantime, the formations of the *SS-Panzer-Korps* rolled from the west by high-speed rail transport which had absolute route priority over all other trains. The journey led via Nantes, Orléans, Froyes, Bainvilles, Luneville, Saarburg, Homburg, Bad Kreuznach, Mainz, Frankfurt am Main, Gemünden, Lichtenfeld, Hof, Zwickau, Olmütz, Lauban, Ratibor, Krakow, Przemysl, Tarnopol and Kasatin to Kiev.

SS-Panzer-Grenadier-Division "Das Reich" rolled at the head of the *SS-Panzer-Korps. SS-Panzergrenadier-Regiment "Der Führer"* was in the lead. *SS-Panzergrenadier-Regiment "Der Führer"* had been the first formation of the division to be withdrawn from the Eastern Front at the close of the defensive fighting at Rshew and to be moved to Fallingbostel for reorganization and refitting.

SS-Panzer-Grenadier-Division "Leibstandarte SS Adolf Hitler" and, somewhat later, *SS-Panzer-Grenadier-Division "Totenkopf"* followed.

In France violets were still in bloom for Christmas season. An extensive glittering cover of snow lay around Kiev — an external change that entirely matched the inner one. The formations of the corps detrained in Kiev and reached the Kharkov area via motor march. The *SS-Panzer-Korps* completed its staging there on 30 January.

***

The first element of *SS-Panzergrenadier-Regiment "Der Führer"* to entrain was the *I./SS-Panzergrenadier-Regiment "Der Führer"* under command of *SS-Hauptsturmführer* Opificius. The battalion was reinforced by the entire *14./SS-Panzergrenadier-Regiment "Der Führer"* (*Flak*) and one platoon of the

16./SS-Panzergrenadier-Regiment "Der Führer" (combat-engineer platoon). It had entrained on 10 January in Rennes.

Since the battalion was committed separately from the division, its operations will be presented in outline form in the following account.

Operations of the Reinforced I./SS-Panzergrenadier-Regiment "Der Führer" in the Stalino – Woroschilowgrad Area

Sub-Section a)

Defensive Fighting in the Donez Area (I./SS-Panzergrenadier-Regiment "Der Führer): 23-24 January

On 20 January 1943 the following Teletype arrived for the *SS-Panzer-Korps* at the military government area headquarters at Stalino (excerpt):

1.) By order of *Oberkommando des Heeres* the elements of *SS-Panzer-Grenadier-Division "Das Reich"* that have already been transported via Kiev are to be employed to protect Woroschilowgrad. After the main body of the division arrives they will again be returned to the division.

2.) *Armee-Abteilung Fretter-Pico* is to bring those units forward in direct coordination with the *SS-Panzer-Korps* (via military government area headquarters at Donez and Stalino) and commit them accordingly.

3.) To be reported: …

***

The *SS-Panzer-Korps* passed that order on to *SS-Panzer-Grenadier-Division "Das Reich"* which selected the *I./SS-Panzergrenadier-Regiment "Der Führer"* for that operation.

The *SS-Panzer-Korps* order ended with the words:

I wish the *Kampfgruppe* complete success in its first mission.

/signed/ Hausser

***

The *I./SS-Panzergrenadier-Regiment "Der Führer"* under *SS-Hauptsturmführer* Opificius entrained in Rennes during an uncommonly warm spell of 26 degrees Celsius (77 degrees Fahrenheit). The battalion rolled through France, Germany and Poland to the southern sector of the Eastern Front by high-speed rail transport. A dangerous crisis existed in the Woroschilowgrad area of operations, and the German defensive front urgently needed help against heavy Russian pressure.

After a 10-day trip, the reinforced *I./SS-Panzergrenadier-Regiment "Der Führer"* arrived in Awdejewka and detrained in a temperature of -38 degrees

Celsius (-36 degrees Fahrenheit). That was a difference of 64 degrees Celsius (113 degrees Fahrenheit) from the departure area in France. The battalion commander reported to *Armee-Abteilung Fretter-Pico* in Woroschilowgrad.

The battalion was brought forward in motor march with the *14./SS-Panzergrenadier-Regiment "Der Führer"*, one platoon of the *16./SS-Panzergrenadier-Regiment "Der Führer"*, two batteries of *SS-Panzer-Artillerie-Regiment 2 "Das Reich"* and one battery of *SS-Flak-Abteilung 2 "Das Reich"*. This meant a journey of 265 kilometers in biting frost. It was completed without significant losses — a good performance by the inexperienced drivers.

On 22 January the battalion staged in the Woronesh area and, on 23 January, assembled for an attack in the Alexandrowka — Sabowka area.

On 24 January there was an unlikely change of weather. Rain and a thaw set in. With armored support from the *6. Panzer-Division*, *Kampfgruppe Opificius* attacked hills 165.7 and 168.1. The enemy, who had forward positions there, was forced back a distance of 12 kilometers.

During the night of 25 January 1943 the temperature went through another surprise change, dropping suddenly to -28 degrees Celsius (-18 degrees Fahrenheit)! Because of the warm weather of the thaw, some of the men had left their winter clothing back on the vehicles. The men had a hard time dealing with the cold and an icy wind. Woe to those who wore felt boots that were soaked with water and froze to their legs in the night. They all became frostbite casualties. The good old *Knobelbecher* (hob-nailed boot) proved itself in the situation as the most practical footgear in these wild temperature swings.

The aggressively led attack had cost sweat. Rain and thaw did the rest, so that the men were thoroughly soaked when it was over. The decision of the battalion commander that was reported by radio, to let elements of the battalion mount up on the attached tanks in order to reach the assigned objective was prohibited. The battalion was ordered to hold in the positions it had reached, on an open plateau in an icy wind.

The losses due to frostbite were frighteningly high and, in that one night, the combat power of the battalion was reduced to about 50 percent. There were horrible scenes. A motorcycle messenger had to go to the dressing station: His hands had frozen to the handlebars when the thoroughly sodden gloves froze as thick lumps of ice by the sudden onset of bitter cold. They had to be cut loose from the handlebars — a casualty of frostbite.

Repeated requests of the battalion commander to remain in motion, either toward the objective of the attack — the battalion's reconnaissance had not resulted in any enemy contact — or by falling back to the departure position were denied. Only after night fell was the battalion pulled back and relieved by two army companies.

It was tragic that the first successful attack suffered from such extremely unfavorable weather conditions.

By 31 January 1943 the *I./SS-Panzergrenadier-Regiment "Der Führer"* had reorganized itself with the attached regimental units. It was reinforced by bringing up *Feldersatz-Bataillon 304* (minus staff and trains). At the same time, a 100-watt radio station for communications with *SS-Panzer-Grenadier-Division "Das Reich"* was provided. A 10.5-cm gun from the army and two 5-cm *Pak* were also brought forward. A volunteer company which had been assembled through the initiative of *SS-Obersturmführer* Dahl, from men who had become separated from their units in all branches of the *Wehrmacht,* was also attached to the battalion. It fought with exemplary courage.

On 28 January 1943 all these elements were combined under the command of *SS-Standartenführer* Schuldt, the former commander of *schnelles SS-Schützen-Regiment "Langemarck"*. It was committed as *Kampfgruppe Schuldt.* All the formations were staged in the Woroschilow area by 30 January 1943. Aircraft reported that the enemy had constructed ice bridges over the Donez.

During the night of 31 January / 1 February 1943, the Soviets attacked in regimental strength with armored support. At 0300 hours the main thrust was directed at Woroschilow, defended by the main body of the battalion, and against Petrowka, to its northwest, which was defended by the reinforced *1./SS-Panzergrenadier-Regiment "Der Führer"* (with one platoon of the *14./SS-Panzergrenadier-Regiment "Der Führer"* [2-cm *Flak* mounted on self propelled chassis] and a 5-cm *Pak*). The 2-cm *Flak* and the *Pak* formed the backbone of the defense at Petrowka. *SS-Rottenführer* Heider knocked out five enemy tanks with his *Pak.* He was awarded the Iron Cross, First Class at the command post and, shortly thereafter, was promoted to *SS-Unterscharführer.* The armorer of the *1./SS-Panzergrenadier-Regiment "Der Führer"*, *SS-Oberscharführer* Sepp Kammerer, blew up with a *Teller* mine a T 34 tank that had broken through. He was also decorated with the Iron Cross, First Class.

The enemy attacked the battalion's positions in Woroschilow in vain. The attached platoon of the *16./SS-Panzergrenadier-Regiment "Der Führer"*, under *SS-Oberscharführer* von Eberstein, excelled in particular. At the same time, attacks to the right and left were repulsed with heavy losses to the enemy. On the left was the *3./SS-Panzergrenadier-Regiment "Der Führer"* under *SS-Hauptsturmführer* Lex; on the right was the volunteer company of *SS-Obersturmführer* Dahl.

During the night of 1/2 February 1943, the battalion was pulled back to Wodjanoi. The enemy continued to exert pressure on the positions with massed artillery and mortar fire, with armor and with support by low-level attack aircraft. In spite of the unfavorable terrain, the *Panzergrenadiere* clawed out positions in houses, foxholes and trenches and repulsed all the enemy attacks. The tankers of the *6. Panzer-Division* and the *Stuka* pilots who brought relief and assistance in the most dangerous situations earned special gratitude for their self-sacrificing service. The commander of the *4./SS-Panzergrenadier-Regiment "Der Führer"*, *SS-Hauptsturmführer* Hocke, was killed during this fighting due to a direct hit on the battalion command post.

On 14 February the *I./SS-Panzergrenadier-Regiment "Der Führer"* was pulled out of its previous positions and, with the attached weapons, moved to the Krasnodonsky area via Samsonoff. The days that followed were filled with screening missions, immediate counterattacks and attacks with limited objectives.

On 17 February 1943 the battalion arrived at a rest position in the Krasnaja Swesda area. In a comradely fashion, a maintenance section of *SS-Panzer-Grenadier-Division "Wiking"* supplied the urgently needed fuel to the battalion.

On 21 February 1943 the battalion adjutant, *SS-Obersturmführer* Pahnke, was sent with an extensive report to the division in the Pawlograd area. His objective was to get the battalion pulled out of the lines and sent back to the regiment.

On 23 February the battalion commander himself was ordered by radio to report to *SS-Panzer-Grenadier-Division "Das Reich"*. In the meantime, the commander of the *3./SS-Panzergrenadier-Regiment "Der Führer"* assumed acting command of the battalion.

Until 7 March 1943 there were insignificant actions north of Debalzewo. The battalion commander, *SS-Hauptsturmführer* Opificius, brought the order from the division that the *I./SS-Panzergrenadier-Regiment "Der Führer"* was to immediately return to the regiment via Pawlograd — news that was received with great joy by all of the men.

The march to the regiment suffered particularly from a shortage of fuel. It was only through the "procurement" talents of all officers and men that this difficulty could be surmounted. The movement back to the regiment was via Grischino, Nikolajowka, Nowomoskowsk, Pawlograd, Krasnograd, Liubotin and Kharkov to the billeting area to the east of Kharkov.

After a veritable odyssey the battalion commander reported back to the commander of the regiment with his reinforced *I./SS-Panzergrenadier-Regiment "Der Führer"*. After reorganizing into two rifle companies (*SS-Haupsturmführer* Lex and *SS-Obersturmführer* Pahnke) and one heavy company (*SS-Obersturmführer* Rudolph), the battalion participated in the further fighting of the regiment.

The employment of the reinforced *I./SS-Panzergrenadier-Regiment "Der Führer"* was extremely unfortunate. As a separate *Kampfgruppe,* the battalion had spent the previous weeks under different commands, always at the hotspots of the defense at the critical point in the Woroschilowgrad area. Employed everywhere as a "fire brigade", the nearly impossible was frequently demanded — and was delivered by the officers and men of the battalion.

Sub-Section b)

OKH Reserve in the Heeresgruppe B Area: 25 - 28 January 1943

Let us now return to the staging area of the *SS-Panzer-Korps* in and around Kharkov.

In a Teletype classified secret that was simultaneously directed to *Heeresgruppe Don*, the *SS-Panzer-Korps* and *SS-Panzer-Grenadier-Division "Das Reich"*, the German Army High Command directed as follows:

Elements of *SS-Panzer-Grenadier-Division "Das Reich"* proceeding by motor march are to initially reach the Kharkov area via Military Route V.

Continued movement from Kharkov will not take place without permission of the *OKH. SS-Panzer-Grenadier-Division "Das Reich"* is to report the composition of the march serials to the operations section before the start of the movement, the points reached daily by the march serials and the intended objectives for the ensuing day. (*OKH Gen. St. d. H. Op. Abt. I Nr. 904/43 g. Kdos.*)

As a result, the SS-Panzer-Korps was directly subordinated to the Oberkommando des Heeres.

On 23 January 1942 the *SS-Panzer-Korps* was temporarily attached to *Armee-Abteilung Fretter-Pico* (command post in Woroschilowgrad).

On 24 January 1943 the following Teletype from the *Oberkommando des Heeres* arrived via *Heeresgruppe Don*:

Headquarters, *SS-Panzer-Korps*, is to proceed immediately to Kharkov by motor march and there assume command of the arriving elements of *SS-Panzer-Grenadier-Divisionen "Leibstandarte SS Adolf Hitler"* and *"Das Reich"*.

Headquarters, *SS-Panzer-Korps*, must remain available by telephone through *Heeresgruppe B*. It is to report the time of its arrival in Kharkov to the *Oberkommando des Heeres*. (*OKH Gen. St. d. H./Op. Abt. Ib Nr. 1058/43 g. Kdos.*)

The main body of *SS-Panzer-Grenadier-Division "Das Reich"* and additional elements of *SS-Panzer-Grenadier-Division "Leibstandarte SS Adolf Hitler"* arrived by 28 January 1943. The corps headquarters was located in Makejewka.

On 29 January the corps headquarters assumed command of the initial elements of the two divisions and over the Kupiansk — Wolokomowka sector on the Oskol River.

The missions for the days that followed were terrain reconnaissance and establishing contact with the withdrawing formations east of the Oskol under the commander-in-chief of the Italian Eighth Army, *General* Garibaldi (von

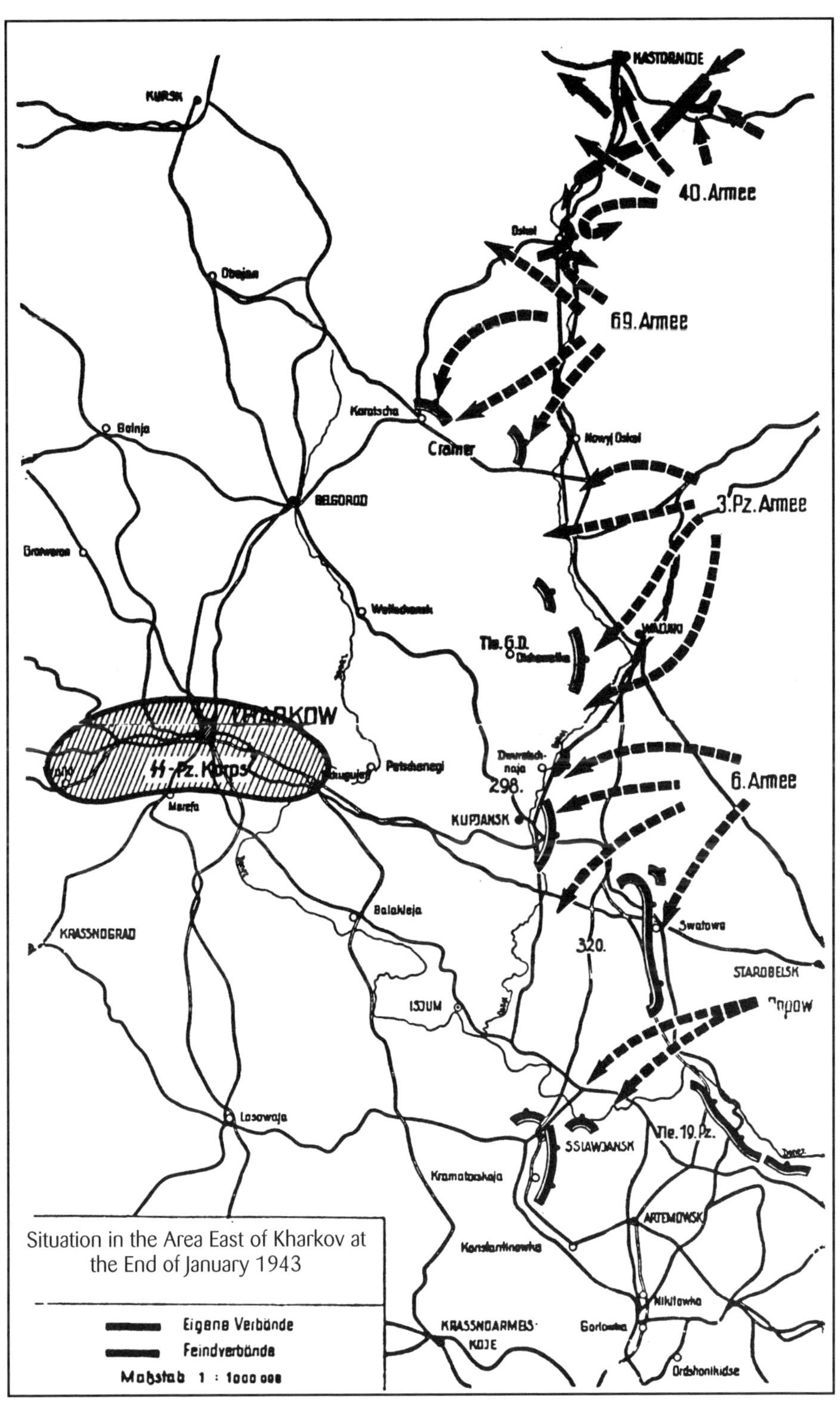

Situation in the Area East of Kharkov at the End of January 1943

Tippelskirch), as well as with elements of the *298.* and *320. Infanterie-Divisionen* and separate police units.

The situation had, in the meanwhile, developed as follows: At the end of January 1943 the Russians had reached the line; Donez at Woroschilowgrad — Starobelsk — Waluiki — upper Oskol. They had closed up their formations for a continued eastward advance.

As for friendly units, the *320. Infanterie-Division* was at Sswatowo. The *298. Infanterie-Division,* which had been badly battered during its fighting retreat, assembled in Kupjansk. Elements of *Infanterie-Division (mot.) "Großdeutschland* screened west of Waluiki. In the Kordiska area *Korps Kramer* gathered up and made use of elements of the battered German and Hungarian formations that came from the upper Don.

Great gaps yawned between the formations. Command in the area was held by von Tippelskirch, who was the senior German general with the staff of the headquarters of the Italian Eighth Army.

The *SS-Panzer-Korps* that was being brought in from the west was the only operational reserve in the *Heeresgruppe B* area.

At the end of January the *SS-Panzer-Korps* had staged in the Kharkov area with its headquarters, the main body of *SS-Panzer-Grenadier-Division "Das Reich"* and combat elements of *SS-Panzer-Grenadier-Division "Leibstandarte SS Adolf Hitler".* The latter division organized for defense on the Donez on both sides of Tschugujew. *SS-Panzer-Grenadier-Division "Das Reich"* was west of Kharkov.

The intention of the German Army High Command to commit the *SS-Panzer-Korps* as a whole for a counterattack was thwarted by the rapid Soviet advance. An attack into the corps area of concentration had to be prevented. In addition, Kharkov's importance as a transportation, industrial, economic and political center meant that it could not be lost.

SS-Panzergrenadier-Regiment "Der Führer", the first regiment of the division to arrive in Kharkov, was initially to remain there for several days to await the arrival of the other division formations. However, as outlined above, the *I./SS-Panzergrenadier-Regiment "Der Führer"* went right into action in the Woroschilowgrad area. As a result, it was not available for the impending operations.

***

Corps Order No. 2 for 29 January 1943 stated:

1.) The enemy has advanced over the Oskol at Nowyi Oskol. *Infanterie-Division (mot.) "Großdeutschland"* is temporarily attached to *Korps Kramer* to force back the enemy west of Nowyi Oskol.

2.) *SS-Panzer-Grenadier-Division "Das Reich"* is to screen the area between the Oskol and Donez in the sector whose southern boundary is Smijew — Kupjansk (inclusive) and northern boundary Schebekino — Wolokonowka (inclusive).

3.) Effective immediately, reconnaissance is to be conducted to the Oskol. Contact is to be established with the screening forces of *Infanterie-Division (mot.) "Großdeutschland"*. Crossing the Oskol to the east is forbidden.

4.) The Kupjansk strongpoint is to be held by elements of the *298. Infanterie-Division*. They are to remain there and Kupjansk can be bypassed.

5.) A reinforced regiment of *SS-Panzer-Grenadier-Division "Das Reich"* is to be moved to the area southeast of Woltschansk on 30 January. The regiment's mission is to force the enemy that is advancing to the west back across the Oskol in local attacks.

FOR THE CORPS HEADQUARTERS:
Chief of Staff
(for the chief of staff) Müller

***

On 29 January the *SS-Panzer-Korps* also received the following order from the headquarters of *Heeresgruppe B*:

To the *SS-Panzer-Korps*:

Oberkommando des Heeres orders:

Those elements of *SS-Panzer-Grenadier-Division "Das Reich"* that are employed in the sector of *Heeresgruppe Don* are to be pulled out as the 335. Infanterie-Division arrives and sent back to their division. *Heeresgruppe Don* is to report when the release will be effective.

***

On the same day the following Teletype arrived at the corps from the *Oberkommando des Heeres*

To the *SS-Panzer-Korps*:

It remains the intention of *OKH* to employ the formations of the *SS-Panzer-Korps* as a whole for a counterattack. It is therefore of great importance that the formations not be split up before that operation and the minimum possible forces be employed for the task of securing the staging area.

With that in mind, the corps headquarters is to secure the Kupjansk — Wolokonowka sector west of the Oskol with the least forces possible.

Heeresgruppe B is to issue the necessary tactical orders to accomplish that task. It is to report to the *OKH* which elements will be employed for that task.

The direct attachment of the *SS-Panzer-Korps* to *OKH* remains unaffected by the above. (*OKH Gen. d. H./Op. Abt. I, Nr. 1290/43 g. Kdos.*)

***

On 30 January 1943 elements of *SS-Panzer-Grenadier-Division "Das Reich"* had to be sent forward to screen in the area west of Waluiki. The elements of *Infanterie-Division (mot.) "Großdeutschland"* that had been screening there were needed on the northern wing of *Korps Kramer*. The division reported that heavier attacks than in previous days against the built-up areas west of Borki and Kosinka had been repulsed.

SS-Panzer-Grenadier-Division "Das Reich" was employed securing the Oskol with the following elements:

The *III./SS-Panzergrenadier-Regiment "Deutschland"* relieved elements of *Infanterie-Division (mot.) "Großdeutschland"* at Kosinka in the afternoon. The staff of the regiment...(and the remaining two battalions)...are at the Prikolotnoje railroad station. The *15./SS-Panzergrenadier-Regiment "Deutschland"* is en route to Kamenka.

Reinforced *SS-Aufklärungs-Abteilung 2 "Das Reich"* has been in Alexandrowka, 15 kilometers west of Wolokonowka, since 0930 hours. There are no reports concerning enemy contact.

The relief of elements of *Infanterie-Division (mot.) "Großdeutschland"* west of Borki by the *III./SS-Panzergrenadier-Regiment "Deutschland"* has been completed. In the division's sector reinforced reconnaissance has been sent forward to the Oskol in preparation for presumably forcing the enemy west of Waluiki back over the Oskol on 1 February. (Daily report of the *SS-Panzer-Korps* for 30 January 1943)

***

In the final days of January *SS-Panzergrenadier-Regiment "Der Führer"* was sent forward into the Bely Kolodes — Woltschansk — Weliki Burluk area, and the *II./SS-Panzergrenadier-Regiment "Der Führer"*, under *SS-Sturmbannführer* Stadler, was employed defensively on the Oskol. *Regiment Witt* of *SS-Panzer-Grenadier-Division "Leibstandarte SS Adolf Hitler"* was the friendly force on the right in the Kupjansk sector. The extremely thin line of defense could not prevent the enemy from infiltrating with powerful motorized elements.

31 January 1943

The enemy attacked the *298. Infanterie-Division* at Petropawlowka from the east and north with two weak regimental groups in the sector of the *SS-Panzer-Korps* during the morning hours. The enemy had no more than weak artillery. The attack from the east was repulsed. The attack from the north reached Kutschelowka. An immediate counterattack is in progress.

The *15./SS-Panzergrenadier-Regiment "Deutschland"* attacked weak enemy forces in the woods southwest of Kamenka. The enemy probed the front of *SS-Panzergrenadier-Regiment "Deutschland"* with combat patrols west of Borki and Kosinka. They were driven off. The enemy facing *SS-Aufklärungs-Abteilung 2 "Das Reich"* at Krassny Paccar is inactive.

SS-Panzergrenadier-Regiment "Deutschland" is committed in the sector: woods southwest of Kamenka — hills west of Borki — Kosinka — Olowatka.

The defensive sector of the *298. Infanterie Division* was reinforced for a limited time by provision of an artillery battalion from *SS-Panzer-Grenadier-Division "Das Reich"*.

Combat-patrol operations were conducted in the direction of Borki and the high ground east of Kosinka. (From the daily report of the *SS-Panzer-Korps* for 31 January 1943.)

***

Stalingrad

The *6. Armee* surrendered in Stalingrad on 31 January 1943 after the failure of the relief attempt by *Armeegruppe Hoth*. The last fighting continued until 2 February 1943.

1 February 1943

General der Gebirgstruppen Lanz assumed command of the sector formally commanded by the Italian 8th Army in the Kharkov — Bjelgorod area. His command was referred to as *Armee-Abteilung Lanz* and it retained most of the original German staff that had augmented the Italian 8th Army.

That same day the Russians continued their attack on a broader front after inserting the 3rd Tank Army at Waluiki. The *320. Infanterie -Division* was forced back to the Oskol.

***

The **daily report** of *SS-Panzer-Grenadier-Division "Das Reich"* for 1 February 1943 read as follows:

The *15./SS-Panzergrenadier-Regiment "Deutschland"* was initially employed against the Kamenka woods with the mission of forcing back weak enemy forces and occupying Kamenka. A strong enemy attack on Dwuretschnaja presented the threat that the company would be cut off. By order of the corps, it was attached to the Dwuretschnaja strongpoint with the order to hold the strongpoint.

At 1700 hours the strongpoint was enveloped from north and south. Roads to the west were still free of the enemy. There was strong enemy combat reconnaissance in front of the *III./SS-Panzergrenadier-Regiment "Deutschland"*. Around noon, enemy armor was reported for the first time at Babka.

The enemy attack on Babka was repulsed. Reconnaissance determined that the woods south and southwest of Karabinowo were held by the enemy. Work on fortifications was identified on the high ground four kilometers east of Borki. There was heavy enemy traffic, including horse-drawn enemy artillery, on the roads leading to the north and from the east.

There were attacks in battalion strength from the northeast on Kosinka and Kasnatschejewka in the sector of the *II./SS-Panzergrenadier-Regiment "Deutschland"* during the morning. The enemy was repulsed at Kosinka. By midday the enemy penetrated the northern portion of Kasnatschejewka, but the *6./SS-Panzergrenadier-Regiment "Deutschland"* was able to hold the southern outskirts.

During the midday hours heavy attacks in battalion strength continued against Kosinka from the south and east. Kosinka was encircled with the forces there. Strong enemy forces were also brought in from the southeast to Michailowka (five guns and

Stalin organs). Five Soviet ground-attack planes joined in the fighting. At 1600 hours the *6./SS-Panzergrenadier-Regiment "Deutschland"* was able to clear the enemy out of Kasnatschejewka. One platoon of the *3./SS-Panzergrenadier-Regiment "Deutschland"*, which had been brought forward, supported the *II./SS-Panzergrenadier-Regiment "Deutschland"* in the fighting at Kosinka. Around 1400 hours the enemy was still in the northern portion of Kosinka. The rest of Kosinka was clear of enemy. Strong attacks continued against Kosinka.

Enemy forces that had been responsible for killing seven wounded German soldiers in Obignajawere were in Konawaloff.

In the sector of *SS-Aufklärungs-Abteilung 2 "Das Reich"* there was an attack at 0200 hours against the Werch Lubjanka strongpoint. The attack by one battalion from the east was repulsed. Enemy reconnaissance (60 men) from the west was similarly repulsed.

Friendly reconnaissance determined: Enemy occupation of the high ground south, east and northwest of Werch Lubjanka. A friendly patrol was fired on in the woods north of Krassny Paccar. It was not possible to establish contact with friendly forces to the north.

General impression: The enemy is fighting moderately well to well. The strength of the enemy attacking the *II./* and *III./SS-Panzergrenadier-Regiment "Deutschland"* is estimated to be approximately one division. The sector that was assumed was held until 1700 hours. Withdrawal of the (infantry) battalions and the reconnaissance battalion prepared as ordered. Relief of *SS-Aufklärungs-Abteilung 2 "Das Reich"* by *SS-Kradschützen-Bataillon 2 "Das Reich"* was prepared.

The main body of the *I./SS-Panzergrenadier-Regiment "Deutschland"* was employed to support the *II./SS-Panzergrenadier-Regiment "Deutschland"*.

Operational: 66 *Panzer III's*; 60 *Panzer IV's*; 4 *Panzer VI's* (all subject to the arrival of winter tracks or winter cleats!)

Snow conditions east of the Donez: Average 25 centimeters deep; heavy snowdrifts.

/signed/ Keppler
SS-Gruppenführer

***

On 1 February 1943 *Armee-Abteilung* Lanz received the following order from the headquarters of *Heeresgruppe B*:

To dispel any doubt it is again emphasized that the *SS-Panzer-Korps* remains at the disposal of the *OKH*. Only the following forces are available from the *SS-Panzer-Korps* for the conduct of mobile screening operations between the Oskol and the Donez:

> *SS-Aufklärungs-Abteilung 2 "Das Reich"* and one reinforced grenadier regiment of *SS-Panzer-Grenadier-Division "Das Reich"*.

These forces have been reported to the *OKH*.

Any employment of additional forces of the *SS-Panzer-Korps* east of the Donez requires permission in advance from the *OKH*. Therefore, in the event that such becomes necessary, it must be requested in advance from the *OKH*.

Fragmentation of the combat power of the *SS-Panzer-Korps* must be avoided under all circumstances. (*Oberkommando der Heeresgruppe B, Ia Nr. 506/43 g. Kdos.* for 1 February 1943)

Sub-Section c)

Defensive Fighting in the Kharkov Area of Operations: 2 - 18 February 1943

2 February 1943

In order to avoid encirclement, the bridgehead over the Oskol in the Kupjansk — Wolokomowka area had to be evacuated after heavy enemy attacks.

Despite this, the Russians were able to cut off the *320.* and *298. Infanterie-Divisionen* and the *15./SS-Panzergrenadier-Regiment "Deutschland"* from their routes of withdrawal. They had to fight their way through on unbeaten paths in heavy fighting and with the loss of significant materiel.

SS-Panzer-Grenadier-Division "Das Reich" had been holding its position in the Olchowatka area since 1 February. It initially had the mission of pinning the enemy east of the Donez in order to later counterattack to the southeast in conjunction with *SS-Panzer-Grenadier-Division "Leibstandarte SS Adolf Hitler"* (following the completion of its concentration).

However, the critical development of the situation inexorably continued. *SS-Panzer-Grenadier-Division "Das Reich"* was bypassed on both sides and had to fall back to the west in a mobile defense.

At the same time, *Armee-Abteilung Lanz* ordered a withdrawal to the Donez. *SS-Panzer-Grenadier-Division "Leibstandarte SS Adolf Hitler"* defended in the Petschenegi area and conducted a passage of lines along a broad front for the force pulling back.

It then became clear that the *SS-Panzer-Korps* had been brought forward from France too late to be able to assemble in the Kharkov area and then be committed as an entire corps in a counterattack. Instead of this, elements of the corps continually had to be shoved into the penetrated front and inserted into the existing gaps. Thus, the only *OKH* reserve was committed piecemeal before completion of its concentration and, to some extent, pinned along the front.

3 February 1943

On the preceding day the *I./schnelles SS-Schützen-Regiment "Langemarck"* (*SS-Kradschützen-Bataillon 2 "Das Reich"*) had reached Sziwo after a motor march of 160 kilometers via Woltschansk and Marien. It relieved *SS-Aufklärungs-Abteilung 2 "Das Reich"* in the afternoon. The battalion screened south of Alexandrowka. One platoon, led by *SS-Untersturmführer* Riotte, was employed as a combat outpost in the village five kilometers farther south.

SS-Kradschützen-Bataillon 2 "Das Reich" received orders to break contact with the enemy, who was exerting strong pressure on the *1./SS-Kradschützen-Bataillon 2 "Das Reich"*. The combat outpost under Riotte was attacked during the night from three sides after civilians had assisted the Russian soldiers. *SS-Untersturmführer* Riotte and eight men were killed, two men were wounded and two men were missing. *SS-Oberscharführer* Wolf was able to withdraw with what was left of the platoon.

At 1010 hours the *SS-Panzer-Korps* received the following order from *Armee-Abteilung Lanz*:

> Enemy advance from the Waluiki area via Burluk railroad station toward Artemowka requires immediate countermeasures in order to secure the assembly of the *SS-Panzer-Korps*.
>
> I have therefore transmitted by telephone the following order to the commanding general of the *SS-Panzer-Korps*:
>
> 1.) Delay the enemy advance with reinforced screening elements along the Kupjansk — Woltschansk road.
>
> 2.) Hold the Donez line in the event of an enemy attack. For that purpose I have released *SS-Panzer-Grenadier-Division "Das Reich"*... (*Nr. 141/43 g. Kdos.*)

***

The *III./SS-Artillerie-Regiment 2*, which had been temporarily employed with the *298. Infanterie-Division*, was set in march to Kharkov by order of the corps and directed to support *SS-Panzergrenadier-Regiment "Deutschland"*.

4 February 1943

In the sector of *SS-Panzergrenadier-Regiment "Der Führer"* the *III. (gep.)/SS-Panzergrenadier-Regiment "Der Führer"* was also brought forward to the Bely Kolodes — Woltschansk — Weliki Burluk area. Together with *SS-Panzer-Regiment 2 "Das Reich"*, it was to force the enemy back the next day.

The 2. (gep.)/SS-Aufklärungs-Abteilung 2 "Das Reich" Attacks

SS-Aufklärungs-Abteilung 2 "Das Reich" repulsed strong Russian attacks in the area north of Jefremowka on the road from Woltschansk to the northeast.

At 0600 hours a standing patrol of the *3./SS-Aufklärungs-Abteilung 2 "Das Reich"* returned from the village five kilometers east of the main line of resistance and reported the approach of a Russian battalion. It prepared to defend. At about 0700 hours the leading elements of the Russian battalion moved out of the village to the east.

At almost the same time *SS-Hauptsturmführer* Kämpfe showed up with his *2./SS-Aufklärungs-Abteilung 2 "Das Reich"* — a *SPW* company — to relieve the *3./SS-Kradschützen-Bataillon 2 "Das Reich"*.

The *SPW* positioned themselves behind a gentle knoll at the edge of the village on both sides of the road along which the Russians were approaching. When the lead elements of the Russians were only a few meters away, the heavy machine guns of the *3./SS-Kradschützen-Bataillon 2 "Das Reich"* forced the enemy to take cover on the broad snow-covered open area. Then the *SPW* made a pincers attack and destroyed the entire Russian battalion, including its trains. The trains attempted to escape into the village behind them. The *2./SS-Aufklärungs-Abteilung "Das Reich"* then took over the positions of the *3./SS-Kradschützen-Bataillon 2 "Das Reich"*, which went back into position at the point of some woods south of the main supply route.

5 February 1943

The newly organized *SS-Panzer-Regiment 2 "Das Reich"* under *SS-Standartenführer* Vahl launched its first armored attack together with the *III. (gep.)/SS-Panzergrenadier-Regiment "Der Führer"* against the northern flank of the greatly superior enemy.

In the extremely broken terrain and in spite of deep snow, it was possible to destroy the wedge that the enemy attempted to drive between the main body of the division and *SS-Aufklärungs-Abteilung 2 "Das Reich"*. That made it possible for what was left of the *298. Infanterie-Division* to pass through the front.

However, this temporary relief did not delay the enemy's westward advance for long.

The Russians had already forced the combat outposts in front of *SS-Panzer-Grenadier-Division "Leibstandarte SS Adolf Hitler"* back from the east bank of the Donez and were in front of its positions. Heavy defensive fighting began, particularly intense around the key position at Petschenegi. In spite of the thin manning of the main line of resistance — the sector of *SS-Panzer-Grenadier-Division "Leibstandarte SS Adolf Hitler"* had a width of 90 kilometers — the Russians achieved no more than temporary penetrations which could immediately be cleaned up in immediate counterattacks that inflicted-heavy casualties upon the enemy.

The *IV./SS-Artillerie-Regiment 2 "Das Reich"* particularly excelled in the heavy defensive fighting under its extremely flexible and unconventional young commander, *SS-Sturmbannführer* Karl Kreutz. Kreutz commanded that battalion until 18 March 1943, when he assumed command of the entire regiment, replacing *SS-Standartenführer* Kurt Brasack. His intense concentrations of fire in front of the division's sector were a great help to the infantry. His forward observers and their radio operators, who directed the fire from the foremost positions of the grenadiers, were practically an organic component of the individual battalions. All the men of *SS-Panzer-Grenadier-Division "Das Reich"* agreed that they had never known better artillery support than that of their own *SS-Panzer-Grenadier-Division "Das Reich"*.

6 February 1943

The *III. (gep.)/SS-Panzergrenadier-Regiment "Der Führer"* advanced to Olchowatka and forced the enemy back from his positions to a depth of about ten kilometers. While pursuing the enemy, the *SPW* battalion and the *I./SS-Panzer-Regiment 2 "Das Reich"* ran into a strong concentration of anti-tank fronts in Weliki Burluk. The tank battalion suffered regrettable losses. Falling darkness assisted in breaking off the fight.

The enemy, the Soviet 179th Tank Brigade and the 1245th Antitank Regiment under Colonel Rudkin, had taken advantage of favorable terrain in constructing a strong antitank front.

***

An overview of the larger situation gives the following picture:

The groups that were desperately defending themselves in the areas in front of Kharkov and Bjelgorod — including remnants that had fought their way back from positions that the Russian advance had long since left behind — were forced back to the Donez, east of Kharkov, along with the divisions of the *SS-Panzer-Korps* that had originally been intended for the relief of the *6. Armee*. In the process a gap formed between the army group and the Isjum area, through which the Soviet Armored Group "Popov" crossed the Donez to the south before the armored divisions that were on their way from Rostow via bottomless roads could intervene.

With that, the doorway to the lower Dnjepr in the rear of the Donez basin was forced open.

The Eastern Front was thus faced with a catastrophe of the highest order when Hitler, on 6 February, ordered the commanders-in-chief of *Heeresgruppen Don* and *Mitte*, along with *General* Lanz, to report to him at *Führer* headquarters in East Prussia.

There, certain requests for a "withdrawal" as a basis for an imminent counteroffensive could be met. This resulted in the following plan:

Withdrawal of *Heeresgruppe Don* to the Mius river. Move *Panzergruppe Hoth* from Rostow to the left wing.

In addition, there was a change in command relationships. The headquarters of *Heeresgruppe B* (the former Italian Eighth Army headquarters) was eliminated. *Armee-Abteilung Lanz* was attached to *Heeresgruppe Don* — henceforth designated *Heeresgruppe Süd* — commanded by *Generalfeldmarschall* von Manstein. (A. Philippi and F. Heim, *Der Feldzug gegen die Sowjet-Union*, ? Stuttgart: Kohlhammer-Verlag, ?)

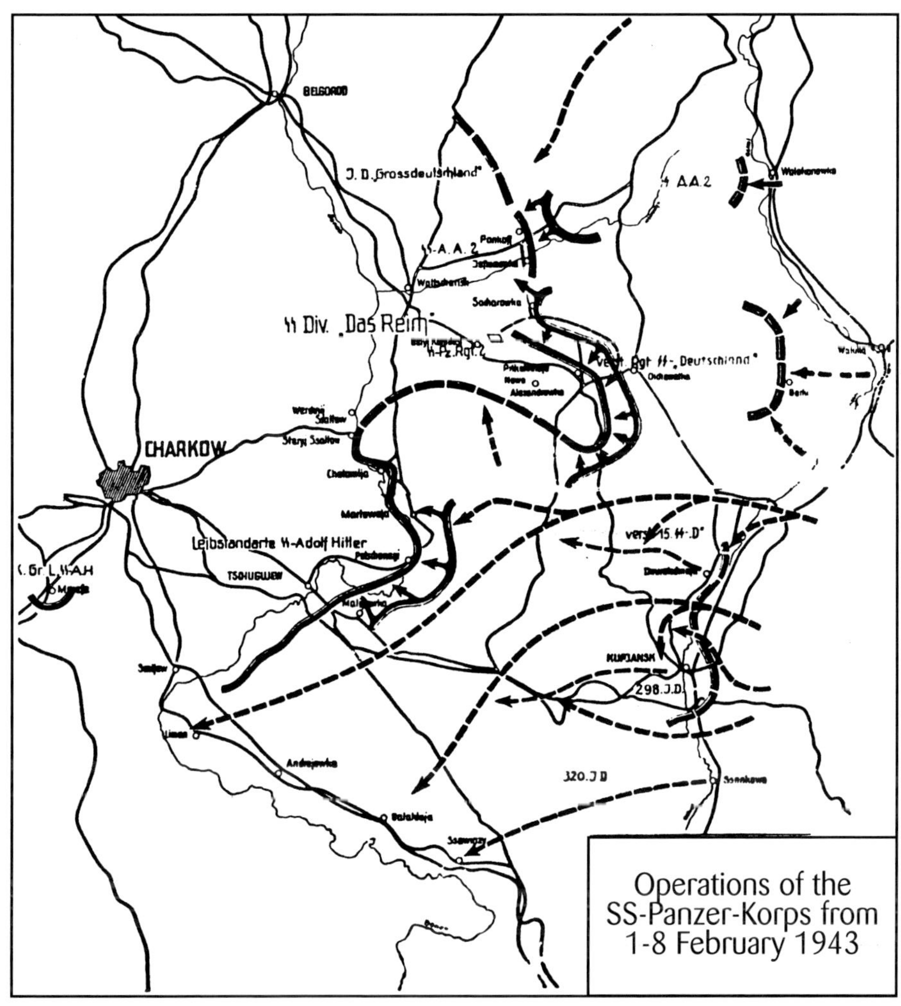

Operations of the SS-Panzer-Korps from 1-8 February 1943

7 February 1943

Following the relief of *SS-Panzer-Regiment 2 "Das Reich"* by *Infanterie-Division (mot.) "Großdeutschland"*, the *III. (gep.)/SS-Panzergrenadier-Regiment "Der Führer"* renewed its relief attacks and again forced the enemy back. The *10./, 11./,* and *12./SS-Panzergrenadier-Regiment "Der Führer"* in a rapid advanceforced the Soviets back to the northwestern outskirts of Weliki Burluki.

Going it alone, the *9./SS-Panzergrenadier-Regiment "Der Führer"* advanced to Gotschino and forced the enemy back.

As a result of these extremely aggressive, lightning-fast attacks the enemy advance was hindered. However, continuation of the friendly advances to the southeast was no longer possible.

8 February 1943

A crisis grew on both flanks of the *SS-Panzer-Korps* as a result of the threatened envelopment by two Russian armies. To the south, the *320. Infanterie-Division* was pulled back from the Oskol too late. It had been slowly fighting its way back, on deeply snowbound roads without outside contact, since 5 February.

The Russians probed the front of *SS-Panzer-Grenadier-Division "Leibstandarte SS Adolf Hitler"* and found the southern wing at Smijew. A gap of 40 kilometers yawned between it and the *320. Infanterie-Division*. The Russian advance there threatened the southern flank of the corps at Merefa.

A small armored *Kampfgruppe* of *SS-Panzer-Grenadier-Division "Leibstandarte SS Adolf Hitler"* was hastily sent toward Merefa with the mission of blocking the road there toward Kharkov. *SS-Kradschützen-Bataillon "Langemarck"* of *SS-Panzer-Grenadier-Division "Das Reich"* was attached to assist in this operation.

Encirclement of Kharkov Appears Imminent

The northern flank was also exposed. The numerically extremely weak *Korps Kramer* was fighting northeast of Bjelgorod and had already been outflanked. The operational envelopment of Kharkov had begun and could not be prevented with the forces available.

Accordingly, sooner or later, the evacuation of the city — or its encirclement — loomed.

There could be no talk of the massed employment of *SS-Panzer-Grenadier-Divisionen "Das Reich"* and *"Leibstandarte SS Adolf Hitler"*.

At the same time, the Soviet command prepared the advance into the north flank of the Donez basin. In addition to the attack on the Bjelgorod — Kharkov line, it was evident that the enemy intended to cut the lines of communication of the German Front that was still holding in the Donez basin between the Sea of Asov and Slawansk. It would seize these lines of communications in a *coup de main* and then destroy the German forces there.

The deadly thrust was to advance via Barwenkowo, Losowaja and Pawlograd to Dnjepropetrowsk and Saporoshje. Five tank corps and three rifle corps had been staged north of Slawjansk for the operation.

Following the evacuation of Isjum, the Soviet 1st Guards Army poured into the area that had opened up to the southwest without meeting any resistance. The Soviet 6th Guards Army closed up to the attack on the right wing after cutting off the *320. Infanterie-Division*.

If that operation succeeded, *Heeresgruppe Süd* would be cut off from its lines of communications, the Dnjepr left open to enemy attack, the route to the western Ukraine open and the campaign in the east lost.

The situation was extremely serious.

In the sector of *SS-Panzer-Grenadier-Division "Das Reich"* the Russians conducted strong attacks against the left wing of the division.

General der Gebirgstruppen Lanz and *SS-Obergruppenführer* Hausser personally visited the division command post to get a better picture of the situation. As a result, *General* Lanz was convinced that a withdrawal behind the Donez, which was still held by *SS-Panzer-Grenadier-Division "Leibstandarte SS Adolf Hitler"*, was inevitable.

The commanding general of the *SS-Panzer-Korps* established contact with *General* Hörnlein, the commander of *Infanterie-Division (mot.) "Großdeutschland"*.

The Russian envelopment operation became increasingly evident.

9 February 1943

The prerequisites no longer existed for a German counteroffensive east of the Donez. In response to an urgent request of the *SS-Panzer-Korps*, *General* Lanz ordered that *SS-Panzer-Grenadier-Division "Das Reich"* be pulled back behind the Donez. He issued this order on his own initiative without prior permission of the German Army High Command. He would soon learn what this entailed. *SS-Panzer-Grenadier-Division "Das Reich"*, however, was indebted to him for what was still a timely, complete withdrawal behind the Donez and for avoiding the first threat of envelopment.

The city of Kharkov was placed under the command of the *SS-Panzer-Korps*.

Through deep snowdrifts, on laboriously cleared roads, constantly fighting enemy forces that were already on the flanks and in the rear, the division managed to withdraw from its former positions to behind the Donez. The Donez was to be held by the *SS-Panzer-Korps*.

However, that position was also already threatened in its deep flanks at the time it was occupied. An additional withdrawal had to be considered. The enemy followed closely on the heels of the withdrawal movement, was present all along the Donez and, above all, was advancing through the gap between the right flank of *SS-Panzer-Grenadier-Division "Leibstandarte SS Adolf Hitler"* and the *320. Infanterie-Division* with such strong forces that decisive measures had to be taken there.

The situation necessitated either an immediate attack against the enemy forces enveloping the city from the south and the evacuation of Kharkov or a tighter concentration of all forces for all-around defense of the city, which meant encirclement.

As a result, the withdrawal of the front from the Donez to a position east of Kharkov was ordered on 9 February. That withdrawal of the front also took place without permission and approval from Hitler and the Army High Command. It was simply based on the development of the situation as forced by the enemy.

Around noon *Armee-Abteilung Lanz* received orders that elements of the *SS-Panzer-Korps* were to eliminate the danger of envelopment from the south by offensive operations to the south, in spite of renewed enemy attacks against the entire corps front to the east and northeast.

10 February 1943

After withdrawing from the Donez with both divisions to the Mirgorod — Konstantowka — Lisogubowka — Rogan — Priwolje — Russkije Tischky line to shorten the front, elements could be freed up by both divisions and staged near Merefa. Yet another attempt would be made to prevent the encirclement of Kharkov by attacking to clear the right flank.

The advance to Artemowka was ordered for 11 February. This required blocking the attack against the left wing of *SS-Panzer-Grenadier-Division "Das Reich"*, pulling the front back in the area east of Kharkov and regrouping for the advance to the south.

It would have taken too much time to withdraw a complete division from the front. Accordingly, a *"Divisions-Kampfgruppe"* was formed from elements of both divisions and placed under the command of *SS-Panzer-Grenadier-Division "Leibstandarte SS Adolf Hitler"*, *SS-Obergruppenführer* Sepp Dietrich. The continued defense by the remainder of the two divisions remained under the commander of *SS-Panzer-Grenadier-Division "Das Reich"*, *SS-Gruppenführer* Keppler. Also defending were *Korps Raus — Infanterie-Division (mot.) "Großdeutschland"* — and the remnants of *Korps Kramer.*

Could the front be held there? The situation was openly discussed with *Armee-Abteilung Lanz* and also passed to the Army High Command by the corps chief of staff, *SS-Standartenführer* Ostendorff.

Without the assignment of an aviation element (*Fieseler Storch*), it would have been impossible to maintain contact with the forces on the ground and with the adjoining units due to the widely separated areas of operation. This was the only way to gain personal insight, maintain a discussion of the situation and transmit orders.

The corps command post moved to Merefa. Orders for the attack were issued there early on 10 February.

In addition to *SS-Kradschützen-Bataillon "Langemarck"*, *SS-Panzergrenadier-Regiment "Der Führer"* was pulled out of the front, set in march to Merefa and attached to *SS-Panzer-Grenadier-Division*

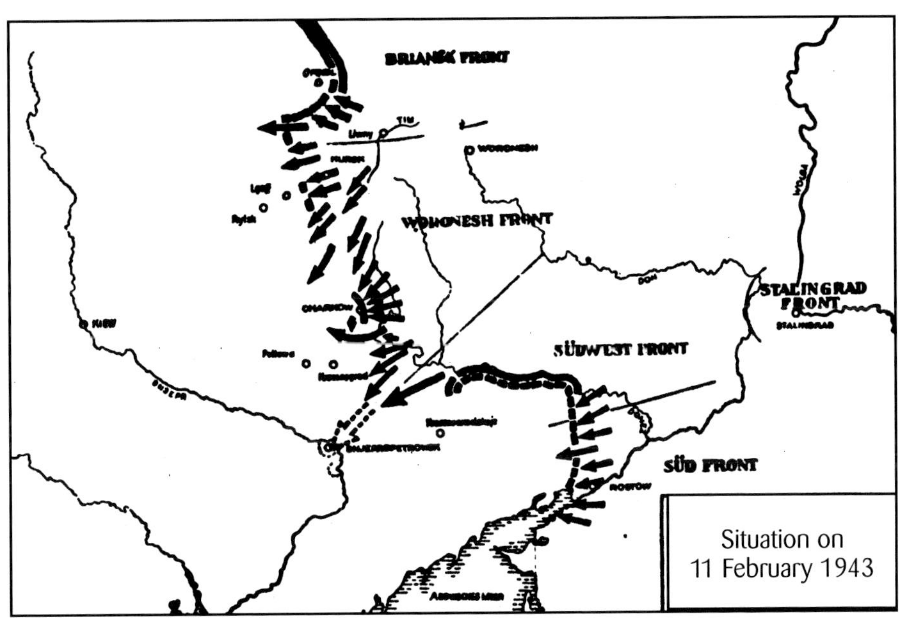

Situation on 11 February 1943

"Leibstandarte SS Adolf Hitler" for the advance to the south.

In its place, a regiment of *SS-Panzer-Grenadier-Division "Leibstandarte SS Adolf Hitler"* was provided to *SS-Panzer-Grenadier-Division "Das Reich"*. It was to stabilize the situation east of Kharkov as best it could, given increasing enemy attacks.

Deep snow delayed the approach march for the attack. The unavoidable mingling of the formations complicated the staging for the attack.

That day the commander of *SS-Panzer-Grenadier-Division "Das Reich"* suffered a recurrence of a previous attack of meningitis and had to turn the command of the division over to *SS-Oberführer* Vahl, the commander of *SS-Panzer-Regiment 2 "Das Reich"*. *SS-Sturmbannführer* von Reitzenstein, the commander of the *I./Panzer-Regiment 2 "Das Reich"*, assumed command of the tank regiment. The army supply dump at Merefa was opened up for the friendly troops.

Advance South from Merefa

11 February 1943

In spite of all the difficulties, three assault groups set out from the Merefa bridgehead to the south:

Right: *SS-Aufklärungs-Abteilung 1 "Leibstandarte SS Adolf Hitler"* under *SS-Sturmbannführer* Meyer (nicknamed: *Panzermeyer*)

Center: *SS-Panzergrenadier-Regiment "Der Führer"*, directed to coordinate with *SS-Panzer-Regiment 1 "Leibstandarte SS Adolf Hitler"*.

Left: *SS-Regiment Witt* (*SS-Panzergrenadier-Division "Leibstandarte SS Adolf Hitler"*)

The temperature was -20 degrees Celsius (-4 degrees Fahrenheit). Thirty centimeters of snow cover significantly interfered with the movement. The terrain, which was cut by deep *Balkas,* made the employment of tanks nearly impossible.

The attack, which came as a surprise to the enemy, started successfully and *Stoßgruppe Meyer* (Assault Group "Meyer") was able to reach Starowerowka via Nowaja — Wodolaga on the first day.

The other two *Stoßgruppen* experienced hard, but successful operations.

The forces defending north and east of Kharkov also experienced hard fighting. Two reinforced regiment groups — one regiment of *SS-Panzer-Grenadier-Division "Leibstandarte SS Adolf Hitler"* and the reinforced *SS-Panzergrenadier-Regiment "Deutschland"* with the main body of *Artillerie-Regiment 2 "Der Führer"* — were involved in heavy defensive fighting.

The Soviets started massed attacks with strong armored forces on the 11 February against the east side of the defensive ring around the city of Kharkov. Smijew, which had been attacked from three sides, had already been lost on 10 February. There was strong enemy pressure on Ternowoje. The thin German line at Rogan held against extremely strong attacks continually driven home by newly introduced forces.

Farther north, Priwolje and the high ground west of Michaelowski were temporarily lost. Ongoing immediate counterattacks with weak reserves cleaned up the penetrations and exacted heavy losses from the enemy. Regardless, the enemy continued to attack and constantly brought forward new masses of forces.

It would have been practically impossible to hold the positions without the outstanding support of the division's own artillery, which stopped many enemy attacks, before they started, with its tight concentrations of fire.

SS-Sturmbannführer Tychsen and his *II./SS-Panzer-Regiment "Das Reich"* and *SS-Hauptsturmführer* Zens Kaiser particularly distinguished themselves. The last reserves, *SS-Aufklärungs-Abteilung 2 "Das Reich"*, had to be committed on 11 February following an enemy penetration in the sector adjoining on the left (*213. Sichrungs-Division*). As a result, the thinly held front east of the city lacked any reserves worth mentioning. However, the men continued to hold their positions, unshaken.

Nevertheless, the decisive Russian advance to encircle the city from the east and north took place there.

Lead Elements of SS-Panzer-Grenadier-Division "Totenkopf" Arrive

A ray of hope appeared with the arrival of the lead elements of *SS-Panzer-Grenadier-Division "Totenkopf"*. *SS-Panzergrenadier-Regiment "Thule"* of that division was hastily sent forward when it detrained at Kiev to secure Krassnograd and its critical road junctions. As of 12 February *SS-Panzergrenadier-Regiment "Thule"* held the eastern outskirts of the city. In addition, it screened the deep southern flank of the *SS-Panzer-Korps* by reconnaissance.

12 February 1943

On that day the German southward advance captured Nowaja Wodolaga. *Stuka-Geschwader 77*, whose air/ground control officer moved with the staff of *SS-Panzergrenadier-Regiment "Der Führer"*, provided outstanding support for the aggressively advancing battalions. The attack made good overall progress.

The Crisis Reaches Its Climax

The events of 13 and 14 February 1943 signaled the climax of the crisis at Kharkov.

As a result of the thin manning of the defensive positions, enemy penetrations required commitment of the very last reserves to interdict them.

In the north, an enemy army advanced deep into the area northwest of Kharkov after capturing Bjelgorod. Direct attacks toward the city from the east and northeast remained as strong as ever while other formations advanced past the city to the west. Their intent was to turn inwards if any gaps were discovered. The main supply route from Poltawa was threatened.

Infanterie-Division (mot.) "Großdeutschland", which was fighting its way back from the Bjelgorod area, had to be committed to defending Kharkov to the northwest. With that, the original intention of *Armee-Abteilung Lanz* to free up the elements of *SS-Panzer-Grenadier-Division "Das Reich"* which remained defending east of Kharkov, in order to reinforce the attack to the south by relieving them with units of *Infanterie-Division (mot.) "Großdeutschland"* was thwarted.

Once again, the old comrades-in-arms of *Infanterie-Division (mot.) "Großdeutschland"* fought shoulder-to-shoulder with the men of *SS-Panzer-Grenadier-Division "Das Reich"*, just as they had in the campaign in Yugoslavia and in the bloody defensive fighting in the Jelnja salient.

The *213. Sicherungs-Division* that adjoined *SS-Panzer-Grenadier-Division "Das Reich"* to the north was exceedingly limited in its combat power.

Its individual formations were later divided between *SS-Panzer-Grenadier-Division "Das Reich"* and *Korps Kramer*.

Because the defensive front continually extended farther to the west, it was only possible to hold strongpoints on the access roads to the north and northwest of the city.

By the morning of 13 February the Kharkov defensive front had extended its left wing from Russkije — Tischky — north of Russkije via the Jemzow railroad station to Feski.

The cut-off *320. Infanterie-Division* fought its way back toward Smijew from the Andrejewka area with 1,500 wounded. The entire *SS-Panzer-Korps* medical and supply capabilities, as well as a portion of the transportation means of the *SS* divisions, were standing by to care for the superbly fighting division. Rations were prepared for the severely famished soldiers.

The *SPW* battalion of *SS-Panzer-Grenadier-Division "Leibstandarte SS Adolf Hitler"* had established contact with the *320. Infanterie-Division* at the Donez crossing east of Smijew and dispersed enemy forces south of Wodjanoje on 12 February. As a result, the *320. Infanterie-Division* would make a passage of lines during the following day — 15 February — through the friendly front.

During the morning of 13 February the *SS-Panzer-Korps* received an order from the *Führer* through *Armee-Abteilung Lanz* to unconditionally hold the city of Kharkov.

The corps reported that it would not be possible to continue to hold the city past 14 February. Appropriate route reconnaissance missions in preparation for a withdrawal were issued. The *320. Infanterie-Division* under the outstanding leadership of *General* Postel came back with its 1,500 wounded after tremendous hardships and heavy fighting. It made a passage of lines through the *SPW* battalion of *SS-Panzer-Grenadier-Division "Leibstandarte SS Adolf Hitler"*. Evacuation of the wounded was undertaken and the entire logistical requirements of the severely tested and especially proven division were immediately met by the *SS-Panzer-Korps* and the two *SS* divisions.

During the night of 13/14 February an additional tightening of the Kharkov defensive front was carried out in order to pull reserves out of the front. The new line ran via Lisogubowka — Rogan railroad station — road fork southeast of Lossewo — Sankin to Bolschaja Danilowka.

During the evening of 13 February the corps pointed out that this line could only be held until 14 February, since the city had already been enveloped. *General* Raus also fully agreed with that evaluation of the situation. The corps then made recommendations for regulating the continued withdrawal. The divisions were assigned route-reconnaissance missions to accomplish this.

Sub-Section d)

Evacuation of the City of Kharkov: 15 February 1943

The danger of encirclement was already acute on 14 February. Once more, an attack to the southeast of the city by Jochen Peiper's battalion — the *SPW* battalion — of *SS-Panzer-Grenadier-Division "Leibstandarte SS Adolf Hitler"* provided a little breathing space.

On 14 February at 1330 hours *Armee-Abteilung Lanz* again issued written orders that the positions around Kharkov must be held. Demolitions of all supply dumps and facilities of military or economic importance were prepared.

In the morning the enemy was able to break through the thin line of strongpoints north of the Rogan railroad station and north of Satischje. An enemy armored attack with 40 tanks at Rogan also led to a breakthrough. It was feared that the attack would continue to the Lossewo tractor factory. Weak forces formed a blocking position. The enemy also found gaps in the front of *Infanterie-Division (mot.) "Großdeutschland"* northwest of the city and occupied the wooded terrain directly northwest of the city outskirts during the course of the day.

With that, significant formations of *Korps Raus* — *Generalleutnant* Raus had assumed command of *Korps Kramer* — were already cut off from their communications with Kharkov. The enemy controlled the Poltawa — Kharkov supply road with fire and held Olschany.

At 1645 hours, *SS-Obergruppenführer* Hausser acted on his own initiative and issued the order to evacuate Kharkov and fall back behind the Udy River during the night of 14/15 February — he also notified *Korps Raus* of his decision.

At 1750 *General* Lanz again ordered that the positions were to be held to the last man.

Yet again, Hausser deferred his decision — proof of how he had struggled with himself to bring conscience and obedience into alignment.

Late in the afternoon of 14 February, enemy units that had broken through from the southeast penetrated into the Osnowa section of the city. The *SPW* battalion of *SS-Panzergrenadier-Division "Leibstandarte SS Adolf Hitler"*, which had been sent in an immediate counterattack, became decisively engaged in nighttime fighting. It was unable to clear that part of the city from the constantly growing enemy forces. In the city itself, civilians began to commit armed rebellion. Columns marching through were fired on from the houses.

In the evening of 14 February *Armee-Abteilung Lanz* ordered that the corps attack group halt the attack to the south and hold the terrain that had been captured.

How had the attack south from Merefa progressed up to that time? The after-action report of the *SS-Panzer-Korps* states:

The attack surprised the enemy and started successfully. *Kampfgruppe* Meyer (*Panzer*-Meyer) of *SS-Panzer-Grenadier-Division "Leibstandarte SS Adolf Hitler"* succeeded in reaching Starowerowka via Nowaja — Wodolaga on 11 February and, in the days that followed, to advance to Alexejewka along with *Angriffsgruppe Witt* (*SS-Panzer-Grenadier-Division "Leibstandarte SS Adolf Hitler"*). *Kampfgruppe* Kumm (*SS-Panzergrenadier-Regiment "Der Führer*) captured Borki and Ochotschaje in hard fighting. The Soviet 6th Guards Cavalry Corps was completely dispersed with heavy losses in the Ochotschaje — Taranowka — Borki area with heavy losses.

The commander of *SS-Panzergrenadier-Regiment "Der Führer"*, *SS-Obersturmbannführer* Kumm, wrote the following concerning the fighting:

The first two days brought hard fighting but great success rewarded hard work. Nowaja Wodolaga fell on 12 February and, on 13 February, the *III./SS-Panzergrenadier-Regiment "Der Führer"* captured the village and railroad station of Borki.

In the immediate pursuit by the regiment from Borki to Rjabuschino, which was outstandingly supported by *Stuka-Geschwader 77*, the *9./SS-Panzergrenadier-Regiment "Der Führer"* got hopelessly stuck in the deeply snow-covered terrain with its *SPW*. The enemy immediately launched heavy attacks against the immobilized company. Summoned by radio, help arrived a short while later in the form of the regiment's maintenance officer, *SS-Obersturmführer* Herbst, who arrived with the courageous men of his maintenance section and three 12-ton tank recovery vehicles. Under covering fire from the company, the *SPW* were hauled out.

The regiment spent the night of 13/14 February in Rjabuschino. The next attack objective was Ochotschaje, about ten kilometers farther south. The reconnaissance of the *10./SS-Panzergrenadier-Regiment "Der Führer"* led by *SS-Untersturmführer* Nickmann, reported that Ochotschaje was held by the enemy.

During the night the regiment — with the *III./SS-Panzergrenadier-Regiment "Der Führer"* in the lead and the *II./SS-Panzergrenadier-Regiment "Der Führer"* initially in reserve — occupied jump-off positions for the attack: A patch of woods about 4.5 kilometers north of Ochotschaje. It staged there for the attack. The attack was to be supported by a tank company of *SS-Panzer-Grenadier-Division "Leibstandarte SS Adolf Hitler"* and a battery of the *II./SS-Artillerie-Regiment "Das Reich"*.

Advancing along the Rjabuschino — Ochotschaje road, the *III./SS-Panzergrenadier-Regiment "Der Führer"* quickly reached the first houses of the built-up area with the *10./* and *11./ SS-Panzergrenadier-Regiment "Der Führer"* alongside each other. They were directly west of the northward flowing stream. The tankers and artillery men fired round after round over open sites, thus giving the attack good support. Unfortunately, both were soon out of ammunition and dropped out of the main phase of the fight, which was then joined in earnest.

The mounted *9./SS-Panzergrenadier-Regiment "Der Führer"* had worked its way to within one kilometer of Ochotschaje. Its mission was to break through the built-up area and across the Berestowaja River to the south. At the moment that the company advanced and showed itself on the wide expanse of open terrain, the enemy suddenly opened extraordinarily heavy fire with machine guns, antitank guns, mortars and tanks. The companies, particularly the *9./SS-Panzergrenadier-Regiment "Der Führer"*, suffered heavy losses. The rear elements of the companies fell back while the leading platoons sought cover in the protection of the houses and took up the fight. (Otto Weidinger, *Kameraden bis zum Ende"*, p. 127. Göttingen: Plesse-Verlag, 1962)

***

The battalion commander, *SS-Sturmbannführer* Horn, was wounded in the arm by a fragment. The commander of the *9./SS-Panzergrenadier-Regiment "Der Führer"*, *SS-Hauptsturmführer* Schober, assumed acting command of the battalion.

***

On receipt of that report the regimental commander immediately went forward to the edge of the village and realized that the forces were ready to give way to the far superior enemy. The commander of the *III./SS-Panzergrenadier-Regiment "Der Führer"*, two company commanders and numerous officers, noncommissioned officers and men were killed or wounded. (Otto Weidinger, *Kameraden bis zum Ende"*, p. 127. Göttingen: Plesse-Verlag, 1962)

***

SS-Untersturmführer Schmager, who at that moment assumed command of the *9./SS-Panzergrenadier-Regiment "Der Führer* from *SS-Hauptsturmführer* Schober, wrote the following concerning the fighting:

Bloody Sunday in Ochotschaje

A powerful Soviet counterattack collapsed in the face of the last friendly forces...In a makeshift fashion *SS-Obersturmführer* Werner organized his *10./SS-Panzergrenadier-Regiment "Der Führer* and I the elements of the *9./SS-Panzergrenadier-Regiment "Der Führer* for defense. It was our duty, after all, to at least recover the wounded.

Our weakness was quickly recognized. The Ivans fired on us from every nook and cranny.

"*Untersturmführer*, shoot me!" cried *SS-Sturmmann* W. with his last strength as he writhed in pain in the snow. "Shut your trap!" I told him, pulling myself together. "There is the medic's *SPW* and Molz will help you."

"*Jawohl, Untersturmführer*", was the answer...

"What's wrong with you?" I called to little H., the radio operator in my platoon.

"Not so bad, *Untersturmführer*. Help the others first!" And, with every word, a stream of blood flowed from his mouth. Molz, my loyal shadow and messenger, also dragged that barely 17-year old youth to the medic's *SPW.*

Should I relate more?

In the meantime, firing like madmen, all the wounded were evacuated and, meter by meter, the Ivans forced us back until we completely broke contact. When the companies assembled at the jump-off position my company numbered exactly 21, including myself; the others were certainly no better off. Even if those numbers looked a little better a few hours later, those of us who were once in the *III. (gep.)/SS-Panzergrenadier-Regiment "Der Führer"* will never forget that bloody Sunday in Ochotschaje.

***

SS-Obersturmbannführer Kumm continues regarding Ochotschaje:

In spite of that situation: If the battalion stopped the fight in falling darkness it could scarcely withstand another attack. The regiment's adjutant, *SS-Hauptsturmführer* Holzer, assumed command of the *III./SS-Panzergrenadier-Regiment "Der Führer"* by order of the regimental commander. His mission was to start the attack again and carry it on under any circumstances.

At the same time the *II./SS-Panzergrenadier-Regiment "Der Führer"* under *SS-Sturmbannführer* Stadler mounted on the *SPW* of the *III./ SS-Panzergrenadier-Regiment "Der Führer"* and attacked Ochotschaje from the east via Popowka. It was determined that the enemy had positioned thirty tanks, as well as antitank guns in Ochotschaje. They were skillfully camouflaged as haystacks, and they opened fire from all barrels. The fighting continued well into the night. Then the enemy was forced out and Ochotschaje was in the regiment's hands. Unfortunately, most of the enemy tanks escaped.

The real victory that day, however, was primarily that the *III./SS-Panzergrenadier-Regiment "Der Führer"*, under pressure of extremely concentrated enemy fire, had pulled itself together again after a moment of weakness and renewed the attack. The young men had quickly won back confidence in their own abilities and never again lost it.

The self-sacrificing actions of all medical personnel were indeed extraordinary in that fight. The battalion's surgeon, *SS-Hauptsturmführer Dr.* Spielberger, advanced with his men to the forward-most lines and brought out the wounded without regard for the furious enemy fire. (Otto Weidinger, *Kameraden bis zum Ende*", p. 127. Göttingen: Plesse-Verlag, 1962)

***

The order cited above from *Armee-Abteilung Lanz* in the evening of 14 February — to stop the southward attack of the division-sized force of the *SS-Panzer-Korps* from Merefa; to hold the terrain that had been captured in order to free up forces to reinforce the defense of Kharkov; and, to send an armored group to Walki in order to recapture enemy-held Olschany and keep the supply road free — could not be executed. The staging of those formations would have taken two days under existing road conditions.

***

SS-Obergruppenführer und General der Waffen-SS Hausser wrote the following in his personal notes:

Reorganization, creation of reserves and continued action was only possible in the south for the attack group of SS-Panzer-Grenadier-Division "Leibstandarte SS Adolf Hitler". That necessitated evacuation of Kharkov. To stand fast meant being surrounded. That view was reported.

Armee-Abteilung Lanz turned it down and, at 1800 hours, passed on Hitler's categorical order:

"Kharkov is to be held to the last man!"

In the evening the commanding general again outlined the situation in order to elicit the order to evacuate Kharkov. — In vain. —

He would wait until 15 February, especially since the passage of lines had not yet been completed by the *320. Infanterie-Division.*

In the meantime, the situation worsened on both wings of the corps:

During the night of 14/15 February the enemy had already penetrated on the left wing of *Kampfgruppe "Das Reich"* and at *Korps Raus* in the northwest sector and, on the right wing, at the airfield south of Kharkov behind our troops and into the southeast part of the city.

However, the *320. Infanterie-Division* was safe.

***

A tank battalion of *SS-Panzer-Grenadier-Division "Das Reich"* was able to exact heavy losses from the enemy in an immediate counterattack in the northwestern part of the city. The enemy advance was temporarily stopped. Once again the *SS-Panzer-Korps* reported the gravity of the situation to *Armee-Abteilung Lanz*. The attempt by the commanding general to fly to Lanz in a *Fieseler Storch* on 15 February and meet with him was unsuccessful. By noon on 15 February there was still no decision.

***

SS-Obergruppenführer und General der Waffen-SS Hausser continues:

The development of the situation forced a withdrawal to the south. That was the only way to make possible the operation Manstein had planned.

***

At that last possible moment — at 1250 hours on 15 February — the commanding general of the *SS-Panzer-Korps* issued the order to *Divisionsgruppe "Das Reich"* to fight its way back behind the Udy River. With armored support it was still just possible to bring the forces back through Kharkov and past the city to the southeast. As a result, it was possible to avoid the encirclement of one and a half divisions.

At 1300 hours that decision was reported to *Armee-Abteilung Lanz* and passed on to *Korps Raus*.

At 1600 hours the army order calling for the unconditional defense of Kharkov was renewed. — it had been overtaken by events. The withdrawal had succeeded!

The Lonely Decision

George Berger, at that time the assistant operations officer at the headquarters of the *SS-Panzer-Korps*, outlined the immediate circumstances of *SS-Obergruppenführer* Hausser's decision to evacuate Kharkov:

In his book, *"Verbrannte Erde"*, Paul Carell wrote of "the judicious disobedience of a German general." By that he meant the decision of the commanding general of the *SS-Panzer-Korps*, Paul Hausser, to evacuate his corps from the city of Kharkov in the face of an explicit *Führer* order to the contrary. In so doing, he laid the cornerstone for Manstein's offensive on the southern front that led to the destruction of the Russian 6th Army and other Russian formations, as well as to the recapture of Kharkov.

That decision to disobey a *Führer* order was something rare in the history of World War II and demonstrated the courage of the most important officers of the *Waffen-SS*.

On 11 February 1943 the *SS-Panzer-Korps* with *SS-Panzer-Grenadier-Divisionen "Leibstandarte SS Adolf Hitler"* and *"Das Reich"* was nearly encircled in Kharkov. It was faced with the same fate that had overtaken the *6. Armee* at Stalingrad unless the order to withdraw and evacuate the city arrived at the last moment.

On 13 February Russian armored formations broke through as far as the city limits. Only the road leading to the southwest to Poltawa could be kept open. As the assistant operations officer at the corps headquarters, I experienced the terrible hours before the breakout from Kharkov and personally watched the moral dilemma into which Hausser was plunged by a senseless order from the *Führer*.

Plainly and simply, the *Führer* order of 13 February stated: "Kharkov must be held." In a situation report to *Armee-Abteilung Lanz* Hausser requested permission to evacuate. His request was refused with reference to the order from the *Führer*. After several telephone conversations with the commander-in-chief of the army, *General* Lanz, the latter gave Hausser permission to personally talk with the commander-in-chief of the army group, *Generalfeldmarschall* von Manstein.

After many technical difficulties, I put that connection through in the evening of 13 February. Unfortunately, it was impossible to gain von Manstein's approval since it dealt with an explicit order from the *Führer*. However, *Generalfeldmarschall* von Manstein gave Hausser permission to turn directly to the *Führer* headquarters in order to personally present his case.

I was also able to connect to the *Wolfsschanze*. The chief of the general staff of the Army, *General* Zeitzler, promised Hausser that he would try again to elicit a different decision from the *Führer* in the situation conference with him that was scheduled for 0200 hours.

***

In the meantime, on 14 February, the orders for withdrawal had long since been written for *SS-Panzer-Grenadier-Divisionen "Leibstandarte SS Adolf Hitler"* and *"Das Reich"* and the division liaison officers were waiting impatiently at the door of the corps command post for the orders to be issued.

Late in the afternoon of 14 February Paul Hausser stepped out of the squat peasant hut into the biting frost and silently walked back and forth. All of a sudden he told me, quite calmly: "Please issue the withdrawal orders to the divisions." For a moment my breath stopped. Then I dared to raise an objection: "*Obergruppenführer*, the order from the *Führer* specifically states....". Paul Hausser interrupted me. "My old head does not matter, but I cannot do that to the youngsters outside. Simply issue the corps order."

***

As a result of the evacuation of Kharkov, a shortened line of resistance could be established for which the available forces were adequate. The enemy's continued advance could be halted by an orderly defense.

On 16 February the rearguards of *SS-Panzer-Grenadier-Division "Das Reich"* fought their way back through the city.

The Battle of Kharkov From the Russian Viewpoint

The Soviet Colonel W. P. Morosow wrote regarding the fighting in and around Kharkov during the period from 11 to 14 February 1943 in his book, *"Westlich von Woronesch"* as follows (excerpts):

On 11 February at 0820 hours the forces received their specific missions for the capture of Kharkov. According to the plans of General Rybalko, the 6th Guards Cavalry Corps was to unite with the 40th Army, block the Kharkov garrison from the west and, thus, cut it off completely. It was to build the outer encirclement front along the Peressetschnaja — Ljubotin — Rakitnoje line, twenty-five kilometers from the inner encirclement front. All formations received the orders that they were not to force the fascist troops out of the city of Kharkov but, instead, that they were to destroy them inside the city.

The enemy had brought the main bodies of *SS-Panzer-Grenadier-Divisionen "Das Reich"* and *"Leibstandarte SS Adolf Hitler"* from the northern Donez — in the case of *SS-Panzer-Grenadier-Division "Das Reich"* the main body at that point consisted only of *SS-Panzergrenadier-Regiment "Der Führer"*, minus the *I./SS-Panzergrenadier-Regiment "Der Führer"*! — They were concentrated west of Merefa. The enemy launched a counterattack from the Msha River against the cavalry formations. On 11 February the cavalrymen repulsed the attack, but still had to withdraw to the Borki — Ordiwka area.

In light of the situation, the commander of the Guards Cavalry Corps, General Sokolow, decided to pull his troops back to the south to the Ochotschaje — Melichowka area. He would regroup them there, launch a surprise attack into the flank of the advancing enemy group and penetrate into their rear in the Ljubotin area.

In the morning of 13 February the cavalry units, supported by the 21st Armored Brigade, organized an all-around defense in the Ochotschaje and Melichowka areas and held a favorable position in relation to the grouping of enemy armor. On 14 February the cavalry formations were involved in heavy defensive fighting in that area.

***

On 15 February *SS-Panzergrenadier-Regiment "Der Führer"* continued the attack. Within a few kilometers it had reestablished enemy contact. By then, however, the enemy was battered and the resistance was broken in a rapid advance.

In the meantime *SS-Panzer-Aufklärungs-Abteilung 1 "Leibstandarte SS Adolf Hitler"* captured Bereka in an aggressive advance to the south but was then encircled there by far superior enemy forces. The *II./SS-Panzergrenadier-Regiment "Der Führer"* was set in march to Bereka on the *SPW* of the *III./SS-Panzergrenadier-Regiment "Der Führer"* and was able to break the encirclement in a dashing attack. The enemy forces that were located there were then completely defeated by *SS-Panzer-Aufklärungs-Abteilung 1 "Leibstandarte SS Adolf Hitler"* and the *II./SS-Panzergrenadier-Regiment "Der Führer"*.

During the morning of 17 February alarming news reached the regiment from the friendly forces on the left, *Regiment Witt* of *SS-Panzer-Grenadier-Division "Leibstandarte SS Adolf Hitler"*. It was under flank attack from the east by strong enemy forces. *Regiment Witt* then consisted of only one reinforced battalion and was in a critical situation. The *SPW* of the *III./SS-Panzergrenadier-Regiment "Der Führer"* were sent to *Regiment Witt*. Mounted, the battalion launched an attack to the east that relieved the pressure. The attack also resulted in a decisive victory. In the afternoon, *Regiment Witt* could organize its troops for defense in the line designated in the orders, without significant losses.

The enemy's intentions were totally brought to naught. The cavalry corps whose mission was to cut the Kharkov — Poltawa supply road and close the ring around the city of Kharkov had been smashed by the greatly inferior German forces. It was a short, hard and successful opening note for the coming offensive operations of the *SS-Panzer-Korps.*

It had to be considered a success that the evacuation of Kharkov prevented the encirclement and destruction of one and one-half fully combat worthy *SS* divisions and made it possible for the defense to be conducted along a significantly shortened front. The decisive significance, however, was in freeing the main body of the *SS-Panzer-Korps* to carry on the attack to the south to establish contact with *Heeresgruppe Süd*, to which *Armee-Abteilung Lanz* had been attached since the elimination of *Heeresgruppe B.*

In this section on Kharkov the question has come up repeatedly of why the commanding general of the *SS-Panzer-Korps* had to take upon himself the thankless task and heavy burden of premeditated disobedience to an order from the *Führer*. Why was it that neither his superior, *General* Lanz nor, even more importantly, the commander-in-chief of *Heeresgruppe Süd, Generalfeldmarschall* von Manstein, accepted this responsibility?

Today it is a known fact that both superiors were of the same opinion as *SS-Obergruppenführer* Hausser. Indeed, Manstein even had a special interest in the preservation of the *SS-Panzer-Korps*. It would be his only operational reserve for future operations.

Manstein may always had a strained relationship with his supreme commander. Lanz had already made himself unpopular with Hitler by his order to withdraw *SS-Panzergrenadier-Division "Das Reich"* to the Donez and, again, to the area east of Kharkov. Apparently, both of them believed that an *SS* general would be the best one to refuse to carry out a *Führer* order. In any case, *Generalfeldmarschall* von Manstein did not ultimately cover Hausser's decision with respect to the *Führer* headquarters.

On 20 February Lanz was relieved of his position and replaced by *General der Panzertruppen* Werner Kempf. The justification was that Lanz was a *General der Gebirgstruppen* and that this action required a *Panzer* commander.

"The Judicious Disobedience of a German General"

Paul Carell outlined the dramatic events in the battle for Kharkov between 11 and 16 February 1943 as follows:

The Soviet "Woronesh Front", "Southwest Front" and "South Front" received orders, "to pursue the withdrawing enemy without regard to supply or enemy rearguards, to reach the Dnjepr before the start of the spring mud season and to cut off Manstein's retreat to the river."

The 11 February 1943 STAVKA order to "Southwest Front" stated: "You are to prevent the enemy from retreating to Dnjepropetrowsk and Saporoschje, force the enemy forces back to the Crimean peninsula, block access to the Crimea and, in so doing, cut off the German southern group."

There it was: The bold venture! That was the risk that Stalin had decided to take and on which Manstein had speculated.

One event especially caused the Soviet high command to err, a dramatic event: Namely, the judicious disobedience of a German general. It had the effect of a brilliant trick and yet it was no trick at all.

Hitler had issued strict orders on 11 February to *Armee-Abteilung Lanz* — which still belonged to *Heeresgruppe B* and was not yet attached to Manstein at the time — to hold Kharkov, although the city had already been operationally outmaneuvered by two Soviet armies and was facing encirclement.

The fateful mission of defending Kharkov fell to the newly formed *SS-Panzer-Korps* under *General der Waffen-SS* Paul Hausser that had just arrived from France.

The two elite divisions, *SS-Panzer-Grenadier-Division "Das Reich"* and *SS-Panzer-Grenadier-Division "Leibstandarte SS Adolf Hitler"*, belonged to that corps.

The order to hold Kharkov was foolish and informed by the apparent loss of prestige if the city were to fall. Manstein attempted to dissuade Hitler from it. Far more important than holding a city was the necessity of interdicting the enemy advancing south of Kharkov. The enemy had to be defeated and finally stopped. That would relieve the pressure on the left flank of *Heeresgruppe Süd* and prevent a Soviet breakthrough to and across the Dnjepr.

Hitler, however, did not want to give up the industrial and political metropolis of the Ukraine. Kharkov became a matter of prestige to him, as had Stalingrad before, in spite of all prior bad experiences. And he was prepared to send outstanding combat formations such as *SS-Panzer-Grenadier-Divisionen "Leibstandarte SS Adolf Hitler"* and *"Das Reich"* to the same fate that had overtaken the forces at Stalingrad.

Even on 13 February Hitler reiterated the strict order to hold Kharkov and, if necessary, set up an all-around defense there. Lanz passed the order on to Hausser. The obstinate *Führer* was reassured; he counted on the unconditional obedience of the *Waffen-SS* corps and overlooked the sober judgement, the operational wisdom and the moral courage of its commanding general, Paul Hausser.

And then something happened that proves false the legend that has been attached to the solders of the *Waffen-SS* and their officers, namely, that they had become unthinkingly obedient party forces.

On 14 February the impending encirclement of the city became clear. Packs of Soviet armor broke through the northern, northwestern and southeastern blocking positions and penetrated to the city limits of Kharkov. The Poltawa — Kharkov main supply route was under Soviet artillery fire. Hausser requested permission to break out from *General* Lanz. His sober evaluation of the situation is in the corps war diary for 14 February 1943 under entry 138/43. It reads:

> The enemy facing the east and northeast Kharkov front has been significantly strengthened on 14 February. Attacks on the Tschugujew and Woltschansk roads have been repulsed with the last reserves. There is a penetration twelve kilometers deep from the southern airfield to Ossonowa. Clearing that up is in progress with inadequate forces. *Infanterie-Division (mot.) "Großdeutschland"* has no forces to block the enemy breakthrough northwest of Kharkov. All attacking forces to the south are currently pinned by the enemy. The *320. Infanterie-Division* has not yet passed through the main line of resistance. Based on the conditions reported by the operations officer, offensive operations are ruled out for the next few days.
>
> Mobs are firing on soldiers and vehicles in Kharkov. There are no forces available to deal with that situation since all are at the front. The city, including railroad, rations supplies and ammunition dumps have been effectively destroyed in accordance with army orders. The city is on fire. A deliberate withdrawal becomes less probable each day. Prerequisites for the operational significance of Kharkov no longer appear to exist. A new Führer decision is required as to whether Kharkov should be held to the last man.

***

Above: East of Kharkov. **Below**: Hausser, the commanding general of the *II. SS-Panzer-Korps*, Lanz, the commander-in-chief of *Armee-Abteilung Lanz*, and Keppler, commander of *SS-Panzer-Grenadier-Division "Das Reich"* at the command post of *SS-Panzergrenadier-Regiment "Deutschland"* at Bely Kolodes during the encirclement of Kharkov.

General Lanz understood Hausser's appeal. However, he refused to override the order to hold the city in light of the clear order that Hitler had given him a few hours earlier as his definitive decision. Lanz' decision was made easier for him since the *320. Infanterie-Division*, which had been fighting its way back for weeks from the area of the shattered Hungarian 2nd Army, still had not made it to safety.

Paul Hausser — a wartime veteran and general staff officer of the *Kaiser's* army who retired from the pre-war German Army in 1932 as a *Generalleutnant* and who then transferred over to the *Waffen-SS* — was not content. Orders, even orders from the *Führer*, were not the commandments for him. He called Lanz and implored him. However, the general remained firm in his denial. Thereupon, Hausser radioed one more time to *Armee-Abteilung Lanz*:

"Decision regarding withdrawal required by 1200 hours. Signed: Hausser."

Lanz refused.

***

The *SS-Panzer-Korps* then reported in the afternoon:

> ...at 1645 hours on 14 February the order was issued to evacuate Kharkov and withdraw behind the Udy River during the night of 14/15 February. Message was passed on to *Korps Raus* at the same time. Evaluation of the situation follows in writing.

***

In light of the strict instructions from Hitler, Lanz, a mountain-troop general, was in an extremely difficult situation. Although he and his staff were at heart on Hausser's side, he ordered the following in radio message number 624 at 1725 hours:

> **The armored corps is to hold its present positions on the east side of Kharkov to the last man in accord with the Führer order.**

In the evening of 14 February *General* Lanz even ordered that the corps' attack forces that had gone over to the defensive to the south of the city were to give up formations for the defense of the city. At the same time, they were still to force the enemy out of Olschany to the south of the hotly contested city. The radio order from *Armee-Abteilung Lanz* read:

> *Führer* decision:
>
> 1.) The eastern defensive positions of Kharkov are to be held.
>
> 2.) The large *SS* formations that are arriving are to be employed to clear the lines of communications to Kharkov as well as to strike the enemy forces exerting pressure on Kharkov from the northwest.

An order that could not possibly be carried out!

***

In the center of the city the partisans were already openly in arms. Hausser, who had again conferred with his chief of staff, Ostendorff, and his operations officer, *Oberstleutnant i.G.* Müller, telephoned Lanz again that evening. However, the commander-in-chief of the army detachment again turned down the request for evacua-

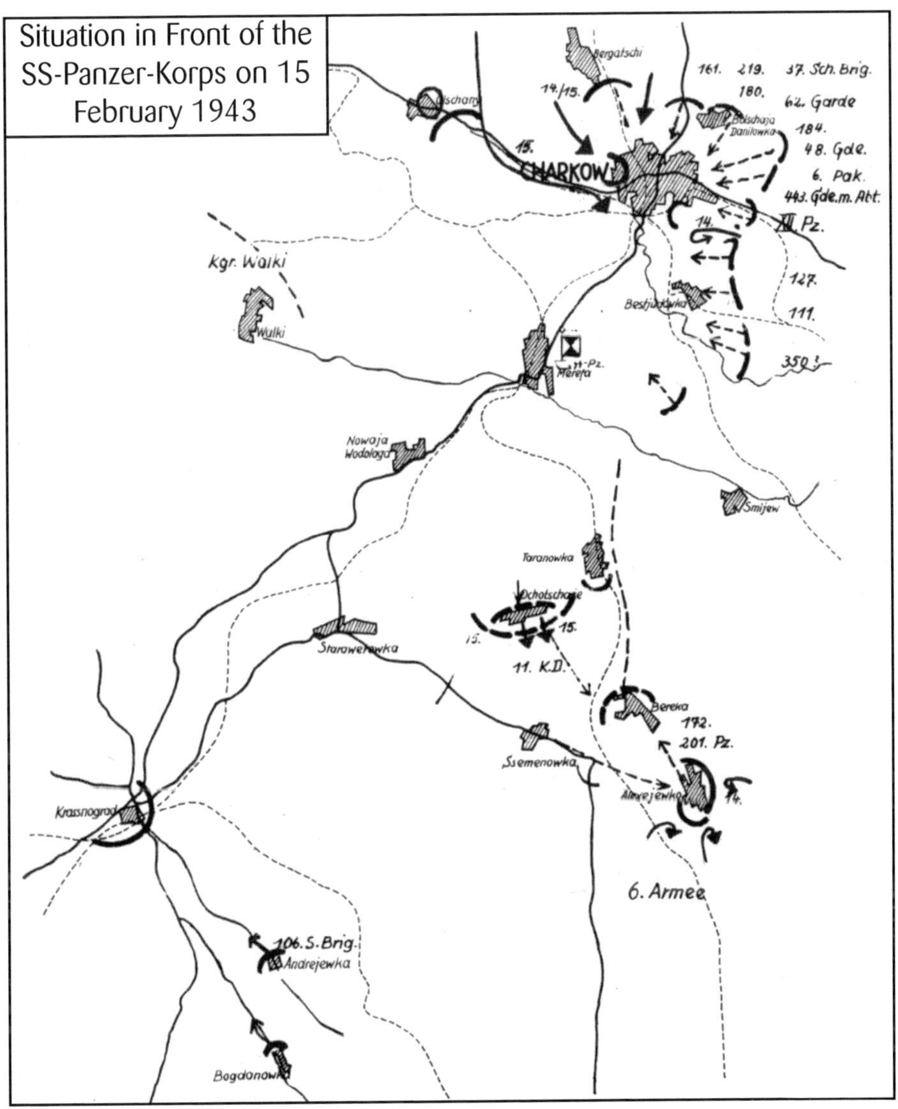

Situation in Front of the SS-Panzer-Korps on 15 February 1943

tion by referring to the order of the *Führer*. Stalingrad!

During the night of 14/15 February the Russians penetrated into the northwest and southeast portions of the city. A tank battalion of *SS-Panzer-Grenadier-Division "Das Reich"* was once more committed in an immediate counterattack.

On 15 February the Russians attacked again at noon. Only a tiny gap was still open southeast of the city. If that was closed, Hausser's corps and also *Infanterie-Division (mot.) "Großdeutschland"* in the northern part of the city would be lost. Stalingrad!

In that situation Hausser, in agreement with the neighboring *Korps Raus*, to which *Infanterie-Division (mot.) "Großdeutschland"* was attached, issued the orders to his divisions that the logic of the military art, the responsibility of the troop leader and the courage of the soldier called for: Evacuate their positions and fight their way back. Stalingrad did not take place!

At 1300 hours Hausser reported the decision to *Armee-Abteilung Lanz* with the following radio message:

> In order to prevent encirclement of troops and save equipment, the order was issued at 1300 hours to clear a way through behind the Udy River at the outskirts of the city. Breakthrough currently in progress. Street fighting in the southwestern and western parts of the city.

The message went into the ether. The refusal of obedience to an order from the *Führer*. What would happen?

At 1530 hours Hausser's signals section received the strict order from *General* Lanz: "Kharkov is to be defended under all circumstances!"

But Hausser did not let that concern him; he did not answer. He broke out to the southwest. The tanks opened the way for the grenadiers. Artillery, *Flak* and combat engineers covered the flanks, interdicted the pursuing enemy and then turned around at the Udy River. Twenty-four hours later the rearguards of *SS-Panzer-Grenadier-Division "Das Reich"* fought their way through the burning city.

At the road intersections, in the flickering light of the burning buildings, were the powerful assault guns of *Infanterie-Division (mot.) "Großdeutschland"*. They awaited the rearguards of their division. After Hausser's breakout order, *General* Hoernlein's division evacuated its positions northwest of Kharkov and fought its way back through the city. The battle followed the logic of the front, not the unrealistic order from Rastenburg.

The veteran *Infanterie-Division (mot.) "Großdeutschland"* also had the most difficult defensive fighting behind it.

During the morning hours, the last messengers and *SPW* of Remer's battalion dashed through the streets. Russians who had infiltrated already fired on them from windows and ruins. Partisans raised a giant red flag at Red Square.

And what happened in the *Wolfschanze*? Pale with rage, Hitler received the report of the disobedience of his *SS-Panzer-Korps*. However, before it was clear what he should do to Hausser, it already began to become evident how correct Hausser's decision had been. Two indispensable, fully equipped and veteran mechanized infantry divisions as well as *Infanterie-Division (mot.)"Großdeutschland"* were saved for the decisive phase of the defensive fighting.

Moreover, the resistance offered by the defenders of Kharkov and their counterattack had also made possible the passage of lines of *Generalmajor* Postel's *320. Infanterie-Division* to *Armee-Abteilung Lanz*. The temporary evacuation of Kharkov, despite all fears to the contrary, had worked out to be a good move from an operational standpoint.

However, what no one on the German side could perceive was the psychological effect of the evacuation of Kharkov on Stalin and his general staff, as is confirmed today from Soviet sources. The liberation of Kharkov, the fourth largest city of the Soviet Union, did more than just heighten the Soviet mood of victory. Far more important, Stalin saw in it a confirmation for the presumption that the Germans planned to withdraw. He knew Hitler and he considered it unimaginable that his "Praetorian Guard" would evacuate Kharkov unless a general retreat had been ordered.

Logically thought out! And yet false. For Stalin had not included the unwavering moral courage of one man. (Paul Carell, *Verbrannte Erde*, pp. 159-163. Frankfurt am Main / Berlin (West): Verlag Ullstein GmbH, 1966)

***

SS-Obergruppenführer und General der Waffen-SS Hausser wrote the following in his personal notes concerning his decision at Kharkov:

My personal opinion is that the decision of the commanding general of the *SS-Panzer-Korps* to evacuate Kharkov and, in so doing, to strengthen Manstein's decisive left wing was an essential fundamental prerequisite for Manstein's success.

In the work by A. Philippi and F. Heim, *Der Feldzug gegen Sowjetrußland 1941-45 — ein operativer Rückblick,* that is clear between the lines but is otherwise unmentioned.

***

By 17 February the southern attack group had reached Tanarowka. *SS-Obergruppenführer* Hausser checked out the situation with the *Kampfgruppe* of *SS-Panzer-Grenadier-Division "Leibstandarte SS Adolf Hitler"* in his *Fiesler Storch* and then flew to *Armee-Abteilung Lanz*. He there received new instructions that the *SS-Panzer-Korps* was to continue its withdrawal on 17 February behind the Mscha River. In the Krassnograd area the corps would be reorganized for its decisive employment as part of Manstein's operational plans.

With a total of three fully combat-ready *SS-Panzer-Grenadier-Divisionen* — *SS-Panzer-Grenadier-Division "Totenkopf"* had arrived and assembled in the meantime — the *SS-Panzer-Korps* was ready for new employment.

SS-Panzergrenadier-Regiment "Der Führer", which had been attached to *SS-Panzer-Grenadier-Division "Leibstandarte SS Adolf Hitler"*, was released from its attachment, set in march to Krassnograd and again attached to *SS-Panzer-Grenadier-Division "Das Reich"*.

The brilliant and decisive operations that followed under *Generalfeldmarschall* von Manstein showed how correct and decisive the evacuation of Kharkov was. These operations saved the southern front. They would not have been possible without the decisive employment of the *SS-Panzer-Korps*.

APPENDICES

Appendix 1:
Major Operations of the Division from 19 August 1941 to 18 February 1943

19 August - 1 September 1941: Army group reserve for *Heeresgruppe Mitte*

4 - 18 September 1941: Pursuit in the battle of Kiev

20 - 24 September 1941: Fighting in area east of Kiev

2 - 4 October 1941: Breakthrough through the Desna position

8 - 13 October 1941: Advance via Gshatsk

14 - 26 October 1941: Breakthrough through the Moscow defense position

27 October - 16 November 1941: Defensive fighting west of Moscow

17 November - 4 December 1941: Capture of Istra and Solnechnogorsk

5 - 21 December 1941: Defensive fighting outside of Moscow

22 - 31 December 1941: Defensive fighting in the Rusa and Wolokolamsk positions

1 - 17 January 1942: Defensive fighting in the winter positions of the *9. Armee*

19 - 20 February 1942: Winter battle of Rshew (only *SS-Infanterie-Regiment "Der Führer"*)

19 January - 7 February 1942: Offensive fighting northwest of Sytschewka (Division minus *SS-Infanterie-Regiment "Der Führer"*)

9 - 20 February 1942: Defensive fighting in Volga bend west of Rshew (Division minus *SS-Infanterie-Regiment "Der Führer"*)

25 February - 13 March 1942: Offensive operations between Rshew railroad — Olenino — Ossugo (*Kampfgruppe "SS-Reich"*)

17 March - 8 April 1942: Defensive fighting in Volga bend west of Rshew (*Kampfgruppe "SS-Reich"*)

9 - 10 April 1942: Defensive fighting in Olenino — Nelidowo area (*Kampfgruppe "SS-Reich"*)

15 April - 24 July 1942: Employment on the home front

25 July - 7 November 1942: Occupation duty in northern France

6 - 20 November 1942: Staging at the demarcation line

21 - 28 November 1942: Occupation of remainder of France

27 November 1942: Coup de main against Toulon (Only *SS-Kradschützen-Bataillon "Das Reich"*)

29 November - 19 December 1942: Coastal defense of Mediterranean (Only *SS-Kradschützen-Bataillon "Das Reich"*)

20 December 1942 - 15 January 1943: Occupation duty in France

23 - 24 January 1943: Defensive fighting in the Donez area (Only *I./SS-Panzergrenadier-Regiment "Der Führer"*)

25 - 28 January 1943: *OKH* reserve in *Heeresgruppe B* (Division minus *I./SS-Panzergrenadier-Regiment "Der Führer"*)

29 January - 1 February 1943: Defensive fighting and fighting retreat between the Don and Oskol Rivers (Division minus *I./SS-Panzergrenadier-Regiment "Der Führer"*)

2 - 18 February 1943: Defensive fighting in the Kharkov area of operations (Division minus *I./SS-Panzergrenadier-Regiment "Der Führer"*)

14 - 15 February 1943: Evacuation of city of Kharkov (Division minus *I./SS-Panzergrenadier-Regiment "Der Führer"*)

Appendix 2:
Operational Attachments of the Division from 19 August 1941 to 18 February 1943

5 June - 1 September 1941: *XXXXVI. Panzer-Korps* (*General der Panzertruppen* von Vietinghoff)

1 - 7 September 1941: *Panzergruppe 2* (*Generaloberst* Guderian)

7 - 24 September 1941: *XXIV. Panzer-Korps* (*General der Panzertruppen* von Schweppenburg)

24 September - 3 October 1941: *LVII. Panzer-Korps* (*General der Panzertruppen* Kuntze)

3 October - 13 December 1941: *XXXX. Panzer-Korps* (*General der Panzertruppen* Stumme)

13 December 1941 - 15 January 1942: *4. Panzer-Armee* (*Generaloberst* Hoepner) and *9. Armee* (*Generaloberst* Model)

15 January - 18 February 1942: *VI. Armee-Korps* (*9. Armee*) (*General der Infanterie* Biehler) (Only *SS-Infanterie-Regiment "Der Führer"*)

25 January - 9 February 1942: *XXXXVI. Panzer-Korps* (*General der Panzertruppen* von Vietinghoff) (Division minus *SS-Infanterie-Regiment "Der Führer"*)

8 - 12 February 1942: *VI. Armee-Korps* (*General der Infanterie* Biehler) (Staff of *SS-Infanterie-Regiment "Deutschland"* and the I./*SS-Infanterie-Regiment "Deutschland"*)

9 - 18 February 1942: *VI. Armee-Korps* (*General der Infanterie* Biehler) (Divisional staff and *SS-Kradschützen-Bataillon "Reich"*)

18 February - 1 June 1942: *XXXXVI. Panzer-Korps* (*General der Panzertruppen* von Vietinghoff) (*Kampfgruppe "SS-Reich"*)

15 April - 1 June 1942: Fallingbostel Training Area and the *SS* Main Office (Division minus *Kampfgruppe "SS-Reich"*)

1 June - 24 July 1942: Fallingbostel Training Area and the *SS* Main Office (All of division)

1 - 24 July 1942: *7. Armee* (*Generaloberst* Dollmann) (*SS-Infanterie-Regiment "Der Führer"*)

24 July - 12 August 1942: *7. Armee* (*Generaloberst* Dollmann) (Entire division)

12 August 1942 - 18 February 1943: *SS-Panzer-Korps* (*SS-Obergruppenführer* Hausser)

20 January - 7 March 1943: *Armee-Abteilung Fretter-Pico* (*I./SS-Panzergrenadier-Regiment "Der Führer"*)

Appendix 3:
Organizational Charts of the Division as SS-Panzergrenadier-Division "Das Reich" in 1942

Kriegsgliederung der SS-Division DAS REICH
als Panzer-Grenadier-Division, 1942

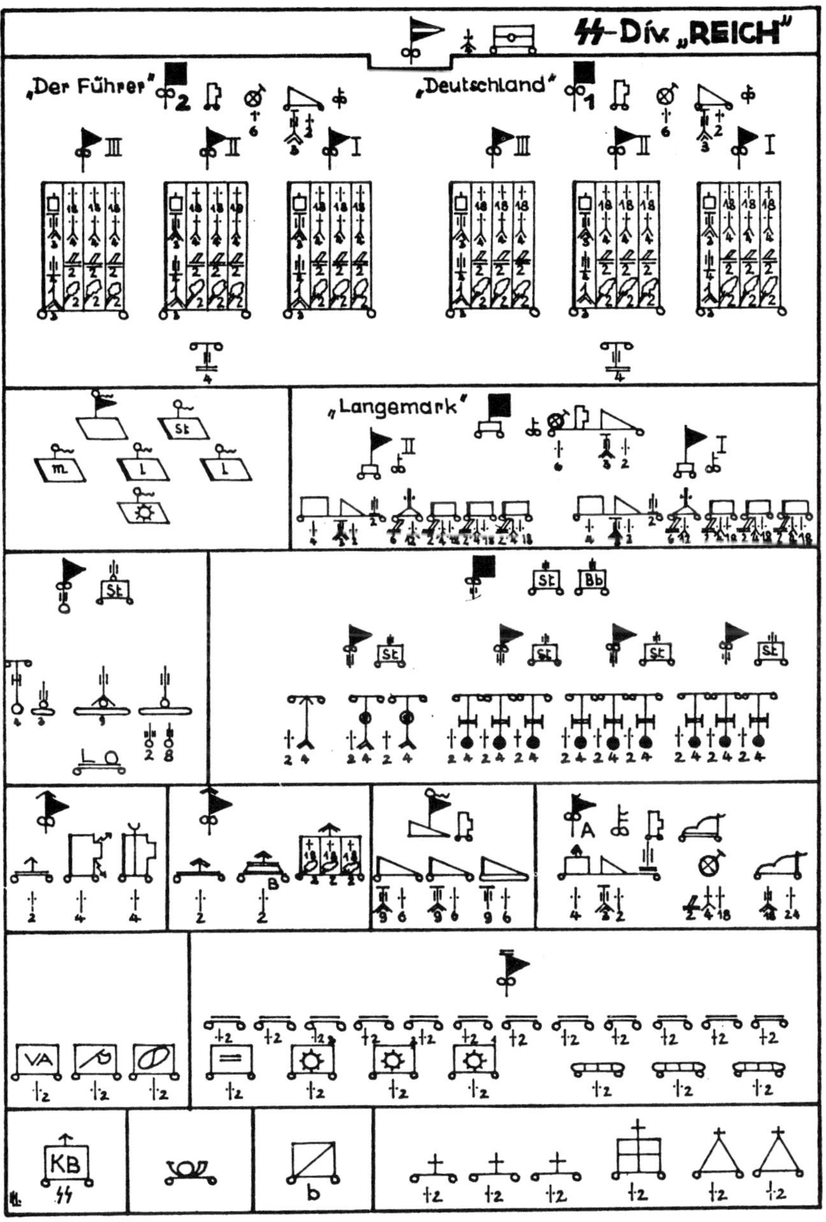

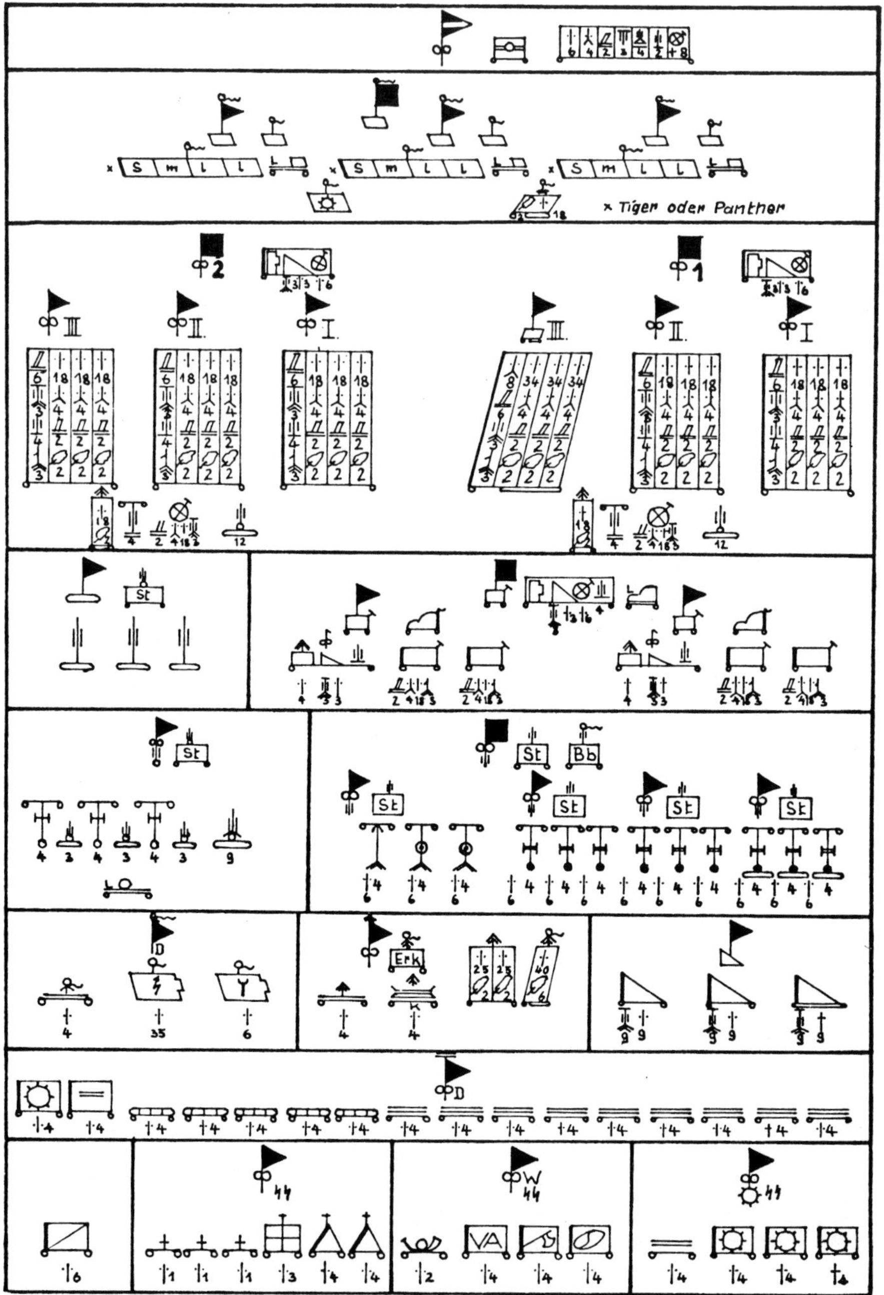
× Tiger oder Panther

Tactical Signs

Telegraph construction company

Field-cable company

Radio company

Radio section

Backpack radio section

Division Staff

Regimental staff, Panzer-Grenadier-Regiment

Regimental staff, Panzer-Regiment

Regimental staff, artillery regiment

Battalion staff, Panzer-Grenadier-Regiment

Battalion staff, artillery regiment

Battalion staff, combat engineer battalion

Battalion staff, tank battalion

Battalion staff, antitank battalion

Supply section

Fuel section

Maintenance company

Provost service; military police

Field post office

Medical company

Ambulance platoon

Field hospital

Butcher company

Field bakery company

Tactical Signs

Light machine gun

Heavy machine gun

Light infantry gun (75 mm)

Heavy infantry gun (150 mm)

Light mortar (50 mm)

Heavy mortar (80 mm)

Light Pak (37 mm)

Medium Pak (50/75 mm)

Defensive position

Light field howitzer (105 mm)

Heavy field howitzer (150 mm)

SP light field howitzer (105 mm)

Heavy Flak (88 mm)

Light Flak (quad 20 mm)

Medium Flak (37 mm)

SP light Flak (20 mm)

Antitank company

Reconnaissance company

Tank company

Motorcycle company

Light engineer section

Bridging section

Signals company

Telephone company

Appendix 4:
A Farewell to SS-Oberstgruppenführer und Generaloberst der Waffen-SS Paul Hausser (1880-1972), the First Divisional Commander

His motto: " I serve!"

A Farewell to Paul Hausser, *SS-Oberstgruppenführer und Generaloberst der Waffen-SS*

During the morning hours of 21 December 1972 *Generaloberst der Waffen-SS* Paul Hausser died in Ludwigsburg near Stuttgart shortly after his 92nd birthday. The death of *Papa* Hausser, as all his old soldiers respectfully and trustingly called him, symbolized to a special degree the end of an epoch that spanned from the *Kaiser's* Imperial Empire of the 19th century to our own day. What a shattering historical allegory: On the same day that the first commander of *SS-Division "Das Reich"* closed his eyes forever, the empire that von Bismarck founded was finally destroyed in the divided capital city of Berlin...(a reference to the legal recognition by the Federal Republic of Germany of the German Democratic Republic as a separate state).

The news of the death of the general — generally ignored by the daily press — traveled like wildfire throughout German-speaking countries, indeed, through all of Europe. The sad news made it to wherever men of the deceased army leader's troops lived, often by word of mouth. Even though the Christmas holidays were imminent and many were on the road, when the news arrived they did their best to meet the "Senior" of the *Waffen-SS* one more time, to pay him final respects and accompany him on his final journey.

The first arrived in the city early in the morning of 28 December. Among them were comrades from Vienna and Salzburg who had traveled by private automobile and by bus. And the stream of mourners did not let up. The vehicles with license plates of many countries assembled on the large parking lot at the city hall, frequently draped with signs of mourning. Others arrived by rail. They came from all points of the compass, from all of the federal republic, from Austria, Flanders, Switzerland, France, Holland, even from Sweden and Finland.

In the early afternoon hours a cold, pale blue sky arched over Ludwigsburg. The destination of the many mourners was the New Cemetery, where Sepp Dietrich had also rested for the past six years.

More and more people continued to arrive until, finally, more than three thousand assembled as a huge mass of people. The small memorial hall could hold barely two hundred persons, but on the square outside, on the paths between the rows of graves, there they stood, silently mourning. Old and young stood beside each other, men injured in the war, fathers with their sons, a few wearing the uniform of the *Bundeswehr.* There were old men, gray haired, marked by the years and the scars of the war alongside widows of fallen comrades. Men blinded in the war, arm in arm with their wives or carefully led by comrades. Here and there a Knight's Cross shone in the light of the winter sun. Weathered faces of men in traditional costumes who had hastened from the mountains, their countenances evidencing their pain and their feelings. More than half an hour before the start of the ceremonies they already stood silent and waiting, as if they wanted, together, to mount one final guard for their honored *Papa* Hausser — united in mourning the great man and comrade who was laid out there in the hall.

Twelve Knight's Cross recipients formed a guard of honor inside the memorial hall at the closed coffin, which was covered with splendid flowers. At the side stood the highly decorated bearers of the boxes holding his decorations. From one of the boxes shimmered the Knight's Cross with Oakleaves and Swords. Motionless, like statues, the bearers of the Knight's Cross stood watch. All of them in their military careers had once served in units that were under the command of the deceased military leader.

The funeral service in the chapel was broadcast by loudspeakers to the tightly pressed thousands who waited in silence. The Evangelical pastor based his sermon on the biblical verse, "Be faithful unto death and I shall give you the crown of life." They were the words that had accompanied the deceased and his wife on their life's path since those words had initiated a marriage lasting sixty years.

Then, in accord with the wishes of the deceased general, the only speaker, retired *General* Otto Kumm, offered the eulogy, the final salute to the deceased. His striking words came directly from the heart of the old soldier, and among all the thousands of veterans present, it is likely that there was not one who was unmoved. In the name of all, he took leave of the dead commander:

Highly honored *Herr Generaloberst,*
Dear *Papa* Hausser.

For the last time we stand gathered around you…your old comrades-in-arms at the side of your most venerated family. We cannot and will not let you leave us. Each of us leaves a void behind him when he is summoned to the great army — larger or smaller, depending on his influence on his fellow human beings. After a period of mourning and of rebellion against fate, the void is closed. Others walk in our place.

However, the void that you, *Herr Generaloberst*, have left behind will never close!

The sublime greatness of your personality, the influence of your intellect and character were too great, the love and affection of all your soldiers too deep! Thus you shall live on for all time in our ranks. — There is hardly a gathering of our comrades without your presence as the radiant central point. We do not wish to thus rob you of the rest that you have been granted after a long and difficult path. No — but just as we were ready at all times to do our duty for you, thus would we also remain in the future, as one man, inspired by your strength and following your will.

When you, *Herr Generaloberst,* after a distinct military career from the cadet school through the First World War to infantry commander in Magdeburg and

SS-Oberstgruppenführer und Generaloberst der Waffen-SS
Paul Hausser (1880-1972)

DISOBEDIENCE

Is it permissible, at this point in a book of reminiscences, to examine the concept at least superficially? There will always be a legitimate variety of opinions regarding the estimate of a situation. Orders end the discussion. Without obedience no armed forces can exist. If the subordinate feels that an order is wrong, he must report his opinion, explain his reasons and request that the order be changed. If the superior command holds to its original concept, the subordinate must obey. If he believes that he cannot carry out the order and operates on his own initiative, then he must take the consequences. If a newsmagazine declares that disobedience is a sign of "initiative", then it overlooks one of the obligations of a troop commander: *"responsibility for the forces under his command!"* The threat of destruction of his troops must awaken the commander's conscience! That is how it was at Kharkov! The decision to disobey does not come lightly to a responsible man, especially with regard to an order that has been repeated three times by the supreme command. The feeling that all the intermediate levels of command were in secret agreement was a help! In addition there was the cautionary example of "Stalingrad", which had just ended in catastrophe about two weeks earlier. The intermediate levels of command, however, cannot be measured with the same scale. The decision to disobey could NOT be demanded of them. Only the immediate commander who daily shares the experience of his troops in combat and also listens to them is in that position. Essential to correct judgement are education, human experience and, probably, also a bit of courage.

Generalleutnant in the *Reichswehr*, came to our young force in 1934, a new day began for that force. As commander of *Junkerschule Braunschweig* you first trained and educated the new generation of officers to be professionals. Then, as inspector, you formed the young battalions and, in so doing, laid the foundation stone for later victories. As commander of *SS-Division "Das Reich"* — in the west and in the east — your art of leadership, outstanding courage, your endurance — which was a daily wonder to us all — and your undemanding personality left its deep impress in all our hearts. When you were seriously wounded in front of the Moscow defensive position — in the immediate vicinity of our regiment's command post — a tremor shook the entire division and many a hard heart softened.

One year later, as a commanding general, you united our three oldest divisions in your *Panzer-Korps Hausser*. It was then clear to us all that, in so doing, your would cut a particularly deep notch in the tree of history. And that did not take long to happen.

After the fateful blow of Stalingrad and the nearly complete collapse of the southern wing of the Eastern Front — the corps had fallen back before vastly superior enemy forces to the city limits of Kharkov — the exceeding greatness of your personality made itself evident. Contrary to the repeated order of the *Führer* that Kharkov was to be defended to the last man, you withdrew the corps from the city. In so doing you saved it from destruction and gave *Heeresgruppe Manstein* the opportunity to stop the Soviet offensive in a large-scale counterattack and restore the front in the south. That was a deed — comparable to Taurrogen (an allusion to another incident of disobedience in German military history) — that, for you personally, entailed the possibility of the direst consequences and, to this day, has yet to find suitable recognition in the history of the Second World War. We shall ensure that this great deed receives the recognition it deserves. Until now, your proverbial modesty has held us back. With the courageous deed at Kharkov every last grenadier of your forces was forever bonded to you. Thus it is understandable how joyful your oldest troop units were a year later to have brought you — wounded again, it is true, but alive — out of the Falaise pocket.

After the operations in Normandy as commander-in-chief of the *7. Armee* came your last call to duty as commander-in-chief of *Heeresgruppe Süd*, in which soldiers of all branches of the military were subordinated to you. With that you were recognized as a truly great military commander. Your high decorations from both world wars — above all, the Knight's Cross with Oakleaves and Swords — are only small visible signs of your great military accomplishments.

How dark, then, was your lot when you had to spend precious years of your life in shabby American clothing on a wretched sack of straw. And yet, there more than ever, you radiated true chivalry. You bore yourself in such a manner that demanded admiration from all and helped hundreds of thousands who shared that fate to survive that time unbroken. In that difficult time you became a legendary father figure and, in every new prison camp, the first question of our comrades was: "How is *Papa* Hausser?" — Uncompromising, you pursued your course. Before the great court of justice you defended the innocence and fairness of your troops. You took up the pen and, in two works and innumerable letters, you fought for equal treatment for our soldiers — Soldiers Like the Rest [the title of one of Hausser's books] — for whom you felt personally responsible to the highest degree. For that we thank you. The responsibility is now taken from you and we shall attempt to carry that forward, following the path you have charted. We shall requite your unshakeable loyalty to us as we solemnly pledge that your deeply revered wife, your daughter, your grandchildren and great grandchildren shall never be forsaken. So long as a single one of us lives, they shall remain under our protection. We shall carry on your work, most venerated *Generaloberst*: The vindication of the honor of our soldiers. We shall carry on the *HIAG* (*Hilfsgemeinschaft auf Gegenseitigkeit* = Mutual Aid Society = the non-governmental welfare organization for former *Waffen-SS* personnel) and the social work that bears your revered name as our mission from you. Your entire life had one theme, to serve the fatherland. In spite of the spirit of the times and hostile circumstances, we will also hold high the concept of the fatherland. *Herr Generaloberst,* greet our dead comrades for us!

***

Though all become unfaithful, we shall yet remain true!

***

Without a word and deeply moved, the great family in mourning of the faithful of old stood. The words that had just been spoken echoed for a long time.

Then the mourners moved from the memorial hall to the crematorium a hundred meters away. The procession was led by the city orchestra of Ludwigsburg — Ossweil that intoned the measured steps of Chopin's funeral march. Then came the countless wreaths accompanied by the representatives of the formations and the veterans' associations. Behind them walked the bearers of the boxes with the decorations. The coffin of the dead *Generaloberst* Paul Hausser was escorted by Knight's cross recipients of all branches of the military, followed by the family and close friends of the deceased. *Papa* Hausser's final journey led through innumerable ranks of men and women pressed tightly along the path.

Silently they saluted their old comrade, all the comrades from greater and often more difficult times. Here and there among the crowd soldiers and officers of the *Bundeswehr* silently raised their hand to their cap. They also honored the great field captain and man one more time. And it was not without a certain bitterness. Those men of the *Bundeswehr*, by order from the highest places, had to take part in the funeral as "private" individuals. The state denied one of its greatest sons the final respects. No wreath was placed by the army...

In accord with long-standing military tradition, the coffin arrived to the strains of the "Prussian Presentation March". There the speakers of the organizations, soldiers' associations and veterans' groups said farewell for the last time and placed their wreaths. That was accompanied by brief, incisive words that expressed all the more clearly the close connection with the deceased.

Who could cite all the names — a few shall represent the whole. There were the former Hungarian volunteers, the comrades from *SS-Division "Reich"*, those from the *I.* and *II. Panzer-Korps,* the association of the *Ritterkreuzträger*, the association of German soldiers, the *Stalhelm* and the *Kyffhäuserbund*, the social work that bore the name of the deceased, the *HIAG* and, naturally, the comrades from Austria. But there were also French companions in arms from *Division "Charlemagne"*. Their Danish and Dutch comrades stood, moved, at the coffin of the man who, for them, decades earlier had been not only a German, but also a European general in whose formations men of the entire continent had fought shoulder to shoulder.

***

The casket of the *Generaloberst* slowly sank into the grave to the strains of the soldiers' song, *"Ich hatte einen Kameraden..."* After a moment of silence, the impressive melody of the German national anthem, rose loud and clear over the breadth of the great cemetery. All joined, deeply moved, in singing the verses.

***

The funeral was over, but no one stirred. From nearly three thousand throats the old song of loyalty rose on high, sung from passionate hearts. And, like an oath, it resounded over the men: "Though all become unfaithful, we shall yet remain true, so that there shall always be a banner for you on earth..."

Then the great body of mourners silently went their separate ways. But the old soldiers, hastily convened from all of Europe, sat together for a long time in the city hall of Ludwigsburg. Thoughts flew back to the time that they had shared together whose fire, joys and passion were the foundation of the close comradeship existing to the present day. And each took with him on his way home the certainty that the word of honor — loyalty — had lost nothing of its strength and would continue to live on — until sod covered the very last of them.

Walter H. Hefti

Appendix 5: Author's Thanks to his Collaborators

The author thanks all who have collaborated in this third volume of the history of the division, including:

Generaloberst a. D. Paul Hausser (deceased) for turning over his valuable handwritten notes.

Herr Oberarchivrat Dr. Stahl, director of the Bundesarchiv/Militärarchiv Freiburg/Breisgau and *Herr Archivamtmann Ziggel* for their friendly support in the archival work.

Herr Dr. Arenz of the *Militärgeschichtlichen Forschungsamt Freiburg/Breisgau* for his advice on all technical questions

Former company commander Heinz Lindner for drawing the numerous sketch maps as well as for drawing the routes of march and operations of the division.

Former company commander Gert Schmager (deceased) for procuring files and the initial treatment of the "The Winter Fighting at Rshew".

Former adjutant of SS-Kradschützen-Bataillon "Reich" Hermann Buch for his personal diary entries and writings, for his cooperation in the reconstruction of the routes of march and operations of the division and for providing photographs.

Former "regimental photographer" Ferry Fendt of Vienna, who made available a large number of the photographs.

Member of the SS-Panzergrenadier-Regiment "Der Führer" Association Walter Schallowetz for the print of the memorial page for *Generaloberst a. D.* Paul Hausser (see appendices) and for his generous support.

Members of the SS-Panzergrenadier-Regiment "Der Führer" Association Burkhardt, Lindner and Schallowetz for their support and cooperation.

SS-Panzergrenadier-Regiment "Der Führer" Association for financing the procurement of all the documents and all the costs that arose.

All of the commanders, officers, noncommissioned officers and enlisted men of all formations of the division who have made their contribution to the division history by offering their diaries, reports, sketch maps and pictures.

Appendix 6:
Whereabouts of the Wartime Files of the Waffen-SS

The author has been given the following notarized, sworn declaration of former *SS-Hauptscharführer* Georg Streicher dated 15 May 1970 regarding the whereabouts of the wartime files of the *Waffen -SS* — evidently including the war diaries of the division.

Sworn Declaration

I, the undersigned, Georg Streicher, born on 16 November 1919 in Aalen/Württemberg, declare under oath that on 9 May 1945 in the village of Gottesgab in the Erz Mountains about 10-12 kilometers east of Johanngeorgenstadt, seven trucks — two Fords and five captured French Berliths — were set on fire by myself. Those trucks were loaded with containers whose contents were wartime files.

Those trucks were escorted by an *SS-Oberscharführer* Maier or Meier with an "e". With them were also four *SS-Rottenführer*, two *SS-Sturmmänner* and four *SS-Männer* as drivers and armed escort. The *SS-Oberscharführer* was known to me from the Wildflecken Training Area and was at that time also a member of the newly activated *SS-Panzer-Abteilung "Wiking"*.

On 9 May 1945 I arrived via Kaaden — Schmiedeberg in the village of Gottesgab at 1500 hours and wanted to go to Johanngeorgenstadt. I met the column with the seven trucks at the outskirts of the village about 200 meters below the church on a meadow and joined it. In the course of the conversation it came out that the cargo came from a castle east of Prague at Kolin. The men had loaded the containers on the trucks early in the morning and were to bring them to Bavaria. Furthermore, the soldiers did not know that the war was already over.

There was no longer any possibility of making it through to the south. For those reasons we decided to destroy the entire cargo. Also our vehicles and all of our possessions. I still had about a thousand liters of diesel oil and 200 liters of gasoline. We drove the trucks together and doused everything with fuel. We had unloaded a few containers so that they would burn better. In so doing I discovered labels on the chests such as *Standarte Germania* and *Deutschland.*

Since I was formerly with *Germania* I inspected the contents and determined that they were war diaries of the field units. I took with me the [diaries that covered the] French campaign in which I had taken part and later read them. In part they were signed by Demelhuber and by Dörffler-Schuband.

I destroyed them too at Rautenkranz. There was nothing left of the trucks. The others and I remained there until 9 May and slept in the open by the fire. We separated near Hof; north Germans going toward Thuringia and Saxony. We south Germans went toward Nuremberg. That *SS-Oberscharführer* was, as I recall, from near Magdeburg. One of the *SS-Rottenführer* was later with me in Prison Camp 73 at Kornwestheim, barracks A. I do not know what happened to him subsequently because I was moved to the prison at Schwäbisch-Hall, then to Mannheim and then Heilbronn.

I can swear to all of the above and declare that I have made all statements correct to the best of my knowledge and recollection. The fact that I have not spoken of the files and the like until today is because I read in the book by *Herr* Weidinger that these files were not to be found. For that reason I have made this declaration because I did not know that these records were being sought.

Georg Streicher
Former *SS-Hauptscharführer*

Sources and Bibliography

Unpublished Sources

Bundesarchiv/Militärarchiv Freiburg/Breisgau:

Gen. Kdo. XXXXVI. Pz.-Korps, Bestand-Nr. 30241/2: 20 - 23 August 1941; 25 January - 9 February 1942; 18 February - 1 June 1942

Gen. Kdo. XXIV. Pz.-Korps, Bestand-Nr. 21363/19 and *6*: 7 September - 24 September 1941

Gen. Kdo. XXXX. Pz. Korps, Bestand-Nr. 31093/1: 3 October - 13 December 1941

Gen. Kdo. VI. AK with appendices

In addition:

Gen. Kdo. SS-Pz. -Korps, Microkopie-Nr. T-354, Rollen 116 and *119*

Private Sources:

War diary, *SS-Infanterie-Regiment "Deutschland"*, Microkopie T-354, Roll 121

Generaloberst a. D. Paul Hausser, personal handwritten notes

Otto Kumm, personal notes

Armee-Oberkommando 9 after-action report (reprint): *"Die Winterschlacht von Rshew"*

XXXXVI. Panzer-Korps, Errinerungsschrift für Kommandeure: "Die Winter-Kesselschlacht von Sytschewka, 25.1 - 12.2. 1942", 15 December 1942, *Abt. Ic Nr. 242/42 geh.*

XXXXVI. Panzer-Korps, Errinerungsschrift: "Abwehrschlacht im Wolgabogen", 15 April 1942, *Abt. Ic Nr. 800/42* (reprint)

SS-Panzer-Korps, Zusammenfassender Bericht: "SS-Panzer-Korps in der Schlacht zwischen Donez und Dnjepr" (reprint)

War diary of *SS-Sturmgeschütz-Batterie "Reich"*

War diary of *SS-Kradschützen-Bataillon "Reich"*

War diary of the *4./SS-Kradschützen-Bataillon "Reich"*

Hermann Buch, former adjutant of *SS-Kradschützen-Bataillon "Reich"*, personal diary entries and after-action reports

Oberstleutnant Freiherr von Reccum, materials for the divisional history of the *251. Infanterie-Division*

Oberst a. D. Walter Straub, *Geschichte des Panzerregiments 7* (mimeograph)

Published Sources

Burdick, *Prof. Dr. Furchtlos und treu (zum 75. Geburtstag von General der Gebirgstruppen Hubert Lanz)*. Cologne: Markus-Verlagsgesellschaft GmbH, 1971.

Carell, Paul. *Unternehmen Barbarossa*. Frankfrut am main / Berlin (West): Verlag Ullstein GmbH, 1963.

——-. *Verbrannte Erde*. Frankfrut am main / Berlin (West): Verlag Ullstein GmbH, 1966.

Cerff, Karl. *Die Waffen-SS im Wehrmachtbericht*. Osnabrück: Munin Verlag, 1971.

Guderian, Heinz. *Erinnerungen eines Soldaten*. Heidelberg: Kurt-Vowinckel-Verlag, 1960.

Günther, Helmut. *Heiße Motoren — Kalte Füße*. Neckargemünd: Kurt-Vowinckel-Verlag, 1963.

Haupt, Werner. *Heeresgruppe Mitte*. Bad Nauheim: Podzun-Pallas-Verlag, 1968.

Hausser, Paul. *Waffen-SS im Einsatz* (7th edition). Preußisches Oldendorf: K.W. Schütz Verlag KG, 1973.

——-. *Soldaten wie andere auch*. Osnabrück: Munin Verlag, 1966

Klietmann, *Dr.* Kurt-Gerhard. *Die Waffen-SS — eine Dokumentation*. Osnabrück: Munin Verlag, 1965.

Krätschmer, Ernst-Günther. *Ritterkreuzträger der Waffen-SS*. Göttingen: Plesse-Verlag, 1965.

Payk, Ernst. *Die Geschichte der 206. Infanterie-Division*. Bad Nauheim: Podzun-Pallas-Verlag, ?

Phillipi, A. and F. Heim. *Der Feldzug gegen die Sowjetunion*. Stuttgart: Verlag W. Kohlhammer, ?

Rendulic, *Dr.* Lothar. *Soldat in stürzenden Reichen*. Munich: Damm Verlag, 1965.

Schukow, G.K. *Erinnerungen und Gedanken*. Stuttgart: Deutsche Verlagsanstalt, 1969.

Stein, George H. *Geschichte der Waffen-SS*. Düsseldorf: Droste-Verlag, 1967.

Stoves, Rolf. *Geschichte der 1. Panzer-Division*. Bad Nauheim: Podzun-Pallas-Verlag, ?

Weidinger, Otto. *Kameraden bis zum Ende*. Göttingen: Plesse-Verlag, 1962.

Werth, Alexander. *Krieg in Rußland, 1941-45*. Munich: Droemersche Verlagsanstalt, ?

Rank Comparisons

Enlisted

US Army	*German Army*	*Waffen-SS*
Private	*Schütze*	*SS-Schütze*
Private First Class	*Oberschütze*	*SS-Oberschütze*
Corporal	*Gefreiter*	*SS-Sturmmann*
(Senior Corporal)	*Obergefreiter*	*SS-Rottenführer*
(Staff Corporal)	*Stabsgefreiter*	(None)

Noncommissioned Officers

US Army	*German Army*	*Waffen-SS*
Sergeant	*Unteroffizier*	*SS-Unterscharführer*
Staff Sergeant	*Feldwebel*	*SS-Oberscharführer*
Sergeant First Class	*Oberfeldwebel*	*SS-Hauptscharführer*
Master Sergeant	*Hauptfeldwebel*	*SS-Sturmscharführer*
Sergeant Major	*Stabsfeldwebel*	(None)

Officers

US Army	*German Army*	*Waffen-SS*
Lieutenant	*Leutnant*	*SS-Untersturmführer*
First Lieutenant	*Oberleutnant*	*SS-Obersturmführer*
Captain	*Hauptmann*	*SS-Hauptsturmführer*
Major	*Major*	*SS-Sturmbannführer*
Lieutenant Colonel	*Oberstleutnant*	*SS-Obersturmbannführer*
Colonel	*Oberst*	*SS-Oberführer or SS-Standartenführer*
Brigadier General	*Generalmajor*	*SS-Brigadeführer*
Major General	*Generalleutnant*	*SS-Gruppenführer*
Lieutenant General	*General der Panzertruppen* etc.	*SS-Obergruppenführer*
General	*Generaloberst*	*SS-Oberstgruppenführer*
General of the Army	*Feldmarschall*	*Reichsführer-SS*